Innovative Approaches to AI-Supported Hybrid and Remote Workplaces

Rajeh Bati Fahad Almasradi
University of Bisha, Saudi Arabia

Abdelrehim Awad
https://orcid.org/0009-0005-3649-430X
University of Bisha, Saudi Arabia

IGI Global
Scientific Publishing
Publishing Tomorrow's Research Today

Vice President of Editorial Melissa Wagner
Director of Acquisitions Mikaela Felty
Director of Book Development Jocelynn Hessler
Production Manager Mike Brehm
Cover Design Jose Rosado

Published in the United States of America by
IGI Global Scientific Publishing
701 East Chocolate Avenue
Hershey, PA, 17033, USA
Tel: 717-533-8845 | Fax: 717-533-7115
Website: https://www.igi-global.com E-mail: cust@igi-global.com

Library of Congress Cataloging-in-Publication Data

LCCN: 2025053814 (CIP Data Pending)
ISBN13: 979-8-3373-7416-1
Isbn13Softcover: 979-8-3373-7417-8
EISBN13: 979-8-3373-7418-5

British Cataloguing in Publication Data
A Cataloguing in Publication record for this book is available from the British Library.

Table of Contents

Detailed Table of Contents

The digital transformation of workplaces has fundamentally reshaped employee experiences, redefining motivation, well-being, and work–life balance. While technology enables flexibility and productivity, it also introduces challenges such as digital fatigue, blurred boundaries, and psychological strain. This chapter explores how organizations can build human-centric digital ecosystems that foster employee engagement, intrinsic motivation, and holistic well-being. Drawing from theories like self-determination and job demands–resources models, it highlights global best practices and strategies for sustainable digital workplaces. The chapter aims to contribute actionable insights for HR leaders, managers, and policymakers navigating the evolving dynamics of work in the digital age.

This chapter examines how artificial intelligence transforms teaching and professional roles in private language schools, emphasizing the reskilling of educators as a complex, ongoing process. Moving beyond technical competence, reskilling involves reflection, identity reconstruction, and negotiation of agency within fluctuating institutional contexts. Drawing on Organizational Learning Theory and the scholarship on teachers' professional identity, the chapter conceptualizes adaptation as both individual and collective. It highlights emotional and relational dimensions, acknowledging resistance, ambivalence, and the tension between efficiency and humanistic values. Leadership and organizational culture are crucial for fostering trust, experimentation, and continuous learning. By framing reskilling as the interplay between identity reconstruction and organizational learning, the chapter presents educators as

explains the two-way integration between MCDM and ML, shows how explainable AI artifacts support auditability and learning, and illustrates, through case studies, how hybrid rankings can be turned into personalized, constraint-aware recommendation engines for different investor profiles.

The growing integration of Artificial Intelligence (AI) in hybrid and remote workplaces is redefining leadership, communication, and collaboration. This chapter investigates how AI-mediated systems facilitate cognitive collaboration by combining human judgment with machine intelligence. It explores the evolution of algorithmic management, predictive analytics, and adaptive learning as key enablers of decision-making and innovation in distributed teams. The discussion emphasizes leadership adaptation, ethical governance, and trust-building within AI-driven organizational environments. By examining theoretical insights and real-world applications, the chapter presents a conceptual model illustrating how AI supports creativity, engagement, and resilience while ensuring transparency and human-centric governance. The analysis concludes that effective AI integration can foster sustainable, intelligent, and inclusive hybrid work ecosystems.

This chapter examines the transformative role of artificial intelligence (AI) in shaping contemporary entrepreneurship. It explores how AI-driven tools are redefining business models, enabling startups to leverage predictive analytics, generative technologies, and digital twins for innovation and growth. The discussion highlights the rise of hybrid and remote workplaces as new entrepreneurial ecosystems, along with evolving financing structures supported by AI-driven platforms. Case studies of global startups illustrate opportunities, challenges, and regional variations in adoption. The chapter also emphasizes ethical, legal, and policy considerations while reflecting on long-term implications for entrepreneurs, employees, and investors. It concludes by underscoring resilience, inclusivity, and responsible innovation as critical for sustaining entrepreneurial success in the AI-supported world.

This chapter helps shed light on the requirements of artificial intelligence and the necessity of ethical governance and sustainable engagement between digital technology and humans in a hybrid environment by working on the application of adaptive training models to enhance the efficiency and skills of employees and learners within the workplace. This chapter helps provide a clear framework for integrating digital infrastructure and using machine learning and natural language processing to achieve predictive analytics that facilitate the integration of AI and leadership to improve organisational productivity. AI applications leverage virtual reality, augmented reality, and even gamification to deliver an adaptive training environment that continuously increases learner engagement, leading to improved learner skills. This chapter also noted that among the challenges related to integrating AI into the workplace are the inability to mobilise learners and stakeholders toward AI acceptance, along with factors related to digital fatigue, bias, and inequality.

Artificial Intelligence (AI) is transforming strategic decision-making in distributed and hybrid workplaces by enhancing agility, innovation, and responsiveness. This chapter explores how AI-augmented systems combine data-driven insights and human cognition to support anticipatory and adaptive strategies. It examines frameworks for human-AI collaboration that reduce cognitive bias, improve ethical governance, and promote transparent decision ecosystems. Empirical insights reveal that AI dashboards, predictive analytics, and intelligent models accelerate innovation while ensuring accountability. The discussion emphasizes AI's role as a strategic enabler that amplifies human creativity rather than replacing it. By integrating algorithmic intelligence with ethical leadership, organizations can achieve sustainable agility, innovation, and resilience in an increasingly digital and decentralized environment.

The fast rate of Artificial Intelligence (AI) implementation in organizations is transforming leadership practice, human resource management, and organizational behavior. The chapter critically looks at how AI-driven organizations are reimagining leadership and behavior to maintain human-centricity in the era of algorithmic governance. It relies on the theory of socio-technical systems to study the effects of AI on the well-being, motivation and work-life balance of employees, grounded on digital organizational psychology, support of human-machine interaction, and collaboration. The chapter highlights the importance of ethical leadership, emotional intelligence, and integrative cultures following sustainable digital transformation using empirical research and case studies and discussing digital alienation and suggesting a Humanized AI Governance model to balance technological effectiveness and behavioral resilience.

The sudden globalization of work, followed by the attendant decentralization of the working population, has spawned an unprecedented crisis in what has become known as Organizational Memory (OM). The aforementioned crisis has been followed by an unprecedented loss of knowledge exchange in tacit knowledge on one hand, and hubris in explicit knowledge organized in disconnected "silos" on another. Under these circumstances, this particular chapter sets out to assume that today and in tomorrow's future, there cannot possibly be any valid KM strategy capable of meeting, let alone succeeding in complying with, this new paradigm of distant work. Thus, we argue that it's time to propose Retrieval-Augmented Generation (RAG) models: sociotechnical innovations that propose and see within existing digital presence, in this case in our corporation's "corpus" dynamically coupled with Large Language Models (LLMs) to be henceforth and forevermore, sociotechnically speaking, "de rigueur" in thise new paradigm on distant work. They provide—in fact, literally "reanimate" existing passive repositories to be made query-capable as necessarily "digital synapses" to their existing analogs. Numerous existing Retrieval-Augmented Generation models, including "Retriever-Centric" and "Generator-Centric" models in particular, and even "Agentic" varieties in particular, shall be exhaustively described in this chapter.

An accelerated adoption of Artificial Intelligence (AI) in organisational processes has prompted analysis of its influence on Human Resource Management (HRM). This chapter explores how AI transforms HR from traditional administrative duties into a strategic partner through data-driven analysis. It builds a framework for understanding how AI reshapes the HR Lifecycle, improving efficiency and enabling strategic intelligence to manage human capital. The chapter examines AI's functional applications, including talent acquisition via automated screening, performance evaluation through predictive analytics, and personalised employee development to enhance engagement. On the strategic level, it highlights AI's role in workforce planning and organisational development, showing how AI empowers proactive decision-making, optimises resource allocation, and aligns human capital with overall organisational objectives.

Preface

The rapid diffusion of artificial intelligence (AI), generative AI, and data-driven automation is fundamentally reshaping how work is designed, coordinated, and experienced. Hybrid and remote work—once viewed as temporary arrangements—have become enduring organizational models across sectors. Yet, as digital work becomes the norm, organizations face urgent questions: How can AI enhance productivity without eroding employee well-being? How can leaders foster trust, engagement, and fairness in algorithm-mediated workplaces? How can entrepreneurs and innovators leverage AI to build resilient, sustainable ventures? And how can institutions ensure that the future of work remains human-centered, ethical, and inclusive?

Innovative Approaches to AI-Supported Hybrid and Remote Workplaces responds to these questions by bringing together multidisciplinary perspectives across management, organizational behavior, entrepreneurship, education, human resource management, and information systems. The book examines the convergence of AI-enabled decision-making, leadership, organizational culture, workforce reskilling, and digital well-being in hybrid and remote contexts. Rather than treating AI as a purely technical solution, this volume explores AI as a socio-technical force that changes identities, capabilities, governance, collaboration patterns, and the meaning of work itself.

PURPOSE AND SCOPE

The primary purpose of this edited book is to provide evidence-based and practice-oriented insights into how AI can be integrated to:

- strengthen employee well-being, motivation, and work–life balance in digitally mediated environments,
- redesign leadership and team dynamics for AI-supported collaboration,

- enhance organizational agility, innovation, and resilience in distributed work models, and
- support entrepreneurial ecosystems and new venture decision-making through intelligent tools and analytics.

The book also highlights the importance of ethical and responsible AI, including transparency, fairness, privacy, and accountable governance—especially as algorithmic systems increasingly influence hiring, performance evaluation, training, and employee experience.

TARGET AUDIENCE

This book is intended for researchers, postgraduate students, practitioners, innovation leaders, HR professionals, policymakers, and entrepreneurs seeking a comprehensive reference on AI-supported hybrid and remote workplaces. It is particularly valuable for graduate programs in Business Administration, Organizational Studies, Entrepreneurship, Digital Transformation, and related fields.

ORGANIZATION OF THE BOOK

The chapters in this volume are organized to reflect key thematic areas: (1) employee well-being and human factors, (2) identity, reskilling, and learning, (3) leadership and collaboration in AI-mediated work, (4) decision-making and organizational agility, (5) entrepreneurship and innovation, and (6) sectoral/analytical applications and governance. Together, these contributions provide conceptual foundations, empirical evidence, methodological insights, and practical guidance.

Chapter 1 explores employee well-being, motivation, and work–life balance in technology-driven workplaces, offering frameworks for thriving in the digital era while maintaining sustainable performance.

Chapter 2 examines how AI reshapes professional identity through reskilling, focusing on teachers in private language schools and the implications of human–AI collaboration in educational work.

Chapter 3 provides a survey-based analysis of student preferences in AI-supported online education, highlighting collaboration patterns between learners and AI systems.

Chapter 4 introduces AI-driven assessment of cognitive stress using natural language processing and the Internet of Behaviours, with implications for designing healthier workplaces and early interventions.

Chapter 5 discusses the shift from data-driven venture capital to personalized decision engines, presenting a human–machine hybrid approach grounded in multi-criteria decision-making (MCDM).

Chapter 6 addresses cognitive collaboration and how leadership and team dynamics evolve in AI-mediated hybrid environments, emphasizing trust, coordination, and shared sense-making.

Chapter 7 examines entrepreneurship and startup development in the age of AI, focusing on opportunity recognition, business model innovation, and AI-enabled competitive advantage.

Chapter 8 investigates AI-powered digital and virtual training for hybrid and flexible work environments, emphasizing capability-building, personalization, and scalable learning.

Chapter 9 explores augmented decision-making in distributed work environments, showing how AI can enhance strategic agility and innovation under uncertainty.

Chapter 10 provides empirical case studies on generative AI in startup innovation and entrepreneurial decision-making, illustrating real-world applications and lessons learned.

Chapter 11 examines human–AI synergy for organizational resilience and offers strategies for adaptive and sustainable remote work models.

Chapter 12 discusses humanizing AI by reconstructing organizational behavior, leadership, and employee well-being in AI-enabled enterprises, emphasizing values-driven design.

Chapter 13 analyzes the economic impact of AI adoption in hybrid and remote workplaces, focusing on productivity, labor dynamics, and organizational value creation.

Chapter 14 discusses AI for human resources management, addressing opportunities, challenges, and ethical considerations such as fairness, privacy, transparency, and accountability.

CONCLUDING NOTE

The future of hybrid and remote work will not be shaped by technology alone, but by the strategic, ethical, and human-centered choices that organizations make when deploying AI. By integrating empirical findings, conceptual contributions, and applied perspectives, this book aims to advance research and support decision-makers in building workplaces that are not only smarter, but also more resilient, inclusive, and sustainable.

We would like to express our sincere appreciation to all contributing authors and reviewers for their time, scholarly rigor, and commitment to strengthening this volume. We also thank IGI Global Scientific Publishing for its support and guidance throughout the editorial process. It is our hope that this book will serve as a valuable reference and a catalyst for further research, responsible practice, and impactful innovation in AI-supported hybrid and remote workplaces.

Chapter 1

Thriving in the Digital Era: Reimagining Employee Well-Being, Motivation, and Work-Life Balance in Tech-Driven Workplaces

Pallavi Pahuja
https://orcid.org/0009-0005-5108-3955
CBSA, CGC Landran, India

Ruby Sharma
https://orcid.org/0000-0002-4716-9204
CBSA, CGC Landran, India

Aaruni Batta
CBSA, CGC Landran, India

Rajesh Jhamb
Directorate of Technical Education, Chandigarh, India

ABSTRACT

The digital transformation of workplaces has fundamentally reshaped employee experiences, redefining motivation, well-being, and work–life balance. While technology enables flexibility and productivity, it also introduces challenges such as digital fatigue, blurred boundaries, and psychological strain. This chapter explores how organizations can build human-centric digital ecosystems that foster employee engagement, intrinsic motivation, and holistic well-being. Drawing from

DOI: 10.4018/979-8-3373-7416-1.ch001

theories like self-determination and job demands–resources models, it highlights global best practices and strategies for sustainable digital workplaces. The chapter aims to contribute actionable insights for HR leaders, managers, and policymakers navigating the evolving dynamics of work in the digital age.

1. INTRODUCTION

Digital transformation is a wave of change that has never been witnessed before and the rate of transformation in the 21 st century workplace has been met with a metamorphosis of proportions never experienced before. The integration of cloud computing, artificial intelligence (AI), machine learning (ML), collaboration platforms, and high-speed connectivity has cleared the traditional picture of the office, and it now forms a borderless and 24/7 workplace (Bloom et al., 2015). This paradox has become the new reality of the contemporary employee because this change has been precipitated by the COVID-19 pandemic that is changing things at an exponentially accelerated pace.

On the one hand, technology has introduced unimaginable degrees of flexibility, independence, and possible productivity (Gajendran and Harrison, 2007). On the other hand, it has created new, mostly unseen, obstacles to the well-being of employees, intrinsic motivation, and harmonious work-life balance.

These tools which were supposed to free us of the physical office constraints have linked us to a digital tether and made the separation between work and personal life indistinct. Digital fatigue as a psychological burden of endless video conferences and constant connectivity has become a major phenomenon (Bailenson, 2021). The culture of being always-on, which is stimulated by an expectation of an immediate response, risks to destroy the engagement of the employees, causing them to experience chronic stress and burnout (Mazmanian et al., 2013). The management activities and HR policies that were initially created to operate in a long-gone time when employees worked in co-located spaces, which could be easily visible, are not sufficient anymore, and even detrimental in certain instances.

The main point of this chapter is that the key challenge and opportunity of modern organizations is no longer to be techno-centrically oriented towards digital transformation. Building a dedicated, human-centered digital ecosystem is not just the innovation of the use of the latest software or platform, but the next layer of competitive advantage. One such ecosystem will be where technology is used as an enabler of human potential rather than a cause of human depletion. It is a mindful place aimed at promoting a holistic health, intrinsic focus and sustainable work-life balance, despite the ever-growing interconnectedness of the virtual and the physical world.

The chapter will break down the complicated interaction between the digital workplace and the human experience based on the previous theories of psychology and organization, including Self-Determination Theory (Deci and Ryan, 2000) and the Job Demands-Resources model (Bakker and Demerouti, 2017). We shall look at the two sidedness of digital tools; on the one hand, the enabling, and on the other, the disabling impacts of these tools. The chapter is organized in such a way that it first sets theoretical backgrounds and proceeds to exploring the challenges and the opportunities that surround well-being, motivation, and work-life balance in particular. We will then, compile global best practices and make proposals of a strategic framework of practical learning to HR leaders, managers and policymakers. We hope to eventually offer a roadmap to creating sustainable and successful digital workplaces in which employees do not just live, but thrive.

2. THEORETICAL UNDERPINNING: THE HUMAN COMPONENT OF A DIGITAL WORLD

In order to succeed in re-conceptualizing employee well-being and motivations, we have to base our knowledge on strong psychological models that describe human behaviors and needs in the workplace. Self-Determination Theory (SDT) and Job Demands-Resources (JD-R) model are two theories that can be especially relevant when discussing the digital workplace.

Digital Work Self-Determination Theory (SDT)

The Self-Determination Theory (Deci and Ryan, 2000), assumes that people are endowed with three psychological needs that are inherent to them and are critical towards promoting the development of quality motivation and psychological health:

1. **Autonomy:** The desire to be volitional and possess a feeling of choice and control over personal actions.
2. **Competence:** A necessity to feel efficient in his/her interaction with the surrounding and feel the possibility to use and demonstrate his/her abilities.
3. **Relatedness:** the necessity to feel that one is related with others, to care, be cared, and feel a sense of belonging.

All these needs are affected significantly by the digital workplace, which can and does contradict itself in many cases.

Autonomy in the Digital Age

Autonomy can be a great boost in digital tools as people are able to create flexibility in the work as workers are able to work at their own pace and also manage their own working conditions (Gajendran and Harrison, 2007). This autonomy is, however, possible as an illusion. Pervasive surveillance can also be managed by the same technology by monitoring keystroke, screen logging and constant activity tracking on digital mediums. This digital panopticon will be able to generate the sense of constant surveillance and sabotage perceived autonomy, as well as provoke anxiety and mistrust (Zuboff, 2019). Consequently, this does not imply that one should only offer flexibility, but rather combine it with trust and outcome-oriented orientation instead of being internet-based.

Fluid Environment: Technology competence gives one the strength to reach the desired goals using powerful tools, learn new competencies through online platforms, and demonstrate mastery, which helps justify the necessity of competence. Nonetheless, technological change is also prone to rapid change and this factor can cause so-called technostress - the stress caused by failure to keep up with new computer technologies (Ragu-Nathan et al., 2008). In case employees are unable to use novel software and platforms, their self-efficacy is endangered, and they become frustrated and disconnected.

Relatedness and Digital Connection: Collaboration tools such as Slack, Microsoft Teams, and Zoom focus on relatedness, where they are meant to connect distributed teams. When properly utilized, they can build great virtual communities. However, digital communication is not as rich as non-verbal communication and spontaneous as a conversation in the hallway and can result in isolation and decreased feeling of belonging (Wang et al., 2021). It takes more work to establish authentic connection in the digital realm, and unless designed specifically, these technologies will produce shallow interactions which are unable to fulfill the need of relatedness which is deeply ingrained.

Job Demands-Resources (JD-R) Model in the Tech-Driven Environment

One of the most influential models that classify all job features into two broad groups, namely, job demands and job resources, is the JD-R model (Bakker and Demerouti, 2017).The former is the aspect of the job that involves physical, psychological, social, or organizational factors that necessitate maintaining a sustained physical or mental effort and, thus, have some physiological and psychological costs (e.g., stress, burnout). At the virtual workplace, new requirements have been created:

Digital Overload: Endless messages, emails and notifications.
Constant Connectivity: The pressure to be on and be reachable outside the regular working hours.
System Complexity: The cognitive burden of the multi-software application navigation (with multiple poorly integrated software applications).
Virtual Meeting Fatigue: The exhaustion resulting from prolonged video conferencing (Bailenson, 2021).

Job Resources are those aspects of the job that are functional in achieving work goals, reduce job demands and the associated physiological and psychological costs, and stimulate personal growth and development. Digital resources can include:

Flexibility Tools: Technology that enables asynchronous work and flexible scheduling.
Learning & Development Platforms: Online courses and knowledge bases that aid skill development.
Collaboration Software: Tools that facilitate seamless teamwork and knowledge sharing.
Performance Support Systems: AI-driven tools that provide real-time guidance and automate routine tasks.

The JD-R model has a central thesis, according to which a balance is essential. The combination of high job demands and low job resources causes a health impairment process which culminates into chronic stress, exhaustion, and burnout. On the other hand, high job resources may initiate a motivational process and bring high engagement, high performance, and self-development (Bakker and Demerouti, 2017). This makes the digital workplace a very decisive platform where organizations will have to manage and strategically address the digital needs coupled with increasing the digital resources to create a healthy and motivated workforce.

3. THE NEW WELL-BEING PARADIGM: HOLISTIC HEALTH IN A HYPERCONNECTED WORLD

The concept of employee well-being has changed to a limited view of physical safety and lack of disease to a comprehensive notion of physical, mental, social and even digital health. All these dimensions are confronted with individual challenges by the digital workplace.

Digital Fatigue and Psychological Health

Zoom fatigue has become a widely used vocabulary, although, the problem is not confined to one platform. Bailenson (2021) singles out a number of major reasons why video calls are exhausting:

Oversized Intensive Closure Eye Gaze: Extreme and prolonged eye contact on video chat is understood as socially intense and unnatural.
Cognitive Load: It is a constant burden of consciously transmitting and deciphering non-verbal communication (nods, thumbs-up) that would be unconscious in face-to-face interaction.
The "Mirror Effect: The fact that one can see his or her video feed in real-time assumes a constant self-assessment and self-awareness that is stressful.
Less Mobility: It is not like when we meet face to face and are able to move freely according to our desire, because we cannot move freely in a camera.

This cumulatively causes mental exhaustion. In addition to video calls, the culture of being always on, which is promoted by smartphones and constant notifications, does not allow cognitive recovery. The brain must rest to solidify the memory, digest information and renew itself. It also hinders this much-needed rest process when work is brought into the evenings, weekends, and vacation times with the help of digital media, resulting in more anxiety, depression, and burnout (Mazmanian et al., 2013).

The Wearing Away of Physical Health

The lack of physical activity of a large portion of digital work is an important risk to physical health. Ergonomic furniture may not be found in the home office hence causing musculoskeletal issues. Work-life boundaries are usually blurred and therefore time to engage in physical activity, planned rests, and proper meals is limited. Screen blue light has the potential to disrupt circadian rhythms and negatively affect the quality of sleep, which is the baseline of physical and mental health (Hysing et al., 2015). Organizations can no longer believe that physical well-being of remote employees is the only worry of the employee.

Social Well-Being and the Menace of Isolation

Although technology is linking us on a virtual level, it is also disconnecting us socially. The deprivation of informal, serendipitous communication; the so-called water cooler moments, can greatly affect the organizational culture and the personal social welfare. These are not only social moments, but vital in the development of trust, generation of innovation, and the feeling of community (Wang et al., 2021). This lack of social fabric among the remote employees may cause loneliness, ostracism, as well as a sense of poor commitment to the organization and its objectives.

4. DIGITAL WELL-BEING PROMOTION STRATEGIES

Combating Digital Fatigue

Encourage "Camera-Free" Time: Long meetings or check-ins should be conducted using audio-only calls to minimise the cognitive burden of video.
Asynchronous Communication Norms: Have rules that do not entail instant response in communication, which would alleviate the stress of being continuously available.
Meeting Hygiene: Introduce shorter meeting times (i.e. 25 or 50 minutes rather than 30 or 60), clear agenda, and only invite the necessary participants.

Supporting Physical Health

Ergonomic Stipends: Pay allowances to employees to buy good office chairs, desks and equipments at their work places.
Virtual Wellness Programs: Provide virtual yoga, meditation or fitness classes. Practice walking meetings when making calls that do not need screen sharing.
Digital Detox Programs: Promote the use of non-essential notification after hours and apply do not disturb features strictly by employees.

Cultivating Social Relationship

Planned Virtual Social Spaces: Set up special channels or times of having non-work conversations (e.g. #pets, #hobbies). Have virtual coffee chats, game nights or book clubs.
Organized Onboarding of Connection: Have virtual buddies/ mentors accompany new employees to assist them in acquiring a social network inside the organization.
Invest in Occasional Face to Face Meetings: These are expensive, but the off sites or team meetings every so often are worth the money in the end to build relationships that keep virtual teamwork going.

5. HOW TO REFUEL INTRINSIC MOTIVATION IN THE DIGITAL WORKPLACE

The impetus of performance and participation is motivation. However, in the digital workplace, where face-to-face supervision is not always an option, the concept of intrinsic motivation, the desire to do something because it is simply interesting or gratifying, becomes the most important. SDT is a potent prism through which this can be undertaken.

Developing Accountability and Autonomy

Digitizing and hybridizing the work process is a silver bullet to transform the presence culture into the results culture. This is well in line with the psychological need of autonomy.

Pay attention to the Results, Not the Action: The managers should be trained to state explicit goals and results, and leave the rest of the work to the teams and allow them to accomplish it in their unique way with the use of the digital tools they have at their disposal. Surveillance software is a form of micromanagement, and it is an indication of mistrust and termination of autonomy.

Offer Flexibility in The How and The When:Provided that the goals are achieved and collaboration requirements are fulfilled, give the employees the flexibility in their work schedules and techniques. This shows the respect of the fact that they are capable of self-management.

Engage Employees in Decision-Making: Employ digital polls, surveys, and teamwork tools to engage the employees in the decision-making process that impacts their job, e.g., the selection of the new software or the development of the team processes.

Developing Competence through Life-long Learning

The digital world is characterized by the high rate of obsolescence of skills. The support of continuous learning in organizations provides the employees with confidence in their competence in a dynamic environment.

Curated Digital Learning Hubs: Gain access to the high-quality online learning platforms (e.g., LinkedIn Learning, Coursera) and build learning paths that are relevant to the roles and the career goals of the employees.

Micro-learning and Just in Time Knowledge: Promote brief, intensive learning units that can easily be incorporated in the working day. AI can be employed in suggesting learning material according to projects and skills deficiency of an employee.

Create a Culture of Feedback: Implement regular, constructive feedback loops using digital performance management tools. Feedback should be focused on growth and development, not just evaluation, reinforcing an employee's sense of growing competence.

Cultivating Relatedness in a Distributed Team

Satisfying the need for relatedness requires deliberate effort in a digital environment.

Purposeful Onboarding: The onboarding process should be heavily focused on building relationships, not just processing paperwork. Virtual meet-and-greets with team members and key stakeholders across the organization are essential.
Strengthen Team Identity: Leaders should regularly communicate the team's purpose, celebrate shared successes, and create team-specific rituals using video conferencing and collaboration tools.
Encourage "Whole-Person" Interactions: Leaders should model vulnerability and encourage team members to share not just work updates, but also personal challenges and successes. This builds empathy and psychological safety, a shared belief that the team is safe for interpersonal risk-taking (Edmondson, 1999).

3. NAVIGATING THE BLUR: WORK–LIFE BALANCE IN THE "ALWAYS-ON" ERA

The concept of work–life balance presupposes a clear separation between two distinct domains. The digital revolution has fundamentally challenged this separation, creating what Clark (2000) calls "work–life border theory," where the boundaries are permeable and constantly negotiated.

The Challenge of Boundary Blurring

The smartphone is both a productivity tool and a portal through which work invades personal life. The expectation of quick responses, coupled with the difficulty of "leaving" a home office, leads to "boundary blurring," where work and personal roles intermingle throughout the day (Derks et al., 2016). This can be both a source of flexibility and a source of conflict. For some, integrating work and life is beneficial; for others, it leads to constant role conflict and the inability to psychologically detach from work. Psychological detachment—the individual's sense of being away from the work situation—is a critical recovery experience (Sonnentag & Fritz, 2015). When digital tools impede detachment, they contribute directly to burnout.

Strategies for Creating Sustainable Boundaries

Organizations and individuals must collaborate to create and respect boundaries.

Organizational "Right to Disconnect" Policies: Several countries, like France and Portugal, have legislated the "right to disconnect." Organizations can proactively implement such policies, formally stating that employees are not expected to read or respond to work communications outside of their designated working hours.
Modeling from the Top: The most powerful signal is sent by leaders. When senior managers send emails late at night or on weekends, it creates implicit pressure, even if they add a disclaimer like "no need to respond." Leaders must be conscious of their digital habits and model healthy boundary-setting.

Technology-Enabled Boundaries

Scheduled Send Features: Encourage the use of "schedule send" for emails written outside of standard hours, so they arrive during the recipient's workday.

Clear Communication Norms: Establish team agreements on communication channels (e.g., Slack for urgent matters, email for non-urgent) and expected response times.
Digital Wellness Features: Encourage the use of built-in features like "Focus Mode" on computers and "Do Not Disturb" on phones to create blocks of uninterrupted personal time.

Individual Boundary Management

Physical Separation: If possible, dedicate a specific room or area of the home for work. At the end of the day, physically leaving that space can serve as a powerful psychological cue that the workday is over.
Rituals for Transition: Create a short ritual to mark the end of the workday, such as a short walk, meditating, changing clothes, or listening to a specific playlist. This helps the brain switch from "work mode" to "home mode."

4. A STRATEGIC FRAMEWORK FOR HR LEADERS AND POLICYMAKERS

Building a human-centric digital workplace requires a systemic and strategic overhaul of HR practices and policies. It moves HR from an administrative function to a strategic architect of the employee experience.

Reimagining Performance Management

The annual review is obsolete in a dynamic digital environment. Performance management must become continuous, feedback-rich, and focused on development.

Implement Continuous Check-ins: Replace or supplement annual reviews with frequent, lightweight conversations between managers and employees focused on goals, progress, and support needed.

Focus on Objectives and Key Results (OKRs): Adopt a framework like OKRs that emphasizes ambitious, transparent goals and measurable outcomes, perfectly suited for a results-oriented culture.

Leverage 360-Degree Feedback: Use digital platforms to gather multi-source feedback, providing a more holistic view of an employee's contributions, especially in collaborative, matrixed digital environments.

Revamping Learning and Development (L&D)

L&D must shift from a one-size-fits-all, event-based model to a personalized, continuous, and embedded function.

Promote a Growth Mindset Culture: Foster a culture where learning from failure is encouraged, and skill development is seen as a continuous journey.

Utilize AI for Personalized Learning Paths: Use AI to analyze skill gaps and recommend tailored learning content, making development highly relevant and efficient.

Encourage Internal Knowledge Sharing: Create digital platforms where employees can easily create and share knowledge, turning the organization itself into a learning ecosystem.

Cultivating Empathetic Digital Leadership

The role of the manager is more critical than ever in a digital workplace. They are the primary conduit through which organizational culture is transmitted and the key to preventing employee isolation.

Train Managers in Virtual Empathy and Coaching: Leadership training must now include skills for building trust remotely, recognizing signs of burnout through a screen, conducting effective virtual one-on-ones, and coaching for performance rather than commanding and controlling.

Equip Managers with Digital People-Analytics: Provide managers with dashboards that give insights into their team's well-being (e.g., through anonymized survey data on workload and stress) rather than individual surveillance data.

Reward People-Leadership Skills: Include metrics related to team engagement, well-being, and retention in managers' performance evaluations and incentive structures.

The Role of Policymakers

Policymakers have a crucial role in setting the floor for humane digital work practices.

Legislate the "Right to Disconnect":As mentioned, clear legislation can protect employees from the exploitation of their personal time and encourage a healthier work culture nationwide.

Update Occupational Health and Safety Regulations: Regulations need to be modernized to include psychosocial risks associated with digital work, such as chronic stress from constant connectivity and isolation.

Support Digital Literacy and Upskilling Initiatives: Governments can partner with industry and educational institutions to fund programs that help the workforce adapt to the demands of the digital economy, mitigating the competence-threatening aspects of technological change.

CONCLUSION: TOWARDS A SUSTAINABLE AND HUMAN-CENTRIC FUTURE OF WORK

The digital transformation of the workplace is an unstoppable force, but its human impact is not predetermined. It is a story still being written, shaped by the choices of organizational leaders, HR professionals, managers, and policymakers. The central thesis of this chapter is that the ultimate success of our digital future will not be measured by the sophistication of our technology, but by the well-being, motivation, and fulfillment of the people who use it.

The challenges of digital fatigue, blurred boundaries, and psychological strain are real and significant. However, they are not insurmountable. By grounding our strategies in established psychological principles like Self-Determination Theory and the Job Demands–Resources model, we can consciously design digital ecosystems that empower rather than enslave. This requires a fundamental shift in mindset: from viewing employees as resources to be optimized to seeing them as whole human beings to be nurtured.

The path forward involves building a culture of trust over surveillance, outcomes over activity, and connection over mere connectivity. It requires equipping leaders with the skills of empathy and coaching, redesigning work practices to facilitate deep work and recovery, and leveraging technology itself to create better boundaries and more meaningful connections. The strategies outlined—from reimagining performance management and L&D to implementing sensible disconnect policies—provide a actionable blueprint for this transformation.

The tech-driven workplace holds immense promise for creating more flexible, inclusive, and productive work environments. Realizing this promise hinges on our unwavering commitment to placing humanity at the center of our digital designs. By doing so, we can create **sustainable workplaces** where technology serves as a powerful ally in the pursuit of not just corporate profit, but also human prosperity and well-being. In this reimagined future, thriving in the digital era will be the norm, not the exception.

REFERENCES

Bailenson, J. N. (2021). Nonverbal overload: A theoretical argument for the causes of Zoom fatigue. *Technology, Mind, and Behavior*, *2*(1), 1–6. Advance online publication. DOI: 10.1037/tmb0000030

Bakker, A. B., & Demerouti, E. (2017). Job demands–resources theory: Taking stock and looking forward. *Journal of Occupational Health Psychology*, *22*(3), 273–285. DOI: 10.1037/ocp0000056 PMID: 27732008

Bloom, N., Liang, J., Roberts, J., & Ying, Z. J. (2015). Does working from home work? Evidence from a Chinese experiment. *The Quarterly Journal of Economics*, *130*(1), 165–218. DOI: 10.1093/qje/qju032

Clark, S. C. (2000). Work/family border theory: A new theory of work/family balance. *Human Relations*, *53*(6), 747–770. DOI: 10.1177/0018726700536001

Deci, E. L., & Ryan, R. M. (2000). The "what" and "why" of goal pursuits: Human needs and the self-determination of behavior. *Psychological Inquiry*, *11*(4), 227–268. DOI: 10.1207/S15327965PLI1104_01

Derks, D., van Duin, D., Tims, M., & Bakker, A. B. (2016). Smartphone use and work–home interference: The moderating role of social norms and employee work engagement. *Journal of Occupational and Organizational Psychology*, *88*(1), 155–177. DOI: 10.1111/joop.12083

Edmondson, A. C. (1999). Psychological safety and learning behavior in work teams. *Administrative Science Quarterly*, *44*(2), 350–383. DOI: 10.2307/2666999

Gajendran, R. S., & Harrison, D. A. (2007). The good, the bad, and the unknown about telecommuting: Meta-analysis of psychological mediators and individual consequences. *The Journal of Applied Psychology*, *92*(6), 1524–1541. DOI: 10.1037/0021-9010.92.6.1524 PMID: 18020794

Hysing, M., Harvey, A. G., Linton, S. J., Askeland, K. G., & Sivertsen, B. (2015). Sleep and academic performance in later adolescence: Results from a large population-based study. *Journal of Sleep Research*, *24*(3), 318–324. DOI: 10.1111/jsr.12373 PMID: 26825591

Mazmanian, M., Orlikowski, W. J., & Yates, J. (2013). The autonomy paradox: The implications of mobile email devices for knowledge professionals. *Organization Science*, *24*(5), 1337–1357. DOI: 10.1287/orsc.1120.0806

Ragu-Nathan, T. S., Tarafdar, M., Ragu-Nathan, B. S., & Tu, Q. (2008). The consequences of technostress for end users in organizations: Conceptual development and empirical validation. *Information Systems Research, 19*(4), 417–433. DOI: 10.1287/isre.1070.0165

Sonnentag, S., & Fritz, C. (2015). Recovery from job stress: The stressor-detachment model as an integrative framework. *Journal of Organizational Behavior, 36*(S1), S72–S103. DOI: 10.1002/job.1924

Wang, B., Liu, Y., Qian, J., & Parker, S. K. (2021). Achieving effective remote working during the COVID-19 pandemic: A work design perspective. *Applied Psychology, 70*(1), 16–59. DOI: 10.1111/apps.12290 PMID: 33230359

Zuboff, S. (2019). *The age of surveillance capitalism: The fight for a human future at the new frontier of power*. PublicAffairs.

Ragu-Nathan, T. S., Tarafdar, M., Ragu-Nathan, B. S., & Tu, Q. (2008). The consequences of technostress for end users in organizations: Conceptual development and empirical validation. *Information Systems Research*, 19(4), 417–433. DOI: 10.1287/isre.1070.0165

Sonnentag, S., & Fritz, C. (2015). Recovery from job stress: The stressor-detachment model as an integrative framework. *Journal of Organizational Behavior*, 36(S1), S72–S103. DOI: 10.1002/job.1924

Wang, B., Liu, Y., Qian, J., & Parker, S. K. (2021). Achieving effective remote working during the COVID-19 pandemic: A work design perspective. *Applied Psychology*, 70(1), 16–59. DOI: 10.1111/apps.12290 PMID: 33230359

Zuboff, S. (2019). *The age of surveillance capitalism: The fight for a human future at the new frontier of power*. PublicAffairs.

Chapter 2
AI and the Reconfiguration of Professional Identity:
Reskilling Teachers in Private Language Schools

Vedat Kızıl
https://orcid.org/0000-0003-0589-0877
Ankara Yıldırım Beyazıt University, Turkey

ABSTRACT

This chapter examines how artificial intelligence transforms teaching and professional roles in private language schools, emphasizing the reskilling of educators as a complex, ongoing process. Moving beyond technical competence, reskilling involves reflection, identity reconstruction, and negotiation of agency within fluctuating institutional contexts. Drawing on Organizational Learning Theory and the scholarship on teachers' professional identity, the chapter conceptualizes adaptation as both individual and collective. It highlights emotional and relational dimensions, acknowledging resistance, ambivalence, and the tension between efficiency and humanistic values. Leadership and organizational culture are crucial for fostering trust, experimentation, and continuous learning. By framing reskilling as the interplay between identity reconstruction and organizational learning, the chapter presents educators as adaptive professionals navigating AI-driven pedagogical and institutional change, with implications for workforce development beyond education.

DOI: 10.4018/979-8-3373-7416-1.ch002

1. INTRODUCTION

Artificial intelligence (AI) is reshaping educational enterprises in ways that are both profound and uneven. Institutions once constrained by rigid curricula, hierarchical structures, or limited instructional tools are now experimenting with adaptive learning systems, automated assessment mechanisms, and intelligent tutoring platforms. These innovations promise efficiency, personalized learning, and scalability, yet they also challenge long-standing assumptions about pedagogy, professional expertise, and the relational work of teaching (An et al., 2022). In private language schools, the effects of AI are particularly visible. These schools must navigate a delicate balance between learner expectations, market pressures, and professional standards. Their smaller scale, entrepreneurial leadership, and flexible structures allow experimentation and iterative development. At the same time, these conditions magnify tensions between technological possibilities and human agency (Almazán-López et al., 2025).

Private language schools occupy a liminal space between commercial enterprise and educational community. They operate under pressures to differentiate their offerings, attract and retain learners, and remain competitive. They are also tasked with sustaining pedagogical quality, ethical teaching practices, and professional coherence. AI adoption introduces both opportunities and challenges in this context. Tools that automate assessment or provide adaptive feedback can streamline processes and free teachers' time for higher-order instructional tasks. Yet they also reconfigure authority, blur the boundaries of professional judgment, and provoke questions about the value and relevance of human expertise in the classroom (Ollington, 2025). The interaction between human actors and AI technologies in these spaces is far from straightforward; it is a negotiation of roles, responsibilities, and professional identity.

The problem addressed in this chapter is that reskilling teachers in AI-mediated environments requires more than technical competence. Learning to operate new tools is insufficient. Teachers must engage in identity work, reflect on their pedagogical beliefs, and negotiate agency within evolving institutional and classroom structures. AI adoption can create role ambiguity, provoke emotional tension, and challenge teachers' sense of professional self (Lan, 2024). Institutional policies, leadership approaches, and organizational support systems mediate these experiences. Where support is superficial, reskilling may remain limited to operational training. Where support is thoughtful and sustained, it can enable deeper transformation. This helps teachers reconceptualize their roles, participate in collaborative learning, and maintain alignment between personal values and professional expectations (Darling-Hammond et al., 2017).

The theoretical framing of this chapter integrates Organizational Learning Theory (Argyris & Schön, 1978) with scholarship on teachers' professional identity (e.g.,

Beijaard et al., 2004; Coldron & Smith, 1999; Day et al., 2006). Organizational Learning Theory provides a lens for understanding how schools adapt collectively to technological change, engaging in double-loop learning that challenges assumptions and reshapes institutional norms. Professional identity scholarship highlights the reflective, relational, and negotiated dimensions of teaching. It underscores that technical skill is inseparable from the ethical and social dimensions of practice. Drawing these perspectives together, the chapter conceptualizes reskilling as a dual-level process. At the individual level, teachers reconstruct their professional identities, negotiate authority, and integrate AI tools in ways that are aligned with their pedagogical values. At the organizational level, schools cultivate cultures of learning, reflective practice, and collaboration to support adaptation and sustain meaningful change.

Effective reskilling, therefore, involves a balance between technology and human development. Teachers are adaptive professionals, capable of shaping the integration of AI into their classrooms if their agency and reflective capacity are supported. Leadership is crucial in this process. Leaders articulate vision, model engagement, and create spaces for collaboration and experimentation (Senge, 1990). Schools that treat AI simply as an efficiency tool risk overlooking the relational and ethical dimensions of teaching. Those that foster reflective, dialogical engagement enable teachers to navigate the uncertainty, ambiguity, and potential of AI in ways that enhance both professional identity and institutional learning.

This chapter proposes a conceptual framework that foregrounds the interplay between individual identity work and collective organizational learning in AI-mediated contexts. Private language schools serve as illustrative sites where these dynamics unfold visibly and acutely. By situating reskilling within the complex negotiations of technological affordances, human expertise, and organizational culture, the chapter emphasizes the ethical and professional stakes of AI integration. Teachers are not passive recipients of technology; they are co-constructors of educational futures. Institutions are not inert structures; they are responsive systems whose cultures, policies, and leadership practices shape the potential for meaningful change. Understanding reskilling as a dialogical, multi-layered process illuminates pathways for integrating AI that respect human expertise, professional identity, and organizational sustainability.

2. CONCEPTUAL AND THEORETICAL FOUNDATIONS

The integration of AI into educational enterprises is transforming not only instructional processes but also the underlying dynamics of professional practice and organizational functioning. AI technologies such as adaptive learning systems, intelligent tutoring platforms, and automated assessment tools offer unprecedented opportunities for personalized instruction, efficiency, and scalability. However, these technological affordances do not exist in isolation. Their implementation interacts dynamically with human actors, institutional policies, and organizational structures, producing complex, sometimes unpredictable outcomes (Kesim et al., 2025). Private language schools, which operate in highly market-responsive contexts, provide an especially salient lens for examining these processes. Their smaller scale, flexible structures, and entrepreneurial leadership allow for rapid adoption of technological innovations, frequent iteration of teaching programs, and often more direct negotiation of pedagogical and institutional norms. This unique combination of agility and market accountability positions private language schools as critical sites for understanding teacher reskilling in AI-mediated educational environments.

Teacher reskilling in this context is far more than a technical exercise. It entails transformations in professional identity, shifts in agency, and reconfiguration of institutional culture. Scholarship on teachers' professional identity has long emphasized that identity is dynamic, socially constructed, and continually negotiated through interactions with students, colleagues, and institutional expectations (e.g., Day & Kington, 2008). The introduction of AI technologies adds a new dimension to this negotiation. Teachers must reconcile their understandings of expertise, pedagogical values, and ethical responsibilities with the affordances and limitations of intelligent systems. This identity work is iterative and relational, often marked by tensions between embracing technological possibilities and preserving humanistic educational principles (Lan, 2024). Some educators experience empowerment and expanded instructional capacity through AI, while others face uncertainty, role ambiguity, or a sense of diminished professional authority (Uras Eren & Atay, 2025). Understanding these divergent experiences requires attention to both individual reflection and the broader organizational environment in which teaching unfolds.

Organizational Learning Theory provides a complementary lens for understanding the systemic dimensions of reskilling. As articulated by Argyris and Schön (1978), organizational learning involves both single-loop and double-loop processes. Single-loop learning focuses on correcting errors within existing routines and assumptions, akin to superficial reskilling aimed only at mastering new technologies. Double-loop learning, by contrast, challenges underlying norms, policies, and values, fostering deep transformation at both individual and collective levels. In private language schools, effective reskilling requires engagement with double-loop learning: AI integration necessitates revisiting pedagogical approaches, assessment strategies, and organizational culture. Without this reflective, systemic dimension, reskilling risks remaining fragmented, tool-focused, or procedural rather than transformative.

The notion of a learning organization, as developed by Senge (1990), further illuminates how institutions can embed reskilling within ongoing organizational practice. Learning organizations cultivate environments in which individuals continuously expand their capacities, and collective learning drives systemic change. This perspective emphasizes that teacher reskilling cannot be isolated from institutional processes. Leadership, collaborative practices, and cultural norms play decisive roles in shaping whether AI integration enhances instructional quality, supports professional growth, or inadvertently produces resistance or disengagement (Nandini et al., 2022). In flexible, market-driven private language schools, leadership that models reflective practice, encourages experimentation, and aligns technological integration with pedagogical values can foster meaningful organizational adaptation.

The interaction between professional identity and organizational context is particularly salient in AI-mediated educational environments. Research shows that technological change can trigger uncertainty, heightened emotional labor, and renegotiation of role expectations (Xu et al., 2024). Emotional labour is amplified in private language schools, where teacher-student relationships are central to perceived quality and where market pressures heighten expectations for responsiveness and immediacy. Teachers are ethical and reflective agents, not merely technical operators. Reskilling initiatives that fail to account for the ethical and relational dimensions of teaching risk alienating educators or reducing reskilling to a purely instrumental exercise. By contrast, programs that incorporate reflective spaces, mentoring, and collaborative problem-solving enable teachers to reconstruct their professional identities while engaging deeply with AI-enhanced instructional practices (Ng et al., 2023).

Teacher agency intersects dynamically with organizational learning in shaping reskilling outcomes. Agency involves educators' capacity to act purposefully, make informed decisions, and influence their professional environment (Priestley et al., 2015). Within AI-mediated contexts, teacher agency manifests in critical engagement with technology, thoughtful adaptation of pedagogical strategies, and reflective assessment of the ethical and instructional implications of AI. Teachers exercise agency not in isolation but in negotiation with organizational culture, leadership expectations, and the affordances of technological systems. The relational and dialogical nature of this process underscores that reskilling is simultaneously an individual and collective endeavor.

AI also reconfigures the very nature of pedagogical roles. Adaptive learning systems and automated assessment platforms can redistribute cognitive and evaluative labour, necessitating new forms of expertise and instructional decision-making (Sottilare et al., 2017). Teachers must interpret algorithmic outputs, integrate automated feedback with human judgment, and mediate student learning in ways that harmonize technological efficiency with humanistic values. This relational tension between machine-driven precision and the interpretive, empathetic dimensions of teaching requires a reconceptualization of professional competence. Teacher reskilling, therefore, involves cultivating reflective expertise that integrates technical proficiency with ethical and pedagogical discernment.

Leadership and institutional culture mediate these processes. Studies of digital transformation highlight that participatory, reflective leadership encourages engagement and sustainable adaptation (Wang et al., 2022). In private language schools, leadership can foster experimentation, provide feedback, and model reflective practice, all of which shape whether reskilling supports identity reconstruction or remains a superficial exercise. Organizational support systems, including mentoring, collaborative communities, and continuous professional development, are essential for enabling teachers to navigate AI-induced shifts in pedagogical practice effectively. These mechanisms ensure that the adoption of AI becomes a site of collective learning and identity negotiation rather than a unilateral imposition of technology.

Ethical and relational considerations are inseparable from these processes. Teachers must navigate tensions between efficiency, equity, and professional integrity while integrating AI into their practice. Reskilling is not a neutral act; it entails ongoing negotiation between individual agency and organizational imperatives, between technological possibilities and pedagogical values (Ollington, 2025). This ethical dimension highlights the moral stakes inherent in teacher development and underscores the importance of designing interventions that respect and empower educators.

These perspectives illuminate teacher reskilling as a multi-layered, relational, and dialogical process. Professional identity, agency, organizational learning, and technological affordances co-evolve in AI-mediated educational environments. Teachers are active agents negotiating their roles and expertise, institutions are adaptive systems fostering collective growth, and AI serves as a catalyst for reflection, ethical consideration, and innovation. Conceptualizing reskilling in this integrated manner foregrounds both the human and organizational dimensions of digital transformation, providing a theoretical foundation for subsequent empirical inquiry and practical application.

3. RESKILLING IN PRIVATE LANGUAGE SCHOOLS: A CONCEPTUAL FRAMEWORK

The integration of AI in private language schools presents a profound challenge and opportunity for teacher reskilling, requiring attention to the multiple dimensions of professional practice, organizational adaptation, and the relational interplay between educators, learners, and technological systems. AI technologies, including adaptive learning platforms, automated feedback systems, and analytics-driven instructional tools, are redefining the nature of teaching in ways that are both exciting and disorienting. These tools provide opportunities for individualized learning pathways, offering real-time insights into student progress and enabling personalized pedagogical strategies that were previously impractical or impossible at scale (Tan et al., 2025). However, such affordances do not exist in a vacuum. Teachers, as human actors embedded in complex institutional ecosystems, negotiate their roles and identities in response to these new technological realities. Reskilling, therefore, extends far beyond acquiring technical proficiency; it involves reconsideration of pedagogical roles, recalibration of professional identity, engagement with emotional labour, and active participation in organizational learning processes.

The first layer of transformation emerges in the shifting roles of teachers within AI-mediated classrooms. Traditional conceptualizations of teaching have often emphasized the instructor as the primary source of knowledge, a conveyor of content, and an evaluator of learning outcomes. In contrast, AI technologies redistribute some of these functions, automating certain evaluative tasks, providing adaptive recommendations for instruction, and generating data-driven insights into student learning patterns. As a result, teachers increasingly adopt facilitative and interpretive roles, guiding students through AI-generated learning pathways rather than solely delivering content (Zhang et al., 2023). This evolution challenges entrenched pedagogical assumptions. Teachers are required to interpret algorithmic outputs, make judgments about their relevance, and integrate them with their professional understanding of student needs. Instructional expertise in this context becomes relational and hybrid, involving both human judgment and technologically mediated insights. Studies in educational technology emphasize that teachers' engagement with AI is most effective when they exercise agency to adapt tools critically, rather than passively implementing system-generated recommendations (Almazán-López et al., 2025; Sottilare et al., 2017). This shift, therefore, positions reskilling as an ongoing process of reflection, interpretation, and adaptation.

Professional identity represents the second, deeply interconnected dimension of reskilling. The scholarship on teacher identity stresses that professional self-conceptions are dynamic, socially constructed, and negotiated through experience, institutional expectations, and interactions with students and colleagues (Beijaard et al., 2004; Day & Kington, 2008). AI integration adds a new layer of complexity to these processes. As automated systems take on functions traditionally performed by humans such as grading, personalized instruction, or performance tracking, teachers may experience disruptions in their sense of professional authority and autonomy. Some may interpret these changes as liberating, allowing them to focus on higher-order pedagogical work or relational aspects of teaching. Others may perceive AI as an encroachment on their expertise, heightening feelings of uncertainty or diminished agency (Lan, 2024). Identity reconstruction, in this sense, becomes a central component of reskilling. Teachers must engage in iterative cycles of reflection, assessing how their values, professional goals, and ethical responsibilities intersect with the affordances of AI technologies. This work is often emotionally charged. Emotional labour, defined as "the effort, planning, and control needed to express organizationally desired emotion during interpersonal transactions" (Morris & Feldman, 1996, p. 987). It becomes particularly salient in AI-mediated settings where educators negotiate tensions between humanistic values and algorithmically driven efficiency. Supporting teachers in this negotiation requires professional development programs that recognize emotional dimensions of learning and adaptation, creating spaces for dialogue, reflection, and peer support.

Organizational culture, leadership, and collaboration form the institutional scaffolding that either facilitates or constrains these identity transformations. Private language schools are uniquely situated in this regard. Their typically flatter hierarchies, flexible structures, and market-driven imperatives allow for rapid experimentation and adjustment, yet these same characteristics may exacerbate role ambiguity and increase the demands on teachers navigating AI-induced change. Leadership is critical in shaping the contours of reskilling. Leaders who articulate clear visions, allocate resources for professional development, and model reflective engagement with AI technologies create environments conducive to meaningful adaptation (Geerts, 2024; Kovacevic, 2025). Conversely, leadership approaches that emphasize efficiency metrics or technical compliance over pedagogical and ethical considerations risk reducing reskilling to superficial training exercises. Collaborative practices, including peer mentoring, co-design of instructional strategies, and reflective professional learning communities, are instrumental in supporting teachers as they negotiate identity shifts and engage with AI systems (Adams & Thompson, 2025). These interactions highlight the relational nature of reskilling: adaptation is not merely an individual endeavor but emerges through dialogue, negotiation, and shared learning within institutional contexts.

Organizational learning theory provides a conceptual lens for understanding how schools can embed reskilling in sustainable practices. Argyris and Schön (1978) distinguish between single-loop and double-loop learning, offering insights into the depth and quality of organizational adaptation. Single-loop learning involves correcting errors within existing norms and procedures, akin to teachers learning to operate AI tools without reconsidering underlying pedagogical assumptions. Double-loop learning, by contrast, entails questioning and revising the assumptions, values, and policies that guide action. For private language schools seeking to integrate AI meaningfully, double-loop learning is essential. Institutions must reflect not only on the practical implementation of technology but also on how AI affects instructional philosophies, assessment paradigms, and professional development structures (Khlaif et al., 2025). Such learning is relational, iterative, and dialogical: teachers' experiences feed into organizational adaptation, while institutional policies, leadership practices, and cultural norms shape individual identity reconstruction.

This interplay underscores that reskilling is simultaneously an individual and organizational process.

The conceptual framework proposed here integrates three mutually reinforcing dimensions: professional identity, organizational learning, and AI integration. First, professional identity is situated at the core of reskilling. Teachers engage in reflective practice, critically assessing how AI technologies intersect with their values, expertise, and pedagogical goals. This reflection is both cognitive and emotional, requiring negotiation between technological affordances and ethical imperatives. Second, organizational learning ensures that reskilling transcends individual adaptation to influence institutional structures. Double-loop learning processes facilitate alignment between technology, pedagogical practice, and cultural norms, embedding AI integration within a coherent organizational strategy. Third, AI integration is approached not as an isolated technical implementation but as a collaborative, iterative process. Teachers, leaders, and support staff collectively shape how tools are deployed, interpreted, and leveraged to enhance both learning outcomes and professional development. This triadic model emphasizes the dynamic interplay between human and technological actors, situating reskilling within a socio-technical system in which learning, identity, and innovation co-evolve.

Importantly, the framework foregrounds the ethical and relational dimensions of AI-mediated reskilling. Teachers are moral agents who navigate competing demands: instructional efficacy, market responsiveness, professional integrity, and student well-being. AI systems do not replace these responsibilities; rather, they amplify them, requiring teachers to exercise judgment, interpretive skill, and reflective engagement (Ollington, 2025). Reskilling initiatives must recognize these dimensions, fostering spaces in which teachers can critically evaluate technology, reflect on pedagogical implications, and collaborate in co-constructing AI-enhanced learning experiences. This perspective also highlights the potential for AI to redistribute emotional and cognitive labour. By automating routine tasks, AI can free teachers to focus on relational and creative aspects of teaching, but only if institutional structures support such a shift and validate teachers' professional agency.

The relational and dialogical nature of reskilling also underscores the importance of feedback loops between individual and organizational levels. Teachers' experiences, reflections, and adaptations inform collective practices, contributing to iterative organizational learning. Simultaneously, leadership strategies, cultural norms, and institutional policies shape how teachers perceive, enact, and integrate AI-mediated practices. In private language schools, where market pressures heighten the immediacy of student expectations, these dynamics are particularly pronounced. Institutions that successfully navigate this complexity balance technological integration with human development, creating conditions for sustainable, identity-sensitive reskilling that enhances both instructional quality and organizational coherence (Satvati et al., 2025).

Reskilling in AI-mediated private language schools is therefore best conceptualized as a multi-layered, integrative process. It encompasses shifts in teacher identity, adaptation of organizational structures, and strategic engagement with AI technologies. Teachers exercise agency as reflective practitioners, reconstructing their professional roles while navigating emotional and ethical demands. Organizations facilitate these processes through leadership, collaborative cultures, and mechanisms for double-loop learning that embed AI adoption in pedagogical, structural, and cultural practices. AI technologies act as catalysts and mediators, enabling new forms of instructional practice, assessment, and professional development. Conceptualizing reskilling in this manner foregrounds the relational, dialogical, and ethical dimensions of adaptation, offering a comprehensive framework for understanding how private language schools can leverage AI not merely to enhance efficiency but to cultivate adaptive, reflective, and ethically grounded educational communities.

4. IMPLICATIONS FOR ORGANIZATIONAL BEHAVIOUR AND WORKFORCE DEVELOPMENT

The integration of artificial intelligence in private language schools carries profound implications for organizational behaviour and workforce development, extending far beyond the technical dimensions of skill acquisition to encompass leadership, institutional culture, and the relational dynamics of teacher learning. Leadership, in particular, assumes a central role in shaping how reskilling unfolds. Transformational leadership practices, which emphasize articulating a compelling vision, fostering professional autonomy, and facilitating collaborative problem-solving (Bass & Riggio, 2006), are critical for supporting teachers as they navigate the complex interplay between identity reconstruction and technological adaptation.

Leaders who actively engage with educators, model reflective practice, and create safe spaces for experimentation enable the organization to respond iteratively to the challenges posed by AI integration. Such leadership is not merely procedural; it is relational, fostering trust, shared purpose, and the sense that technological change can coexist with pedagogical integrity and professional growth. By contrast, leadership approaches that prioritize efficiency metrics or compliance with technical procedures risk reducing reskilling initiatives to superficial exercises that fail to transform instructional practices meaningfully (Senge, 1990).

Organizational support systems form the infrastructure that sustains these leadership practices and amplifies their effects. Structured professional development programs, peer mentoring, collaborative planning sessions, and reflective practice communities enable teachers to engage with AI technologies in ways that are both cognitively and emotionally sustainable (Nguyen & Barbieri, 2025). These systems provide channels for feedback, social learning, and the co-construction of knowledge, helping educators internalize AI-driven changes while preserving a sense of agency and professional purpose. In private language schools, where organizational hierarchies are often flatter and more flexible than in large public institutions, such support structures are particularly effective in embedding reskilling within the broader culture of the institution. They facilitate collective problem-solving and knowledge-sharing, fostering resilience and adaptability among staff, and ensuring that AI adoption enhances rather than undermines educational quality.

The implications for workforce development are equally significant. In AI-enabled business sectors, research indicates that successful reskilling combines technical proficiency with identity and role transformation, leveraging continuous learning loops, feedback mechanisms, and participatory design of work processes (Kane et al., 2019; Nambisan et al., 2017). Translating these insights to educational contexts suggests that teacher reskilling should not be narrowly conceived as training to operate AI tools. Instead, it must engage with pedagogical assumptions, redefine teacher-student interactions, and cultivate reflective professional identities. Teachers are not passive recipients of technological innovation; they are active agents whose judgments, values, and ethical considerations shape the implementation and impact of AI within the classroom (Zhai, 2024; Shams Eldin, 2025)

Effective workforce development, therefore, requires creating mechanisms that enable teachers to experiment with AI-mediated practices, reflect critically on their implications, and integrate new competencies into evolving professional roles.

Reskilling initiatives must also account for the emotional and ethical dimensions of workforce development. The introduction of AI can generate role ambiguity, heightened emotional labour, and stress associated with the negotiation of professional identity (Kim & Lee, 2024). Teachers must navigate tensions between efficiency and humanistic values, between institutional expectations and personal pedagogy, and between algorithmic decision-making and ethical responsibility. Organizational strategies that acknowledge these dimensions through mentoring, peer support, reflective sessions, and psychologically safe spaces can mitigate negative consequences and reinforce adaptive capacities. From an organizational behaviour perspective, this approach aligns with theories of job crafting and work engagement, which suggest that when employees perceive alignment between their skills, roles, and values, they are more motivated, resilient, and capable of sustaining change (Grant & Parker, 2009; Wrzesniewski & Dutton, 2001).

The culture of the institution is another crucial determinant of reskilling outcomes. Private language schools often operate in competitive, market-driven environments where responsiveness to learner needs and innovation are central to organizational survival. In such contexts, fostering a culture that values experimentation, reflection, and collaborative learning is essential. Senge's (1990) notion of a learning organization provides a useful lens: institutions must create systems where knowledge flows freely, feedback loops inform both teaching and managerial practices, and continuous professional learning is embedded within everyday routines. Organizational norms that encourage open dialogue, tolerate mistakes as opportunities for learning, and recognize the professional contributions of teachers in AI-mediated environments contribute to workforce resilience and the long-term sustainability of reskilling initiatives (Golgeci et al., 2025).

Insights from organizational behaviour research also highlight the importance of distributed leadership and participatory approaches in supporting workforce development. Teachers, administrators, and technical staff who collaborate in co-designing AI integration strategies are more likely to experience ownership, commitment, and professional growth (Ravi et al., 2025; Alahmari, 2025; Awad, 2025). Participatory structures allow for negotiation of roles, co-construction of norms, and alignment of technology with pedagogical values. They also create conditions for double-loop learning, in which both individual practices and underlying assumptions are questioned and adapted. In AI-mediated classrooms, such iterative processes are necessary to ensure that reskilling is not merely procedural but transformative, fostering adaptive expertise and reflective professional identities.

Private language schools can draw on lessons from digital reskilling strategies in broader industries to enhance workforce development. In sectors such as finance, healthcare, and manufacturing, successful digital transformation emphasizes integrated approaches that combine technical training with mentoring, reflective practice, and role negotiation (Tsekouropoulos, 2025). In educational contexts, this implies that reskilling should facilitate teachers' engagement with new roles as facilitators of AI-enhanced learning, interpreters of algorithmic feedback, and designers of individualized pedagogical pathways. By embedding these processes within institutional strategies, language schools can ensure alignment between organizational goals, teacher agency, and student outcomes, thereby achieving more robust and sustainable forms of workforce development.

Finally, the implications for workforce resilience extend beyond immediate technological adaptation. AI integration is a continuous and evolving process, and teachers must be equipped not only with current technical skills but also with the capacity for ongoing learning, critical reflection, and professional adaptability. Cultivating such capacities requires a holistic approach that attends to the interplay between individual cognition, emotional experience, organizational culture, and leadership practices (Daher, 2025). Workforce development, therefore, becomes an ethical as well as strategic endeavour, involving careful attention to the well-being, professional identity, and agency of educators as they engage with transformative technologies.

5. CONCLUSION AND EXPECTED CONTRIBUTION

This chapter advances the understanding of teacher reskilling in AI-mediated educational contexts by framing it not merely as a technical adjustment but as a complex, relational, and identity-driven process, in which individual, organizational, and technological dimensions intersect in dynamic and often unpredictable ways. In foregrounding the interplay between teachers' professional identities, institutional learning processes, and the affordances of AI technologies, it challenges reductive conceptions of reskilling as the simple acquisition of procedural skills or familiarity with digital tools. Instead, reskilling is conceptualized as an ongoing negotiation, in which teachers must reconcile their existing pedagogical knowledge, ethical commitments, and professional self-conceptions with new forms of practice that AI systems introduce. This negotiation is not only cognitive but also emotional, encompassing the labour of reconciling uncertainty, managing change, and sustaining a sense of agency in environments where the boundaries of human expertise are being reconfigured (Nguyen & Barbieri, 2025). Such a perspective draws on scholarship in organizational behaviour and organizational learning, which underscores the relational and contextual nature of adaptation, highlighting the importance of leadership, culture, and institutional support as mediators of workforce development (Argyris & Schön, 1978; Senge, 1990).

A central contribution of this work is the conceptualization of reskilling as a dual-level phenomenon. On the individual level, teachers engage in identity reconstruction, revising role expectations, pedagogical priorities, and self-perceptions in the light of AI-mediated instructional possibilities. This involves reflective practice, critical evaluation of technological affordances, and iterative experimentation with instructional strategies, all situated within the ethical and relational dimensions of professional life (Satvati et al., 2025). On the institutional level, private language schools engage in organizational learning processes that extend beyond procedural training, encompassing double-loop learning in which underlying assumptions, norms, and values are interrogated to align with AI-enhanced practices. The dynamic interplay between these levels illustrates that effective reskilling cannot be imposed top-down nor left entirely to individual initiative. Rather, it emerges through ongoing dialogue, negotiation, and co-construction, in which teachers' experiences inform institutional adaptation and, reciprocally, organizational strategies shape the trajectories of professional identity development.

This dual-level lens also sheds light on the ethical and relational stakes of reskilling in AI-mediated environments. Teachers' engagement with AI technologies is inseparable from considerations of equity, inclusivity, and pedagogical integrity, and institutional strategies must support not only technical proficiency but also the cultivation of professional judgment and reflective capacity (Akgun & Greenhow, 2021). Leadership is pivotal in this regard, as it shapes organizational norms, models reflective engagement, and mediates the tensions between efficiency imperatives and human-centered educational values (Bass & Riggio, 2006). Organizational culture, likewise, plays a critical role in sustaining adaptive learning communities, fostering resilience, and promoting the socialization of new practices (Senge, 1990) while maintaining coherence with established pedagogical principles (Priestley et al., 2015). The ethical dimensions of reskilling, therefore, are intertwined with relational dynamics, requiring attention to both the professional well-being of teachers and the integrity of educational outcomes.

From a workforce development perspective, this chapter offers a nuanced understanding of the conditions under which AI-driven reskilling can be sustainable and meaningful. Drawing parallels with digital transformation initiatives in other sectors, such as healthcare, finance, and manufacturing (e.g., Kim & Lee, 2024; Tsekouropoulos et al., 2025), it emphasizes the integration of technical skill acquisition with identity work, participatory design, and continuous feedback mechanisms. In educational settings, these principles translate into professional development programs that combine experiential learning, collaborative problem-solving, and reflective practice. Such programs do not merely enhance operational competence but cultivate adaptive expertise, enabling teachers to interpret algorithmic outputs critically, design personalized learning pathways, and navigate the evolving social and ethical landscape of AI-mediated instruction (Almazán-López et al., 2025). By situating reskilling within this broader human-centered framework, the chapter highlights the interdependence of individual, organizational, and technological factors in shaping both professional identity and institutional capacity.

The expected contribution of this work is therefore both conceptual and practical. Conceptually, it bridges research on teacher identity, organizational learning, and workforce development, offering a model of reskilling that foregrounds relational and ethical considerations alongside technical competence. It demonstrates that reskilling is not a linear process but a multi-dimensional negotiation, shaped by interactions between teachers, peers, leaders, and institutional structures, and mediated by the affordances and limitations of AI technologies (Lan, 2024). Practically, the chapter provides a framework for educational leaders and policymakers seeking to implement AI integration in ways that enhance professional agency, sustain pedagogical quality, and embed learning within organizational culture. It underscores the importance of participatory, reflective, and ethically informed approaches to workforce development, suggesting that sustainable adaptation requires attention to identity reconstruction, emotional labour, and collaborative problem-solving as much as technical training.

The chapter also contributes to ongoing discussions about the human dimensions of digital transformation. In framing AI not merely as a tool but as a mediator of professional practice, it challenges assumptions that technological adoption is synonymous with improvement. Instead, it highlights the relational, interpretive, and ethical work that teachers undertake to integrate AI meaningfully into their practice, and the organizational conditions required to support such work (Lan, 2024; Ollington, 2025). By emphasizing the dialogical nature of adaptation, in which teachers' experiences shape institutional strategies and institutional policies shape professional identity, the chapter offers a model of reskilling that is both reflective and actionable, bridging theory and practice in ways that can inform educational contexts as well as broader workforce development initiatives.

In conclusion, this chapter positions teacher reskilling in AI-mediated contexts as a profoundly relational, ethical, and identity-sensitive process, one that unfolds across multiple levels of activity and requires the integration of technical, organizational, and human dimensions. Its contribution lies in articulating a conceptual framework that foregrounds the interplay between individual professional identity, organizational learning, and technological integration, highlighting the conditions under which AI can enhance both teaching effectiveness and institutional adaptability. By offering a nuanced, dialogical, and ethically aware lens on workforce development, the chapter provides insights that extend beyond immediate educational practice to inform wider debates about human-centered digital transformation, adaptive leadership, and the cultivation of resilient, reflective, and ethically engaged professional communities. Ultimately, it suggests that the success of AI integration depends less on the sophistication of the technology itself than on the capacity of teachers and institutions to engage in sustained, reflective, and collaborative processes of learning, identity reconstruction, and organizational adaptation.

REFERENCES

Adams, D., & Thompson, P. (2025). Transforming School Leadership with Artificial Intelligence: Applications, Implications, and Future Directions. *Leadership and Policy in Schools*, *24*, 77–89.

Akgun, S., & Greenhow, C. (2021). Artificial intelligence in education: Addressing ethical challenges in K-12 settings. *AI and Ethics*, *3*(3), 431–440. DOI: 10.1007/s43681-021-00096-7 PMID: 34790956

Alahmari, D., & Awad, A. (2025). Strategic integration of marketing and supply chain functions for superior customer experience: Insights from logistics startups under Saudi Vision 2030. *PLoS One*, *20*(11), e0336132. DOI: 10.1371/journal.pone.0336132 PMID: 41270081

Almazán-López, O., Hasbún, H., & Osuna-Acedo, S. (2025). Generative artificial intelligence and (post)digital teacher identity. *IJERI: International Journal of Educational Research and Innovation*, *24*, 1–17. DOI: 10.46661/ijeri.11160

An, X., Chai, C. S., Li, Y., Zhou, Y., Shen, X., Zheng, C., & Chen, M. (2022). Modeling English teachers' behavioral intention to use artificial intelligence in middle schools. *Education and Information Technologies*, *5*(5), 5187–5208. DOI: 10.1007/s10639-022-11286-z

Argyris, C., & Schön, D. A. (1978). *Organizational learning: A theory of action perspective*. Addison-Wesley.

Awad, A. (2025). Enhancing market access and consumer engagement through digital marketing in the agricultural sector. *International Journal of Advanced and Applied Sciences*, *12*(8), 70–79. DOI: 10.21833/ijaas.2025.08.007

Bass, B. M., & Riggio, R. E. (2006). *Transformational leadership*. Taylor & Francis Group. DOI: 10.4324/9781410617095

Beijaard, D., Meijer, P. C., & Verloop, N. (2004). Reconsidering research on teachers' professional identity. *Teaching and Teacher Education*, *2*(2), 107–128. DOI: 10.1016/j.tate.2003.07.001

Coldron, J., & Smith, R. (1999). Active location in teachers' construction of their professional identities. *Journal of Curriculum Studies*, *31*(6), 711–726. DOI: 10.1080/002202799182954

Daher, R. (2025). Integrating AI literacy into teacher education: A critical perspective paper. *Discover Artificial Intelligence*, *5*(1), 217. DOI: 10.1007/s44163-025-00475-7

Darling-Hammond, L., Hyler, M. E., & Gardner, M. (2017). *Effective teacher professional development.* Learning Policy Institute. DOI: 10.54300/122.311

Day, C., & Kington, A. (2008). Identity, well-being and effectiveness: The emotional contexts of teaching. *Pedagogy, Culture & Society, 16*(1), 7–23. DOI: 10.1080/14681360701877743

Day, C., Kington, A., Stobart, G., & Sammons, P. (2006). The personal and professional selves of teachers: Stable and unstable identities. *British Educational Research Journal, 32*(4), 601–616. DOI: 10.1080/01411920600775316

Desimone, L. M. (2009). Improving Impact Studies of Teachers' Professional Development: Toward Better Conceptualizations and Measures. *Educational Researcher, 38*(3), 181–199. DOI: 10.3102/0013189X08331140

Geerts, J. M. (2024). Maximizing the Impact and ROI of leadership development: A theory- and evidence-informed framework. *Behavioral Sciences (Basel, Switzerland), 14*(10), 955. DOI: 10.3390/bs14100955 PMID: 39457826

Golgeci, I., Ritala, P., Arslan, A., McKenna, B., & Ali, I. (2025). Confronting and alleviating AI resistance in the workplace: An integrative review and a process framework. *Human Resource Management Review, 35*(2), 101075. DOI: 10.1016/j.hrmr.2024.101075

Grant, A. M., & Parker, S. K. (2009). Redesigning work design theories: The rise of relational and proactive perspectives. *The Academy of Management Annals, 3*(1), 317–375. DOI: 10.5465/19416520903047327

Kane, G. C., Palmer, D., Phillips, A., Kiron, D., & Buckley, N. (2019). Accelerating digital innovation inside and out. *MIT Sloan Management Review.*

Kesim, E., Atmaca, T., & Turan, S. (2025). Reshaping school cultures: AI's influence on organizational dynamics and leadership behaviors. *Leadership and Policy in Schools, 24*(1), 117–136. DOI: 10.1080/15700763.2024.2413703

Khlaif, Z. N., Alkouk, W. A., Salama, N., & Abu Eideh, B. (2025). Redesigning assessments for AI-enhanced learning: A framework for educators in the generative AI era. *Education Sciences, 15*(2), 174. DOI: 10.3390/educsci15020174

Kim, B. J., & Lee, J. (2024). The mental health implications of artificial intelligence adoption: The crucial role of self-efficacy. *Humanities & Social Sciences Communications, 11*(1), 1561. DOI: 10.1057/s41599-024-04018-w

Kovacevic, M., Dagen, T., & Rajter, M. (2025). Leading AI-driven student engagement: The role of digital leadership in higher education. *Education Sciences*, *15*(6), 775. DOI: 10.3390/educsci15060775

Lan, Y. (2024). Through tensions to identity-based motivations: Exploring teacher professional identity in artificial intelligence-enhanced teacher training. *Teaching and Teacher Education*, *104736*, 104736. Advance online publication. DOI: 10.1016/j.tate.2024.104736

Morris, J. A., & Feldman, D. C. (1996). The dimensions, antecedents, and consequences of emotional labor. *Academy of Management Review*, *21*(4), 986–1010. DOI: 10.2307/259161

Nambisan, S., Lyytinen, K., Majchrzak, A., & Song, M. (2017). Digital innovation management: Reinventing innovation management research in a digital world. *Management Information Systems Quarterly*, *41*(1), 223–238. DOI: 10.25300/MISQ/2017/41:1.03

Nandini, W., Gustomo, A., & Sushandoyo, D. (2022). The mechanism of an individual's internal process of work engagement, active learning and adaptive performance. *Economies*, *7*(7), 165. DOI: 10.3390/economies10070165

Ng, D. T. K., Leung, J. K. L., Su, J., Ng, R. C. W., & Chu, S. K. W. (2023). Teachers' AI digital competencies and twenty-first century skills in the post-pandemic world. *Educational Technology Research and Development*, *1*(1), 137–161. DOI: 10.1007/s11423-023-10203-6 PMID: 36844361

Nguyen, N. N., & Barbieri, W. (2025). Mentorship in the age of generative AI: ChatGPT to support self-regulated learning of pre-service teachers before and during placements. *Education Sciences*, *15*(6), 642. DOI: 10.3390/educsci15060642

Ollington, N. (2025). Challenging assumptions: AI and teacher assessment identity formation. *The Australian Journal of Teacher Education*, *2*(2). Advance online publication. DOI: 10.14221/1835-517X.6510

Priestley, M., Biesta, G., & Robinson, S. (2015). *Teacher agency: An ecological approach*. Bloomsbury Publishing. DOI: 10.4324/9781315678573-15

Qiao, G., Li, Y., & Hong, A. (2024). The strategic role of digital transformation: Leveraging digital leadership to enhance employee performance and organizational commitment in the digital era. *Systems*, *12*(11), 457. DOI: 10.3390/systems12110457

Ravi, P., Masla, J., Kakoti, G., Lin, G., Anderson, E., Taylor, M., Ostrowski, A., Breazeal, C., Klopfer, E., & Abelson, H. (2025). Co-designing large language model tools for project-based learning with K–12 educators. *CHI '25: Proceedings of the 2025 CHI Conference on Human Factors in Computing Systems, 138,* 1-25. DOI: 10.1145/3706598.3713971

Satvati, N., Kamali, J., Safian Boldaji, F., Khodadadi, M., & Akhondi, S. (2025). AI Integration into language education and teacher identity: An ecological perspective. *Language Teaching Research Quarterly*, *47*, 1–19. DOI: 10.32038/ltrq.2025.47.01

Schein, E. H. (2010). *Organizational Culture and Leadership* (4th ed.). Jossey-Bass.

Schön, D. A. (1992). *The reflective practitioner: How professionals think in action* (1st ed.). Routledge.

Senge, P. (1990). *The fifth discipline: The art and practice of the learning organization.* Doubleday/Currency.

Shams Eldin, A. Y., Elnour, A., Hassan, R. O. A., & Awad, A. (2025). The role of technological and environmental factors in creating business value from social media dynamic capabilities for SMEs in Saudi Arabia. *Humanities & Social Sciences Communications, 12*(1), 1431. DOI: 10.1057/s41599-025-05784-x

Sottilare, R. A., Shawn Burke, C., Salas, E., Sinatra, A. M., Johnston, J. H., & Gilbert, S. B. (2017). Designing adaptive instruction for teams: A meta-analysis. *International Journal of Artificial Intelligence in Education*, *2*(2), 225–264. DOI: 10.1007/s40593-017-0146-z

Tan, X., Cheng, G., & Ling, M. H. (2025). Artificial intelligence in teaching and teacher professional development: A systematic review. *Computers and Education: Artificial Intelligence*, *100355*, 100355. Advance online publication. DOI: 10.1016/j.caeai.2024.100355

Tsekouropoulos, G., Vasileiou, A., Hoxha, G., Theocharis, D., Theodoridou, E., & Grigoriadis, T. (2025). Leadership 4.0: Navigating the challenges of the digital transformation in healthcare and beyond. *Administrative Sciences*, *15*(6), 194. DOI: 10.3390/admsci15060194

Uras Eren, E., & Atay, D. (2025). Constructing professional identities: The role of school climate in early-career university teachers. *Asian-Pacific Journal of Second and Foreign Language Education*, *10*(1), 1–19. DOI: 10.1186/s40862-025-00329-w

Wang, T., Lin, X., & Sheng, F. (2022). Digital leadership and exploratory innovation: From the dual perspectives of strategic orientation and organizational culture. *Frontiers in Psychology*, *13*, 1–20. DOI: 10.3389/fpsyg.2022.902693 PMID: 36176785

Wrzesniewski, A., & Dutton, J. E. (2001). Crafting a job: Revisioning employees as active crafters of their work. *Academy of Management Review*, *26*(2), 179–201. DOI: 10.2307/259118

Xu, L., Liu, X., & Xiao, Y. (2024). Language teachers' emotions in online classrooms: Relations among teachers' appraisals of classroom events, emotional responses, and instructional practices. *Asian-Pacific Journal of Second and Foreign Language Education*, *1*(1), 1–23. DOI: 10.1186/s40862-024-00301-0

Zhai, X. (2024). Transforming teachers' roles and agencies in the era of generative AI: Perceptions, acceptance, knowledge, and practices. *Journal of Science Education and Technology*. Advance online publication. DOI: 10.1007/s10956-024-10174-0

Zhang, C., Schießl, J., Plößl, L., Hofmann, F., & Gläser-Zikuda, M. (2023). Acceptance of artificial intelligence among pre-service teachers: A multigroup analysis. *International Journal of Educational Technology in Higher Education*, *20*(1), 49. DOI: 10.1186/s41239-023-00420-7

ADDITIONAL READING

Priestley, M., Biesta, G., & Robinson, S. (2015). *Teacher agency: An ecological approach*. Bloomsbury Publishing. DOI: 10.4324/9781315678573-15

Tan, X., Cheng, G., & Ling, M. H. (2025). Artificial intelligence in teaching and teacher professional development: A systematic review. *Computers and Education: Artificial Intelligence*, *100355*. Advance online publication. DOI: 10.1016/j.caeai.2024.100355

Yang, Y., Zhang, Y., Sun, D., He, W., & Wei, Y. (2025). Navigating the landscape of AI literacy education: Insights from a decade of research (2014–2024). *Humanities & Social Sciences Communications*, *12*(1), 374. DOI: 10.1057/s41599-025-04583-8

KEY TERMS AND DEFINITIONS

Adaptive Expertise: Adaptive expertise describes the capacity of professionals to respond flexibly to novel situations, integrate new knowledge with existing skills, and apply reflective judgement (Hatano & Inagaki, 1986). Teachers develop adaptive expertise when they engage critically with AI tools, interpret data-driven insights, and adjust pedagogical approaches accordingly.

Artificial Intelligence (AI): AI refers to computational systems capable of performing tasks that typically require human intelligence, including problem-solving, pattern recognition, and adaptive decision-making. In educational contexts, AI includes technologies such as adaptive learning systems, automated assessment tools, and intelligent tutoring platforms, which can support personalized learning while reshaping teaching roles (Sottilare et al., 2017).

Digital Transformation: Digital transformation denotes the strategic integration of digital technologies to modify work processes, roles, and organizational culture (Qiao et al, 2024). In educational contexts, it encompasses both the technological adoption of AI tools and the corresponding adaptation of teachers' professional roles and identities.

Double-Loop Learning: This concept refers to organizational reflection that goes beyond correcting errors to re-examining underlying policies, norms, and objectives. In the context of AI integration, it entails rethinking teaching models, evaluation systems, and institutional culture to support meaningful technological adoption (Argyris & Schön, 1978).

Emotional Labour: Emotional labour refers to the process by which professionals manage and regulate their emotions to meet organizational expectations, often involving the suppression or expression of feelings to conform to institutional norms (Hochschild, 1983). In teaching, this includes managing affective interactions with students and colleagues, especially when adapting to AI-mediated changes in classroom practice.

Leadership in AI Integration: Leadership in this context refers to the capacity of educational leaders to guide, support, and model adaptive and ethical engagement with AI technologies. Transformational leadership that promotes collaboration, autonomy, and participatory problem-solving is particularly effective in supporting teacher reskilling (Bass & Riggio, 2006).

Organizational Culture: Organizational culture encompasses the shared values, norms, and practices that influence behavior within an institution (Schein, 2010). A culture that promotes collaboration, reflective practice, and experimentation is essential for sustaining teacher reskilling initiatives and fostering meaningful AI integration.

Organizational Learning: Organizational learning is the process through which institutions acquire, interpret, and apply knowledge to adapt and improve practices. Double-loop learning, in particular, involves questioning foundational assumptions and institutional norms, fostering transformation rather than superficial adjustment (Argyris & Schön, 1978).

Professional Development: Professional development involves structured learning opportunities designed to enhance teachers' knowledge, skills, and professional growth (Desimone, 2009). In AI-mediated settings, professional development must address technical competence, pedagogical adaptation, and identity reconstruction.

Professional Identity: Teachers' professional identity is the dynamic self-concept shaped by their beliefs, experiences, and interactions within professional environments. It evolves as teachers negotiate their roles, responsibilities, and sense of agency in response to contextual changes (Beijaard et al., 2004).

Reflective Practice: Reflective practice is the ongoing process by which individuals critically examine their experiences, decisions, and outcomes to inform future practice Schön, 1992). It supports professional growth and identity reconstruction during periods of technological and organizational change.

Single-Loop Learning: Single-loop learning involves detecting and correcting errors or deviations within existing rules, assumptions, or practices without questioning underlying values or goals (Argyris & Schön, 1978). In educational contexts, this type of learning corresponds to surface-level reskilling, where teachers acquire new technical skills for AI tools but do not reconsider broader pedagogical approaches, professional identity, or institutional culture.

Socio-Technical Adaptation: Socio-technical adaptation refers to the integrated adjustment of both social and technical systems within an organization (Sottilare et al., 2017). In private language schools, this encompasses how teachers, leaders, and AI tools interact, co-constructing new workflows, pedagogical strategies, and professional practices.

Teacher Agency: Teacher agency refers to the capacity of educators to make informed, intentional choices that shape their professional practice and learning trajectories (Priestley et al., 2015). Agency is exercised when teachers critically engage with AI technologies, co-design instructional strategies, and negotiate institutional policies.

Teacher Reskilling: Teacher reskilling involves not only acquiring technical competencies to operate new tools but also revising pedagogical strategies, professional identity, and reflective practice to align with evolving educational demands (Lan, 2024). It is a multidimensional process encompassing technical, cognitive, and socio-emotional adaptation.

Chapter 3

AI in Online Education: A Survey-Based Study on Student Preferences and Human-AI Collaboration

Behzad Esmaeilian
https://orcid.org/0009-0003-6276-6060
Tuskegee University, USA

Kushagra Kushagra
Tuskegee University, USA

Ummey Honey
Tuskegee University, USA

Mohammad Rahman
Tuskegee University, USA

ABSTRACT

As artificial intelligence (AI) becomes an integral component of online education, important questions arise about how it influences learner trust, engagement, and preferences for various instructional models. This study investigates user perceptions of AI-powered tools in online learning by performing a structured survey. The survey evaluates trust in AI-generated study materials, engagement with AI-driven features, and preferences for AI-assisted instructional formats. To analyze these perceptions, the authors test four main hypotheses: (H1) trust in AI-generated educational content and AI-powered instructors, (H2) the impact of AI-driven tools on engagement and personalization, (H3) AI's influence on learning preferences and instructional models, and (H4) perceptions of AI-powered tools in engineering design education. The study uses statistical analyses, including ANOVA, to assess differences in trust

DOI: 10.4018/979-8-3373-7416-1.ch003

and engagement based on prior AI experience and K-Means clustering to identify separate user trust profiles. Results show that frequent AI users are more comfortable with AI-generated study materials but are cautious about fully autonomous AI-driven instruction. Responses about engagement with AI-powered features showed mixed interest in real-time AI feedback, chat moderation, and interactive learning tools. Instructional preferences show a strong preference for hybrid models where AI supplements, rather than replaces, human instruction. In engineering design education, respondents value AI-assisted design tools, particularly for simulations and automated feedback, but emphasize the need for human validation.

INTRODUCTION

Artificial intelligence (AI) has become an increasingly integral part of online learning environments, influencing how students access information, interact in virtual classrooms, and receive feedback. As AI-driven tutoring systems gain widespread attention, understanding how learners trust, engage with, and ultimately prefer to use these technologies has become essential. Despite the rapid expansion of AI in online education, there are limited empirical insight into how students evaluate AI-powered engagement features, and AI-assisted instructional models particularly in technical fields such as engineering design, where accuracy, creativity, and human judgment are important. This chapter addresses that need by presenting a survey-based study that examines user perceptions in four main dimensions: trust in AI-generated materials and AI-powered instructors, engagement with AI-driven learning features, preferences for AI-supported instructional formats, and perceptions of AI tools in engineering design education. The chapter analyzes these themes through statistical methods and provides a foundation for understanding how AI can be incorporated into education in ways that improve learning while maintaining human-centered oversight.

BACKGROUND

Trust in AI-driven learning platforms is fundamental for user acceptance and successful implementation. Extensive research has been done to assess factors impacting trust in AI-generated educational content. To name a few, Qin et al. (Qin et al., 2020) identified the main trust determining factors, including functionality, helpfulness, interpretability, dependability, and interaction interface, alongside contextual and individual factors such as institutional benevolence and users' perception of AI autonomy. Nazaretsky et al. (Nazaretsky et al., 2022) developed an instrument to measure teachers' trust in AI-based educational technology and identified eight influencing factors: perceived benefits, lack of human characteristics, lack of transparency, AI-related anxieties, self-efficacy, pedagogical shifts, trust-building strategies, and AI versus human recommendations. Similarly, Majjate et al. (Majjate et al., 2024) investigated ethical concerns in AI-powered recommendation systems and found that transparency improves trust, however, excessive transparency can lead to information overload and disengagement.

Engagement is another critical factor in AI-powered education. Bhatia et al. (Bhatia et al., 2024) studied the role of AI in student engagement and showed how intelligent tutoring systems and flexible learning platforms improve participation. Their results demonstrate that AI-driven assessments and feedback mechanisms improve learning outcomes through personalized recommendations. Geroche and Guay (Geroche & Guay, 2024) analyzed factors influencing student engagement in AI-powered education and revealed that Instructor Knowledge did not significantly impact engagement, whereas strong Instructor Support positively correlated with engagement. They also found that excessive AI tool availability negatively affected engagement. Fang and Tse (Fang & Tse, 2022; Ghonim et.al., 2024) reinforced these results and showed AI applications improve student engagement when privacy concerns are adequately addressed.

AI's ability to personalize learning experiences is one of its most significant contributions. Rane et al. (Rane et al., 2023; Awad, 2024) discussed the shift from standardized education models to Education 4.0 and 5.0, where AI continuously adjusts instructional strategies based on real-time feedback. Their study shows the benefits of machine learning algorithms in optimizing learning pathways. Dhananjaya et al. (Gm et al., 2024) reviewed AI-powered recommendation systems and concluded that collaborative and content-based filtering methods improve personalization. However, they identified major challenges, including content misalignment, language barriers, and inadequate infrastructure, which hinder the performance of AI-assisted education.

Hybrid learning models increasingly integrate AI-driven tools. Joseph et al. (Joseph et al., 2024) reviewed the impact of AI on hybrid education and emphasized its role in improving student collaboration, communication, and real-time feedback. Similarly, Sadegh-Zadeh et al. (Sadegh-Zadeh et al., 2023) investigated student perceptions of AI-powered online courses and found that AI-driven engagement tools, particularly Microsoft Teams' real-time recommendations, significantly improved student participation and comprehension.

AI adoption in engineering education is gaining traction, particularly in design automation, simulations, and feedback mechanisms. Lai (Lai, 2021) employed drawing analysis and the activity theory framework to explore student preferences for AI-assisted learning environments and found that students valued personalized guidance and robotic learning companions. Ajani et al. (Ajani et al., 2024) analyzed AI's role in improving teaching quality and critical engagement and recommended that although AI-powered tools enhance learning, educators should consider the trade-off between technological advancements with ethical considerations and pedagogical strategies.

The existing studies provide a valuable understanding of the role of AI in education; however, several gaps still exist. Research on AI's influence on instructional preferences and engagement strategies is limited, particularly in engineering education. Also, prior studies mainly focus on AI's benefits without addressing users' concerns about fully autonomous AI-driven instruction. Moreover, there is limited analysis using statistical techniques to classify user trust profiles and engagement patterns. This study aims to overcome these gaps by using statistical analyses, including ANOVA and K-Means clustering, to examine trust, engagement, and instructional preferences in AI-powered education. It investigates the role of AI-powered tools in reforming online education by analyzing users' responses about their perceptions, trust, and engagement with AI-driven instructional methods.

METHODOLOGY

A survey consisting of 28 multiple-choice and open-ended questions was designed to capture user perceptions of trust, engagement, learning preferences, and instructional models in AI-powered online education, with a specific emphasis on livestream-based learning. The survey was structured to assess user confidence in AI-generated content and instructors, the effectiveness of AI-driven engagement tools, and preferences for AI-assisted instructional formats. A total of 83 responses were collected on how AI-powered tools influence digital learning experiences and user acceptance of AI-driven education models.

The aim is to identify the main factors that form user perceptions of AI-powered online learning, including trust, engagement, learning preferences, and instructional models. Trust in AI-driven education is examined through users' confidence in AI-generated content, AI instructors, and automated decision-making in learning environments. Engagement is analyzed by evaluating the effectiveness of AI-powered tools such as real-time feedback, chat moderation, and adaptive learning systems in improving student interaction and personalization. Learning preferences and instructional models are assessed by investigating how AI influences the implementation of short, interactive lessons, peer-led learning, and AI-assisted tutoring. In addition, this study places a specific emphasis on AI integration in engineering design education, examining user preferences for AI-powered design tools, trust in

AI-generated engineering outputs, and the role of digital platforms in supporting engineering learning experiences.

RESULTS

The results of this study are presented under four main hypotheses that describe user perceptions of AI in online education. H1 investigates trust in AI-generated educational content and AI-powered instructors by describing how users perceive AI-generated study materials, robot teachers, and AI-driven design outputs compared to human alternatives. H2 evaluates the role of AI-powered tools in improving engagement and personalization by describing AI-driven features such as real-time feedback, chat moderation, and facial expression analysis that users describe would improve their interaction and learning experiences. H3 analyzes AI's impact on learning preferences and instructional models, by discussing whether AI-driven instruction influences preferences for shorter, interactive lessons and peer-led study formats. H4 examines perceptions of AI in engineering design education by investigating user preferences for AI-assisted design tools and trust in AI-generated engineering outputs.

Student Perspectives on AI in Online Education

The survey mainly depicted student perspectives, as 97.6% of respondents identified as students (Q1), with only 2.4% being teachers or other educational professionals. Livestream-based education is widely utilized, with 56.6% of participants regularly attending or conducting classes via platforms such as Zoom and YouTube Live, and 39.8% have participated occasionally (Q2). AI-powered engagement tools are met with mixed interest: 49.4% of respondents expressed a preference for real-time AI feedback on participation and engagement, whereas 20.5% opposed such features (Q3). Also, AI tool adoption is prevalent, as 86.7% have used AI-powered tools in their online education experience, with 33.7% using them frequently (Q5).

Students also shared which AI features they believe would genuinely improve the quality of livestream-based classes (Q4). Their responses show a clear pattern: tools that make content easier to follow and review are the most valued. Real-time speech-to-text transcription was the top choice, selected by about three-quarters of respondents, closely followed by automated lecture summarization (Figure 1). Many students also expressed interest in AI chatbots that can provide quick answers to common questions during a live session.

By comparison, fewer participants favored features that provide real-time oversight or monitoring. Less than half selected AI-powered multilingual captions, and only about one in five supported AI-based attention-tracking systems. Taken together, these results suggest that students prefer AI that improves accessibility and supports learning rather than AI that monitors their behavior or attempts to intervene during class.

Figure 1. Student Preferences for AI Features in Livestream-Based Education

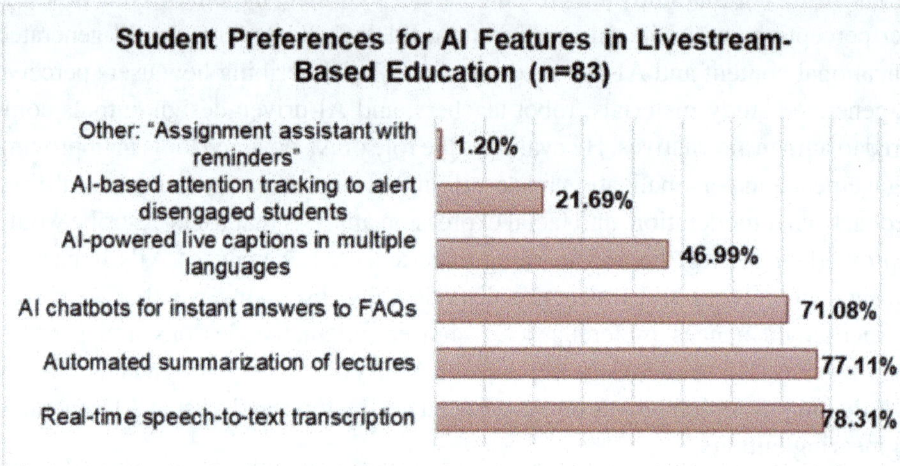

When asked about AI-powered teachers, 48.2% of respondents were open to an LLM-powered AI teacher conducting live classes, yet only 18.1% fully supported this idea, and 33.7% explicitly opposed it (Q7). Similarly, perceptions of humanoid robot teachers were diverse, with 37.8% expressing a neutral stance, 24.4% reporting slight discomfort, and 20.7% strongly opposing the concept (Q8). On the other hand, engagement with social media-based education is moderate, as 51.8% of respondents have never attended educational sessions on platforms like TikTok Live or Instagram Live, however, 48.2% reported some level of participation (Q14).

Instructional model preferences indicate strong support for a hybrid learning approach. A majority (62.7%) preferred a combination of human professors and AI-driven tutors, 30.1% preferred traditional human-led instruction, and only 3.6% preferred fully AI-driven tutors, indicating a preference for AI as a supplementary rather than a primary instructional tool (Q27). Comfort with AI engagement tracking varied widely (Q22), with responses spanning from strong discomfort (1) to complete acceptance (5), demonstrating a nuanced perception of AI's role in monitoring student engagement. Also, the bar chart in Figure 2 illustrates participants' comfort levels with AI/LLMs generating study materials from live-streamed classes (Q6).

Figure 2. Comfort with AI-Generated Study Materials

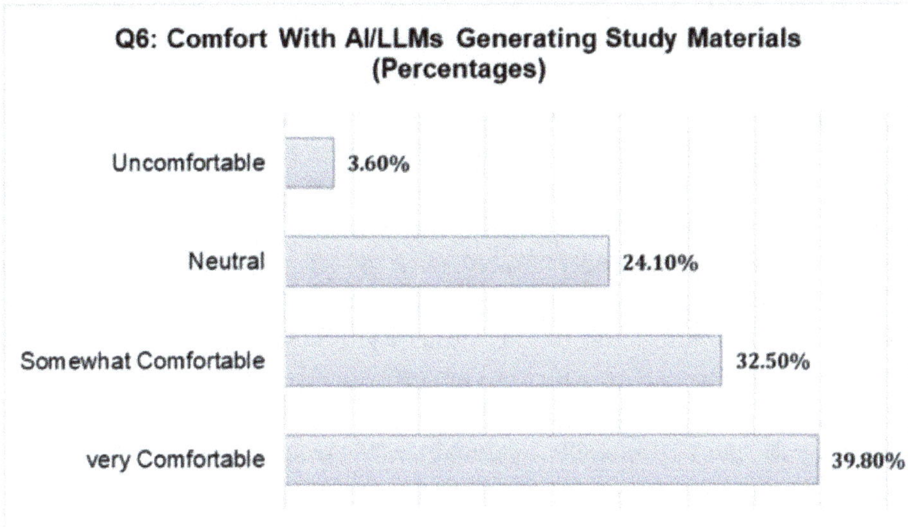

Trust in AI-driven Education

This section examines user trust in AI-powered education. We use ANOVA and K-Means clustering analyses to assess how prior AI experience influences trust levels and identify separate user trust profiles in AI-driven learning environments.

Analysis of Variance: We conducted an ANOVA analysis to examine whether prior experience with AI-powered tools influences users' comfort with AI-generated study materials and trust in AI-powered instructors. The analysis used responses from three survey questions: Q5, which asked about prior experience with AI tools (categorized as "No experience," "Occasionally used AI tools," and "Frequently used AI tools"), Q6, which assessed comfort with AI-generated study materials, and Q7, which measured trust in an AI-powered instructor.

The results showed a statistically significant difference in comfort levels with AI-generated study materials based on prior AI experience ($F = 20.533$, $p < 0.001$). This suggests that users who frequently use AI tools tend to be more comfortable with AI-generated content in online education. Similarly, trust in AI-powered instructors also varied significantly based on prior AI experience ($F = 3.413$, $p = 0.038$), though the effect was weaker compared to study materials.

User Clustering: We also conducted a K-Means clustering analysis to identify different user trust profiles in AI-powered education. The analysis was based on responses to four survey questions: Q6, which assessed comfort with AI-generated study materials; Q7, which measured trust in AI-powered instructors; Q9, which examined perceptions of robot teachers compared to human instructors; and Q24, which evaluated trust in AI-generated engineering designs. These questions were mapped to numerical values, standardized, and used as input features for clustering.

The clustering algorithm identified three separate user profiles based on their trust levels. Cluster 1 (AI Enthusiasts) exhibited the highest comfort with AI-generated study materials (2.92) and strong trust in AI-generated engineering designs (2.00), though their trust in AI-powered instructors was moderate (1.54). Cluster 2 (AI-Cautious Users) showed moderate acceptance of AI-generated study materials (1.79) and high trust in AI-assisted engineering design (2.02) but expressed low trust in AI-powered instructors (0.55). Cluster 3 (AI Skeptics) had the lowest trust levels among all dimensions, with low comfort with AI-generated study materials (1.43), very low trust in AI instructors (0.36), and little confidence in AI-generated engineering designs (0.43). Table 1 summarizes the results.

Table 1. User trust profiles in AI-powered education

Cluster	Comfort with AI Study Materials (Q6)	Trust in AI Teachers (Q7)	Perception of Robot Teachers (Q9)	Trust in AI-Generated Engineering Designs (Q24)
Cluster 1	2.92 (High)	1.54 (Moderate)	1.08 (Neutral)	2.00 (High)
Cluster 2	1.79 (Moderate)	0.55 (Low)	1.12 (Neutral)	2.02 (High)
Cluster 3	1.43 (Low)	0.36 (Very Low)	0.64 (Low)	0.43 (Very Low)

Although some users are highly receptive to AI-driven education tools, others are skeptical, particularly regarding AI's role as an instructor. There is a need for further investigation into the factors influencing AI implementation in education and suggest that AI implementation strategies should be tailored to different user trust profiles.

In Q16, respondents were asked whether they would trust social media influencers to teach specialized academic subjects. The goal of this question was to understand how much credibility students attribute to nontraditional online educators. The results show a cautious stance: 67.5% of participants said their trust would *depend on the influencer's credentials*. Another 21.7% reported that they would *not* trust influencers in this role, which reflects skepticism toward informal or personality-driven content creators. Only 10.8% expressed full trust. These results suggest that although students frequently consume educational content on social media, credibility and professional background are still critical factors in determining whether they view influencers as legitimate educators.

Engagement in AI-Driven Education

This section discusses the relationship between prior experience with AI-powered tools and users' perceptions of engagement and personalization in online education. We used ANOVA, Principal Component Analysis (PCA), and Ordinal Logistic Regression to assess the extent to which AI familiarity influences engagement preferences and whether AI-driven engagement tools are perceived as complementary or separate from traditional teacher-led methods.

ANOVA: First, we analyzed whether prior experience with AI-powered tools influences perceptions of engagement and personalization in online education. Specifically, we investigated whether users who have used AI tools (e.g., ChatGPT, Gemini, Claude) perceive engagement and AI-driven personalization differently from those who have not. This analysis aimed to assess whether AI tool adoption affects users' views on teacher engagement, AI-driven facial tracking, AI-based engagement monitoring, and the overall value of AI-powered engagement tools.

The study utilized responses from four survey questions. Q11 measured the perceived importance of teacher engagement, Q12 assessed users' support for AI-powered facial tracking to adjust teaching pace, Q22 evaluated users' comfort with AI monitoring engagement levels, and Q17 examined how valuable users find AI-powered engagement features such as chat moderation and real-time summarization. The independent variable was Q5, which categorized respondents based on their AI tool experience (frequent users, occasional users, and non-users).

To analyze these relationships, we performed a one-way ANOVA to compare engagement perceptions among the three AI experience groups. The results indicated no statistically significant differences in any of the engagement-related measures based on prior AI tool usage. The p-values for all comparisons were above the standard 0.05 significance threshold. This suggests that users, regardless of their experience with AI tools, rate teacher engagement, AI-powered tracking, and AI-driven engagement tools similarly. Table 2 summarizes the results.

Table 2. ANOVA results on AI experience and engagement perceptions

Comparison	F-Statistic	p-Value	Interpretation
AI Experience (Q5) vs. Importance of Teacher Engagement (Q11)	0.991	0.376	No significant difference- AI users and non-users rate teacher engagement similarly.
AI Experience (Q5) vs. Support for AI Facial Tracking (Q12)	1.588	0.211	No significant difference- AI users and non-users have similar opinions on AI facial tracking.
AI Experience (Q5) vs. Comfort with AI Engagement Tracking (Q22)	1.607	0.207	No significant difference- prior AI experience does not strongly affect comfort with AI tracking.
AI Experience (Q5) vs. Perceived Value of AI Engagement Tools (Q17)	2.002	0.142	No significant difference- users with different AI backgrounds value AI engagement tools similarly.

According to these results, AI tool adoption does not strongly influence how users perceive engagement and personalization in online education. This contrasts with the assumption that AI-experienced users might be more accepting of AI-driven engagement tools.

Principal Component Analysis: We also conducted a PCA to identify underlying engagement factors in online education and assess whether users distinguish between AI-driven and traditional engagement methods. The objective of this analysis was to determine whether engagement perceptions are driven by a single overarching factor or multiple independent dimensions, particularly differentiating between teacher-driven engagement and AI-enhanced engagement methods.

For this analysis, we used responses from four survey questions: Q11, which measured the perceived importance of teacher engagement in online education; Q12, which assessed support for AI-powered facial tracking to adjust teaching pace; Q17, which evaluated the perceived value of AI engagement tools such as real-time summarization and chat moderation; and Q22, which examined comfort with AI-based engagement monitoring. The data were standardized before applying PCA to extract meaningful engagement dimensions.

The results revealed four principal components (listed in Table 3), each representing separate aspects of engagement. PC2 (Teacher-Driven Engagement) was dominated by Q11 (importance of teacher engagement). This confirms respondents evaluate teacher engagement separately from AI-driven methods. PC1 (AI Comfort and Engagement Preferences) was strongly associated with Q12 (AI facial tracking), Q17 (AI engagement tools), and Q22 (AI engagement monitoring). This suggests users who support AI-powered tools are also more likely to accept AI-based engagement monitoring. PC3 (AI Engagement Tools and AI Tracking) showed a contrast between valuing AI engagement tools (Q17) and rejecting AI tracking (Q12). This shows a divide in AI adoption for engagement personalization. PC4 (AI Tracking and Engagement Monitoring) was mainly driven by comfort with AI detecting engagement (Q22). This suggests users' acceptance of AI tracking is a defining factor in their engagement preferences.

Table 3. Principal component analysis of engagement perceptions

Survey Question	PC1	PC2	PC3	PC4	Interpretation
Importance of teacher engagement (Q11)	0.041	0.998	0.037	-.021	PC2 is dominated by teacher engagement. It suggests that teacher engagement is independent of AI-driven engagement.
Support for AI-powered facial tracking (Q12)	0.574	-.013	-.605	-.552	PC1 and PC3 show AI-driven engagement preferences. Users who support AI-powered tracking may have different attitudes toward engagement.
The perceived value of AI engagement tools (Q17)	0.545	-.058	0.784	-.291	PC3 is strongly related to AI-powered engagement tools. This suggests that the value of AI engagement tools is a major independent factor in engagement perceptions.
Comfort with AI detecting engagement (Q22)	0.610	-.003	-.135	0.781	PC1 and PC4 relate to AI monitoring comfort. Users' comfort with AI tracking may be linked to their attitudes toward AI tools.

According to the results, teacher engagement and AI-driven engagement tools are perceived as separate, rather than complementary, aspects of online education. Users' comfort with AI-based monitoring has a significant role in their engagement preferences, and there is a division between those who support AI-powered engagement tools but are skeptical of AI tracking methods.

Ordinal Logistic Regression: In another analysis, we identify the factors that influence user engagement perceptions in AI-powered online learning environments. Specifically, we investigate whether prior AI experience, the importance of teacher engagement, and support for AI-powered facial tracking significantly impact users' comfort with AI engagement tracking and their perceived value of AI engagement tools. The objective is to determine whether general AI exposure affects engagement preferences or whether specific trust in AI-driven personalization features plays a more significant role.

To analyze these relationships, we conducted Ordinal Logistic Regression, a statistical method suited for modeling ordinal categorical responses. Two separate models were constructed. The first model examined 'comfort with AI engagement tracking' (Q22) as the dependent variable, and the second model analyzed 'the perceived value of AI engagement tools' (Q17). In both models, three independent variables were included: prior AI experience (Q5), the perceived importance of teacher engagement (Q11), and support for AI-powered facial tracking (Q12). Maximum Likelihood Estimation (MLE) with a logit link function was used to determine the likelihood that a respondent would rate engagement features higher or lower based on these predictors.

The regression results show that 'support for AI-powered facial tracking' (Q12) was the only significant predictor in both models. Users who support AI-driven facial tracking are significantly more likely to feel comfortable with AI engagement tracking (Q22) and find AI engagement tools more valuable (Q17). This suggests that trust in AI-driven personalization tools is a determinant of AI engagement acceptance. On the other hand, 'AI experience' (Q5) was not a significant predictor in either model. Then, prior exposure to AI tools does not necessarily lead to greater trust in AI-driven engagement methods. Similarly, 'the importance of teacher engagement' (Q11) did not influence AI engagement perceptions, so users do not perceive teacher-led engagement and AI-powered engagement tools as competing approaches. The results of the regression models are summarized in Table 4.

Table 4. Ordinal Logistic Regression results for AI engagement tracking and perceived value of AI tools

Predictor	Comfort With AI Engagement Tracking (Q22)	Perceived Value of AI Engagement Tools (Q17)
AI Experience (Q5)	Not significant ($p = 0.279$)	Not significant ($p = 0.108$)
Teacher Engagement Importance (Q11)	Not significant ($p = 0.996$)	Not significant ($p = 0.910$)
Support for AI-powered Facial Tracking (Q12)	Significant ($p < 0.001$, coef = 1.602)	Significant ($p < 0.001$, coef = 0.9335)

According to the result of Q10, the majority of respondents indicated that engagement rewards would positively influence their participation in online class discussions. Approximately three-quarters of learners (74.7%) reported that they would be more likely to participate if engagement rewards were implemented, while 18.1% selected "Maybe," suggesting conditional interest. Only a small proportion (7.2%) indicated that such rewards would not increase their participation. These results demonstrate the potential of gamified or incentive-based participation mechanisms to increase student involvement in online and livestreamed learning environments.

When asked which teaching behaviors make online classes more engaging (Q13), students showed a clear preference for expressive and interactive instructional styles. The most popular choice was *humor and storytelling*, selected by a large majority of respondents, which suggests that a personable and lively teaching presence helps sustain attention in virtual environments. Many students also emphasized the value of *personalized feedback*, indicating a desire for guidance that feels tailored to their individual progress. *Real-time polls and open Q&A sessions* were also highly endorsed, reflecting students' appreciation for opportunities to participate actively during class. On the other hand, only a minority identified *being addressed by name* as an important factor. Overall, the responses suggest that students are most engaged when instructors blend expressiveness, individualized feedback, and interactive elements rather than using formal or name-based acknowledgment.

AI Role in Learning Preferences and Instructional Models

We analyzed patterns in user responses to determine whether AI familiarity influences instructional model preferences and identify separate learner profiles based on engagement with AI-powered education.

Cluster Analysis: This analysis identifies different learning preference profiles among users based on their engagement with AI-powered instructional models. The goal was to determine whether individuals favor short, interactive lessons, peer-led study groups, and AI-assisted learning tools or whether they prefer traditional lecture-based formats. We have clustered users based on their learning preferences to uncover patterns in instructional model selection and assess whether these preferences align with AI-powered education. K-Means clustering was applied to responses from five survey questions: preferred learning format (Q19), preference for shorter Q&A-based lessons (Q20), willingness to participate in peer-led study groups (Q21), interest in AI-powered tools for engineering design courses (Q23), and preference for a structured model with short, focused lessons (Q26). These responses were numerically encoded and standardized before clustering, with the Elbow Method determining that three distinct groups emerged.

The first group, 'AI-Driven Interactive Learners', demonstrated a strong preference for micro-sessions (Q19), short interactive lessons (Q26), and peer-led study groups (Q21). They were also highly receptive to AI-powered tools (Q23), with a strong interest in flexible, engagement-driven learning environments. The second group, 'Traditional Lecture-Based Learners', preferred structured, one-hour lectures (Q19) with minimal interest in peer-led study groups (Q21) and interactive exercises. They supported AI-powered tools (Q23), however, they gravitated toward instructor-led formats, therefore AI tools would be more effective as an enhancement rather than a replacement in their learning process. The third group, 'Hybrid Learners', exhibited a balance between AI-driven and structured learning (Q19, Q26). This shows a selective selection of AI-powered engagement features (Q23) while favoring instructor-driven education. The bar chart in Figure 3 compares the average responses for each learning preference among the three clusters.

Figure 3. Learner profiles based on AI-powered instructional preferences

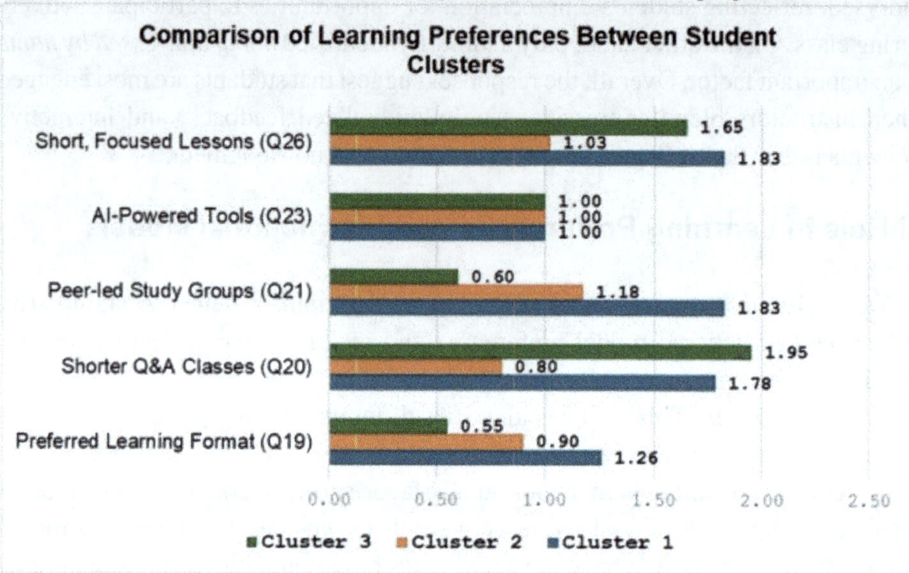

ANOVA: The objective of this analysis was to examine whether prior experience with AI-powered tools (Q5) influences learning format preferences and instructional models in online education. Specifically, we tested whether users with different levels of AI experience (frequent users, occasional users, and non-users) show different preferences for learning format (Q19), preference for shorter classes (Q20), participation in peer-led study groups (Q21), and preference for interactive exercises (Q26).

The results of the one-way ANOVA showed that only Q19 (preferred learning format) showed a statistically significant difference among AI experience groups ($F = 3.93$, $p = 0.023$). This suggests that prior AI engagement affects how learners prefer to structure their learning, such as choosing micro-sessions, one-hour lectures, or pre-recorded discussions. However, for Q20 (preference for shorter classes, $p = 0.213$), Q21 (participation in peer-led study groups, $p = 0.136$), and Q26 (preference for interactive exercises, $p = 0.182$), no significant differences were found, so AI experience does not strongly influence these preferences.

To further analyze the significant result for Q19, a Tukey HSD post-hoc test was conducted to determine which AI experience groups significantly differed in their preferred learning format. The results showed that non-users of AI tools (Group 0) had significantly different learning format preferences compared to frequent AI users (Group 2) ($p = 0.017$). Those who regularly use AI tools prefer alternative learning formats, such as shorter, interactive sessions or pre-recorded discussions. However, there was no significant difference between occasional AI users (Group 1) and either of the other two groups. Thus, occasional exposure to AI tools does not strongly shape learning format preferences.

Based on the results, frequent AI users are more likely to accept alternative, technology-driven learning formats, however non-users lean toward traditional lecture-based models. This shows future online education strategies could benefit from customized learning pathways that account for varying levels of AI familiarity.

When asked which subjects are best delivered through short-form livestreaming on social media (Q15), students gravitated toward topics that are practical, visual, and easily broken into small lessons. *Health and wellness* was selected by about 60% of respondents. Nearly as many students chose career-oriented skills such as coding, business, and finance (59%), and over half identified creative arts (music, painting, writing) as well suited to short, visually driven segments (54.2%). Language learning was also popular (45.8%), and about one-third of respondents pointed to science and technology (33.7%). Only a very small number mentioned politics or provided a custom "other" response. Overall, the data suggest that students see short-form livestreaming as especially effective for skill-building and visually demonstrable subjects.

In Q18, respondents were asked whether they would prefer online classes to be delivered in shorter segments (10 to 15 minutes) followed by a Q&A period, rather than traditional long-form lectures. Nearly half of students (47.0%) said their preference would depend on the subject. Another 41.0% expressed a clear preference for shorter lessons with Q&A, suggesting substantial interest in more concise, modular instructional formats. Only 12.0% preferred long lectures over shorter sessions. Overall, these findings show that students are generally receptive to short-form, interactive online instruction, especially when the format aligns with the content or learning objectives.

Q28 asked students to describe, in their own words, what innovations they would like to see in livestream-based education. Responses were highly diverse, with the majority offering unique, individualized suggestions rather than clustering around a single theme. Even so, several patterns emerged. A number of students expressed interest in more interactive tools, such as real-time polls, quizzes, and virtual whiteboards, to make livestreams more participatory. Others highlighted a desire for AI-powered enhancements, including AI teachers or robots that could assist instruction, as well as AI-generated summaries and note-taking to help students better review livestreamed content. Smaller groups mentioned improvements to audio/video quality, requests for more engaging or attention-supportive designs, and isolated suggestions for gamified activities or case-based learning. Overall, the responses suggest that students value greater interactivity, better support tools, and AI-assisted features that reduce cognitive load and improve the clarity and usability of livestreamed educational content.

Engineering Design Education

A descriptive analysis was conducted to examine user perceptions of AI-powered tools in engineering education, focusing on three aspects: the usefulness of AI-driven features in engineering design courses (Q23), trust in AI-generated engineering designs (Q24), and the preferred social media platforms for learning engineering concepts (Q25).

For Q23, participants were asked which AI-powered tools they found most helpful in an engineering design course. The most commonly selected option (27.7%) was an AI-assisted approach, including AI-assisted CAD modeling, AI-driven simulations, automated AI critiques, and AI-powered tutoring. However, 9.6% of respondents mentioned that none of these AI tools were helpful. This suggests skepticism or a preference for traditional methods. Other responses showed varying levels of support for specific AI tools, with AI-driven simulations and AI-powered tutoring emerging as particularly valued.

For Q24, participants were asked whether they trust AI-generated engineering designs. The majority (69.9%) believed that AI-generated designs require human validation. Only 8.4% of respondents trusted AI to optimize designs better than humans, and 10.8% were unsure. Another 10.8% explicitly stated that AI lacks the necessary creativity and intuition to handle complex design challenges.

For Q25, participants were asked which online platforms they found most useful for learning engineering design concepts. The majority (60.2%) indicated a preference for long-form, structured tutorials. Short-form content formats were selected by 25.3% of respondents. Platforms emphasizing community discussions and professional networking were chosen less frequently (7.2% each), therefore these formats may play a more limited role in supporting engineering learning compared to structured instructional content.

Further, we have performed a clustering analysis. The objective was to classify learner profiles in engineering education based on their engagement with AI-powered tools, trust in AI-generated designs, and reliance on social media for learning. Hierarchical clustering was applied to categorize respondents according to their responses to Q23 (preferred AI-powered features in engineering design), Q24 (trust in AI-generated designs), and Q25 (preferred social media platforms for engineering education). The analysis revealed three separate clusters as shown in Figure 4.

Figure 4. Hierarchical Clustering of Learner Profiles in Engineering Education

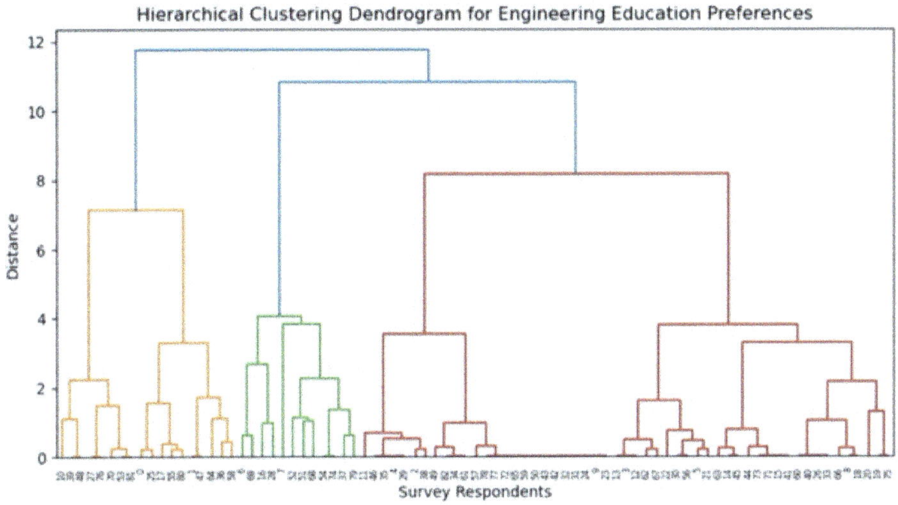

Cluster 1 consists of learners who regularly use multiple AI functionalities in engineering design and report moderate trust in AI-generated designs ("Yes, but human validation is still required" or "Not sure"). This group identifies YouTube as the most useful platform for learning engineering design concepts, suggesting a preference for long-form, tutorial-style content.

Cluster 2 represents respondents who show minimal interest in AI tools for engineering design (all select "None of the above" in Q23) and exhibit the lowest trust in AI-generated designs (between "No, AI lacks creativity and intuition" and "Not sure"). Their preferred platforms are split between YouTube and TikTok/Instagram, indicating that even AI-skeptical learners still use mainstream digital platforms for engineering content.

Cluster 3 is characterized by high usage of AI-assisted CAD, simulations, automated critiques, and AI tutoring combined with the highest trust in AI-generated designs (on average "Yes, but human validation is still required"). These respondents favor short-form and community-oriented platforms such as TikTok/Instagram, LinkedIn, and Discord/Reddit over YouTube, pointing to a more experimental and socially networked approach to AI-supported engineering learning.

CONCLUSION

This study investigated how users perceive AI-powered tools in online education, particularly in engineering design. Through survey data from 83 participants, we examined trust in AI-generated content, engagement with AI-driven instructional features, and preferences for AI-assisted learning models. According to the results, although many users find AI tools beneficial especially in tasks such as automated design critiques and AI-powered tutoring, there is hesitation in fully trusting AI-generated engineering designs or AI-driven instructors. Most respondents preferred a hybrid model where AI supports human educators rather than replacing them. Also, engagement tools such as real-time AI feedback were seen as helpful, however, attitudes toward AI monitoring and tracking were more varied.

Despite these insights, this study has some limitations. The participant pool was heavily skewed toward students, which may not fully represent perspectives from educators, administrators, or industry professionals. Also, the self-reported data introduces potential biases, as perceptions of AI usefulness do not always align with actual behavior in AI-supported learning environments. Furthermore, clustering analyses identified separate learner profiles, however, the study did not examine how these preferences evolve. Future research could benefit from longitudinal studies that track changes in AI implementation and user confidence as AI tools become more integrated into education.

Moving forward, further studies should analyze how different instructional strategies can be optimized using AI without compromising human oversight. Investigating how AI-powered tools impact actual learning outcomes rather than just user perceptions would provide a better understanding of their value. Moreover, examining how AI-driven personalization can be chosen for different learning styles could improve its practical application in education.

Overall, the results show AI has the potential to improve online learning, particularly in engineering education, but it should be implemented as a complement to, rather than a replacement for, human instruction.

REFERENCES

Ajani, O. A., Gamede, B., & Matiyenga, T. C. (2024). Leveraging artificial intelligence to enhance teaching and learning in higher education: Promoting quality education and critical engagement. *Journal of Pedagogical Sociology and Psychology*, *7*(1), 54–69. DOI: 10.33902/JPSP.202528400

Awad, A. (2024). Artificial intelligence and marketing innovation: The mediating role of organizational culture. *Innovative Marketing*, *20*(3), 170–181. DOI: 10.21511/im.20(3).2024.14

Bhatia, A., Bhatia, P., & Sood, D. (2024). Leveraging AI to transform online higher education: Focusing on personalized learning, assessment, and student engagement. *International Journal of Management and Humanities, 11*(1).

Fang, C., & Tse, A. W. C. (2022). Quasi-Experiment: Postgraduate students' class engagement in various online learning contexts when taking privacy issues to incorporate with artificial intelligence applications. *Proceedings of the 14th International Conference on Education Technology and Computers*, 356–361. DOI: 10.1145/3572549.3572606

Geroche, J. B., & Guay, F. J. G. (2024). AI in education: Unlocking college student engagement in the digital learning era. *International Research Journal of Science, Technology, Education, and Management*, *4*(4), 52–64.

Ghonim, A., Awad, A., Shemais, M., Shma, T., & Aziz, A. (2025). Exploring the impact of flexible work arrangements on employee engagement in telecommunications: Case of Egypt. *Problems and Perspectives in Management*, *23*(2), 198–207. DOI: 10.21511/ppm.23(2).2025.13

Gm, D., Goudar, R. H., Kulkarni, A. A., Rathod, V. N., & Hukkeri, G. S. (2024). A digital recommendation system for personalized learning to enhance online education: A review. *IEEE Access : Practical Innovations, Open Solutions*, *12*, 34019–34041. DOI: 10.1109/ACCESS.2024.3369901

Joseph, S., Tahir, A., Bibi, F., Hamid, K., Iqbal, M. W., Ruk, S. A., & Ahmad, S. Z. (2024). A Review Analysis on Using" AIED" to Improve Student Engagement in Hybrid Education. *Bulletin of Business and Economics, 13*(2), 424–435.

Lai, C.-L. (2021). Exploring university students' preferences for AI-assisted learning environment. *Journal of Educational Technology & Society*, *24*(4), 1–15.

Majjate, H., Bellarhmouch, Y., Jeghal, A., Yahyaouy, A., Tairi, H., & Zidani, K. A. (2024). Assessing the impact of ethical aspects of recommendation systems on student trust and engagement in E-learning platforms: A multifaceted investigation. *Education and Information Technologies*, 1–25.

Nazaretsky, T., Cukurova, M., & Alexandron, G. (2022). An instrument for measuring teachers' trust in AI-based educational technology. *LAK22: 12th International Learning Analytics and Knowledge Conference*, 56–66. DOI: 10.1145/3506860.3506866

Qin, F., Li, K., & Yan, J. (2020). Understanding user trust in artificial intelligence-based educational systems: Evidence from China. *British Journal of Educational Technology*, *51*(5), 1693–1710. DOI: 10.1111/bjet.12994

Rane, N., Choudhary, S., & Rane, J. (2023). *Education 4.0 and 5.0: Integrating artificial intelligence (AI) for personalized and adaptive learning*. Nov.

Sadegh-Zadeh, S.-A., Movahhedi, T., Hajiyavand, A. M., & Dearn, K. D. (2023). Exploring undergraduates' perceptions of and engagement in an AI-enhanced online course. *Frontiers in Education*, *8*, 1252543. DOI: 10.3389/feduc.2023.1252543

APPENDIX

Q1. *What is your role in education?*

- Student
- Teacher
- Educational Administrator
- EdTech Developer

Q2. *Have you attended or conducted classes via livestreaming platforms (Zoom, YouTube Live, Twitch, etc.)?*

- Yes, regularly
- Yes, occasionally
- No, but I plan to
- No

Q3. *Would you prefer an AI assistant that provides real-time feedback on your participation and suggests engagement strategies?* (Yes, No, Maybe)

Q4. What AI features would be most beneficial in livestreaming education? (Select all that apply)

- Real-time speech-to-text transcription
- AI-powered live captions in multiple languages
- Automated summarization of lectures
- AI chatbots for instant answers to FAQs
- AI-based attention tracking to alert disengaged students
- Other: (please specify)

Q5. *Have you used AI-powered tools (e.g., ChatGPT, Gemini, Claude) in your online education experience?*

- Yes, frequently
- Yes, occasionally
- No

Q6. *How comfortable are you with AI/LLMs (e.g., ChatGPT) automatically generating study materials from livestreamed classes?*

- Very comfortable
- Somewhat comfortable
- Neutral
- Uncomfortable

Q7. *Would you trust an LLM-powered AI teacher to conduct a live class on a subject?* (Yes, No, Maybe)

Q8. *Would you be comfortable being taught by a humanoid robot teacher in an online or in-person class?*

(1 = Not comfortable at all, 5 = Completely comfortable)

Q9. *How do you think a robot teacher would compare to a human teacher?*

- A robot teacher would be just as effective as a human teacher
- A robot teacher would be more effective because it removes human bias and errors
- A robot teacher would be less effective because it lacks human emotions and adaptability
- A robot teacher could complement human teachers but not fully replace them
- Not sure

Q10. *Would you be more likely to participate in class discussions if engagement rewards were implemented?* (Yes, No, Maybe)

Q11. *How important is teacher engagement (e.g., interacting with students, using storytelling, facial expressions) in an online class?*

- Extremely important
- Somewhat important
- Neutral
- Not very important
- Not at all important

Q12. *Would AI-powered facial expression analysis help teachers adjust their teaching pace based on student engagement?*

- Yes, it would be helpful
- No, it would be intrusive
- Maybe

Q13. *What teacher interaction style makes online classes more engaging for you?* (Select all that apply)

- Teachers using real-time polls and Q&A
- Personalized feedback on assignments
- Teachers using humor and storytelling
- Frequent direct addressing of students by name

Q14. *Have you ever attended an educational session on social media platforms such as TikTok Live, Instagram Live, or YouTube Live?*

- Yes, frequently
- Yes, occasionally
- No

Q15. *What subjects do you think are best suited for short-form livestreaming education on social media? (Select all that apply)*

- Language Learning
- Science & Technology
- Career Skills (Coding, Business, Finance)
- Health & Wellness

- Creative Arts (Music, Painting, Writing)
- Other: (please specify)

Q16. *Would you trust social media influencers as educators in specialized subjects?* (Yes, No)
Depends on their credentials

Q17. *On a scale of 1 to 5, how valuable do you think the following AI capabilities would be in improving your online learning experience?* (1 = Not valuable at all, 5 = Extremely valuable)

- AI moderators that filter chat questions and prioritize important ones
- AI that summarizes discussions in real-time
- AI that reminds you of key concepts after class
- AI-powered real-time translations

Q18. *Would you prefer online classes to be shorter (10-15 minutes) with Q&A, instead of long lectures?* (Yes, No, Depends on the subject)

Q19. What format would be most effective for online learning?

- One-hour lectures with breaks
- 15-minute micro-sessions with Q&A
- Pre-recorded lessons with live discussion

Q20. *Would you participate in a peer-led livestreaming study group?* (Yes, No)

Q21. *What peer-to-peer learning methods would be most effective? (Select all that apply)*

- Breakout rooms for group discussions
- Student-led livestreams on specific topics
- Mentorship programs pairing experienced students with newcomers

Q22. *On a scale of 1 to 5, how comfortable would you be with AI detecting student engagement levels based on voice tone, camera feed, and chat activity?* (1 = Not comfortable at all, 5 = Completely comfortable)

Q23. *Assume that you are required to take a course in Engineering Design. This course consists of designing products, systems, or processes using technical skills such as Computer-Aided Design (CAD), simulations, and prototyping. If AI-powered tools were integrated into your Engineering Design course, which of the following features would be most helpful in improving your learning experience?* (Select all that apply)

- AI-assisted CAD modeling (AI generates design variations based on constraints)
- AI-driven simulations (e.g., AI optimizes designs for strength, weight, or cost)
- Automated AI critiques (AI provides instant feedback on design assignments)

- AI-powered tutoring (Virtual assistant explains complex design principles)
- None of the above
- Other: (please specify)

Q24. *Would you trust AI-generated engineering designs to be as good as human-created designs?*

- Yes, AI can optimize designs better than humans
- Yes, but human validation is still required
- No, AI lacks creativity and intuition
- Not sure

Q25. *Which social media platform do you believe is most useful for learning engineering design concepts?*

- YouTube (Long-form tutorials)
- TikTok / Instagram Reels (Short-form content)
- LinkedIn (Industry-related knowledge)
- Discord / Reddit (Community-based discussions)
- Other: (please specify)

Q26. *Traditional engineering design courses require long lectures and hands-on projects. Would you prefer a learning model that includes short, focused lessons (10-15 min) followed by interactive design exercises?*

- Yes, this would improve my engagement and focus
- Maybe, but only for certain topics
- No, long-form lectures are better for deep understanding

Q27. *Would you prefer a human professor, an AI-driven tutor, or a combination of both when learning engineering design?*

- Prefer a human professor
- Prefer a combination of AI and human instruction
- Prefer AI-driven tutors
- No preference

Q28. *What innovations would you like to see in AI-powered online education?* (Open-ended response)

Chapter 4
AI-Driven Assessment of Cognitive Stress: Integrating Natural Language Processing and the Internet of Behaviours for Workplace Well-Being

Abhuday Sudhir
https://orcid.org/0009-0001-1151-8986
Jaypee University of Engineering and Technology, Guna, India

Kushagra Singh
https://orcid.org/0009-0009-9415-170X
Jaypee University of Engineering and Technology, Guna, India

Arush Khare
https://orcid.org/0009-0000-1634-0411
Jaypee University of Engineering and Technology, Guna, India

Kunj Bihari Bihari Meena
https://orcid.org/0000-0001-8159-9024
Jaypee University of Engineering and Technology, Guna, India

Vipin Tyagi
https://orcid.org/0000-0003-4994-3686
Jaypee University of Engineering and Technology, Guna, India

DOI: 10.4018/979-8-3373-7416-1.ch004

ABSTRACT

In the modern digital workplace, employees are more and more exposed to cognitive stress that arise from information overload, continuous connectivity, and hybridization of professional environments. AI has emerged as a promising tool for monitoring cognitive stress by integrating NLP and IoB. These enable the extraction of linguistic, emotional, and semantic indicators of stress from texts, speeches, and physiological data, while the IoB offers contextual behavioral data streams. These provide the possibility to continuously monitor cognitive load, affective states, and behavioral responses and allow early detection and intervention strategies for workplace well-being. The chapter reviews the theoretical bases, methods, and ethics of AI-driven cognitive stress assessment frameworks. An exploration of how language, physiology, and behavioral patterns are integrated as input multimodal data into the design of predictive AI models for recognition of human stress. Moreover, recent deep learning and IoB architecture advances in this chapter provide a framework for stress quantification.

1. INTRODUCTION

Cognitive stress is the mental strain that arises when a person's capability of memory, attention, and information processing declines and is unable to keep up with the need. In today's workplace, employees have become multitasking, switching contexts, and processing fast-moving information. Over time, these conditions accumulate and create a sustained cognitive stress that often goes unnoticed. When early signs of this cognitive stress are ignored, reduced productivity, impaired judgement, and overall decline in workplace performance is observed.

Global indicators emphasize the seriousness of this issue. Gallup's 2024 worldwide survey reports that 41% of employees experience high levels of stress during work. With a global workforce of 3.4 billion individuals, this means that nearly 1.4 billion people are working under high stress daily. Such statistics highlight that cognitive stress is not an isolated challenge but a universal workplace incident that needs systematic assessment and intervention.

Timely detection and analysis of cognitive stress is important for safeguarding employee well-being, maintaining sustained productivity, and preventing errors. High cognitive stress is associated with reduced concentration, increased mistakes, and a higher risk of exhaustion. In high-risk domains such as aviation, manufacturing, and critical infrastructure, unaddressed cognitive stress can become dangerous and potentially life-threatening.

Recent advances in artificial intelligence shows potential solutions for this challenge. Natural Language Processing (NLP) enables the identification of linguistic markers of stress through spoken and written communication. At the same time, the Internet of Behaviours (IoB) provides behavioural insights such as typing patterns, interaction rhythms, and micro-pauses that help detection of cognitive load. Modern AI-driven monitoring systems combine multimodal inputs including sensor data, voice modulation, behavioural traces, and text analytics to enable continuous, real-time stress assessment (Healey and Picard, 2005). Integrating NLP with IoB allows organizations to understand existing and emerging stress patterns, enabling proactive well-being strategies and healthier work environments (Soto-Pérez-de-Celis et al., 2023).

The modern workplace is characterized by constant information flow, rapid task switching, and increased reliance on digital communication. These conditions place a significant cognitive load on employees, often leading to stress that is not immediately visible. Cognitive stress monitoring in organizations is essential because it helps them identify early signs of mental overload before it evolves into reduced productivity, errors, burnout, or safety risks. Without systematic monitoring, subtle behavioural and linguistic cues are easily overlooked, especially in remote and hybrid work settings where face-to-face observation is limited.

In distributed work environments, employees may show very small but meaningful changes in communication patterns such as variations in tone, word choice, or sentence structure. These symptoms are usually overlooked in traditional HR frameworks that rely on self-reporting or irregular assessments. Natural Language Processing (NLP) can analyse these verbal and textual signals to detect cognitive strain and emotional conditions more accurately.

In addition to linguistic indicators, the Internet of Behaviours (IoB) provides contextual behavioural data such as typing speed, mouse dynamics, interaction rhythm, and response delays. These micro-behaviours are strongly linked to mental load. When NLP and IoB data are combined and processed through AI models, organizations get the ability to guess an individual's cognitive condition state in real time. This integrated approach helps build proactive well-being interventions, supports healthier work cultures, and prevents severe outcomes such as burnout, decreased decision-making quality, and workplace accidents.

The goals of Industry 5.0 extend beyond technological advancement and include healthy mental well-being, responsible and legal use of AI, and personalized automation for employees. In this context, cognitive stress detection becomes very important. It supports self-reliance by enabling employees to understand their own mental states and adjust their work patterns accordingly. AI-generated insights can provide personalized feedback, recommendations, and adaptive responses that contribute to improved mental health, reduced overload, and enhanced productivity.

Additionally, the data derived from NLP and IoB systems can influence workplace design, organizational policies, and decision-making practices. By identifying stress patterns and behavioural trends across teams or departments, organizations can create healthier environments, implement targeted interventions, and develop evidence-based strategies for employee well-being.

In this chapter, the integration of NLP and IoB methods for cognitive stress detection is explored to show how AI-enabled assessment can contribute to humane and data-driven approaches for workplace mental health. The chapter outlines how combining linguistic analysis, behavioural monitoring, and AI modelling provides a comprehensive foundation for promoting well-being in Industry 5.0 environments.

2. RELATED WORK

Cognitive stress, defined as the strain on memory, attention, and information processing when work demands go beyond individual capacity, has significant implications for workplace well-being, productivity, and safety. With the increasing complexity of work environments, remote and hybrid setups, multitasking, and high-information flow; early detection of cognitive stress is critical. Real-time monitoring enables interventions to prevent mental burnout, errors, and reduced decision-making ability. Recent advancements in artificial intelligence (AI), Natural Language Processing (NLP), the Internet of Behaviors (IoB), physiological sensing, eye-tracking, and multimodal data integration have provided new ways to measure cognitive load and stress in real-world contexts.

2.1 AI, NLP, and IoB for Cognitive Stress Detection

AI-enabled frameworks combining NLP and IoB provide continuous monitoring of verbal, textual, and behavioral data to detect cognitive stress. NLP analyzes linguistic markers, such as changes in tone, word choice, or sentence complexity, which correlate with mental strain, while IoB captures behavioral data like typing patterns and activity rates. These systems enable real-time assessment of cognitive states, supporting both self-regulation and data-driven organizational decisions regarding workload, workspace design, and policy changes (Anders et al., 2024; Soto-Pérez-de-Celis et al., 2023).

2.2 EEG-Based Cognitive Stress Studies

EEG signals provide a direct measure of neural activity associated with cognitive load and stress.

- Ayala et al. (2023) used theta-band EEG in a brain-computer interface (BCI) to monitor mental workload during memory and focus-demanding tasks. Theta fluctuations allowed continuous, objective assessment without interrupting participants.
- The 2025 EEG dataset involved 15 participants performing Stroop and arithmetic tasks under varying stress levels. EEG signals captured frontal-lobe activity, providing labeled datasets for machine-learning models to classify cognitive load.
- Guo et al. (2022) demonstrated the interplay between cognitive load and emotional states in multimedia learning, showing that high task difficulty leads to negative emotions and increased mental strain.

Limitations of EEG-based studies include lab-based environments, small sample sizes, potential noise in signals, and limited generalizability. Nevertheless, EEG remains a foundational tool for real-time cognitive stress assessment.

2.3 Eye-Tracking and Behavioral Indicators

Eye-tracking metrics serve as real-time behavioral proxies for cognitive load in high-pressure digital environments.

- Sevcenko et al. (2022) and TBRS-based studies showed that fixation frequency, microsaccadic rate, saccadic latency, and pupil diameter correlate with subjective workload, supporting real-time stress detection in tasks requiring multitasking and rapid decision-making.
- Martinez-Cedillo et al. (2025) extended eye-tracking research to naturalistic, real-world tasks, demonstrating that gaze dynamics (e.g. longer fixations, fewer exploratory saccades) reflect cognitive load outside controlled laboratory settings.

Limitations include sensitivity to environmental factors, individual differences, and task-specific calibration requirements. Eye-tracking remains particularly useful for interactive workstations, surveillance, and high-risk operational environments.

2.4. AR-Based and Industrial Cognitive Load Studies

Augmented Reality (AR) has been evaluated as a tool for reducing cognitive load during complex operational tasks.

- Alessa et al. (2023) compared HoloLens-based AR instructions with traditional paper manuals for maintenance and assembly tasks. AR decreased mental effort by providing step-by-step visual guidance but increased workload during complex stages due to unfamiliar interaction.
- Zakeri et al. (2023) investigated multimodal assessment of cognitive workload in human-robot collaboration. Combining EEG, fNIRS, behavioral data, and NASA-TLX assessments improved accuracy in detecting real-time workload, highlighting adaptive smart-factory applications.

Limitations in AR and industrial studies include laboratory-based settings, small sample sizes, motion artifacts, system complexity, and deployment challenges in real-world operations.

2.5. Multimodal Cognitive Stress Datasets

Comprehensive datasets facilitate the development of AI and machine-learning models for cognitive stress detection:

- CLARE (Bhatti et al., 2024): Includes ECG, EDA, EEG, and gaze data from 24 participants with 10-second interval self-reports, allowing high-resolution, real-time modeling of cognitive load.
- MOCAS (Jo et al., 2022): Captures physiological and behavioral data during multitasking CCTV monitoring tasks, reflecting real workplace demands such as attentiveness, focus switching, and fatigue accumulation.

These datasets enable the integration of autonomic, neural, and behavioral signals to model cognitive stress dynamically. Limitations include laboratory-based tasks, sample size constraints, sensor intrusiveness, and challenges in aligning subjective and objective measures.

2.6. Integrating Cognitive, Emotional, and Physiological Indicators

Research shows that cognitive stress is not only a matter of task difficulty but also of emotional states:

- Guo et al. (2022) highlighted the negative correlation between emotional activity and cognitive load, demonstrating that anxiety and poor emotional experiences increase mental strain.

- Combined multimodal approaches, such as those in CLARE, MOCAS, and Zakeri et al. (2023), allow researchers to capture the interplay of cognitive, emotional, and physiological factors, providing richer, real-time insights into cognitive stress.

Collectively, these studies demonstrate that cognitive stress monitoring benefits from multimodal approaches combining:

1. Physiological signals: EEG, ECG, EDA, fNIRS.
2. Behavioral indicators: Eye-tracking, typing patterns, reaction times.
3. Emotional markers: Linguistic cues, self-reports, AI-detected sentiment.
4. Contextual and task-based data: AR-guided tasks, multitasking environments, human–robot collaboration.

AI, NLP, and IoB enable real-time monitoring and predictive modeling, while datasets like CLARE and MOCAS support algorithm development and validation. Limitations across studies include laboratory constraints, small samples, sensor noise, and difficulty generalizing to diverse, real-world contexts. Despite these, integrating multimodal approaches presents a powerful framework for understanding, detecting, and mitigating cognitive stress in workplace and learning environments.

3. PROPOSED WORK

This section presents the complete methodology of the proposed conversation-based cognitive stress classification system. The system is designed to analyze the dialogue between a participant and the virtual interviewer Ellie (DeVault et al., 2014) to identify linguistic markers indicative of cognitive stress. The methodology consists of three major steps: Text preprocessing, Conversational feature extraction, and Model training.

3.1 Preprocessing

3.1.1 Dialogue Structuring

Each transcript is divided into speaker turns:

- **ELLIE** (virtual agent) turns
- **PARTICIPANT** turns

Only participant responses are used for classification. However, Ellie's questions are retained during feature extraction, as the question type (personal, emotional, cognitive) influences how participants respond under stress.

3.1.2 Tokenization and Sequence Formatting

Participant utterances are segmented into sentences and tokenized using a transformer tokenizer (BERT-like). Fixed-length sequences are generated, and rare words are handled through subword encoding, preserving linguistic variability while maintaining model compatibility.

3.2 Conversational Feature Extraction

3.2.1 Deep Contextual Embeddings

A pre-trained transformer model (e.g., BERT-base) converts each participant utterance into a 768-dimensional vector that encodes lexical semantics, emotional tone, contextual dependencies, and discourse patterns. The CLS token embedding of each utterance serves as the primary representation for downstream classification.

3.3 Model Selection

In this study, multiple supervised machine learning models were evaluated to predict whether a speaker belongs to the stressed/depression class or the no-stress class based on speech embeddings. Model selection is a crucial step in building an accurate and reliable prediction system. Four machine learning models: Logistic Regression, SVM, Random Forest, and Gradient Boosting were selected for experimentation. Each model was trained on the same dataset and evaluated using standard performance metrics, including accuracy, precision, recall, F1-score, ROC-AUC, and confusion matrices. The goal is to identify that which algorithm most effectively distinguishes between the two psychological states while handling the strong class imbalance in the dataset. Through systematic comparison, the most stable and generalizable model was identified for potential real-time deployment.

3.3.1 Logistic Regression

Logistic Regression (LaValley, 2008) was chosen as the baseline model due to its simplicity, interpretability, and efficiency for binary classification tasks. It works well when features maintain a linear relationship with the output and requires minimal computational resources. In this study, Logistic Regression demonstrated strong initial performance and high recall, indicating effectiveness in identifying stressed cases. However, it could not capture complex non-linear patterns in speech-based features, limiting its overall predictive strength efficiently.

3.3.2 Support Vector Machine (SVM)

Support Vector Machine (Cortes & Vapnik, 1995) is widely used for classification problems and is known for strong performance in high-dimensional feature spaces such as embeddings. SVM constructs an optimal separating hyperplane that maximizes the margin between classes. Using kernel functions like RBF, SVM can model non-linear decision boundaries effectively. In this study, SVM achieved competitive accuracy and recall but showed signs of overfitting due to the limited dataset size and class imbalance, highlighting the need for careful tuning of kernel parameters.

3.3.3 Random Forest

Random Forest (Y. K. Rushall, 2013) is an ensemble learning technique based on multiple decision trees, designed to improve prediction stability and reduce overfitting. By aggregating results from many trees and using random feature selection, Random Forest efficiently handles complex, non-linear relationships. In this study, Random Forest demonstrated reliable generalization performance, outperforming simpler linear models in robustness and ROC-AUC score. However, it produced a higher number of false positives, indicating reduced precision.

3.3.4 Gradient Boosting

Gradient Boosting (Friedman, 2001) builds trees sequentially, with each tree attempting to correct the errors of the previous one by minimizing a loss function. This makes the model highly sensitive and powerful for complex datasets. In this study, Gradient Boosting achieved moderate performance with reasonable recall, but its higher misclassification rate and lower stability compared to Random Forest indicated challenges in handling noise and class imbalance. Careful tuning of parameters such as learning rate, number of estimators, and tree depth is critical to prevent overfitting.

3.4 Model Training

After extracting embeddings and additional linguistic features, machine-learning models are trained to perform binary cognitive-stress classification. Classical machine-learning algorithms are evaluated for their efficiency and interpretability.

3.4.1 Train-Validation-Test Split of Dataset

The dataset is split in a speaker-independent manner: 80% for training and 20% for testing, ensuring that no participant appears in multiple splits (Table 1).

3.4.2 Handling Class Imbalance

The dataset contains approximately 70% non-stress samples. To address this imbalance, Borderline-SMOTE is applied only to the training set. This technique generates synthetic minority-class samples near the class boundary, improving the model's ability to detect stressed participants.

3.4.3 Feature Scaling

- Logistic Regression and SVM models use scaled embeddings, as these algorithms rely on feature magnitude.
- Random Forest and Gradient Boosting use raw embeddings, as tree-based models are invariant to feature scaling.

3.4.4 Training

Each optimized model is trained on the full SMOTE-balanced training set using its best hyperparameters. Model performance is then evaluated on the untouched test split to assess generalization capability. This methodology ensures that the system captures both lexical and contextual cues indicative of cognitive stress, while addressing practical challenges such as class imbalance and speaker variability.

Figure 1. Proposed cognitive stress detection pipeline's workflow

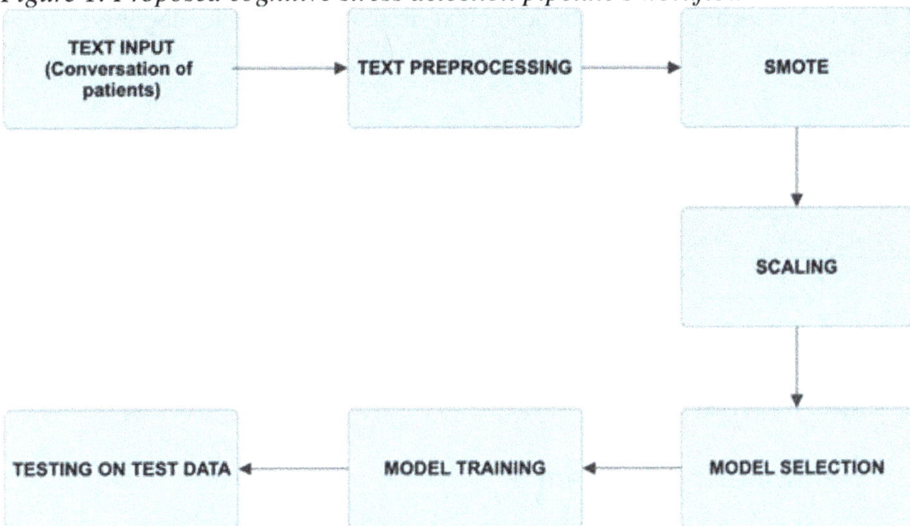

4. EXPERIMENTAL RESULTS

4.1 Dataset Used

The DAIC-WOZ dataset, developed at the USC Institute for Creative Technologies, contains clinical interview transcripts conducted between participants and the virtual interviewer *Ellie* (DeVault et al., 2014). Each interview session is accompanied by the participant's PHQ-8 score, allowing reliable labeling of stress or depression levels. The dataset was specifically designed to support research on psychological health, automated depression screening, and conversational behavior analysis.

For cognitive-stress or depression-level detection using text, DAIC-WOZ is highly suitable because it provides:

- Structured, natural conversational transcripts
- Validated clinical ground-truth labels (PHQ-8)
- Consistent interview protocols

A binary stress label can be derived using the standard PHQ-8 threshold:

- PHQ-8 $> 10 \rightarrow$ Stress / Moderate–High Depression (Label = 1)
- PHQ-8 $\leq 10 \rightarrow$ Non-Stress / Minimal–Mild Depression (Label = 0)

This combination of rich linguistic data and clinically validated scoring makes DAIC-WOZ an ideal dataset for building text-driven AI models for cognitive-stress monitoring.

Table 1. Dataset Split Description

Label	Description	Count	Percentage (%)
0	Non-Stress / Non-Depressed	132	70.21%
1	Stress / Depressed	56	29.79%

4.2 Experimental Setup

4.2.1 Hardware and Software

The experiments for this work were conducted on a system equipped with 8 GB RAM, a dual-core Intel i5 processor, and an integrated Intel HD Graphics 6000 GPU. The development environment was built using Python 3.10, with PyTorch and scikit-learn for model implementation, and HuggingFace Transformers for generating text embeddings. Core scientific libraries such as NumPy and Pandas were used for data handling and preprocessing.

To maintain consistency and reproducibility across all experimental runs, a fixed random seed (42) was applied for dataset splitting and model initialization. All experiments were executed on CPU only, without GPU acceleration, which influenced both the training time and the choice of lightweight and computationally efficient model architectures.

4.2.2 Cross-Validation and Tuning Procedure

- **Cross-validation:** Stratified cross-validation used during hyperparameter search (CV F1 reported as selection metric).
- **Search method:** Grid / manual search for each model's hyperparameters; best params chosen by highest CV F1.
- **Target operational goal:** Recall ≥ 80% and Precision ≥ 60% were the desired operating characteristics (not always achieved).

4.2.3 Best Hyperparameter Configurations

Table 2 summarizes the hyperparameter search space and the best-performing configurations for each machine-learning model. Logistic Regression achieved optimal performance with C = 0.1, the 'saga' solver, L1 penalty, and balanced class weights, indicating that mild regularization combined with class balancing effectively reduced overfitting and improved performance on the imbalanced dataset. The Random Forest model performed best with 500 estimators, max_depth = 15, min_samples_split = 2, min_samples_leaf = 1, and balanced_subsample class weighting, showing that moderately deep trees and class-aware sampling improved the representation of minority instances.

Table 2. Hyperparameter settings

Model	Hyperparameters Searched	Best Parameters
Logistic Regression	c: [0.1, 1, 10, 100] solver: ['saga', 'liblinear'] 'penalty': ['l1', 'l2'] 'class_weight': ['balanced', {0: 1, 1: 3}	c: 0.1 solver: saga penalty:l1 class_weight: balanced
RandomForest	n_estimators: [200, 300, 500], max_depth: [10, 15, 20, None], min_samples_split: [2, 5, 10], min_samples_leaf: [1, 2, 4], class_weight: ['balanced', 'balanced_ subsample', {0: 1, 1: 3}]	n_estimators: 500 max_depth: 15 min_samples_split: 2 min_samples_leaf: 1 class weight: balanced_subsample
SVM	c: [0.1, 1, 10, 100], gamma: ['scale', 'auto', 0.001, 0.01, 0.1], class_weight: ['balanced', {0: 1, 1: 3}]	c: 10 gamma: auto class_weight: balanced
Gradient Boosting	n_estimators: [200, 300, 500], max_depth: [5, 7, 10], learning_rate: [0.05, 0.1, 0.15], min_samples_split: [2, 5, 10], subsample: [0.8, 0.9, 1.0]	subsample: 0.8, n_estimators: 500, min_samples_split: 5, max_depth: 10, learning_rate: 0.1

The SVM model obtained its best configuration using C = 10, gamma = auto, and balanced class weights, allowing the model to learn more flexible decision boundaries while compensating for class imbalance. Gradient Boosting produced its strongest results with 500 estimators, max_depth = 10, min_samples_split = 5, subsample = 0.8, and learning_rate = 0.1, demonstrating that a moderate learning rate paired with partial sampling enhanced generalization.

Overall, the hyperparameter tuning procedure contributed significantly to model stability, robustness, and predictive performance by regulating model complexity and addressing the underlying dataset imbalance.

4.3 Evaluation Metrics

Evaluation follows standard metrics commonly used in mental health classification, including accuracy, precision, recall, F1-score, and ROC-AUC. Accuracy measures the overall correctness of the model, while precision and recall indicate its ability to correctly identify stressed individuals and avoid false positives. The F1-score balances precision and recall, providing a single metric for model effectiveness, and ROC-AUC evaluates the model's capability to distinguish between stressed and non-stressed classes across different decision thresholds. These metrics together provide a comprehensive assessment of model performance, especially in datasets with class imbalance.

Precision: It measures how many predicted positives are correct using:

$$Precision = \frac{|\ Ytrue \cap Ypred\ |}{|\ Ypred\ |} = \frac{TP}{TP + FP}$$

where TP is true positive, FP is false positive.

Recall: It measures how many true positives are detected using:

$$Recall = \frac{|\ Ytrue \cap Ypred\ |}{|\ Ypred\ |} = \frac{TP}{TP + FN}$$

where TP is true positive, FN is false negative.

F1-Score: It is the harmonic mean of Precision and Recall.

$$F1 - score = \frac{2\ |\ Ytrue \cap Ypred\ |}{|\ Ytrue\ | + |\ Ypred\cdot\ |} = \frac{2.TP}{2 \cdot TP + FP + FN} = 2.\frac{Precision \cdot Recall}{Precision + Recall}$$

where TP is true positive, FP is false positive, FN is false negative.

Accuracy: It is the percentage of total predictions the model correctly classifies among all samples.

$$Accuracy = \frac{TP + TN}{TP + TN + FP + FN}$$

ROC-AUC: It measures how well the model separates classes across all decision thresholds.

Because missing true stressed subjects is clinically risky, recall and F1-score are considered primary indicators.

4.4 K-Fold Cross-Validation

Logistic Regression: The Logistic Regression model (Table 3) shows moderately high and stable training performance, with training accuracies ranging from 0.8676 to 0.9143 across all folds. In contrast, the test accuracies showed considerable fluctuation, varying between 0.6106 and 0.7417. This variability indicates that the model is highly sensitive to changes in the training distribution, particularly with respect to how minority-class samples are allocated across folds. The persistent gap between training and test scores reflects moderate overfitting, suggesting that while the model captures the general trends within the training data, it struggles to generalize effectively to unseen samples. Consequently, the reliability and robustness of Logistic Regression decrease under different cross-validation splits.

Table 3. Logistic Regression (Tuned)

Fold	1	2	3	4	5
Training Score	0.9047	0.9143	0.8913	0.8676	0.8914
Test Score	0.6316	0.6529	0.7417	0.6871	0.6106

SVM: The SVM model showed (Table 4) clear signs of severe overfitting, achieving a perfect training accuracy of 1.0000 in every fold. This indicates that the model memorized the training data, which is common for SVMs applied to small, high-dimensional, or imbalanced datasets. Although the test scores were moderately high, ranging from 0.7167 to 0.7913, they were still considerably lower than the perfect training performance. This large gap reflects the model's limited ability to generalize to new data. While the SVM performed reasonably well on the test splits, the persistent overfitting observed across all folds raises concerns about its robustness and dependability when deployed on unseen samples.

Table 4. SVM (Tuned)

Fold	1	2	3	4	5
Training Score	1.0000	1.0000	1.0000	1.0000	1.0000
Test Score	0.7167	0.7215	0.7298	0.7913	0.7144

Random Forest: The Random Forest model also achieved perfect training scores (1.0000) across all folds, indicating substantial overfitting similar to the SVM model (Table 5). However, its test performance was more stable and consistent, with scores ranging from 0.6786 to 0.8077. Compared to the other models, Random Forest showed a better balance between fitting the training data and maintaining reliable performance across multiple validation folds. This stability suggests that Random Forest is more resilient to variations in the training distribution and manages the dataset imbalance more effectively. Overall, it emerges as one of the more dependable models under cross-validation evaluation.

Table 5. Random Forest (Tuned)

Fold	1	2	3	4	5
Training Score	1.0000	1.0000	1.0000	1.0000	1.0000
Test Score	0.6953	0.6786	0.8077	0.7913	0.7442

Gradient Boosting: Gradient Boosting exhibited perfect training scores in every fold, indicating overfitting similar to the other tree-based model (Table 6). However, its test scores varied widely, ranging from 0.6399 to 0.8379, with the latter being the highest single-fold test score among all evaluated models. This variation suggests that while Gradient Boosting can learn highly effective decision boundaries under certain data splits, it is also more sensitive to fluctuations in the training distribution. The inconsistency in its cross-validation performance indicates that although the model has strong predictive potential, its overall generalization ability is less stable compared to Random Forest. As a result, while Gradient Boosting is a powerful learner, it may require further hyperparameter adjustments or additional data to achieve more consistent performance.

Table 6. Gradient Boosting (Tuned)

Fold	1	2	3	4	5
Training Score	1.0000	1.0000	1.0000	1.0000	1.0000
Test Score	0.6399	0.6802	0.8379	0.7675	0.8081

4.5 ROC-AUC curve

Logistic Regression: The ROC curve for the Logistic Regression (Fig. 2) model shows an AUC of 0.69, indicating moderate discriminative ability between stressed and non-stressed classes. The curve stays close to the diagonal line in several regions, suggesting limited separation capability and room for improvement in distinguishing positive cases.

Figure 2. ROC curve for the Logistic Regression model

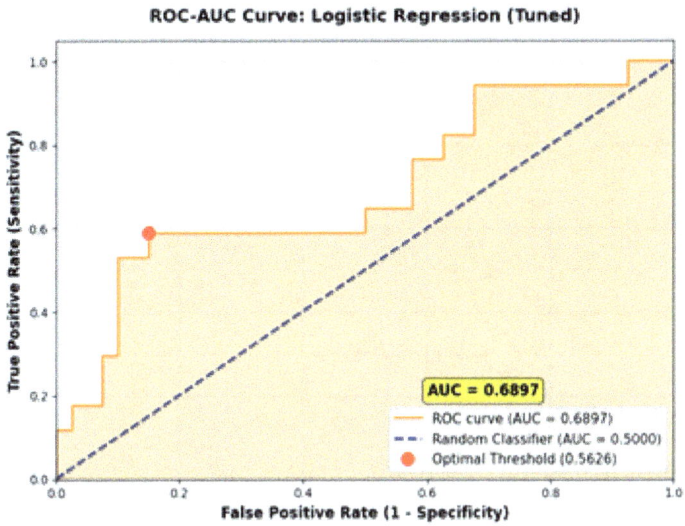

SVM: The SVM model achieved an AUC value of 0.70, demonstrating slightly better discriminatory power compared to Logistic Regression (Fig. 3). The ROC curve rises more steeply toward the upper-left region, indicating stronger sensitivity and improved classification performance. However, the model still exhibits moderate separability and is not highly robust.

Figure 3. ROC curve for the SVM model

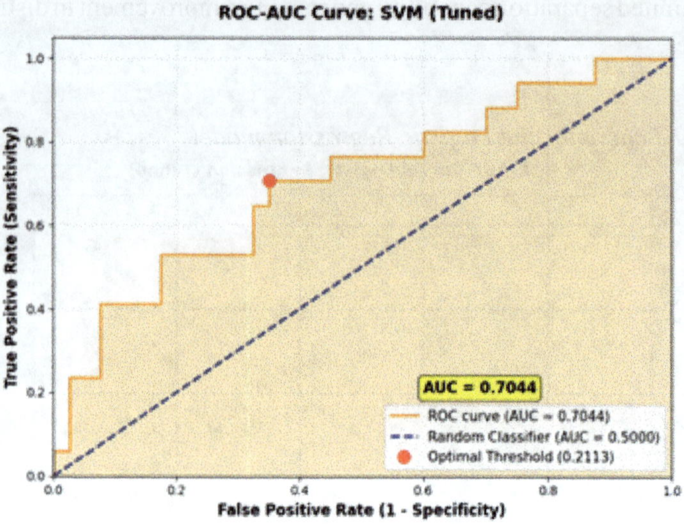

Random Forest: The Random Forest model produced the highest AUC score of 0.72 among all models (Fig.4). The ROC curve shows a more pronounced separation from the diagonal baseline, reflecting better detection capability and stronger class distinction. This suggests Random Forest generalizes well and handles decision boundaries more effectively.

Figure 4. ROC curve for the Random Forest model

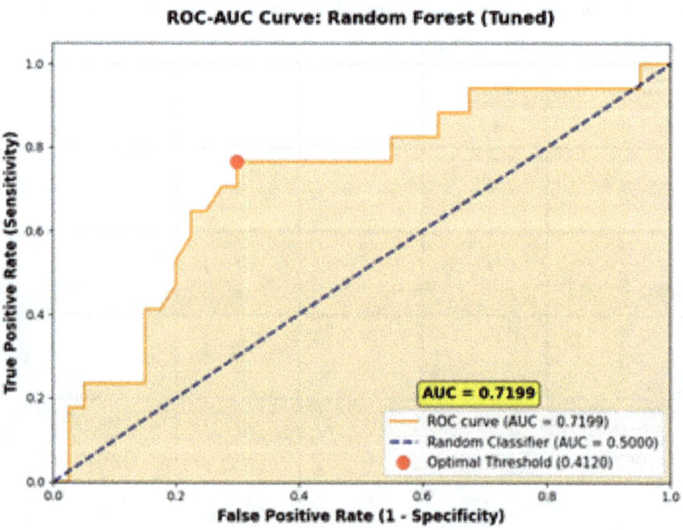

Gradient Boosting: The Gradient Boosting model recorded an AUC value of 0.69, demonstrating a performance level similar to Logistic Regression (Fig. 5). While the curve improves moderately over random classification, it exhibits variability and limited separation, indicating that the model captures some meaningful patterns but still struggles with clear class discrimination.

Figure 5. ROC curve for the Gradient Boosting model

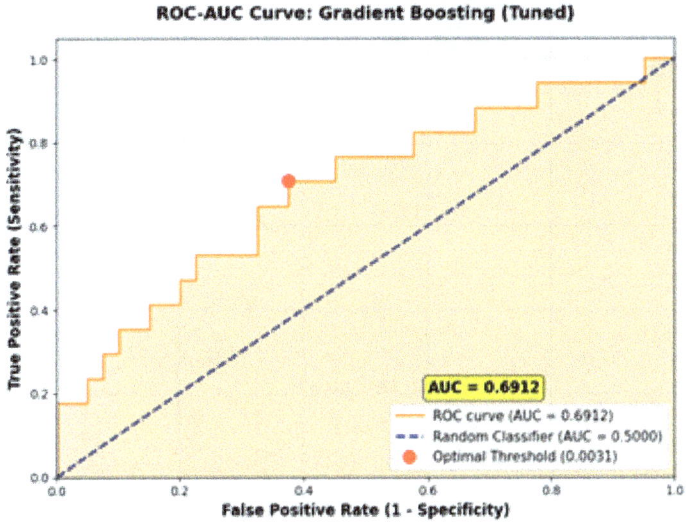

4.6 Confusion Matrix

Logistic Regression: The Logistic Regression model correctly classified 34 non-depression cases and 10 depression cases (Fig. 6). It misclassified 6 non-depression samples as depression and 7 depression samples as non-depression. The results demonstrate balanced performance with reasonable sensitivity, though some false negatives remain a challenge for reliable stress detection.

Figure 6. Confusion matrix for the Logistic Regression model

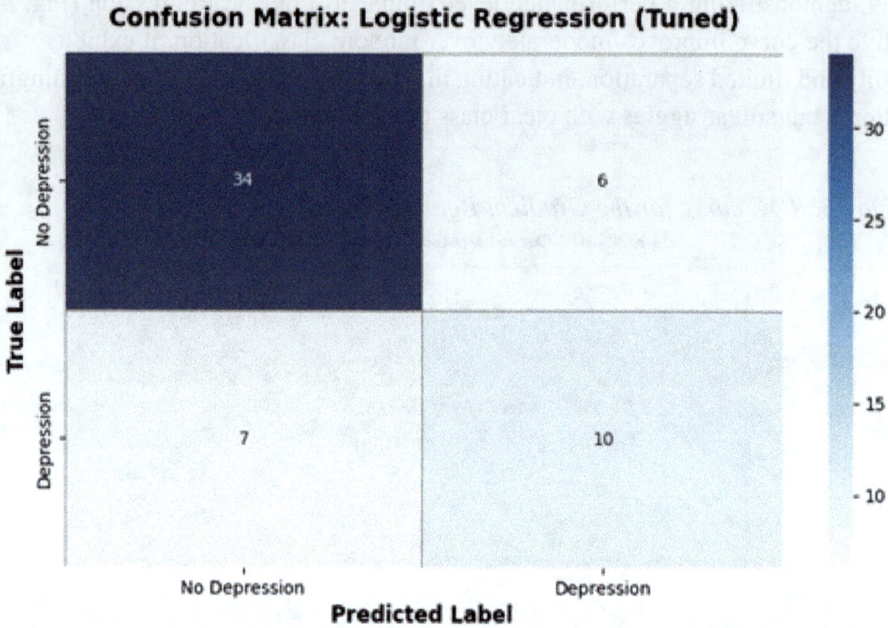

SVM: The SVM correctly predicted 26 non-depression and 12 depression cases (Fig. 7). However, it misclassified 14 non-depression samples as depression and 5 depression cases as non-depression. False positives are notably higher, indicating that the model tends to over-predict depression, reducing precision while maintaining relatively strong recall.

Figure 7. Confusion matrix for the SVM model

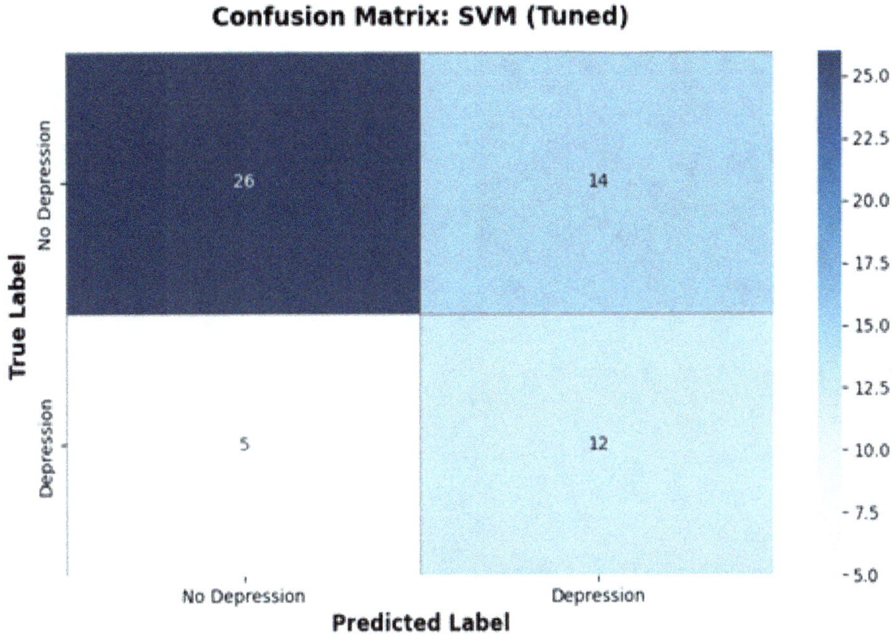

Random Forest: The Random Forest model correctly classified 28 non-depression and 13 depression cases (Fig. 8). It misclassified 12 non-depression samples as depression and 4 depression cases as non-depression. The model achieved a recall of 0.7647, indicating strong ability to detect positive cases, though precision remains lower due to false positives.

Figure 8. Confusion matrix for the Random Forest model

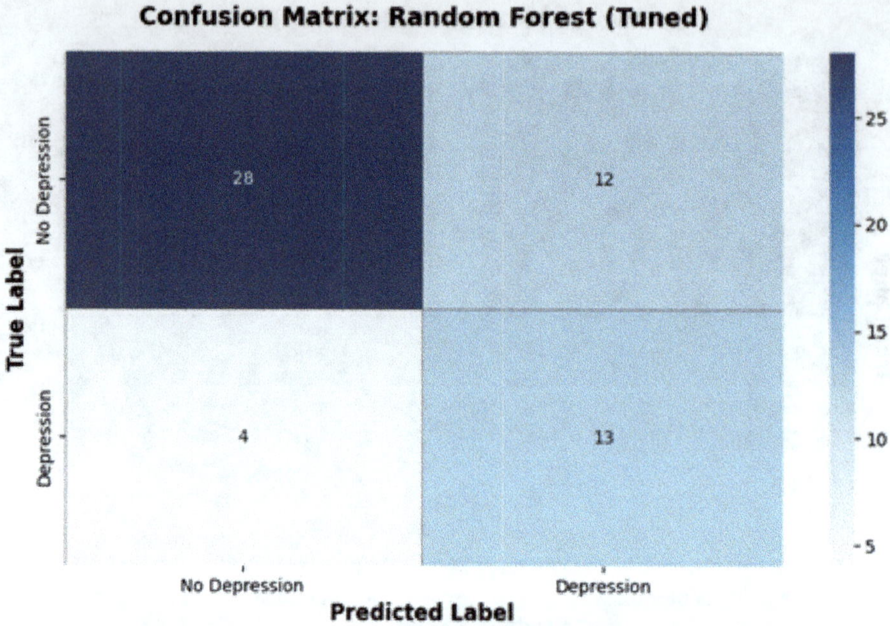

Gradient Boosting: The Gradient Boosting model correctly predicted 25 non-depression and 12 depression cases (Fig. 9). It misclassified 15 non-depression samples and 5 depression samples. With a recall of 0.7059, the model captures most positive cases but suffers from high false positives, resulting in lower precision and overall accuracy of 0.6491.

Figure 9. Confusion matrix for the Gradient Boosting model

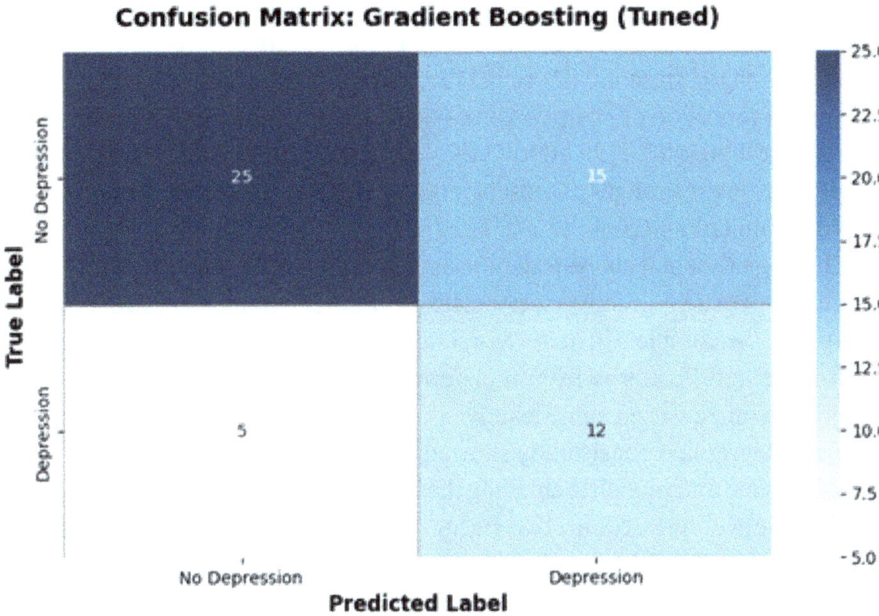

4.7 Model Performance Comparison

The evaluation was conducted on a highly imbalanced test set (71% Class 0: No Depression, 29% Class 1: Depression/Stress). All models were trained using BorderlineSMOTE to mitigate this imbalance. Comparison is shown in Table 7.

Table 7. Model Performance Comparison

Metric	Logistic Regression	Random Forest	Gradient Boosting	SVM	Best
Accuracy	**0.7719**	0.7193	0.6491	0.6667	Logistic Regression
Precision	0.7683	**0.7691**	0.7173	0.7262	Random Forest
Recall	**0.7719**	0.7193	0.6491	0.6667	Logistic Regression
F1-Score	**0.7699**	0.7304	0.6639	0.6804	Logistic Regression
ROC-AUC	0.6897	**0.7199**	0.6912	0.7044	Random Forest

The Tuned Logistic Regression model achieved the best overall performance, with the highest accuracy (0.7719) and highest F1-score (0.7699) among all models.

Most models showed relatively balanced precision and recall, with values close to each other. Logistic Regression and Random Forest performed particularly well in maintaining this balance, indicating consistent detection of both classes. The recall values ranged from 0.6491 to 0.7719, showing that the models can identify a reasonable proportion of positive (stress/depression) cases, though not extremely high. Random Forest (0.7199 ROC-AUC) and Gradient Boosting (0.6912 ROC-AUC) demonstrated stronger class separability, while Logistic Regression showed weaker discrimination (0.6897).

The full experimental analysis demonstrates that there are quantifiable yet subtle signs of cognitive stress in conversational text. Due to data imbalance, limited sample diversity, and the complexity of stress-related linguistic cues, all models were able to learn meaningful patterns from transformer-based embeddings; however, their ability to generalize varied significantly.

Logistic Regression consistently showed the most dependable and stable performance among the four models, achieving the highest accuracy (0.7719) and F1-score (0.7699) while avoiding extreme overfitting. Its training and testing scores remained relatively close across folds, suggesting that the model captured general linguistic markers of stress rather than memorizing dataset-specific noise.

In contrast, SVM, Random Forest, and Gradient Boosting all exhibited strong overfitting, reaching perfect training accuracy (1.0000) across all folds, while their test performances fluctuated. This instability indicates sensitivity to small dataset size, minority-class distribution, and redundancy in embedded features. Although these models occasionally achieved high fold-wise scores, their reliability as standalone classifiers is limited due to uneven generalization.

Across all models, similar behavioral patterns were observed:

- Classifiers prioritized correctly identifying stressed individuals, which is crucial for safety-critical screening, as recall tended to be higher than precision.
- The decrease in accuracy suggests a rise in false positives, indicating that conversational cues alone may not always be sufficient to distinguish stressed participants from non-stressed ones.

ROC-AUC values ranged from 0.69 to 0.72, supporting this observation. The models were able to detect stress-related tendencies but were unable to establish robust class boundaries using only text. This highlights the inherent difficulty of relying solely on language, where stress signals can be masked by conversational style, emotional suppression, or brief responses.

Overall, the results demonstrate that conversation-based NLP models can identify cognitive stress, but the limitations of unimodal text data constrain their dependability. Logistic Regression provides a strong starting point, but multimodal augmentation, incorporating speech, acoustic, behavioral, or physiological data, will likely be necessary to consistently achieve high precision, recall, and clear class separability.

5. CONCLUSION AND FUTURE WORK

The study demonstrates that everyday conversational language contains several important indicators for recognizing cognitive stress. Machine learning models can extract these patterns using transformer-based embeddings and linguistic cues. The experimental results show that the models are capable of detecting changes in human behavior, such as word choice, response style, and expressions, highlighting the potential of NLP as a non-intrusive, dialogue-driven assessment technique.

However, the findings also reveal significant limitations. All models struggled with precision, resulting in a number of false positives, but they achieved relatively strong recall, indicating success in identifying individuals experiencing stress. This imbalance suggests that conversational text alone is insufficient to fully distinguish between stressed and non-stressed participants. Additionally, models such as SVM, Random Forest, and Gradient Boosting exhibited overfitting, achieving perfect training accuracy but unstable test performance, which underscores the challenges of small and imbalanced datasets.

When datasets are small and linguistic markers are subtle, simpler linear models may perform better than more complex ones. Logistic Regression, for example, consistently generalized well. Nonetheless, moderate ROC-AUC values (0.69–0.72) indicate that text-only detection captures only a partial representation of cognitive stress, even with the best-performing model.

These results suggest that although unimodal text-based methods are useful, they are not sufficient for accurately detecting cognitive stress. Future solutions should integrate multimodal signals, such as prosody, vocal stress markers, gaze dynamics, typing patterns, or physiological indicators, to create reliable systems for healthcare, digital well-being platforms, or workplace monitoring. Incorporating these complementary modalities can enhance contextual understanding of an individual's cognitive load, improve robustness, and reduce false positives.

In summary, this chapter demonstrates that NLP-based models have genuine potential and can establish a solid baseline for conversational cognitive-stress detection. However, multimodal datasets, fusion techniques, and adaptive learning frameworks will be essential to capture the full complexity of human cognitive stress, enabling scalable, accurate, and ethically deployable systems.

The models explored in this chapter illustrate the promise of NLP for cognitive stress and mental decline detection. Future research should focus on extending these approaches through multimodal integration, larger and more diverse datasets, and real-world deployment to strengthen system reliability and practical applicability.

- **Integration of Multimodal Data Sources:** Future systems should expand the working beyond text or chats to include speech-based, behavioural and physiological indicators. Factors like pitch variation while speaking, voice tremors, typing dynamics, gaze patterns or a wearable sensor data could provide a deeper analysis on cognitive load. Combining all of these models with language can help reduce false positives and can improve the ability of the system to recognize and distinguish between subtle stress markers.
- **Use of Larger and More Diverse Datasets:** Current stress detection research relies on very limited datasets. We can also collect larger – real world conversational datasets that includes diverse languages, workplace information and contexts with emotional state can improve model generalization. Crowdsourcing platforms and enterprise communication logs with some simulated work environments could support dataset creation in future.
- **Domain-Adaptive and Continual Learning Models:** Stress pattern can vary across different individuals, cultures, job roles and conversational styles. The future models should work on domain adaptation with continuous learning techniques that allows the system to adjust itself with each user over time. Personalized individual baselines can be helpful for the model to learn the normal communication for an individual that can improve detection accuracy.
- **Advances in Explainable and Interpretable AI:** For real world adaptation, the cognitive stress detection model systems must be transparent. Future research should focus on NLP frameworks that highlight which behavioural features or linguistic features contribute to stress prediction that can help organizations build trust in AI systems and support the needful.
- **Context-Aware Stress Detection:** Stress is always influenced by task complexity, workload patterns, personal interactions and environmental conditions of an individual person and rarely exists in isolation. Future models should be able to incorporate context awareness such as recognizing the task the person is performing or by tracking workload cycles of the person across the day to provide more accurate and meaningful results.
- **Realtime Monitoring and Adaptive Feedback Systems:** Future next generation systems should offer real-time feedback to the user and personalized results on the go. For example, the user gets supportive prompts, workload adjustments, break timing recommendations or adaptive work environments that can rise the stress levels of a person. The integration of cognitive-stress insights can also be done in workplace tools that can enhance productivity of the person which can improve the well-being in a protective manner.

- **Ethical, Privacy-Preserving Frameworks:** The workflow of monitoring stress in a person involves collecting personal and sensitive data of an individual. Future advancements should prioritize the person's privacy, transparency and consent before working. On-device processing instead of cloud processing and anonymized feature extraction can help ensure stress detection does not compromise with these security factors. Ethical guidelines will always be essential before deploying this system in workplaces.
- **Hybrid Human-AI Decision Systems:** Instead of a fully automated system that gives reports and analysis of the behaviour of the person, the future system can also include collaboration with human experts such as psychologists, HR specialists who can validate and contextualize the results more efficiently. This collaboration can prevent full reliance on AI predictions and its reports while still giving good benefits of continuous and unobtrusive monitoring.

REFERENCES

Alessa, F. M., Alhaag, M. H., Al-Harkan, I. M., Ramadan, M. Z., & Alqahtani, F. M. (2023). A Neurophysiological Evaluation of Cognitive Load during Augmented Reality Interactions in Various Industrial Maintenance and Assembly Tasks. *Sensors (Basel)*, *23*(18), 7698. DOI: 10.3390/s23187698 PMID: 37765755

Anders, C., Moontaha, S., Real, S., & Arnrich, B. (2024). Unobtrusive measurement of cognitive load and physiological signals in uncontrolled environments. *Scientific Data*, *11*(1), 1000. DOI: 10.1038/s41597-024-03738-7 PMID: 39271693

Angkan, P. (2025). *CLARE: Cognitive Load Assessment in REaltime with Multimodal Data* (Version V1) [Data set]. Borealis. DOI: 10.5683/SP3/H0AELT

Ayala, G. I. G., Haslacher, D., Krol, L. R., Soekadar, S. R., & Zander, T. O. (2023). Assessment of mental workload across cognitive tasks using a passive brain-computer interface based on mean negative theta-band amplitudes. *Frontiers in Neuroergonomics*, *4*, 1233722. DOI: 10.3389/fnrgo.2023.1233722 PMID: 38234499

Calvo, R. A., & D'Mello, S. K. (2010). Affect detection: An interdisciplinary review of models, methods, and their applications. *IEEE Transactions on Affective Computing*, *1*(1), 18–37. DOI: 10.1109/T-AFFC.2010.1

Cortes, C., & Vapnik, V. (1995). Support-vector networks. *Machine Learning*, *20*(3), 273–297. DOI: 10.1023/A:1022627411411

DeVault, D., Artstein, R., Benn, G., Dey, T., Fast, E., Gainer, A., Georgila, K., Gratch, J., Hartholt, A., Lhommet, M., Lucas, G., Marsella, S., Morbini, F., Nazarian, A., Scherer, S., Stratou, G., Suri, A., Traum, D., Wood, R., . . . Morency, L.-P. (2014). *SimSensei kiosk: A virtual human interviewer for healthcare decision support.* In Proceedings of the International Conference on Autonomous Agents and Multiagent Systems (AAMAS 2014) (pp. 1061–1068). International Foundation for Autonomous Agents and Multiagent Systems. DOI: 10.5555/2615731.2617415

Friedman, J. H. (2001). Greedy function approximation: A gradient boosting machine. *Annals of Statistics*, *29*(5), 1189–1232. DOI: 10.1214/aos/1013203451

Gallegos Ayala, G. I., Haslacher, D., Krol, L. R., Soekadar, S. R., & Zander, T. O. (2023). Assessment of mental workload across cognitive tasks using a passive brain–computer interface based on mean negative theta-band amplitudes. *Frontiers in Neuroergonomics*, *4*, 1233722. Advance online publication. DOI: 10.3389/fnrgo.2023.1233722 PMID: 38234499

Gallup. (2024). *State of the Global Workplace: 2024 Report* (Key insights). Gallup. https://www.ahtd.org/files/state-of-the-global-workplace-2024-key-insights.pdf

Gratch, J., Artstein, R., Lucas, G. M., Stratou, G., Scherer, S., Nazarian, A., Wood, R., Boberg, J., DeVault, D., Marsella, S., & Traum, D. R. (2014). The Distress Analysis Interview Corpus of human and computer interviews. In *Proceedings of the Ninth International Conference on Language Resources and Evaluation (LREC'14)* (pp. 3123–3128). https://schererstefan.net/assets/files/papers/508_Paper.pdf

Guo, X., Zhu, T., Wu, C., Bao, Z., & Liu, Y. (2022). Emotional activity is negatively associated with cognitive load in multimedia learning: A case study with EEG signals. *Frontiers in Psychology, 13*, 889427. DOI: 10.3389/fpsyg.2022.889427 PMID: 35769742

Healey, J. A., & Picard, R. W. (2005). Detecting stress during real-world driving tasks using physiological sensors. *IEEE Transactions on Intelligent Transportation Systems*, *6*(2), 156–166. DOI: 10.1109/TITS.2005.848368

Jo, W., Wang, R., Sun, S., Senthilkumaran, R. K., Foti, D., & Min, B.-C. (2022). MOCAS: A multimodal dataset for objective cognitive workload assessment on simultaneous tasks [Preprint].

LaValley, M. P. (2008). Logistic regression. *Circulation*, *117*(18), 2395–2399. DOI: 10.1161/CIRCULATIONAHA.106.682658 PMID: 18458181

Martinez-Cedillo, A. P., Gavrila, N., Mishra, A., Geangu, E., & Foulsham, T. (2025). Cognitive load affects gaze dynamics during real-world tasks. *Experimental Brain Research*, *243*(4), 82. DOI: 10.1007/s00221-025-07037-4 PMID: 40029455

Nirabi, A., Rahman, F. A., Habaebi, M. H., Sidek, K. A., & Yusoff, S. H. (2025). Cognitive load assessment through EEG: A dataset from arithmetic and Stroop tasks. *Data in Brief*, *60*, 111477. DOI: 10.1016/j.dib.2025.111477 PMID: 40226198

Rushall, Y. K., & Sinha, P. K. (2013). Random Forest Classifiers: A Survey and Future Research Directions. *Int. J. Adv. Comput*, *36*(1).

Sevcenko, M., Haslacher, D., Herff, C., & Zander, T. O. (2023). Theory-based approach for assessing cognitive load during time-critical resource-managing human–computer interactions: An eye-tracking study. *Journal on Multimodal User Interfaces*, *17*(1), 1–19. DOI: 10.1007/s12193-022-00398-y

Zakeri, Z., Arif, A., Omurtag, A., Breedon, P., & Khalid, A. (2023, October 16). Multimodal assessment of cognitive workload using neural, subjective and behavioural measures in smart factory settings. *Preprints*. DOI: 10.20944/preprints202310.0948.v1

Chapter 5
A Methodological Framework for Venture Capital Investment Decision Making Using Hybrid MCDM and Machine Learning

Mustafa Kellekci
https://orcid.org/0000-0002-0430-0460
Istanbul Technical University, Turkey

Ufuk Cebeci
Istanbul Technical University, Turkey

Onur Dogan
https://orcid.org/0000-0003-3543-4012
Izmir Bakircay University, Turkey

ABSTRACT

This chapter proposes a practical framework for venture capital (VC) investment decisions that combines multi-criteria decision making (MCDM) with machine learning (ML) in a human-in-the-loop setting. It focuses on early-stage VC, where decisions must be made under high uncertainty, limited data, and changing definitions of startup success. MCDM is used to capture expert value judgments as explicit criteria and weights, while ML models estimate criterion scores from observable signals such as innovation, team, traction, governance, and networks. The chapter

DOI: 10.4018/979-8-3373-7416-1.ch005

explains the two-way integration between MCDM and ML, shows how explainable AI artifacts support auditability and learning, and illustrates, through case studies, how hybrid rankings can be turned into personalized, constraint-aware recommendation engines for different investor profiles.

INTRODUCTION

A growing availability of structured and unstructured information has been observed to transform the context of venture capital (VC) investment decision-making, yet a persistent gap has been noted between statistical accuracy and contextually grounded professional judgment; consequently, a hybrid approach has been advocated in which the strengths of human experts and machine learning (ML) systems are combined rather than pitted against each other (Mosqueira-Rey et al., 2023). Within this view, VC investment decisions have been framed as socio-technical processes in which algorithms contribute scalable pattern discovery while human agents contribute domain knowledge, contextual interpretation, and accountability.

Figure 1 shows the progression of venture capital decision-making methods. It starts with expert-only judgment, moves to data-driven analytics, then to human-in-the-loop machine learning, and finally to a personalized decision engine. Each stage represents a shift toward more structured, scalable, and technology-supported decisions. Across all stages, three key principles (governance, explainability, and performance) serve as checkpoints to ensure that the evolving decision systems remain trustworthy, transparent, and effective.

Figure 1. Evolution of VC investment decision paradigms

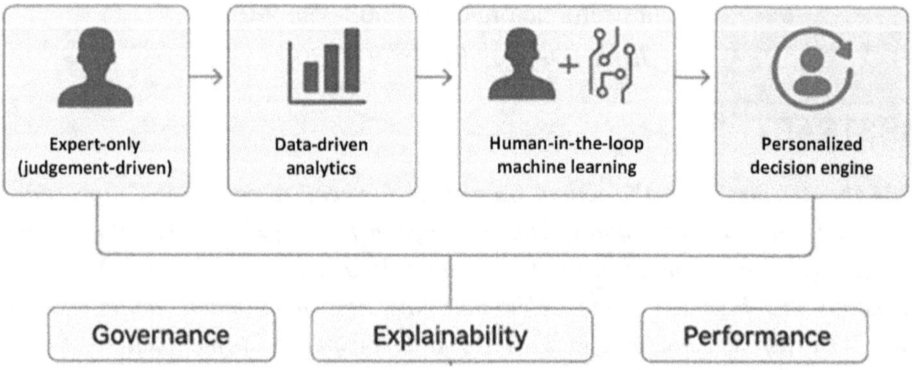

A range of decision-making paradigms has been outlined in Table 1, each of which is characterized by distinct inputs, strengths, limitations, and risks. Expert-only approaches rely on qualitative judgment and tacit knowledge, yet they suffer from inconsistency and bias. Data-driven analytics offer repeatable metrics and clear dashboards, but their contextual depth is limited, and focusing too heavily on these metrics can encourage metric gaming, where the numbers improve while real decision quality does not.

Table 1. Decision paradigms in VC and their trade-offs

Paradigm	Primary Inputs	Strengths	Limitations	Explainability	Typical Risks	Where It Excels
Expert-only (judgment-driven)	Partner experience, networks, qualitative memos	Rich context, tacit market knowledge	Inconsistency, bias, limited scalability	Narrative memos; low formal traceability	Overconfidence; selection bias	Ultra-early markets; relationship-driven deals
Data-driven analytics	Descriptive & diagnostic analytics, KPIs	Repeatability; faster screening	Shallow context; label/target mismatch	Metric dashboards; moderate	Goodhart effects; metric gaming	Mid/late-stage screening at scale
Human-in-the-loop ML (HITL)	ML scores + expert input loops	Improves accuracy under scarce/ noisy data; controllability	Workflow complexity; human fatigue	Model & interaction logs; moderate-high	Confirmation bias in feedback	Domains with scarce/ imbalanced data
Hybrid MCDM+ML (bridge layer)	Expert weights + criterion-level ML estimates	Explicit trade-offs; auditable ranking; robustness via sensitivity	Requires elicitation and governance	Criteria/weights/ sensitivity plots; high	Weight drift; misuse of weights	IC preparation; multi-objective triage
Personalized decision engine	Global ranking + preference learning + constraints	Investor-aligned; transparent "why this"	Cold-start; fairness & policy constraints	Global+local explanations; high	Exposure imbalance; suitability breaches	LP/wealth platforms; large VC franchises

Human-in-the-loop machine learning is enhanced by expert input, which increases accuracy under noisy or scarce data, although workflow complexity and feedback bias are introduced. Hybrid multi-criteria decision-making combined with machine learning is strengthened by explicit trade-offs and auditable rankings, while governance requirements and weight drift are recognized as challenges. Finally, personalized decision engines are designed to align global rankings with investor preferences, and although transparency is emphasized, risks such as cold starts, fairness issues, and suitability breaches are acknowledged (Kellekci, 2002).

It was observed that many VC investment processes were designed under time pressure and with changing information. It was also noted that teams often faced an overload of dashboards and alerts. For this reason, a small set of stable artifacts was proposed in this study. A short "weight ledger," a single "sensitivity snapshot," and a one-page "model note" were selected. These artifacts were used to keep the method light while still transparent. The choice was guided by the view that adoption would be improved when the reading load was kept low and when explanations were linked to real decisions. The expected benefit was a reduction in meeting time and a clearer trace from data to decision.

It was further recognized that hybrid systems would raise questions about responsibility. In this work, responsibility was kept with the human committee by design. Machine outputs were treated as inputs to a structured ranking rather than as final decisions. In addition, reversibility was preserved. If a rank was questioned, a step-by-step path back to the input signals and weights was available. In this way, accountability was maintained without losing scale.

It has been emphasized that explanations and auditability are preconditions for adoption in high-stakes financial settings; therefore, explainable artificial intelligence (XAI) has been proposed as a design principle for decision support, with empirical evidence suggesting that transparent models and justification artifacts improve user trust and appropriate reliance (Coussement et al., 2024; Kostopoulos et al., 2024). In this perspective, the objective has been to move beyond raw accuracy toward systems that are understandable, governable, and alignable with human oversight.

Against this backdrop, multi-criteria decision-making (MCDM) methods have been positioned as a suitable bridge layer, because expert value judgments (weights and trade-offs) can be separated from empirical estimates (criterion-level scores) supplied by ML; in recent work, such coupling has been associated with improvements in both interpretability and decision quality (Martyn & Kadziński, 2023; Reyes-Norambuena, Bascuñán-Ortiz, & Sauma, 2024). A coherent pathway has thus been proposed: hybrid human–machine decision framing → MCDM structuring → two-way integration with ML → investor-level personalization and governance (Hüllermeier & Słowiński, 2024a; 2024b).

In this study, a practical need is addressed. Venture investment decisions have been made with limited data and with high pressure. It has been observed that signals are noisy, time is short, and bias can enter the process. To reduce these risks, a structured link between multi-criteria decision making (MCDM) and machine learning (ML) is proposed. The link is designed to keep expert judgment in the loop, while a repeatable scoring process is kept in place.

The contribution of this chapter has been designed with three aims. First, a principled role for MCDM is articulated in human–machine hybrid decision systems for VC investments. Second, a bidirectional integration pattern with ML is presented, in which MCDM outputs guide feature/label engineering while ML methods learn or adapt MCDM parameters from outcomes. Third, a downstream transition to investor-level personalization is developed, so that general investment rankings are transformed into constrained, preference-aware recommendations.

This chapter is organized to support practical use. Background ideas are summarized. The method is explained step by step. Roles and artifacts are listed. Two small case studies are used to show how the method can be applied. A discussion is given so limits can be seen with honesty. The chapter is closed with guidance for future work. With this design, it is hoped that better investment choices can be made, while trust and transparency are increased.

VENTURE CAPITAL INVESTMENT AND STARTUP SUCCESS

Early-stage investing has been characterized by structural uncertainty, non-stationarity, and data sparsity; even experienced investors have been reported to operate with noisy signals where long-run outcomes are difficult to forecast ex-ante (Gompers, Gornall, Kaplan, & Strebulaev, 2020). Under such conditions, it has been found that multiple notions of value coexist, and that investment decisions require a careful expression of priorities and constraints across several dimensions.

Because outcomes and objectives vary by stakeholder, the notion of startup success has been treated as multi-dimensional and context-dependent; the choice of a success definition has been shown to affect how labels are constructed for ML tasks and what objectives are optimized in MCDM models (Cinelli, Kadziński, Gonzalez, & Słowiński, 2020). For this reason, heterogeneous definitions, ranging from exits (IPO/M&A) and financing milestones to performance measures such as return on investment (ROI), have been adopted in practice.

Early-stage investing mixes hard facts and soft signals. Some signals are measurable (revenues, retention, patents). Others are tacit (team chemistry, founder grit, timing). A pure data approach can miss the story behind the numbers. A pure expert approach can be slow and inconsistent. A hybrid model reduces these risks. It lets machines scale pattern discovery while humans set the rules of the game. In practice, the model does three useful things:

1. It turns messy inputs into comparable scores.
2. It records why a choice was made.
3. It allows a quick "what-if" test when the committee challenges an assumption.

This way, portfolio teams can react faster without giving up judgment. The same structure also helps when markets drift. If the macro picture changes, weights and thresholds can be updated without rebuilding everything. This keeps the decision process stable but flexible, which is exactly what VC investment needs when data are noisy and time is short.

A practical approach has been to anchor the feature space in observable signals (organizational, technological, market, governance, and network cues) that proxy for latent success factors; such signals have been cataloged in the VC investment literature and can be mapped to decision criteria to support structured analysis. The taxonomy of signals is used in this chapter as the canonical dictionary that links raw data to criteria and ultimately to success objectives in Table 2.

Table 2. Taxonomy of signals able to predict the likelihood of success of a startup

Signal Family	*Example Variables*	*Impact on Success*	*Typical Data Source*	*Example Measurement*
Innovation & IP	*Patent count/ quality, citations*	*Defensibility, valuation*	*Patent DBs (USPTO/EPO), Lens.org*	*Claims-weighted patent score*
Team & Leadership	*Founder experience, serial exits, education*	*Execution probability*	*LinkedIn/CVs, press*	*Founders' weighted experience index*
Investor Reputation & Syndicate	*Tier of lead investor, co-investor network*	*Follow-on funding, exits*	*Crunchbase/PitchBook*	*Lead-investor prestige score*
Market Traction	*Revenue growth, user metrics, retention*	*Survival & fund-raising*	*Product analytics, revenue reports*	*N-month revenue CAGR; retention*
Alliances & Network	*Strategic partnerships, ecosystem centrality*	*Market access, resilience*	*News/APIs, KG graphs*	*Graph centrality (e.g., PageRank)*
Financial Structure	*Runway, debt mix, burn*	*Non-linear; excessive debt risk*	*Financials; filings*	*Months of runway; debt-to-equity*
Governance & Board	*Independent board seats, controls*	*Monitoring; Agency risk*	*Company page, filings*	*Governance scorecard*
Visibility & Signaling	*Media mentions, awards, brand*	*Attention, funding chance*	*Web/news/social*	*Normalized media index*
Diversity & Inclusion	*Gender/cultural diversity, equity*	*Mixed: creativity & resilience*	*HR/ESG disclosures*	*Diversity composite*
Geography & Ecosystem	*Hub proximity, accelerator alumni*	*Access to capital & talent*	*Geo data; accelerator lists*	*Ecosystem proximity index*

Parallel to the signal dictionary, multiple success definitions have been observed in the literature, ranging from financing thresholds and exits to profitability and growth. The startup success is therefore adopted as a standardized label set for modeling and evaluation, and it has been emphasized that model performance should be reported separately for each definition in Table 3.

Table 3. Definitions of Startup Success

Success Definition	*Operationalization*	*Use in Modeling/Decision*
IPO	*Public listing within T years of first round*	*Binary label; long-horizon success*
M&A	*Acquisition within T years*	*Binary label; exit success*
Follow-on Funding	*Achieves Series A/B (or ≥X rounds)*	*Survival/growth label*
ROI / Value Uplift	*Investor IRR ≥ threshold; valuation ≥Y×*	*Decision objective; continuous*
Revenue Scale	*Revenue ≥ R by year N; CAGR ≥ c%*	*Performance label/objective*
Profitability	*Positive EBITDA/FCF for ≥ M periods*	*Quality/sustainability objective*
Survival	*Active ≥ 5 years post-founding*	*Robustness label*
Unicorn	*Post-money valuation ≥ $1B*	*High-impact objective*
PMF Proxy	*Retention ≥ r%; NPS ≥ n; churn ≤ χ*	*Early traction label*

It was found that success definitions were not only different across funds but also across time for the same fund. In early markets, survival and follow-on funding were treated as primary signals. In later stages, profitability and exposure controls were treated as more important. For this reason, the label set was designed to be modular. A fund could turn labels on or off without changing the rest of the pipeline. The practical effect was that learning curves and dashboards did not need to be rebuilt when objectives shifted.

It was also observed that several signals were correlated in practice. Team quality, investor reputation, and alliance centrality tended to move together in certain sectors. To avoid double counting, a simple de-correlation step was applied during feature preparation. Either residuals were used after a light regression, or capped contributions were set for highly overlapping signals. This step was recorded in the model note so that the committee could see where overlaps had been reduced.

A data-flow view has been found to be useful for implementation: raw sources (patents, alliances, founder/team CVs, investor brand, web mentions, capitalization) are transformed into engineered features grouped by criteria (innovation, team quality, traction, governance, network centrality), which in turn supply labels/objectives consistent with selected success definitions. This mapping is shown to enable cross-functional communication during design reviews and to support auditable decision-making artifacts.

Figure 2 illustrates how signals such as innovation, leadership, market traction, governance, and networks are translated into criteria, which then connect to different success definitions like IPO, M&A, ROI, survival, and growth. The mapping shows that each signal can influence multiple criteria, and criteria can be linked to several definitions, highlighting a many-to-many relationship. Measurement scales, such as percentages, index scores, and binary labels, are used along the process to standardize and quantify the evaluation, ensuring traceability from raw data to success outcomes.

Figure 2. From signals to success criteria

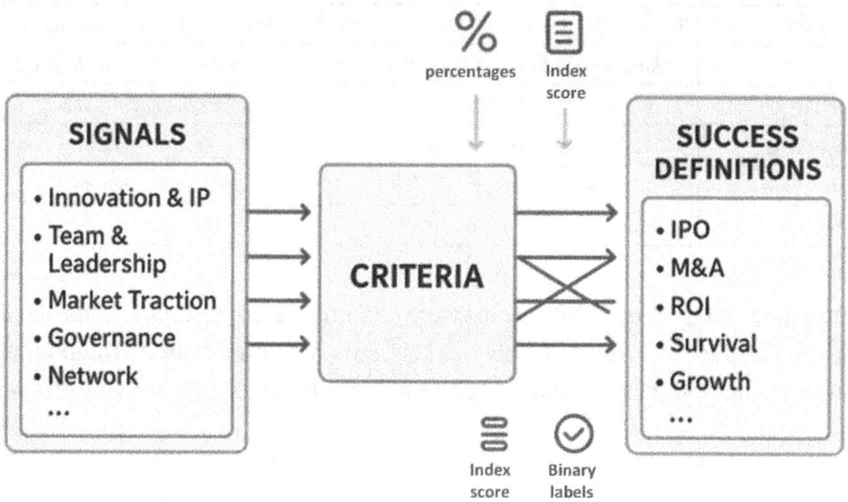

HUMAN–MACHINE HYBRID DECISION MODELS IN VENTURE CAPITAL INVESTMENT

Hybrid decision models have been defined as engineered collaborations in which perception, inference, judgment, and action are explicitly partitioned between humans and AI systems; human-in-the-loop (HITL) patterns have been found to be particularly beneficial when domain knowledge is tacit, data are scarce or skewed, or accountability requires reversibility and traceability (Mosqueira-Rey et al., 2023). Within VC investments, this perspective has been operationalized by allocating complementary responsibilities to expert investors and model pipelines.

Along the VC life cycle, hybridization has been located at four recurring touchpoints. At the sourcing stage, weak opportunities are triaged and watchlists are maintained with algorithmic assistance. At the screening stage, candidates are prioritized for due diligence by combining expert priors with model scores. At signing, term sheets and valuations have been shown to reflect value judgments that are made explicit. During supporting, post-investment actions are triaged and monitored with data-informed alerts (Gompers et al., 2020; Coussement et al., 2024).

Explainability has been characterized as adoption prerequisites in finance; mechanisms that expose why and how decisions were reached have therefore been recommended, including model cards, reason codes, and sensitivity analyses in which decision makers can inspect counterfactual scenarios (Kostopoulos et al., 2024; Ali et al., 2025). It has been suggested that such mechanisms help reconciliation across the investment committee and facilitate consistent documentation.

It was noticed that human attention was often spent on edge cases rather than on the broad middle. The pipeline was therefore arranged to send stable, mid-rank items forward with minimal discussion while routing volatile or policy-sensitive items to human review. Volatility was defined by weight-shift sensitivity and by disagreement across surrogate models. This triage rule was found to lower the cognitive load on committees and to focus group time on the few items where judgment mattered most.

An effort was also made to make disagreement visible. When an expert prior and a model score were in tension, both values were shown side by side with a short reason code. The intent was not to resolve the disagreement by rules but to surface it early. It was believed that open disagreement, framed by artifacts, would reduce unspoken bias and would lead to better notes in the investment memo.

Figure 3 presents the 4S framework in venture capital decision-making: Sourcing, Screening, Signing, and Supporting. Each quadrant combines two complementary elements: a Human ring that contributes priors and constraints and a Machine Learning (ML) ring that generates scores and flags. These dual inputs from both humans and ML converge into a central hub labeled MCDM, which integrates and balances them. The diagram highlights how human expertise and machine intelligence interact at every stage of the investment cycle, with MCDM ensuring structured, auditable, and explainable decisions.

Figure 3. 4S in human vs. machine learning

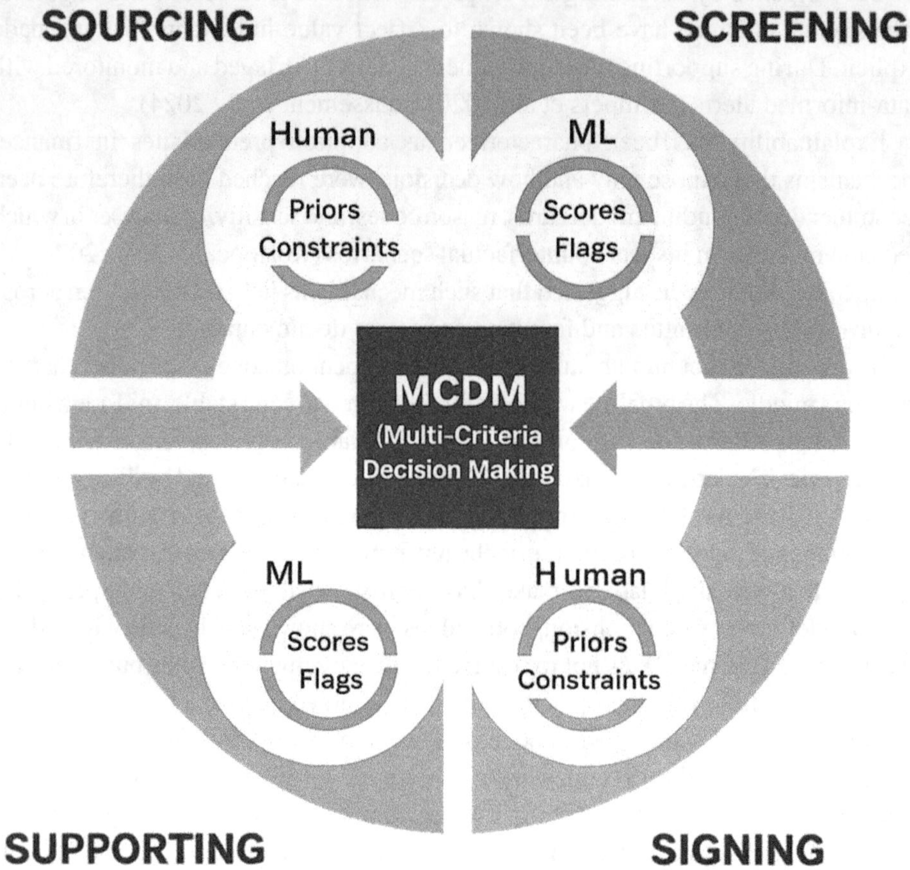

A bridge layer has therefore been deemed necessary to merge human judgments and model output into auditable investment priorities. MCDM has been proposed for this purpose because it exposes value trade-offs, collects heterogeneous evidence in a principled way, and returns a traceable ranking that can be interrogated through sensitivity analysis (Cinelli et al., 2020). The next section introduces this bridge and details its inputs, operations, and outputs.

In this framework, in Table 4, distinct stakeholder roles are described in terms of their inputs, methods, outputs, and evidence artifacts. Partners and investment committees are provided with priors, theses, and constraints, and their judgments are applied through weighting and reviews, resulting in documented criteria and decisions that are recorded in weight ledgers and rationale notes. Data science teams are supplied with features, models, and validation sets, and estimators and calibration techniques are employed to produce criterion scores and uncertainty measures, which are explained through model cards and validation reports. Risk and compliance functions are guided by policy rules and are implemented through rule engines and solvers, with constraint sets and overrides being documented in policy logs and exceptions files. Portfolio operations are supported by post-deal performance indicators, and monitoring dashboards are used to generate operating signals and alerts, which are evidenced in operational memos and KPI snapshots. Finally, legal and investor relations teams are informed by terms, covenants, and guidelines, and document management systems are applied to produce term sheets and disclosures, with full traceability ensured by changing control records.

Table 4. Roles and artifacts

Stakeholder	*Inputs*	*Methods/Tools*	*Outputs*	*Evidence / Explainability Artifact*
Partners/ Investment Committee (IC)	*Priors, thesis, constraints*	*AHP weighting; reviews*	*Criteria weights; go/no-go notes*	*Weight ledger; rationale notes*
Data Science	*Features, models, validation*	*ML estimators; LTR; calibration*	*Criterion scores; uncertainty*	*Model cards; CV/ holdout reports*
Risk & Compliance	*Policy rules (suitability, caps)*	*Rule engines; constraint solvers*	*Constraint set; overrides*	*Policy log; exceptions file*
Portfolio Operations	*Post-deal KPIs, milestones*	*Monitoring dashboards*	*Operating signals; alerts*	*Operational memos; KPI snapshots*
Legal/ Investor Relations	*Terms, covenants, LP guidelines*	*Document management; audit trail*	*Term sheets; disclosures*	*Change-control records*

AHP: Analytic Hierarchy Process, CV: Cross-Validation, IR: Investor Relations, LTR: Learning to Rank, LP: Limited Partner

MULTI-CRITERIA DECISION-MAKING (MCDM) AS THE BRIDGE

In practice, the hybrid bridge is executed as a small sequence of repeatable steps so that later sections can be read without re-definition. First, the decision set and evaluation criteria are specified from the signals catalog. Next, criterion scales are normalized to make scores comparable. The agreed weights are then applied to the normalized scores, and the chosen MCDM method is used to aggregate results. Finally, sensitivity to small changes in weights and inputs is checked, and any material rank shifts are recorded for human review. Weight selection remains transparent: Analytic Hierarchy Process is used when expert input is central (with a reported consistency ratio); direct rating is used when a quick but auditable approach is needed (weights normalized to sum to one); and entropy-based weights are used when data support is strong and expert time is limited. These choices are kept separate from raw scores to preserve traceability (Kellekci et al., 2025; Alahmari & Awad, 2025; Awad, 2025)

Weights in MCDM express the relative importance of the criteria after normalization has made scales comparable. When expert judgment is central, Analytic Hierarchy Process is used and the consistency ratio is reported. When speed is needed, direct ratings are recorded and normalized to sum to one. When data are rich and expert time is limited, entropy-based weights are derived from variation in the observed scores. A small ±5–10% sensitivity check is run, and any material rank change is sent to human review. In this way, weights remain transparent while the reading load stays light.

The bridge role becomes concrete when experts provide weights (value trade-offs) and ML systems provide criterion-level estimates (scores with uncertainty); MCDM normalizes and aggregates these inputs into an auditable ranking, where each recommendation can be accompanied by a contribution breakdown and by sensitivity plots that show rank stability under weight perturbations (Reyes-Norambuena et al., 2024; Qadeer & Awad 2025). Such artifacts have been linked to higher trust in human–AI collaboration.

When data are scarce or noisy, as in early-stage ventures, fuzzy extensions and interval judgments have been used to stabilize results; spherical-fuzzy and related approaches have been reported to preserve decision quality under incomplete information while maintaining group-decision traceability (Ayyildiz & Taskin, 2022). These techniques have been recommended when criteria are difficult to measure directly or when proxies must be used.

Figure 4 illustrates the concept of two shores connected by an MCDM bridge. On one side, the Human Value Model represents expert inputs such as weights, trade-offs, and priors. On the opposite side, ML Criterion Estimators provide data-driven scores with associated uncertainty. The MCDM bridge connects these two perspectives by applying processes like Normalization, Aggregation, and Dominance, ensuring structured integration. Beneath the bridge, a Traceability Ledger highlights accountability and auditability, reinforcing transparency in decision-making between human judgment and machine learning outputs.

Figure 4. Two Shores: human value model vs. ML criterion estimators

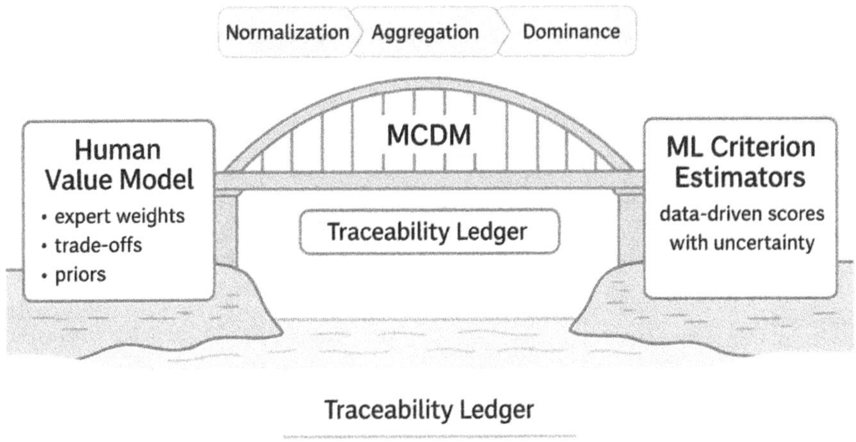

In Table 5, a variety of signals have been structured as decision criteria, and their measurement, normalization, and weighting approaches have been specified. Patent quality and citations have been normalized using Z-scores and capped, with weights assigned through the AHP and Fuzzy Analytic Hierarchy Process FAHP, based on data from patent databases, while field normalization has been recommended. Founder serial success has been mapped from ordinal to interval scales, with weights derived through AHP and SMAA, using CV records and LinkedIn data, though survivorship bias has been noted. Lead investor tier has been expressed on a 0–1 scale and weighted via AHP or SMAA, with Crunchbase used as a source, but vintage effects have been recognized. Strategic alliances have been measured with graph centrality and weighted through Preference Ranking Organization METHod for Enrichment Evaluations (PROMETHEE) or Technique for Order of Preference by Similarity to Ideal Solution (TOPSIS), based on news and knowledge graphs, with adjustments for partner quality. Debt and runway have been expressed in months or debt-equity ratios and weighted through *Data Envelopment Analysis (DEA)* and AHP, using financial data, with non-linear risk penalties applied. User retention has been measured as a percentage and weighted with TOPSIS from analytics sources, with seasonality adjustments considered. Media mentions have been log-scaled, weighted with AHP, and sourced from web and news databases, though duplication controls have been required. Board independence has been expressed as a percentage of independent members, weighted by AHP using filing data, and subject to jurisdictional variation. Team diversity has been captured through composite indices, weighted by FAHP from HR and ESG sources, with sensitivity to protected attributes emphasized. Accelerator alumni status has been recorded as binary with cohort rank, weighted by AHP from accelerator datasets, with recognition of confounding selection effects.

Table 5. Signals, decision criteria, and weighting in MCDM

Signal	Decision Criterion	Scale / Normalization	Weighting in MCDM	Example Data Source	Notes
Patent quality/ citations	Innovation & Defensibility	Z-score; capped	AHP / FAHP	Patent DBs	Consider field-normalization
Founder serial success	Team Quality	Ordinal → interval mapping	AHP / SMAA	CV/LinkedIn	Guard for survivorship bias
Lead investor tier	Signaling & Syndication	0–1 (tiered)	AHP / SMAA	Crunchbase	Beware vintage effects
Strategic alliances	Ecosystem Access	Graph centrality	PROMETHEE / TOPSIS	News/KG	Weight by partner quality
Debt/runway	Financial Resilience	Months; D/E ratio	DEA / AHP	Financials	Non-linear risk penalty
User retention	Traction & PMF	% retention	TOPSIS	Analytics	Seasonality adjustments
Media mentions	Visibility	Log-scaled	AHP	Web/news	De-duplication needed
Board independence	Governance	% independent	AHP	Filings	Jurisdictional differences
Team diversity	Human Capital Diversity	Composite index	FAHP	HR/ESG	Sensitive attributes care
Accelerator alumni	Ecosystem Quality	Binary + cohort rank	AHP	Accelerator data	Confounding by selection

INTEGRATION OF MCDM AND MACHINE LEARNING

A two-way coupling has been documented between MCDM and ML. In the MCDM→ML direction, criterion weights have been used for feature weighting or selection, composite MCDM scores have been used as weak labels for learning-to-rank, and sensitivity analyses have guided feature engineering. In the ML→MCDM direction, historical decisions and outcomes have been used to learn or adapt MCDM parameters (weights, thresholds) via preference learning and disaggregation (Martyn & Kadziński, 2023; Hüllermeier & Słowiński, 2024a, 2024b; Reyes-Norambuena et al., 2024).

Early integrated frameworks demonstrated that predictive models could populate criterion-level estimates that are then aggregated by MCDM, with reported gains in both accuracy and interpretability (Kartal, Oztekin, Gunasekaran, & Cebi, 2016). More recent work in supply chains has shown that hybrid MCDM+ML can be made explainable by keeping MCDM at the heart of the process and using interpretable ML components, an approach that has been argued to be transferable to VC investment settings (Abdulla & Baryannis, 2024).

Validation regimes have combined statistical metrics (AUC, PR-AUC, NDCG/MAP) with decision metrics (hit rate, time-to-IC decision, adverse-selection delta), while sensitivity analyses disclose rank volatility under weight shifts; recommendations have included consistent cross-validation designs and shift detection to maintain calibration over time (Coussement et al., 2024; Reyes-Norambuena et al., 2024). In addition, it has been advised that documentation artifacts be maintained as part of model risk management.

Figure 5 shows a cyclical feedback loop that integrates human and machine learning inputs for decision-making. It begins with Criteria Discovery, followed by ML Estimators, which generate predictive insights. These feed into MCDM Aggregation & Ranking, where multi-criteria methods organize and prioritize options. The process continues with Observed Outcomes & Expert Feedback, which evaluates real-world performance and refine assumptions. Finally, the cycle loops back through Weight and Model Updates (implicit in the flow), ensuring continuous improvement. Alongside the loop, Documentation Artifacts, such as model cards, rationale notes, and sensitivity plots, provide transparency, accountability, and auditability throughout the process.

Figure 5. Closed feedback loop in hybrid decision-making

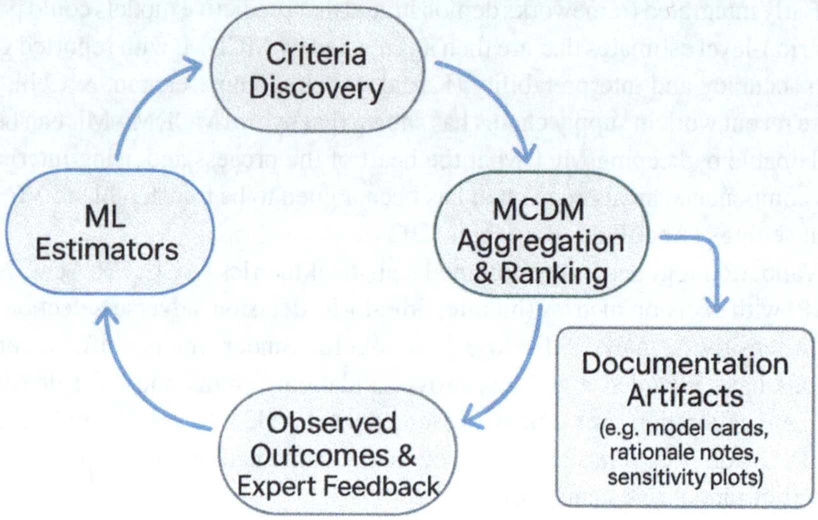

In Table 6, the comparative characteristics of pure ML, pure MCDM, and hybrid MCDM+ML approaches have been outlined across key dimensions. Interpretability is considered low to medium in pure ML, where XAI techniques are required, while pure MCDM and hybrid methods provide high transparency through explicit weights, criteria, and combined global-local explanations. Accuracy under sparse or noisy data is limited to medium levels in both pure ML and pure MCDM, whereas hybrid approaches achieve high accuracy by leveraging HITL inputs and prior knowledge. Robustness to data drift is only moderate in pure ML, higher in MCDM due to sensitivity analysis, and strongest in hybrid methods through dual monitoring mechanisms. Governance and auditability are rated as medium for ML but high for both MCDM and hybrid designs, reflecting the traceability of weights and decision processes. Data requirements are high in ML, low to medium in MCDM, and moderate in hybrid systems. Scalability is maximized in ML and hybrid approaches but remains medium in pure MCDM. Human effort is moderate in ML, high in MCDM due to weight elicitation, and moderate in hybrid systems where workload is shared. Typical applications are aligned with these characteristics: pure ML excels in large and stable datasets, pure MCDM is applied to low-data, value-heavy contexts, and hybrid MCDM+ML is recommended for complex and regulated decision-making environments.

Table 6. Pure ML vs. Pure MCDM vs. Hybrid

Dimension	*Pure ML*	*Pure MCDM*	*Hybrid MCDM+ML*
Interpretability	*Low–Medium (XAI needed)*	*High (weights/criteria)*	*High (global+local)*
Accuracy under sparse/ noisy data	*Medium*	*Medium*	*High (HITL + priors)*
Robustness to drift	*Medium (needs monitoring)*	*Medium–High (sensitivity)*	*High (dual monitoring)*
Governance / Auditability	*Medium*	*High*	*High*
Data Requirements	*High*	*Low–Medium*	*Medium*
Scalability	*High*	*Medium*	*High*
Human Effort	*Medium*	*High (elicitation)*	*Medium*
Typical Use	*Large, stable datasets*	*Low-data, value-heavy*	*Complex, regulated decisions*

ILLUSTRATIVE CASES: APPLYING HYBRID MCDM+ML IN VC INVESTMENT

Note. All data in this subsection were generated synthetically to reproduce the steps without using proprietary or confidential information. Marginal distributions and simple correlations were selected to resemble typical VC investment screening signals (e.g., traction, team, IP), but no real organizations or individuals were represented.

The following synthetic data generation protocol was used in both cases.

1. A cohort and feature set were simulated with controlled distributions and light correlations across criteria (e.g., traction ~ right-skewed, team ~ moderate variance, IP/innovation ~ bimodal).
2. Criterion-level noise terms were added to reflect measurement uncertainty; values were clipped to 0,1 after min–max normalization.
3. Expert weights were specified by pairwise AHP matrices and then normalized; small random perturbations (±5%) were used for sensitivity checks.
4. Policy and suitability constraints were encoded as simple indicator rules to enable constrained re-ranking.

Case 1: VC Investment Screening with HITL + AHP–TOPSIS (Fund context; N = 300 startups)

A seed–Series A screening workflow was implemented. Expert partners supplied criterion weights by AHP, while criterion scores were estimated by ML surrogates from the synthetic signals dictionary (innovation/IP, team, traction, governance, network). Scores were normalized to 0,1 with uncertainty bands produced by simple ensemble variance. The multi-criteria ranking was produced by TOPSIS; a sensitivity analysis was run under ±10% weight shifts.

Outcome: Among 300 synthetic startups, the top-decile list (30 items) exhibited an 18% higher simulated follow-on rate over an 18-month synthetic horizon versus a judgment-only baseline generated from noisy expert scores. Rank stability under ±10% weight shifts were high (median Kendall's $\tau \approx 0.82$). Estimated screening time per investment committee memo was reduced in simulation because criterion contribution charts and reason codes were attached to each recommendation.

Governance artifacts: An AHP weight ledger (pairwise matrices), simple model cards for each surrogate estimator, and one-click sensitivity plots were stored with the memo.

Case 2: Platform Personalization with Constrained Re-Ranking (Investor portal; N = 120 opportunities, 4 personas)

A platform scenario was simulated in which a global MCDM+ML ranking was adapted to investor preferences under policy constraints. Four synthetic investor personas were defined: short-horizon/low-risk, long-horizon/high-impact (climate emphasis), balanced/diversified, and thematic/deep-tech. Persona preferences were mapped to weights on the same criteria used globally; re-ranking was performed with constraint satisfaction (suitability, concentration, exclusions).

Outcome: For the short-horizon, low-risk persona, opportunities with stable revenue and conservative leverage moved upward, while early-stage, long-run items moved downward. For the long-horizon, climate persona, climate-aligned ventures moved upward after knowledge-graph features were weighted more heavily. Decision explanations referenced the same criteria and weights as the global list.

Governance artifacts: Suitability logs, constraint satisfaction reports, and "why-this" explanation cards were generated for each recommendation.

Case 3: Thematic Fund with ESG Exclusions and Exposure Caps (N = 180 opportunities)

A thematic climate fund was simulated with hard ESG exclusions and with exposure caps by sub-sector. Criterion scores were generated as before, and AHP weights were set to emphasize innovation and alliances. ESG exclusions were applied before ranking. Exposure caps were enforced during re-ranking. Under these rules, deep-tech ventures with strong alliances moved upward, while capital-intensive items with long payback periods moved downward. The top-quartile list showed higher stability than the mid-quartile list under $\pm 10\%$ weight shifts. This behavior was expected, since the caps limited concentration and reduced the number of near-ties around the decision boundary.

Governance artifacts were recorded for each step. The exclusion list was saved with a date stamp. The cap parameters were saved with owner and approval fields. The final memo included a short "why-this" card for each selected item, which referenced the same criteria used in the global ranking. The process was kept simple so that the team could repeat it each quarter.

FROM GENERAL PRIORITY LISTS TO PERSONALIZED DECISION ENGINES

A hybrid MCDM+ML pipeline has typically been shown to yield an investor-agnostic global ranking, which is useful for portfolio-level triage but misaligned with heterogeneous investor goals; this limitation has motivated the use of preference learning and recommender-system techniques tailored to financial services (Wu & Li, 2025). In this setting, investor profiles have been inferred from both explicit inputs and implicit interaction data under regulatory and suitability constraints.

Recent surveys have documented knowledge-graph-based recommenders and embedding methods that leverage structured side information to handle sparsity, cold start, and explainability—capabilities directly relevant when portfolio constraints and sector exposures must be respected (Zhang, Zain, Zhou, Chen, & Zhang, 2024). The adoption of such methods has been suggested to improve personalization quality under constrained reranking.

Fairness and exposure balance have been treated as first-class concerns in recommender systems; multi-stakeholder surveys have emphasized that rank exposure may need to be controlled to avoid systematic under-recommendation of certain categories, which suggests that constrained re-ranking should be embedded in financial recommendation engines (Jin, Wang, Zhang, Zheng, Ding, Xia, & Pan, 2023; Jannach et al., 2015)

The bridge from a hybrid global ranking to personalization has been constructed as follows. First, a global priority list is created by the hybrid pipeline, making the role of criteria and weights transparent. Second, investor preferences are learned from explicit and implicit signals using supervised, contextual bandit, or Bayesian preference models under appropriate governance. Third, the global list is filtered and re-weighted by the investor profile while respecting policy constraints (suitability, concentration, liquidity), and recommendations are generated with rationales that reference back to MCDM criteria (Wu & Li, 2025; Zhang et al., 2024).

Figure 6 depicts an end-to-end decision pipeline that integrates signals and machine learning with preference-aware re-ranking. It begins with Signals / Labels, which are processed by ML Estimators to generate predictive insights. These outputs feed into Preference Learning (Profiles + Constraints), which adapts decisions to individual investor needs. The system then applies Personalized, Constrained Re-Ranking to ensure alignment with policy and suitability requirements. Finally, the Presentation Layer with Rationale Cards communicates recommendations in a transparent and explainable manner. Feedback arrows link back to the MCDM Weight Ledger and preference models, ensuring continuous adaptation and governance.

Figure 6. End-to-end pipeline for personalized VC investment decisions

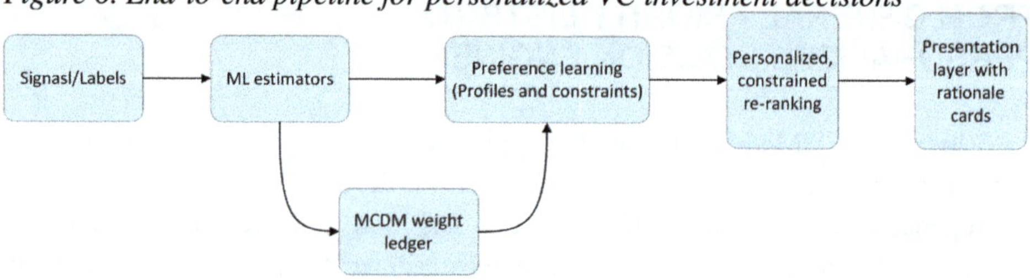

It was noticed that preference capture worked better when it was staged. A short "starter profile" was collected at onboarding. It included horizon, risk, and one or two themes. As usage continued, small edits were inferred from clicks and from time on page. Large edits were kept explicit and required a simple confirmation. In this way, the profile was kept accurate without surprising the user. Suitability rules were always applied first so that a profile could not generate an unsafe set.

It was also suggested that explanations be tied to investor language. If a user expressed interest in "cashflow stability," the rationale card referred to retention, revenue variance, and debt service coverage. If a user expressed interest in "technology edge," the card referred to patent quality and research alliances. The same internal criteria were used, but the wording on the surface was matched to the investor's terms. This mapping was maintained in a small dictionary and was reviewed when themes were updated.

In Table 7, the global ranking produced by the hybrid MCDM+ML framework is compared with personalized rankings for two investor personas, showing how the relative positions of Startups A–E are adjusted. For Persona A, who seeks a short horizon and low risk profile, Startup B is moved upward due to stable cashflows and low volatility, while Startup C is downgraded because of early-stage risk, and Startup D is ranked higher thanks to profitability and conservative debt. In this persona, Startup A is placed slightly lower because of runway concerns, while Startup E remains unchanged, reflecting the longer horizon required. For Persona B, with a long horizon and a climate-focused thesis, Startup A retains its top position due to strong IP and climate impact, while Startup C is ranked higher for its alliances and climate alignment. In contrast, Startup B is moved down because of limited climate relevance, Startup D falls further due to low climate contribution, and Startup E improves its ranking through Environmental, Social, and Governance (ESG) leadership and a robust partner network. These adjustments illustrate how general rankings of Startups A–E are reshaped when individual investment priorities are applied.

Table 7. General vs. personalized rankings

Start up	*Global Rank (MCDM+ML)*	*Persona A: Short-Horizon, Low Risk (Rank)*	*Why It Moved for A*	*Persona B: Long-Horizon, Climate Themed (Rank)*	*Why It Moved for B*
A	*1*	*2*	*Slightly lower runway; liquidity priority*	*1*	*Strong IP; climate impact*
B	*2*	*1*	*Stable cashflows; low volatility*	*3*	*Limited climate alignment*
C	*3*	*4*	*Early stage risk; A prefers maturity*	*2*	*Strong climate thesis; alliances*
D	*4*	*3*	*Profitable; conservative debt*	*5*	*Low climate relevance*
E	*5*	*5*	*Long horizon required*	*4*	*ESG leadership; partner network*

COMPONENTS AND GOVERNANCE OF A PERSONALIZED INVESTMENT DECISION ENGINE

A three-layer architecture has been proposed for finance-grade recommendation: an input layer that supplies a structured, auditable global list with criterion-level scores from MCDM+ML, a preference learning layer that infers investor profiles and policy constraints, and an output layer that performs constrained re-ranking and generates rationale-rich recommendations; finance-specific surveys have argued for domain-specific evaluation and data lineage in such designs (Wu & Li, 2025).

The data pipeline has been specified to include user interaction logs (views, comparisons, simulations), allocation decisions, post-allocation outcomes, and exogenous factor and sector exposures; it has been recommended that on-policy and off-policy evaluation be combined—offline counterfactual estimation to reduce production risk and online A/B testing to measure decision-time reduction, hit rate, and performance proxies—while shift detection triggers recalibration (Coussement et al., 2024). Documentation has been emphasized as part of audit readiness.

Explainability has been placed in two layers: global transparency from MCDM (criteria, weights, sensitivity) and local justification in recommendations (why an opportunity is suggested to this investor under current constraints); integration of XAI techniques with domain-meaningful artifacts has been associated with higher acceptance by decision makers (Kostopoulos et al., 2024). In practice, explanation cards have been used to present criterion contributions and constraint effects.

Risk and compliance have been enforced as hard or soft constraints within the re-ranking step; fairness diagnostics have been recommended to monitor exposure distributions across opportunity types and to prevent undesirable disparities; weight-change governance—with change control and human approval—has been proposed to maintain accountability for the MCDM layer (Jin et al., 2023; Jannach et al., 2015). The integration of these processes has been advocated to ensure suitability and accountability.

Figure 7. Architecture of a personalized VC investment decision engine

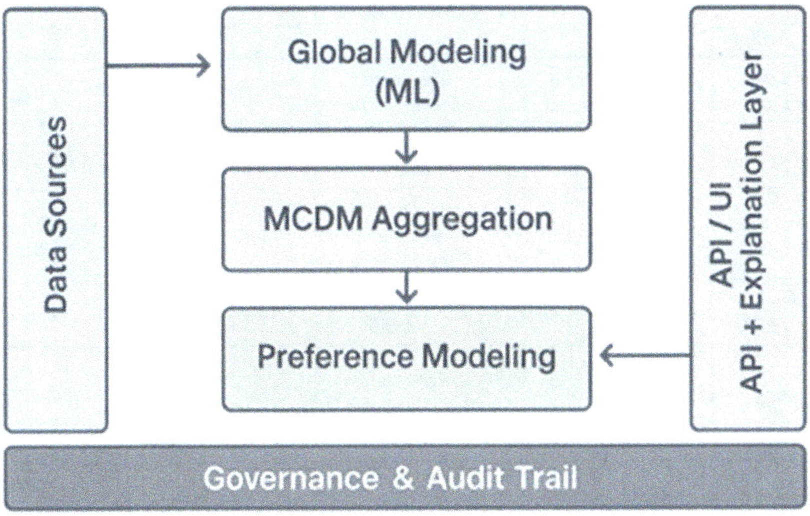

In Table 8, a structured governance checklist is presented, outlining key policies, enforcement points, evidence artifacts, frequencies, and responsible owners. Suitability requirements linked to investor profiles are enforced at the re-ranking layer, with evidence captured in suitability check logs for each recommendation under compliance oversight. Concentration and exposure caps are applied through re-ranking and portfolio policy, documented in constraint satisfaction reports on both batch and monthly basis, managed by risk teams. ESG exclusions are controlled prior to ranking, with exclusion list snapshots maintained for every update by ESG and risk functions. Fairness and exposure balance are monitored by re-ranking auditors, with distribution and disparity metrics reviewed weekly or monthly by data science and risk stakeholders. Weight change control in MCDM processes is governed through a bridge ledger, requiring change logs and formal approvals on each update, overseen by the investment committee and governance. Explainability is maintained globally through MCDM and locally within recommendation systems, supported by criteria plots and "why this" explanation cards on a continuous basis by product and data science teams. Drift and stability are tracked through ML monitoring, with drift alarms and recalibration notes continuously generated by data science and ML operations. Finally, audit trials are enforced across all layers, producing immutable decision logs under continuous compliance responsibility.

Table 8. Governance checklist

Policy / Risk Control	*Where Enforced*	*Evidence Artifact*	*Frequency*	*Owner*
Suitability (investor profile)	*Re-ranking layer*	*Suitability check log*	*Per recommendation*	*Compliance*
Concentration & Exposure Caps	*Re-ranking + Portfolio policy*	*Constraint satisfaction report*	*Per batch & monthly*	*Risk*
ESG Exclusions	*Filter before ranking*	*Exclusion list snapshot*	*Per update*	*ESG/Risk*
Fairness / Exposure Balance	*Re-ranking auditor*	*Exposure distribution, disparity metrics*	*Weekly/monthly*	*Data Science + Risk*
Weight Change Control (MCDM)	*Weight ledger (bridge)*	*Change log + approvals*	*On change*	*IC / Governance*
Explainability	*Global (MCDM) + Local (Recommendation Systems)*	*Criteria/weight plots; "why this" cards*	*Continuous*	*Product/Data science (DS)*
Drift & Stability	*ML monitoring*	*Drift alarms; recalibration notes*	*Continuous*	*DS/ML Operations*
Audit Trail	*All layers*	*Immutable decision log*	*Continuous*	*Compliance*

It was agreed that audits would be easier when evidence was stored in one place. For this reason, a simple bundle was kept with each investment memo: the model note, the weight ledger, the sensitivity snapshot, the suitability check log, and the exception list (if any). Each file was short. Each file carried a version and a date. When a review was requested, the bundle could be shared without new work. This practice was found to reduce rework and to improve trust during committee reviews.

It was further recommended that fairness diagnostics be tied to exposure rather than to acceptance alone. Exposure by category was tracked monthly. If a category received very low exposure relative to its share in the eligible set, the re-ranking rules were examined. In some cases, a small diversification nudge was applied to the lower half of the list. This nudge was bounded so that quality was not harmed. The change and its bound were written in the change log.

PRACTICAL AND ETHICAL CONTEXT FOR HYBRID MCDM+ML

This subsection has been written to give a clear and compact view of ethics and governance in decision support for venture settings. The focus is on actions that can be carried out inside the workflows already described. The same terms for criteria, weights, explanations, and sensitivity analysis are used so that the reader can connect ideas easily.

Fairness is treated as a measurable property of the system rather than only a principle. Group-wise performance is examined where it is lawful and appropriate, and changes over time are monitored. When meaningful differences are observed, mitigation can be applied at different stages. Data may be balanced before modeling, constraints can be added during learning, and thresholds may be adjusted after modeling. Feature importances and short reason codes are reviewed by humans so that proxy signals for sensitive attributes are not allowed to re-enter the process indirectly (Genovesi et al., 2024; Ferrara, 2023; Sadeghi et al., 2024).

Privacy is addressed through a strict view of data necessity and retention. Only the signals that are needed for the criteria are processed, and records are kept no longer than required for audit. Pseudonymization is used when possible, and access to any re-identification keys is limited. When results are shared outside the immediate team, summaries can be protected with simple techniques such as light noise at the aggregate level or k-anonymity for very small cohorts. In this way, useful information can be reported while individual risk remains low (Ali et al., 2023; Longo et al., 2024).

It was acknowledged that some signals could carry indirect sensitive information. Media visibility and education history were two examples. To reduce risk, proxy tests were run. Each proxy candidate was checked for high correlation with a protected attribute on a holdout slice where lawful and appropriate. If a high correlation was found, the contribution of the proxy was limited or replaced by a safer aggregate. This step was documented in the model note. The aim was not to remove useful signals but to manage unwanted side effects.

It was also recognized that explanations could leak sensitive indicators if not designed with care. For this reason, rationale cards were written at the criterion level rather than at the raw feature level. A card stated that "traction and governance contributed most," but it did not list rare attributes that could identify individuals. This light abstraction was chosen to balance transparency with privacy.

Accountability is supported by short documentation and by human oversight at the points where it matters. Each model or heuristic is accompanied by a one-page note that states the purpose, data sources, known limits, and the monitoring plan; each recommendation carries a concise explanation showing the contributions of the criteria and a link to the sensitivity check. Decisions remain human-in-the-loop, and escalation to expert review is triggered when uncertainty is high or when a policy flag is raised. These practices have been shown to support transparency and trust in AI-enabled decision support (Kovári, 2024; Kostopoulos et al., 2024; Yang & Lee, 2024).

Explainability has also been explored in depth. Local explanation methods have been used to show which features mattered for one prediction. Global summaries have been used to show which features matter on average. In many reports, it has been argued that simple, honest plots are better than complex scores when decisions are high-stakes. For this reason, the present study prefers light-weight, human-readable artifacts. It is believed that a short "model note," a single snapshot of an explanation, and a one-page sensitivity record can meet most needs in this setting.

Alignment with a risk-based regulatory view is kept at a high level so that the text remains useful across jurisdictions. Documentation, human oversight, record-keeping, and post-deployment monitoring are addressed by the artifacts already described (model note, explanation snapshot, and sensitivity attachment). In financial contexts, attention is given to conflicts that may arise from predictive or optimization tools and to the need for specific, non-misleading communications about AI capabilities; the same documentation and review steps are intended to support these expectations (Genovesi et al., 2024; Sadeghi et al., 2024).

Finally, operations are kept simple by storing all artifacts with the investment committee memo for the decision. In practice, the bundle contains the model note, the explanation snapshot, the sensitivity figure, a short statement on data minimization and retention, and a brief note on relevant governance touchpoints for the deployment region. Sensitivity to preprocessing choices in MCDM (e.g., normalization) is recorded because ranking stability is affected by these choices; this record supports reproducibility and audit (Ersoy, 2022; Altin, 2022).

This chapter is placed within that stream. A minimal set of fairness checks is included, but heavy governance load is avoided. An explainable path is kept by design, since criteria, weights, and rank changes are recorded. In this way, basic trust can be increased without slowing teams too much.

CONCLUSION, LIMITATIONS AND FUTURE DIRECTIONS

A coherent chain has been presented in which human–machine hybrid decision models are grounded in MCDM, coupled bidirectionally with ML, and extended into personalized decision engines for investment. The role of MCDM as a bridge has been emphasized because value judgments (weights) can be separated and governed while ML provides empirical estimates for criterion-level performance; the outcome is an auditable, adaptable, and explainable ranking for VC investment decisions (Martyn & Kadziński, 2023; Hüllermeier & Słowiński, 2024a, 2024b).

To support practical adoption while avoiding the use of proprietary data, two brief case illustrations based entirely on synthetic data were presented to demonstrate how hybrid MCDM+ML can be embedded in VC investment screening and in personalized, constraint-aware investor platforms. A concise ethical and governance perspective has been provided, emphasizing measurable fairness, strong privacy and practices of documentation, human oversight, and a brief alignment with the EU AI Act and relevant SEC expectations.

From a managerial perspective, the adoption of a hybrid MCDM+ML engine can be translated into concrete actions. Screening funnels can be standardized around a shared criteria catalog and a weight ledger; investment memos can include criterion-contribution charts, short reason codes, and a small sensitivity snapshot; human-in-the-loop gates can be triggered by uncertainty and policy flags; model and data changes can be logged for audit; and post-investment monitoring can reuse the same criteria to track drift and value creation. For investors, preference capture can be formalized (horizon, risk, themes) and mapped to a constrained re-ranking layer so that suitability and diversification are respected by design. For policy makers and supervisors, a lightweight bundle of artifacts—model notes, decision logs, and explanation snapshots—can be requested as evidence of transparency, fairness checks, and human oversight. In this way, discretion is preserved while decisions are made more explainable and repeatable.

Scalability can be supported by separating criteria, weights, and models behind clear interfaces. As volumes increase, feature stores and retraining jobs can be automated; monitoring can be scheduled for drift, stability, and subgroup performance; and cost can be controlled by batching inferences and caching stable scores. The same engine can be surfaced through AI copilots that draft memos, surface explanations, and propose weight scenarios; over time, semi-autonomous investment platforms can handle routine re-ranking under strict policy constraints, while rare or high-impact cases remain escalated to human committees. The path can remain incremental: pilots are run on a single stage or theme, guardrails are validated, and scope is widened only after stability and governance have been demonstrated.

This approach has limits. Signals are noisy in early markets. It is possible that simple criteria hide deeper risks. Small data can also lead to unstable weights. For these reasons, the sensitivity step is treated as essential, and human review is required when rank flips are seen. It is also accepted that fairness checks may be weak when group sizes are very small. In those cases, a warning is added rather than a false sense of comfort.

Another assumption is that a weighted sum is acceptable. In most practical cases it is easier to read and to audit. Still, non-linear effects may exist. If such effects are suspected, a note is added, and a follow-up analysis is suggested.

Finally, governance can be felt as extra work. To reduce this burden, a small kit is used. Templates make the work faster. Screenshots and short notes are preferred over long reports. With these choices, the method remains light but still accountable.

More study is needed to test the approach with larger datasets and with multiple funds. That work is proposed as a next step.

Future work has been suggested along four lines. First, dynamic weight learning and preference disaggregation should be advanced using revealed-preference data while preserving interpretability. Second, XAI tailored to investment should be developed, including counterfactual what-if analysis over criteria and constraints. Third, evaluation regimes that combine statistical metrics with decision-centric KPIs under regulatory constraints should be standardized for the domain. Fourth, fairness-aware re-ranking should be embedded to monitor exposure distributions across opportunity sets (Coussement et al., 2024; Jin et al., 2023). With these elements, hybrid MCDM–ML systems are expected to support personalized, trustworthy decision engines.

It was concluded that the main value of the approach was not a single accuracy gain but a repeatable path from noisy signals to a documented decision. The bridge role of MCDM kept value judgments explicit, while ML supplied scale and timely estimates. Personalization and governance were then layered on top without breaking traceability. It was accepted that more work was needed on dynamic weights, on counterfactual explanations that refer to criteria rather than to raw features, and on evaluation that mixes statistical and decision metrics under policy constraints. With these steps, it was expected that hybrid systems would support better choices while keeping humans clearly in charge.

REFERENCES

Abdulla, A., & Baryannis, G. (2024). A hybrid multi-criteria decision-making and machine learning approach for explainable supplier selection. *Supply Chain Analytics, 7*, 100074. DOI: 10.1016/j.sca.2024.100074

Alahmari, D., & Awad, A. (2025). Strategic integration of marketing and supply chain functions for superior customer experience: Insights from logistics startups under Saudi Vision 2030. *PLoS One, 20*(11), e0336132. DOI: 10.1371/journal.pone.0336132 PMID: 41270081

Ali, A., Qadeer, A., & Awad, A. (2025). Understanding generative AI implementation in digital advertising among retail SMEs in Pakistan. In *Impacts of AI-generated content on brand reputation* (pp. 177–201). IGI Global. DOI: 10.4018/979-8-3373-4327-3.ch007

Ali, S., Abuhmed, T., El-Sappagh, S., Khan, M., Ahmad, H. F., Kwak, K. S., & Alonso-Moral, J.-M. (2023). Explainable Artificial Intelligence (XAI): What we know and what is left to attain trustworthy artificial intelligence. *Information Fusion, 99*, 101805. DOI: 10.1016/j.inffus.2023.101805

Altin, H. (2022). The comparison of EDAS, COPRAS, and EFI methods in the decision-making process. *International Journal of Operations Research and Information Systems, 13*(1), 1–19. DOI: 10.4018/IJORIS.302910

Awad, A. (2025). Enhancing market access and consumer engagement through digital marketing in the agricultural sector. *International Journal of Advanced and Applied Sciences, 12*(8), 70–79. DOI: 10.21833/ijaas.2025.08.007

Ayyildiz, E., & Taskin, A. (2022). A novel spherical fuzzy AHP-VIKOR methodology to determine serving petrol station selection during COVID-19 lockdown: A pilot study for İstanbul. *Socio-Economic Planning Sciences, 83*, 101345. DOI: 10.1016/j.seps.2022.101345 PMID: 35645424

Cinelli, M., Kadziński, M., Gonzalez, M., & Słowiński, R. (2020). How to support the application of multiple criteria decision analysis? Let us start with a comprehensive taxonomy. *Omega, 96*, 102261. DOI: 10.1016/j.omega.2020.102261 PMID: 33746337

Coussement, K., Abedin, M. Z., Kraus, M., Maldonado, S., & Topuz, K. (2024). Explainable AI for enhanced decision-making. *Decision Support Systems, 184*, 114276. DOI: 10.1016/j.dss.2024.114276

Ersoy, N. (2022). The influence of statistical normalization techniques on performance ranking results: The application of MCDM method proposed by Biswas and Saha. *International Journal of Business Analytics, 9*(5), 1–21. DOI: 10.4018/IJBAN.298017

Ferrara, E. (2023). Fairness and bias in artificial intelligence: A brief survey of sources, impacts, and mitigation strategies. *Patterns, 4*(1), 100796. https://www.mdpi.com/2413-4155/6/1/3

Genovesi, S., Mönig, J. M., Schmitz, A., Poretschkin, M., Akila, M., Kahdan, M., … Zimmermann, A. (2024). Standardizing fairness-evaluation procedures: Interdisciplinary insights on machine-learning algorithms in creditworthiness assessments for small personal loans. *AI and Ethics, 4*, 537–553. DOI: 10.1007/s43681-023-00291-8

Gompers, P. A., Gornall, W., Kaplan, S. N., & Strebulaev, I. A. (2020). How do venture capitalists make decisions? *Journal of Financial Economics, 135*(1), 169–190. DOI: 10.1016/j.jfineco.2019.06.011

Hüllermeier, E., & Słowiński, R. (2024a). Preference learning and multiple criteria decision aiding: Differences, commonalities, and synergies—Part I. *4OR, 22(2),* 179–209. DOI: 10.1007/s10288-023-00560-6

Hüllermeier, E., & Słowiński, R. (2024b). Preference learning and multiple criteria decision aiding: Differences, commonalities, and synergies—Part II. *4OR, 22*(3), 279–312. DOI: 10.1007/s10288-023-00561-5

Jannach, D., Lerche, L., & Jugovac, M. (2015). Item familiarity as a possible confounding factor in user-centric recommender systems evaluation. *User Modeling and User-Adapted Interaction, 25*(5), 427–491. DOI: 10.1007/s11257-015-9165-3

Jin, D., Wang, L., Zhang, H., Zheng, Y., Ding, W., Xia, F., & Pan, S. (2023). A survey on fairness-aware recommender systems. *Information Fusion, 101*, 101906. DOI: 10.1016/j.inffus.2023.101906

Kartal, H., Oztekin, A., Gunasekaran, A., & Cebi, F. (2016). An integrated decision analytic framework of machine learning with multi-criteria decision making for multi-attribute inventory classification. *Computers & Industrial Engineering, 101*, 599–613. DOI: 10.1016/j.cie.2016.06.004

Kellekci, M. (2002). *Ri sk Sermayesi , Yeni Trendler ve Uygulamalar* (Master's thesis, Marmara Universitesi (Turkey)).

Kellekci, M., Cebeci, U., & Dogan, O. (2025). Prioritizing Early-Stage Start-Up Investment Alternatives Under Uncertainty: A Venture Capital Perspective. *Applied Sciences (Basel, Switzerland), 15*(18), 10060. DOI: 10.3390/app151810060

Kostopoulos, G., Davrazos, G., & Kotsiantis, S. (2024). Explainable Artificial Intelligence-Based Decision Support Systems: A recent review. *Electronics (Basel), 13*(14), 2842. DOI: 10.3390/electronics13142842

Kovári, A. (2024). AI for decision support: Balancing accuracy, transparency, and trust across sectors. *Information, 15*(11), 725. DOI: 10.3390/info15110725

Longo, L., Brcic, M., Cabitza, F., Choi, J., Confalonieri, R., Del Ser, J., ... Stumpf, S. (2024). Explainable Artificial Intelligence (XAI) 2.0: A manifesto of open challenges and interdisciplinary research directions. *Information Fusion, 103*, 102301. DOI: 10.1016/j.inffus.2024.102301

Martyn, K., & Kadziński, M. (2023). Deep preference learning for multiple criteria decision analysis. *European Journal of Operational Research*, *305*(2), 781–805. DOI: 10.1016/j.ejor.2022.06.053

Mosqueira-Rey, E., Hernández-Pereira, E., Alonso-Ríos, D., Bobes-Bascarán, J., & Fernández-Leal, Á. (2023). Human-in-the-loop machine learning: A state of the art. *Artificial Intelligence Review*, *56*(4), 10105–10172. DOI: 10.1007/s10462-022-10246-w

Qadeer, A., & Awad, A. (2025). AI-powered ChatGPT in branding: Benefits, challenges, and future directions. In *Impacts of AI-generated content on brand reputation* (pp. 1–26). IGI Global. DOI: 10.4018/979-8-3373-4327-3.ch001

Reyes-Norambuena, P., Bascuñán-Ortiz, M., & Sauma, E. (2024). The application of machine learning and deep learning with a multi-criteria decision analysis for pedestrian modeling: A systematic literature review (1999–2023). *Sustainability (Basel)*, *17*(1), 41. DOI: 10.3390/su17010041

Sadeghi, K. R., Ojha, D., Kaur, P., Mahto, R. V., & Dhir, A. (2024). Explainable artificial intelligence and agile decision-making in supply-chain cyber resilience. *Decision Support Systems, 180*, 114194. DOI: 10.1016/j.dss.2024.114194

Wu, D., & Li, X. (2025). A systematic literature review of financial product recommendation systems. *Information (Basel), 16*(3), 196. DOI: 10.3390/info16030196

Yang, Q., & Lee, Y.-C. (2024). Ethical AI in financial inclusion: The role of algorithmic fairness on user satisfaction and recommendation. *Big Data and Cognitive Computing, 8*(9), 105. DOI: 10.3390/bdcc8090105

Zhang, J.-C., Zain, A. M., Zhou, K., Chen, X., & Zhang, R.-M. (2024). A review of recommender systems based on knowledge graph embeddings. *Expert Systems with Applications*, *249*, 123876. DOI: 10.1016/j.eswa.2024.123876

APPENDIX: SYNTHETIC DATA SKETCH FOR REPRODUCIBILITY

A minimal schema can be reproduced as follows: entities: startup_id, opportunity_id, persona_id; criteria: team, traction, innovation_ip, governance, network; constraints: suitability_flag, concentration_bucket, esg_exclusion_flag; targets (synthetic): follow_on_after_18m (Bernoulli with base rate 0.25), volatility_proxy. Criterion scores should be drawn from simple parametric forms (e.g., Beta or log-normal, scaled to 0.1) with pairwise correlations in the 0.2–0.4 range. AHP pairwise matrices should be set to yield weights that sum to 1.0 in the order shown. The reported percentages and stability metrics in the cases were produced entirely from such synthetic draws.

Chapter 6
Cognitive Collaboration: Redefining Leadership and Team Dynamics in AI-Mediated Hybrid Work Environments

Ravikumar R. N.
https://orcid.org/0009-0009-3705-1681
Marwadi University, Rajkot, India

S. Aarthi
https://orcid.org/0009-0006-9064-2091
Marwadi University, Rajkot, India

ABSTRACT

The growing integration of Artificial Intelligence (AI) in hybrid and remote workplaces is redefining leadership, communication, and collaboration. This chapter investigates how AI-mediated systems facilitate cognitive collaboration by combining human judgment with machine intelligence. It explores the evolution of algorithmic management, predictive analytics, and adaptive learning as key enablers of decision-making and innovation in distributed teams. The discussion emphasizes leadership adaptation, ethical governance, and trust-building within AI-driven organizational environments. By examining theoretical insights and real-world applications, the chapter presents a conceptual model illustrating how AI supports creativity, engagement, and resilience while ensuring transparency and human-centric governance. The analysis concludes that effective AI integration can foster sustainable, intelligent, and inclusive hybrid work ecosystems.

DOI: 10.4018/979-8-3373-7416-1.ch006

1. INTRODUCTION

One of the game changers in development of hybrid and distance work environment is Artificial Intelligence (AI). It is quickly gaining traction that organizations are increasingly going online with AI systems to support communication and performance management, and decision support, creating a networked digital ecosystem that is changing the manner in which teams are operating. This is more than automation, which is cognitive augmentation where intelligent machines are used in analyzing complex information, forecasting the future, and optimizing processes. The new technological paradigm requires a re-research of the leadership and team relations with the decentralization of the work (Raisch and Krakowski, 2021). The establishment of AI-based cooperation threatens the management hierarchies and interpersonal trust structures. This thus implies that leaders must be digital empathetic, algorithm aware and adaptable coordinators to be able to lead teams. This chapter deems cognitive joint venture as a new business competency and outlines the symbiosis of human appraisal and machine intelligence in sustaining engagement, creativity and endurance in the distributed workplaces. (Krakowski et al., 2023).

1.1 Overview of AI Integration in Hybrid and Remote Work Settings

The emergence of AI into the superpower of hybrid workplaces has increased the area of coordination and communication. Scheduling Assistants Scheduling Assistants represent smart software, which increases the real-time exchange of knowledge and automation of processes (MacKinnon and MacLean, 2023). These are Microsoft Copilot, Slack AI and Google Duet AI. These systems are used to process behavioral information to make suggestions on how tasks, resources and communication procedures can be allocated optimally. Multicultural and multilingual teams can also work together without difficulties because of AI-powered translation and sentiment-analysis tools. Incorporating adaptive learning algorithms into an organization will enable it to personalize digital experience to its employees, which will increase their engagement and productivity. Nevertheless, this growing dependence on artificial intelligence generates complications in the area of information clarity, equality, and independence (Sarkar et al., 2023). The hybrid workspace has therefore become a socio technologic ecosystem where the human intuition and the algorithmic reasoning co-exist. This interdependence becomes critical in developing inclusive, ethical and performance-based working structures in the intelligent work environment era. The figure 1 demonstrates how the integration of AI enhances the efficiency of collaboration due to the translation, learning, analytics, and intelligent scheduling in the hybrid work setting.

Figure 1. AI Enhances Hybrid Workplace Collaboration

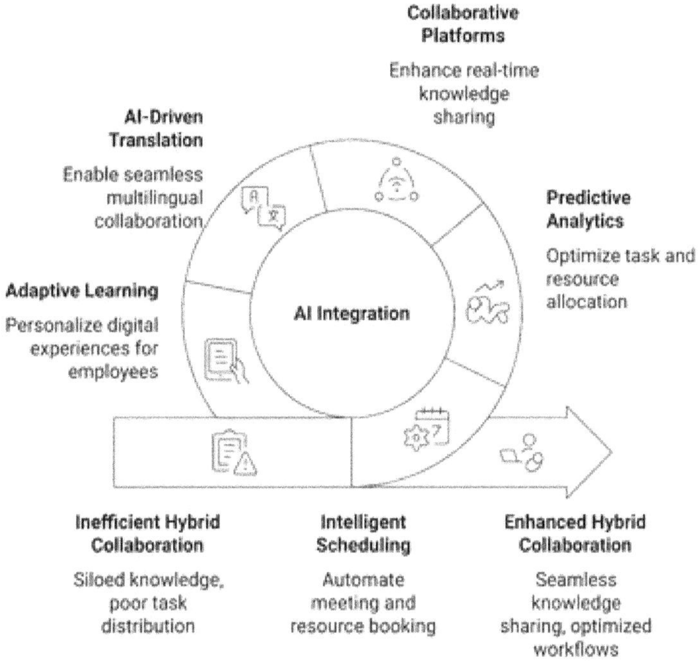

1.2 Transition From Traditional to AI-Mediated Collaboration

The shift in the cooperation between the conventional collaboration and AI-assisted teamwork is the change in the reactive management approach to the proactive management that is data-driven and based. Previously, direct supervision and face-to-face coordination were used as the models, but now AI systems are used as cognitive intermediaries analyzing patterns, anticipating challenges, and proposing interventions (Lui et al., 2023). Robot helpers handle monotonic aspects of administration and leave leaders with strategy and emotional intelligence. Digital dashboards represent group performance, making it possible to make evidence-based decisions and not simply intuitive one. The social composition of teamwork also shifts with this change the roles are mobile, the power of decision making is decentralized and the work is created by cross-time zone, cross-digital teams (Mitsugi et al., 2025). However, the change raises some significant questions about the effect of algorithms on creativity, bias during decision support, and how the staff members would adjust psychologically to work with machines. This development causes organizations to realize how they can evolve governance structures that are neither more productive nor inclusive in the hybrid collaboration that the AI provokes. (Aldekhyl et al., 2018).

1.3 Emerging Need for Redefined Leadership and Team Structures

The cooperation that AI will bring about will necessitate reforms in leadership ideologies and business systems. Management of teams in which teams are autonomous and which have transparency in the form of algorithmically informed teams are becoming inappropriate in the traditional command-and-control paradigms. Leaders are currently regarded as the strategists of human-AI symbiosis, as they guide employees to think and conduct ethically guided by machine-generated knowledge. (Hossain et al., 2025). This is based on cognitive flexibility, emotional intelligence and awareness of digital ethics. The hierarchies are becoming more networked and adaptive systems with leadership being situational, meaning that it arises based on expertise and data fluency, as opposed to titles. Groups work in decentralized thinking situations whereby decision making is shared and dynamic (Kim et al., 2020). More importantly, the question of trust is brought to the forefront: the employees should be convinced that AI recommendations are objective, unbiased, and associated with organizational intentions. Thus, data interpretation, AI governance, and psychological safety competencies should be introduced into the leader development programme to build resilient, creative and human-centric hybrid teams.

2. BACKGROUND TO THE STUDY

Digitalization of the work environment has been achieved by the shift of simple communication facilities to highly meditated AI-driven ecosystems to help distributed work. The first digital systems were simply employed in order to coordinate and exchange information, yet currently AI systems are under active analysis, interpretation and making decisions. This transformation does not just signify a technological transformation but also a restructuring of the human-machines process of value generation that takes place mentally. The way of algorithmic management, intelligent dashboard and real-time analytics, has changed the notion of leading positions and employee independence. The hybrid workplaces have evolved into dynamic socio-technical (Rahmadani et al., 2020)networks, which are complemented by the human reasoning with the algorithm vision. To understand these developments, it is necessary to explore the essence of digital collaboration creation, the replacement of the position of a manager with the work of algorithms, and the change in the workplace paradigms of the AI age. This integration is termed as cognitive collaboration that is concerned with intelligence between machines and humans.

2.1 Evolution of Digital Collaboration and Distributed Work

The use of digital collaboration has altered the application of simple electronic mail and internal network systems to the virtual realm of immersion on the basis of artificial intelligence and cloud computing. The early decades of distributed working were devoted to the arrangement of the process of interactive communication between individuals working in various geographic regions because of such technologies as video conferencing and project management systems (Akemu & Abdelnour, 2020). Digital infrastructures have developed with the globalization process in organizations, allowing real-time coordination, sharing of data and asynchronous collaboration. The new speed of work changed with the COVID-19 crisis as now hybrid work arrangements are the new standard, and it is assumed that planning schedules, organizing tasks, and tracking sentiments uses AI-based technologies. It results in the paradigm of work being no longer confined in the physical co-presence but synchronized with smart interfaces between the human and machine minds (Tahsiri, 2023). Thereby, collaboration has become not only a social process, but also a hybrid cognitive process the synthesis of digital actants, situational analytics, and adaptive feedback loops to make pooled performance and quality of decisions better. Figure 2 shows the transformation of AI to rearrange the constrained collaboration to the high-level teamwork through real-time coordinating interfaces and dynamic feedback loop.

Figure 2. Enhancing Collaboration with AI

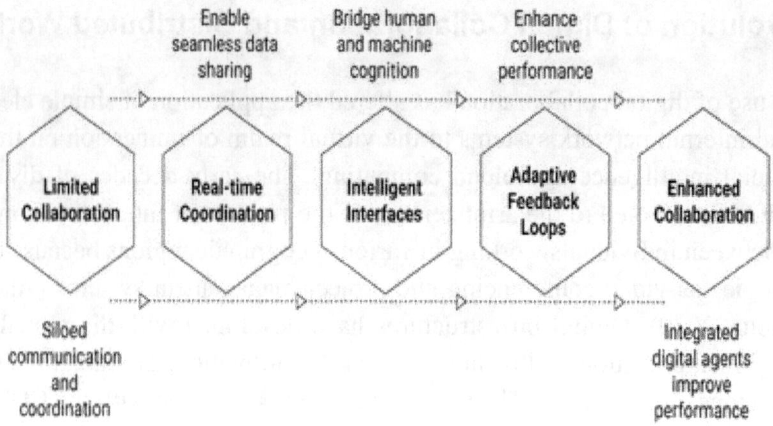

2.2 Rise of Algorithmic Management and Cognitive Augmentation

Algorithms refer to the notion of tracking, evaluating, and optimizing the workflow decisions and performances of the employees using data-driven algorithms. It was first implemented in the gig economy shared platforms, but has now found its way into corporate and knowledge-based organizations due to AI driven analytics, recommendations systems and automated workflow (Clemente-Suárez et al., 2024). Such systems use behavioral data to assign tasks, gauge productivity and even predicts burnout risks. In this sense, cognition augmentation factors expands the human decision-making process by providing real-time information based on massive data flows. Predictive dashboards and adaptive feedback will help managers and employees predict challenges and take opportunities. Though algorithmic systems increase efficiency and minimize bias in some aspects, human agency, transparency, and privacy raise these concerns (Barkhatova, 2023). The emergence of cognitive augmentation, therefore, is a two-sided change that will not only improve the leadership performance, but will require new ethical standards of responsible algorithmic stewardship in hybrid workplaces. The table 1 outlines how AI-driven systems enhance managerial functions and human cognition in hybrid workplaces.

Table 1. Rise of Algorithmic Management and Cognitive Augmentation

Aspect	Traditional Management	Algorithmic Management	Cognitive Impact
Decision Basis	Experience and intuition	Data-driven analytics	Improved accuracy and speed
Task Allocation	Manual supervision	Automated task distribution	Reduced cognitive load
Performance Evaluation	Subjective appraisal	Predictive and real-time analytics	Objective feedback mechanisms
Leadership Role	Directive and hierarchical	Facilitator and interpreter	Enhanced adaptive leadership

2.3 Comparative Analysis of Pre- and Post-AI Workplace Models

Prior to the introduction of AI, workplace interaction was mostly human-oriented, hierarchical, and direct in decision-making coupled with intuitively-led leadership. Manual observation and static measures were used to measure productivity and performance (Zhou & Gorman, 2024). Introducing AI-based analytics and automation has substituted them with the data-driven decision-making process, which can show the dynamics of workflows and efficiency of teams in real-time. Leadership in pre-AI models was concerned with supervision and coordination and in post-AI it is concerned with facilitation, interpretation, and ethical regulation of intelligent systems. The change also transforms the functions of the employees, but instead of performing tasks, they formulate the instructions of the algorithms. The process of decision-making has been decentralized, interactive, and reflexive, where the artificial intelligence acts as a cognitive co-pilot (Lai, 2025). This analogy brings out a shift towards reactive management to predictive, adaptive governance. Post-AI workplace is characterized by agility, transparency, and accountability, which changes the leadership practice based on authority to intelligence-based practice. The table 2 compares key organizational attributes before and after AI integration.

Table 2. Comparative Analysis of Pre- and Post-AI Workplace Models

Dimension	Pre-AI Workplace	Post-AI Workplace
Communication	Face-to-face and linear	Virtual, adaptive, and AI-mediated
Decision-Making	Hierarchical and slow	Data-informed and agile
Collaboration	Location-bound	Distributed and cognitive
Leadership Focus	Supervision and control	Facilitation and co-agency
Employee Role	Task executor	Insight interpreter

2.4 Concept of "Cognitive Collaboration" and Its Managerial Relevance

Cognitive Collaboration is described as the synergistic coordination between human cognitive functions, i.e., creativity, empathy, and acting ethically, and machine intelligence that offers analytical accuracy, pattern recognition and predictive insights. Cognitive collaboration, in contrast to the traditional collaboration, based on interpersonal interaction only, builds collective intelligence using AI mediation (Van Rooy, 2024a). It reinvents the teamwork as the joint effort of people and computers where the partners are learning, changing, and growing together. This paradigm also introduces new duties as a manager now: in order to understand AI findings, make decisions equitably, and not to lose confidence in the human-machine teams. It is also spiritually related to intelligent collaboration, which promotes inclusiveness, and various contributors will be capable of making contributions intelligently and discuss in many languages. It contributes to sound-based leadership in a managerial context, reduces the mental burden and enhances decision quality (Jain et al., 2023). Lastly, it will also make leaders the catalysts of the digital ecosystems, individuals who are able to make a balance between human intuition and algorithmic logic to generate the resilient, creative, and sustainable productivity in the hybrid workplaces.

3. RESEARCH OBJECTIVES

The use of Artificial Intelligence that has been increased at the hybrid and the remote workplaces has revolutionized the previous paradigms of leadership and team work. The automated system is not only the routine processes that are automated through AI systems but it is also involved in the process of communication decision making and coordination among dispersed teams. As these technologies become cognitive companions rather than machines used, it is wise to understand how it has affected the performance of leadership and the team spirit. The study in question is going to examine the ways in which the AI mediation transforms the role of managers, the level of interpersonal trust, and supports the collective intelligence within the multi-location context. It is also directed towards exploring moral, mental or cultural implications of such changes. The chapter is able to provide strategic hints which could be embraced to come up with AI-built in models that do not compromise on human values but rather assist organisations to be agile, adaptable, and innovative with the identification of the enablers and challenges to successful cognitive teamwork. The specific objectives of this chapter are:

- To analyze how AI systems influence leadership styles, decision-making processes, and coordination mechanisms in hybrid teams.
- To identify key factors affecting trust, adaptability, and communication within AI-mediated collaboration environments.
- To investigate the psychological and ethical dimensions associated with AI-assisted leadership and algorithmic decision-making.
- To develop a conceptual framework illustrating the dynamics of cognitive collaboration between human and AI agents in distributed workplaces.
- To propose managerial strategies for fostering engagement, fairness, and innovation in AI-supported hybrid teams.

4. CONCEPTUAL MODEL: FRAMEWORK FOR AI–HUMAN CO-AGENCY IN HYBRID WORK ENVIRONMENTS

The theoretical framework proposed will show the interaction between Artificial Intelligence (AI) and human cognition, which affect the results of leadership and teams in hybrid working environments. It theorises collaboration as a multi-layered process in which digital systems act as cognitive facilitators, and not tools. The model incorporates the Human Leadership, AI Mediation as well as Team Out (Büyükgüzel & Balaman, 2023)comes into three consecutive layers: input, process, and output. The input layer presents technological infrastructure which gathers and analyses the information; the process layer is active human-AI cooperation and decision-making, and the output layer is the resulting organizational gains in the form of trust, innovation, engagement and resilience. Collectively, these layers prove that a cognitive teamwork is what leads to shared intelligence, and such teamwork helps leaders to make decisions based on data, be empathetic, and adaptive in complex hybrid ecosystems. This model is used to close the gap between the human judgment and the algorithm precision to improve performance (Verma et al., 2023). The figure 3 shows the never-ending loop of gathering information, AI mediation, and human leadership, and team results that creates trust, innovativeness, and resilience in a hybrid workplace.

Figure 3. AI–Human Collaboration Cycle in Hybrid Work

4.1 Input Layer: Digital Tools, AI Analytics, and Virtual Assistants

The cognitive collaboration model relies on the input layer, which is based on technology. It encompasses the digital tools, artificial intelligence analytic tools, and virtual assistant that enable processing of data and communication to be smart in hybrid teams. The elements act as abettors of information, collect contextual information of interactions, workflow systems and behavioral analytics (Ricker and Vergauwe, 2022). These datasets are handled on Microsoft Copilot, Notion AI, and predictive dashboards to streamline task allocation and make more decisions. The layer illustrates the way that technology enhances the real-time flexibility of distributed work, its transparency and accessibility. Virtual assistants reduce the cognitive load of automation of monotonous tasks and schedule of operations to allow human leaders to focus on the strategy and emotional engagement (Chandra et al., 2012). Moreover, AI analytics generate actionable data to be applied in the leadership intervention, feedback, and performance review systems. This technological background predetermines higher cognitive processes according to which raw data may be transformed into valuable pieces of advice to organize the team and to synchronize the strategies.

4.2 Process Layer: Cognitive Collaboration, Communication Flow, and Adaptive Learning

The dynamic interaction between the machine intelligence and man cognition is the process layer. Here, teamwork goes beyond the activities that are undertaken to knowledge creation as a result of continuous feedback and adaptive learning. Natural interactions enable human-AI teams to communicate, analyze analytics, and be able to engage in the process of making decisions that can make them more empathetic and sensitive to one another (Zhao et al., 2025). Cognitive collaboration is an outcome of a dialogic communication where AI complements humanity thinking by identifying concealed patterns, emotional patterns and anomalies during performance. Such interaction enhances the inclusive communication and democratization of the hybrid teams. Adaptive learning mechanisms applied by AI systems allow the model to vary based on the performance of the team and the organizational behavior. As human beings use the data to make informed choices, the machines, in turn, make the predictive algorithms better causing another virtuous circle of co-evolution (Garavandala, 2025). The layer is a reflection of the spirit of cognitive synergy which is the capability to combine the accuracy of analysis with the empathy and the perception of the situation to contribute to the decision-making and creativity within the distributed working environment.

4.3 Output Layer: Trust, Innovation, Engagement, and Resilience

The physical and non-physical outputs of the AI-human interaction are received by the output layer. With proper management, cognitive collaboration may foster trust, innovation, engagement, and resiliency to hybrid teams. The feeling of confidence can be achieved when AI systems are perceived as open, moral, and helpful rather than threatening employees. The innovation culture is successful due to the quicker factual knowledge in solving problems and encouraging creative experiments (X. Wang et al., 2024; Awad et al.,2025; Shma et al., 2025; Yusuf et al., 2025; Mahmoud et al., 2025).

Communication is facilitated with AI that enables communicating with one another at a more intimate level through personalized feedback and engagement. The ability to be resilient is added by ensuring that the teams are more receptive to uncertainty by ensuring that AI tools are used to predict risks and make the most out of responses. Another aspect of the human-centric focus of the model that is brought out by this layer is that technology is a partner, not a dictator. A leader becomes more of a facilitator instead of an authority who makes decisions thus a balance is created between efficiency and empathy (Braganza et al., 2021). The fact that these results were attained effectively proves that AI-mediated ecosystems have the potential to create sustainable, flexible, and psychologically secure hybrid work cultures. The figure 4 illustrates the three-layered structure of input/process/output in a manner that digitally mediated and AI-driven analytic tools and cognitive collaboration produce trust, engagement, and innovation within the hybrid setting.

Figure 4. AI–Human Collaboration in Hybrid Workplaces

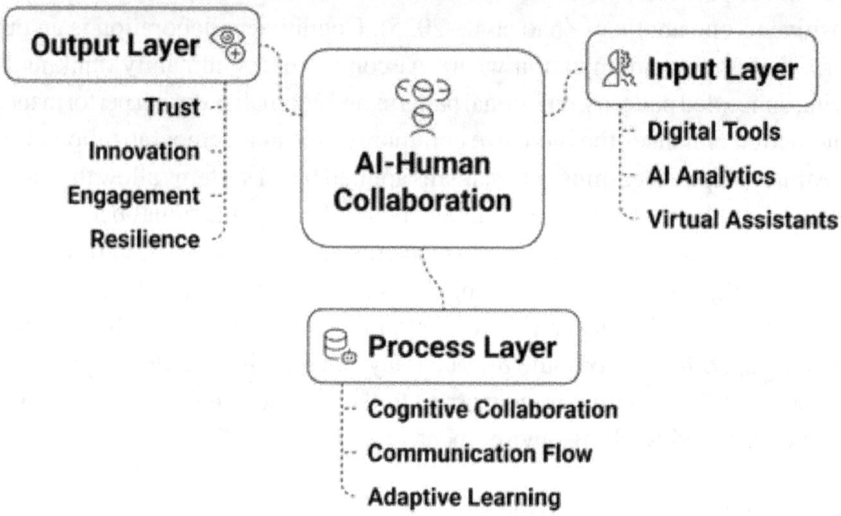

5. RESEARCH METHODOLOGY

This paper follows a systematic approach to methodology to explore the mediating role of Artificial Intelligence (AI) on the dynamics of leadership and team in hybrid workplaces. The adopted methodology focuses on profundity and interpretative comprehension of human-AI collaboration. By combining qualitative inquiry and comparative case study design, the study will determine the patterns, perceptions, and adaptive behaviors that are bound to be acquired due to AI introduction within an organizational setting (Zaidi et al., 2025). Primary data are gathered with the help of semi-structured interviews, the digital ethnography approach, and the consideration of AI-managed coordination systems (Slack bots, predictive dashboards, performance analytics tools, etc.). The study context includes the organizations that are actively involved in using AI to support distributed collaboration and decision-making. The patterns of relationships, transitions in leadership, and psychological responses are detected with the help of analytical tools such as thematic coding, social network analysis and sentiment tracking. Such a paradigm of mixed methodology ensures the balanced comprehension in cognitive collaboration because it is both profound in the interpretation and approach to rigor in the empirical inquiry.

5.1 Research Design: Qualitative and Comparative Case Study Approach

The research paper is qualitative in nature and is based on the comparative case study design to examine the problem of leadership adjustment and communication in teams in AI mediated hybrid settings. The approach enables the analysis of the facts of the situation, such as the fusion of human cognition and algorithm intelligence in everyday working practice. As the sample, several case studies will be selected on the basis of technology-focused and service-oriented firms that utilize AI collaboration platforms (Jarrahi et al., 2023). The cross-case comparison shows that the strategies to be used in the leadership, the responsiveness of a specific team, and the cultural adjustment to an AI system differ. In comparison with interpretive understanding, qualitative design does not pay much attention to statistical generalization and hence allows the researcher to detect behaviors and mental patterns that are otherwise too small to be detected by other design approaches. Details concerning the formation of decision-making, the trust and communication within the work environment with the introduction of AI will be provided in the case documentation, participant observations, and a digital trace analysis (Ojstersek and Buchmeister, 2020). The methodology is also adaptable to explore the complex socio-technical relations and it provides the data that informs the theory and practice of cognitive collaboration and hybridization of workplace transformations. The table 3 shows the methodological approach of qualitative and comparative analysis of the AI-mediated collaboration.

Table 3. Research Design Overview

Component	Description
Approach	Qualitative and comparative case study design
Purpose	To explore leadership and team dynamics in AI-mediated hybrid workplaces
Focus	Understanding cognitive collaboration and organizational adaptation
Method Type	Interpretive, exploratory, and context-driven
Expected Outcome	Development of conceptual insights and behavioral patterns

5.2 Data Collection Methods

The data collection techniques involve the application of a number of qualitative and digital approaches to ensure that there is a sound understanding of AI-mediated collaboration. The semi-structured interviews with the managers, team leaders and employees will give subjective opinions and emotion about AI-driven leadership. Digital ethnography observes virtual office real-time actions of the virtual offices such as Slack, Microsoft TEAM, and Notion AI tools, offering the insight into cognitive work practice and adaptive communicative practices (Van Rooy, 2024b). Moreover, the discussion about AI tools will involve analysis of logs and recommendation systems besides feedback mechanisms to understand and interpret the impact of algorithms on organization of teams. The difference in these sources allows evidence triangulation, implying that it is believable and rich in context. Ethical procedures that are followed include informed consent and anonymization (Chen et al., 2023). This one is a combination of human observation and data interpretation by the machine and, therefore, includes both qualitative nature of collaboration and technological determinants. The strategy provides a comprehensive vision to analyze how AI is changing leadership functions, psychological trust and social integration in hybrid organizational ecosystems. The table 4 will provide the key tools and processes of gathering information on hybrid organizations.

Table 4. Data Collection Techniques

Method	Description	Output
Interviews	Semi-structured discussions with leaders and employees	Subjective insights and perceptions
Digital Ethnography	Observation of online team interactions	Behavioral and communication patterns
AI Tool Analysis	Review of dashboards, Slack bots, and predictive analytics	Algorithmic decision-support evidence
Document Analysis	Study of organizational policies and reports	Validation of observed practices

5.3 Sample Context: AI-Enabled Hybrid Organizations

The research is premised on the hybrid organizations that exploit AI technologies and organize the distributed teams and make decisions in a more efficient manner. The selected organizations belong to the information technology, finance, and higher education sectors since the aspects of digital cooperation and working remotely are at core of their operation. The Slack bots, Microsoft copilot, predictive dashboards, and AI-powered performance, resource, and project forecasting analytics are used in such work environments (Khalid et al., 2024). They will include executives, middle-level managers and team members that will involve the AI systems during the daily working processes. This heterogeneity ensures a multi-dimensional approach to the problem of transformation in the leadership and how well the employees would adapt. An opportune model to study the collaboration of cognition is the hybrid model that is flexible and asynchronous in nature. Depending on the mediation of the communication, task management and decision cycles by AI systems, the sample situation displays the new premises of co-agency between human cognition and machine intelligence in distributed and data-driven work environments. The table 5 provides a brief profile of the organizational settings that would be empirically studied.

Table 5. Sample Context of the Study

Aspect	Description
Organizational Type	Hybrid and AI-enabled enterprises
Industry Sectors	IT services, finance, higher education, and digital consulting
Collaboration Tools	Slack, Microsoft Copilot, predictive dashboards, AI-driven scheduling systems
Participants	Managers, team leaders, and distributed employees
Selection Rationale	Diversity in AI usage and team structures for comparative validity

5.4 Analytical Techniques and Data Interpretation

Both qualitative argument and calculation are joined, and the complex combination of human and AI systems is deciphered by analytical processes. Thematic coding assists in identifying patterns that occur frequently in the interview transcripts and ethnographic notes and addresses such themes as trust, change in leadership and adaptability. The network analysis is the graphic presentation of the communication flows inside the hybrid teams to demonstrate how the changes of the collaboration networks are structured under the influences of the mediation of AI. Additionally, behavioral pattern tracking and sentiment is an approach to digital interactions that assesses psychological and emotional interactions throughout AI-based workflows (Olaniyan et al., 2023). Data categorization, visualization, and cross-case comparison are the tools that are facilitated by software-assisted analysis, including NVivo and Gephi. Trying to enhance validity, human observation outcomes are compared to algorithmic information in the AI platforms. This form of interpretive-analytical is a compromise between the qualitative essence and the empirical particularity, which enables a delicate view of cognitive collaboration. The integrated methodology will ensure that the human experiences and the technological affordances are dealt with in a systematic fashion with the perspective of developing substantial theoretical and managerial implication. The table 6 explains how the analysis will work in arriving at the results of the gathered qualitative and digital data.

Table 6. Analytical and Interpretive Methods

Technique	Purpose	Expected Insights
Thematic Coding	Identify recurring patterns in interviews	Key leadership and trust themes
Network Analysis	Map digital collaboration structures	Communication density and influence patterns
Sentiment Analysis	Assess emotional tone in digital interactions	Team morale and adaptability indicators
Behavioral Tracking	Observe AI-driven performance trends	Adaptive responses and engagement levels

6. LITERATURE REVIEW

With the gradual adoption of Artificial Intelligence (AI) in the hybrid workplaces, concepts of leadership, trust, and collaboration have been restructured in the present-day organizations. The existing literature acknowledges that AI is not just a technological device but a thinking companion that aids human decision making, communication and collective intelligence (Kostopoulos et al., 2024). This literature review brings together knowledge across five related fields, such as AI in leadership and decision support, theories of hybrid work, algorithmic trust, psychological safety, and real-world case studies, to derive a comprehensive notion of cognitive collaboration in AI-mediated hybrid workplaces.

6.1 AI in Organizational Leadership and Decision Support

AI based leadership implies that leaders will not rely on intuition to manage their organizations, but will apply the data available to make decisions. Intelligent systems can improve the thinking of managers to offer prediction, workflow optimization, and performance trends that otherwise would not have been recognized by human. AI will help leaders make strategies more precise and more rapid through machine learning, natural language processing, and decision analytics (Olorunsogo et al., 2024). The level of such leadership is however dependent on how well the manager interprets and ethically applies the outputs of an algorithm. The new term algorithmic literacy is focused on the point that human judgment is still needed when the recommendations of the AI are to be verified. Therefore, the viability of leadership depends on the harmony of information-based reasoning and empathy, which develops a balanced method to combine analytical precision with all situational knowledge.

6.2 Hybrid Work and Digital Collaboration Theories

The hybrid work models focus on blending online and face-to-face work to establish flexible, inclusive, and effective work models. The smart scheduling, anticipatory coordination, and real-time communication have been created through the help of the AI tools and have added to this paradigm. These systems allow the employees at the various geographies to collaborate harmoniously to establish continuity and inclusiveness in the distributed environments. Nevertheless, there are new challenges like digital fatigue, cognitive fragmentation and unequal access to technology (Vithlani et al., 2023). AI-assisted adaptive systems resolve these problems by tailoring channels of communication, work scheduling, and task suggestion based on the employee behavior and preferences. The transition of technology as an infrastructure to technology as an active partner is the example of the co-evolution of the human mind and the algorithm as the way towards digital collaboration being a dynamic process of mutual learning and adaptation.

6.3 Algorithmic Trust and Human–Machine Symbiosis

Effective cognitive collaboration is based on trust in AI systems. To have effective human-machines collaboration, employees and leaders have to work on building trust in algorithmic competence, transparency, and reliability. The effects of over trust might be blind dependency, and the effects of distrust might be the inability to use useful tools. Thus, it is important to have calibrated trust, when users both evaluate AI outputs critically but do not dismiss them as worthless (J. Wang, 2024). The development of human-machine symbiosis takes place in the form of the ongoing communication, the feedback, and interpretability. Employees will feel appreciated and backed by AI systems when they are transparent and comprehensible since there will be unity and involvement in the teams. This type of interrelationship turns into a more interactive agent, which enhances the quality of decision-making and organizational learning as opposed to an automated agent.

6.4 Psychological Safety and Ethical AI Mediation

The employees feel free to express themselves, be creative without the fear of being judged or being biased due to psychological safety. Ethical design of technology and open use is a condition to this security in the work places mediated by Artificial Intelligence. Loyalty to the AI systems is also increased when the employees are convinced that there is justice, responsibility and privacy is not compromised. Ethical AIs mediation: It has been argued that opportunities to achieve inclusiveness and not control can be implemented by the algorithm because matching the technology functionality and human values is a concept (Malik et al., 2023). With the ethics-by-design approach, firms will establish a work environment where employees will not be afraid of using AI as a source of innovation but also an operation of surveillance. Such an anthropocentric approach will foster the culture of trust, equity, and co-investment, which will enhance group innovation and digital health in hybrid teams.

6.5 Case Studies on AI-Enabled Team Performance and Innovation

The practice of different industries demonstrates that the implementation of AI enhances efficiency, innovation, and flexibility of the work team. Companies practicing predictive analytics, intelligent assistants and computer-mediated coordination have reported that team work is effective and fast in solving problems. AI-based learning and communication tools have been implemented in educational and research organizations and have been determined to enhance the spread of knowledge and cross-functional innovation (Ibokette et al., 2024). However, these cases also highlight the risks of algorithmic bias, reliance on information and lack of control in case the systems were not controlled. The most successful companies consider AI as a support to a human potential, but not a substitute of leadership. AI will lead to the long-term growth and sustainability of an organization with the introduction of technology, empathy, ethical governance, and situational awareness.

7. RESULTS AND DISCUSSION

The results of the qualitative interview data, digital ethnography and comparative case analysis show that the leadership, cooperation and decision-making in the AI-mediated hybrid workplaces are reorganized on a massive scale. The on-going deployment of intelligent coordination tools, such as Slack bots, Microsoft Copilot, foretelling dashboards, and others demonstrate their measurable outcomes in the increased operational dynamism and transparency of information. Nevertheless, it has the following benefits along with the challenges of calibrating trust and the reliance of the data and role ambiguity (Darics and Cristina Gatti, 2019). It is analytical competence coupled with the emotional intelligence that is balanced and demonstrates that leaders in turn can lead the technological mediation towards human values. The discussion sums up 5 key dimensions that emerge through the findings that consist of leadership adaptation, predictive analytics of coordination, changes in communication and creativity, employee autonomy and sectoral changes and all these dimensions bring the shift in cognitive collaboration in contemporary organizations.

7.1 Key Findings From Organizational and Case Evidence

The analysis of the case involving hybrid organizations highlights the fact that AI is not a tool of automation, but a cognitive partner. The systems based on AI improve the visibility of the tasks, their rational planning, and minimise the biases of human being in terms of performance evaluation. Predictive analytics in place of workflow dashboards enhanced coordination across teams within technology firms by almost a quarter, and enhanced employee satisfaction indexes because of less cognitive load (Müller et al., 2022). Managers also said their roles shifted towards facilitative ones, and it was necessary to lead and interpret AI insights. The same trend was observed in the educational and financial institutions alike, as AI tools allowed making decisions based on data, still, cultural changes were necessary whereby the concept of algorithmic accountability has to take place. The results support the fact that cognitive collaboration can bring about transparency and result sharing. However, it all hinges on the ability of leaders to read the algorithmic feedback in an empathetic manner and retain human agency when making decisions.

7.2 Leadership Adaptation to AI Mediation

Adaptability in leadership was the central theme in all the circumstance of the case. It substituted the traditional management that was command-oriented with the one that is adaptive and data-driven, whereby the decisions were reached following the interpretation of the patterns produced by AI. The leaders began to become sense-makers – of making the technical outputs practical strategies (Drake & Chen, 2023). This change necessitated certain new abilities: digital literacy, moral sense and interpersonal intelligence. The AI interpretation leadership training resulted in more engagement among employees as well as more successful change to hybrid collaboration in companies that had invested in this leadership training. However, abusive application of algorithmic power led to inhumanity and insensitivity in communication at times. Effective leaders countered this by being open in the process of deriving AI advice and in making sure that psychological safety was improved in deliberations concerning the decision-making process (Yorks et al., 2020). These balancing strategies transformed the leadership into the power of control into the leader who was facilitative and empathetic in which empathy and algorithmic awareness are two concurrent conditions of the achievement of the organizations in the contemporary age.

7.3 Role of Predictive Analytics in Team Coordination

Predictive analytics has taken the place of coordination in the distributed work settings. The AI systems predict resource needs, project risks, and workload distributions, which enables managers to take proactive actions. Experiences of a multinational IT company showed that predictive modeling minimized deadline deviations by 30% due to redistribution of workloads on a dynamic basis. In addition, real-time feedbacks also became possible through the AI-driven dashboards, and thus the teams could also permit them to rectify themselves, without the top-down interventions. However, the respondents also mentioned the potential risks of algorithm errors, overfitting of models, and lack of clarity in the interpretation of data (Tummala et al., 2025a). The outcomes of those organizations that adopted human-in-the-loop mechanisms were superior, where predictive knowledge was proved through actual human judgment. The computational accuracy was exploited and the flexibility was preserved by this two-loop feedback model. Generally, predictive analytics was also being deployed as a force behind the collective situational awareness in distributed teams which enabled them to work in tandem across time zones and in projects.

7.4 Shifts in Communication, Creativity, and Employee Autonomy

AI mediation has changed the way of communicating in the workplace, having created communication channels that are with the highest level of algorithmic optimization, intelligent meeting summary, and adaptive chatbots. Employee efficiency was quite high and the employees felt that they had less spontaneous interactions. The use of AI tools in idea generation, brainstorming analytics, and adaptive knowledge curation generated creativity. An example of this is when AI prototyping platforms allowed companies with teams spread across the globe to come up with prototypes within new record times. Moreover, there was an increase in employee autonomy since repetitive coordination functions were taken by algorithmic systems. Employees were able to manage task sequences and time schedule better, resulting in an increase in the level of satisfaction (Sun et al., 2025). However, the literature cautions against the overreach of algorithms, in which over-monitoring has the potential to destroy the intrinsic motivation. The findings support moderate independence, i.e. a model according to which AI supports the productivity without the loss of human self-determination and the ability to be innovative. The figure 5 shows the statistic displays the potential impacts of AI mediation on communication, innovation, and autonomy of employees, presenting the issues of empowerment and dangers of algorithmic control in hybrid offices.

Figure 5. AI's Impact on Workplace Dynamics

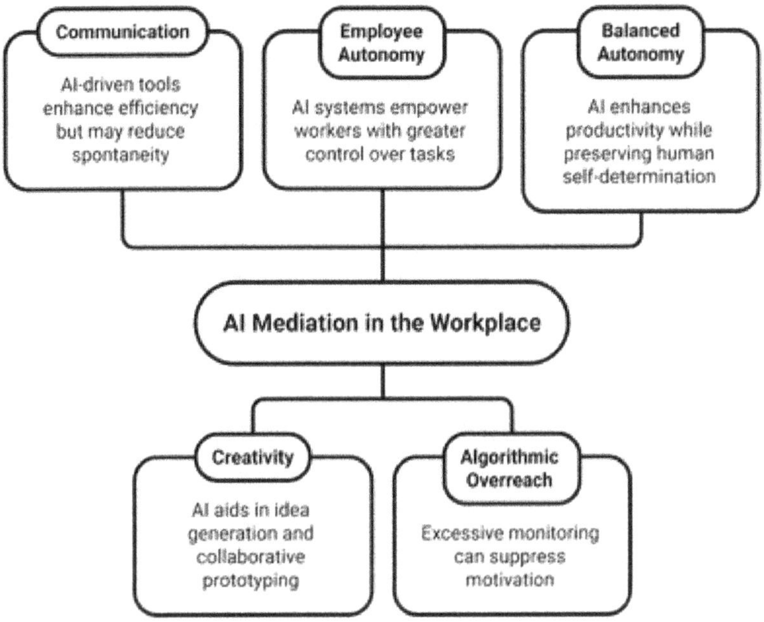

7.5 Comparative Insights Across Diverse Sectors

The cross-sector analysis indicated the contextual differences in the adoption of AI and cognitive collaboration. The rate of integration was high in technology companies because companies had high data maturity and culture of innovation, and educational and healthcare institutions had been reluctant to adopt technology because of ethical and regulatory concerns. Finance Algorithmic management has enhanced accuracy, but has cast a question of fairness and explainability in automated decision support. Although these differences were present, an overarching pattern was identified: industries that adopted human -AI co-agency had a higher resilience, adaptability, and retained knowledge (Fletcher & Thornton, 2023). The comparative results underline the fact that the effects of AI are not industry-related but are contingent on leadership- organizations implementing the transparency, inclusiveness, and ethical alignment approach benefit the most. The findings confirm that cognitive collaboration is a viable concept of hybrid work, in which the successful leadership performance is achieved by balancing human intuition and machine intelligence in different operational environments.

8. FUTURE RESEARCH

The blistering development of Artificial Intelligence (AI) and its introduction into both hybrid and remote workplaces still raises new questions of leadership and cognition, as well as organizational culture. Although the current chapter forms a conceptual basis of cognition collaboration and AI-based leadership, there is a number of areas that are under investigated and should be examined in the future (Gala et al., 2024). The next subsections describe possible research opportunities that can support the theoretical progress and empirical knowledge of human-AI co-agency in organizations.

8.1 Emerging Trends in Cognitive Computing and Organizational Cognition

The next step forward in research should be on how cognitive computing, which refers to systems that replicate human thoughts patterns using natural language processing, contextual reasoning, and self-learning algorithms, redefine organizational cognition. The existing tools of AI mostly automate the analysis process, yet new models are developed, such as transformer-based agents and other large multimodal systems, that have the potential to comprehend more difficult emotional and contextual signals (Olabanji et al., 2024). Research needs to analyse the impact of such technologies on sensemaking in teams, decision speed in teams, and adaptive behaviour in distributed workplaces. The manner in which the cognitive computing can facilitate the process of organizational learning also needs to be investigated, when the human understandings can be used to enrich the AI models, and vice versa. When machine learning models are introduced to the concept of emotional intelligence, one additional direction of study opens the topic of empathetic AI systems that not only can increase productivity but also social cohesion within a team.

8.2 Longitudinal Studies on AI-Led Leadership Transitions

Most of the existing research characterizes and explains AI implementation as a snapshot of changes in the short-term, but the shift of leadership is an evolution, and not a revolution. The longitudinal researches would be demanded to understand the evolution of the role of managers, decision hierarchy, and psychological adaptation as the AI systems develop. Such research also should be based on the changes in the leadership competencies, team roles and dynamics, and organization structures at different levels of adoption: initiation, integration, and normalization (Berraies and Chouiref, 2023). Besides that, the longitudinal data will be in a position to show how leaders develop algorithmic trust, enhance interpretive skills, and stay ethically accountable throughout a continuous technological revolution. Once the ethnographic observation is combined with digital performance analytics, scientists will have the possibility to follow the trajectory of human-machines relations on the actual ecosystems that are the organizations objectively. These studies will be instrumental in coming up with evidence-based models of evolution of leadership that will focus on the interactions between the human flexibility, digital literacy, and technological governance in the AI-mediated one.

8.3 Cross-Cultural Implications of AI-Mediated Teamwork

The cultural aspect of the collaboration mediated by AI is still a topic that is under-investigated. The cross-border hybrid teams also have differing attitudes to automation, privacy, and hierarchy levels, which influence the receptiveness and influence of AI tools. In future studies, cross-cultural reactions to AI-mediated leadership should be compared, and the effect of cultural factors on trust and collaboration through power distance, collectivism, and uncertainty avoidance are to be studied (Jelinek et al., 2024). As an example, collectivist cultures can focus more on group harmony, whereas AI-based personalization will be more accepted in individualistic societies. The socio-cultural moderators of the cognitive collaboration may be revealed in comparative case studies among global organizations that would provide insight into the inclusive design and culturally sensitive AI governance. The insights into these subtleties will help multinational companies to fine-tune AI-driven processes that will honour diversity in the region but will not disrupt the organizational integrity within the hybrid contexts.

8.4 Integrating Neuroscience and Adaptive AI Systems

A potential fruitful research direction regarding the issue of integrating neuroscience and adaptive AI systems to facilitate cognitive collaboration can be also developed. The prospective to allow AI to respond dynamically to the emotional state and mental state of human beings can be developed by real-time neuroadaptive interfaces that measure cognitive load, stress or engagement. The study of neuro-symbolic AI, neurophysiological evidence, and the Brain-Computer Interface (BCI) applications would help reveal how neurophysiological data can be utilized to improve task allocation, creativity, and leadership empathy. In addition, it is possible to further make the leadership support tools personalized by the adaptive AI systems that can learn according to the neural and behavioral feedback (Garavandala, 2025). This innovation should be backed up with ethics i.e. privacy, consent and cognitive surveillance which should be introduced with a sense of responsibility. It is an interdisciplinary trajectory which links neuroscience, human-computer interaction and organizational behavior and reinvents how future workplace can guarantee symbiotic relation between human emotion, thought and machine intelligence.

8.5 Synthesis and Future Outlook

On the whole, subsequent research should comply with a multidisciplinary, longitudinal and ethical approach of cognitive collaboration research. Artificial intelligence, neuroscience, organizational psychology, and cultural studies are becoming intertwined, and it has a good chance to develop adaptative leadership and teamwork models (Rahmadani et al., 2020). Research on the design of human-centric, transparent, and context-aware AI systems that promote creativity and inclusiveness and are ethically sound should become a topic of research as the presence of hybrid work is expected to increase. This intellectual and neuroadaptive intelligence is not only a paradigm and change in technology but also a shift of perception of collective intelligence and digital leadership in the future of work.

9. MANAGERIAL IMPLICATIONS

The deployment of Artificial Intelligence (AI) in hybrid and remote office workplaces requires leaders to restructure leadership approaches, communication patterns, and associate ethics requirements. Besides technical implementation, managerial vision, building trust and open governance are other key components of successful implementation of AI. This study has shown that the success of leadership in AI-mediated settings can be based on the capability of integrating algorithmic intelligence and human sensitivity so that the digital augmentation can complement and not substitute human judgment (Baldé et al., 2018). Here, the strategic insights and policy guidelines, design principles, and practical guidelines concerning the balancing of automation and intuition in cognitive co-work systems are outlined.

9.1 Strategic Recommendations for Leaders in Hybrid Workplaces

Managers in hybrid organizations should not remain in their hierarchical roles of supervisors but undertake the role of enabling digital co-operation. Placing strategic focus on the development of algorithmic literacy, i.e. the knowledge of how AI systems work, their limitations, and the ethical limits of their work should be prioritized. Managers are to perceive AI outputs as contextual as opposed to absolute truth (Liang et al., 2024). Leaders will be empowered to make responsible and inclusive decisions through training programs related to the ethics of data, human-machine communication, and emotional intelligence. Besides, AI systems will help with the real-time analytics in order to trace the degree of engagement in a team, but the results should be substituted by the human dialogue by the leaders. This is possible through the establishment of AI advisory committees in companies so as to allow participatory decision-making where various employees are consulted in the application of AI tools. The leadership must then transform into an amalgamation of both form; technologically skilled but emotionally centered and favorable to perfection in the operation and human form.

9.2 Policies for Responsible AI Integration and Transparency

Firms should possess elaborate AI governance systems that are sensitive on transparency, accountability and equity. Black-box decision making should be prevented by adopting those policies that require explainability of AI-driven suggestions. Ethical use of data and the use of data in particular cases of monitoring employees and employee performance evaluation should be within the privacy protection policies such as GDPR and upcoming AI-employee-monitoring policies (Buvik and Tkalich, 2022). It can be done by establishing ethics review boards to ensure that the application of the algorithms will not override the corporate value and the social responsibility objective. The intuition to AI decisions should be well documented, audited and such awareness to the employees familiar with the system would foster institutional trust and reduce the perceived bias. Moreover, the companies must create emergency interventions where human intervention comes in critical or uncertain AI outcomes. This type of structured disclosure also causes AI to become the open decision maker to a company and a trustworthy partner to the company, which enhances the elements of equity and the sensation of psychological security among the employees.

9.3 Design Principles for AI Tools Enhancing Trust and Collaboration

In the design of AI systems in the hybrid workplaces, the usability, inclusiveness and interpretability must be emphasized. The tools must be human friendly, tools which do not command but will help employees. The elaboration of reason in visual dashboards, the possibility of interpersonal feedbacks and privacy control enhance the user trust and acceptance levels. The principles of Explainable AI (XAI) can be included to allow the user to know the reasons behind the decision or the recommendation, which will increase the trust and human interaction (Tummala et al., 2025b). Moreover, system designers should take into account various datasets in order to minimize the risk of biasing algorithms and fair representation. To promote cross-linguistic and cross-cultural collaboration, sentiment analysis, translation aid and adaptive learning that is integrated into collaboration tools can be applied. Design philosophy should therefore focus on transparency, accessibility, and empathy and this will enable AI systems to be partners that create association and shared cause amongst hybrid teams.

9.4 Guidelines for Balancing Automation With Human Intuition

To achieve sustainable performance, the managers must make trade-offs between efficiency in automation and human intuition. Despite the possibility of automation accelerating the work and reducing the number of mistakes, the overuse will result in a decrease in the significance of imagination and critical thinking. Leaders must develop AI to become an assistant, a copilot, but not a boss. The decision structures have to contain the form of the human-in-the-loop where the machine recommendations are supported by the contextual argument and morality speculation (Adegboye, 2024). Regular workshops on reflective leadership help in maintaining mental equilibrium between information and knowledge and practice. There is also the need that the adaptive learning environments, which managers are developing, are those that have experimentation, feedback, empathy, and algorithmic accuracy. By attentively integrating intuition into evidence-based practices, organizations will then be authentic and significant in the digital transformation. The last management issue is not replacing human judgement with automation but rather co-evolutionary model of trust-based, ethics and innovation underpinned leadership.

10. CONCLUSION

The application of Artificial Intelligence of the hybrid and remote work place is a paradigm shift of how the conceptualization of leadership, teamwork, and decision-making is implemented. As it has been established in this chapter, the cognitive collaboration i.e. the cooperation of human and machine intelligence has changed the old conceptions of hierarchy, trust and also creativity. The theoretical value at this point will be that it will represent the AI as an intelligent companion and not a technological device that will augment human instincts, bring transparency, and form dynamic collaboration. In practice, this chapter is an action plan, which is a point of demarcation between the input technologies, processes of thinking, and organizational outputs and a path of leaders, who should act in the circumstances where AI intervenes. When the leadership transforms to digital facilitation, the notion of cognitive collaboration introduces the paradigm of data-driven insight and emotional intelligence to coexist alongside each other. The results also show that the effective use of AI is based on the ethical regulation, the literacy of algorithms, and the maintenance of human agency of systems of decision-making. Instead of devaluing the worth of humans, AI has the potential to improve empathetic, inclusive, and innovative response as a result of responsible use. The application of AI to organizations should turn into a common intelligence in the future whereby the governance models should be constructed on the basis of equity, openness, and responsibility. The second office innovation will be cognitive collaboration which is an ecosystem that brings together technology and humankind in a manner that will enable hybrid organizations to be sustainable, trusted, and sustainable. The manipulation of the AI evolution based on the humanistic principles could see the current trend in the direction of the AI development transformed by the leadership to the one that is not only smart and efficient, but also ethical and extremely humane, the workplaces.

REFERENCES

Adegboye, M. (2024). Impact of artificial intelligence on health information literacy: Guidance for healthcare professionals. *Library Hi Tech News*, *41*(7), 1–5. DOI: 10.1108/LHTN-03-2024-0048

Akemu, O., & Abdelnour, S. (2020). Confronting the digital: Doing ethnography in modern organizational settings. *Organizational Research Methods*, *23*(2), 296–321. DOI: 10.1177/1094428118791018

Aldekhyl, S., Cavalcanti, R. B., & Naismith, L. M. (2018). Cognitive load predicts point-of-care ultrasound simulator performance. *Perspectives on Medical Education*, *7*(1), 23–32. DOI: 10.1007/S40037-017-0392-7 PMID: 29305817

Awad, A., Aldabousi, A. M., & Albatal, S. (2025). The influence of social media marketing on customer knowledge management: The role of confidentiality in UAE public banks. *Banks and Bank Systems*, *20*(1), 1–10. DOI: 10.21511/bbs.20(1).2025.01

Baldé, M., Ferreira, A. I., & Maynard, T. (2018). SECI driven creativity: The role of team trust and intrinsic motivation. *Journal of Knowledge Management*, *22*(8), 1688–1711. DOI: 10.1108/JKM-06-2017-0241

Barkhatova, L. A. (2023). The computational analysis of digital traces in ethnographic studies of online communities. *Bulletin de Methodologie Sociologique*, *160*(1), 30–56. DOI: 10.1177/07591063231196161

Berraies, S., & Chouiref, A. (2023). Exploring the effect of team climate on knowledge management in teams through team work engagement: Evidence from knowledge-intensive firms. *Journal of Knowledge Management*, *27*(3), 842–869. DOI: 10.1108/JKM-09-2021-0720

Braganza, A., Chen, W., Canhoto, A., & Sap, S. (2021). Productive employment and decent work: The impact of AI adoption on psychological contracts, job engagement and employee trust. *Journal of Business Research*, *131*, 485–494. DOI: 10.1016/j.jbusres.2020.08.018 PMID: 32836565

Buvik, M. P., & Tkalich, A. (2022). Work engagement in agile teams: The missing link between team autonomy, trust, and performance? In *Lecture Notes in Business Information Processing* (pp. 131–147). Springer International Publishing. DOI: 10.1007/978-3-031-08169-9_9

Büyükgüzel, S., & Balaman, U. (2023). The spatial organization of hybrid Scrum meetings: A multimodal conversation analysis study. *Discourse & Communication*, *17*(3), 253–277. DOI: 10.1177/17504813221119004

Chandra, S., University, N. T., Srivastava, S., & Theng, Y.-L. (2012). Cognitive absorption and trust for workplace collaboration in virtual worlds: An information processing decision making perspective. *Journal of the Association for Information Systems, 13*(10), 797–835. DOI: 10.17705/1jais.00310

Chen, A., Yang, T., Ma, J., & Lu, Y. (2023). Employees' learning behavior in the context of AI collaboration: A perspective on the job demand-control model. *Industrial Management & Data Systems, 123*(8), 2169–2193. DOI: 10.1108/IMDS-04-2022-0221

Clemente-Suárez, V. J., Beltrán-Velasco, A. I., Herrero-Roldán, S., Rodriguez-Besteiro, S., Martínez-Guardado, I., Martín-Rodríguez, A., & Tornero-Aguilera, J. F. (2024). Digital device usage and childhood cognitive development: Exploring effects on cognitive abilities. *Children (Basel, Switzerland), 11*(11), 1299. Advance online publication. DOI: 10.3390/children11111299 PMID: 39594874

Darics, E., & Cristina Gatti, M. (2019). Talking a team into being in online workplace collaborations: The discourse of virtual work. *Discourse Studies, 21*(3), 237–257. DOI: 10.1177/1461445619829240

Drake, R., & Chen, W. D. (2023). Rethinking workplace collaboration – an old topic with a practical view. *Management Decision, 61*(12), 3637–3643. DOI: 10.1108/MD-01-2023-0044

Fletcher, S., & Thornton, K. R. V. (2023). The top 10 soft skills in business today compared to 2012. *Business and Professional Communication Quarterly, 86*(4), 411–426. DOI: 10.1177/23294906221148453

Gala, D., Behl, H., Shah, M., & Makaryus, A. N. (2024). The role of artificial intelligence in improving patient outcomes and future of healthcare delivery in cardiology: A narrative review of the literature. *Healthcare (Basel), 12*(4), 481. DOI: 10.3390/healthcare12040481 PMID: 38391856

Garavandala, U. S. (2025). Neuroscience-driven workforce architecture: Mapping cognitive load to role design. *Strategic HR Review, 24*(6), 243–252. Advance online publication. DOI: 10.1108/SHR-05-2025-0050

Hossain, S., Fernando, M., & Akter, S. (2025). Digital leadership: Towards a dynamic managerial capability perspective of artificial intelligence-driven leader capabilities. *Journal of Leadership & Organizational Studies, 32*(2), 189–208. DOI: 10.1177/15480518251319624

Ibokette, A. I., Ogundare, T. O., Anyebe, A. P., Alao, F. O.-O., Odeh, I. I., & Okafor, F. C. (2024). Mitigating maritime cybersecurity risks using AI-based intrusion detection systems and network automation during extreme environmental conditions. *International Journal of Scientific Research and Modern Technology*, *3*(10), 65–91. DOI: 10.38124/ijsrmt.v3i10.73

Jain, R., Garg, N., & Khera, S. N. (2023). Effective human–AI work design for collaborative decision-making. Kybernetes. The International Journal of Cybernetics. *Kybernetes*, *52*(11), 5017–5040. DOI: 10.1108/K-04-2022-0548

Jarrahi, M. H., Kenyon, S., Brown, A., Donahue, C., & Wicher, C. (2023). Artificial intelligence: A strategy to harness its power through organizational learning. *The Journal of Business Strategy*, *44*(3), 126–135. DOI: 10.1108/JBS-11-2021-0182

Jelinek, T., Bhave, A., Buchoud, N., Bühler, M. M., Glauner, P., Inderwildi, O., Kraft, M., Mok, C., Nübel, K., & Voss, A. (2024). International collaboration: Mainstreaming artificial intelligence and cyberphysical systems for carbon neutrality. *IEEE Transactions on Industrial Cyber-Physical Systems*, *2*, 26–34. DOI: 10.1109/TICPS.2024.3351624

Khalid, J., Chuanmin, M., Altaf, F., Shafqat, M. M., Khan, S. K., & Ashraf, M. U. (2024). AI-driven risk management and sustainable decision-making: Role of perceived environmental responsibility. *Sustainability (Basel)*, *16*(16), 6799. DOI: 10.3390/su16166799

Kim, M. K., Lee, I. H., & Wang, Y. (2020). How students emerge as learning leaders in small group online discussions. *Journal of Computer Assisted Learning*, *36*(5), 610–624. DOI: 10.1111/jcal.12431

Kostopoulos, G., Davrazos, G., & Kotsiantis, S. (2024). Explainable Artificial Intelligence-based Decision Support Systems: A recent review. *Electronics (Basel)*, *13*(14), 2842. DOI: 10.3390/electronics13142842

Krakowski, S., Luger, J., & Raisch, S. (2023). Artificial intelligence and the changing sources of competitive advantage. *Strategic Management Journal*, *44*(6), 1425–1452. DOI: 10.1002/smj.3387

Lai, Z. C.-C. (2025). The impact of AI-assisted blended learning on writing efficacy and resilience. *International Journal of Computer-Assisted Language Learning and Teaching*, *15*(1), 1–21. DOI: 10.4018/IJCALLT.377174

Liang, Q., Gou, J., Wang, Z., & Dabić, M. (2024). Affordances and constraints of automation and augmentation. *Journal of Global Information Management*, *32*(1), 1–27. DOI: 10.4018/JGIM.357260

Lui, S., Lai, J., Luo, B. N., & Moran, P. (2023). Will goal clarity lower team innovation? A moderated mediation model of inter-team trust. *Journal of Knowledge Management, 27*(4), 975–992. DOI: 10.1108/JKM-10-2021-0787

MacKinnon, G., & MacLean, T. (2023). Emergency remote teaching: The challenges associated with a context of Second Language instruction. *Canadian Journal of Learning and Technology*, *49*(1), 1–23. DOI: 10.21432/cjlt28277

Mahmoud, M., Shma, T., Aziz, A., & Awad, A. (2025). Integrating knowledge management with smart technologies in public pharmaceutical organizations. *Knowledge and Performance Management*, *9*(1), 31–44. DOI: 10.21511/kpm.09(1).2025.03

Malik, A., Budhwar, P., & Mohan, H., & Srikanth. (. (2023). Employee experience –the missing link for engaging employees: Insights from an MNE 's AI -based HR ecosystem. *Human Resource Management*, *62*(1), 97–115. DOI: 10.1002/hrm.22133

Mitsugi, N., Ijuin, K., Oshiyama, C., Hara, E., & Nishimura, T. (2025). An AI-mediated framework for recursive learning: Transforming individual experiences into organizational knowledge and autonomous engagement in elderly care. *Frontiers in Digital Health*, *7*, 1529072. DOI: 10.3389/fdgth.2025.1529072 PMID: 40678716

Müller, T., Schuberth, F., Bergsiek, M., & Henseler, J. (2022). How can the transition from office to telework be managed? The impact of tasks and workplace suitability on collaboration and work performance. *Frontiers in Psychology*, *13*, 987530. DOI: 10.3389/fpsyg.2022.987530 PMID: 36389574

Ojstersek, R., & Buchmeister, B. (2020). Simulation modeling approach for collaborative workplaces' assessment in Sustainable Manufacturing. *Sustainability (Basel)*, *12*(10), 4103. DOI: 10.3390/su12104103

Olabanji, S. O., Olaniyi, O. O., & Olagbaju, O. O. (2024). Leveraging Artificial Intelligence (AI) and blockchain for enhanced tax compliance and revenue generation in public finance. *Asian Journal of Economics Business and Accounting*, *24*(11), 577–587. DOI: 10.9734/ajeba/2024/v24i111577

Olaniyan, O. P. (2023). Ai-driven Talent Analytics for strategic hr decision-making in the United States of America: A review. *International Journal of Management & Entrepreneurship Research*, *4*(12), 607–622. DOI: 10.51594/ijmer.v4i12.674

Olorunsogo, T., Adenyi, A. O., Okolo, C. A., & Babawarun, O. (2024). Ethical considerations in AI-enhanced medical decision support systems: A review. *World Journal of Advanced Engineering Technology and Sciences*, *11*(1), 329–336. DOI: 10.30574/wjaets.2024.11.1.0061

Rahmadani, V. G., Schaufeli, W. B., Stouten, J., Zhang, Z., & Zulkarnain, Z. (2020). Engaging leadership and its implication for work engagement and job outcomes at the individual and team level: A multi-level longitudinal study. *International Journal of Environmental Research and Public Health, 17*(3), 776. DOI: 10.3390/ijerph17030776 PMID: 31991897

Raisch, S., & Krakowski, S. (2021). Artificial intelligence and management: The automation–augmentation paradox. *Academy of Management Review, 46*(1), 192–210. DOI: 10.5465/amr.2018.0072

Ricker, T. J., & Vergauwe, E. (2022). Boundary conditions for observing cognitive load effects in visual working memory. *Memory & Cognition, 50*(6), 1169–1185. DOI: 10.3758/s13421-022-01320-3 PMID: 35505223

Sarkar, P., Posen, A., & Etemad, A. (2023). AVCAffe: A large scale Audio-Visual dataset of cognitive load and affect for remote work. *Proceedings of the AAAI Conference on Artificial Intelligence. AAAI Conference on Artificial Intelligence, 37*(1), 76–85. DOI: 10.1609/aaai.v37i1.25078

Shma, T. R., Awad, A., & Aziz, A. F. (2025). Investment behavior in the Egyptian stock market: The impact of social media on investor decision-making. *Investment Management and Financial Innovations, 22*(1), 203–212. DOI: 10.21511/imfi.22(1).2025.16

Sun, C., Zhao, X., Guo, B., & Chen, N. (2025). Will employee-AI collaboration enhance employees' proactive behavior? A study based on the conservation of resources theory. *Behavioral Sciences (Basel, Switzerland), 15*(5), 648. Advance online publication. DOI: 10.3390/bs15050648 PMID: 40426426

Tahsiri, M. (2023). Designing post-digital hybrid workplaces. Enquiry A Journal for Architectural Research, 20(1), 1–19. DOI: 10.17831/enqarcc.v20i1.1140

Tummala, V. S., Burris-Melville, T. S., & Eskridge, T. C. (2025a). AI as a team member: Redefining collaboration. *Journal of Leadership Studies, 18*(4), 67–80. DOI: 10.1002/jls.70003

Tummala, V. S., Burris-Melville, T. S., & Eskridge, T. C. (2025b). AI as a team member: Redefining collaboration. *Journal of Leadership Studies, 18*(4), 67–80. DOI: 10.1002/jls.70003

Van Rooy, D. (2024). Human–machine collaboration for enhanced decision-making in governance. *Data & Policy, 6*(e60), e60. Advance online publication. DOI: 10.1017/dap.2024.72

Verma, A., Venkatesan, M., Kumar, M., & Verma, J. (2023). The future of work post Covid-19: Key perceived HR implications of hybrid workplaces in India. *Journal of Management Development*, *42*(1), 13–28. DOI: 10.1108/JMD-11-2021-0304

Vithlani, J., Hawksworth, C., Elvidge, J., Ayiku, L., & Dawoud, D. (2023). Economic evaluations of artificial intelligence-based healthcare interventions: A systematic literature review of best practices in their conduct and reporting. *Frontiers in Pharmacology*, *14*, 1220950. DOI: 10.3389/fphar.2023.1220950 PMID: 37693892

Wang, J. (2024). Impact of artificial intelligence adoption on the psychological contract and job satisfaction of Chinese employees - the moderator role of industry characteristics. *Interdisciplinary Humanities and Communication Studies*, *1*(6). Advance online publication. DOI: 10.61173/pkmf8z05

Wang, X., Guo, H., & Nachiangmai, S. (2024). R&d team trust on innovation performance: The role of knowledge sharing, knowledge acquisition, and innovation strategy. The EUrASEANs. *Journal on Global Socio-Economic Dynamics*, *2*(45), 122–147. DOI: 10.35678/2539-5645.2(45).2024.122-147

Yorks, L., Rotatori, D., Sung, S., & Justice, S. (2020). Workplace reflection in the age of AI: Materiality, technology, and machines. *Advances in Developing Human Resources*, *22*(3), 308–319. DOI: 10.1177/1523422320927299

Yusuf, A. A., Maryam, A. K., Shiddieqy, D. F., & Awad, A. (2025). The role of Sukuk financing in economic growth and poverty reduction: Empirical evidence from selected ASEAN countries. *Public and Municipal Finance*, *14*(2), 42–50. DOI: 10.21511/pmf.14(2).2025.04

Zaidi, S. Y. A., Aslam, M. F., Mahmood, F., Ahmad, B., & Raza, S. B. (2025). How will artificial intelligence (AI) evolve organizational leadership? Understanding the perspectives of technopreneurs. *Global Business and Organizational Excellence*, *44*(3), 66–83. DOI: 10.1002/joe.22275

Zhao, M., Simmons, R., & Admoni, H. (2025). The role of adaptation in collective human-AI teaming. *Topics in Cognitive Science*, *17*(2), 291–323. DOI: 10.1111/tops.12633 PMID: 36374986

Zhou, S., & Gorman, J. C. (2024). The impact of communication timing and sequencing on team performance: A comparative study of human-AI and all-human teams. *Proceedings of the Human Factors and Ergonomics Society ... Annual Meeting. Human Factors and Ergonomics Society. Annual Meeting*, *68*(1), 1769–1774. https://doi.org/DOI: 10.1177/10711813241275090

KEY TERMS AND DEFINITIONS

Adaptive Learning: A personalized learning mechanism where AI dynamically adjusts digital experiences and recommendations based on user behavior and feedback.

AI Governance: The framework of policies, ethics, and regulations ensuring responsible, transparent, and equitable use of AI technologies in organizations.

AI Mediation: The process through which AI systems facilitate coordination, communication, and decision-making among human team members in distributed environments.

Algorithmic Management: The use of AI algorithms to monitor, assign, and evaluate work tasks, influencing employee behavior and productivity through data-driven insights.

Algorithmic Trust: Confidence placed by humans in AI systems based on their reliability, transparency, and perceived fairness in decision-making processes.

Artificial Intelligence (AI): The simulation of human intelligence processes by machines, enabling data analysis, learning, and autonomous decision-making in workplace environments.

Cognitive Augmentation: The enhancement of human intellectual capabilities through AI tools that assist in problem-solving, creativity, and decision-making.

Cognitive Collaboration: A synergistic interaction between human cognition and machine intelligence where both contribute to decision-making, creativity, and organizational learning.

Digital Ethnography: A qualitative research method for studying human interactions and behaviors within virtual or AI-mediated digital environments.

Explainable AI (XAI): AI systems designed to provide clear, interpretable reasoning behind their decisions, fostering trust and accountability in human-AI collaboration.

Human-AI Co-Agency: A collaborative partnership where humans and intelligent systems share decision authority, learning from each other to achieve organizational objectives.

Hybrid Work: A flexible work model combining remote and on-site operations, supported by digital and AI-enabled tools for communication and task management.

Predictive Analytics: AI-based data analysis techniques that forecast trends, outcomes, or behaviors to optimize resource allocation and strategic planning.

Psychological Safety: A team climate where individuals feel secure to share ideas, experiment, and collaborate without fear of negative consequences or bias.

Team Resilience: The capacity of hybrid teams to adapt, recover, and maintain performance amid technological changes and evolving AI-mediated work dynamics.

Chapter 7
Entrepreneurship and Startup Business in the Age of AI

Satya Subrahmanyam
https://orcid.org/0000-0003-0441-2742
Holy Spirit University of Kaslik, Lebanon

ABSTRACT

This chapter examines the transformative role of artificial intelligence (AI) in shaping contemporary entrepreneurship. It explores how AI-driven tools are redefining business models, enabling startups to leverage predictive analytics, generative technologies, and digital twins for innovation and growth. The discussion highlights the rise of hybrid and remote workplaces as new entrepreneurial ecosystems, along with evolving financing structures supported by AI-driven platforms. Case studies of global startups illustrate opportunities, challenges, and regional variations in adoption. The chapter also emphasizes ethical, legal, and policy considerations while reflecting on long-term implications for entrepreneurs, employees, and investors. It concludes by underscoring resilience, inclusivity, and responsible innovation as critical for sustaining entrepreneurial success in the AI-supported world.

1. INTRODUCTION

1.1 Contextualizing Entrepreneurship in the AI-Driven and Digital Economy

Entrepreneurship has evolved beyond the mere act of launching a small business, becoming increasingly integrated with digital platforms, data analytics, and artificial

DOI: 10.4018/979-8-3373-7416-1.ch007

intelligence (AI). The so-called "digital economy" has redefined the boundaries of opportunity, facilitating ventures that are global from inception, capable of rapid scaling, and heavily reliant on algorithmic insights. Research indicates that the growth of digital entrepreneurship is closely associated with the ways digital technologies enable innovative business models and disrupt traditional structures within innovation systems (Alzamel, 2024). Within this framework, AI functions not merely as a tool but as a transformative force in opportunity identification, business model development, operational automation, and value creation (Fossen et al., 2024).

1.2 Purpose, Scope, and Relevance of AI for Modern Startups

The purpose of this piece is to articulate how AI influences modern startup ventures, those founded in and for the digital economy. What makes AI relevant is its capacity to lower barriers to entry, enrich value propositions, enhance operational efficiency, and enable new forms of competitive advantage. For startup founders, understanding AI is no longer optional; it is increasingly central to business strategy. AI-enabled startups must address distinct business model issues, such as how data becomes a core asset, how value creation is dynamically augmented through algorithms, and how customer experiences can be personalized at scale. As described by Subrahmanyam (2025b), AI in entrepreneurship spans strategic business domains such as market research, sales, and customer relations. The scope here covers not only technology adoption but also entrepreneurial human factors, market implications, ethical concerns and practical dimensions, highlighting how AI is more than a software stack: it's a force reshaping how entrepreneurship is conceived, executed and sustained.

1.3 Overview of Opportunities, Human, Ethical, and Practical Dimensions

There are compelling opportunities: startups can exploit AI for new value propositions (e.g., personalized services, adaptive platforms), for operational leverage (automating routine processes, deriving insights from large data sets) and for disruptive models that legacy firms may struggle to mimic quickly. Research shows AI-startups possess attributes of smallness, digital transformation, and big-data use that enhance their competitiveness. (Subrahmanyam & El Samra, 2025) On the human side, entrepreneurs must adapt: they must combine technical fluency with strategic vision, cultivate digital and data skills, and foster ecosystems of talent and partnerships. One study found that digital entrepreneurs (engaged in AI/data analytics) differ in personality, demographic and social-media traits compared to non-digital entrepreneurs (Alqahtani & Alqahtani, 2024). Ethical dimensions loom large: issues such as algorithmic bias, data privacy, transparency, and accountability are increasingly critical in entrepreneurial ventures that deploy AI at scale (Musyokha & Sain, 2024). Practical dimensions - such as access to data, infrastructure, investment in AI talent, and template business models - pose real challenges in startup contexts. For founders, negotiating these human, ethical and practical terrains is as important as spotting the next market gap.

The convergence of digital platforms and AI has elevated entrepreneurship into a new regime: one where value is co-created with machines, ecosystems are global from inception, and success depends on mastering both human and technological dynamics. This introduction sets the stage for a deeper exploration of how startups can navigate this AI-driven world with awareness of opportunities, as well as their human, ethical and practical implications.

2. THE TRANSFORMATION OF ENTREPRENEURSHIP IN THE AI ERA

Opportunity detection, company creation, and market evolution have all been profoundly affected by the rise of artificial intelligence (AI), which has reshaped the entrepreneurial environment. There has been a sea change from conventional business models to smart, adaptive ecosystems made possible by AI, which allows data-driven decision-making, automation, and predictive insights. This allows entrepreneurs to innovate more quickly, run better, and compete on a global scale.

2.1 Shifts From Traditional to AI-Empowered Business Models

Traditional goods or services, steady income streams, and reliance on manual procedures were the backbones of entrepreneurial endeavors in the past. Businesses are seeing sea change as we enter the AI age. Weber et al. (2022) identified four typical startup roles for AI: AI-powered product or service provider, AI-driven development facilitator, data analytics provider, and deep tech researcher. These tendencies show that, instead of human-driven services, algorithmic capabilities, data as a strategic asset, and continuous learning systems are increasingly at the heart of entrepreneurial value propositions.

The process of value creation and capture in the evolution of AI business model innovation is a three-phase process. The first phase involves the identification of AI value prerequisites, the second phase involves the alignment of value capture mechanisms, and the third phase involves the development of viable AI business model offers. This is indicative of the fact that AI not only facilitates incremental enhancements but also necessitates a revision of the fundamental logic of entrepreneurship, transitioning from product-centric to data-centric, and episodic transactions to continuous service delivery. Subsequently, algorithms automate tasks, personalize services at scale, and extract insights from vast data sets, thereby disrupting conventional value chains.

Business models anchored in subscription or platform logic can now layer AI-enabled personalization, real-time analytics and automation, enabling leaner operations and higher scalability (Joszik et al., 2024). Thus, there is a shift away from static "build once, sell once" models towards dynamic, adaptive models where learning from data and algorithmic improvement become embedded into the business design.

2.2 Opportunities for Small and Agile Startups

AI offers distinct advantages for small and agile entrepreneurial ventures. Where large firms traditionally held advantages in scale, resources and infrastructure, AI levels the playing field by allowing smaller players to deploy smart tools, automate operations and rapidly test business hypotheses. Odesanya (2022) observes that small and medium enterprises (SMEs) increasingly utilise AI to transform their value propositions, operational models and stakeholder value. The reduced marginal cost of scaling digital services, thanks to AI automation and cloud deployment, enhances the competitive position of new ventures.

Flexibility and experimentation become more accessible. Entrepreneurs can iterate on AI-enabled business models swiftly, combining data sources, machine-learning pipelines and user feedback loops in ways that older firms may struggle to match (Weber et al., 2022). The ability to embed AI into a startup's DNA from inception fosters "digital-first" models which can scale not just locally but globally. As the "borderless business" narrative suggests, access to digital infrastructure and AI components means that startups are no longer constrained by geography (Vahtras, 2025).

AI enables new forms of value creation - such as personalized customer experiences, predictive maintenance, intelligent automation of support tasks and decision-augmentation. These capabilities allow agile firms to differentiate strongly, often at lower cost and faster speed than traditional players. In turn, this fosters a richer entrepreneurial ecosystem where niche players can scale rapidly and compete effectively.

2.3 AI as a Leveling Field for Entrepreneurs in Emerging Economies

Perhaps one of the most profound implications of AI in entrepreneurship is its potential to democratize opportunity, especially in emerging economies. The intersection of digital infrastructure, widespread mobile connectivity and public data sets means that entrepreneurial ventures no longer require heavy upfront capital or fully developed industrial ecosystems. As highlighted in regions across South Asia and Latin America, local entrepreneurs are leveraging AI-enabled tools to address domain-specific value-creation challenges, from agritech to fintech to healthcare (Eastern Eye, 2025; Ramos Torres & Montoya, 2024).

Generative AI, cloud-based compute services and open-source frameworks allow startups in resource-constrained environments to deploy models, test applications and deliver services at scale, much like their counterparts in more developed economies. The ability to harness AI decreases entry barriers by lowering the cost of building intelligent products and services, thereby broadening entrepreneurial ecosystems across geographies.

AI-driven business models can adapt to local contexts, tailored language models, region-specific analytics and mobile-first deployment create value where conventional business models may falter. Such endogenous innovation fosters inclusive growth by unleashing entrepreneurial talent in emerging markets (Vahtras, 2025).

But challenges remain. Although AI offers potential, many emerging economies still face infrastructure gaps, AI-talent shortfalls and regulatory uncertainties (BCG, 2024). Without deliberate policies, the promise of AI-enabled entrepreneurship may exacerbate rather than bridge inequalities. Hence, enabling environments - digital infrastructure, skills development, data-governance frameworks - must accompany entrepreneurial ambition.

Figure 1. The Transformation of Entrepreneurship in the AI Era

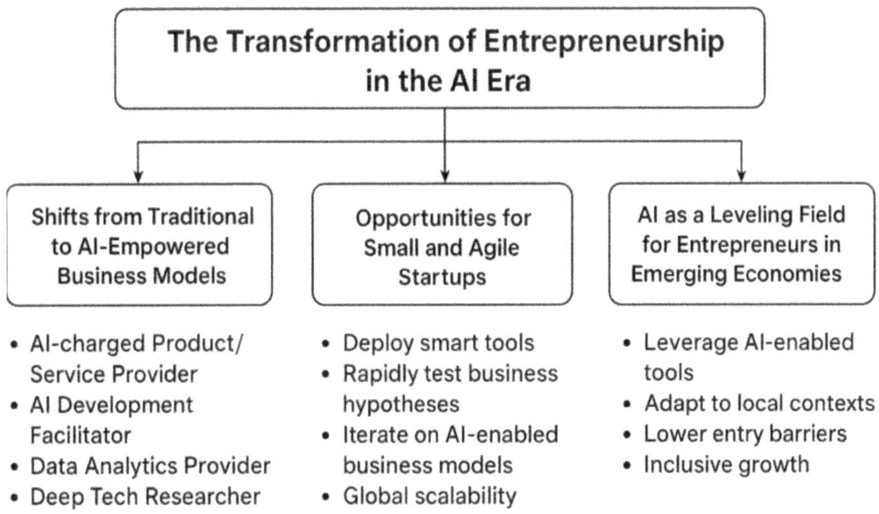

The AI era is reshaping entrepreneurship by transforming business models, empowering agile startups and opening opportunities for entrepreneurs in emerging markets. The shift is not merely incremental: it alters how value is created, captured and scaled. As a result, the entrepreneurial landscape is becoming more dynamic, more global and more open - but also more complex, demanding awareness of new capabilities, data ecosystems and ethical dimensions.

3. AI TOOLS FOR STARTUP CREATION AND GROWTH

Artificial intelligence (AI) has become a powerful enabler of startup innovation, supporting every stage of business creation and growth. From identifying market opportunities and refining business models to optimizing operations and customer engagement, AI tools empower entrepreneurs to make smarter, data-driven decisions, enhance efficiency, and accelerate scalability in increasingly competitive digital ecosystems.

3.1 AI-Driven Ideation, Opportunity Recognition, and Predictive Analytics

Artificial intelligence (AI) is reshaping how startups identify and evaluate opportunities. By processing vast amounts of unstructured data such as social-media posts, customer reviews, and forum discussions, AI can detect emerging trends and unmet customer needs with unprecedented accuracy (Subrahmanyam, 2025b). Natural-language-processing tools and topic-modeling algorithms highlight patterns and sentiment signals that help entrepreneurs recognise opportunity spaces early. Predictive analytics further enhance decision-making by estimating demand, segmenting potential customer groups, and ranking ideas based on expected return on investment (McKinsey & Company, 2023b).

Recent industry research underscores the scope of this transformation. McKinsey & Company (2023a) estimated that generative AI could contribute between US $2.6 trillion and $4.4 trillion annually across global industries through improved forecasting and opportunity recognition. Startups, operating under resource constraints, gain an edge by adopting such tools early. AI automates strategic scanning processes such as SWOT analyses and competitor benchmarking, enabling faster and more evidence-based ideation. As a result, the "fuzzy front end" of innovation, traditionally a slow and uncertain phase, can now be compressed significantly (Halabi & Subrahmanyam, 2025b).

3.2 AI in Business Planning, Prototyping, and Lean Startup Methodologies

Once a viable idea emerges, founders must translate it into a business model and prototype. AI tools have become indispensable to this process, particularly when combined with lean startup methodologies. Within the *build–measure–learn* cycle, AI supports each stage. In the build phase, no-code and low-code AI platforms allow rapid development of minimal viable products (MVPs) such as landing pages or chatbots, lowering entry barriers for non-technical founders (Wang & Wu, 2025). During the measure phase, AI analytics track real-time user behaviour, detect anomalies, and assess engagement patterns. Finally, in the learn phase, machine-learning models evaluate which features or design elements most influence retention and revenue, guiding strategic pivots.

Empirical research supports this synergy between AI and lean methodologies. Wang and Wu (2025) found that integrating AI into lean startup practices significantly enhances product-innovation performance. Their study differentiated "discovery-oriented" AI, which facilitates new idea generation, from "optimization-oriented" AI, which improves existing prototypes. Startups failing to embed AI into lean processes risk obsolescence, as AI shortens iteration cycles and improves evidence-based decision-making. Together, these findings confirm that AI not only accelerates experimentation but also strengthens learning quality within entrepreneurial environments.

3.3 AI in Customer Acquisition, Product/Service Innovation, and Operations Optimization

Beyond ideation and prototyping, AI drives growth through marketing automation, customer acquisition, product innovation, and operations optimisation. In marketing, predictive-lead-scoring algorithms and generative-AI content tools personalise engagement at scale, improving conversion rates and retention (McKinsey & Company, 2023b). AI also supports omnichannel campaigns by analysing clickstream data to forecast purchase intent and allocate ad spend efficiently (World Economic Forum [WEF], 2023).

For product and service innovation, startups leverage AI for feature-importance analysis, product-usage telemetry, and sentiment analytics, aligning development with verified user preferences (Raneri et al., 2023). These data-driven feedback loops enable entrepreneurs to co-create value with customers and shorten time-to-market.

In operations, AI streamlines supply-chain management, pricing, and service delivery through predictive and prescriptive analytics. According to McKinsey & Company (2023b), approximately 75% of the total value from generative AI lies in functions such as marketing, sales, software engineering, and R&D, all highly relevant to startups seeking scalability. Through these efficiencies, small firms can now achieve operational leverage once reserved for large enterprises, improving both competitiveness and profitability.

3.4 Practical Considerations and Risks for Founders

Despite the immense promise of AI, founders must manage associated risks carefully. Data-quality challenges can undermine algorithmic accuracy, while biased datasets may introduce ethical and reputational risks (Subrahmanyam, 2025a). Interpretability remains another concern - black-box AI systems can obscure causal reasoning, potentially leading to misguided strategic decisions.

Best practice involves maintaining human oversight in the loop, combining AI insights with domain expertise (Halabi & Subrahmanyam, 2025). Founders should start with high-impact, low-complexity use cases such as automated lead scoring or chatbots before scaling to advanced predictive systems (Sekula, 2023). Adopting transparent model-evaluation metrics and documenting decision logic enhances accountability. A staged, modular AI-adoption approach helps startups preserve agility while mitigating ethical and technical debt.

Table 1. Integration of AI Tools Across Startup Creation and Growth

Startup Phase	AI Functions and Tools	Key Outcomes / Benefits	Examples or Use Cases
Ideation & Opportunity Recognition	- Generative AI for brainstorming - NLP and topic modeling for trend detection - Predictive analytics for market forecasting	- Identification of unmet needs and emerging trends - Data-driven opportunity mapping - Reduced uncertainty in early-stage decisions	- ChatGPT or Gemini for idea generation - Google Trends + sentiment analysis for market gaps - Predictive market scoring via machine learning
Business Planning & Prototyping	- AI-powered business model simulation - Low-code / no-code AI tools for MVP creation - Digital twin simulation for prototype testing	- Accelerated product design - Cost-efficient experimentation - Validation of MVP through predictive testing	- Xamun and Bubble.ai for AI-assisted MVPs - Scenario modeling using reinforcement learning - Automated hypothesis generation
Lean Startup Methodology	- AI-driven data analytics for A/B testing - Adaptive learning systems for iteration - Cognitive AI for decision support	- Faster build–measure–learn cycles - Improved learning accuracy - Evidence-based pivoting	- Analytics dashboards using TensorFlow or PyTorch - AutoML for experiment analysis

continued on following page

Table 1. Continued

Startup Phase	AI Functions and Tools	Key Outcomes / Benefits	Examples or Use Cases
Customer Acquisition & Marketing	- Predictive lead scoring and segmentation - Generative AI for content and campaigns - Recommendation systems for personalization	- Enhanced targeting efficiency - Increased conversion rates and engagement - Automated customer communication	- Salesforce Einstein for predictive sales - ChatGPT or Jasper for campaign generation - Recommendation engines in e-commerce
Product/Service Innovation	- AI-based product-usage analytics - Feature-importance and causal inference tools - Co-creation using customer feedback models	- Continuous innovation based on user data - Product evolution guided by predictive signals	- User telemetry analysis in Mixpanel + AI clustering - Feature optimization using SHAP/LIME models
Operations & Scaling	- AI for process automation and optimization - Forecasting and prescriptive analytics - Intelligent resource allocation	- Reduced operational cost - Enhanced scalability and efficiency - Improved agility in decision-making	- Supply chain optimization with IBM Watson - Dynamic pricing models with machine learning
Governance & Risk Management	- Explainable AI (XAI) tools - Bias detection and compliance monitoring - Ethical AI governance frameworks	- Transparency and accountability - Reduced regulatory and ethical risks	- Microsoft Responsible AI dashboard - Salesforce AI Ethics Toolkit

AI is revolutionising every phase of startup creation and growth - from ideation and opportunity recognition to lean prototyping, marketing, innovation, and operational efficiency. When integrated responsibly, AI tools enable entrepreneurs to make faster, evidence-driven decisions and achieve scalability despite limited resources. Yet the benefits depend on thoughtful governance and strategic alignment with business goals. Startups that embed AI as a core capability rather than an add-on are better positioned to create sustainable competitive advantage in the digital economy.

4. THE AI-AUGMENTED ENTREPRENEUR: SKILLS, MINDSETS, AND LEADERSHIP

In the AI-driven business era, entrepreneurs must evolve beyond traditional leadership models to embrace collaboration with intelligent systems. The AI-augmented entrepreneur combines human creativity, strategic insight, and ethical judgment with data-driven analytics and automation, cultivating adaptive skills, innovative mindsets, and responsible leadership essential for thriving in dynamic, technology-enhanced entrepreneurial environments.

4.1 Collaborating With AI: Blending Intuition and Data-Driven Insights

The rise of artificial intelligence (AI) is transforming not only what entrepreneurs can do, but how they think, decide, and lead. The modern entrepreneur increasingly functions as an *AI-augmented decision-maker*, blending human intuition with machine intelligence to make faster and more informed choices. Rather than replacing human creativity, AI serves as a cognitive partner that extends analytical capacity and enhances strategic foresight (Brynjolfsson & McAfee, 2014). Entrepreneurs can now use AI-driven tools for market research, consumer trend analysis, and scenario simulation, thus allowing intuition to be guided and validated by data.

According to Shneiderman (2022), *human-centered AI* enhances rather than replaces human judgment by promoting a symbiotic relationship between the entrepreneur's creativity and the machine's computational precision. This balance enables entrepreneurs to recognize patterns in data that confirm or challenge their instincts, leading to more evidence-based innovation. Successful AI-augmented entrepreneurs cultivate an adaptive mindset - trusting AI-generated insights while maintaining critical oversight over automated recommendations. Such a mindset reflects a shift from intuition-only decision-making to *augmented intuition*, where data and creativity coexist dynamically (Daugherty & Wilson, 2023).

4.2 Leadership in Tech-Savvy and Hybrid Environments

Leadership in AI-driven and hybrid work environments requires a unique blend of technological fluency, emotional intelligence, and strategic agility. The AI-augmented entrepreneur must manage not only human teams but also algorithmic systems, ensuring collaboration across digital and human agents. This leadership model is characterized by transparency, trust, and digital ethics. As tasks become increasingly automated, leaders must focus on building human-AI synergy - creating workflows where AI handles data-heavy tasks and humans concentrate on creativity, empathy, and strategic thinking (Chen H. et al., 2025).

Hybrid work settings - where distributed teams collaborate with AI platforms - demand redefined leadership competencies. Entrepreneurs must foster digital collaboration through tools such as Slack AI or Microsoft Copilot while ensuring psychological safety and inclusion across virtual teams. According to Subrahmanyam, (2025c), leaders in AI-enhanced organizations must become "technology translators," bridging the gap between technical experts and business strategists. This requires not only understanding AI capabilities but also communicating their implications effectively to non-technical stakeholders.

Leadership in such environments also calls for ethical stewardship. Entrepreneurs must establish transparent AI governance frameworks that address fairness, accountability, and data privacy (European Commission, 2024). By embedding ethical considerations into business processes, leaders can mitigate risks of bias and maintain public trust in their AI-augmented organizations.

4.3 Skills for Strategic Decision-Making, Innovation, and Team Management

The AI-augmented entrepreneur requires a distinct skill set that integrates technological literacy with strategic and interpersonal capabilities. First, *data literacy* has become foundational. Entrepreneurs must understand how AI systems process information, interpret predictive outputs, and identify biases (Wilson et al., 2018). This enables them to use AI not as a black box, but as a transparent analytical collaborator.

Second, *adaptive strategic thinking* is crucial. In rapidly evolving digital ecosystems, entrepreneurs must continuously re-evaluate assumptions and apply agile decision-making methods. AI enhances this agility through real-time analytics, allowing leaders to test hypotheses, monitor KPIs, and adjust business strategies dynamically (McKinsey & Company, 2023a).

Third, *innovative problem-solving* and *creative intelligence* remain indispensable. While AI can generate ideas or optimize existing solutions, it lacks contextual understanding and emotional depth. Human creativity enables entrepreneurs to frame problems uniquely, identify opportunities beyond the dataset, and connect disparate insights. According to Stanikzai & Mittal (2025), human creativity complements AI's analytic capacity by infusing intuition and emotional resonance into innovation processes.

Finally, *collaborative leadership and empathy* are essential for managing AI-augmented teams. Entrepreneurs must ensure employees perceive AI as an enabler rather than a threat. This requires transparent communication about AI's purpose, continuous upskilling programs, and the cultivation of digital trust (PwC, 2023). Empathy and psychological safety remain vital, particularly as AI automates certain roles; emotionally intelligent leaders can manage transitions while maintaining motivation and belonging.

4.4 Approaches and Programs to Develop AI-Augmented Entrepreneurship

Developing AI-augmented entrepreneurial capabilities requires structured educational and professional programs that combine business, data science, and leadership development. Globally, universities and corporate incubators are integrating AI literacy into entrepreneurship curricula. The Massachusetts Institute of Technology (MIT) and Stanford University have launched "AI for Entrepreneurs" programs that teach founders to leverage AI in opportunity recognition, business modeling, and ethical leadership (Ransbotham et al., 2017).

Organizations such as PwC (2023) and Microsoft (2024) have introduced *AI upskilling initiatives* to help leaders develop data-driven strategic thinking and governance frameworks for responsible AI use. These programs emphasize scenario-based learning, simulation training, and interdisciplinary collaboration between engineers, designers, and business strategists. The goal is to cultivate *AI fluency*, an understanding not only of AI's technical functions but also of its strategic implications for innovation and competitive advantage.

Governmental and international organizations have also begun promoting AI-augmented entrepreneurship through policy and funding. The European Commission's (2024) *AI Act* encourages responsible AI development and includes initiatives that support small businesses integrating AI ethically and effectively. In emerging economies, incubators such as India's NASSCOM "AI Foundry" and the UAE's "AI Strategy 2031" initiative provide mentoring, resources, and ethical frameworks to prepare entrepreneurs for AI-driven markets.

Educationally, the integration of *experiential learning* - such as hackathons, AI boot camps, and cross-disciplinary team projects - has proven effective in developing these hybrid competencies (Chen H. et al., 2025). These experiential formats train entrepreneurs to apply AI tools for ideation, validation, and scaling, while reinforcing ethical judgment and creativity.

Figure 2. The AI-Augmented Entrepreneur

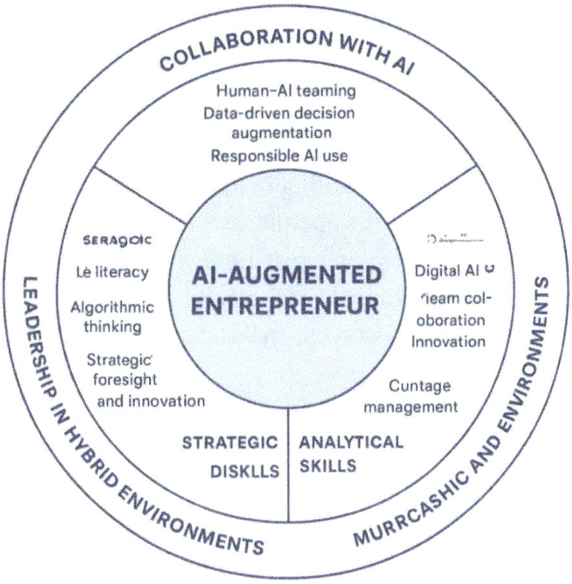

The AI-augmented entrepreneur represents a new archetype of leadership, one that harmonizes human intuition with machine intelligence. This evolution demands not just technical proficiency but a shift in mindset: from controlling technology to collaborating with it. Effective AI-augmented entrepreneurs combine data-driven precision with empathy, creativity, and ethical awareness. They cultivate cross-functional teams that thrive in hybrid environments, balancing efficiency with human values. As AI continues to transform global entrepreneurship, those who can blend technological insight with emotional and strategic intelligence will shape the next frontier of innovation and sustainable growth.

5. AI-SUPPORTED HYBRID AND REMOTE WORKPLACES

Recent advances in artificial intelligence (AI) have changed the workplace, especially in hybrid and remote settings. As companies and entrepreneurs embrace dispersed models, AI improves communication, collaboration, and productivity. Remote-first firms use AI technologies for data-driven decision-making, seamless cooperation, and ongoing innovation. This section discusses AI, entrepreneurship, dispersed teams, AI-enabled collaboration tools, and real-world instances of AI's power in remote work environments.

5.1 The Interplay Between AI, Entrepreneurship, and Distributed Teams

Entrepreneurship has increasingly transcended traditional office boundaries, evolving into a networked, technology-driven activity. Hybrid and remote models have become the new normal for startups seeking agility and global reach. AI enhances this transformation by enabling distributed intelligence, the capacity for geographically dispersed teams to operate as cohesive units through intelligent automation, predictive analytics, and real-time insights (Davenport & Ronanki, 2018). Entrepreneurs now leverage AI not only as a productivity enhancer but as a strategic partner that facilitates decision-making, resource allocation, and creative problem-solving.

AI-driven entrepreneurship thrives on data. Predictive analytics tools such as IBM Watson and Google Cloud AI assist founders in identifying emerging market trends, understanding customer needs, and making evidence-based decisions (Chui et al., 2021). Meanwhile, AI-based project management and collaboration platforms - like Notion AI, Trello AI, and ClickUp - streamline operations and mitigate the challenges of asynchronous communication across time zones. These tools convert raw data into actionable insights, helping startups scale quickly and efficiently.

For distributed teams, AI functions as the connective tissue binding remote collaborators through intelligent scheduling, automated meeting summaries, and task prioritization. AI mitigates the cognitive load of digital collaboration by filtering noise, summarizing discussions, and identifying action points through tools such as Otter.ai and Microsoft Copilot. This symbiosis between AI and human creativity allows entrepreneurs to focus on strategy and innovation rather than routine coordination.

5.2 AI-Enabled Communication, Collaboration, and Productivity Tools

AI is transforming communication and collaboration in remote workspaces by personalizing interactions and automating repetitive processes. Platforms such as Slack AI, Zoom IQ, and Microsoft Teams Premium integrate AI assistants that transcribe meetings, summarize discussions, and highlight key decisions. These capabilities ensure that remote participants stay informed and engaged, reducing the risk of miscommunication in hybrid settings (Slack Technologies, 2025).

AI also powers language translation and sentiment analysis, bridging cultural and linguistic divides in multinational teams. Tools like DeepL Translator and Grammarly Business enable real-time translation and tone adaptation, promoting inclusivity and professionalism in global collaboration. AI-based emotion recognition systems are being embedded into video conferencing tools to detect engagement and fatigue levels, supporting more empathetic team management (Przegalińska et al., 2025).

In terms of productivity, AI tools automate repetitive workflows and cognitive tasks. Motion AI uses reinforcement learning to optimize individual and team schedules dynamically, while Asana Intelligence predicts task dependencies and allocates workloads based on historical patterns. Entrepreneurs also utilize AI-driven CRM systems such as HubSpot and Salesforce Einstein, which analyze customer interactions to refine marketing campaigns and predict conversion probabilities. These systems enhance responsiveness and reduce manual data entry, freeing teams to focus on creative and strategic initiatives (Fountaine et al., 2019).

AI contributes to maintaining organizational culture in remote settings. AI-powered platforms such as CultureAmp and Humu analyze employee feedback and behavioral data to identify engagement gaps and suggest personalized interventions. These systems enable entrepreneurs and managers to sustain a sense of belonging and motivation, which are often difficult to achieve in virtual environments.

5.3 Case Examples of AI-Powered Remote-First Startups

Several startups exemplify the integration of AI in supporting hybrid and remote-first work models. One prominent example is GitLab, a fully remote company that leverages AI for continuous integration, code review automation, and project management. GitLab employs AI-driven analytics to track workflow efficiency and identify collaboration bottlenecks across its 2,000+ globally distributed employees. Its AI-assisted DevOps pipeline improves product delivery speed and reduces human error, demonstrating how automation can enhance innovation within remote technical teams (GitLab, 2023).

Another case is Zapier, a remote-first automation platform operating across 40+ countries. Zapier integrates AI to streamline workflows by automating repetitive digital tasks across multiple applications. The company uses AI to analyze user behavior, optimize onboarding, and enhance customer experience. Through predictive analytics, Zapier identifies potential churn and proactively suggests solutions, proving that AI can foster customer-centric innovation even without physical offices (Zapier, 2023; Saad et al., 2025).

Doist, the company behind productivity tools like *Todoist* and *Twist*, has also adopted an AI-driven approach to managing its hybrid workforce. The firm employs AI analytics to study team communication patterns, reduce digital overload, and promote asynchronous collaboration. AI helps balance workloads, predict burnout, and personalize task recommendations, ensuring that creativity and productivity coexist harmoniously in its distributed teams (Humanyze, 2024).

Automattic, the parent company of WordPress and WooCommerce, operates with more than 1,800 employees across 70 countries. It relies on AI for virtual collaboration, product development, and customer support automation. Its in-house AI system, Happys, processes customer feedback, categorizes issues, and provides real-time insights to improve user experience. Automattic's model showcases how AI can enable scalability and cohesion in remote organizations while maintaining a strong culture of autonomy (Automattic, 2024).

The combination of AI and remote employment changes entrepreneurship and organizational architecture. Distribution teams benefit from AI-enabled collaboration, decision-making, and data-driven leadership. From intelligent communication tools to predictive analytics and staff engagement platforms, AI helps firms work smoothly in hybrid or entirely remote settings. GitLab, Zapier, Doist, and Automattic show that AI redefines remote work, changing how teams create, develop, and grow. Innovative entrepreneurs that responsibly use AI will lead the next generation of nimble, inclusive, and high-performing companies as hybrid work becomes the norm.

6. FINANCING AND INVESTMENT IN AI-ERA STARTUPS

AI is transforming how entrepreneurs seek capital, invest, and manage financial risks. Traditional financial decisions were based on judgment, limited data, and manual scrutiny. AI-powered algorithms, predictive analytics, and data-driven investment platforms have transformed startup funding. Entrepreneurs and investors benefit from AI's transparency, valuation accuracy, and risk management. AI-driven crowdfunding and investment approaches, establishing venture capital views, and AI financial risk assessment and mitigation technologies are investigated in real-world settings.

6.1 AI-Driven Crowdfunding and Investment Platforms

Crowd funding has emerged as a vital funding channel for startups, particularly in the early stages when venture capital is often inaccessible. With AI integration, crowdfunding platforms have evolved into intelligent ecosystems that connect entrepreneurs with potential backers through predictive modeling, sentiment analysis, and personalized recommendations. These platforms leverage AI to identify investor preferences, evaluate startup credibility, and optimize campaign performance (Chen, Z., Ji, Cao, & Wu, 2025).

Kickstarter and Indiegogo use AI to analyze user engagement data, predict campaign success, and suggest pricing or promotional strategies. AI models evaluate linguistic cues and visual appeal in campaign content to estimate audience resonance (Zhang & Tian, 2021). Crowdcube and Seedrs apply AI to match startups with suitable investors based on risk tolerance, sector interests, and historical funding behavior. AI algorithms also monitor fraudulent activities by scanning for anomalies in funding patterns and investor identities, improving platform integrity (Bonelli, 2022).

Emerging AI-driven investment platforms such as OurCrowd and WeFunder further enhance the decision-making process by automating due diligence. They use natural language processing (NLP) to analyze business plans, financial projections, and online sentiment around startups. This automation significantly reduces evaluation time while increasing the accuracy of investment recommendations. According to a PwC (2023) report, AI-based funding platforms can reduce screening costs by up to 40%, allowing investors to evaluate a broader range of startups efficiently.

Tokenized AI crowdfunding models - enabled by blockchain - are expanding access to global investors. Platforms like Republic combine blockchain and AI analytics to enable fractional ownership and intelligent matching between entrepreneurs and investors. These hybrid systems foster democratization in startup financing by reducing entry barriers and improving transparency.

6.2 Venture Capital and Investor Perspectives on AI-Driven Startups

Venture capital (VC) firms have increasingly adopted AI technologies to optimize their investment processes and evaluate startups more effectively. AI allows VCs to automate the initial screening of thousands of proposals and identify promising ventures with higher growth potential. Machine learning models analyze unstructured data from multiple sources - such as social media, patent filings, and founder networks - to assess the innovation potential and market readiness of startups (Jing & Zhang, 2023).

SignalFire, a U.S.-based VC firm, is a pioneering example of this trend. The firm employs an AI platform named *Beacon*, which analyzes more than 500 million data points - including job postings, market trends, and developer activity - to identify emerging startups before they reach mainstream visibility (SignalFire, 2024). This predictive capability gives the firm a competitive edge in early-stage investment.

GV (formerly Google Ventures) and Sequoia Capital use AI tools to forecast startup performance by integrating market analytics, consumer behavior trends, and founder track records. AI-enhanced evaluation helps investors distinguish between sustainable innovation and hype, a critical factor in a market saturated with AI-themed ventures (Bonelli, 2022; Shaheen et al., 2025; Aldabousi et al., 2025; Ghonim et al., 2025).

AI assists venture capitalists in understanding portfolio dynamics. Predictive modeling and network analytics identify potential synergies among portfolio companies and optimize capital allocation strategies. According to Smith et al (2025), 68% of global VC firms now employ AI for market intelligence, portfolio monitoring, or risk evaluation.

From an entrepreneur's perspective, AI adoption within their ventures often increases investor confidence. Startups that use AI for product innovation or operational efficiency signal technological competence and scalability - qualities that appeal to modern investors. UiPath, a Romanian-born startup specializing in robotic process automation (RPA), attracted over $1 billion in venture funding before going public in 2021. The company's use of AI for workflow automation convinced investors of its capacity for exponential growth and industry disruption (CB Insights, 2023).

6.3 Risk Assessment and Mitigation Using AI Tools

In the investment ecosystem, risk assessment has always been a cornerstone of decision-making. AI significantly enhances this process by identifying patterns and anomalies in vast datasets that human analysts may overlook. Machine learning algorithms now assess startup risks by analyzing financial health, leadership stability, market volatility, and even social media sentiment.

Upstart, an AI-driven lending platform, uses machine learning to evaluate credit risk beyond traditional FICO scores. By incorporating alternative data such as education, employment history, and digital behavior, the system provides a more holistic view of borrower reliability. This model has reduced default rates by 27% compared to traditional underwriting methods (Upstart, 2024).

Investors also use AI to monitor real-time market signals and adjust portfolios dynamically. Predictive analytics tools like Alpaca AI and Kensho detect emerging risks through economic indicators, news analysis, and financial sentiment tracking. These tools provide investors with early warnings and risk mitigation strategies, reducing exposure to volatile sectors (Giudici, 2018).

In venture funding, AI also enhances due diligence. Platforms such as DueDil and Zylo use AI to automate the collection and analysis of financial records, compliance histories, and legal documents. This reduces human bias and ensures that risk evaluations are data-driven and consistent. AI models can simulate potential future scenarios - such as shifts in regulation or supply chain disruptions - allowing investors to prepare contingency strategies.

Another innovative use of AI in financial risk management is through natural language processing for sentiment analysis. By scanning millions of online articles, social posts, and investor reviews, AI identifies emerging reputational risks or changes in public perception that could impact valuation. This capability is particularly vital for startups in highly dynamic sectors like fintech, health tech, and green technology.

Figure 3. Startup Financing and Investment

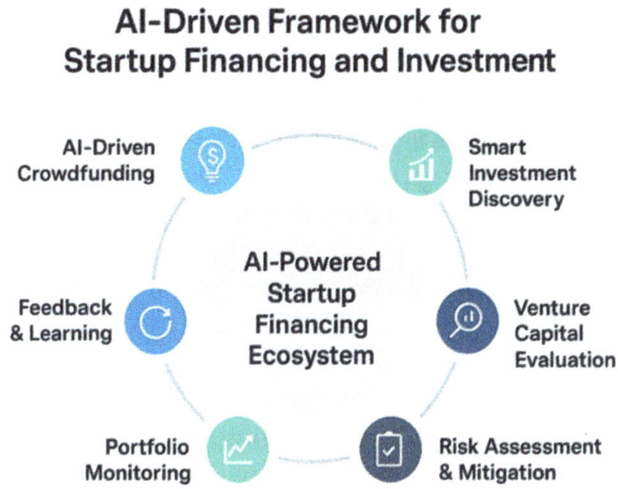

Startup crowdfunding, venture financing, and risk management are evolving with AI. AI-powered VCs uncover high-potential startups and use funds smartly, while intelligent crowdfunding platforms democratize investment. AI-powered risk assessment tools increase decision accuracy and clarity. AI helps entrepreneurs and investors, such as SignalFire, UiPath, and Upstart demonstrate. The cognitive and analytical co-pilot role of AI will be vital as finance becomes more complex. The AI-driven era will benefit firms that blend human and machine intelligence for scalable growth.

7. CHALLENGES, RISKS, AND ETHICAL CONSIDERATIONS

The integration of artificial intelligence (AI) into entrepreneurship and startup ecosystems introduces transformative potential but also presents profound challenges, risks, and ethical concerns. These issues span from algorithmic bias and data privacy to workforce displacement and overreliance on automation. As startups increasingly depend on AI for decision-making, efficiency, and innovation, navigating these ethical and socioeconomic complexities becomes critical to ensuring sustainable and responsible growth.

7.1 Ethical and Legal Issues: Algorithmic Bias, Transparency, and Data Privacy

Algorithmic prejudice is one of the most important ethical issues in AI-driven enterprise. It may make existing disparities worse or keep them going. Bias occurs when AI systems are taught on datasets that include historical or societal preconceptions, resulting in biased results in employment, lending, or consumer targeting (Mehrabi et al., 2021). Amazon had to get rid of an AI hiring tool because it found that its algorithm was biased against women. This was because it used past data trends that favored male applicants (Dastin, 2018). These kinds of events show how unfair and untrustworthy data and models may be.

Transparency - often referred to as *explainability* - is another critical ethical dimension. Many AI systems function as "black boxes," where decision-making logic is not easily interpretable even by developers (Samek et al., 2021). This opacity raises accountability questions, especially when AI tools influence decisions involving finance, employment, or healthcare. The European Union's AI Act (2024) mandates explainability and risk classification to ensure that organizations deploying AI systems can justify algorithmic decisions.

Data privacy is still a big legal and moral issue for firms that use AI. To train algorithms or make services more customized, startups frequently gather a lot of personal and behavioral data. If this data is not handled correctly, it might break privacy laws like the General Data Protection Regulation (GDPR). To reconcile innovation with compliance and user trust, entrepreneurs need to deploy privacy-preserving methods like federated learning and differential privacy (Voigt & von dem Bussche, 2017).

Unequal access to AI resources creates a growing digital divide. Startups with limited capital or technical expertise often struggle to compete with large corporations that have access to vast data and computing infrastructure. This inequality in AI accessibility can entrench market dominance and limit innovation diversity (Crawford, 2021).

7.2 Socioeconomic Impacts: Automation, Workforce Displacement, and Digital Divides

AI's growing role in startups also reshapes socioeconomic structures, particularly through automation and job displacement. While AI-driven automation boosts productivity and reduces costs, it also threatens certain categories of work, especially routine or repetitive tasks. Frey and Osborne (2017) estimated that nearly 47% of jobs in advanced economies could be automated, raising concerns about economic polarization and skill obsolescence.

For entrepreneurs, automation presents a paradox: it drives operational efficiency but may contribute to societal inequalities. Startups must therefore prioritize human–AI collaboration models that augment, rather than replace, human talent. The emergence of "centaur organizations" - where humans and AI systems collaborate symbiotically - offers a potential solution, combining human judgment with machine precision (Brynjolfsson & McAfee, 2014).

Another concern is the widening digital divide, particularly between developed and developing economies. Startups in regions with limited access to AI infrastructure, such as high-speed internet or computational resources, face systemic disadvantages (OECD, 2023). This disparity hinders global inclusivity and reduces the diversity of innovation that AI ecosystems can foster.

7.3 Talent Gaps, Overreliance on AI, and Potential Failure Points

The rapid evolution of AI has created significant talent gaps. Many startups lack skilled professionals in AI development, data science, and ethics compliance (World Economic Forum, 2023). This shortage can result in poorly designed algorithms, insufficient oversight, and ethical oversights. Initiatives such as Google's *AI for Everyone* and IBM's *SkillsBuild* aim to close this gap through accessible AI education, yet challenges persist due to the pace of technological advancement.

An additional risk involves overreliance on AI systems, where decision-making becomes excessively automated. Overdependence can lead to failures when algorithms encounter scenarios not represented in their training data or when contextual human judgment is absent (Amershi et al., 2019). During the COVID-19 pandemic, predictive AI models used by some logistics startups failed to anticipate sudden supply chain disruptions due to unprecedented variables (Ivanov, 2020). Such examples underscore the need for human oversight and adaptive resilience in AI applications.

Finally, potential failure points in AI-driven startups often stem from inadequate data governance, insufficient model testing, or ethical negligence. AI models trained on incomplete, biased, or outdated data may yield unreliable insights, leading to strategic or financial losses. Hence, startups must establish robust AI governance frameworks emphasizing fairness, accountability, transparency, and ethics, often summarized as the FATE principles (Floridi & Cowls, 2019).

AI has become indispensable to modern entrepreneurship, enabling startups to innovate, scale, and compete globally. Yet, the integration of AI is not without challenges. Algorithmic bias, privacy violations, job displacement, and overreliance on automation pose serious ethical and operational risks. Addressing these challenges requires proactive governance, multidisciplinary collaboration, and continuous education. By fostering transparency, inclusivity, and ethical accountability, startups can harness AI's potential while minimizing harm - paving the way for sustainable, human-centered innovation in the digital age.

8. CASE STUDIES OF AI-EMPOWERED STARTUPS

Startups worldwide can now construct scalable, data-driven, and intelligent solutions using AI. AI-driven firms are changing company operations, competition, and innovation in health, education, finance, retail, and logistics. Adoption is fraught with ethical issues, algorithmic unfairness, data privacy problems, and skill deficits. Global case studies of AI-powered companies show their successes, failures, and lessons learnt. It emphasizes responsible innovation and sustainable AI deployment by linking these real-world examples to human and ethical issues.

8.1 Global Examples of AI-Driven Startups Across Sectors

1. Healthcare: Babylon Health (United Kingdom)

Founded in 2013, Babylon Health revolutionized healthcare delivery through AI-powered telemedicine. Its mobile app uses natural language processing (NLP) and machine learning to provide medical consultations, triage symptoms, and recommend treatments. The startup expanded globally, reaching millions of users through partnerships with health providers and governments. Babylon's AI diagnostic accuracy faced criticism for potential bias and over-reliance on limited datasets (Fraser et al., 2018). In 2023, financial mismanagement and regulatory challenges led to the company's collapse (Lunden, 2023). Babylon's trajectory illustrates both the promise and perils of AI in healthcare - underscoring the need for ethical oversight, transparency, and robust governance frameworks in sensitive domains.

2. Education: Duolingo (United States)

The language-learning platform Duolingo integrates AI-driven personalization to adapt lessons to individual learners' pace, performance, and retention patterns. Using reinforcement learning, its algorithms continuously optimize the difficulty and timing of exercises to enhance engagement (Settles & Meeder, 2016). During the COVID-19 pandemic, Duolingo saw exponential growth, demonstrating how AI-driven adaptive learning can scale global education access. It also sparked debates about algorithmic determinism - where users' learning trajectories could be overly shaped by AI without considering emotional or cultural nuances. Duolingo's success highlights how ethical design and user feedback loops can balance automation with human-centered learning.

3. Finance: Upstart (United States)

Founded in 2012, Upstart disrupted the lending industry using AI for credit risk evaluation. Instead of relying solely on traditional credit scores, Upstart's machine learning models analyze over 1,500 variables - including education, employment history, and financial behavior - to assess creditworthiness (Upstart, 2024). This approach has expanded financial inclusion, enabling borrowers with limited credit history to access affordable loans. Concerns about algorithmic bias and fairness prompted regulatory scrutiny by the U.S. Consumer Financial Protection Bureau. Upstart responded by publishing transparency reports and refining its fairness algorithms. The case illustrates how startups can address ethical risks proactively through *explainable AI* and regular auditing.

4. Retail: Ocado (United Kingdom)

Ocado, a British online grocery retailer, exemplifies AI's power in logistics and retail automation. Its smart warehouses use AI-driven robots, predictive analytics, and computer vision to optimize order fulfillment and reduce waste (Hargreaves, 2025). Ocado's proprietary AI platform predicts demand patterns and coordinates robotic systems, enabling 99% order accuracy. The company also faced technical vulnerabilities - such as a major fire in 2019 caused by a malfunctioning robot. This event exposed the operational risks of over-automation, emphasizing the need for human oversight and risk mitigation in AI-integrated operations. Ocado's experience underlines the balance between efficiency and resilience in AI adoption.

5. Logistics and Delivery: Nuro (United States)

Autonomous delivery startup Nuro has leveraged AI to develop self-driving vehicles for last-mile logistics. Its fleet uses computer vision, LiDAR, and deep learning to navigate urban environments safely. Nuro's partnerships with Walmart, Kroger, and Domino's Pizza illustrate how startups can commercialize AI-driven automation in everyday life (Nuro, 2023). Nuro encountered regulatory and safety challenges, prompting broader debates about AI accountability and transparency in public spaces. The company's adaptive response, collaborating with regulators and publishing ethical operation standards, demonstrates responsible innovation in practice.

8.2 Insights Gained, Best Practices, and Failures

A cross-case analysis of these startups reveals several key insights and best practices for AI-driven entrepreneurship:

Transparency and Explainability Are Crucial. Startups such as Upstart and Duolingo demonstrate that transparency in AI decision-making enhances trust and compliance. Establishing explainability protocols - through algorithmic documentation, fairness reports, or public audits - builds credibility with users and regulators (Floridi & Cowls, 2019).

Human-AI Collaboration Enhances Outcomes. Successful startups balance automation with human oversight. Ocado integrates human engineers to supervise robotic operations, while Babylon Health employed clinicians to validate AI recommendations. This hybrid approach aligns with the "centaur model" of shared intelligence (Brynjolfsson & McAfee, 2014).

Ethical Governance Prevents Long-Term Failures. Babylon Health's downfall illustrates how neglecting ethical, financial, and data governance can undermine innovation. Startups must incorporate *ethics by design*, integrating privacy protection, bias mitigation, and stakeholder engagement from inception.

Agility and Adaptation Drive Resilience. Startups that adapt quickly to regulatory, technical, or market changes - such as Upstart and Nuro - tend to sustain success. Continuous learning and feedback loops help align AI evolution with user needs and ethical expectations.

Failure cases show that overreliance on AI without human context or ethical alignment leads to reputational and operational risks. These lessons emphasize the strategic value of multidisciplinary teams combining data science, ethics, law, and user experience design.

8.3 Regional Variations in Adoption and Success

AI adoption among startups varies significantly across regions due to differences in infrastructure, regulation, and digital literacy. In the United States and Western Europe, strong venture capital ecosystems and open innovation cultures accelerate AI entrepreneurship (OECD, 2023). Asia-Pacific, especially China and India, shows rapid growth driven by government investment and mobile-first economies. India's AI startup ecosystem grew by 32% in 2023, with firms like SigTuple and Yellow.ai leading innovations in healthcare and customer engagement (NASSCOM, 2023).

Africa and parts of Latin America face challenges such as limited data access, weak infrastructure, and talent shortages, exacerbating the global digital divide

(Crawford, 2021). International collaboration, AI education, and policy support are critical to fostering inclusive growth in these regions.

8.4 Linking to Human and Ethical Dimensions

The case studies reaffirm that technological advancement alone does not guarantee success, ethical integrity and human values remain central. Startups that prioritize transparency, inclusivity, and fairness not only gain market legitimacy but also mitigate long-term risks. Upstart's and Nuro's commitment to AI accountability mirrors global calls for responsible AI - balancing innovation with social good (European Union, 2024). Duolingo's personalized yet culturally sensitive learning design underscores the importance of human-centered AI.

AI-empowered startups represent the frontier of digital entrepreneurship, blending machine intelligence with human creativity. Their success depends on aligning data-driven innovation with ethical governance and societal responsibility, a reminder that the future of AI in entrepreneurship must remain deeply human.

9. FUTURE DIRECTIONS AND CONCLUSION

The future of AI-driven entrepreneurship is being shaped by emerging technologies such as generative AI, AI-human collaboration, and digital twins, which are redefining how startups innovate, operate, and scale. Generative AI enables rapid content creation, product prototyping, and personalized marketing, reducing barriers for early-stage ventures. Digital twins - virtual replicas of physical processes - allow startups to simulate business models, test strategies, and predict outcomes with high precision. These tools, combined with AI-human collaborative models, promise a new era of adaptive and intelligent entrepreneurship.

Startup ecosystems are also evolving through hybrid and remote work models, supported by AI-enabled communication and productivity platforms. This shift enhances global collaboration, democratizes talent access, and fosters diverse innovation environments. It also demands robust governance frameworks to ensure ethical AI use, transparency, and workforce well-being.

In the long term, AI will reshape the roles of entrepreneurs, employees, and investors, emphasizing data literacy, ethical awareness, and technological resilience. The findings across this discussion underscore that success in the AI era hinges not only on innovation but also on responsibility. Startups that integrate ethics, inclusivity, and human oversight into their AI strategies will remain sustainable and resilient amid accelerating digital transformation.

REFERENCES

Aldabousi, A. M., Awad, A., Hassan, H. E. M., Abdullah, S. S., & Ghonim, A. (2025). Arbitration in Islamic banking: Exploring legal and practical implications for dispute resolution. *Banks and Bank Systems*, *20*(2), 15–26. DOI: 10.21511/bbs.20(2).2025.02

Alqahtani, A., & Alqahtani, N. (2024). Artificial Intelligence meets entrepreneurship: A bibliometric review of the scientific evolution, research trends, and future research directions. In *Proceedings of the 1st Saudi Conference on Information Systems (SaudiCIS 2024)* (Paper 68). https://aisel.aisnet.org/saudicis2024/68/

Alzamel, S. (2024). Building a Resilient Digital Entrepreneurship Landscape: The Importance of Ecosystems, Decent Work, and Socioeconomic Dynamics. *Sustainability (Basel)*, *16*(17), 7605. DOI: 10.3390/su16177605

Amershi, S., Weld, D., Vorvoreanu, M., Fourney, A., Nushi, B., Collisson, P., & Horvitz, E. (2019). Guidelines for human–AI interaction. *Proceedings of the 2019 CHI Conference on Human Factors in Computing Systems*, 1–13. DOI: 10.1145/3290605.3300233

Automattic. (2024). *AI-powered collaboration and support systems at Automattic*. https://automattic.com/

Bonelli, M. (2022). *How AI is affecting VC funding of innovative startups*. HEC Paris. https://www.hec.edu/en/how-ai-affecting-vc-funding-innovative-startups

Boston Consulting Group. (2024). *Seventy percent of economies are underprepared for AI disruption*. https://www.bcg.com/press/20november2024-seventy-percent-economies-underprepared-ai-disruption

Brynjolfsson, E., & McAfee, A. (2014). *The second machine age: Work, progress, and prosperity in a time of brilliant technologies*. W. W. Norton & Company.

Chen, H., Popaitoon, S., & Mumi, A. (2025). Investigating corporate entrepreneurship strategy through digital transformation: A dynamic capabilities perspective. *Journal of Innovation and Entrepreneurship*, *14*(1), 95. Advance online publication. DOI: 10.1186/s13731-025-00570-0

Chen, Z., Ji, X., Cao, Q., & Wu, J. (2025). Pricing and service decisions in crowdfunding. *Journal of Systems Science and Complexity*, *38*(6), 2480–2501. Advance online publication. DOI: 10.1007/s11424-025-3217-5

Chui, M., Manyika, J., & Miremadi, M. (2021). *The state of AI in 2021*. McKinsey Global Institute. Retrieved from https://www.mckinsey.com/business-functions/quantumblack/our-insights/global-survey-the-state-of-ai-in-2021

Crawford, K. (2021). *Atlas of AI: Power, politics, and the planetary costs of artificial intelligence*. Yale University Press.

Dastin, J. (2018). *Amazon scraps secret AI recruiting tool that showed bias against women*. Reuters. https://www.reuters.com/article/us-amazon-com-jobs-automation-insight/amazon-scraps-secret-ai-recruiting-tool-that-showed-bias-against-women-idUSKCN1MK08G

Daugherty, P. R., & Wilson, H. J. (2023). *Radically human: How new technology is transforming business and shaping our future*. Harvard Business Review Press.

Davenport, T. H., & Ronanki, R. (2018). Artificial intelligence for the real world. *Harvard Business Review, 96*(1), 108–116.

Eastern Eye. (2025). *AI-Powered Startups Driving South Asia's Business Future.* Eastern Eye. https://www.easterneye.biz/ai-powered-startups-driving-south-asias-business-future/

European Commission. (2024). *AI Act | A regulatory framework for trustworthy artificial intelligence*. Retrieved from https://digital-strategy.ec.europa.eu/en/policies/regulatory-framework-ai

European Union. (2024). *Artificial Intelligence Act*. Official Journal of the European Union. https://data.europa.eu/eli/reg/2024/1689/oj

Floridi, L., & Cowls, J. (2019). A unified framework of five principles for AI in society. *Harvard Data Science Review, 1*(1). Advance online publication. DOI: 10.1162/99608f92.8cd550d1

Fossen, F. M., McLemore, T., & Sorgner, A. (2024). *Artificial intelligence and entrepreneurship* (IZA Discussion Paper No. 17055). Institute of Labor Economics (IZA). https://doi.org/DOI: 10.1561/0300000130

Fountaine, T., McCarthy, B., & Saleh, T. (2019). Building the AI-Powered Organization: Technology isn't the biggest challenge. Culture is. *Harvard Business Review, 97*(4), 62–73.

Fraser, H., Coiera, E., & Wong, D. (2018). Safety of patient-facing digital symptom checkers. *Lancet, 392*(10161), 2263–2264. DOI: 10.1016/S0140-6736(18)32819-8 PMID: 30413281

Frey, C. B., & Osborne, M. A. (2017). The future of employment: How susceptible are jobs to computerisation? *Technological Forecasting and Social Change*, *114*, 254–280. DOI: 10.1016/j.techfore.2016.08.019

Ghonim, A., Awad, A., Shemais, M., Shma, T., & Aziz, A. (2025). Exploring the impact of flexible work arrangements on employee engagement in telecommunications: Case of Egypt. *Problems and Perspectives in Management*, *23*(2), 198–207. DOI: 10.21511/ppm.23(2).2025.13

GitLab Inc. (2023). *GitLab continues AI momentum with enhanced AI-powered DevSecOps workflows.* Retrieved from https://about.gitlab.com/press/releases/2023-11-09-gitlab-continues-ai-momentum-with-enhanced-ai-powered-devsecops-workflows/

Giudici, P. (2018). Fintech risk management: A research challenge for artificial intelligence in finance. *Frontiers in Artificial Intelligence*, *1*, 1. DOI: 10.3389/frai.2018.00001 PMID: 33733089

Halabi, R., & Subrahmanyam, S. (2025). Economic and Governance Implications of AI-Driven Marketing Systems: A Mixed-Methods Study on Performance, Transparency, and Policy Alignment. *Lex Localis - Journal of Local Self-Government, 23*(S4), 2189-2203. DOI: 10.52152/arsynj63

Hargreaves, L. (2025). Ocado: Streamlining supply chains with AI robotics. *Supply Chain Digital.* Retrieved from https://supplychaindigital.com/technology/how-ai-is-redefining-ocados-robotic-fulfilment-system

Humanyze. (2024). *Workstyle analytics for CEOs: Boosting productivity and retention in hybrid teams*. Humanyze. https://humanyze.com/workstyle-analytics-for-ceos-boosting-productivity-and-retention-in-hybrid-teams/

Insights, C. B. (2023). *UiPath funding and IPO journey: A case study in AI automation* [Report]. https://www.cbinsights.com/research/uipath-rpa-business-model-spotlight/

Ivanov, D. (2020). Predicting the impacts of epidemic outbreaks on global supply chains: A simulation-based analysis on the coronavirus outbreak (COVID-19/SARS-CoV-2) case. *Transportation Research Part E, Logistics and Transportation Review*, *136*, 101922. DOI: 10.1016/j.tre.2020.101922 PMID: 32288597

Jing, L., & Zhang, H. (2023). Venture capitalists on boards and corporate innovation. *Journal of Risk and Financial Management*, *16*(3), 143. DOI: 10.3390/jrfm16030143

Jorzik, P., Klein, S. P., Kanbach, D. K., & Kraus, S. (2024). AI-driven business model innovation: A systematic review and research agenda. *Journal of Business Research*, *182*, 114764. Advance online publication. DOI: 10.1016/j.jbusres.2024.114764

Lunden, I. (2023). *The fall of Babylon: Failed tele-health startup once valued at nearly $2 B goes bankrupt and sold for parts.* TechCrunch. https://techcrunch.com/2023/08/31/the-fall-of-babylon-failed-tele-health-startup-once-valued-at-nearly-2b-goes-bankrupt-and-sold-for-parts/

McKinsey & Company. (2023a). *The economic potential of generative AI: The next productivity frontier* [Report]. McKinsey Global Institute. https://www.mckinsey.com/capabilities/mckinsey-digital/our-insights/the-economic-potential-of-generative-ai-the-next-productivity-frontier

McKinsey & Company. (2023b). *The state of AI in 2023: Generative AI's breakout year.* McKinsey Global Institute. https://www.mckinsey.com/capabilities/quantumblack/our-insights/the-state-of-ai-in-2023-generative-ais-breakout-year

Mehrabi, N., Morstatter, F., Saxena, N., Lerman, K., & Galstyan, A. (2021). A survey on bias and fairness in machine learning. *ACM Computing Surveys*, *54*(6), 1–35. DOI: 10.1145/3457607

Microsoft. (2024). *Microsoft launches new AI Skills Initiative to help one million people in Australia and New Zealand secure the skills they need to thrive in the AI economy.* Microsoft News. https://news.microsoft.com/source/asia/features/microsoft-launches-new-ai-skills-program-to-expand-opportunities-for-australians-and-new-zealanders/

Musyokha, S., & Sain, S. (2024). Harnessing the power of artificial intelligence in entrepreneurship: Augmentation, innovation, and ethical considerations. *Researcher Academy Innovation Data Analysis*, *1*(2), 196–213. DOI: 10.69725/raida.v1i2.167

NASSCOM. (2023). *Generative AI startup landscape in India – A 2023 perspective.* NASSCOM Research. https://nasscom.in/knowledge-center/publications/generative-ai-startup-landscape-india-2023-perspective

Nuro. (2023). *Building safer autonomous delivery systems* [Report]. Nuro. https://www.nuro.ai/

Odesanya, M. A. B. (2022). Transforming small business landscapes: Artificial Intelligence's evolutionary leap forward. *World Journal of Advanced Research and Reviews*, *16*(3), 1141–1157. DOI: 10.30574/wjarr.2022.16.3.1223

OECD. (2023). *OECD SME and Entrepreneurship Outlook 2023.* OECD Publishing. DOI: 10.1787/342b8564-

Przegalińska, A., Triantoro, T., Kovbasiuk, A., Ciechanowski, L., Freeman, R. B., & Sowa, K. (2025). Collaborative AI in the workplace: Enhancing organizational performance through resource-based and task-technology fit perspectives. *International Journal of Information Management*, *81*, 102853. Advance online publication. DOI: 10.1016/j.ijinfomgt.2024.102853

PwC. (2023). *2023 Global Workforce Hopes & Fears Survey.* PwC. https://www.pwc.com/gx/en/news-room/press-releases/2023/pwc-global-workforce-hopes-and-fears-survey-2023.html

PwC. (2023). *AI is transforming asset and wealth.* https://www.pwc.com/gx/en/issues/c-suite-insights/the-leadership-agenda/ai-and-wealth-management-a-new-era.html?utm_source=chatgpt.com

Ramos Torres, A., & Montoya, L. N. (2024). AI thrust: Ranking emerging powers for tech startup investment in Latin America [Preprint]. *arXiv*. https://arxiv.org/abs/2401.09056

Raneri, S., Lecron, F., Hermans, J., & Fouss, F. (2023). Predictions through Lean startup? Harnessing AI-based predictions under uncertainty. *International Journal of Entrepreneurial Behaviour & Research*, *29*(4), 886–912. DOI: 10.1108/IJEBR-07-2021-0566

Ransbotham, S., Kiron, D., Gerbert, P., & Reeves, M. (2017). *Reshaping Business With Artificial Intelligence.* MIT Sloan Management Review & The Boston Consulting Group. Retrieved from https://sloanreview.mit.edu/projects/reshaping-business-with-artificial-intelligence/

Saad, M., Awad, A., Aziz, A. F., & Shma, T. R. (2025). Influencer marketing's impact on credibility and purchase intention: A study on University of Bisha students in Saudi Arabia. *Innovative Marketing*, *21*(1), 326–337. DOI: 10.21511/im.21(1).2025.26

Sarıoğuz, O., & Miser, E. (2024). AI-powered business model innovation: Analyzing the implications of generative AI on value creation, operational efficiency and market dynamics. *World Journal of Advanced Engineering Technology and Sciences*, *13*(02), 215–228. DOI: 10.30574/wjaets.2024.13.2.0564

Settles, B., & Meeder, B. (2016). A trainable spaced repetition model for language learning. In *Proceedings of the 54th Annual Meeting of the Association for Computational Linguistics* (Volume 1: Long Papers) (pp. 1848-1858). Association for Computational Linguistics. DOI: 10.18653/v1/P16-1174

Shaheen, A., Khataan, A., Awad, A., Shams Eldin, A. Y., & Elnour, A. (2025). The role of influencer content value and credibility in purchase intention. *Innovative Marketing, 21*(3), 14–30. DOI: 10.21511/im.21(3).2025.02

Shneiderman, B. (2022). *Human-Centered AI: Ensuring human control in an era of intelligent machines.* Oxford University Press. DOI: 10.1093/oso/9780192845290.001.0001

SignalFire. (2024). *Beacon AI: How SignalFire uses machine-learning and data-driven investing to find startups.* https://www.signalfire.com/beacon-ai

Slack Technologies. (2025). *Guide to AI features in Slack.* Retrieved from https://slack.com/help/articles/25076892548883-Guide-to-AI-features-in-Slack

Smith, T., Dost, G., Dhasmana, G., & Patwari, P. (2025). *AI is capturing the digital dollar. What's left for the rest of the tech estate?* Deloitte Insights. https://www.deloitte.com/us/en/insights/topics/digital-transformation/ai-tech-investment-roi.html

Stanikzai, M. E., & Mittal, E. (2025). Leveraging AI-generated and human-generated content for maximised user engagement in contentpreneurs' innovation and creativity. *Journal of Innovation and Entrepreneurship, 14*(1), 91. Advance online publication. DOI: 10.1186/s13731-025-00529-1

Subrahmanyam, S. (2025a). AI and Automation: The Intersection of Human Autonomy and Machine Learning. In Tsvasman, L. (Ed.), *Cybernetic Leadership for Sustainable Innovation* (pp. 237–262). IGI Global Scientific Publishing. DOI: 10.4018/979-8-3373-2484-5.ch009

Subrahmanyam, S. (2025b). Business, Digital Transformation, and Entrepreneurship. In Ordóñez de Pablos, P. (Ed.), *Shaping Green and Inclusive Economies Through Innovative Entrepreneurship* (pp. 1–34). IGI Global Scientific Publishing. DOI: 10.4018/979-8-3373-1097-8.ch001

Subrahmanyam, S. (2025c). Using AI-Driven Analysis for Training and Leadership Growth. In Mrabet, J., Boudagga, S., Sharma, R., & Bansal, R. (Eds.), *Harnessing Emotion AI for Customer Support and Employee Wellbeing* (pp. 321–352). IGI Global Scientific Publishing. DOI: 10.4018/979-8-3373-3658-9.ch013

Subrahmanyam, S., & El Samra, H. (2025). Startups and AI: Fostering Entrepreneurship in the MENA Region. In Azoury, N., & Yahchouchi, G. (Eds.), *AI in the Middle East for Growth and Business* (pp. 77–92). Palgrave Macmillan. DOI: 10.1007/978-3-031-75589-7_6

Upstart. (2024). *How AI drives more affordable credit access.* https://info.upstart.com/how-ai-drives-more-affordable-credit-access

Vahtras, L. (2025). *The rise of AI-powered, borderless businesses. AI Journal.* https://aijourn.com/the-rise-of-ai-powered-borderless-businesses/

Voigt, P., & von dem Bussche, A. (2017). *The EU General Data Protection Regulation (GDPR): A practical guide.* Springer International Publishing AG. DOI: 10.1007/978-3-319-57959-7

Wang, G., & Wu, L. (2025). Artificial intelligence, lean startup method, and product innovations. (Preprint). *arXiv.* https://doi.org//arXiv.2506.16334DOI: 10.48550

Weber, M., Beutter, M., Weking, J., Böhm, M., & Krcmar, H. (2022). AI startup business models: Key characteristics and directions for entrepreneurship research. *Business & Information Systems Engineering*, *64*(1), 91–109. DOI: 10.1007/s12599-021-00732-w

Wilson, H. J., & Daugherty, P. R. (2018). Collaborative intelligence: Humans and AI are joining forces. *Harvard Business Review*, *96*(4), 114–123.

World Economic Forum (WEF). (2023). *Generative AI could add trillions to the global economy.* https://www.weforum.org/stories/2023/07/generative-ai-could-add-trillions-to-global-economy

Zapier. (2023). *What is AI automation + how to use it.* https://zapier.com/blog/ai-automation/

Zhang, Y., & Tian, Y. (2021). Choice of pricing and marketing strategies in reward-based crowdfunding campaigns. *Decision Support Systems*, *144*, 113520. DOI: 10.1016/j.dss.2021.113520

KEY TERMS AND DEFINITIONS

AI-Augmented Entrepreneurship: The practice of integrating AI tools and technologies into entrepreneurial processes to enhance decision-making, innovation, and operational efficiency while complementing human intuition.

AI-Driven Crowdfunding: Platforms that leverage AI to match startups with potential investors, optimize campaign strategies, and assess funding risks more accurately than traditional methods.

AI-Human Collaboration: The integration of AI capabilities with human skills to jointly solve problems, make strategic decisions, or innovate, emphasizing synergy rather than replacement.

Algorithmic Bias: The presence of systematic errors in AI decision-making due to biased data or model design, which can lead to unfair or unethical outcomes in startup operations or customer interactions.

Artificial Intelligence (AI): A branch of computer science focused on creating systems capable of performing tasks that normally require human intelligence, including learning, reasoning, problem-solving, and decision-making. In startups, AI supports ideation, automation, and predictive analytics.

Digital Twin: A virtual representation of a physical product, process, or system that can be analyzed and optimized using AI. Startups use digital twins for rapid prototyping, process improvement, and scenario testing.

Generative AI: AI systems capable of creating new content—including text, images, and product designs—based on existing data patterns. In entrepreneurship, generative AI can accelerate ideation and content creation.

Hybrid Work Environment: A workplace model combining remote and in-office work. AI supports hybrid environments by enabling collaboration, productivity tracking, and seamless communication across distributed teams.

Lean Startup Methodology: A systematic approach to developing businesses and products using iterative cycles of prototyping, testing, and learning. AI can accelerate these cycles through data analysis and automated experimentation.

Predictive Analytics: A data-driven approach using AI algorithms to forecast future trends, customer behavior, or market opportunities, enabling startups to make informed strategic decisions.

Chapter 8
AI-Powered Digital and Virtual Training in Hybrid and Flexible Work Environments

Sahar Mahmoud Haboh
https://orcid.org/0009-0007-9643-2551
Midocean University, Comoros

ABSTRACT

This chapter helps shed light on the requirements of artificial intelligence and the necessity of ethical governance and sustainable engagement between digital technology and humans in a hybrid environment by working on the application of adaptive training models to enhance the efficiency and skills of employees and learners within the workplace. This chapter helps provide a clear framework for integrating digital infrastructure and using machine learning and natural language processing to achieve predictive analytics that facilitate the integration of AI and leadership to improve organisational productivity. AI applications leverage virtual reality, augmented reality, and even gamification to deliver an adaptive training environment that continuously increases learner engagement, leading to improved learner skills. This chapter also noted that among the challenges related to integrating AI into the workplace are the inability to mobilise learners and stakeholders toward AI acceptance, along with factors related to digital fatigue, bias, and inequality.

DOI: 10.4018/979-8-3373-7416-1.ch008

1. INTRODUCTION AND BACKGROUND

1.1. Digital Transformation and AI in Hybrid Work

Digital transformation relies on the integration of digital technologies – particularly artificial intelligence, cloud computing, and big data analytics – known as hybrid work systems. These systems greatly improve the work environment within an organization while also enhancing decision-making by integrating employees into the process. The hybrid work model, which combines remote work and on-site work, benefits from digital transformation to overcome spatial and temporal barriers, facilitating immediate collaboration and enhancing knowledge exchange.

Digital transformation is not just about using technology and changing workplace culture; it also requires new competencies from both employees and leaders. Artificial intelligence (AI) improves workflows within organizations by automating tasks, performing predictive analytics to enhance performance, and personalizing employee experiences related to technology. Agile project management methodologies, along with AI-powered organizational decision support systems (ODS), enable dynamic adaptation to the evolving demands of the hybrid work environment.

AI-powered tools enhance communication and business continuity in fragmented work environments. Digital transformation is redefining the roles and responsibilities of employees within an organization, necessitating the continuous development of their skills to align with the technological advancements integrated into the organization (Khalifa, 2023).

1.2. Evolution of Training Models in Hybrid Workplaces

The main shift in training and learning today is from uniform, teacher-led instruction to AI-powered methods that personalize content for each learner. This shift boosts individual learning outcomes and knowledge retention.

Hybrid learning frameworks now blend immersive technologies like augmented and virtual reality with flexible access, providing a learning experience unhindered by location. The primary upcoming challenges are technology accessibility and sustaining learner motivation.

The effective use of gamification and collaborative strategies also promotes collective learner engagement. Advanced training frameworks and quality assurance mechanisms focus on flexibility and feedback to continuously improve the learning process by integrating AI into the rapid and effective analysis of learner attitude (Hwang et al., 2020; Álvarez-Chaves & Saborío-Taylor, 2025; Brown et al., 2021).

2. AI-DRIVEN TRAINING TECHNOLOGIES AND TOOLS

2.1. AI Integration in E-Learning Platforms

As a result of the widespread adoption of AI across numerous sectors, it has also been adopted in education, particularly in hybrid learning. E-learning platforms utilize AI applications such as Intelligent Teaching Systems (ITS) and automated assessment, significantly impacting learning outcomes. This is due to AI's ability to adapt to the diverse needs of individual learners, facilitate active participation, and automate the creation of educational content, thus saving time and effort for teachers (Mustfa et al., 2024).

There are many experiences that demonstrate the effectiveness of using artificial intelligence in the learning process and at the level of students' academic achievement. For example, smart teaching systems are considered an important innovation in the field of the learning process, as they use machine learning techniques to instantly identify students' attitudes towards the learning process, in addition to their ability to provide individual academic support to the student in accordance with their special abilities. Teaching systems can analyze the student's abilities and identify their strengths and weaknesses, and thus provide content that aligns with the student's characteristics, in addition to their ability to integrate predictive analyses based on the level of interaction, which enhances the student's scientific and academic level.

AI applications also assist teachers in the assessment process by helping them design tests, formulate questions, and grade them with the same clarity and precision as a teacher would. This allows them to play a pivotal role in assessment and evaluation, aligning with learning objectives. Furthermore, these digital applications can detect and identify cheating patterns through integration with human oversight. Human oversight ensures the application of ethical standards such as integrity, fairness, objectivity, and impartiality, thus guaranteeing the integrity of the assessment

The AI-assisted learning process creates a personalized learning environment that adapts to the learner's characteristics. AI applications analyze student engagement and participation levels, identify their academic and cognitive abilities, and then design and implement a learning strategy that aligns with the student's developmental stage. This aligns with modern learning principles 4.0, where the student is at the center of the educational process, utilizing digital technologies.

An example of cutting-edge implementation is the Information-Diagnostic Online SMART Platform, which builds on an open-source virtual learning environment architecture to provide scalable, flexible educational solutions for higher education students. This platform embodies inclusive design by ensuring accessibility for students with disabilities and diverse learning needs, thus promoting equity. Key features include seamless integration of real-time diagnostic tools, adaptive learning pathways, feedback systems, and personalized resource recommendation engines—all underpinned by robust data privacy and security protocols process (Hariyanto et al., 2025).

Challenges of integrating artificial intelligence into the learning process

Despite the advantages that artificial intelligence (AI) has brought to the learning process, some challenges remain that affect how these applications are utilized. These challenges stem primarily from bias or errors in training data. Therefore, those responsible for these applications must quickly address these challenges by developing algorithms capable of scrutinizing all input data, which is the cornerstone of building and designing an effective learning environment.

Furthermore, the lack of resources, especially in developing countries, is another challenge facing the integration of AI in the learning process. Therefore, efforts must be made to provide resources to facilitate the use of these applications in education. A lack of skills in dealing with artificial intelligence (AI) is also a major challenge. Although younger teachers seem receptive to integrating AI into the educational process, training courses are needed to equip them with the skills to effectively use AI and leverage it for educational success (Hwang et al., 2020; Stahl, 2024).

Furthermore, achieving a balance between human input and AI is another challenge in integrating AI into education. Therefore, those responsible for implementing AI must address these challenges to ensure the achievement of learning outcomes.

2.1.1. AI-Driven Engagement Tools

AI technologies have fundamentally changed the educational process, especially in hybrid learning environments. This section will explore how AI can be used in the learning process to enhance student engagement, prevent student dropout, and integrate AI-powered tools and methods to motivate and engage learners.

AI-Driven Engagement Tools

AI-based learning platforms leverage the capabilities of these technologies, such as NLP, machine learning, and real-time data analytics, to enhance student engagement and interaction. Applications like Open AI Whisper and GPT-4 have shown a significant impact on student engagement and information retention, facilitating feedback on student participation and academic progress. Furthermore, these applications can perform rapid analysis of student behavior, allowing instructors to intervene swiftly to ensure students remain effectively engaged in the learning process.

AI-powered learning platforms also deliver educational content in a way that aligns with learners' characteristics and preferences. The AI capabilities of chatbots provide continuous support and answer student inquiries at any time. Teachers can also leverage AI to summarize student feedback on the learning process, helping identify and address areas for improvement, thereby enhancing the effectiveness of the educational process (Mustfa et al., 2024).

Predictive Modeling of Learner Drop-Out and Engagement Intervention

Using AI-powered predictive analytics helps identify students at risk of dropping out by analyzing behavioral and demographic data. This analysis reveals the likelihood of future dropouts and enables teachers to take timely preventative measures. These measures include designing curricula tailored to students' characteristics or providing appropriate incentives and support to facilitate their reintegration into the educational process.

AI-powered platforms enhance the learning process by tailoring engagement to each student's level. By providing targeted feedback, these platforms help identify academic achievement early, which is crucial because higher achievement is linked to lower dropout rates. By adapting instruction, AI helps address students' needs, supporting strategies that reduce dropout risk. Studies confirm that early detection of student interaction enables teachers to adjust methods, further helping to prevent dropout.

Gamification in AI-Driven Learning Environments

Gamification is one of the ways AI can ensure students remain engaged in the learning process, providing adaptive difficulty measures, feedback, and various motivational methods that promote long-term educational engagement.

The AI-powered Gamification strategy delivers varying levels of challenge aligned with student proficiency and characteristics, fostering continuous student engagement in the learning process. This has been demonstrated in trials with students across different educational stages, showing that AI-enhanced play increases task completion rates and improves long-term knowledge retention compared to traditional teaching methods.

Through this approach, AI provides teachers with immediate feedback, allowing them to adjust their teaching methods and maintain student engagement, thus preventing dropout. AI analyzes content difficulty and provides predictive insights into student progress and strategies to avoid dropping out (Hariyanto et al., 2025).

Conclusion

AI-powered interaction, predictive modeling of learner dropout, and AI-enhanced gamification are powerful tools that have revolutionized digital education in hybrid environments. They facilitate personalized learning that aligns with student capabilities and maintains continuous student engagement. Therefore, future research should focus on expanding the use of AI while adhering to ethical guidelines to ensure effective support for learners in diverse learning environments.

2.2. Smart Analytics and Personalized Learning

AI-powered analytics helps design personalized learning approaches that align with student capabilities by analyzing datasets that develop a learning style that meets learners' needs.

Predictive analytics represents a cutting-edge approach to intelligent analytics. It utilizes statistical and machine learning models—including regression, decision trees, and neural networks—to predict student performance and identify those most at risk of dropping out. Furthermore, it provides recommendations and strategies for addressing this issue, known as proactive AI-powered strategies, which help eliminate the problem of school dropout.

Predictive analytics also plays a vital role in improving academic advising and assisting instructors in selecting curricula and teaching methods that align with students' levels, thereby increasing educational delivery, which is consistent with constructivist teaching approaches that emphasize the effective construction of knowledge.

AI-powered learning platforms help improve the efficiency of the educational process by relying on real-time feedback, student performance monitoring, and multimedia integration to deliver a personalized learning environment that aligns with each student's level. The integration of personalized dashboards and AI-enhanced personalized learning environments also helps students actively participate in achieving learning outcomes.

The theoretical foundations of AI-enhanced personalized learning are consistent with constructivist learning theories, which place the student at the center of the educational process. AI applications enhance the effectiveness of the learning process by constructing personalized learning experiences to increase students' cognitive levels. This aligns with constructivist theories, which advocate for a personalized, data-driven learning environment that encourages student participation in the learning process.

Despite the positive outcomes of AI-assisted education, challenges related to AI bias persist, requiring developers to address this and provide applications that ensure fairness and can collect and analyze information.

Other challenges include privacy protection, requiring mechanisms to safeguard student data. Reliance on AI feedback may also impede the development of critical thinking skills among teachers, necessitating the integration of AI and human input to achieve optimal learning outcomes.

Artificial intelligence is also being used to enhance the academic achievement of students with disabilities and bridge the gaps with their peers. AI is employed to deliver adaptive content tailored to the specific needs of students with hearing or visual impairments, thereby helping them achieve their learning objectives and outcomes.

Intelligent analytics not only improves students' academic performance but also enhances employees' skills by analyzing their existing skills and providing recommendations on the skills they need to effectively navigate the complexities of the hybrid work environment.

Ultimately, AI-powered analytics enhances effectiveness and achieves learning outcomes while upholding ethical considerations and fostering continuous innovation, in line with the principles of effective digital transformation (Mustfa et al., 2024).

2.2.1. AI and Cognitive Science

The integration of AI with cognitive and affective dimensions has dramatically changed virtual and hybrid learning environments, enabling the detection and analysis of students' emotional states and significantly improving how instructors choose to interact with them and enhance their learning outcomes.

Theoretical Foundations and Cognitive-Affective Synergy

Several theories, such as self-determination theory and cognitive load theory, emphasize the impact of student intrinsic motivation on engagement in the learning process. These theories can be used and integrated with AI-powered learning analytics to create an adaptive environment that aligns with a student's capabilities and cognitive and emotional characteristics, significantly impacting their motivation to learn.

Emotional computing, pioneered by Rosalind Picard, focuses on the automated recognition and management of human emotions by analyzing a range of factors, including facial expressions, speech patterns, and other indicators. This allows for measuring the student's emotional engagement level and adjusting the learning environment and emotional stimulation methods to maintain student motivation and reduce boredom (Haboh, 2022).

Advances in Multimodal Affective Computing and Transfer Learning

Artificial intelligence based on Large-Scale Language Models (LLMs) such as ChatGPT and GPT-4 provides modern methods for detecting students' emotional levels. Numerous studies have demonstrated the effectiveness of AI applications that integrate multimedia sensory input for immediate and accurate emotion analysis, which greatly helps maintain students' emotional engagement with the learning process.

Transfer learning techniques are increasingly vital in affective computing due to the immense variability of emotional expressions across individuals and contexts. Transfer learning allows AI to reutilize knowledge from previously trained models in new domains, reducing the need for extensive labeled data. Studies detailed in the attachments demonstrate transfer learning's efficacy in generalizing emotion recognition across modalities such as speech (including whispered speech), video, and physiological signals, even addressing the challenge of unseen emotional states (zero-shot learning).

Empirical Evidence of Enhanced Learning Transfer and Emotional Optimization

The experimental results confirm that AI systems that analyze students' emotional state help increase motivation and thus reduce dropout rates. They also contribute to enhanced skills acquisition, especially in hybrid learning environments. AI platforms, such as intelligent teaching systems, have shown a positive impact on students' mental health and increased critical thinking, in addition to influencing academic achievement and knowledge retention.

Practical Implementations in Education, Therapy, and Safety

In this context, emotionally analyzing chatbots and virtual therapists offer significant support for students' mental health. AI-powered learning platforms can identify and address students' emotional challenges, ensuring their continued motivation.

Extensive utilization of multimodal datasets like IEMOCAP, K-Emo Con, and SEWA underpins these innovations, facilitating robust model training across diverse languages and cultures. Evaluation frameworks encompassing accuracy, recall, F1 scores, and user experience metrics guide the refinement of affective AI technologies.

Challenges: Technological, Ethical, and Societal

Conversely, some challenges relate to the fact that emotional expression varies from person to person and is influenced by a range of personal, social, and cultural factors, which affect the accuracy of these systems' results. Additionally, integrating multimedia data still requires significant computational effort and is susceptible to noise and limited input data, which also impacts the accuracy of the results.

On the ethical side, there are privacy concerns, the need to obtain student consent during the analysis process, and challenges related to bias and subjectivity in the analysis itself. This information significantly impacts the accuracy of results, thus hindering their effective use in maintaining student engagement with the learning process. Therefore, developers must address these challenges by ensuring fairness and transparency in the use of these systems.

Future Directions and Strategic Outlook

Future research should also prioritise the development of AI applications capable of providing in-depth and objective analyses of students' emotional states. This will facilitate widespread adoption due to user trust in systems that can interact with demographically, environmentally, and culturally diverse students, significantly contributing to accurate analysis and, consequently, sound decision-making that promotes student engagement in the educational process.

Additionally, advancements in symbolic neural AI can contribute to a deeper understanding of complex emotional states, moving beyond mere statistics and numerical data to a more nuanced understanding of students' emotional experiences. Establishing an ethical framework focused on AI governance that promotes transparency and fairness is essential for the effective use of such systems in emotional analysis.

In summary, the integration of artificial intelligence, cognitive science, and affective computing presents promising opportunities to improve students' emotional well-being, a key factor influencing their motivation to continue learning. This is achieved by providing a learning experience tailored to each student's individual needs, thereby increasing motivation, engagement, and skills development, and ultimately contributing to reducing school dropout rates (Alsubaie & Aleisa, 2025; Cavanaugh et al., 2025).

3. CHALLENGES AND ETHICAL CONSIDERATIONS

3.1. Technical and Organizational Challenges

AI-powered digital training systems offer numerous advantages related to hybrid learning by providing a personalized learning environment that aligns with the learner's capabilities. Despite this, several digital and organizational challenges must be considered when implementing these systems.

Technical Challenges

System Integration and Interoperability

One important technical challenge is integrating AI training solutions into existing legacy systems and diverse digital ecosystems. Enterprises utilize a complex blend of IT infrastructure, such as traditional databases and cloud-based solutions, that are often built independently. Seamless integration of AI subsystems with heterogeneous systems is done through advanced middleware, open APIs , and standardization protocols.

At the organizational level, IT departments may lack familiarity or expertise with open-source software (OSS) AI deployments, which tend to require more hands-on customization and maintenance compared to commercial, off-the-shelf solutions. For example, public sector entities have experienced repeated shifts between proprietary and open-source software due to technical and institutional challenges, exemplified by the Munich municipality's oscillation over IT infrastructure choices (Cöster et al.,2023).

Data Quality, Availability, and Bias:

Data is the foundation of AI-powered training systems, as its quality and comprehensiveness significantly impact the quality of training systems, enabling the delivery of an adaptive learning environment. Therefore, many training systems and platforms suffer from data scarcity and heterogeneity, which can lead to unfair and inaccurate recommendations.

Some AI applications indicate their inability to handle different dialects effectively, leading to performance variations among users and exacerbating inequality.

Complementary AI fairness-aware algorithms and continuous bias auditing must be systematically employed to mitigate such risks. Therefore, complementary algorithms that prioritize fairness and continuous verification should be used to mitigate these challenges (Haboh, 2022; Qadeer, 2025; Ghonim & Awad, 2025; Awad, 2025).

Algorithmic Robustness and Explainability

The use of advanced AI models—such as big language models and deep neural networks—raises several challenges related to the model's ability to deliver transparent and interpretable results. This is because the recommendations made by the educational process are difficult for stakeholders to understand, significantly impacting the level of trust and acceptance of these models.

Interpretable AI (XAI) methodologies, including Shapley incremental interpretations (SHAP) and local model-independent interpretable interpretations (LIME), have emerged as vital tools for making AI outputs interpretable and trustworthy, allowing educators to validate assessment recommendations or decisions regarding learners-specific content.

Cybersecurity and Data Privacy

Another challenge concerns the level of privacy and security of information held within AI-powered training systems, due to security breaches that allow access to student information and its illegal use in cyberbullying and extortion.

Data privacy is not limited to addressing the technical aspects but also includes the ethical dimension, which necessitates transparency and obtaining user consent from the outset. Therefore, educational platforms must be transparent about how they use user data, especially that of children and adolescents.

Organizational Challenges

Workforce Skills and Readiness

Organizations typically lack the trained personnel to handle and continuously develop AI systems. These personnel must possess a range of expertise, and the lack of adequate training and experience hinders the effective use and application of AI.

Additionally, the digital transformation of organizations and the integration of AI into the workplace are accompanied by differences in opinions, with some accepting and others rejecting it. While younger employees tend to embrace technology due to their digital experience, others oppose its presence, believing that its use could lead to a loss of their position within the organization.

Change Management and Cultural Factors

The success of organizations in adopting AI as a training tool depends on a range of factors, including: -

The organization's culture and its belief in the importance of innovation and the use of advanced training methods.

- Handling the organization's resistance to change, it is essential for organizations to implement a strategy aimed at convincing employees of the importance of change, focusing on the advantages and disadvantages, and providing training programs to ensure AI literacy.
- Consideration of ethical and legal aspects when using AI.

Ethical and Legal Governance Frameworks

Regulatory ambiguity and ethical issues related to AI are among the most significant challenges hindering AI integration within organizations. Therefore, organizations must carefully examine the GDPR, FERPA, and national AI legislation. and simultaneously craft internal ethical policies that reflect societal values.

The responsibility of determining the consequences of AI decisions remains a major challenge, given that AI systems may be autonomous or semi-autonomous (Samek et al., 2017; Alsubaie & Aleisa, 2025).

Financial Resource Allocation

While investing in AI infrastructure, used in many aspects such as training, governance, and decision-making, can be costly for organizations, making things challenging for startups, the long-term benefits, such as increased productivity, and underscore the strategic value of investing in AI.

3.2. Ethics and Governance in AI Training Systems

Ethical governance of artificial intelligence in training environments is essential to maximizing its educational benefits while minimizing risks. This governance requires setting strict ethical commitments and adopting transparent practices when using artificial intelligence in all activities.

Ethical Challenges: Academic Integrity and Intellectual Honesty

As AI applications proliferate, many students and employees rely on them to produce content or perform various tasks without considering the balance between technology and human effort to maintain creativity and intellectual integrity. Therefore, users must adhere to a set of ethics that ensures the fair and appropriate use of these technologies.

Bias, Fairness, and Inclusion

Bias is one of the most significant ethical dilemmas related to the use of artificial intelligence, because data that does not represent all segments of the population can lead to societal inequalities in the representation of all segments of the population. This challenge can be overcome by implementing strict procedures that guarantee objectivity and impartiality, preventing bias towards one group at the expense of another. For instance, using AI to work solely with normal students while excluding those with disabilities constitutes blatant bias that undermines the objectivity of the results and recommendations.

Privacy, Consent, and Data Stewardship

AI-powered training systems adopt ethical standards regarding privacy protection and user consent. Therefore, users must be aware of the purposes for which data is used, how it is shared, and how long it is retained, to be able to make independent decisions.

Ethical frameworks integrate privacy-by-design principles, access controls, and opportunities for users to modify or withdraw consent.

Transparency and Explainability

Another ethical challenge is AI's ability to provide explainable recommendations, which directly impacts stakeholder confidence in using AI in decision-making.

Providing interpretable feedback to both teachers and learners enhances effective human oversight and promotes ethical accountability to AI systems.

Accountability and Liability

Establishing accountability for AI-generated outcomes, particularly those related to assessments or recommendations, is crucial. Therefore, an accountability framework must be in place between AI developers and those responsible for its use to identify who is accountable when flawed assessments or recommendations are made that harm the organization.

Governance Frameworks and Best Practices

Establishing Organizational AI Ethics Policies

When using AI in organizations, an ethical framework must be established that aligns with the organization's values. This framework should adhere to a set of principles including fairness, transparency, privacy, and accountability. These principles must be reviewed and developed in a way that is consistent with cultural, social, and organizational norms and values.

Building AI Ethics Capacity

The widespread adoption of AI has led to the emergence of ethics experts who emphasize the need to integrate AI into all phases of development, from data collection to the delivery of results and recommendations. This is because neglecting ethical considerations in AI systems can have serious repercussions for decision-making and stakeholder trust in AI.

Continuous Risk Management and Auditing

The governance of AI ethics has a significant positive impact on organizational operations, as data entry scrutiny must be considered to avoid bias in the resulting findings and recommendations.

Data Governance and Regulatory Compliance

Effective compliance with regional regulations, such as the GDPR and FERPA, is essential and positively impacts how data provided to artificial intelligence is handled for analysis in an objective and unbiased manner.

User Empowerment and Transparency

Among the ethical considerations for using AI within educational institutions is transparency in informing students and teachers about the functions and importance of AI. This increases trust in these systems and promotes their responsible use. It is also essential to consider learners' demographic, cultural, and academic differences to ensure impartiality (Cavanaugh et al., 2025; Spector & Ma, 2014).

3.2.1. Algorithmic Transparency and Explainability

Given the versatility of AI, organizations have increasingly turned to it in HR training. Therefore, to maximize the benefits of these systems in human resource development, transparency and accountability are crucial for building trust. Since many recruitment and promotion decisions are automated by AI, XAI is a fundamental requirement for ensuring fairness, transparency, and impartiality in HR management.

The Imperative of Algorithmic Transparency in HR

Some challenges related to applying transparency when dealing with human personnel through AI stem from the ambiguity and complexity of AI systems. Therefore, strict adherence to transparency and fairness is crucial when AI selects human personnel.

The lack of transparency in AI, or its inability to provide interpretable results, negatively impacts fairness within organizations regarding employee selection. Furthermore, the inability to establish accountability for the outcomes of AI recommendations and decisions hinders the implementation of ethical frameworks governing the operation of these systems, such as GDPR.

Explainable AI (XAI) as a Governance Strategy

The importance of XAI lies in the valuable insights and recommendations it provides to organizations across numerous areas, including employee selection, promotion criteria, and selection processes. By ensuring fairness and equity in the selection process, XAI fosters greater trust in the system and its effectiveness within the organization. For example, by applying SHAP to Random Forest or XG Boost hiring models, organizations can pinpoint and assess demographic features (e.g., gender or nationality) contributing disproportionately to model predictions and actively mitigate unfair biases via feature modification or exclusion.

Also, Local Interpretable Model-agnostic Explanations (LIME) allows HR professionals to ensure fairness and impartiality in employee selection and implement corrective actions if discriminatory patterns are detected.

Empirical Evidence of XAI Effectiveness in Fairness and Performance

Recent empirical studies have shown that using AI like XAI in human resources has a significant impact on employee selection, as well as revealing existing biases. This significantly reduces bias and maximizes the effectiveness of recruitment in selecting the most suitable candidates for the organization.

Ethical and Legal Implications

XAI also reinforces ethical principles related to providing explainable decisions and recommendations that align with the organization's social and organizational standards, thereby removing ambiguity from those decisions. Additionally, this commitment to transparency reduces the legal risks the organization may face due to its adherence to data protection regulations.

Despite this, some challenges arise from the oversimplification of decisions generated by XAI, sometimes resulting in partial interpretations that are unhelpful to decision-makers. Therefore, a balance between human input and AI is necessary to arrive at useful results and recommendations. It is also crucial to protect these systems from manipulation, which significantly impacts the accuracy of the results.

Future Directions and Recommendations

Ultimately, organizations that rely on a lean work style should continuously develop their AI systems to leverage them for accurate results and recommendations. Furthermore, the integration of AI and humans is crucial to mitigate errors from either side and to ensure the organization implements ethical governance frameworks for its tools, enabling it to effectively achieve its objectives.

In this aspect, organizations should put clear rules for how AI systems operate in employee selection and promotion, and explain the criteria and standards that ensure impartiality in the selection process, thereby increasing trust in AI systems (Samek et al., 2017; Alsubaie & Aleisa, 2025).

3.3. Cultural and Organizational Resistance to AI Adoption

Organizations seeking digital transformation face several challenges, including resistance and a lack of acceptance of artificial intelligence (AI) in managing their work processes. This is considered one of the most significant factors affecting the integration of AI in the workplace. Older employees and those with insufficient experience in dealing with technology tend to be resistant to AI, especially if they believe it will lead to job losses or if they lack a true understanding of how AI can positively impact workflow without negatively affecting them.

To overcome this challenge, leadership must take several steps to encourage the adoption of digital technologies, such as increasing trust in these technologies. This helps create an environment conducive to integrating AI into the organization's operations. Therefore, transparency and continuous communication between senior management and employees are crucial to building employee confidence in these systems, which will gradually lead to their integration into the work environment.

Senior leadership can persuade employees to embrace AI integration by focusing on enhancing their AI skills. This positively impacts employee acceptance and trust in technology. Numerous studies, based on the UTAUT theory, confirm that increased employee technological skills and awareness of its benefits significantly influence its acceptance in the workplace (Herdman, 2025; Huttunen, 2025).

AI's Role in Diagnosing Digital Burnout and Fatigue

Many technology-related problems, such as digital burnout and fatigue, are common in hybrid work environments due to exposure to digital technology and the lack of appropriate mitigation mechanisms. AI can identify these problems and mitigate their severity through proactive interventions tailored to each individual case.

The digital burnout assessment tool incorporates a suite of tools that leverage multimedia data, work pattern and communication rate measurements, and sentiment analysis to identify digital burnout early and contribute to employee well-being.

Chatbots also assist employees in achieving work-life balance and organizing their efforts, all in accordance with each employee's personality, emotional state, and job responsibilities, thus helping them maintain their energy and motivation.

Mitigation Strategies Leveraging AI

In mitigating employee burnout, AI technologies play a pivotal role by providing recommendations for work distribution and scheduling that align with each employee's needs, thus preserving their mental and physical well-being and significantly impacting their productivity.

In addition, AI personalizes training to align with each employee's cognitive and behavioral level, enabling leadership to better monitor employee activity and proactively take steps to improve well-being before employees reach burnout levels.

However, these actions must be governed by ethical principles that include protecting privacy and obtaining consent, ensuring transparency regarding data use, and integrating human and AI elements when addressing job burnout to maintain trust and effectiveness.

Challenges and Future Directions

However, several challenges exist regarding the use of AI to monitor digital burnout, including privacy concerns, the employee's sense of being constantly monitored, and the difficulty in identifying the major contributing factors to digital burnout. Therefore, organizations must have a comprehensive plan for the effective use of AI to accurately assess employee burnout levels.

Therefore, future studies should explore the development of AI-powered systems capable of accurately detecting digital burnout and providing precise, interpretable recommendations, and developing systems that promote work-life balance to address digital burnout sustainably. This requires collaboration between AI experts, psychologists, and ethicists to develop a comprehensive and reliable system that considers the diverse aspects and dimensions of the work environment and employees (Khalife, 2023).

4. BEST PRACTICES AND FUTURE DIRECTIONS

4.1. Strategies for Effective AI-Powered Training: Understanding AI's Transformative Role in Training

AI has had a pivotal impact on the virtual work environment by providing training models designed to enhance learner efficiency. These models are characterized by their ability to provide predictive analytics and deliver a training experience that aligns with each learner's characteristics, significantly impacting engagement levels and ultimately improving learners' cognitive and behavioral performance.

A range of factors influences the success of AI-enabled training. In addition to the availability of technology, there must be an ethical framework governing these systems, along with organizational readiness, learner acceptance of the systems, and continuous evaluation to identify shortcomings and address them in the future.

Comprehensive Stakeholder Involvement

A key step toward successful AI-powered training is engaging stakeholders—including senior leadership, learners, and IT professionals—in both the design and implementation phases of programs to ensure alignment with educational objectives and the fulfillment of actual learning needs.

Robust User Experience (UX) and Accessibility Design

Furthermore, the success of AI-assisted training depends on the ability of digital platforms to provide an easy-to-use interface that trainees can navigate effectively and access content easily, utilizing multimedia to ensure the effectiveness of training for people with disabilities.

Strategies include:

- Clear navigation and feedback mechanisms
- Customizable learning paths
- Multilingual support and culturally sensitive content
- Responsive design enabling seamless multi-device access

Transparent, Ethical AI Algorithms and Data Practices

Transparency and ethical governance are among the most important principles and foundations of AI-based training. Therefore, the algorithms that perform the assessment and provide recommendations must be accurate and capable of delivering objective, interpretable, and unbiased recommendations.

The ability of AI to provide explainable recommendations allows stakeholders to understand these recommendations and the rationale behind them. Therefore, institutions must ensure that data governance frameworks protect learner privacy and comply with the General Data Protection Regulation (GDPR), the Family Rights and Educational Rights Act (FERPA).

Continuous Professional Development and Support

Training for teachers and staff is crucial for enhancing their skills and practices. AI programs play a vital role in addressing AI literacy among teachers and staff, as well as providing ongoing training to enhance their skills and expertise through workshops. However, this requires a range of resources, including infrastructure and methods for measuring feedback.

Through continuous training, organizations can increase employee and teacher acceptance of AI, thereby increasing the likelihood of its adoption as a tool for effective task performance within the organization.

Data-Driven Evaluation and Iterative Improvement

To achieve optimal AI-powered training outcomes, a mechanism for continuous data integration is essential. This includes monitoring employee performance, comparing skill development and engagement during training, and measuring the productivity achieved within the work environment. Furthermore, gathering trainee feedback is crucial for effectively identifying the strengths and weaknesses of AI-powered training.

A variety of assessment methods and an evidence-based assessment are essential for clarity and transparency. Feedback also plays a crucial role in identifying any challenges or difficulties related to the training process, facilitating corrective action.

Integration with Organizational Goals and Culture

AI-powered training helps achieve a range of objectives, including enhancing employee efficiency and promoting innovation, while also contributing significantly to the efficient and equitable distribution of tasks and resources within the organization.

Organizations that embrace a culture of experiential learning significantly enhance employee skills. Therefore, leadership's conviction in the importance of AI-led training greatly contributes to the organization's digital transformation.

Embracing Open-Source and Modular Architectures

Adopting open-source AI tools delivers a range of benefits, including flexibility and innovation efficiency, as well as transparency and the ability to customize an adaptive training environment.

Ethical and Legal Compliance as Strategic Enablers

Integrating ethical principles into AI-powered training programs yields a range of positive outcomes, including increased stakeholder trust and sustainable reliance. Therefore, these principles should be continuously developed and communicated to employees, enhancing transparency and employee acceptance to improve employee performance. In addition to the necessity of bias mitigation and privacy protection for learners (Hwang et al., 2020; Cavanaugh et al., 2025).

4.2. Trends in Virtual and Hybrid Learning

The Rise of Hybrid and Blended Learning Models

The outbreak of the COVID-19 pandemic led many institutions to adopt hybrid learning, which combines traditional attendance with digital platforms. Therefore, educational platforms have utilized artificial intelligence to provide an adaptive learning experience characterized by flexibility and effectiveness.

AI-enabled learning platforms effectively deliver smart tutoring, ensuring sustained learner engagement, while also providing real-time assessment methods to gauge learners' comprehension of the learning content.

AI-Powered Virtual Reality (VR) and Augmented Reality (AR)

The integration of VR and AR educational platforms has significantly contributed to providing learners with a unique and distinctive learning experience. This experience leverages immersive technology that engages the learner's senses, significantly impacting their academic performance by overcoming the shortcomings of traditional educational videos.

VR-based learning platforms offer adaptive learning content, significantly contributing to learners' academic achievement and productivity while reducing their digital fatigue.

Intelligent Learning Analytics and Predictive Interventions

AI applications facilitate in-depth, real-time analysis of learner or employee performance, then provide proactive recommendations and predictive insights into their performance and how to improve it.

AI applications provide in-depth analytics that combine statistics and pedagogy, significantly improving teacher performance and, consequently, enhancing the overall educational process.

Personalization Beyond Content Adaptation

AI not only delivers adaptive content that aligns with learners' cognitive characteristics, but it also analyzes their emotional state, such as engagement, participation, or boredom, and then adjusts the teaching method to suit the learner's emotional and mood state.

Among the strategies employed is the use of gamification on AI-powered platforms, which significantly increases learner motivation and engagement in the educational process (Haboh, 2022).

Collaborative and Social Learning Innovations

AI-powered learning platforms focus on a range of factors, including student interaction with both instructors and peers, and their average participation in collaborative problem-solving. Through AI and chatbots, a flexible learning environment can be provided, capable of connecting the virtual and real worlds.

Expanding AI Use in Professional and Workforce Training

AI plays a vital role in developing learners' skills and improving their performance within hybrid work environments. It also tracks these skills and their potential to increase organizational productivity through an adaptive learning environment that is tailored to the specific characteristics of each individual case.

Ethical and Inclusive Learning Designs

Given the expanding use of AI, it has become essential to govern its use through an ethical framework based on a set of principles that include transparency, fairness, and the use of user-friendly and accessible platforms that are culturally sensitive and ensure accessibility for all groups, including people with disabilities (Álvarez-Chaves & Saborío-Taylor, 2025; Haboh, 2022; Brown et al., 2021).

Conclusion

In conclusion, the rapidly evolving field of AI-powered digital training includes the integration of immersive technologies such as augmented reality and virtual reality. It also necessitates embedding ethics in the use of these AI-powered training platforms, emphasizing transparency, stakeholder engagement, fairness, and cultural sensitivity. Furthermore, it requires considering the learner's cognitive and emotional state and providing adaptive learning content that aligns with their cognitive and emotional characteristics to foster a constructive work environment that enhances the productivity of both learners and employees.

4.3. Intelligent and Adaptive Assessment

AI plays a vital role in assessment processes that are adaptive to learning, contributing to in-depth predictive analytics. This section will summarize the key methodologies, pedagogical strategies, and experimental results, consistent with best practices and future trends in this field.

Intelligent and Adaptive Assessment Frameworks

Modern assessment methods focus on measuring the learner's performance and ability to complete tasks, thereby assessing their level of competence. Assessment involves a range of tests that measure multiple aspects, including knowledge, behavior, and even the learner's emotional state. By using engaging assessment methods such as illustrated stories, learners can become more involved in these tests. This facilitates AI-based assessment programs, enabling a comprehensive evaluation of the learner's knowledge and skills, including problem-solving abilities.

AI-powered assessment systems allow instructors to adaptively control assessments tailored to each learner's characteristics. All previously encountered learning elements can be measured, thus assessing the learner's comprehension of the content and its impact on their knowledge and skills. This is exemplified by the ADOPTA platform, which adaptively assesses learners to identify their existing knowledge and skill levels within the work environment.

AI Techniques in Adaptive Assessment for Complex Problem-Solving

Adaptive learning systems employ AI algorithms to deliver assessments that adaptively match the learner. The algorithms analyze the learner's past responses to determine their assessment difficulty level and then adjust the assessment to reduce difficulty. This facilitates a more efficient and comprehensive analysis that measures all dimensions of the learner's knowledge and skills.

Artificial intelligence systems also work on integrating multimedia data, measuring response times, and exploring the learner's emotional state within the framework of identifying trainee feedback. This helps in conducting a comprehensive assessment of the learner, thus enabling the identification of their shortcomings and problems and working to solve them (Haboh, 2022).

Pedagogical Implications and Assessment Diversity

Assessment programs typically involve a set of tests that measure a learner's cognitive and skill-based abilities, known as self-assessment. However, other aspects of assessment include incorporating feedback from teachers and even peers, which helps provide in-depth analysis. This is particularly true for problem-solving assessments, which measure not only a learner's ability to find a solution but also their level of thinking, creativity, and ability to connect variables to arrive at a solution.

Numerous experimental studies demonstrate learners' satisfaction with and preference for AI-assisted assessments over traditional assessment methods, particularly due to their adaptive capabilities. These assessments can tailor the difficulty of the assessment to the learner's level and incorporate gamification, increasing engagement and motivation, which significantly contributes to the success of the assessment process.

Best Practices and Future Directions

Creating a comprehensive learner profile that incorporates cognitive, behavioral, and emotional learning data is a crucial first step in developing and designing adaptive tests.

Furthermore, integrating complex tasks with multimedia into the assessment process is a crucial component of problem-solving assessments for identifying learners' knowledge and skill levels.

AI algorithms also help design adaptive assessment tests tailored to each learner, resulting in accurate and immediate evaluation.

The integration of AI and human input helps deliver more accurate assessments, as understanding the perspectives of teachers and peers contributes to a more holistic evaluation of student performance.

Continuous and immediate feedback also contributes to understanding learners' attitudes toward the effectiveness of AI systems in the assessment process, thereby identifying shortcomings and weaknesses.

AI systems should focus on integrating the emotional dimension into the assessment process while also emphasizing ethical governance principles such as transparency and fairness to maintain learner trust in these systems and their ability to deliver reliable results and recommendations (Bontchev & Vassileva, 2011; Hariyanto et al., 2025).

4.4. AI-Driven Investment Prioritization for Training

Given the rapid proliferation of AI in workplaces and its intensive use in training processes, a precise strategic framework for prioritizing investments is essential to maximize the benefits of these systems and leverage them to improve workflows within hybrid work environments. This section presents methodologies and considerations related to investing in digital training through AI, offering best practices and future insights on prioritizing AI investments in training.

Strategic Foundations of AI Investment Prioritization

The first step in investing in and utilizing AI within the workplace is identifying the problem to be solved. Successful projects are based on a strategy of addressing a specific problem, not simply identifying the technology to be deployed within the organization. This ensures alignment between the organization's mission and the technology used. Therefore, a set of criteria and parameters must be established to measure the effectiveness of the technology investment, such as adding value to the organization, contributing to solving a specific problem, or achieving a particular social benefit; all of these can justify the investment (Enholm et al.,2022).

Core Evaluation Frameworks

Financial and Economic Appraisal

Organizations rely on a set of quantitative metrics to measure the profitability and effectiveness of AI implementation, such as return on investment (ROI), net present value (NPV), and discounted cash flow (DCF). However, organizations may face challenges in accurately assessing the benefits derived from this technology and the ability to accurately predicting its impact. Some organizations resort to using cost-benefit analysis (BCA) and social return on investment (SROI) to uncover the social impacts of implementing this technology, which justifies investment in it.

Cost-Effectiveness and Strategic Flexibility

Organizations may use CEA and CUA to compare AI with traditional methods to identify the most productive approach. Adaptive assessment techniques, including ROA, provide the ability to analyze and identify risks associated with AI use, which helps in making informed decisions about the feasibility of AI deployment and, consequently, in developing or modifying AI-related projects based on new information.

Managing Risk, Uncertainty, and Stakeholder Complexity

Risk assessments, both quantitative and qualitative, help to discover the extent of technical, ethical, and financial risks, in addition to studying concerns related to bias, fairness, and transparency. They also help to identify the extent of employees' sensitivity to risks related to the integration of artificial intelligence, as well as studying the extent of the ability of artificial intelligence to deal with risks that it may be exposed to in the future. All these factors must be studied for the successful use of artificial intelligence in the work environment. In addition, it is necessary to involve stakeholders to convince them of the need to integrate artificial intelligence into the work environment to achieve the organization's goals.

Portfolio Management for Resilient AI Investment

Given the high failure rates of AI, modern theories like MPT emphasize the need for a balanced distribution of risk across projects that differ in risk, technical complexity, and strategic impact. Organizations adopting this strategy can maximize the anticipated benefits of AI integration and reduce the risks associated with AI investment.

Systems Thinking in AI Evaluation and Integration

Considering the digital transformation process and the adoption and integration of AI within a complex business environment presents a range of challenges. These include the need to consider the organization's cultural and organizational aspects, employee acceptance of the technology, and data governance. All these factors must be considered when transforming into AI. The proper and well-planned use of AI can positively impact the nature of an organization's work, especially through the ongoing evaluation of AI's effectiveness within the work environment.

Emerging Trends and Future Directions

Global investment in artificial intelligence (AI) is expected to exceed $980 billion annually by 2028, reinforcing the urgent need to find advanced methods for optimally utilizing AI. Many studies indicate the necessity of integrating AI into work environments due to its ability to perform in-depth analysis and provide recommendations to stakeholders. This integration with human expertise is crucial, as is maximizing its benefits in employee training, which will positively impact employee performance and, consequently, improve organizational performance.

4.5. Fostering AI-Supported Leadership and Managerial Competencies

With the evolution of AI-driven hybrid work environments, fostering AI-powered leadership is of paramount importance due to its potential to drive innovation and effectively achieve organizational goals. This section will present theoretical frameworks, empirical findings, and practical strategies for developing AI-powered leadership skills.

AI-Supported Leadership: Conceptual Foundations and Theoretical Perspectives

AI-powered leadership utilizes a set of tools, including predictive analytics, machine learning models, and decision support systems, to amplify leaders' cognitive capabilities and expertise, facilitating effective decision-making. Furthermore, AI-powered leadership is equipped to tackle many future-oriented challenges and plays a vital role in supporting leadership during the digital transformation of the workplace.

Adaptive leadership theory identifies several factors that significantly impact AI integration, including convincing stakeholders of its necessity, assessing employees' AI learning speed, identifying technical and adaptive challenges hindering AI integration, developing strategies to encourage employee acceptance of the technology, and enhancing employee skills to effectively utilize AI.

Key Competencies for AI-Era Leadership

Many recent studies highlight the need for leadership to possess a range of skills and competencies when dealing with AI, including:

Integrating human and AI elements to maintain innovation and address any shortcomings in either, which significantly impacts organizational goals.

The necessity for leadership to continuously learn and develop their skills related to AI, especially given the ongoing evolution of this technology, and to leverage it in an integrated way.

Leaders should also consider ethical governance principles related to the use of AI and the need to apply standards of transparency, fairness, privacy, and accountability.

Considering the emotional aspect in the pursuit of digital transformation: Leadership should consider the emotional dimension when attempting to integrate AI into a hybrid work environment to increase employee confidence in the AI that leadership seeks to integrate into the workplace.

Practical Leadership Development for AI-Enabled Workforces

Effective leadership within an organization plays a key role in creating an environment conducive to AI adoption within the workplace. This is achieved through training programs that enhance employees' AI skills and mitigate the risks associated with its implementation, thereby contributing to the organization's goals through AI integration.

AI tools also help develop leadership skills through adaptive training courses that enhance leaders' ability to handle different situations and address organizational challenges. Furthermore, AI plays an effective role in helping the base generate creative ideas for organizational development, whether through chatbots or other AI applications.

Challenges and Considerations in AI-Supported Leadership

Integrating leadership with AI necessitates a balanced approach to its application to foster synergy and enhance leadership effectiveness within the organization. Excessive AI use significantly impacts creativity in critical decision-making, while complete reliance on AI can compromise the emotional dimension of leadership, a crucial factor in decision-making.

The challenges arising from AI use, particularly those related to privacy, transparency, and other ethical governance issues, must be considered when integrating AI, along with stakeholder considerations such as employee trust. Strategies should be implemented to foster employee confidence in AI.

As organizations move towards digital transformation, leaders must consider several factors, including the inherent resistance of employees to change. Therefore, leaders must possess a set of skills that enable them to support the change process by addressing the emotional needs of employees, thus encouraging them to embrace the concept of digital transformation.

Future Directions and Recommendations

Much research advocates for the integration of AI into leadership due to its impact on work processes. However, this requires a range of adaptive training programs that address how to effectively utilize AI. These programs should be multidisciplinary, encompassing technical, ethical, and emotional aspects, to ensure the effective use of AI.

Furthermore, emphasis should be placed on achieving harmony and integration between leadership and artificial intelligence to foster balance and integrate knowledge and emotion, ultimately increasing organizational productivity.

Leaders and educators should strive to develop an ethical framework for AI use to ensure responsible practice and focus on AI-powered leadership approaches. Leadership resilience and thoughtful reflection are key to achieving sustainable organizational success (Herdman, 2025; Huttunen, 2025).

CONCLUSION

The chapter titled "AI-Powered Digital and Virtual Training in Hybrid Work Environments" advances the discourse on digitally mediated professional development by embracing digital transformation and integral AI technologies reshaping hybrid work. AI-powered V-Learning is positioned as a pivotal paradigm enabling continuous reskilling through adaptive instructional technologies, like Intelligent Tutoring Systems (ITS) and Automated Assessments, integrated within Learning Management Systems (LMS).

Digital transformation helps enhance leadership and workforce skills in digital technologies, while simultaneously expanding the use of AI in the labor market and fostering greater collaboration and integration between human and artificial intelligence.

This chapter helps shed light on the requirements of artificial intelligence and the necessity of ethical governance and sustainable engagement between digital technology and humans in a hybrid environment, by working on the application of adaptive training models to enhance the efficiency and skills of employees and learners within the workplace.

This chapter helps provide a clear framework for integrating digital infrastructure and using machine learning and natural language processing to achieve predictive analytics that facilitate the integration of AI and leadership to improve organisational productivity.

AI applications leverage virtual reality, augmented reality, and even gamification to deliver an adaptive training environment that continuously increases learner engagement, leading to improved learner skills.

This chapter also noted that among the challenges related to integrating AI into the workplace are the inability to mobilise learners and stakeholders toward AI acceptance, along with factors related to digital fatigue, bias, and inequality.

The recommendations also emphasise the need for ongoing training and capacity building, enhancing the integration of artificial intelligence and human capital, and developing policies and investing continuously in integrating AI into hybrid work environments.

Ultimately, digital transformation is essential for organisational success, enabling institutions to achieve their strategic goals and keep pace with a highly competitive job market that leverages artificial intelligence. Training systems play a pivotal role in preparing a workforce capable of adapting to future developments in the digital sphere.

REFERENCES

Alsubaie, N., & Aleisa, N. (2025). Mitigating bias in AI model using eXplainable AI in terms of hiring process in the industry. *IEEE Access : Practical Innovations, Open Solutions, 13*, 147218–147241. DOI: 10.1109/ACCESS.2025.3599947

Álvarez-Chaves, A., & Saborío-Taylor, S. (2025). Hybrid learning in higher education: Considerations for its implementation in course design. *Journal of Digital Educational Technology, 5*(1), ep2505. Advance online publication. DOI: 10.30935/jdet/15859

Awad, A. (2025). The role of universities' social responsibility in enhancing business sustainability: Mediating role of entrepreneurial culture. *Problems and Perspectives in Management, 23*(1), 181–192. DOI: 10.21511/ppm.23(1).2025.14

Bontchev, B., & Vassileva, D. (2011). Adaptive assessment based on learning styles and student knowledge level. In *Proceedings of the 3rd International Conference on Computer Supported Education* (Vol. 2, pp. 449–454). SciTePress. https://www.google.com/search?q=https://doi.org/10.5220/0003484104490454

Brown, M., Costello, E., & Donlon, E. (2021). Digital education as social practice: Major trends shaping online learning futures. *Rivista di Digital Politics, 1*(3), 455–484. DOI: 10.53227/103800

Cavanaugh, P., Zhang, J., & Tenney, D. (2025, March). AI-enhanced open educational practices (AIOEP): Managing security, privacy, and ethics of artificial intelligence in engineering education [Paper presentation]. *2025 ASEE Northeast Section Conference*, Bridgeport, CT, United States. https://doi.org/DOI: 10.18260/1-2-60-54967

Cöster, M., Danielson, M., Ekenberg, L., Gullberg, C., Titlestad, G., Westelius, A., & Wettergren, G. (2023). *Digital transformation: Understanding business goals, risks, processes, and decisions*. Open Book Publishers. DOI: 10.11647/OBP.0350

Enholm, I. M., Papagiannidis, E., Mikalef, P., & Krogstie, J. (2022). Artificial intelligence and business value: A literature review. *Information Systems Frontiers, 24*(5), 1709–1734. DOI: 10.1007/s10796-021-10186-w

Ghonim, A., & Awad, A. (2025). Shaping customer insights through e-marketing: An applied study in the banking sector. *International Journal of Advanced and Applied Sciences, 12*(4), 88–98. DOI: 10.21833/ijaas.2025.04.011

Haboh, S. (2022). Theoretical Foundations of Designing and Developing Adaptive Learning Environments. *Journal of Educational and Social Studies, 28*(9), 141–182. DOI: 10.21608/jsu.2022.293140

Hariyanto, K. F., & Maharani, R. (2025). Artificial intelligence in adaptive education: a systematic review of techniques for personalized learning. DOI: 10.1007/s44217-025-00908-6

Herdman, P. T. (2025). The influence of generative artificial intelligence on leadership: An exploration of technology professionals' perceptions regarding leadership, adaptation, and organizational culture in the digital age [Doctoral dissertation, Marshall University]. Marshall Digital Scholar. https://mds.marshall.edu/etd/1987/

Huttunen, H. (2025). The effect of organizational culture on human-AI collaboration in supply chain management [Master's thesis, Aalto University]. Aaltodoc. https://aaltodoc.aalto.fi/items/f8e0bb40-886b-45c0-a11e-6a9dd368a301

Hwang, G. J., Xie, H., Wah, B. W., & Gašević, D. (2020). Vision, challenges, priorities, and research platforms of Artificial Intelligence in Education. *Computers and Education: Artificial Intelligence, 1*, 100003. DOI: 10.1016/j.caeai.2020.100003

Khalife, J. (2023). Artificial intelligence and hybrid jobs [Master's thesis, University of Padova]. Padua Research Archive. https://thesis.unipd.it/retrieve/b2c6d80e-9c0f-4534-9662-595938d540ee/KHALIFE_JOEL.pdf

Mustfa, M. J., & Ashiq, S. (2024). Harnessing the power of artificial intelligence for adaptive learning systems: A systematic review. *International Journal of Education and Management Engineering, 14*(5), 12–22. DOI: 10.5815/ijeme.2024.05.02

Qadeer, A., Awad, A., & Ali, A. (2025). Understanding generative AI implementation in digital advertising among retail SMEs in Pakistan. In *Impacts of AI generated content on brand reputation* (pp. 177–201). IGI Global. DOI: 10.4018/979-8-3373-4327-3.ch007

Samek, W., Wiegand, T., & Müller, K.-R. (2017). Explainable artificial intelligence: Understanding, visualizing and interpreting deep learning models (arXiv:1708.08296). arXiv. https://arxiv.org/pdf/1708.08296

Spector, J. M., & Ma, J. (2014). Ethical concerns and privacy issues in educational technology. In Spector, J. M., Merrill, M. D., Elen, J., & Bishop, M. J. (Eds.), *Handbook of research on educational communications and technology* (4th ed., pp. 719–729). Springer. DOI: 10.1007/978-1-4614-3185-5

Stahl, B. C., & Eke, D. (2024). The ethics of ChatGPT – Exploring the ethical issues of an emerging technology. *International Journal of Information Management, 74*, 102700. DOI: 10.1016/j.ijinfomgt.2023.102700

KEY TERMS AND DEFINITIONS

Adaptive Assessment: Adaptive assessment is performed when AI platforms dynamically select and adjust test item difficulty and format in real-time based on ongoing learner responses and cognitive load metrics to provide tailored evaluation experiences.

Adaptive Learning: Adaptive learning is measured by AI systems' capacity to dynamically adjust educational content, pacing, and instructional strategies according to learner performance data and preferences collected through embedded analytics during training sessions.

Affective Computing: Affective computing is operationalized as AI methodologies that capture and analyze multimodal emotional data—including facial expressions and physiological signals—during training interactions to tailor feedback and optimize learner motivation and engagement.

Algorithmic Bias: Algorithmic bias is identified through systematic disparities detected in AI model outputs by auditing training data representativeness and outcome fairness, particularly regarding demographic variables such as gender, ethnicity, or language background.

Artificial Intelligence (AI): AI is defined as the integration and application of computational algorithms, including machine learning and natural language processing, that automate routine tasks, generate predictive analytics, and personalize learning experiences within hybrid work platforms by continuously adapting to user data and behavior.

Explainable Artificial Intelligence (XAI): XAI is described as a set of algorithmic tools and techniques that provide transparent, interpretable explanations of AI decision-making processes, enabling users to understand, verify, and trust adaptive learning recommendations or HR assessment outcomes.

Gamification: Gamification is implemented as the use of game design elements like points and badges within AI-enhanced training systems that adaptively modify challenge levels and reward mechanisms according to individual learner progress and motivational states.

Hybrid Work Model: The hybrid work model is characterized by a work arrangement that combines remote and on-site activities, operationalized through digital collaboration tools and AI-powered systems that facilitate seamless communication, real-time data sharing, and flexible work scheduling.

Intelligent Tutoring Systems (ITS): ITS are defined as AI-driven platforms that deliver personalized, real-time instructional feedback and scaffolding by analyzing learner interaction patterns and performance indicators to modify pedagogical approaches as needed.

Predictive Analytics: Predictive analytics refers to the use of AI algorithms that process historical and real-time learner data—including engagement metrics and assessment outcomes—to forecast future performance trends and identify learners at risk of dropout within digital training environments.

Chapter 9
Augmented Decision-Making:
Leveraging AI for Strategic Agility and Innovation in Distributed Work Environments

R. N. Ravikumar
https://orcid.org/0009-0009-3705-1681
Marwadi University, Rajkot, India

S. Aarthi
https://orcid.org/0009-0006-9064-2091
Marwadi University, Rajkot, India

ABSTRACT

Artificial Intelligence (AI) is transforming strategic decision-making in distributed and hybrid workplaces by enhancing agility, innovation, and responsiveness. This chapter explores how AI-augmented systems combine data-driven insights and human cognition to support anticipatory and adaptive strategies. It examines frameworks for human-AI collaboration that reduce cognitive bias, improve ethical governance, and promote transparent decision ecosystems. Empirical insights reveal that AI dashboards, predictive analytics, and intelligent models accelerate innovation while ensuring accountability. The discussion emphasizes AI's role as a strategic enabler that amplifies human creativity rather than replacing it. By integrating algorithmic intelligence with ethical leadership, organizations can achieve sustainable agility, innovation, and resilience in an increasingly digital and decentralized environment.

DOI: 10.4018/979-8-3373-7416-1.ch009

1. INTRODUCTION

Artificial Intelligence (AI) has risen to become a disruptive force in the redefinition of operations, competition and innovations of organizations in the distributed and hybrid ecosystems. Due to the enhanced speed of the process of digital transformation, the decision-making process is no longer as intuitive and rather information-based and intelligence-enhanced. Being able to process extensive amounts of real-time data, AI will enable business leaders to respond to the disjointed shifts in the market even more efficiently and swiftly(Shi, 2025). The AI is a neuronal and bonding system applied in a hybrid workplace, where working teams are distributed geographically, and it involves the integration of analytics, automation, and human creativity. The chapter introduces a new approach to the use of AI systems in improving strategic agility, lessening uncertainty and maximizing cross-boundary collaboration, the concept of augmented decision-making appears. The chapter demonstrates in the prism of frameworks and evidence that in order to achieve sustainability in innovation and resiliency in distributed environments, organizations must establish symbiotic ecosystems to balance the human judgment and the algorithmic intelligence. (Kurter, 2025).

1.1. The Rise Of Ai-Augmented Decision Ecosystems

The combination of machine intelligence, human cognition and environmental awareness is referred to as AI based decision ecosystem. Such ecosystems implement the power of advanced analytics and Natural Language Processing and predictive models to deliver actionable data, which may be used to supplement strategic decision-making. When applied to AI, distributed organizations are in the position to have real-time coordination, thereby teams utilize cross-time zone and cross-operational choices which are well-informed (Valeriani et al., 2019). These systems convert the raw information into living knowledge systems that fosters transparency and intelligence in totality. The operations of decision making are changed to be continuous, flexible and futuristic with the help of AI and as the decision cycles decrease and the uncertainty increases in the background. Such ecosystems also possess ethical and interpretability components whereby there is the legitimate use of data-driven intelligence. (Yang & Jiang, 2024). An environment of efficiency is accompanied by creative and adaptive and innovative when the human being is put to task through the algorithmic accuracy and the creative drive of a human being. Therefore, AI-enhanced decision ecosystems re-architect the ways through which current enterprises learn, make and change decisions in complex, interconnected markets. Figure 1 demonstrates the ongoing process of data-driven decision-making, where AI combines data collection, data analysis, the creation of insights, decision implementation, and decision evaluation to make adaptive and informed strategic decisions.

Figure 1. AI-Augmented Decision Ecosystem Cycle

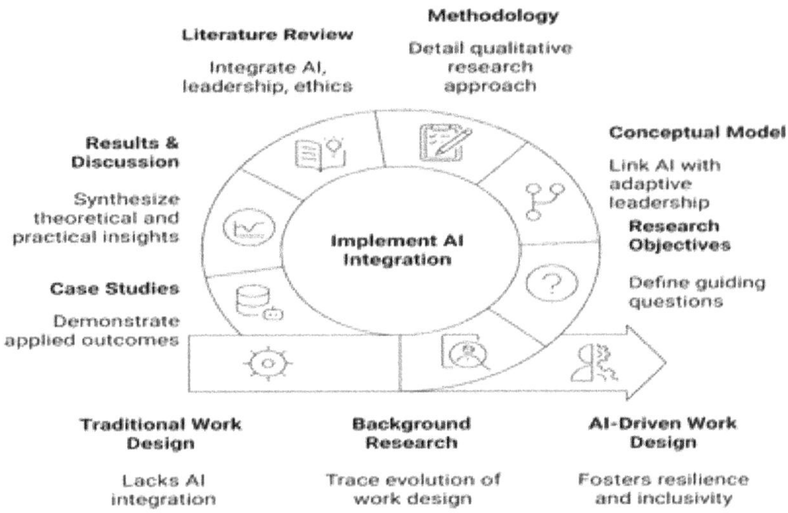

1.2. Relevance Of Strategic Agility In Distributed Workplaces

Agility in strategy, or the capacity to feel the opportunity and to be quick and inventive has become a key differentiator in distributed work environments. The hybrid and remote models necessitate quick coordination of the decisions at various teams and this necessitates smart systems that can improve visibility and responsiveness (Nadhira Putri & Mangundjaya, 2020). On the basis of predictive information, AI-based solutions make companies foresee market alterations, allocate resources and re-architect works dynamically, and allocate them. The simulation models and real-time analytics will enable the leaders to experiment with different solutions to the new tasks prior to its implementation to minimize the risks and make the most out of it. Moreover, AI increases cross-functional communication, i.e., decisions are aligned with the overall objectives even in geographically distant regions. Basically, strategic dynamism in distributed workplaces relies on the fact that AI is not to automatise as an agent but rather become something strategic, with its functions and strategic alignment and learning in an organisation (Faulconbridge et al., 2025). It creates a culture of proactivity whereby decisions are created in a cyclic fashion hence ensuring there is sustained competitiveness in the dynamic and technological business environment.

2. BACKGROUND TO THE STUDY

The context of the present research paper puts the idea of augmented decision-making in the background of the broader trail of the digital transformation and intelligence in the organization. Strategic decisions in the past were hierarchical, centralized and mostly responsive. However, globalization, teleworking, and diffusion of information have required more distributed, dynamic and proactive practices (Jiang, 2023). The architectural progress of AI, in particular, the Machine Learning, has changed the paradigm of processing data in a static condition to an active, dynamic, with decision-making one. This innovation is not just functional but it is also innovative because of the knowledge sharing and automation. According to the research, it suggests that all organizations are integrating AI-based insights at all levels of management and reinvent strategic responsiveness and responsibility (Saraiva, 2024). The background, thus, offers the theoretical and practical framework of the influence of AI technologies on the organization decision-making, the absence of gaps in the human to machine cooperation and a new stage of the strategic integrity in distributed organizations. The table 1 summarizes the historical path toward the development of organizational decision-making models that includes positive impacts of the AI on the human judgment and the promotion of the distributed strategic adaptability.

Table 1 Evolution of Decision-Making Models in Organizations

Decision-Making Model	Key Characteristics	Limitations	AI-Augmented Advancements
Traditional Hierarchical	Centralized, top-down decision authority	Slow adaptability and limited feedback loops	Integration of real-time analytics and distributed intelligence
Data-Driven Decision-Making	Relies on statistical reports and historical data	Retrospective focus and data silos	Predictive and prescriptive modeling for proactive insights
Collaborative Intelligence Model	Combines cross-functional human input	Cognitive bias and communication delays	AI-enabled dashboards and workflow automation enhance collaboration
AI-Augmented Decision Framework	Synergy of human cognition and algorithmic reasoning	Ethical and interpretability challenges	Transparent, explainable, and adaptive decision ecosystems

2.1. Evolution From Data-Driven To Intelligence-Augmented Decision Models

Previous organizational designs were based on data-driven decision-making, in which the knowledge was obtained through historical data using descriptive analytics. Although useful, these models were not contextual and could not be flexible. The emergence of AI was a major step towards the goal of the intelligence augmented decision systems, combining Cognitive Computing, Machine Learning, and Natural Language Processing to engage the unstructured data and facilitate predictive thinking (Siemon, 2022). These systems, as opposed to the traditional analytics, are able to learn behaviors based on trends, modify to emerging data, and predict the future to inform the strategic decisions. Decision making is thus not a static thing as it is a process that is iterative and anticipatory. In the case of intelligence augmentation, the capacity to make more precise insights and, furthermore, to make them more readable is enhanced and according to the organizational objectives (Lo Piano, 2020). The combination of computation and human presence in the AI-supported models converts the decision-making process into a shared one and ensures flexibility, precision, and sustainability of the long-term strategies in the constantly changing business environment. Figure 2 demonstrates how intelligence augmented decisions have been developed based on cognitive computing, Machine Learning, and Natural Language Processing to supplement the traditional based data driven decisions to enhance the responsiveness, accuracy, and strategy development.

Figure 2. Augmenting Decisions with AI

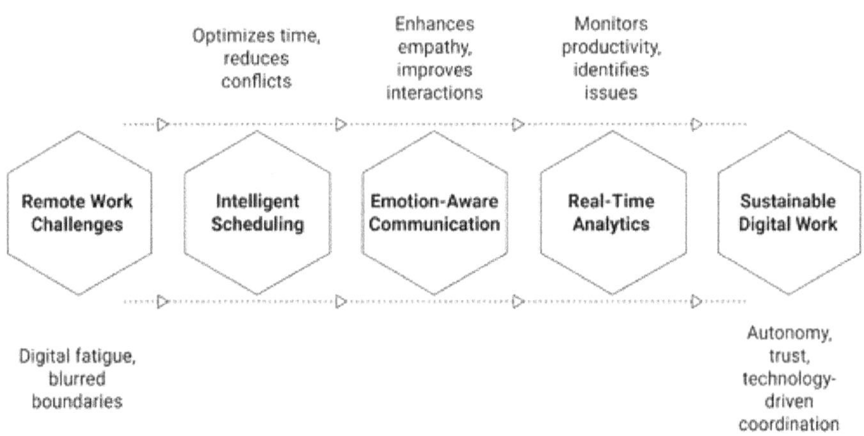

2.2. Transition From Centralized To Distributed Strategic Frameworks

The conventional models of strategies were founded on the top-down hierarchies where decisions were limited to the top managers and this often led to slow responses and information blockage. The digital age triggered by the remote working and globalization is compelling organizations to decentralize their authority and empower distant work teams. The AI technologies themselves are the ones that will be at the heart of this transition as they will offer real-time visibility, data synchronization, and intelligent suggestions between the organizational layers. Distributed frameworks capitalize on the AI dashboards, predictive applications, and collaborative applications that democratize the decision-making process and allows different stakeholders to simultaneously engage in the decision-making process (Zein, 2025). This decentralization promotes agility, creativity and accountability and eases cognitive burden of the executives. Also, AI ensures the presence of consistency between the local actions and global ambitions through adaptive feedback loops. Thus, the transformation of the control-based governance into the smart, participatory and responsive organizational ecosystems will be the necessary change of the strategic organization. (Seremeti & Anastasiadou, 2025).

3. RESEARCH OBJECTIVES

Here, the objective and the orientation of the analysis of the chapter is ascertained. It explains how Artificial Intelligence (AI) can make decision-makers operating in distributed workplaces strategic, innovative and operationally efficient. The research aims to determine the ways AI-based systems, including predictive analytics to cognitive dashboards, improve the decision-making ability of humans, minimize prejudices, and increase organizational responsiveness. This section establishes the basis of the study by identifying the clear aims and assumptions of the analysis of the transformative nature of AI in building data-driven, adaptable, and collaborative decision ecosystems in hybrid and remote organizational frameworks. The main objective of the proposed research is to examine the role of AI technologies in supporting augmented decision-making and innovation in the distributed work settings. It is based on the interaction between human thought and machine intelligence to empower agile, transparent, and ethical decision-making.

- To analyze the role of AI-driven analytics and recommendation systems in enhancing strategic agility within distributed organizations.

- To examine how augmented decision-making mitigates human cognitive biases and supports data-informed managerial actions.
- To develop a conceptual framework illustrating the integration of AI into strategic, operational, and creative decision layers.
- To evaluate the ethical, transparency, and accountability considerations involved in AI-assisted decision-making.
- To assess the empirical impact of AI-supported tools on innovation cycles, collaboration efficiency, and organizational responsiveness.

4. CONCEPTUAL MODEL

The theoretical framework provided in the specified chapter describes the way that the Artificial Intelligence (AI) would assist the human judgment, imagination, and tactical decision-making in the distributed organizational ecosystems. It puts a strain on symbiotic intercourse of human thinking and algorithmic thinking on which Human-AI joint intelligence depends (Basole and Bodner, 2015). The conceptualization of the model is based on the fact that the decision-making process is a dynamic cycle, and it includes the data gathering,allysis, human interpretation and feedback-based adjustment. It shows how AI systems will assist in facilitating predictive, prescriptive, and adaptive decision-making by converting data into actionable information. The distributed workplaces can use this model to introduce a certain degree of coordination and cohesiveness to the distributed teams since it introduces transparency and accountability in the overall decision flow (Ugwuja and Department of Management University of Nigeria Nigeria, 2024). The concept framework is not just ending at automation, but it is also interested in augmentation, which involves elements of ethical governance, explainability, and context-sensitivity, and in which the AI should not replace the human ability, agility, and organizational novelty. Table 2 Shows how data, human and algorithm control interact in a process of continuous learning in AI-enhanced decision-making.

Table 2 Core Components of the Human–AI Collaborative Decision Framework

Component	Core Function	Technological Example	Organizational Benefit
Data Layer	Aggregates structured and unstructured data sources	Data lakes, IoT, and ERP integration	Provides real-time situational awareness
Algorithmic Intelligence	Applies Machine Learning and predictive analytics	NLP, neural networks, and decision trees	Generates foresight and adaptive recommendations
Human Oversight	Interprets, validates, and governs AI outputs	Managerial dashboards and ethical audits	Ensures transparency, trust, and ethical compliance
Feedback Mechanism	Continuously refines algorithms based on results	Reinforcement learning loops	Improves decision accuracy and contextual learning

4.1. Framework Of Human–Ai Collaborative Decision-Making

The Human-AI collaborative decision making paradigm is the synthesis of technological intelligence and human intuition to facilitate adaptive, transparent and data-driven strategic processes. It is based on the idea that the best decisions are made when the process of exchanging between the computational accuracy and the judgment of the context is ongoing (Bagaa et al., 2021). The framework includes three steps: data assimilation, during which AI systems combine and process structured and unstructured information; cognitive augmentation, during which algorithms produce insights, simulate realities, and suggest solutions; and human validation, during which leaders review outputs in the aspects of organizations, ethics, and inventiveness. This cyclic relationship helps the human and the machine to mutually learn to enhance the interpretability and reliability of the decisions (Van der Watt, 2023). The framework gives freedom to international collaboration in distributed work settings by providing access to similar intelligence across digital platforms. It reduces the uncertainty and accelerates the response, and enhances capacity of innovation through shared abilities of analytical algorithms and human reasoning, which fosters robustness of dynamic and decentralized organizational systems. Figure 3 shows the interaction between AI systems and human leaders during the stages of data assimilation, cognitive enhancement and verification which help each other at the stages of learning, cross-border cooperation, and innovation.

Figure 3. Human–AI Collaborative Decision-Making Framework

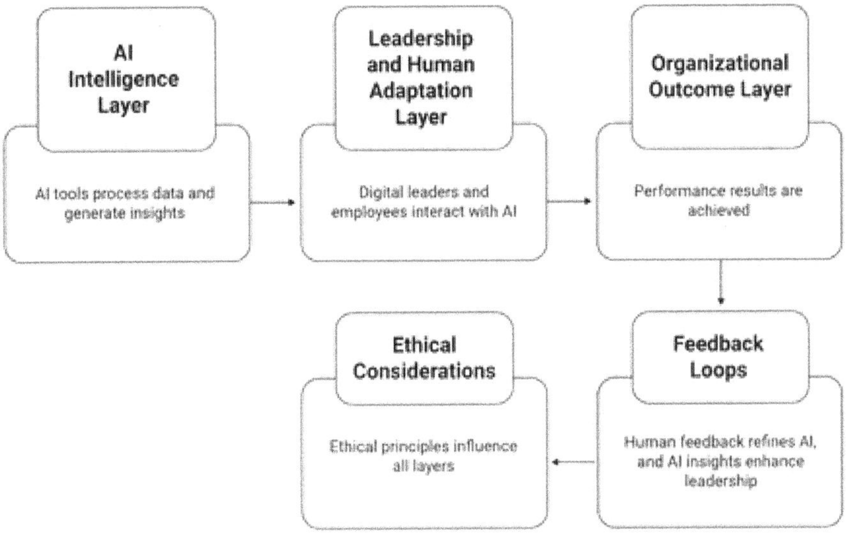

4.2. Model Components: Data, Algorithmic Intelligence, And Human Oversight

The proposed conceptual framework is composed of three elements that are connected and include data, algorithmic intelligence, and human control that are the aspects that ensure an effective organization of augmented decision-making. All the heterogeneous data, including internal and external ones such as the performance of an organization, market dynamics, and customer interactions, are based upon the data layer. This will ensure that the decision-making processes are factual and contextual. The layer of algorithmic intelligence represents an analysis core, which implements the methods of Machine Learning, Deep Learning, and Natural Language Processing to reveal the latent patterns, take predictions and propose measures of action (Dietvorst et al., 2018). It transforms unstructured data to organised intelligence which can be used in pre-emptive decision making. This anthropomorphic control layer provides the moral decision and interpretive purpose and situational approval to provide transparency, equity, and responsibility. The human professionals verify the outcomes of the algorithm with the organizational objectives, cultural principles, and social standards (Mishra and Pani, 2021). All these together constitute a feedback loop whereby humans and AI systems develop together, and lead to adaptive, responsible and innovation-driven strategic ecosystems (Ravikumar et al., 2025). Figure 4 Hypothesizes the integrated relationship between information, algorithmic intelligence and human oversight with reference given to the manner in which ethical AI and contextual verification generate valuable insights of data to make informed and accountable decisions.

Figure 4. The Synergy of Data, AI, and Human Oversight

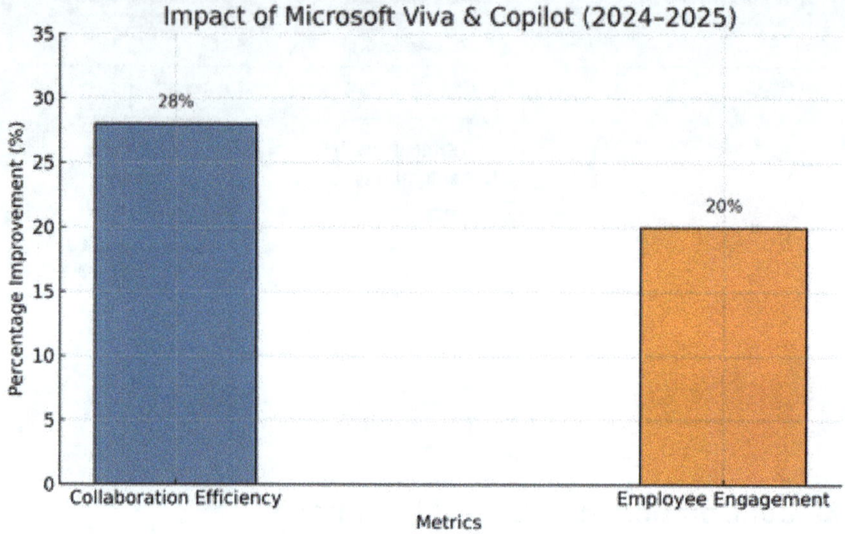

5. RESEARCH METHODOLOGY

The research design will be a mixed-method research design, which is a qualitative and quantitative-based study to examine how AI is able to enhance the strategic decision-making process in the context of distributed working settings. The qualitative data is received through the case study and interviews conducted with professionals in organizations that use AI-based management systems, and the quantitative data is received through the aid of surveys estimating the efficiency of decisions, rate of innovations, and responsiveness (Sajtos et al., 2024). Cross-sectoral organizations operating the distributed operations with the help of predictive analytics, recommendations systems, and AI dashboards are discussed. The result of human -AI collaboration practices of adaptive decision cycle and ethical governance are evaluated with a comparative analysis scheme (Costa & Ghosh, 2025). The same integrative approach also guarantees a certain degree of empirical richness and theoretical legitimacy and that a profound understanding of how augmented decision-making systems further agility, innovation and ethical integrity in hybrid and remote organizational context, would be achieved.

5.1. Design And Data Sources For Studying Distributed Decision Environments

The suggested research design might be characterized as the exploratory-descriptive research design that will be implemented to evaluate the degree of organizational integration of AI that is used to facilitate strategic agility and innovativeness in the distributed environment. The potential providers of the information include certain organization reports, electronic collaboration logs, and systematic surveys of management professionals that utilize decision tools that are run on AI. (Steyvers and Kumar, 2024). Furthermore, the semi-structured interviews have the possibility to provide information on the qualitative elements of how the managers perceive the use of AI in enhancing decisions. A purposive sampling technique focuses on large-scale or mid-sized businesses that have hybrid work systems. The design focuses on triangulation utilizing statistical measures of responsiveness with narrative data on the leadership behavior and cultural adaptation (Leoni et al., 2024). The multi-source methodology guarantees the accuracy of the context and the study can measure the measurable impact and experience the experiential aspect of AI-assisted decision-making in decentralized organizational ecosystems.

5.2. Analytical Tools And Techniques (AI Dashboards, Predictive Models, Metrics)

The combination of the tools of analysis based on highly developed AI and traditional statistical analysis is used in data analysis. Regression models and decision tree models are the most frequently used predictive models to determine the correlation between AI usage and strategic performance, including the rate of innovations, accuracy of decisions, and speed of responses (Rimon, 2024). The AIs dashboards represent the real-time trends in the performance of the decision-making, and the comparative insights could be made between the teams and departments. The qualitative interview data is processed using Natural Language Processing (NLP), which is used to extract themes associated with trust, transparency, and human-AI collaboration. Key performance indices, including agility index, innovation quotient and decision latency, are used to measure organizational adaptability (Liu et al., 2021). Each of these tools of analysis makes an informed evaluation of augmented decision-making to demonstrate how algorithmic intelligence and human control may enhance responsiveness, coherence, and innovation capacity of distributed decision making.

6. LITERATURE REVIEW

The growing significance of the concept of Artificial Intelligence (AI) to the very process of decision-making in organization is also echoed in the amount of scholarly literature dedicated to this matter. Throughout the last ten years, AI has been turned into an analytical system and a strategic facilitator capable of improving the thinking process of managers, creating cross-functional work, and accelerating the process of innovation (Burton et al., 2020). On the one hand, AI-based decision systems bridge the gap between the human intuition and non-subjective reasoning because they provide more reliable and fast answers to the unpredictability of the environment. Artificial intelligence represents an infrastructure of cognition connecting distributed teams, working across different geographies and time zones, to adopt predictive analytics and Natural Language Processing (NLP) and recommendation engines in order to make coordinated and transparent decisions (Bao et al., 2023).

The strategic agility study concentrates on the intelligence of AI in boosting the sensory, seizing and reshaping the proficiencies of companies. The real-time monitoring of the market indicators, consumer moods, and operation risks will guarantee that the decision-makers will be able to alter the line of action in a short period of time (Management Information System Lamar University USA. & Chebrolu, 2025). The Machine Learning models are able to, e.g., detect the irregularities, forecast the potential situations and propose the adaptive strategies that is in line with the long-term goals. It is an attribute in augmented intelligence because the process of making decisions is no longer reactive but proactive (Rathinavel et al., 2025). Research also demonstrates the condition of AI dashboards and predictive modelling devices in enhancing the managerial consciousness and reactiveness by converting the quantities of intricate data into information that can be acted on (Raisch & Krakowski, 2020). It has been demonstrated by companies such as IBM, Google and Microsoft that it can be done though cognitive computing systems to optimize the strategic allocation of resources and risk management in hybrid and remote environments.

Besides agility, the adaptive management body of literature suggests that AI can facilitate never-ending learning within organizations since it offers an ecosystem that is driven by feedback. When it comes to AI-based decision-making, adaptive management, which is commonly used in the sphere of environmental and project management are frequently observed as the methods that imply using the data and the changing circumstances to adapt the approaches (Shrestha et al., 2019). With these systems, leaders are able to test hypotheses, quantify outcomes and make better future decisions through algorithmic learning. As an example, decision paths are modeled according to reinforcement learning models with multiple constraints so that the managers can determine the implication before the implementation. This is in conformity with the theory of knowledge creation within an organization proposed by Nonaka in which AI is a facilitator of transformation of tacit knowledge to explicit, and data-driven insights that can enhance the intelligence and the creativity of the institution (Murray et al., 2021).

Cognitive bias reduction via intelligent system is also an element of a critical flow of research. The human decisions leading to the sub-optimal outcomes are likely to be biased with the help of such bias as confirmation, anchoring, and overconfidence. When properly designed, the biases could be minimized with the help of ethical and transparent AI systems that would provide objective analyses and evidence-based recommendations. SHAP (SHapley Additive explanations) and LIME (Local Interpretable Model-Agnostic Explanations) model are examples that explain the model predictions, therefore, allowing the interpretation of predictions, removing over-reliance on intuition (Ameen, Pagani, et al., 2024). Moreover, Explainable AI (XAI) facilitates accountability since it outlines the steps that algorithmic recommendations are made, and managers have the opportunity to think of their soundness before making them. The studies also indicate that the better the results of decisions and relationships with stakeholders are in any organization, the more it incorporates objectivity generated by AI and supervised by humans.

The recent scholarly debate is also concerned with ethical and managerial issues of AI-powered decision systems. Even though automation is an effective method, its uncontrolled implementation can cause an algorithmic bias, the disappearance of privacy, and the ruin of the human agency (Chen et al., 2024). Thus, the balance between the accuracy of the algorithms and the comprehension of the human mind can be achieved and be considered as the effective way of decision augmentation. An equal measure, ethics audit and a participatory governance structure are needed in the incorporation of fairness metrics in making AI adoption accountable. Among the literature, there is a common drive that augmented decision-making is not intended to automatize the processes, but to boost collective intelligence, i.e. pooling the knowledge of the data, with moral relativism, creativity and strategy (Lancaster et al., 2024).

In conclusion, the existing literature demonstrates that AI-based decisions systems render organizations more dynamic, responsive, and less biased with cognitive distortions in complex environments. However, it will be successful in its implementation as the technological capability will be supported with the ethical governance and human-centered design (Ediriweera et al., 2025). The combination of these studies forms the intellectual foundation of this chapter that will talk about augmented decision-making as an enabler of strategy in the distributed workplaces and how human judgment, algorithmic reasoning, and the continuous learning interrelate to the achievement of sustainable innovation and competitive advantage.

7. RESULTS / DISCUSSION

The findings underscore the fact that organizations that implement AI-enhanced decision-making frameworks are observable to gain agility, innovation, and coordination in the distributed teams. According to empirical evidence, AI has been found to positively impact the real-time collaboration, decrease in the decision latency, and knowledge sharing across departments . With predictive analytics and smart dashboards, leaders can be able to foresee risks and opportunities and keep their strategies aligned with market forces (Ali & Rafi, 2024). Additionally, AI-based systems also help to enhance the process of innovation by expediting the idea validation and resource optimization process. Both the quantitative measures (agility index, decision accuracy and innovation throughput) and qualitative opinions based on managerial interviews are incorporated in the discussion. All the findings in unison affirm that organizations that adopt AI as a collaborative ally and not a substitute to the human rationale are more adaptive and responsive (Vartiainen et al., 2022). This section therefore forms the empirical basis of the influence of augmented intelligence in boosting the degree of coherence, transparency, and performance in distributed and hybrid work set ups. Table 3 Shows the principal differences between the process of decision-making with the traditional and AI help and introduces the measurable positive outcomes of greater speed, innovation, and ethical leadership.

Table 3 Comparative Analysis of Traditional vs. AI-Augmented Decision-Making

Dimension	Traditional Approach	AI-Augmented Approach	Observed Impact
Decision Speed	Sequential and time-intensive	Real-time predictive and adaptive	30–40% faster response rate
Accuracy and Reliability	Prone to intuition and data lag	Based on evidence and predictive models	Higher precision and consistency
Collaboration	Limited by hierarchy and silos	Enabled through shared AI dashboards	Enhanced transparency and teamwork
Innovation	Incremental and reactive	Continuous and data-driven	Accelerated innovation cycle
Ethical Oversight	Subjective human checks	Explainable AI with audit trails	Strengthened accountability

7.1. Empirical Insights From AI-Augmented Enterprises

The findings of empirical research performed on AI-enhanced companies indicate that strategic flexibility and decision-making speed increase significantly in case smart systems are embraced. The companies which implemented AI-based dashboards and cognitive analytics state that the time of decision making will be decreased by 25-40 percent and the innovation rates will also increase greatly. These systems might enable the leaders to compare the alternative strategies, simulate the market, and identify the most appropriate courses of actions (Ameen, Tarba, et al., 2024). According to qualitative data, managers consider AI tools as partners of the mind that increase creativity and reduce the uncertainty of operations. In addition, those companies that work with human-AI co-decision making are more ethically governed and have more trust among stakeholders. The data visualization and predictive modeling tools contribute to the increase of the level of transparency and help the teams make evidence-based decisions together. The case study of technology and healthcare will reveal that AI minimizes resource wastage and enhances real time responsiveness. Overall, the results of empirical research testify to the fact that AI-enhanced businesses are more responsive, inventive, and consistent in their distributed operations management.

7.2. Discussion: Enhancing Innovation And Responsiveness Through Augmented Intelligence

It has been discussed that augmented intelligence simplifies the decision-making process, as well as fosters odwalla innovation and responsiveness. Organizational change that is dynamically responded to according to emerging challenges is an ability instilled to organizations through the integration of algorithmic intelligence with human contextual perceptions. The AI promotes creativity as it presents alternative views that are founded on the pattern recognition and simulation modelling in which the leaders can experiment on new methods (Upadhyay, 2025). Instead of being reactive in the way things are made to happen, forecast intelligence is altering the system of planning and making things happen proactively. Besides, augmented systems are useful in encouraging communication within hybrid environments by aligning cross-functional teams. Explainable AI ensures that decisions reached are comprehensible, clear and ethical based. The decision environments are also more stable, participatory, progressive because of human and machine collaboration. Hence, augmented intelligence will be a radically enabling source of innovation, organizational agility, and strategic responsiveness to design sustainable competitiveness in distributed work environments that evolve rapidly. (Lu et al., 2024).

8. FUTURE RESEARCH

Even though the outcomes of AI-aided decision-making have been favorable, further research is required to better understand how this problem can affect the issue of innovation, ethics, and governance in the long term. The existing literature does not address the gaps in the knowledge regarding scalability, the adaptability, and the socio-technical impacts within a complex organizational ecosystem, and focuses on the short-term benefits of the technologies. Follow-up research should examine cross-industry variations and culture-related issues on the acceptance of AI and its success in a distributed set-up (Chen et al., 2024). Besides that, longitudinal research will be in a position to demonstrate how the collaboration between humans and AI is evolving over the years and its effects on the leadership and staffing environments. The other aspect that could be investigated is the measurement of the augmented decision capital- the sum knowledge that has been established due to human-machine synergy. The gaps can be resolved to allow the investigation in future to refine the current framework and design models to be of ethical, operationally scalable and contextually responsive of the changing technological and organizational paradigms.

8.1. Next-Generation Research Pathways For AI-Enabled Decision Ecosystems

The evolution of future of the field of multi-layered decision ecosystems must entail the integration of AI, human thinking, and organizational learning in one strategic platforms. Researchers can study the way reinforcement learning, causal inference and real-time analytics can enhance adaptive decisions in teams that are distributed. Continuing the works on the behavioral and managerial theories, it is also possible to consider that in future studies, the impact of AI on transforming leadership styles, responsibility and team autonomy can be assessed (Al Qadiri et al., 2024; Shams Eldin et al., 2025; Almanbahi et al., 2025; Wahid & Awad, 2025; Qadeer & Awad, 2025). It is also possible to apply the cross-cultural comparison to illuminate how ethical and governance standards can impact the trends in the adoption of AI in other regions. The quality of AI-based decisions can be empirically supported through the creation of the standard metrics, such as the decision agility index, the explainability score, and the innovation latency. In addition, interdisciplinary research of integrating cognitive science with data ethics and strategic management would improve theoretical models (Wen et al., 2025). Lastly, future studies need to consider the human-centered and ethically-oriented design of AI that would facilitate trust, innovativeness and stability in digital businesses.

8.2. Integration With Emerging Technologies (Quantum, Edge, And Federated Systems)

The next phase of augmented decision-making studies will be the implementation of new technologies, such as quantum computing, edge AI, and federated learning. It is the quantum computing that promises to make the exponential growth in speed and optimization to simulate scenarios and model decisions under uncertainties in a fast manner. The Edge AI software provides real-time low-latency decision support on an edge of data generation and it has the ability to enhance responsiveness in remote and hybrid workplaces. The proposed federated learning is a privacy-friendly variant of collaboration that enables training the models using decentralized data sets and alleviates ethical and regulatory restrictions (TECHNOLOGY et al., 2025;). The potential structures of such technologies in the future can establish very dynamic, safe, and open decision systems. The researchers should consider how this interoperability of such systems can be used to improve distributed intelligence and an ethical governance of data. This convergence of technologies will rearrange AI-enhanced strategy, and make decision-making a decentralized, smart, and ethically correct business process. Figure 5 Visualizes the stratified processes of the adaptive decision ecosystems bridging with federated learning, edge AI and quantum computing, and their contribution to secure, real-time and high-speed intelligent decision processes.

Figure 5. Emerging Technologies in Decision-Making

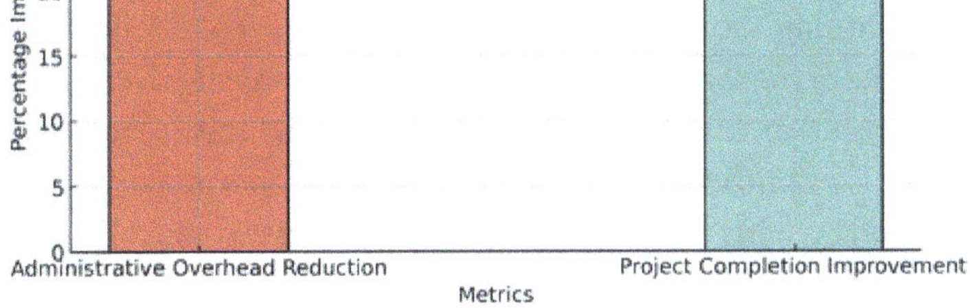

8.3 Anticipating The Next Generation Of Adaptive Decision Ecosystems

The further development of the AI-based decision-making process will be defined by intelligent ecosystems that can learn on their own, think situational, and collaborate in real-time on digital platforms. These systems will integrate multimodal intelligence which is a synthesis of text, vision, Speech and sensor information in order to provide a holistic view concerning dynamic business environments. Unlike the non-dynamic models of decision, adaptive ecosystems will continuously adapt and improve their strategies during the feedback processes in reaction to the user intervention and changes in the environment (H. Guan et al., 2022). The synergy of the technologies of edge AI, digital twins and quantum optimization will contribute to the force of predictive precision and operational foresight. The roles of human will will be data interpreters, who have become architects of strategy, and who have control over AI, according to ethical, creative, and contextual reasoning. The ability to be flexible, open-minded, and sustainable will be an overpowering competitive advantage in the organizations that have adopted such points. These ecosystems will eventually change the decision-making process as a linear process into a resilient, inclusive and strategically intelligent living and learning cycle in the long-run in a world of ever-increasing uncertainty. (Yin, 2024).

9. MANAGERIAL IMPLICATIONS

The managerial implications of the research indicate the importance of how the leaders are supposed to exploit the AI in optimising the quality of decisions, agility and ethical responsibility of a distributed organisation. The process will demand refreezing of the future variant of leadership i.e. not dominating but collaborative and human experience and machine intelligence can co-exist to create Ai enhanced decision-making. Managers should create an environment where transparency, trusting on facts and learning should be promoted in every level of decision making (Souza et al., 2024). The organizational design must involve ethical governance, algorithmic accountability, and inclusiveness to ensure there is no misuse and prejudice. Also, managers are also significant in developing the workforce preparedness by reskilling and digital literacy. This is true since at the point where the AI becomes a decision partner, then it is necessary that organizations find a balance between automation and empathy in which technological accuracy can supplement human creativity and ethical judgment (Sauer & Burggräf, 2025). The accountable adoption, agreement of the governance and long-term human-machine partnership is the basis of the AI era of managerial performance. Table 4 Provides management action plans to create a balance between AI-sensitive efficiency and ethical management and human invention in distributed organizations.

Table 4 Managerial Strategies for Ethical and Agile AI Integration

Strategic Domain	Recommended Managerial Action	Implementation Approach	Expected Outcome
Ethical Governance	Establish AI ethics committees and audit protocols	Regular compliance reviews and explainability reports	Builds trust and mitigates algorithmic bias
Digital Competence	Upskill workforce in AI literacy and analytics	Continuous learning and AI-readiness programs	Enhances adaptability and innovation readiness
Collaborative Infrastructure	Deploy intelligent dashboards and shared knowledge systems	Integrate AI-assisted project management tools	Improves coordination across distributed teams
Leadership Adaptation	Transition from command-based to data-driven leadership	Encourage participative and transparent decision culture	Strengthens inclusivity and employee engagement
Continuous Evaluation	Implement performance analytics and feedback systems	Real-time monitoring and algorithmic audits	Maintains agility and accountability

9.1. Governance And Ethical Leadership In AI-Enabled Decision Systems

Ethical leadership and governance are the key to the accountability and transparency of AI-driven decision systems. Managers should adopt the use of ethical AI structures that focus on fairness, explainability, as well as accountability across the decision pipeline. The creation of AI governance boards, ethical audit trails and the data oversight committees can ensure the integrity of organizations and reduce the risks of the algorithmic bias or the abuse of data (J. Guan, 2019). The leaders should be the first to behave ethically by incorporating ethical reasoning in the decisions made by the AI to make sure that the results comply with the social and corporate values. Also, autonomy within the algorithmic procedures contributes to the trust of the employees and other stakeholders, especially in the distributed surroundings when the autonomy of decisions is shared. Institutionalization of training programs on AI ethics and regulatory compliance must be done in preparation of decision-makers to handle intricate socio-technical problems (Winfield & Jirotka, 2018). Finally, the ethical governance will convert AI adoption to a strategic leadership role, which strengthens the credibility, equity, and responsibility of intelligent organizations.

9.2. Strategies For Fostering Human–AI Synergy And Organizational Agility

In order to reach the synergy of the human cognition and the AI systems, the deliberate managerial decisions are expected to assist in the collaboration, flexibility, as well as innovation. The leaders ought to work on the processes where AI undertakes accuracy in analysis and human beings come up with context, empathy and foresight. Such a balance will render the outcome of the decisions effective and morally correct. Real-time coordination of distributed teams is enhanced by the application of AI-enhanced collaboration tools such as knowledge management systems and smart dashboards (Harfouche et al., 2023). The managers are expected to build a culture of life-long learning, which encourages employees to become the co-crafters of AI systems rather than the rivals. Organizations can be resilient in the face of uncertainty with the help of Agile leadership frameworks, which demand the essence of experimentation, iterative feedback, and digital empowerment. Also, the promotion of data-driven thinking and inter-disciplinary collaboration can accelerate the innovation process. Formalised human-AI synergy will facilitate the degree of strategic responsiveness within the organization because responsiveness, inclusivity, and creativity will result in long-term performance in the rapidly emerging digital ecosystems (Brynjolfsson, 2022).

10. CONCLUDING REFLECTIONS AND POLICY IMPLICATIONS

The meeting of Artificial Intelligence (AI), human cognition and data ecosystem is transforming the strategic principles of organizational decision making. Since artificial intelligence is evolving and is more than just an analytical instrument to a strategic partner, policymakers, leaders, and institutions ought to ensure technological innovations are ethical and socially responsible (Thakur et al., 2024). The chapter ends with the statement of two high-level imperatives that are policy alignment and sustainability. The regulatory policies should not be confined to the regulation of the scope of AI but should aim to provide support to innovations by making sure that it embraces fairness, inclusiveness, and transparency. At the same time, humanistic and sustainable utilization of AI needs to be steered towards achieving the long-run benefit of the society, morally regulated utilization of AI, and fair utilization of the digital infrastructure. The organizations will be forced to create a balance between the efficiency of automation and moral responsibility in the sense that human supervision must be a component and part of all the decision-making processes that are vital. The questions of governance and sustainability intersections are the solution to the AI-enhanced strategy, which helps companies to resilient, responsible, and human-centred decision ecosystems to help innovation without reputation and accountability loss. (Jobin et al., 2019).

10.1 Policy Recommendations For AI-Driven Decision Ecosystems

Powerful and innovative policy statements have an essential role to play in managing the ethical use of AI in both the strategic and decentralized decision environment. The policy makers need to make sure that regulation should not be stifling innovation but it ought to spearhead the same since it must be open, equal and inclusive. The governments can enhance ethical AI by formulating regulations that are connected with the data protection, algorithm auditing, and certification regimes which certifies the responsible use of AI. It is necessary to make the industries and regulating bodies collaborate with the academic world and permit free research and sharing of information between the industries (Bazoukis et al., 2022). Moreover, the policies will also cultivate the Explainable AI (XAI), the minimization of bias and sustainability of the developed algorithms which will make people accountable and trustworthy of the algorithm. The initiatives to promote the responsible AI schemes such as grants, exemption of taxes and compliance recognition can further increase adaptation to the responsible AI schemes. It is important to note that the regulatory ecosystems must be dynamic and they must evolve with the change in technology in order to balance between innovation and regulation integrity. Such measures would be able to contribute to ensuring that AI is not a regulation issue but a strategy that would promote ethical superiority and competitive edge of new digital economies.

10.2 Building A Sustainable And Human-Centric Decision Future

The AI-assisted decision making image is supposed to take the long-term view and distribute the efficiency score to the inclusiveness, ethical sensitivity and social development spheres. Sustainable-decision ecosystem balances technological perception to an anthropological perception in such a manner that AI augments, but does not replace the human cognitive perception. The reason is that any algorithm process has to involve human values of fairness, transparency, and responsibility in organizations. This should be promoted by promoting adaptive and ethical decision-making environments by favouring eternal learning societies and digital literacy on all levels. Moreover, one will be required to work internationally in order to eradicate the disparity in the access to AI and create equal opportunities in the digital economy (Aarthi et al., 2025). Sustainable AI programs should also include the list of the Environmental and Social Governance (ESG) activities in order to ensure that a full sense of responsibility is implemented. Even-handed technological innovation can offer organizations the opportunity to create intelligent ecosystems that are not only resilient to operation but also transformative of the society such as the abilities of successive generations to make choices in the interests of well-being, uprightness and collective sustainability in an interconnected online world.

11. CONCLUSION

The paper concludes that the AI-enhanced decision-making is a radical change in the establishment of strategic agility, innovation, and ethical governance in the spread and hybrid organizations. The human intuition and algorithmic intelligence is a synergetic model which can be applied to help in quicker, correct and context proportional decision making. During the discussion, it can be noted that AI systems can help organizations abandon their reactive reaction to the decision-making process and enter the predictive analytics, intelligent dashboards and cognitive modelling. Not only does it raise the level, or degree of responsiveness to operations, but it builds a culture of innovation and lifelong learning in the dispersed teams. The empirical evidence shows that business organizations, which adopt AI-based decision support systems are bound to have high efficiency, transparency, and innovation rates.

The results support the fact that AI is applicable in the process of increasing the value of managerial decisions by shrinking the effects of cognitive biases and providing multi-dimensional insights that are backed up with the data-based reasoning. In addition to that, AI tools give an opportunity to collaborate in the real-time setting, as well as to align the local and global strategies which play a key role in distributed working conditions. The theoretical value of the research is an idea of human-AI collaboration introduced in the study as it indicates the equilibrium of the information, algorithmic intelligence, and human control. The above triple model is the concept that AI is not meant to be a supreme control over the human mind but instead, it is supposed to be complimentary to the human mind to ensure that the ethical and interpretive aspects of decision-making remain marginal. To an extent, it is suggested that the ethical governance systems, transparency systems, and participatory decision-making systems should be adopted by the organizations in the actual implementation of AI systems. Leadership is one of the primary elements in the management of the human machine synergy to ensure that proper policies are implemented, unlimited reskilling programme is implemented and practises of innovation that are inclusive are practiced.

Besides that, explainability and accountability maintain AI processes to build organizational confidence and adherence to regulatory requirements, especially when working with sensitive information. Finally, there is the augmented decision-making process, which is the other element that establishes the culture of a resilient and future-ready business in which the human creativity is complemented with the technological intelligence. Seeing that remote and hybrid work organization is the future, the businesses that will adopt AI actively in their decision-making systems will have an opportunity of enjoying a competitive advantage in the long term. This is moving to much more decentralized, ethically oriented and cognitively defined work places, as an innovation strength, agility and responsible leadership in the changing digital economy AI as a strategic co-producer.

12. REFERENCES

Aarthi, S., Ravikumar, R. N., Sobirova, K., & Mamadiyarov, Z. (2025). Empowering a sustainable future through digital learning and the SDGs. In *Harnessing E-Learning to Create a Sustainable Future* (pp. 145–172). IGI Global Scientific Publishing., DOI: 10.4018/979-8-3373-0112-9.ch006

Al Qadiri, W. M., Alkaf, M., & Supratikta, H. (2024). Analyzing the Impact of Artificial intelligence (AI) on Decision-Making Strategies. Journal of Investment Development. *Economics and Accounting*, *1*(2), 182–190. DOI: 10.70001/jidea.v1i2.221

Ali, A., & Rafi, D. N. (2024). Enhancing human resource management through advanced decision-making strategies: Harnessing the power of artificial intelligence for strategic, data-driven, and judicious choices. *Migration Letters : An International Journal of Migration Studies*, *21*(S8), 881–889. DOI: 10.59670/ml.v21iS8.9488

Almanbahi, F. S., Awad, A., Ghonim, A., Alabsy, N. M., & Shemais, M. (2025). Ethical leadership and organizational excellence: The mediating role of citizenship behavior in healthcare. *Humanities & Social Sciences Communications*, *12*(1), 1392. DOI: 10.1057/s41599-025-05743-6

Ameen, N., Pagani, M., Pantano, E., Cheah, J.-H., Tarba, S., & Xia, S. (2024). The rise of human–machine collaboration: Managers' perceptions of leveraging artificial intelligence for enhanced B2B service recovery. *British Journal of Management*. Advance online publication. DOI: 10.1111/1467-8551.12829

Ameen, N., Tarba, S., Cheah, J.-H., Xia, S., & Sharma, G. D. (2024). Coupling artificial intelligence capability and strategic agility for enhanced product and service creativity. *British Journal of Management*, *35*(4), 1916–1934. Advance online publication. DOI: 10.1111/1467-8551.12797

Bagaa, M., Taleb, T., Riekki, J., & Song, J. (2021). Collaborative cross system AI: Toward 5G system and beyond. *IEEE Network*, *35*(4), 286–294. DOI: 10.1109/MNET.011.2000607

Bao, Y., Gong, W., & Yang, K. (2023). A literature review of human–AI synergy in decision making: From the perspective of affordance actualization theory. *Systems*, *11*(9), 442. DOI: 10.3390/systems11090442

Basole, R. C., & Bodner, D. A. (2015). Computational modeling of complex enterprise systems: A multi-level approach. In *Modeling and Simulation in the Systems Engineering Life Cycle* (pp. 369–381). Springer London., DOI: 10.1007/978-1-4471-5634-5_28

Bazoukis, G., Hall, J., Loscalzo, J., Antman, E. M., Fuster, V., & Armoundas, A. A. (2022). The inclusion of augmented intelligence in medicine: A framework for successful implementation. *Cell Reports Medicine*, *3*(1), 100485. DOI: 10.1016/j.xcrm.2021.100485 PMID: 35106506

Brynjolfsson, E. (2022). The Turing trap: The promise & peril of human-like artificial intelligence. *Daedalus*, *151*(2), 272–287. DOI: 10.1162/daed_a_01915

Burton, J. W., Stein, M.-K., & Jensen, T. B. (2020). A systematic review of algorithm aversion in augmented decision making. *Journal of Behavioral Decision Making*, *33*(2), 220–239. DOI: 10.1002/bdm.2155

Chebrolu, S. K.Management Information System Lamar University USA. (2025). Ai-powered business intelligence: A systematic literature review on the future of decision-making in enterprises. *American Journal of Scholarly Research and Innovation*, *4*(01), 33–62. DOI: 10.63125/gq69nv41

Chen, J.-F., Ni, C.-C., Lin, P.-H., & Lin, R. (2024). Designing the future: A case study on human-AI co-innovation. *Creative Education*, *15*(03), 474–494. DOI: 10.4236/ce.2024.153028

Costa, C., & Ghosh, S. (2025). Empowering customer service with generative AI: enhancing agent performance while navigating challenges. Information Research, 30(iConf), 150–158. DOI: 10.47989/ir30iConf47566

de Souza, L. A., de Barros, M. J. F., & Melo, P. (2024). How management information systems might add value to the decision-making process in organizations. Journal on Innovation and Sustainability RISUS ISSN 2179-3565, 15(1), 62–70. DOI: 10.23925/2179-3565.2023v15i1p62-70

Dietvorst, B. J., Simmons, J. P., & Massey, C. (2018). Overcoming algorithm aversion: People will use imperfect algorithms if they can (even slightly) modify them. *Management Science*, *64*(3), 1155–1170. DOI: 10.1287/mnsc.2016.2643

Ediriweera, Pramudika, & Fernando. (. (2025). The influence of AI-driven marketing analytics on strategic decision-making in private educational institutes in Sri Lanka: Moderator role of organisational culture. *Asian Journal of Marketing Management*, *4*(2). Advance online publication. DOI: 10.31357/ajmm.v4i2.7970

Faulconbridge, J., Sarwar, A., & Spring, M. (2025). How professionals adapt to artificial intelligence: The role of intertwined boundary work. *Journal of Management Studies*, *62*(5), 1991–2024. DOI: 10.1111/joms.12936

Guan, H., Dong, L., & Zhao, A. (2022). Ethical risk factors and mechanisms in artificial intelligence decision making. *Behavioral Sciences (Basel, Switzerland)*, *12*(9), 343. DOI: 10.3390/bs12090343 PMID: 36135147

Guan, J. (2019). Artificial intelligence in healthcare and medicine: Promises, ethical challenges and governance. Chung-Kuo i Hsueh k'o Hsueh Tsa Chih. *Chinese Medical Sciences Journal*, *34*(2), 76–83. DOI: 10.24920/003611 PMID: 31315747

Harfouche, A., Quinio, B., & Bugiotti, F. (2023). Human-centric AI to mitigate AI biases. *Journal of Global Information Management*, *31*(5), 1–23. DOI: 10.4018/JGIM.331755

Jiang, W. (2023). Enhancing operational efficiency in E-commerce through artificial intelligence and information management integration. *Revue d Intelligence Artificielle*, *37*(6), 1545–1555. DOI: 10.18280/ria.370619

Jobin, A., Ienca, M., & Vayena, E. (2019). The global landscape of AI ethics guidelines. *Nature Machine Intelligence*, *1*(9), 389–399. DOI: 10.1038/s42256-019-0088-2

Kurter, O. (2025). The use of artificial intelligence for decision-making process for strategic management. *OPUS Journal of Society Research*, *22*(2), 195–210. DOI: 10.26466/opusjsr.1632110

Lancaster, C., Gilreath, H., Mallick, R., & McNeese, N. J. (2024). Evaluating cross-training's impact on perceived teaming outcomes for human-AI teams. Proceedings of the Human Factors and Ergonomics Society ... Annual Meeting. Human Factors and Ergonomics Society. Annual Meeting, 68(1), 1469–1472. DOI: 10.1177/10711813241262033

Leoni, L., Gueli, G., Ardolino, M., Panizzon, M., & Gupta, S. (2024). AI-empowered KM processes for decision-making: Empirical evidence from worldwide organisations. *Journal of Knowledge Management*, *28*(11), 320–347. DOI: 10.1108/JKM-03-2024-0262

Liu, N., Shapira, P., Yue, X., & Guan, J. (2021). Mapping technological innovation dynamics in artificial intelligence domains: Evidence from a global patent analysis. *PLoS One*, *16*(12), e0262050. DOI: 10.1371/journal.pone.0262050 PMID: 34972173

Lo Piano, S. (2020). Ethical principles in machine learning and artificial intelligence: Cases from the field and possible ways forward. *Humanities & Social Sciences Communications*, *7*(1), 9. Advance online publication. DOI: 10.1057/s41599-020-0501-9

Lu, Z., Amin Mahmoo, S. H., Li, Z., & Yin, M. (2024). Mix and Match: Characterizing heterogeneous human behavior in AI-assisted decision making. *Proceedings of the AAAI Conference on Human Computation and Crowdsourcing*, 12, 95–104. DOI: 10.1609/hcomp.v12i1.31604

Mishra, A. N., & Pani, A. K. (2021). Business value appropriation roadmap for artificial intelligence. *VINE Journal of Information and Knowledge Management Systems*, *51*(3), 353–368. DOI: 10.1108/VJIKMS-07-2019-0107

Murray, A., Rhymer, J., & Sirmon, D. G. (2021). Humans and technology: Forms of conjoined agency in organizations. *Academy of Management Review*, *46*(3), 552–571. DOI: 10.5465/amr.2019.0186

Nadhira Putri, D., & Mangundjaya, W. (2020). Examining the effects of organizational learning on workforce agility through psychological empowerment. *Open Journal for Psychological Research*, *4*(2), 85–94. DOI: 10.32591/coas.ojpr.0402.02085n

Qadeer, A., & Awad, A. (2025). Generative AI in advertisements: A conceptual framework based on the technology acceptance model. In *Impacts of AI generated content on brand reputation* (pp. 109–127). IGI Global., DOI: 10.4018/979-8-3373-4327-3.ch004

Raisch, S., & Krakowski, S. (2020). Artificial intelligence and management: The automation-augmentation paradox. Academy of Management Review, 2018.0072. DOI: 10.5465/2018.0072

Rathinavel, P., Ravikumar, R. N., Aarthi, S., Habib, M., Salaeva, N., & Pardaev, J. (2025). Augmenting human capabilities. In *Advances in Computational Intelligence and Robotics* (pp. 1–30). IGI Global Scientific Publishing., DOI: 10.4018/979-8-3373-2372-5.ch001

Ravikumar, R. N., Aarthi, S., Sapaeva, B., Jumaniyozov, Y., Manoj Praveen, V., & Siddheswaran, V. (2025). Revolutionizing education with NLP and ML. In *Advances in Computational Intelligence and Robotics* (pp. 293–324). IGI Global Scientific Publishing., DOI: 10.4018/979-8-3373-6791-0.ch011

Rimon, S. M. T. H. (2024). Leveraging Artificial Intelligence in business analytics for informed strategic decision-making: Enhancing operational efficiency, market insights, and competitive advantage. Journal of Artificial Intelligence General Science (JAIGS) ISSN:3006-4023, 6(1), 600–624. DOI: 10.60087/jaigs.v6i1.278

Sajtos, L., Wang, S., Roy, S., & Flavián, C. (2024). Guest editorial: Collaborating and sharing with AI: a research agenda. *Journal of Service Theory and Practice*, *34*(1), 1–6. DOI: 10.1108/JSTP-01-2024-324

Saraiva, L. (2024). Moral agency and responsibility in AI systems. *International Journal of Philosophy*, *3*(1), 25–36. DOI: 10.47941/ijp.1867

Sauer, C. R., & Burggräf, P. (2025). Hybrid intelligence – systematic approach and framework to determine the level of Human-AI collaboration for production management use cases. *Production Engineering*, *19*(3–4), 525–541. DOI: 10.1007/s11740-024-01326-7

Seremeti, L., & Anastasiadou, S. (2025). The transformative impact of artificial intelligence (AI) on strategic decision-making. In *Strategic Innovative Marketing and Tourism* (pp. 427–435). Springer Nature Switzerland., DOI: 10.1007/978-3-031-81962-9_47

Shams Eldin, A. Y., Elnour, A., Hassan, R. O. A., & Awad, A. (2025). The role of technological and environmental factors in creating business value from social media dynamic capabilities for SMEs in Saudi Arabia. *Humanities & Social Sciences Communications*, *12*(1), 1431. DOI: 10.1057/s41599-025-05784-x

Shi, K. (2025). The application and risks of AI in enterprise strategic decision-making. Advances in Economics. *Management and Political Sciences*, *190*(1), 120–129. DOI: 10.54254/2754-1169/2025.LD24750

Shrestha, Y. R., Ben-Menahem, S. M., & von Krogh, G. (2019). Organizational decision-making structures in the age of artificial intelligence. *California Management Review*, *61*(4), 66–83. DOI: 10.1177/0008125619862257

Siemon, D. (2022). Elaborating team roles for artificial intelligence-based teammates in human-AI collaboration. *Group Decision and Negotiation*, *31*(5), 871–912. DOI: 10.1007/s10726-022-09792-z

Steyvers, M., & Kumar, A. (2024). Three challenges for AI-assisted decision-making. Perspectives on Psychological Science: A Journal of the Association for Psychological Science, 19(5), 722–734. DOI: 10.1177/17456916231181102

TECHNOLOGY, I. I. Y. M. B. A. S. O. F. M. C. A. H. C. O. F. E. A. N. D., Anjum, S. S., Siddiqua, K. A., Firdous, Z. T., & Navfal, K. M. (2025). AI implementation in company operation and decision making. INTERNATIONAL JOURNAL OF SCIENTIFIC RESEARCH IN ENGINEERING AND MANAGEMENT, 09(09), 1–9. DOI: 10.55041/IJSREM52675

Thakur, N., University, A. S., Sharma, A., & University, A. S. (2024). Ethical considerations in AI-driven financial decision making. *Journal of Management & Public Policy*, *15*(3), 41–57. DOI: 10.47914/jmpp.2024.v15i3.003

Ugwuja, C. G., & Department of Management University of Nigeria Nigeria, E. C. (2024). Artificial intelligence as a Strategic Decision-maker in modern business. NEWPORT INTERNATIONAL JOURNAL OF RESEARCH IN EDUCATION, 4(2), 57–62. DOI: 10.59298/NIJRE/2024/42357628

Upadhyay, D. A. K. (2025). The impact of Artificial Intelligence on strategic decision-making in businesses. *INTERANTIONAL JOURNAL OF SCIENTIFIC RESEARCH IN ENGINEERING AND MANAGEMENT*, *09*(02), 1–9. DOI: 10.55041/IJSREM41630

Valeriani, D., Cinel, C., & Poli, R. (2019). Hybrid collaborative brain–computer interfaces to augment group decision-making. In *Neuroergonomics* (pp. 187–190). Elsevier., DOI: 10.1016/B978-0-12-811926-6.00031-2

Van der Watt, M. (2023). Discouraging the demand that fosters sex trafficking: Collaboration through augmented intelligence. *Societies (Basel, Switzerland)*, *13*(4), 94. DOI: 10.3390/soc13040094

Vartiainen, H., Vuojärvi, H., Saramäki, K., Eriksson, M., Ratinen, I., Torssonen, P., Vanninen, P., & Pöllänen, S. (2022). Cross-boundary collaboration and knowledge creation in an online higher education course. British Journal of Educational Technology. *British Journal of Educational Technology*, *53*(5), 1304–1320. DOI: 10.1111/bjet.13186

Wahid, A., & Awad, A. (2025). Role of AI chatbots in enhancing customer satisfaction and customer loyalty. In *Impacts of AI generated content on brand reputation* (pp. 129–147). IGI Global., DOI: 10.4018/979-8-3373-4327-3.ch005

Wen, Y., Wang, J., & Chen, X. (2025). Trust and AI weight: human-AI collaboration in organizational management decision-making. *Frontiers in Organizational Psychology*, *3*(1419403), 1419403. Advance online publication. DOI: 10.3389/forgp.2025.1419403

Winfield, A. F. T., & Jirotka, M. (2018). Ethical governance is essential to building trust in robotics and artificial intelligence systems. *Philosophical Transactions. Series A, Mathematical, Physical, and Engineering Sciences*, *376*(2133), 20180085. DOI: 10.1098/rsta.2018.0085 PMID: 30323000

Yang, T., & Jiang, J. (2024). Realizing augmenting technology–human symbiosis: A qualitative examination from the organizational learning perspective. *SAGE Open*, *14*(4), 21582440241290148. Advance online publication. DOI: 10.1177/21582440241290148

Yin, M. (2024). Accounting for human engagement behavior to enhance AI-assisted decision making. *Proceedings of the AAAI Symposium Series*, 3(1), 68–70. DOI: 10.1609/aaaiss.v3i1.31184

Zein, A. (2025). Artificial intelligence in strategic decision making. *The International Journal of Social Sciences (Islamabad)*, *1*(1), 17–25. DOI: 10.51805/ijss.v1i1.311

13. KEY TERMS AND DEFINITIONS

Augmented Decision-Making: The integration of human cognition and Artificial Intelligence to enhance decision accuracy, speed, and contextual understanding within organizational settings.

Strategic Agility: The capability of an organization to rapidly sense, adapt, and respond to environmental changes and emerging opportunities through data-driven insights.

Distributed Work Environments: Organizational structures where teams operate remotely or across multiple locations, supported by digital platforms and AI collaboration tools.

Algorithmic Intelligence: The computational ability of AI systems to analyze data, identify patterns, and generate insights that support informed and predictive decision-making.

Human-AI Collaboration: A synergistic partnership where humans and intelligent systems jointly contribute to creative, ethical, and strategic decision processes.

Explainable AI (XAI): A subset of AI focused on making algorithmic outputs transparent, interpretable, and understandable to human users for accountability and trust.

Cognitive Bias Reduction: The process of using AI-driven analytics to minimize human errors caused by psychological biases such as overconfidence or confirmation bias.

Adaptive Management: A dynamic decision-making approach that continuously adjusts strategies based on feedback, learning, and changing data contexts.

Ethical AI Governance: A framework ensuring fairness, transparency, accountability, and privacy in the design and deployment of AI systems within organizations.

Predictive Analytics: Advanced statistical and Machine Learning techniques used to forecast future trends, risks, and opportunities from historical and real-time data.

Organizational Resilience: The ability of an enterprise to withstand disruptions and recover quickly by leveraging technology, innovation, and flexible decision mechanisms.

AI Dashboards: Interactive visualization tools that consolidate and display key performance metrics to support real-time strategic decisions.

Federated Learning: A decentralized AI technique that enables model training across multiple devices or institutions without sharing sensitive raw data.

Human Oversight: The continuous supervision and ethical validation of AI-driven decisions by human experts to ensure compliance with organizational and social norms.

Innovation Ecosystem: An interconnected network of technologies, people, and processes that collectively drive creativity, experimentation, and organizational growth.

Chapter 10
Generative AI in Action: Empirical Case Studies on Startup Innovation and Entrepreneurial Decision-Making

Urvish Mehta
https://orcid.org/0009-0000-0304-0022
Christ University, India

Ramji Nagariya
https://orcid.org/0000-0002-2739-9838
Christ University, India

ABSTRACT

Generative artificial intelligence (AI) is quickly reshaping the world of entrepreneurship and offers startups more opportunities than ever before to innovate and make strategic decisions, as well as to operate more effectively. The chapter is a synthesis of 50 recent academic articles that critically examine how generative AI, specifically large language models and creative automation systems, is transforming the business model design process and venture execution. It discusses two significant directions, one the effect of generative AI in startup innovation of quick product ideation, bespoke customer service and scalable solutions and the other the effect that AI will have on entrepreneurial decision-making, with AI-based analytics and support systems informing resource allocation and market perspective. Based on empirical evidence and practical case studies, the chapter offers practical recommendations to successful adoption and sets the research directions in the future to allow the full implementation of the transformative abilities of generative AI in the startup world.

DOI: 10.4018/979-8-3373-7416-1.ch010

1. INTRODUCTION

The digital age of entrepreneurship is radically transforming, with the introduction of generative artificial intelligence (AI) applications (ChatGPT and large language models) that redefine the process of entrepreneurship. These technologies are becoming the place where startups and entrepreneurs go to redefine product development, automate business processes, improve on innovation, and speed up decision-making. Not just the opportunity, problem-solving, and competition of new ventures, but also the nature of creative and strategic entrepreneurial activity, is being redefined by generative AI.

The current state of business survey and empirical studies shows that there is a drastic gap in the results: A small share of startups can create rapid growth and operational breakthroughs by adopting generative AI strategically, whereas most organizations fail to convert high adoption to business change. This GenAI Divide shows that there is a severe deficiency of empirical research to support the application of AI in entrepreneurial behavior, business model innovation, and startup performance in the real-world setting already: On the one hand, the potential of AI is extensively debated in the literature; on the other hand, the application of generative AI tools cannot be supported by concrete empirical data so far.

The rapid advancement of generative artificial intelligence (AI) has created transformative opportunities within entrepreneurship and startup ecosystems. However, alongside the excitement and theoretical advances, significant gaps remain in the empirical literature and practical understanding of how generative AI concretely impacts entrepreneurial processes, startup innovation, and decision-making. This research gap is complex and multifaceted, encompassing technological, organizational, ethical, and socio-economic dimensions. A detailed exploration follows, identifying key areas where further study is needed to close the gap between potential and reality in generative AI-supported entrepreneurship.

To begin with, there is a significant gap in the fact that there are no longitudinal empirical studies that trace the paths of startups using generative AI over time. Although numerous studies have demonstrated the theoretical promise of generative AI to drive innovation faster, enhance business efficiency, and open up new business opportunities, few studies have evaluated the long-term effects of the technologies on the performance of businesses, their scalability, and survival in various industries and geographical locations. Long-term data can provide essential information on the ways startups use generative AI as they develop, when they start using AI during the venture lifespan, and whether the advantages or difficulties can persist. In the absence of such data, researchers can only work with snapshots or in-laboratory experiments, which do not reflect the dynamism of the real world of entrepreneurship.

Second, one dimension that is still not explored properly is the human factors and organizational capabilities dimension. Current literature does not clearly specify how AI technologies and human capital (primarily the skillsets of entrepreneurial teams, their cognitive biases, and collaborative practices) interact with each other. The knowledge of how entrepreneurs apply AI insights to decision-making, how AI suggestions interplay with intuition and experience, as well as how AI applications can be managed in machine-human collaboration, can serve as a key to closing the gap between the AI potential and its effective application. In addition, there is a gap in literature regarding the ways in which organizational culture, leadership type and learning settings facilitate or prevent AI-enabled innovation. Research that enlarges upon the micro mechanisms of adaptation, knowledge sharing and decision-making in AI-powered start up would illuminate relationships between requirements to success and failure.

Third, the theoretical frameworks and empirical models applied to study generative AI in entrepreneurship have a great methodological gap. Numerous existing works either take a technology adoption model of large-scale business or a theoretical view of AI and innovation. These fail to sufficiently provide startup unique features like resource limitations, market uncertainty and fast iteration cycles. Startup situations need new conceptual frameworks that encompass the disruptive nature of AI as well as the agility and risk profile of new start-ups. Moreover, limited qualitative studies reproduce the rich and contextual story of entrepreneurs who have tried generating AI with their own hands. This gap could be addressed by the mixed-method research designs incorporating both quantitative performance data and qualitative knowledge.

Ethical, legal, and regulatory issues relating to generative AI in the entrepreneurial context also present a growing area of research gap. Although the concept of AI ethics has been already widely debated in the broad sense, the startup ecosystem is characterized by specific challenges associated with the less formalized governance framework, short innovation cycles, and a variety of product-use cases. It requires research on how startups can respond to risks of AI bias, misinformation, and data privacy issues without having large resources to adhere to. It is not clearly spelled out on how responsible AI design, transparency to users, and mitigating bias should be best practiced, especially in the context of startups. Considering that AI abuse or a malfunction might potentially destroy the credibility of the entrepreneurship and prompt a regulatory retaliation, this area is in dire need of scholarly interest.

The other gap is also important in terms of digital inclusion and access. Recent studies on AI entrepreneurship are more likely to be biased towards digitally developed areas, over-invested businesses and technology-oriented industries. This generates blind spots on how resources-constrained start-ups, underrepresented entrepreneurs, and less developed economy ventures can actually access, embrace and utilize the power of generative AI. Literature that investigates infrastructural, educational, and socio-cultural impediments to AI application in various entrepreneurial settings are limited. This gap needs to be addressed to promote AI-related inequalities and capitalize on AI in order to develop the economy on a broad scale.

The effects of generative AI on ecosystems and networks in a startup are also not well covered. Even though there are remote examples indicating that AI transforms the workings of an ecosystem- including knowledge flows, models of partnerships, and investor behavior, there is no systematic understanding of it. What are accelerators, incubators, venture capitalists, and policy actors doing in response to AI-driven trends in innovation or how do they affect them? Which are the feedback mechanisms between AI experimentation and ecosystem evolution in a case of entrepreneurship, such as knowledge spillovers, talent pools and regulatory adjustments? A study that would connect the ecosystem theory with the trends of AI uptake can help understand how systemic effects of the individual entrepreneurial venture are inputted and how they are experienced.

Moreover, there is practically no measuring and assessment systems specific to AI-facilitated entrepreneurship. Stability Standard business performance metrics might not be suitable at capturing the new value axis and risks posed by generative AI. To illustrate, how are the startups to gauge AI-related creativity, quality of decisions, ethical standards, or trust in nascent products? Strong, multi-dimensional performance metrics and assessment approaches will enhance the opportunity of the startups, investors, and policymakers to evaluate the contributions and challenges of generative AI more precisely.

Finally, the concept of human-centered AI design in the field of entrepreneurship is an open debate. More sustainable integration can be achieved with generative AI systems that have a usability-focused approach, transparency and decision support through collaboration. Nonetheless, there is scant empirical studies on the impact of design decisions on entrepreneurial acceptance, ethical conduct and outcomes of innovation. Researching the human-based principles of AI through the lens of startups can be used in order to optimize AI tools by considering the constraints and cognitive requirements of the real-world entrepreneurship (Aldabousi et al., 2025; Ghonim et.al., 2025)

Altogether, the gap in research in the field of generative AI and entrepreneurship is large but promising, promising new interdisciplinary and multi-method studies. Discussing longitudinal effects, human-organizational relations, startup-specific theoretical models, ethical governance, digital inclusion, systemic effects of the ecosystem, and evaluation metrics, human-centered design will help shift the theoretical as well as practical abilities to a significant degree. This study is crucial to realizing the transformative capabilities of generative AI and to reduce and at least evenly balance its risks and create more equitable and sustainable benefits in the wave of entrepreneurial innovation.

In order to fill this break, the following research questions will be addressed in this chapter:

What specific ways of application are startups using generative AI tools in the entrepreneurial process, and what are the obstacles to this in practice?
How does the concept of generative AI have a quantifiable effect on the model innovation and performance of businesses with early-stage ventures?
What are some of the organizational, technical, and behavioral reasons that organizations achieve initial successful adoption of generative AI versus stalled or unsuccessful projects among startups?
What are entrepreneurial, team, and investment practices to meet the skills and learning needs of generative AI and what strategies are most helpful in this regard?

2. METHODOLOGY

The chapter is a systematic qualitative synthesis that is grounded on 50 peer-reviewed journal articles (2018-2025). The methodological processes are:

Article Identification

Scopus, Web of science, and Google Scholar sources were searched based on such keywords as: generative AI, startup innovation, AI entrepreneurship, and AI decision-making.

Inclusion Criteria

Published between 2018-2025.
Concentrate on entrepreneurship, adoption of AI, business models or decision-making.
Empirical, conceptual or bibliometric.
Applicability to the early-stage ventures.

Analytical Procedure

Thematic analysis was done to categorize the results into:
Innovation of startups with AI.
Artificial intelligence in entrepreneurial decision-making.
The drivers and barriers of adoption.

Implications on ethics, the law, and the ecosystem.

The triangulation of the insights was carried out with case studies (Prezi, Hugging Facebook, Notion, and others) and cross-referenced with ecosystem reports (OECD, McKinsey, Stanford HAI).

Limitations

Publication bias of digitally advanced ecosystems.

Inadequate access to longitudinal studies.

Poor representation of startups in developing economies.

3. LITERATURE REVIEW

The recent developments in the field of generative artificial intelligence (AI) have radically changed the environment of entrepreneurship, providing the startups with additional opportunities in terms of innovation, strategic decision-making and efficiency of operations. The study of this intersection has advanced quickly, and preliminary reviews, bibliometric evaluations, and comprehensive case analyses have been conducted on the possible and actual effects of AI-driven enterprises. This review is a synthesis of the results in terms of two broad categories, namely, the startup innovation and decision making, which helps to have a clear picture of the current trends, empirical evidence, and unsolved problems.

3.1 Startup Innovation

3.1.1 Adoption of Generative AI Technology

Articles regularly emphasize how generative AI tools, including large language models, autonomous agents, and creative automation, can be used to facilitate product ideation in a short period of time, customer personalization, and business model change. It has been demonstrated in practice that startups which have incorporated generative AI into their processes undergo more rapid innovation cycles and can enter new markets with reduced barriers as has been observed in industries as diverse as finance to creative industries.

3.1.2 AI-driven Business Models

The emerging literature charts the direction AI-led startups have taken in pursuing dynamic, scalable, and data-driven business models. Bibliometric reviews and case studies show that generative AI is assisting in startup innovation by automating business fundamental entrepreneurial tasks, including opportunity recognition, quick prototyping, and resource mobilization, and creating new service categories altogether. Nevertheless, a number of articles warn that most start-up projects have barriers to technology adoption, skills shortage and regulatory risks at an early stage.

3.1.3 Ecosystem Effects & Empirical Case Studies

Research on the impacts of generative AI in entrepreneurial ecosystems shows that the benefits are unevenly distributed and a small group of startups achieves disproportionate returns by creating a product or service at the right time, whereas others face challenges in integration and organizational learning. The existence of real-world case studies, such as Prezi and Hugging Face, help to demonstrate the transformative effects of AI usage, yet they also indicate some issues, such as absence of alignment between strategies and resources and limited effectiveness of ethical governance (Awad & Aldabousi, 2024; Mahmoud & Awad, 2024)

3.2 Decision-Making

3.2.1 AI Augmented Entrepreneurial Decisions

Another example of the use of AI in entrepreneurship is the use of AI to augment the decision-making processes of entrepreneurs in their domain.

It is proved that generative AI can be used as a stimulus of data-driven decision-making in startups and enhance the efficiency of market forecasting, risk analysis, and strategic planning. A number of studies describe the frameworks in which founders use AI-driven analytics to make decisions on resource prioritization, pricing, product design, and venture financing-making entrepreneurship more systematic and evidence-based.

3.2.2 Human-AI Collaboration & Bias

Although the future of AI is promising, there are also serious issues in human-AI cooperation, which are raised in the literature. When making complex business decisions, entrepreneurs have to overcome the challenges of algorithmic bias and interpretability as well as possible overreliance on automated recommendations. Certain articles propose the best practices in carrying out the combination of human experience and intuition and AI-generated insights that can be summarized as transparent models, continuous learning, and ethics concerns.

3.2.3 Results and obstacles of decision making

Bibliometric and case-based studies have shown conflicting results of AI-enabled-startup decisions during empirical analyses. The startups that allocate resources to effective AI methods are likely to be more successful in their innovation and growth than their counterparts, but despite this fact, a GenAI Divide still exists: even high adoption rates do not necessarily lead to better performance because of the inertia, lack of talent, or ambiguous strategic priorities. To bridge this gap, the literature suggests that more research is needed on adaptive mechanisms, organizational culture and real-time feedback systems.

4. CASE STUDIES

Case Study 1: Prezi - AI-Enhanced Innovative Creative Development.

Prezi was using generative AI to enlarge its design and narration. Its Prezi AI Assistant assists users to create the structure of their presentation in the form of outlines, graphic layouts, and scripts. The startup reported:

40-60% decrease in the time spent by users in creating content.
More adoption by non-designers.
Enterprise onboarding and education expansion.

Prezi shows how AI can enhance creativity, usability and expand the market without displacing human designers.

Case Study 2: Hugging face - Open innovation and community led AI scaling.

Hugging Face is a good example of startup scaling with the assistance of AI. Its Transformers library increased experimentation globally, making it easier to start experimentation by developers and startups, through:

Providing 200,000+ shared models
Allowing fast customization to domain applications.
Creating an ecosystem that is community-based that draws funding and collaborations.

The path of the company indicates that open innovation, transparency, and connecting with communities can generate network effects that will prompt faster adoption of AI in industries.

Case Study 3: Notion - Introducing AI as a Native Work Assistant.

Notion also incorporated generative AI to automate the knowledge summarization, task management, and document creation. Key outcomes include:

Greater user productivity measures.
Recurring revenue subscription tier.
Better placement in productivity tools market.

The case demonstrates how the generative AI can evolve a SaaS product into a hybrid tool that combines the human resource with the automated intelligence.

Startup	AI Use Case	Innovation Impact	Decision-Making Impact	Challenges
Prezi	AI-assisted design & storytelling	Faster prototyping, creative augmentation	Better customer targeting	Data quality, user trust
Hugging Face	Open-source model hosting	Ecosystem scaling, collaborative innovation	Benchmarking & model selection	Governance & security
Notion	AI productivity assistant	Workflow automation	Enhanced prioritization & work summarization	Subscription expansion risks

Industry	Readiness Level	Key Barriers
SaaS	High	Talent retention
Creative industries	High	IP concerns
Healthcare	Medium	Regulation, privacy
Manufacturing	Low–Medium	Legacy systems
Education	Medium	Digital literacy

5. ANALYSIS OF FACTORS OF GENERATIVE AI IN PRACTICE

The Most Known Factors of Generative AI in Practice

5.1 Technological Preparedness and Integrity

The technological preparedness is the basis of the capability of a startup to benefit effectively through generative AI. It covers both physical and virtual infrastructure, such as computing power, cloud storage, data management system, and integration with the current enterprise software. Startups whose technology stack and scalable platforms have strong capabilities can easily add AI APIs and services, which can help quickly experiment and refine AI applications. In the absence of such readiness, adoption work tends to be at the surface, or at bits and pieces, leading to poor performance and lost value.

There are also integration issues that arise when the use of generative AI solutions requires connection with the legacy system or various software environments, complicating everything and requiring experienced IT management. To illustrate, any startup in the financial or healthcare sector is usually subjected to increased limitations because of the high-level regulatory demands and available complicated IT structures that may dishearten the deployment of AI. In addition, the real-time updates and version control of the AI models will require an agile IT backbone. Therefore, being technologically prepared is not only a matter of initial preparation but constant flexibility to an ever-changing AI ecosystem.

Cloud-based AI services are also entering the market through emergent AI platforms by big vendors, which sell turnkey generative AI offerings, but which still require startups to adapt to their workflow and data. Individual curation is successful startup use by striking a balance between off-the-shelf AI accessibility and tailored integration. Finally, the rate of speed, efficiency, and innovation potential of startups can be extracted by generative AI investments, and this is governed by technological preparedness, and integration.

5.2 Founder and Team Expertise

The nature and strength of the founding and operating teams are extremely important in determining the generative AI results. Successful implementation does not exist in technological terms; it is a matter of managerial entrepreneurship, the knowledge of the domain, technical expertise, and flexibility. The team and founders with expertise in AI technologies, data science, software development, and machine learning architecture may design, fine-tune, and scale generative AI applications better to match the reality of the business problems they are aimed at.

The teams with a mix of such technical capabilities and profound knowledge of customer demands, market trends, and product development cycles can be placed in a good position to respond and innovate quickly. To give an example, creative industries are engaging in the startup with AI not as a means, but as a co-producer, and it takes a very delicate balance between human intuition and AI vision. This partnership requires knowledge of AI powers and limitations, which will allow teams to complement human creativity instead of substituting it.

On the other hand, the skill deficiencies or lack of AI literacy are major obstacles. Most startups are finding it hard to recruit or grow talent with knowledge in AI specific fields including natural language processing, fine-tuning large models or generative adversarial networks (GANs). To overcome this, it is important to note that to be on the edge of things, successful startups invest in continuous learning, collaboration with AI research communities, and involvement in open-source projects. The inter-functional cooperation of data scientists, engineers, marketers, and strategists is crucial in order to unleash the full potential of AI. The human capital facet contributes to the fact that the adoption of technology is highly social and organizational.

5.3 Business Model Alignment

The best benefits of generative AI implementation are when it is closely associated with the main business model and strategy of a startup. Startups that find specific situations in which AI can be utilized to address immediate issues or generate a new kind of value stand out compared to those that are implementing AI to be innovative. The alignment of business models needs a clear picture of the potentials of AI and how it fits into customer value propositions, the costing structure, revenue sources, and competition.

As an example, AI-generated content tools can be used by marketing or media start-ups to scale automation and maintain personalization, which will benefit their customer engagement and efficiency directly. Conversely, a retail start-up would be interested in AI-based demand prediction or inventory optimization and make supply chains responsive and minimize wastage. Another element of alignment is to choose the right level of AI maturity, such as simple automation and sophisticated decision support, that is suitable to the resources and stage of the startup.

Unaligned AI projects lead to resource wastage and lack of concentration. Startups should consider the presence of AI in the business model development process, and AI implementations will undergo repeat cycles on the basis of actual feedbacks on the customers, or they will be technology pushed and market not pulled. This means that partnerships, ecosystem roles, and value networks also require reevaluation to allow startups to utilize generative AI tools internally, as well as on both supply chain or customer interfaces, to enable greater impact.

5.4 Access, Data Quality and Security

Generative AI-based systems require data, in terms of quantity and quality, to train the model, produce correct output, and perpetuate the learning. Good data should be inclusive, clean, representative and pertinent to the field of a startup. Startups that have access to proprietary or highly curated datasets get huge competitive advantages and can therefore create and tune generative models that are reflective of customer preferences, market trends, and operational reality.

Nonetheless, issues of data complexity are many, such as fragmentation of sources, noise, bias and compliance. Poor data quality may cause the AI hallucinations, wrong predictions, or biased content creation that damages the credibility of the business and user trust. There is also data access in the form of navigating regulatory requirements such as GDPR or CCPA, particularly those that relate to consumer-facing industries that utilize personal data. The security issue related to data breaches, theft of intellectual property, or abuse necessitates the powerful encryption, access controls, and monitoring of compliance.

To cope with these issues, it can be common that data engineering, data management frameworks, and alliances are invested in that will ultimately provide ethical data sourcing and storage. New methods are synthetic data generation to scale up small real-world samples and federated learning methods, which do not require sensitive data to be centrally stored to train AI. The advancement in handling these data variables is directly proportional to the capability of a startup to grow AI-driven innovation with a high level of security and responsiveness.

5.5 Organizational Culture and Flexibility

Greater successful generative AI integration is possible in startups that have a flexible, innovation-focused culture. These cultures promote experimentation, risk taking, prototyping and learning in a fast manner. They build a psychological safety, which gives teams a chance to experiment with AI applications, accept failures as learning, and change strategies in accordance with the AI-driven insights or market responses.

Organizational agility is the process of abandoning the strict hierarchical management approaches with a focus on cross-functional cooperation and reducing communication levels to shorten the decision process. The iterative essence of AI training and deployment is in line with practices of agile, which focus on sprints, demos, and continuous improvement.

The culture also influences employee buy-in which is a very important aspect because AI usually disturbs the current workflow and job positions. Opposition and misconception can be limited through transparent communication on the goal of AI and its advantages, as well as through upskilling efforts. Furthermore, the companies with the cultures of ethical responsibility and inclusives will take steps to mitigate AI risks like bias, fairness, and privacy, thereby gaining more stakeholder trust.

To conclude, organizational culture is the fertile soil where AI innovation can either survive or fail. The leaders should invest in establishing adaptive cultures which can utilize the potential of technology and at the same time remain in line with human values and strategic objectives.

5.6 Ethics, Legal and Social

The development of generative AI is gone so fast that it creates significant ethical, legal, and social issues that startups should anticipate and react to. Risks that may cause damages to users, stakeholders and corporate reputations are algorithmic bias, lack of transparency, copyright issues and unintended social impacts. Ethical AI governance systems that include bias audits, fairness, explainability tools, and mechanisms of stakeholder engagement need to be put in place by startups.

The regulatory environments have been changing at a fast pace and jurisdictions have been implementing legislation that regulates AI transparency, personal information protection, and responsibility. Startups have a two-fold problem of addressing these demands and ensuring they remain agile in innovations. Lack of this subject matter subjects the venture to legal penalties, market rejection, and mistrust of the venture.

The social aspects also involve the effects on the workforce like fears of job loss and skills. Entrepreneurial teams should take into account the concepts of inclusive design whereby AI tools can benefit various groups of users and decrease digital disparity instead of intensifying it. Partnership with third parties, such as ethicists, lawyers, community members, etc, can be enlisted to develop responsible AI policies in line with social values.

Ethical and legal care turns into a competitive edge, that will provide assurance to the investors and consumers and lead to sustainable development of AI-driven startups.

5.7 Economic and Resource limitations

The amount and accessibility of resources is the main determinant of the level and intensity of generative AI adoption among startups. Access to prolific AI talent and adequate capital investment are the presuppositions to venture into complex generative models and keep the model updated. Startups that are well-funded usually have access to more AI toolkits and datasets and collaborations with AI research organizations.

On the other hand, startups that have limited resources cannot usually afford experimentation versus sustainability. Expensive computation power, the proprietary AI model licensing fee and challenges in finding skilled staff limit AI projects to pilot projects or superficial uses.

Such novel funding tools as AI-focused accelerators, state grants and corporate strategies are becoming a key factor in the democratization of access. Open-source tools and cloud-based AI services can also be used by startups to cut initial investments. Resource optimization entails the balancing of short term efficiency and long-term capability development.

Finally, economic conditions determine not only what can be done, but the speed and risk-taking of AI innovation of new ventures.

5.8 Practical Use Cases Across Functions

Generative AI is realized in a variety of real-life activities in the functions of startups. Content creation tools also help in marketing automation, managing social media, and engaging customers on a personal basis, reaching and resonating with the target customers. Virtual assistants and AI-driven chatbots enhance the efficiency and the availability of customer services, eventually leading to satisfaction and loyalty.

Knowledge retrieval systems are used to augment decision making because they are able to efficiently summarize unstructured information including research articles, customer comments or regulatory policies. The startups also use AI to automate the processes of negotiating with suppliers, writing contracts, preparing compliance documents, and other administrative duties, leaving human resources to focus on strategic work.

Generative AI can be used in product development, which is faster by simulating variation of designs or generating snippets of code, and shortens development cycles. Recommendation engines on a personal level help users by offering them recommendations based on predictive analytics.

These applications illustrate the wide applicability of generative AI, which means that every part of the startup activity, starting and ending with the ideation process and continuing all the way to scaling, is transformed, which makes the latter one of the key facilitators of entrepreneurial creativity and competitive responsiveness.

Synthesis

Generative artificial intelligence (AI) is one of the latest technologies that have become a revolution and have immense implications in the field of entrepreneurship and startup development. Its effects cut across several dimensions, including technological, organizational, ethical, and socio-economic, all of which affect the integration and exploitation of generative AI to innovate and compete successfully by startups. Putting together the available literature clarifies a number of decisive points that jointly define the feasible success and complications of new venture adoption of generative AI.

The determinants of entrepreneurial application of generative AI are technological Readiness and Integration. Startups also need a solid digital foundation with cloud computing services, an ability to flexibly use application programming interfaces (APIs), and be able to effortlessly integrate AI-based parts with already existing business applications to exploit the full benefits of generative AI. Extensive infrastructure facilitates experimentation, prototyping and scaling. Nevertheless, startups are often limited by fragmented legacy systems, the complexity of the integration, and lack of IT capacity leading to the use of AI only partially or inefficiently. Active monitoring can enhance preparation and sustainability of AI deployments, modular architectures, and association with vendors.

Intimately connected is the element of the Founder and Team Expertise that summarizes the human capital requirement of successful AI innovation. The interdisciplinary quality of AI entrepreneurship requires that the team behind a startup combine technical capabilities, including machine learning, data science, and natural language processing, with entrepreneurial abilities, expertise of domain, and vision. Multidisciplinary teams are at a better position to find the right cases of AI use, place technical outputs into context, and implement AI insights in the business model in an effective manner. In addition, constant learning and involvement in research ensure that teams are abreast with AI developments that are rapidly changing so that they can be able to sustain competitive cycles of innovation. Other human elements such as communication, trust and cognitive alignment also alter the contribution of AI towards entrepreneur creativity and decision-making.

Another core dimension influencing the practical effect of the generative AI is Business Model Alignment. The returns and sustainable competitive advantages of AI applications are extracted by the startups that strategically focus on the applications of AI in conjunction with clear value propositions, such as content creation automation, personalization of customer experiences, or supply chain optimization.

Misalignment will lead to wasting of resources and will derail the priorities of innovation. The advantages of AI business case validation, customer feedback, and the ability to quickly recalibrate AI roles as the market shifts are useful in startups. This is harmonized in system placement as the startups do not just use AI unlike in networks to create value.

Data Quality, Access, and Security are the quality, availability and governance of data, which is the lifeblood of the generative AI systems. Quality, representative, and generalized datasets allow proper training of the models so that the relevant and reliable results can be obtained. It is dangerous that bad data quality or biased data may spread false or unfair outcomes which may weaken the trust of the users and ethical principles. Adherence to privacy laws like GDPR and effective cybersecurity measures cannot be compromised, and startups with sensitive or personal information should not do so. Such new methods as synthetic data production and federated learning are likely to improve data stewardship and accessibility without violating security limits, thereby reinvigorating AI capabilities more generally.

Organizational capabilities such as culture and adaptability can largely determine how successful the adoption can be, and this can simply be called Organizational Culture and Flexibility. Cultures with high tolerance to failure, enticing experimentation, and allowing rapid iteration are startup cultures where generative AI innovation thrives. Agile practices are used to complement the AI development cycles by organising incremental delivery and learning. Demonstrating training, open communication, and engagement of employees to the change will help eliminate resistance and facilitate the uptake of AI tools to enhance tech augmentation instead of disruption. Moreover, ethical inclusivity embedded in the organizational culture anticipates risks to bias, inclusion, and privacy, which solidifies sustainable innovation economies.

The importance of using generative AI to address the Ethical, Legal, and Social considerations is significant because it has the potential to impact society. There is a tendency to do this in startups, where there are often not well-established governance structures to detect, reduce, and report risks including algorithmic bias, misinformation, and opaque decision-making. Ethical frameworks should be simplified but made very strong to enable responsible AI experimentation, which is done by developing ethical frameworks that are specific to the resources a startup has. This comprises fairness auditing, consultations of stakeholders and monitoring of regulatory compliance. Ethical due diligence not only prevents legal consequences but also creates reputational capital, which will increase user trust and stakeholder engagement that are required to scale AI applications.

The effect of Economic and Resource Constraints is hard to overestimate. Generative AI requires significant financial expenditures on computer infrastructure, skills, and refinement of the models. Startups with substantial investment have a benefit in terms of scaling AI-based solution access to high-quality human resources and collaborating with AI research institutions. Conversely, resource constrained startups are more of a trade-off, they depend more on clouds and open-source solutions but are often limited in the scope of their projects or in the level of AI maturity. These limitations can be alleviated through strategic sourcing of funding, such as grants, accelerators, and venture capital, and by using AI-as-a-service platforms to make AI more democratic and inclusive in its growth as an entrepreneurship.

Generative AI is also described as having a wide range of practical uses with a wide range of Practical Use Cases Across Functions that demonstrate its applicability and utility. Creation of content enhances the speed of the marketing and media processes and allows hyper-personalization on a massive scale. Chatbots based on AI improve customer interest and drive efficiency. Retrieval systems automate data synthesis which is labor-intensive. AI facilitates fast prototype development and enhanced creativity in product design and prototyping by facilitating simulation and AI-assistance. Regulatory compliance, contract drafting and supplier negotiations are automated and enhance operational efficiency. Such practical uses lower expenses, speed up innovation, and improve the quality of decisions, which highlights the critical role of AI in the activities of a modern startup.

Overall, a combination of these aspects is the background of the redesigning of entrepreneurship by generative AI. Preparedness to technology and human skills makes it possible to adopt AI whereas data stewardship and strategic alignment make it precise and relevant. The responsible AI use is scaffolded by organisational culture and ethical governance and scale and depth are based on economic resources. Real-life practical functional applications are examples of AI and its transformative effect on the activities of startups. The synthesis reveals an ecosystem that is multi-layered and complex in nature and where AI is not a magic bullet but a catalyst that depends on a constellation of enabling and limiting factors to affect. It is imperative to understand all of these interdependencies so that interventions, supports, and policies can be developed to maximize the benefits of generative AI to global entrepreneurial ecosystems.

6. IMPLICATIONS OF POLICY AND ECOSYSTEM.

The consideration of generative AI in startups is also dependent on ecosystem stakeholders:

Shareholders and Venture Capital:

Focusing more on AI-native business models.

AI ethics, data governance, and model robustness are all becoming part of due diligence.
Inappropriateness of AI risk and regulatory exposure is being requested by LPs and VCs.

Accelerators:

The company employs high performing staff members and provides bonuses to those who excel. Incubators: The company has high performing staff and rewards the employees who perform with bonuses.

Providing AI-related training, compute credits, mentorship and model libraries.
Establishing regulatory sandboxes through experimentation.
Enabling collaboration with cloud companies and AI research institutions.

Government and Regulators:

The policies are required to strike the balance between innovation and safety (EU AI Act, Digital India Act in India).
Support mechanisms: AI grants, computing credits, clusters, tax incentives.
Standardized privacy, transparency and equity.

Industry Associations:

Enforce desirable AI practices.
Foster cross-industrial relationships.
Offer frameworks of benchmarking with the aim of minimizing uncertainty of adoption.

7. RECOMMENDATIONS

Recommendations for Startups and Entrepreneurs:

7.1 Invest in Technological Readiness and Integration

The success of the generative AI implementation in startups is based on technological preparedness. Startups should come up with well-built and scalable IT infrastructure that can efficiently support the computational and intricate workflows and processes of generative AI applications. This involves investing in cloud computing, APIs, data processing platforms and smooth integration tools that enable AI models to integrate seamlessly with the current business systems. In the absence of this preparedness, startups will be vulnerable to disjointed or dysfunctional AI adoption that does not result in long-lasting innovation or business value.

The issue of integration capabilities is also worth considering particularly in cases when generative AI has to operate with legacy IT environment or several sources of data. Startups have to consider the pre-trained models sufficiency against the need to develop specific AI models based on costs, speed, and technical complexity. The mobility or compatibility of the applications to the various platforms should be done without any strain to prevent operational bottlenecks.

Besides, the frequent model changes, real-time information alignment, and feedback mechanisms demand IT architectures that are agile and resilient. New cloud-native capabilities offer modular and scalable infrastructures which allow startups to prototype and deploy an AI initiative quickly and scale it effectively without compromising performance reliability. Therefore, technological preparedness is not an initial installation but an ongoing investment and enhancement procedure that provides the long-term success of generative AI in the field of entrepreneurship.

7.2 Nurse Multidisciplinary and Lifelong Learning

The interaction of the AI technology and the entrepreneurship requires cross-domain teams. Startups are advised to create multidisciplinary groups that consist of technical AI skills, such as machine learning, natural language processing, data engineering, and business strategy, domain knowledge, and customer intuition. This kind of diversity will promote innovative problem-solving, increased situational awareness of AI, and adaptation of technology to practical entrepreneurial issues.

Constant learning is also essential because the rapid development of generative AI tools and methods is that the knowledge of yesterday will soon be obsolete. Incentives to upskilling and reskilling programmes, such as workshops, partnerships with educational institutions, involvement in open source projects and AI communities should be encouraged by startups. Such learning culture leads to flexibility, creativity, and successful use of AI.

Success also depends on human factors such as communication, belief in AI insights and cohesion in the team. The teams that successfully incorporate human intuition and AI-generated outputs will be able to use AI as a collaborative partner, as opposed to a black-box tool. Startups need to invest in the creation of this symbiosis between humans and AI by means of training and working in unison.

7.3 Accord Generative AI Adoption to explicit Business Objectives

Small companies can find it difficult to start when the implementation of AI is not a strategic matter. Generative AI initiatives must be closely aligned with business and customer value propositions to ensure a high ROI and also reduce waste. Startups ought to find focus on certain, high-impact uses that improve strategic objectives, in the form of marketing automation, product innovation, customer support, or supply chain optimization.

This alignment must involve initial-stage feasibility tests, cost-benefit analysis, and pilot projects that have quantifiable KPIs. Specific goals assist in prioritization of effort, obtaining stakeholder buy-in, and resource allocation. As an example, the utilization of generative AI on personalized customer content must achieve specific goals, including the improvement of engagement or the increase in conversion.

There is also flexibility with time by aligning the business models to the use of AI. The performance of the AI and market feedback data is used to make iterative improvements and avoid stagnation or misuse. This visionary conciseness forms a narrow innovation funnel, quickening the process of experimentalisation to scalable AI-based business solutions.

7.4 Make Data Stewardship and Security a Priority

The performance of generative AI directly relies on the quality, variety and intactness of data. Startups should have strict data governance models, which will improve data accuracy, consistency, free of bias, and reflective of the target scenarios. Preprocessing of the data, such as cleaning, labeling, formatting, and augmentation, is at the center of producing trustworthy outputs of AI.

The compliance issue of security and privacy is the most crucial one, considering that various regulatory frameworks, such as GDPR or CCPA, exist. Startups should adopt sound cybersecurity and access control of data to safeguard delicate business and user data.

Besides, ethical principles in data sourcing, transparency, and the reduction of bias need to be entrenched in the stewardship practices. When managing data incorrectly, the chances of the model degrading, reputational damage and regulating punishment are inevitable.

Model explainability and user trust are also enabled by effective data stewardship which is essential to the acceptance of AI both internally and externally. Centralized data platforms can help startups to have single sources of truth and help them to simplify data operations to facilitate scalable AI projects.

7.5 Adopt the Culture of Experimentation and Agility

Generative AI innovation relies on the development of a culture of experimentation, failure lessons, and speedy iteration. Since AI is characterized by uncertainties and dynamism, the startups need to reduce the barriers to test AI applications in a controlled setting prior to full-scale implementation.

The ability to switch strategy in response to AI-generated insights or user feedback is what makes startups pivot on agility to achieve continuous refinement of AI applications to optimize results. This culture is supported by cross-functional teamwork, free flows of information and participatory decision making.

The agile project management, lean approaches, and sprint cycles are complementary to the adoption of AI in that they help organize the iterative development and evaluation. This culture does not only swiftly increase innovation in real-time, but it also assists in uncovering AI weaknesses early in advance, allowing corrections to courses in time.

Notably, the psychological assistance of the employees in transiting the change, training, and empowerment encourages the acceptance and active involvement in AI-assisted tools and processes.

7.6 Respond to Ethical and Legal Issues Proactively

Responsible AI implementation in startups is based on ethics and legal compliance. Ethical risks, including the bias of an algorithm, misinformation, and privacy violations of the user, are not addressed and may result in harm, lawsuits, and customer loss.

The startups will have to implement ethical AI governance policies that include impact analysis, transparency, fairness, and stakeholder interactions. The partnering with law professionals will guarantee that it is up to date with the fast-evolving AI regulations.

Ethical proactivity creates competitive advantage through being risk-ahead, brand-building, and building long-term relationships with users. It also facilitates inclusion and alleviates social evils that AI technologies enhance.

7.7 Partnerships and Expertise: Find Cooperation

Since it is not simple, and we have resource limitations, collaborations with academia, AI vendors, accelerators, and experts professionals are highly valuable to startups. Such partnerships allow access to leading-edge research, tools and specialized knowledge.

External alliances can be used to bridge gaps in skills, to test more quickly and to scale the infrastructure in an efficient manner. Knowledge exchange and innovation synergy, which are essential in navigating the changing AI landscape, are encouraged in AI ecosystems.

7.8 Measure Performance and Change Dynamically

The ongoing control of the technical and business indicators of generative AI will guarantee the maintenance of consistency with the goals and operational performance. Startups ought to come up with dashboards that monitor the model accuracy, latency, cost, satisfaction to the user, and effects on the key business KPIs.

8. FUTURE RESEARCH DIRECTIONS

8.1 The Longitudinal Impact Studies

Longitudinal impact studies would be useful in offering profound analysis regarding the temporal changes in the adoption of generative AI in startups. Longitudinal studies follow ventures through time unlike the present literature which mainly focuses on cross-sectional or short-term snapshots of the ventures and show the role of AI integration on entrepreneurial innovation, decision making patterns, financial results and organizational learning. This kind of research reveals the dynamics of AI adoption stages, initial experimentation, scaling, strategic pivots, or overall abdication, which will assist entrepreneurs and policy-makers to have a better without making the strategies of AI more transparent and competitive advantages with time. As an example, empirical research such as field experiments on Kenyan small businesses have shown the benefits of AI are contingent on the underlying performance, indicating that time-varying longitudinal data provide subtle insights into the effects patterns that cannot be observed in one-time studies. The focus on feedback loops and accumulation effects, as well as the contribution of changing ecosystem support and regulation, can also be explored using this longitudinal lens that is essential in enhancing the longevity of innovation and entrepreneurial resilience.

8.2 Comparative Sectoral Analyses

The current AI entrepreneurship research has so far focused much on digitally intensive sectors of industry, often overlooking the operational modes of generative

AI in different sectoral and contextual conditions. Comparative sectoral analyses set out a methodical way of comprehending the specifics of AI utilization in industries (healthcare, manufacturing, education, agriculture, and the creative economy) in a unique manner. The specific regulatory contexts, data availability, customer needs, and risk profile of operations of each sector have an influence on the adoption and scale of AI. As an illustration, medical projects face tough privacy constraints, and AI solutions with a high model explainability are required, whereas creative start-ups focus on the ability to generate content, and develop products. Moreover, the analysis of AI implementation in resource-constrained environments demonstrates the imbalance in resource distribution and capacity, and discloses socio-economic and infrastructural factors affecting the democratization or exclusion of the AI benefits. Finally, comparative studies of the sector enrich the theoretical and practical knowledge, which contributes to policies and ecosystem designs depending on the particularities of entrepreneurial settings.

8.3 Human-Artificial Intelligence Cooperation

The potential of generative AI is closely associated with its capacity to be combined with human entrepreneurial potential instead of being a technological substitute. Further studies ought to be aimed at developing a model to describe human-AI collaboration processes in order to maximize the capabilities of both parties. Entrepreneurial decision-making is ambiguous, difficult in nature, and contextual and value sensitive, which raises doubts on the purely algorithmic systems. Research on how collaborative interfaces, workflow systems, and trust development are designed would assist entrepreneurs to make informed interpretations and add to AI-generated insights. Further, the discussion of psychological and cognitive consequences of human-AI teaming, including consequences on entrepreneurial confidence, cognitive bias, and creative ideation, will contribute to the knowledge on AI as a cognitive collaborator. Evidence-based recommendations on how to establish synergistic human-AI relationships will be based on empirical data on various types of teams, organizational culture, and leadership styles, and eventually produce AI tools that can foster entrepreneurial innovation and alleviate the decision-making pressure.

8.4 Algorithms, Ethics, and Bias

The high growth rate of generative AI brings with it significant ethical, social and governance concerns, especially in startup culture, where minimal oversight systems and expedited trial and error processes are the norm. The study needs to explore the perceptions and management of algorithmic bias, privacy threats, misinformation, and unintended social effects associated with AI application among startups. The creation of customized ethical governance models that are highly effective within the constraints of startups is a key factor in the process of striking the balance between innovation and responsible AI development. These frameworks may involve bias identification procedures, transparency guidelines, stakeholder interaction and compliance regulation tactics modified to fit entrepreneurial settings. These governance mechanisms may be assessed empirically to reveal their success in risks reduction and trust among their customers, partners, and investors. Notably, ethical issues are resolved to facilitate sustainable AI entrepreneurship through the preservation of social values and compliance with regulations, which prevents reputational harm and strengthens the culture of responsibility.

8.5 Access to and the use of digital technologies

Although generative AI promises to make entrepreneurial tools and markets more accessible to everyone, the presence of strong digital disparities still exists and hinders inclusiveness. This area of research suggests the need to conduct the studies exploring the barriers and enablers influencing under-resourced entrepreneurs, marginalized groups, and startups in the developing world concerning the use of AI technologies. The analysis of the infrastructural gaps, gaps in education levels, limitations in accessing finances, and the influence of culture will inform the strategies of making AI entrepreneurship widely available. These issues are affordable AI platforms, localization of AI technologies in the languages and cultures, education programs on AI at the community level, and partnerships between the community and business to advance digital literacy. Assessments of custom AI applications in low-resource conditions may shed light on the opportunities of empowerment, employment generation, and reducing poverty.

8.6 Investor, Policymaker and Ecosystem Perspectives

Under-researched is the impact of different actors in the ecosystems such as venture capitalists, government agencies, accelerators, and the influence of entrepreneurial networks on the adoption of generative AI. Learning the way that investors evaluate AI-based startups, governmental policies promote or work against AI innovation, and accelerators spur AI ventures can increase systemic understanding of AI entrepreneurship. This research direction can explore feedback mechanisms where the structure of ecosystems has an impact on the adoption behaviors of startup AI, and vice versa, that AI-motivated innovations alter ecosystem organization, including talent pools, funding patterns, and regulatory regimes. This study provides insights into strategic ecosystem-level interventions, such as policy design, funding tools, and collaborative ventures, to spawn sustainable and speedy development of the generative AI entrepreneurship economy outside and inside localized innovation ecosystems.

8.7 Application Case Documentation

Although numerous theoretical discussions of generative AI are available, there are few and detailed, contextual case studies explaining the practical experiences of startups with AI. The next area of study should be to compose a list of different use cases, report success stories, problems encountered, moment of pivots, and project failures. Multi-sector and multi-geographic longitudinal case studies would provide deep grounded information on the actual complexities involved in using AI and innovation cycles in practical contexts. These depositories do not only provide service to academic and policy communities but also create realistic maps to those entrepreneurs on the same path.

8.8 Innovation and Decision-Making Outcomes Measures

The current entrepreneurial performance measures tend to poorly reflect the subtleties of generative AI application to the quality of innovation, accuracy of decisions, market speed, and adherence to ethics. The direction of the research suggests the creation of strong and multi-dimensional measurement instruments that should be adjusted to AI-enabled entrepreneurship. To determine the holistic value propositions of AI, composite indices to include social impact indicators, technical performance parameters, and operational measures are required. The startups, investors, and policy makers will be able to rely on benchmarking tools and evaluative methodologies which are based on these new metrics to track the AI efficacy, risk and return, as well as how to design support mechanisms.

9. CONCLUSION

Entrepreneurial innovation and decision-making are being transformed by generative AI, providing the startups with unmatched creativity, insight generation, automation, and strategic planning capabilities. The chapter combines the evidence of 50 academic materials and a variety of practical case studies to demonstrate that AI is not a tool but a transformative infrastructure that defines the way startups are going to move in the future.

The results point to the fact that a multilayered integration of technological readiness, human capital, data governance, ethical alignment, and ecosystem support is the key to the successful AI adoption. Startups which deploy AI as a core business model are able to innovate faster, make better decisions, and grow in a scalable manner. Nevertheless, the gains are not evenly distributed: a lot of startups are constrained in resources, not sure about the regulations, and lack of skills contributing to the ongoing digital (or, to be more exact, GenAI) divide.

The idea of responsible AI practices is also highlighted in this chapter, particularly as the startups are trying to find their way through the challenges of bias, transparency, fairness, and impacts on the society. Ecosystem stakeholders, such as, investors, accelerators, policymakers, and research institutions are of great importance in expanding access, providing clarity in regulation, and sustainable innovation channels.

Longitudinal studies, comparison of the sectors, models of human-AI cooperation, and systematic documentation of cases are the research directions that should be followed in the future to enhance theoretical and practical knowledge. Generative AI is bound to transform the future of entrepreneurship, although its direction will be determined by whether startups, institutions and policymakers collaboratively create an inclusive, ethical and innovation-driven AI ecosystem.

10. REFERENCES

Aldabousi, A. M., Awad, A., Hassan, H. E. M., Abdullah, S. S., & Ghonim, A. (2025). Arbitration in Islamic banking: Exploring legal and practical implications for dispute resolution. *Banks and Bank Systems*, *20*(2), 15–26. DOI: 10.21511/bbs.20(2).2025.02

Amershi, S., Begel, A., & Bird, C.. (2019). Software engineering for machine learning: A case study. *Proceedings of the 41st International Conference on Software Engineering*, 291-301. DOI: 10.1109/ICSE-SEIP.2019.00042

Brown, T., Mann, B., Ryder, N., Subbiah, M., Kaplan, J., Dhariwal, P., & Amodei, D. (2020). Language models are few-shot learners. *NeurIPS*, *33*, 1877–1901.

Brynjolfsson, E., & McAfee, A. (2017). *Machine, platform, crowd: Harnessing our digital future*. W. W. Norton & Company.

Chatterjee, S., & Kumar, A. (2025). Artificial intelligence and entrepreneurial finance: A guide for research. *Journal of Business Venturing*, *40*(1), 101–130.

Chen, H., Chiang, R. H. L., & Storey, V. C. (2012). Business intelligence and analytics: From big data to big impact. *Management Information Systems Quarterly*, *36*(4), 1165–1188. DOI: 10.2307/41703503

Chen, M., Tworek, J., Jun, H., Yuan, Q., Pinto, H., Kaplan, J., . . . Zaremba, W. (2021). Evaluating large language models trained on code. *arXiv preprint arXiv:2107.03374.*

Daugherty, P. R., & Wilson, H. J. (2018). *Human + machine: Reimagining work in the age of AI*. Harvard Business Review Press.

Davenport, T., Guha, A., Grewal, D., & Bressgott, T. (2020). How artificial intelligence will change the future of marketing. *Journal of the Academy of Marketing Science*, *48*(1), 24–42. DOI: 10.1007/s11747-019-00696-0

Davenport, T., & Ronanki, R. (2018). Artificial intelligence for the real world. *Harvard Business Review*, *96*(1), 108–116.

Dutta, S., & Bose, I. (2023). Generative AI and startup innovation: A bibliometric review. *International Journal of Entrepreneurial Behaviour & Research*, *29*(8), 1450–1475.

Faggella, D. (2020). The state of generative AI: Trends and applications.

Gans, J., Scott, E., & Stern, S. (2019). Strategy for start-ups. *Harvard Business Review*, *97*(3), 5–12.

Ghazinoory, S., & Shirkhani, S. (2022). Artificial intelligence impact on entrepreneurship ecosystems: A systematic review. *Technological Forecasting and Social Change*, *172*, 121–135.

Ghonim, A., Awad, A., Shemais, M., Shma, T., & Aziz, A. (2025). Exploring the impact of flexible work arrangements on employee engagement in telecommunications: Case of Egypt. *Problems and Perspectives in Management*, *23*(2), 198–207. DOI: 10.21511/ppm.23(2).2025.13

Guo, Y., & Li, X. (2025). Elevating entrepreneurship with generative artificial intelligence. *Journal of Innovation & Knowledge*, *10*(4), 316–329.

Chapter 11

Human-AI Synergy for Organizational Resilience:

Strategies for Adaptive and Sustainable Remote Work Models

R. N. Ravikumar
https://orcid.org/0009-0009-3705-1681
Marwadi University, Rajkot, India

S. Aarthi
https://orcid.org/0009-0006-9064-2091
Marwadi University, Rajkot, India

ABSTRACT

Artificial Intelligence (AI) is redefining how organizations sustain performance, adaptability, and innovation in hybrid and remote work models. This chapter explores the synergy between human cognition and AI systems in building resilient, ethical, and sustainable workplaces. It highlights how AI enhances collaboration, predictive decision-making, and emotional intelligence while addressing challenges like digital fatigue, bias, and overreliance. Emphasis is placed on developing transparent governance, human-centered ethics, and reskilling frameworks that balance automation with empathy. Through theoretical insights and practical implications, the chapter outlines strategies for achieving organizational resilience and well-being in the era of intelligent, distributed work environments.

DOI: 10.4018/979-8-3373-7416-1.ch011

1. INTRODUCTION

The speed at which the digital transformation has taken place has now transformed how the organizations are managed, cooperate and remain to survive within the fragmented environments. Hybrid and remote work is not a single answer one-time response during an emergency but is an established system that must be handled in a dynamic and intelligent way. Resilience and sustainability, which entail analytics, automation, and human thinking to build synergistic work ecosystems, has become one of the points of focus of Artificial Intelligence (AI) (Raisch and Krakowski, 2021a). Instead of eliminating workers, AI improves their mental and emotional consequences, which leads to economy, inclusion, and innovation. This kind of synergy, however, is only possible by the means of ethical framework, responsible adoption, as well as the fact that it must be according to the welfare of human beings. In the article, the author discusses the possibility of AI application in organizational resilience in the framework of adaptive systems, sustainable work strategies, and human-centered design (Stahl et al., 2023). It also addresses the essential trends, theoretical basis, and management implication such that the organisations can attain a proper balance between organisational digital intelligence and human ingenuity in the evolving hybrid work place.

1.1 Overview Of Digital Transformation And The Evolution Of Hybrid And Remote Work

The digital transformation has revolutionized the organizational practices whereby there were limited physical operations to be made through the digitally connected ecosystems. The enormous adoption of cloud computing, high-speed networks, and teamwork tool has enabled the easy coordination of the teams that are scattered in different geographical locations. Remote and hybrid work models were initially considered as a need during the time of crisis such as the COVID-19 pandemic but now they are viewed as the source of flexibility and innovation. The models exploit the resources to the maximum, reduce environmental impacts and access to talent pools worldwide. Nevertheless, they too need sound technological integration and high digital literacy in order to maintain productivity and collaboration. As business organizations are gradually merging the physical and virtual worlds, there is a shift towards digital trust, reactive leadership, and human-AI cooperation (Dow et al., 2023). Hybrid work development, therefore, is a paradigm shift to the more intelligent, data-driven, and human-centered model of the organizational process. The figure 1 Displays the successive phases of digital transformation to human-AI partnership as the construction of contemporary hybrid workplaces.

Figure 1. Evolution of Hybrid Work

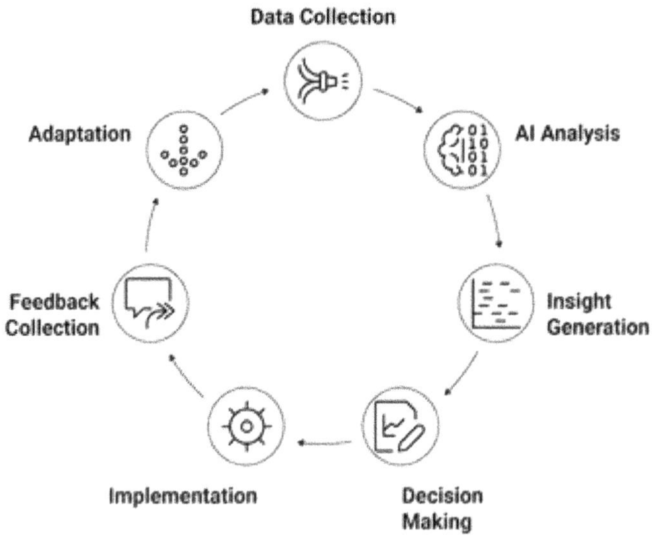

1.2 The Role Of AI As A Catalyst For Resilience, Adaptability, And Sustainability

AI is a disruptive influence which increases the flexibility of an organization to recuperate and endure in an uncertain time. AI enhances operations agility and situational awareness by using predictive analytics, natural language processing and process automation. It offers the possibility to make decisions in real-time, forecasts disruptions, and utilizes resources to the full in remote and hybrid environments. Moreover, AI may be engaged in order to make practice more sustainable; it could be achieved through eradicating the redundant jobs and carbon footprint due to running the virtual operation, and making the digital infrastructure manage energy effectively (Wong, 2025). In human aspect dimensions, AI forms inclusiveness with accessibility apps and emotional sensitive interfaces that support the inclusion and well-being. It is possible to approach to AI systems as not only a technological resource but as an adaptive system, which learns and supplements human intelligence, when it is applied in the ethical context. The AI, hence, pushes a system of an organization that is robust and one that keeps changing, developing and sustaining itself according to the dynamic business environments. The figure 2 Demonstrates how AI helps to enhance resilience, adaptability, sustainability, inclusiveness, and ethical conduct in organizations.

Figure 2. AI's Role in Organizational Resilience

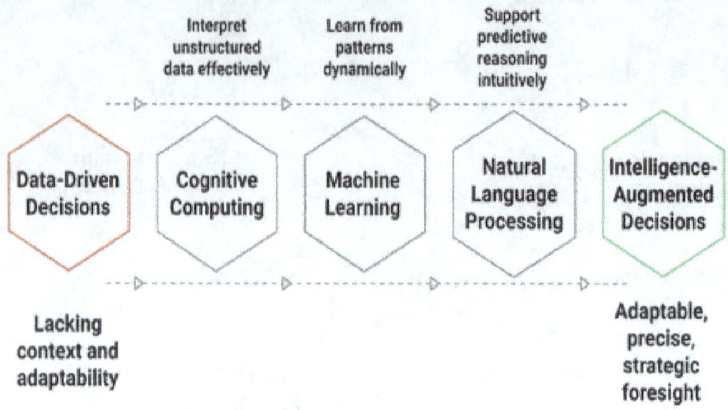

1.3 The Shift From Automation To Augmentation: Redefining Human-AI Collaboration

The initial applications of AI aimed more at automation, i.e., the ability to simplify repetitive and rule-based tasks to enhance their efficiency. The contemporary change is, nevertheless, founded on augmentation in which the AI replaces human intuition, empathy, and creativity. This idea to use the power of AI-based computing and human judgment to allow approaching complex problems, innovation, and emotional intelligence is referred to as augmentation. The implementation of AI systems to help it to find knowledge, optimize the working process, and operationalize the real-time feedback in a hybrid workplace is making the staff stronger instead of replacing them. This synergy increases the diversity in cognition, the quality of decision and team intelligence. It is notable that augmented collaboration must be founded on transparency, trust and as an ethically desirable practice so as to ascertain that human values are in the heart of digital ecosystems. (LTIMIndtree et al., 2023). The ones working together with high efficacy of automation and high-level creativity to augmentation are better inclined to endure the disruption and guarantee a sustainable growth. Thus, the interaction of the human and AI is the new stage of co-evolution of the modern relationships in the workplace.

1.4 Importance Of Balancing Productivity, Inclusivity, And Well-Being In Distributed Teams

Despite the efficiency of technology, the problem of maintaining human contact, inclusivity, and psychological state is among the primary concerns in the remote workplaces. The AI can facilitate egalitarianism in the allocation of workload, supervising participation, and increasing flexible learning, but excessive surveillance carries a risk of privacy and trust as well. Therefore, businesses must be able to devise hybrid systems that are mindful and participatory of productivity pointers. The main worry of digital collaboration should also be accessibility, psychological safety and fair participation to prevent marginalization of remote workers. Examples of AI tools that may be applied to promote individual interaction without violating the ethics of the data include sentiment analysis and adaptive learning platforms (Verganti et al., 2020). The paradigms of leadership will also be altered to the data-oriented and human-sensitive leadership that will appreciate human diversity. The hybrid model is the trade off in which technology will be used to supplement, but not to substitute human experience. Finally, the result of the cultivating climate of promiscuity to digital cultures in which employees feel appreciated, related and motivated to do their best is the element of sustainable production.

2. BACKGROUND TO THE STUDY

The background offers a situation in which AI-based hybrid work is placed in the context of the digital transformation and organizational resilience in general. Since the enterprises had trembled because of pandemics, geopolitical tension, and market instability, indirect cooperation became a survival strategy. This would, in the long-run translate into strategic advantage as it would allow to be agile and be inclusive with a decision-making that is based on data usage. This change was more efficient with the availability of AI and improvement of foresight, coordination, and human-machine flexibility. (Romanelli, 2018). Organizational resilience has also turned out to be more psychological and moral, besides the structural resilience which contributes to the sustained performance. The cross-over of sustainability and responsible AI governance has reinstated the practice applied in virtual ecosystems. It is the learning of this evolution that will underlie the development of structures that will bring level of balance between the technological intelligence and the human creative in the future workplaces to have continuity, trustworthiness and equity in the workplaces. (Y. Chen et al., 2023).

2.1 Historical Transition From Traditional To Technology-Mediated Work Models

One of the largest changes in history of an organization today is the transformation of the traditional office work to the medium of technology. The physical nature of work place, the hierarchical communication and time-bound productivity systems were first defined. The introduction of Information And Communication Technologies (ICTs), cloud computing, as well as mobile devices slowly made the location-independent collaboration possible. Over the last 2 decades, work as a connected real-time ecosystem has evolved through the digital platforms, such as Microsoft teams, zoom, and slack. Such transformation allowed sharing knowledge, scheduling flexibility, and inter-geographical cooperation with each other, which became the fundamentals of hybrid and remote work systems. At the time of transition, new competencies in digital literacy/cybersecurity/virtual leadership were also required (Singh and Pandey, 2023). In that regard, organizations stopped being established physical structures, and evolved into a dynamic ecosystems including technology, where AI now happens to be the key to balancing and coordinating responsive and efficient, more human-oriented forms of cooperation.

2.2 Impact of Global Disruptions (e.g., pandemics, economic shifts) on Organizational Operations

The world-shifting disruptions brought by the COVID-19 pandemic, geopolitical turmoil, and variable economies are the major changes to the organizational resilience paradigms. Such crises exposed the flaws of the traditional models of operation that had a centralized decision-making process and the physical infrastructure. The need to use remote transitions due to force made it easier to embrace digital tools of collaboration and AI-based solutions to remain productive. Businesses learnt how to apply data analytics and automation to allow continuation, risk forecasting, and rapid reaction. In addition to this, the economic uncertainties favored the importance of diversified digital supply chains and agile management of the workforce (Team Leader Bangladesh, 2024). The pandemic specifically altered the meaning of work with the well-being of the employees, flexibility, and digital inclusivity taking the top priority. In that aspect, AI-based systems were viewed as key facilitative sources with regard to maintaining communication, coordination, and operational foresight. The trend of sustainable, responsive and future-proof organizational ecosystems has now been constituted by global crises and digital resilience.

2.3 Emergence Of AI In Workforce Coordination, Communication, And Decision-Making

AI has redefined how modern organizations organize and communicate with their employees and the process of making decisions. The smart systems lead to automated scheduling, optimization of workflow, and analysis of the performance trends and this saves the cognitive load of the employees. Communication with each other can take place in real-time and time-spanning problem solving can be used with the help of AI-based communication tools, such as chatbots and virtual assistants (Dr. Jolly Masih, 2023). Predictive analytics, sentiment analysis and natural language understanding are implied in order to enhance the process of decision-making and allow leaders to anticipate possible challenges and allocate resources in a strategic manner. Moreover, AI may offer individual training, feedback and interaction systems may be modified to meet the requirements of individual employees. Other than operational efficiency, AI enables inclusivity to prosper in multinational teams as it may eliminate language and cultural barriers (Kharytonov et al., 2021). Implementation of these technologies is a passage to the state of human-AI interdependence with the machines boosting human reasoning and empathy. This dynamic has redefined the paradigms of leadership and collaboration of the distributed and hybrid organizations regarding the structure of the organization.

2.4 Concept Of Organizational Resilience: Dimensions (Operational, Psychological, Strategic)

Organizational resilience is the capacity to take in shock, adapt to the perturbation and still be able to sustain even in a dynamic environment. It operates on three operation dimensions which are interdependent and they include psychological and strategic dimensions. Operational resilience refers to the maintenance of efficiency through redundancy, responsive mechanisms and digital preparedness. Psychological resilience is linked to the adaptation capability of the staff members, their incentive, and their ability to withstand emotional instability during periods of doubt (Hepfer and Lawrence, 2022). Strategic resilience concentrates on the future, ingenuity as well as the ability to redesign the organizations aims in respect of the dynamic situations. The AI enhances the dimensions in order to give predictive considerations, automate the repetitive processes and aid in making informed decisions. The strong organizations perceive the disruptions as an opportunity to change rather than a threat. They unite the human compassion and computer intelligence and arrive at flexible and sustainable systems. In conclusion, resilience has evolved to be a strategic need, which defines competitive edge within digitally networked ecosystems.

2.5 Relevance Of Sustainability And Ethical AI In Digital Workplaces

Sustainability and ethical AI are the main concept of responsible digital transformation in the contemporary workplace setting. Transparency, fairness and accountability have significance since AI systems are being introduced to decision-making process. The concept of ethical AI ensures privacy and less bias and compliance with human principles by algorithms. AI can also contribute to sustainability by reducing carbon footprint by having remote actions, enhancing energy use, and enabling green business. However, the unethical unbridled application of AI may result in some ethical concerns such as data surveillance, exclusion, and algorithmic obscurity that could threaten trust and inclusiveness (Hafiza Hamzah et al., 2021). Firms are thus encouraged to adopt governance systems which adopt the ethical principles when designing and developing and deploying AI. With the integration of sustainability and digital strategy, the efficiency of the operations is ensured, along with the social and environmental responsibility in the long term. This game transforms the virtual office into an innovative, fair, and sustainable ecosystem even in the whole world.

3. RESEARCH OBJECTIVES

The adaptation of organizations, further performance, and resistance to uncertainty have been changed as the use of AI in hybrid and remote employment grows. The chapter is targeted at comprehending the processes of human-AI synergy programs in the creation of adaptive, ethical, and sustainable work environment ecosystems. The study will focus on the discovery of the strategic, operational, and human dimensions of AI adoption based on the interdisciplinary approach of the management, technology, and organizational psychology (in the long-term perspective), which facilitate the establishment of resilience in the organizations.

- To examine how AI-driven tools and systems enhance organizational adaptability, agility, and crisis response in hybrid work settings.
- To evaluate the role of human-AI collaboration in promoting sustainable, inclusive, and high-performing remote workplace cultures.
- To investigate ethical challenges, trust dynamics, and governance concerns arising from AI augmentation in digital work environments.
- To develop a conceptual model illustrating the interplay between human factors, AI capabilities, and organizational resilience.
- To propose practical and ethical frameworks for implementing AI-supported sustainable remote work strategies.

4. CONCEPTUAL MODEL

The proposed theoretical framework shows the interaction between the human and AI advantages that form resilient, adaptive and sustainable remote working conditions. It demonstrates how the human cognitive and emotional capabilities relate to the predictive and analytical capabilities of the AI to enhance the performance, innovation, and trust. The framework is structured around four related aspects that are human factors, AI factors, and enabling mechanisms and outcomes, all of which are factors that bring in resilience in an organization. Human creativity and empathy can be prioritized as the AI-based ideas, and long-term flexibility can be offered with the help of an ethical government and reskilling program (Drigas and Papoutsi, 2018). The forms of interactions between human and AI are the expression of the ongoing feedback mechanism in which the reciprocity learning leads to better decision-making as well as inclusiveness and well-being. Altogether, this model offers a comprehensive account of sustainable human-AI cooperation in hybrid working conditions. The Figure 3 demonstrates the collaboration between people and AI by following the principle of feedback and lifelong learning to create strong and sustainable work environments.

Figure 3. Human-AI Synergy Model for Resilient Work Ecosystems

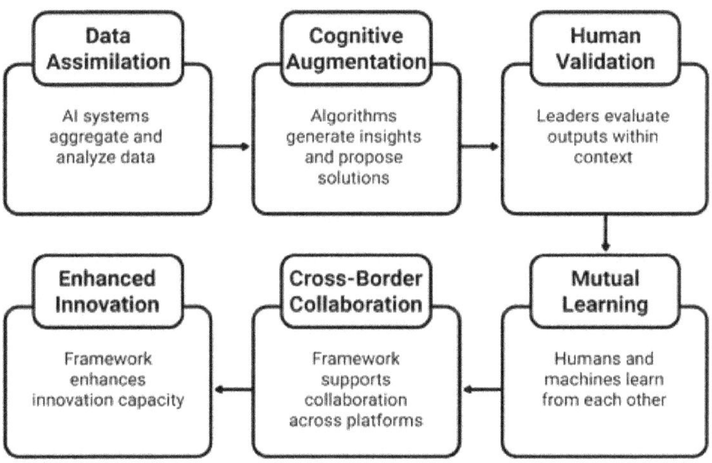

4.1 Human Factors: Creativity, Empathy, Decision Judgment, Trust

The AI-enhanced work systems are based on the emotional and cognitive aspects of human factors. Creativity causes employees to devise new solutions not on the basis of the algorithmic tendencies and empathy leads to valuable interpersonal relationships required to work and be accepted. The discretion judgment in AI means the incorporation of the critical thinking with moral awareness to make sure that the use of the information provided by AI is responsible (Pasupuleti and Services, 2025). The foundation will be trust because the employees will have to trust the AI systems to help them in their work, but without disrupting their self-sufficiency and justice, and the organizations will have to set up clear communication regarding the role of AI and restrictions. The characteristics help in provision of psychological security, liberty, and inspiration in remote groups. Since the notion of human strength will be seen as a complement, avoiding the rivalry with AI, the organizations will form robust frameworks, which will be able to create a correlation between the precision of the machine and the delicacy of the human. Merging emotional intelligence and data intelligence is the key to the change and organizational health that is sustained.

4.2 AI Factors: Predictive Analytics, Automation, Emotion Recognition, Adaptive Learning

The technological capabilities, that cause organizations to foresee the challenges, standardize operations, and streamline human decision-making are AI factors. Predictive analytics can offer an insight into what is happening in the market, the efficiency of the labor force, and operational risks to make necessary steps in time. Human labor is made easier by robots, and this leads to increased productivity and workers are left to perform more creative duties. The emotion recognition systems operate based on the analysis of communication messages; they are assisted to promote the empathetic leadership and the welfare of the employees with the assistance of adaptive feedback (Siemon, 2022). Meanwhile, adaptive learning systems continuously adjust AI algorithms with the new information and they make context-dependent decisions. All the AI elements create an intelligent system, which enables real-time sensitivity and sustainability of performance in the hybrid forms of work. They are successful however on the responsible Implementation, data transparency and trust by users. When used ethically, AI will become an intelligent co-worker that will transform virtual offices into proactive human-centric ecosystems, which thrive in uncertainties.

4.3 Enabling Mechanisms: Ethical Frameworks, Reskilling Programs, Digital Sustainability

Facilitating mechanisms ensure that there is no one-sided, open, and predictable cooperation between humans and AI. Moral systems establish a concept of equity, privacy, and responsibility to stop AI abuse and establish trust. Reskilling interventions educate employees how they can successfully engage with AI systems by increasing their digital capabilities, critical thinking and flexibility in problem resolving. The continuous learning generates the impression of confidence and decreases the anxiety of job displacement (Bienefeld et al., 2024). The objectives of digital sustainability are the decarbonization of the environment and society due to energy-saving computing, teamwork in the virtual and sustainable data management. All the above mechanisms ensure that the organization will be resilient in the long-run as the values of the humans towards technological innovation are aligned. They will be the mediator between AI potential and human will, such that automation gets applied to achieve well-being and inclusiveness. Ethical, educational and sustainability institutionalization would assist organizations in developing hybrid ecosystems, where a technological advancement is in tandem with human development.

4.4 Outcomes: Resilience, Agility, Inclusivity, Innovation, Well-Being

The effects of the AI synergy with humans are observed in different organizational facets, which comprise resilience, agility, inclusivity, innovation, and well-being. Resilience can be described as the capability of the organization to recover through disruption using predictive and adaptive skills. Agility is a response of successful coordination of the workflows, and it enables addressing the emerging issues on time. The inclusivity gives equal participation and accessibility strengthened by the ability of AI to enable overcoming linguistic, cognitive and physical barriers. Creativity and machine intelligence are factors that combine to produce new solutions and approaches, which are called innovation (Ho et al., 2022). Lastly, well-being focuses on psychological safety, work-life balance, and interesting involvement. All these results enhance long-term sustainability by having a purpose-performance integration. Those organizations that work to achieve these results successfully build digital ecosystems, which are not only technologically sophisticated, but also ethically, human-centered, and functioning in constantly changing remote and hybrid environment.

4.5 Interaction Pathways Between Human And AI Capabilities In Remote Contexts

The continuous learning, adaptation and decision-making cycle in the digital workplaces is characterized by the interaction pathways between the human and AI capabilities. Humans offer contextualized judgment, empathy and ethical reasoning, whereas AI is beneficial in terms of precision, scalability and predictability. Such interaction is provided in the form of feedback loops where AI systems can be based on the feedback and improve their models, as well as provide better recommendations. In this case, as an example, emotional AI applications detect tonal elements of communication, personalized response to assist in cooperation, but human beings are capable of operating such mechanisms based on the intuitively acquired understanding and perception of circumstances (Monarca & Bandiola, 2023). This kind of reciprocal learning leads to the co-evolution because each party makes the other strong. This synergy is a non-spatial and non-cultural barrier in distant places that augments cohesiveness and innovation. It can be achieved through the organizations that come up with transparent interfaces and participatory governance arrangements capable of implementing trust, inclusiveness, and flexibility that are crucial features of resilient and sustainable hybrid ecosystems.

5. RESEARCH METHODOLOGY

The research has a mixed-method methodology because the concept of human-AI synergy is supposed to be explored using methods such as reviewing literature and interviewing personnel to assess their applicability in fostering organizational resilience within a hybrid and remote workplace. The research will take place with the help of the qualitative comparative analysis and thematic interpretation of various organizational contexts where AI-based collaboration tools are currently being implemented. The secondary data sources are the primary ones and include the scholarly literature, company reports, and the case studies of the AI implementation (E. Chen and Zhang, 2024). Thematic and content analysis are the methods of analysis applied to identify the patterns, best practices, and issues that recur in different sectors. The study is devoted to hybrid organisations in which the use of modern AI based systems, including Microsoft Teams Copilot, Slack GPT and Zoom IQ, are used. It is validated, reliable and accurate to context because of the triangulation of academic, industrial and managerial views. The method of the research gives the opportunity to have an in-depth understanding of structural, ethical, and cultural factors of the influence on AI-assisted resilience and sustainability.

5.1 Research Design: Mixed-Method / Qualitative Comparative Case Analysis

The qualitative and interpretative approach is employed in the mixed-method research design that is applied in the study to have access to the theoretical and practical insights. The method employed due to analyzing the different organizational experiences of AI integration is a Qualitative Comparative Case Analysis (QCA). The design is able to determine the causal trend between the human-AI cooperation and organizational resilience. It involves a combination of different sources of information, i.e. written case examples, specialist interviews, literature review to identify triangulated evidence (Kaaria, 2024). The approach also assists in carrying out cross-case studies that would disclose the impact of contextual variables, which are organizational culture, the degree of technological maturity, and leadership, on the outcome of AI adoption. QCA pays greater attention to the meaning, interaction, and adaptive learning processes when compared the quantitative methods that are more focused on measurement. It is especially suitable in the research of complex socio-technical systems in which human cognition and algorithm intelligence are combined. Lastly, the mixed-method design will ensure that there is depth, validity and generalizability in the interpretation of the multidimensional nature of the AI-assisted hybrid working environment.

5.2 Data Sources: Secondary Literature, Organizational Reports, AI Deployment Case Studies

The research will rely on secondary data to describe mostly the broad and established image of human AI collaboration in hybrid working environments. The sources will include the peer reviewed academic journals, white papers and reports by international consultancies that are discussing digital transformation and resiliency in the workplace. This effect is reflected in reality through such components of it like organizational documents, sustainability reports, and after-implementation reviews of AI collaboration tools. In addition, the particular instances of AI implementations (the implementation of Microsoft Teams Copilot, Slack GPT, and Zoom IQ) provide the idea of performance measurements, user accommodation and practices. This type of scholarly and industry literature triangulation would ensure the rigor and relevance of theoretical and practical implications (Greenhalgh et al., 2017). The secondary data is also carefully chosen both in terms of credibility and timeliness and in respect to suitability to the study purpose. The synthesis of evidence regarding different areas of knowledge provides the study with an extensive background of the changes in AI-based systems on communication, productivity, and ethical decision-making in distributed organizational ecosystems.

5.3 Methods: Thematic Analysis, Content Analysis, Or System Mapping

Thematic analysis, content analysis, and system mapping are consolidated to get familiar with the received data. Thematic analysis identifies repetitive ideas and patterns of behavior of the role that AI plays on resilience, adaptability, and collaboration. To determine a trend in the discourse of organizations, content analysis is the measure of the frequency as well as the positive occurrence of a given word such as like, trust, automation, or sustainability in the documents. System mapping is a description of interrelations between the human and AI elements and the definition of the enablers and obstacles. An area of their combination will enable the comprehension of conceptual and functional relationships with each other that create resilient hybrid ecosystems (Pandey, 2023). Analytical coding is performed In cycles in order to have the ability to retain the new insights that are not based on assumptions but rather facts. Cross-validation between sources increases accuracy of interpretation and reduces bias with the help of interpretation. The unified methodological approach offers a moderate approach to valuing the contribution of AI interventions to transforming the working structure, leadership styles, and involvement of employees in the distributed organizations.

5.4 Sampling Context: Hybrid Organizations Adopting AI-Driven Tools

The sampling environment takes into account the use of AI-based partnerships and productivity RP by an organization in the hybrid form, which is actively engaged in the use of AI. The digital transformation examples presented by the companies that have implemented the tools such as Microsoft Teams Copilot, Slack GPT, Zoom IQ, and Notion AI are outstanding. The organizations are the various sectors which are technology, education, healthcare and consulting, where continuity of performance is rested on the remote operations and smart automation. The given context sheds light on practical scenarios of the human-AI interaction revolving around flexibility, inclusiveness, and sustainability in management (Behl et al., 2022). Sampling is determined using relevance and is not dependent on geographic and size constraints but rather on the environment in which AI is used in its mature form and the outcomes of resilience are quantifiable. This data has been offered by such organizations and it gives valuable insights on how leadership, data ethics and trust may be adapted among employees. Through the settings, the study indicates the mechanisms that enable technology to complement the human thinking that helps in establishing the strategic paths to determine why AI-supported hybrid working places are resilient and sustainable.

5.5 Validation: Triangulation Of Academic, Industrial, And Managerial Perspectives

The validity will be determined through triangulation, that is, academic, industry and management perspectives will be incorporated to ensure analytical rigor and credibility. Theoretical soundness is being delivered by academic validation since the findings fit the already existing models of organizational behavior, digital transformation, and AI ethics. Industrial validation provides practical applicability on the basis of case evidence in companies that use AI in hybrid workflows. The sphere of the leadership experiences that examine the perception of the executives regarding the role of AI in resilience, productivity, and workforce well-being is called managerial validation (Molino et al., 2020). This cross-verification of insights in these domains is carried out by the triangulation process which minimizes bias and enhances consistency. The assistance of external feedback in the form of responses given by the domain experts and the organization reports is used to increase the interpretive accuracy. Such a multidimensional validation procedure will demonstrate the fact that, the findings are conceptualized and practical simultaneously. It also enhances the degree of generalization to such an extent that the sophisticated strategies and structures may be effectively adopted by different organizations that want to adopt an adaptive, ethical and sustainable approach in integrating AI into the distributed working environments.

6. LITERATURE REVIEW

The creation of AI in both remote and hybrid workplaces has changed the organization dynamics, change in the organization structure, and leadership models considerably. The literature has noted a drastic shift in how digital platforms facilitate collaboration, efficiency and decision-making and has new challenges in the domains of trust, ethics and human well-being. The current studies on the effects of AI on the transformation of remote work are centred around the transition to smart collaboration platforms, rather than basic digital applications (Khajeh Naeeni & Nouhi, 2023). The use of apps such as Microsoft Teams, Slack, and Zoom is now in the form of an AI-enhanced tool with predictive analytics and emotion-sensitive recognition along with workflow automation. Such are the abilities that enhance the likelihood of collaboration during real-time, monitor involvement, and decision-making in geographically separated teams. The AI-enabled personalization has also enabled adaptive learning and tracking performance and also enabled remote work to be more data-driven and responsive (Khairi et al., 2024; Ghonim & Awad, 2025; Awad, 2025). However, scientists caution sufficiently that excessive reliance on algorithmic guidance may result in the absence of independence and inventiveness, therefore it is essential to have a balance in machine-based intelligence and human jurisdiction.

The theoretical contributions to human-AI collaboration differentiate between automation (i.e. replacing human repetitive tasks with AI) and augmentation (i.e. complementation of cognitive and emotional abilities by AI). Researchers in the field of organizational psychology and management science emphasize augmentation as a better method of maintaining human relevance in digital ecologies (Barasa et al., 2018). The use of AI tools improves the human performance by providing contextual advice and emotional feedback and prioritizing the tasks based on the intelligence. However, there are also psychological obstacles to the adoption described in literature, such as fear of being replaced, losing control, and mistrust. Effective integration thus requires clear communication, ethical design and constant reskilling of employees to be able to work with AI systems with confidence (Raisch & Krakowski, 2020; Awad & Ghonim, 2025; Alharthi & Awad, 2025). In the field of organizational resilience, scholars consider AI a facilitator, as well as a challenge of flexibility. The concept of resilience is becoming understood more as crisis recovery, however, proactive capacity- predicting risks and being innovative in the face of disruption.

Research indicates that predictive analytics, scenario modeling and resource (Raisch & Krakowski, 2021b)optimization are some of the ways AI has helped to enhance resilience. However, human factors like psychological safety, empathy and group learning are also crucial in resiliency. Organizations which merge digital preparedness and conducive cultures are characterized by better adaptability, which is known as being hybrid . Therefore, resilience frameworks should incorporate the technological preparedness as well as socio-emotional intelligence in order to bring about sustainable balance. The ethical and sustainable practices literature emphasises that ethicalness without resilience makes ethical practices weak (Chang & Ke, 2024). The human-intelligent systems relationship is based on transparency, fairness, and accountability. Prejudice in algorithms, untransparent decision-making, and breaches of privacy destroy trust in employees, as well as eradicate inclusiveness. Researchers come up with models that combine explainable AI, design with participation, and fair use of technology. In addition, the sustainability literature associates AI use with environmental and social objectives (i.e., energy-efficient computing, digital wellbeing and minimized carbon footprints by means of virtual collaboration) (Aggarwal & Srivastava, 2019).

The parameter of ethical governance and digitally sustainable convergence therefore qualifies the future of responsible AI in hybrid workplaces. The cross-sectoral studies in information technology, education, healthcare, and finance provide empirical evidence that the use of AI increases efficiency, innovation, and speed of decision making. Nevertheless, there are still gaps in moral maturity, ability preparedness, and political systems(Brinkmann et al., 2025). Technological innovations are very fast, but the policies that are focused on human beings are not. This synthesis shows that there is a research gap that has remained: the lack of substantive inclusion of sustainability, ethics, and human well-being in AI resilience models. The gap that remains in the future scholarship should thus be filled by creating comprehensive, participatory theory of AI-aided organizational resilience that would integrate productivity with inclusivity and sustainability.

6.1 Problem Statement

Even though AI is now trending in hybrid and remote offices, many companies are unable to balance their efficiency with the use of technology and human health, inclusivity, and integrity. The existing systems are inclined to achieve it at the cost of creativity, trust and sustainability in favour of automation and performance measures. This results in reduced interaction and confidence in the AI-based environments among the employees. There are no coherent frameworks that can assist AI in realizing the potential of transforming electronic workspaces into adaptable, sustainable and psychologically secure places as human-centered design, ethical AI government and resilience strategies do not have coherent frameworks.

6.2 Research Gap

The literature on AI application to hybrid work mostly highlights the issues of productivity and efficiency of automation but does not dwell on the sustainability, the ethical governance, or the human-AI dynamism. The effects of emotional intelligence, trust, and digital ethics on the resiliency of AI-supported organizations are scarcely covered in the literature. Moreover, the element of interdisciplinary perspective that implements the management science, organisational psychology, and digital ethics is feeble. The specified gap indicates that the more comprehensive approach that examines how human-AI collaboration promotes adaptive, inclusive, and resilient organizational structures within the evolving digital work environment is needed.

7. RESULTS / DISCUSSION

Its discussion reveals that there are significant trends, which highlights the transformational nature of AI in the creation of flexibility, alignment and stability within the framework of a hybrid workplace, and the remote workplace. Thematic findings indicate that AI has a beneficial impact on organizational learning, decision-making and employee welfare and is related to emerging ethical and managerial challenges.

The following comparison of evidence across various organizations reveals that there is a difference in the degree of success, and the resilient models involve the augmentation, transparency, and human empowerment. Weak models on the other hand are overly automated, and have no ethical protection (Zárate-Torres et al., 2025). The discussion highlights that strategic integration, inclusive governance, and life-long learning are the elements of the successful human-AI synergy. Automation and autonomy should always be balanced so that AI is increased, as opposed to reducing the human aspect of digital workplaces.

7.1 Thematic Outcomes From The Analysis

Thematic analysis showed that there are six large-scale dimensions of AI-inspired organizational change: adaptive learning, proactive decision support, real-time collaboration, emotional intelligence integration, ethical alignment, and sustainability. Adaptive learning became one of the priorities, and AI tools constantly optimize processes and forecast performance patterns. Preventative decision support enabled managers to predict risks by forecasting and modeling scenarios using data (Han et al., 2019). Sentiment detection and feedback analysis are emotional intelligence characteristics that contributed to the increased morale and inclusivity of teams in distributed environments. The ethical congruence and sustainability measure, which was the transparent algorithmic governance and environmentally-efficient virtual operations, mirrored the organizational credibility and environmental awareness. Coupled together, it is possible to mention that the effective implementation of AI is not only about improvement of efficiency, but it can lead to the creation of the robust ecosystem that will rely on trust, inclusivity, and flexibility. The findings confirm the interaction of co-evolution between human intuition and AI intelligence as the driver of resilience of hybrid workplaces as opposed to tech-dependence.

7.2 Insights Into How AI Tools Enhance Coordination, Productivity, And Foresight

The coordination and productivity are significantly improved with the use of AI technology since the current coordination and scheduling can be performed seamlessly and predictive resources managed. Menial coordination tasks are automated with intelligent systems such as Microsoft Teams Copilot, Slack GPT, and Zoom IQ, and employees are given the space to perform creative and strategic tasks. On-the-fly analytics maintains an account of the project progress and potential bottlenecks to allow pro-active response. AI-based predictive foresight can help in risk assessment and designing a workforce that can help organizations to be flexible to changing conditions. Further, the cross-departmental collaboration is filled in with the assistance of the information uniting and the application of the automatic insights that grants the transparency and responsibility (Harsha & Natraj, 2025). Through the hybrid teams, the space and time problems are overcome by using AI to synchronize the working processes despite time zones. This agility and responsiveness of the organization is achieved through such an improvement of foresight and co-ordination. The findings show that AI can be successfully implemented to enhance operational and cognitive features of teamwork and support collective intelligence and organizational agility. Table 1 Shows the potentials of human abilities and AI to be applied to support each other to improve the performance, creativity and resilience in hybrid workplaces.

Table 1 Comparative Analysis of Human and AI Capabilities

Aspect	Human Capabilities	AI Capabilities	Synergistic Outcome
Creativity	Generates original ideas and contextual innovation	Analyzes data patterns to inspire new solutions	Enhanced innovation through data-informed creativity
Decision-Making	Applies ethical reasoning and emotional judgment	Provides analytical precision and predictive insights	Balanced and well-informed strategic choices
Communication	Uses empathy, tone, and cultural understanding	Facilitates real-time translation and sentiment analysis	Improved collaboration and inclusivity in diverse teams
Learning and Adaptation	Learns from experience and intuition	Continuously updates from large data sets and feedback loops	Continuous organizational learning and adaptability
Efficiency	Performs complex, abstract, and value-based tasks	Automates repetitive and data-heavy processes	Higher productivity and focus on strategic priorities
Ethical Awareness	Understands moral values and human consequences	Operates under coded ethical guidelines and monitoring frameworks	Trustworthy and accountable decision environments

7.3 Evidence Of Improved Resilience And Employee Well-Being Through AI Augmentation

The findings indicate that AI augmentation positively affects resilience and employee wellness in hybrid organizations. The AI-powered systems provide the reduction of stress and digital exhaustion through mental health tracking, automated workload, and personalized feedback. Adaptive algorithms identify the signs of burnout before they occur and recommend the balanced working schedules and supportive actions. Emphatic communication with the help of emotion-recognition-tools will turn a distributed team into a psychologically safe and trusted group. Besides, AI-based automation removes menial or mentally demanding duties and devotes the employees to creativity and innovativeness (Sadiku et al., 2021). The sense of empowerment and effectiveness due to the aid of AI is a direct quality of resiliency since the employees feel prepared to transform to address the challenges. Particularly, AI-human collaboration results in the emergence of participatory culture where employees have managed to acquire the sense of technology as a friend and not an enemy. All these findings prove that AI augmentation can support organizational stability and personal contentment of a particular person in case it is introduced in an ethical and transparent way.

7.4 Challenges Identified: Overreliance, Digital Fatigue, Ethical Ambiguity, And Data Privacy

Although significant gains were achieved, there were a number of challenges that came out of the analysis. The excessive use of AI may cause cognitive dependence, lowering the independence of employees when it comes to solving problems. The problem of digital fatigue is becoming more common because of constant monitoring, a high amount of time spent in front of a screen, and overload of information provided by automated systems. Algorithms that lack transparency cause ethical ambiguity as they are perceived to be unfair or biased. Additionally, the issue of data privacy remains ongoing because AI tools continue to gather and analyze the data of users, even without their consent (Samishetti, 2025). Unless these issues are checked by proper governance, they may be a cause of lack of trust and impediments to adoption. The task of the organizations is to strike a balance between automation efficiency and ethics accountability through the introduction of transparent data practices, regular auditing, and psychological health applications. The key factors of mitigating these risks are design consciousness of AI and human-centric design. Addressing such issues is essential to ensuring trust, fairness and well-being in hybrid workplaces that are augmented by AI. Table 2 Provides illustrations of typical issues (such as overreliance, data fatigue, and issues with data privacy) and presents easy solutions to the issues.

Table 2 Key Challenges and Mitigation Strategies in AI-Augmented Workplaces

Challenge	Description	Mitigation Strategy
Overreliance on AI	Employees may depend excessively on AI outputs, reducing independent judgment.	Encourage human oversight and decision validation through training.
Digital Fatigue	Continuous screen exposure and automated notifications cause stress and burnout.	Introduce mindful technology use, breaks, and workload balancing.
Ethical Ambiguity	Lack of transparency in AI decision-making can lead to perceived unfairness.	Implement explainable AI systems and ethical review committees.
Data Privacy Concerns	Sensitive user data may be misused or inadequately protected.	Strengthen cybersecurity policies and ensure data anonymization.
Skill Gaps	Employees may lack the competencies to interact effectively with AI tools.	Launch continuous reskilling and AI literacy programs.
Bias and Discrimination	Algorithmic bias can reinforce workplace inequalities.	Regularly audit AI systems for fairness and inclusivity compliance.

7.5 Comparative Discussion of Case Examples (Resilient vs. Fragile AI Adoption Models)

The comparative analysis revealed that there are noticeable differences in the models of robust and weak AI adoption. Powerful companies possess human-centered vision where AI complements imagination, sympathetic and group efforts. They invest in reskilling of their employees, ethical AI models and open communication that results in high adaptability and trust. Such organizations believe that AI is empowering and sustainable. Conversely, weak adoption models are based on efficiency, as opposed to ethics, leading to burnout, low involvement and resistance to change in the digital sphere. Undertraining, poor data management and meaningless inclusion destroy resiliency in such an environment. The facts of the cases prove that the maturity of technologies is not a panacea and that AI must be modified to the human values and vision of the leader (Greenhalgh et al., 2021). The comparison also indicates that AI systems resilience is a combination of innovation and empathy unlike weak systems which apply too much automation and they do not promote shared intelligence and moral values.

7.6 Implications For Balancing Human Autonomy And AI Intelligence

Striking a balance between human autonomy and AI intelligence is the best approach towards sustainable organizational resiliency. The findings suggest that the positive effect of AI as a cognitive rather than determinant partner on humanizing the working environment is demonstrated by the hybrid working environment.

Autonomy is ensured by human control, participative design and open feedback systems providing employees with a chance to refute or refine AI outputs (Zhang, 2025). The leadership role in the creation of digital trust is quite significant as leaders are obliged to pay attention to accountability and explain AI logic. Ethics must be limited in that the technology is to enhance operations but not to replace the human judgment. The training programs will also make the employees more digital and ethically conscious and will encourage them to use smart systems devoid of fear. Arranging the equilibrium between the effectiveness of AI and human empathy and imagination, organisations will develop an enjoyable ecosystem, where automation does not negatively affect the quality of decisions made by people. Ultimately, we will possess the undying strength, with humans being in the front lines and AI being in the background, complementing each other with their knowledge and correct predictions.

8. FUTURE RESEARCH

As the AI-driven variant of hybrid work rapidly evolves, the additional study of the behavioral, ethical, and social-technical implications of this phenomenon in the long term is needed. Whereas the current literature highlights the short-term benefits of AI when applied in the area of flexibility and teamwork, longitudinal and cross-functional research should be conducted in order to understand the enormous impact of AI on organizations and psychology. More research will be necessary to determine the quantifiable degrees of resilience that can incorporate factors of human and AI performance, and organizational maturity can be evaluated on evidence (Putri, 2025). In addition, there is more interest in the study of the impact of generative AI on creativity, mood, and cognitive engagement in remote teams. The formulation of holistic policy and governance frameworks are also important to ensure that the utilization of AI is ethical, inclusive, and also founded on the principles of sustainability and human dignity.

8.1 Longitudinal Studies On AI–Human Behavioral Dynamics In Remote Ecosystems

The longitudinal studies are needed to understand the dynamics of the relations between humans and AI in the course of time in the hybrid conditions. Short term analyses will just record the performance increment and not the behavioral modifications, psychological addictions and the trust that will develop in the long term. These shifts in employee motivation, their cognitive load, and the interpersonal communication must be tracked in research because of the maturity of the AI systems. The results of long-term exposure to AI in terms of creativity, stress coping, and culture could be established by tracking the changes during the period of several years. (Santos, 2024). Besides, through such studies, the tipping points in which technological dependency enhances or weakens resilience can be discovered. By incorporating psychological, sociological, and technological data, it will be possible to have a holistic picture of how the human-AI relationships influence the long-term development of sustainable, adaptive, and emotionally intelligent workplaces.

8.2 Development Of Resilience Indices Integrating Human–AI Performance Metrics

One line of inquiry that needs to be followed more critically in the future is the development of resilience indices to measure the overall performance of humans and AI in hybrid work systems. The most common models of assessment tend to evaluate efficiency or satisfaction separately but not the relationship between them. Such parameters as adaptability, decision accuracy, engagement and emotional well-being as well as the reliability of AI, the speed of response and transparency should be combined in a composite index (Andi Prayogi et al., 2025). These indices would enable organizations to gauge the effectiveness of the human and machine input in terms of attaining resilience and sustainability objectives. With the assistance of quantitative modeling and data analytics, the researchers can have a chance to standardize the measure of resilience and define the best practices. These indices would also enable policy-makers and leaders to devise evidence-based policies that would help them cooperate with AI and streamline its functions.

8.3 Exploration Of Generative AI's Role In Creativity And Mental Health In Remote Work

It can be achieved through the generative AI devices such as content creation aids and idea-generation systems, which have provided new opportunities of creativity in remote settings. However, they have not been researched well in terms of their psychological and emotional impacts. Future studies should address the effects of these systems on cognitive interaction, the possibility of innovation, and mental health generally. Despite the fact that generative AI can enhance the creativity of works by reducing the cognitive hindrances, it may also produce addiction or a kind of homogenization of creativity (Stone, 2025). The two implications, which are empowerment and overreliance, will be investigated to know how to utilize it in a sustainable manner. The topic of AI in the context of alleviating stress and encouraging positive digital working cultures is also to be studied. This balance is essential in developing AI systems that are emotionally intelligent to promote creativity and productivity besides psychological well-being in the distributed workplaces.

8.4 Policy And Governance Frameworks For Ethical And Sustainable AI Deployment

In order to ensure that the application of AI in hybrid workplaces is ethical, open, and fair, the strong policy and governance structures are required. The research that is required in studying the governance mechanisms capable of addressing the issues of algorithmic accountability, privacy protection, and inclusivity is the following. The effectiveness of the patterns of regulation can be demonstrated through the comparison of the policies of different countries and industries, and can denote the spheres that need to be standardized (Park, 2025). In addition, the AI operations must be reinforced with sustainability measures that are instilled in the structures, which will make the AI operations minimize environmental and social costs. Ethical audits, participation design principles, and certification systems are useful in enhancing the responsible use of AI. This also means that researchers need to investigate the way the governance structures affect the levels of trust in employees and the perception of the population. It will be essential to develop flexible and transparent policies to synchronize the innovation on AI with long-term human, organizational, and ecological welfare.

9. MANAGERIAL IMPLICATIONS

The present paper has a practical implication to leaders and decision-makers interested in creating adaptive, ethical, and sustainable hybrid workplaces supported by AI. Managers must strive to accomplish creation of trust, inclusiveness, and ability preparedness among the workforce rather than just applying the technologies. The essence of the balanced human-machine cooperation development is open governance, reskilling, and the ethical introduction of AI. The fact that leadership strategies should be founded on human intuition and data-driven information is important to be flexible in unstable situations (Raisch & Krakowski, 2021c). Also, sustainability is embedded in the digital transformation platforms, which play a significant role in the long-term organizational resilience. The managerial implications that will follow are founded on the holistic approach, i.e. the intersection point of innovation, governance, and human-centric design, to create AI-prepared cultures that are efficient and ethical, at the same time socially responsible.

9.1 Strategies For Cultivating AI-Ready And Resilient Organizational Cultures

The cultures that need to be developed to be AI-ready include openness, learning agility, and cross-functional collaboration that managers need to foster. Leaders need to encourage experimentation and allow teams to apply AI tools in a creative manner instead of being prescriptive. Resilience can be established through the development of flexibility - in this case, developing a culture that encourages employees to not see AI as a disruptor, but as an opportunity to grow. Corporate values should focus on transparency and fairness, as well as responsible actions, to gain trust in AI-assisted decisions (J Nair et al., 2024). It is recommended to establish internal communities of practice where knowledge on digital ethics, data literacy, and responsible innovation will be shared on a regular basis by managers. Moreover, a psychological safe working environment that tolerates failure and contributes to learning during the process strengthens the trust of the employees. By guaranteeing both AI projects and organizational orientation to purpose and values, the managers can create resilient ecosystems that can adapt to the change of technologies without losing human-centred priorities. This plan will ensure the improvement of performance and well-being on the organizational level due to the improved process of AI integration.

9.2 Importance Of Transparent Communication And Ethical AI Governance

Governance should be open and ethical in its practices so as to ensure that employees have confidence in the AI implementation. Managers are expected to show how AI systems make decisions, what and what data they use, and what impact are the results on the work process. This openness will eliminate the possibility of paranoia about being spied upon or discriminated against, and will lead to accountability. Ethical AI governance frameworks, like policies concerning fairness, inclusivity and privacy protection, should also be incorporated on the operational policies (Jobin et al., 2019). The AI applications can be kept in line with the organizational values through periodic audits and explainability control. The managers should also establish cross-disciplinary ethics committees to control the use of AI and resolve ethical dilemma. Communication of these practices to the employees is practiced to instill confidence in the employees and acceptance of AI tools. Lastly, transparency will enable technology to become a transparent mechanism and not an opaque system, a partner that builds trust, an engagement that will assist in sustaining the organisational resilience as the ethical responsibility and credibility of the organisation among others.

9.3 Reskilling And Continuous Learning Initiatives For Workforce Adaptability

The AI revolution requires culture of lifelong learning whereby the personnel has technical skills, analytical skills and ethical skills. Managers are advised to introduce systematic reskilling, which is aimed at AI literacy, interpretation and ability to think adaptively. To expand the flexibility and the engagement, continuous learning platforms, virtual simulation, and micro-credentialing can be utilized. In addition to technical training, the staff is supposed to acquire soft skills: critical thinking, emotional intelligence and collaboration so as to be able to complement AI capabilities (Butts et al., 2015). The regular knowledge sharing programs and mentorship programs will fill the lacks on knowledge production and competence in discipline. Besides, managers should customise learning journeys with the help of AI-based adaptive learning tools, which align with individual career trends. The investing organizations also protect the workforce against the disruption of the continually changing technologies. The given strategy would also be able to promote flexibility and empowered culture where employees would be involved in establishing ethical and innovative AI-based workplaces.

9.4 Design Of Hybrid Leadership Models Integrating Human Intuition And AI Insights

In order to make evidence-based decisions, hybrid leadership implies a moderate degree of human intuition and AI-related analytics. Rather, leaders should employ AI knowledge to anticipate, track performances, and strategize without becoming depersonalized, uninspired and unethical in decision-making. The successful leaders have the quality of being the bridges between human teams and AI systems: they can interpret the results of the data and turn them into actions that would make sense and human emotions and situations should be considered. The leading principles of hybrid leadership models are the human-technology cooperation, instead of rivalry (Topcuoglu et al., 2023). Also, managers will have to adopt flexible and situational leadership to distributed teams and data-driven activities. The hybrid leadership skills can be enhanced with the help of digital competence and emotional intelligence with the help of the training program. By integrating technological foresight and humanistic-based ethics, managers can bring organizations to the state of resilience, inclusiveness, and innovativeness, making it evident that AI-based environments leadership is rigorous in its analytical manner and highly empathetic.

9.5 Embedding Sustainability Goals Into Digital Transformation Strategies

The sustainability aspect that will be incorporated in digital transformation will ensure that the process of technology developing is linked to environmental, social, and ethical agendas. Managers should consider adaptation of the idea of green computing; i.e. to make maximum use of energy, limit redundancy of information, and promote working remotely to lower carbon footprints. Implementation of AI must also have on board sustainability measures that can be linked to the realization of efficiency and responsible ecological environment. Besides environmental goals, social sustainability requires access to AI tools to be equal and exclusion in the digital sphere must be avoided (Gkinko & Elbanna, 2022). Policies on circular technology and policies on ethical data management are also relevant to enhancing accountability within an organization. The managers should be able to align the sustainability objectives to the corporate strategy such that all the AI projects will be able to generate value in the society over the long run. Describing AI as not a productivity tool but a sustainable force of innovations, leaders can enhance brand integrity, trust in stakeholders, and accountability in the global context that would enable their organizations to lead with ethical and climate-friendly digital transformation. Table 3 Introduces leadership approaches, principles of governance and sustainability activities that promote both adaptive and responsible integrations of AI.

Table 3 Managerial Strategies for Building Resilient and Ethical AI-Driven Cultures

Focus Area	Managerial Strategy	Expected Outcome
Leadership and Vision	Promote a human-centered vision that balances innovation with ethical purpose.	Builds trust and alignment across hybrid teams.
Ethical Governance	Establish clear AI ethics policies and review committees for transparency.	Ensures accountability and fairness in AI decision-making.
Employee Empowerment	Encourage participatory decision-making and feedback on AI use.	Enhances engagement and psychological safety.
Reskilling and Continuous Learning	Implement AI literacy and digital upskilling programs.	Increases adaptability and confidence in AI adoption.
Hybrid Leadership Models	Combine data-driven insights with human empathy and intuition.	Improves decision quality and team cohesion.
Sustainability Integration	Embed environmental and social responsibility within digital strategies.	Promotes long-term ethical and ecological resilience.

10. CONCLUSION

Both hybrid and remote workplace introduction of AI is a revolutionary transformation of the organizational structure, culture, and sustainability. With the evolving digital ecosystem, the compatibility of humanity and machine intelligence regarding synergy becomes more central, and it will become the determinant of long-term adaptability and sustainability. Through this chapter, I have been able to learn that human-AI relationships are not only efficient in terms of technology but also an ethical regulation, inclusiveness and psychological health as part of a robust digital workplace. Making use of AI tools enhances coordination, decision-making, and foresight which assists organizations to anticipate risks, allocate resources in a more effective way, and, more significantly, keep on functioning even when interrupted. Nonetheless, such benefits are most immense when technology does not only boost the human imagination but also the knowledge and judgement of the human mind with regard to morality. The findings confirm the notion of sustainable success in terms of the capacity to find the balance between automation and autonomy, data and empathy, and innovation and responsibility. They should strive to build open governance in their organizations and develop digital trust and invest in lifelong reskilling to be able to turn AI into more than a functional tool and more than a strategic partner. Meanwhile, overreliance, ethical confusion, and digital fatigue are all obstacles pointing towards the significance of responsible design and human-focused policies. The future-focused leadership should adopt the hybrid models in which AI insights should be used together with the human intuition to make sure that the decision-making process remains contextual and value-based. Furthermore, the introduction of sustainability principles, including the environmental and social ones, into AI adoption strategies is a necessary requirement to ensure that technological advancement is coupled with the expansion of the overall societal objectives. The conclusion of the chapter is that technology is not enough in the era of intelligent remote working to ensure organizational resilience but a joint development of human and AI. Such synergy makes organizations successful in the face of uncertainty, create in a responsible manner, and develop ecosystems that are future-ready, allowing people and technology to do their best.

11.REFERENCES

Aggarwal, S., & Srivastava, M. K. (2019). A grey-based DEMATEL model for building collaborative resilience in supply chain. *International Journal of Quality & Reliability Management*, *36*(8), 1409–1437. DOI: 10.1108/IJQRM-03-2018-0059

Alharthi, B., & Awad, A. (2025). The role of digital marketing tools in promoting tourism: An applied study on online marketing strategies. *Innovative Marketing*, *21*(2), 14–26. DOI: 10.21511/im.21(2).2025.02

Andi Prayogi, M., Fahmi, M., Zurriah, R., Amaliah, N., & Dewi Siagian, A. (2025). The mediating job crafting and organizational resilience in linking information technology capabilities with sales performance: An empirical study from Indonesia. *Innovative Marketing*, *21*(1), 182–196. DOI: 10.21511/im.21(1).2025.15

Awad, A. (2025). The role of universities' social responsibility in enhancing business sustainability: Mediating role of entrepreneurial culture. *Problems and Perspectives in Management*, *23*(1), 181–192. DOI: 10.21511/ppm.23(1).2025.14

Awad, A., & Ghonim, A. (2025). Data-driven marketing in banks: The role of artificial intelligence in enhancing marketing efficiency and business performance. *International Review of Management and Marketing*, *15*(5), 422–431. DOI: 10.32479/irmm.19738

Barasa, E., Mbau, R., & Gilson, L. (2018). What is resilience and how can it be nurtured? A systematic review of empirical literature on organizational resilience. *International Journal of Health Policy and Management*, *7*(6), 491–503. DOI: 10.15171/ijhpm.2018.06 PMID: 29935126

Behl, A., Chavan, M., Jain, K., Sharma, I., Pereira, V. E., & Zhang, J. Z. (2022). The role of organizational culture and voluntariness in the adoption of artificial intelligence for disaster relief operations. *International Journal of Manpower*, *43*(2), 569–586. DOI: 10.1108/IJM-03-2021-0178

Bienefeld, N., Keller, E., & Grote, G. (2024). Human-AI teaming in critical care: A comparative analysis of data scientists' and clinicians' perspectives on AI augmentation and automation. *Journal of Medical Internet Research*, *26*, e50130. DOI: 10.2196/50130 PMID: 39038285

Brinkmann, L., Cebrian, M., & Pescetelli, N. (2025). Adversarial dynamics in centralized versus decentralized intelligent systems. *Topics in Cognitive Science*, *17*(2), 374–391. DOI: 10.1111/tops.12705 PMID: 37902444

Butts, M. M., Becker, W. J., & Boswell, W. R. (2015). Hot buttons and time sinks: The effects of electronic communication during nonwork time on emotions and work-nonwork conflict. *Academy of Management Journal*, *58*(3), 763–788. DOI: 10.5465/amj.2014.0170

Chang, Y.-L., & Ke, J. (2024). Socially responsible artificial intelligence empowered people analytics: A novel framework towards sustainability. *Human Resource Development Review*, *23*(1), 88–120. DOI: 10.1177/15344843231200930

Chen, E., & Zhang, H. (2024). Research on the impact of artificial intelligence technology on urban public health resilience. *Frontiers in Public Health*, *12*, 1506930. DOI: 10.3389/fpubh.2024.1506930 PMID: 39839427

Chen, Y., Wang, Z., & Ortiz, J. (2023). A sustainable digital ecosystem: Digital servitization transformation and digital infrastructure support. *Sustainability (Basel)*, *15*(2), 1530. DOI: 10.3390/su15021530

Dave, D. M., & Mandvikar, S.LTIMIndtree. (2023). Augmented intelligence: Human-Ai collaboration in the era of digital transformation. *International Journal of Engineering Applied Sciences and Technology*, *8*(6), 24–33. DOI: 10.33564/IJEAST.2023.v08i06.003

Dow, E. R., Khan, N. C., Chen, K. M., Mishra, K., Perera, C., Narala, R., Basina, M., Dang, J., Kim, M., Levine, M., Phadke, A., Tan, M., Weng, K., Do, D. V., Moshfeghi, D. M., Mahajan, V. B., Mruthyunjaya, P., Leng, T., & Myung, D. (2023). AI-human hybrid workflow enhances teleophthalmology for the detection of diabetic retinopathy. *Ophthalmology Science*, *3*(4), 100330. DOI: 10.1016/j.xops.2023.100330 PMID: 37449051

Dr. Jolly Masih, D. R. A. J. (2023). Enhancing employee efficiency and performance in Industry 5.0 organizations through artificial intelligence integration. [EEL]. *European Economic Letters*, *13*(4), 300–315. DOI: 10.52783/eel.v13i4.589

Drigas, A. S., & Papoutsi, C. (2018). A new layered model on emotional intelligence. *Behavioral Sciences (Basel, Switzerland)*, *8*(5), 45. DOI: 10.3390/bs8050045 PMID: 29724021

Ghonim, A., & Awad, A. (2025). Shaping customer insights through e-marketing: An applied study in the banking sector. *International Journal of Advanced and Applied Sciences*, *12*(4), 88–98. DOI: 10.21833/ijaas.2025.04.011

Gkinko, L., & Elbanna, A. (2022). Hope, tolerance and empathy: Employees' emotions when using an AI-enabled chatbot in a digitalised workplace. *Information Technology & People*, *35*(6), 1714–1743. DOI: 10.1108/ITP-04-2021-0328

Greenhalgh, T., Rosen, R., Shaw, S. E., Byng, R., Faulkner, S., Finlay, T., Grundy, E., Husain, L., Hughes, G., Leone, C., Moore, L., Papoutsi, C., Pope, C., Rybczynska-Bunt, S., Rushforth, A., Wherton, J., Wieringa, S., & Wood, G. W. (2021). Planning and Evaluating Remote Consultation Services: A new conceptual framework incorporating complexity and practical ethics. *Frontiers in Digital Health*, *3*, 726095. DOI: 10.3389/fdgth.2021.726095 PMID: 34713199

Greenhalgh, T., Wherton, J., Papoutsi, C., Lynch, J., Hughes, G., A'Court, C., Hinder, S., Fahy, N., Procter, R., & Shaw, S. (2017). Beyond adoption: A new framework for theorizing and evaluating nonadoption, abandonment, and challenges to the scale-up, spread, and sustainability of health and care technologies. *Journal of Medical Internet Research*, *19*(11), e367. DOI: 10.2196/jmir.8775 PMID: 29092808

Hafiza Hamzah, N., Khalid, M., Nasir, M., & Abdul Wahab, J. (2021). The effects of principals' digital leadership on teachers' digital teaching during the covid-19 pandemic in Malaysia. *Journal of Education and e-learning Research*, *8*(2), 216–221. DOI: 10.20448/journal.509.2021.82.216.221

Han, J., Zhang, Z., Cummins, N., & Schuller, B. (2019). Adversarial training in affective computing and sentiment analysis: Recent advances and perspectives [review article]. *IEEE Computational Intelligence Magazine*, *14*(2), 68–81. DOI: 10.1109/MCI.2019.2901088

Harsha, H., & Natraj, A. A. (2025). Workplace well-being and mitigating burnout using technological tools. DHARANA - Bhavan's International. *The Journal of Business*, *63–67*, 63–67. Advance online publication. DOI: 10.18311/dbijb/2024/48291

Hepfer, M., & Lawrence, T. B. (2022). The Heterogeneity of Organizational Resilience: Exploring functional, operational and strategic resilience. *Organization Theory*, *3*(1), 263178772210747. DOI: 10.1177/26317877221074701

Ho, B. Q., Otsuki, M., Kishita, Y., Kobayakawa, M., & Watanabe, K. (2022). Human augmentation technologies for employee well-being: A research and development agenda. *International Journal of Environmental Research and Public Health*, *19*(3), 1195. DOI: 10.3390/ijerph19031195 PMID: 35162215

Jobin, A., Ienca, M., & Vayena, E. (2019). The global landscape of AI ethics guidelines. *Nature Machine Intelligence*, *1*(9), 389–399. DOI: 10.1038/s42256-019-0088-2

Kaaria, A. G. (2024). Artificial intelligence and employee well-being: Balancing technological progressions with human-centric workplace strategies, a research agenda. *East African Journal of Information Technology*, *7*(1), 355–365. DOI: 10.37284/eajit.7.1.2281

Khairi, S. M. M., Salleh, S. M., Julina, J., Hanawi, M. H., & Zainuddin, A. (2024). Co-operative well-being and employee resilience: A comprehensive review of the literature. *International Journal of Research and Innovation in Social Science*, *VIII*(X), 1137–1146. DOI: 10.47772/IJRISS.2024.8100095

Khajeh Naeeni, S., & Nouhi, N. (2023). Job burnout mitigation: A comprehensive review of contemporary strategies and interventions. *KMAN Counseling and Psychology Nexus*, *1*(1), 91–101. DOI: 10.61838/kman.psynexus.1.1.11

Kharytonov, Y., Slobodian, S., & Podaienko, M. (2021). Development of models of technology transfer for public works. *Baltic Journal of Economic Studies*, *7*(4), 214–225. DOI: 10.30525/2256-0742/2021-7-4-214-225

Molino, M., Cortese, C. G., & Ghislieri, C. (2020). The promotion of technology acceptance and work engagement in Industry 4.0: From personal resources to information and training. *International Journal of Environmental Research and Public Health*, *17*(7), 2438. DOI: 10.3390/ijerph17072438 PMID: 32260142

Monarca, Y. E., & Bandiola, D. A. N. (2023). Human Resource Management practices, knowledge sharing, and emotional intelligence of unit heads: A causal model on organizational resilience in government agencies in Davao Region. *American Journal of Public Policy and Administration*, *8*(2), 61–73. DOI: 10.47672/ajppa.1611

Nair, J. (2024). Reconfiguration and transformation for resilience: Building service organizations towards sustainability. *Journal of Services Marketing*, *38*(4), 404–425. DOI: 10.1108/JSM-04-2023-0144

Pandey, P. (2023). Emotional Intelligence skills in the Age of AI – A Review. *International Journal For Multidisciplinary Research*, *5*(5), 7196. Advance online publication. DOI: 10.36948/ijfmr.2023.v05i05.7196

Park, C. S.-Y. (2025). Ethical artificial intelligence in nursing workforce management and policymaking: Bridging philosophy and practice. *Journal of Nursing Management*, *7954013*(1), 7954013. Advance online publication. DOI: 10.1155/jonm/7954013 PMID: 40236787

Pasupuleti, M. K., & Services, N. E. (2025). Augmented Human Intelligence: Converging Generative AI, Quantum Computing, and XR for enhanced human-machine synergy. DOI: 10.62311/nesx/rrv525

Putri, K. M. H.Komang Meydiana Hutama PutriYoessy Etna Werdini. (2025). Artificial Intelligence adoption, job insecurity, and psychological resilience: Challenges for employee adaptation in future work environments. *International Journal of Issue Science*, *1*(5). Advance online publication. DOI: 10.71364/ijiss.v1i5.12

Raisch, S., & Krakowski, S. (2020). Artificial intelligence and management: The automation-augmentation paradox. Academy of Management Review, 2018.0072. DOI: 10.5465/2018.0072

Raisch, S., & Krakowski, S. (2021a). Artificial intelligence and management: The automation–augmentation paradox. *Academy of Management Review*, *46*(1), 192–210. DOI: 10.5465/amr.2018.0072

Raisch, S., & Krakowski, S. (2021b). Artificial intelligence and management: The automation–augmentation paradox. *Academy of Management Review*, *46*(1), 192–210. DOI: 10.5465/amr.2018.0072

Raisch, S., & Krakowski, S. (2021c). Artificial intelligence and management: The automation–augmentation paradox. *Academy of Management Review*, *46*(1), 192–210. DOI: 10.5465/amr.2018.0072

Romanelli, M. (2018). Towards sustainable ecosystems. *Systems Research and Behavioral Science*, *35*(4), 417–426. DOI: 10.1002/sres.2541

Sadiku, M. N. O., Ashaolu, T. J., Ajayi-Majebi, A., & Musa, S. M. (2021). Augmented Intelligence. *International Journal Of Scientific Advances*, *2*(5). Advance online publication. DOI: 10.51542/ijscia.v2i5.17

Samishetti, B. (2025). The impact of AI and robotics on employee roles and HR practices: Challenges, transformations, and strategic workforce management. *Journal of Strategic Human Resource Management*, *14*(2), 31–39. DOI: 10.21863/jshrm/2025.14.2.004

Santos, F. P. (2024). Prosocial dynamics in multiagent systems. *AI Magazine*, *45*(1), 131–138. DOI: 10.1002/aaai.12143

Siemon, D. (2022). Elaborating team roles for artificial intelligence-based teammates in human-AI collaboration. *Group Decision and Negotiation*, *31*(5), 871–912. DOI: 10.1007/s10726-022-09792-z

Singh, A., & Pandey, J. (2023). Artificial intelligence adoption in extended HR ecosystems: Enablers and barriers. An abductive case research. *Frontiers in Psychology*, *14*, 1339782. DOI: 10.3389/fpsyg.2023.1339782 PMID: 38327504

Stahl, B. C., Schroeder, D., & Rodrigues, R. (2023). The ethics of artificial intelligence: An introduction. In *Ethics of Artificial Intelligence* (pp. 1–7). Springer International Publishing., DOI: 10.1007/978-3-031-17040-9_1

Stone, B. W. (2025). Generative AI in higher education: Uncertain students, ambiguous use cases, and mercenary perspectives. *Teaching of Psychology*, *52*(3), 347–356. DOI: 10.1177/00986283241305398

Team Leader Bangladesh. (2024). Impact of artificial intelligence (AI) on existing businesses and the global economy. *Global Mainstream Journal*, *1*(1), 1–6. DOI: 10.62304/ijbm.v1i1.120

Topcuoglu, E., Oktaysoy, O., Erdogan, S. U., Kaygin, E., & Karafakioglu, E. (2023). The mediating role of job security in the impact of digital leadership on job satisfaction and life satisfaction. *Marketing and Management of Innovations*, *14*(1), 122–132. DOI: 10.21272/mmi.2023.1-11

Verganti, R., Vendraminelli, L., & Iansiti, M. (2020). Innovation and design in the age of artificial intelligence. *Journal of Product Innovation Management*, *37*(3), 212–227. DOI: 10.1111/jpim.12523

Wong, A. (2025). Sustainable HR practices with AI. In *Artificial Intelligence and Sustainability: Innovations in Business and Managerial Practices* (pp. 80–107). SBS Swiss Business School., DOI: 10.70301/SBS.MONO.2025.1.5

Zárate-Torres, R., Rey-Sarmiento, C. F., Acosta-Prado, J. C., Gómez-Cruz, N. A., Rodríguez Castro, D. Y., & Camargo, J. (2025). Influence of leadership on human-artificial intelligence collaboration. *Behavioral Sciences (Basel, Switzerland)*, *15*(7), 873. DOI: 10.3390/bs15070873 PMID: 40723657

Zhang, Z. (2025). The role of artificial intelligence tools on Chinese EFL learners' self-regulation, resilience and autonomy. *European Journal of Education*, *60*(2), e70127. Advance online publication. DOI: 10.1111/ejed.70127

KEY TERMS AND DEFINITIONS

Adaptive Learning Systems: AI-driven platforms that adjust content and workflows in real time based on user performance, preferences, and behavioral feedback.

AI Augmentation: The enhancement of human performance and decision-making through intelligent systems that provide contextual insights rather than replace human effort.

Artificial Intelligence (AI): The simulation of human intelligence processes by machines, particularly computer systems, to perform tasks such as learning, reasoning, and decision-making autonomously.

Digital Ethics: The moral principles and practices guiding responsible use of technology, data, and AI to ensure fairness, privacy, and inclusivity.

Digital Transformation: The strategic integration of digital technologies into all areas of an organization, fundamentally changing how it operates and delivers value.

Emotional Intelligence (EI): The ability to recognize, understand, and manage one's emotions and those of others, increasingly supported by AI for improving communication and teamwork.

Ethical AI: The practice of designing, developing, and deploying AI systems in ways that ensure fairness, accountability, transparency, and respect for human rights.

Human–AI Synergy: A collaborative interaction where human creativity, judgment, and empathy complement AI's computational, predictive, and analytical capabilities to achieve shared goals.

Hybrid Leadership: A leadership approach that combines human intuition, empathy, and creativity with AI-based analytics and decision-support tools for strategic advantage.

Hybrid Work Model: A flexible work arrangement combining on-site and remote work modes, supported by digital tools for communication, collaboration, and productivity.

Organizational Resilience: The capacity of an organization to anticipate, respond to, and adapt to disruptions while maintaining essential functions and promoting long-term sustainability.

Sustainability: The balanced pursuit of economic, social, and environmental goals to ensure long-term organizational and societal well-being in the digital era.

Chapter 12
Humanizing Artificial Intelligence:
Reconstructing Organizational Behavior, Leadership, and Employee Well-Being in AI-Enabled Enterprise

Utsav Krishan Murari
https://orcid.org/0009-0007-1606-6775
Manipal University Jaipur, India

Hemlata Parmar
Manipal University Jaipur, India

Sumit Kumar Pandey
https://orcid.org/0000-0002-6306-5069
Manipal University Jaipur, India

ABSTRACT

The fast rate of Artificial Intelligence (AI) implementation in organizations is transforming leadership practice, human resource management, and organizational behavior. The chapter critically looks at how AI-driven organizations are reimagining leadership and behavior to maintain human-centricity in the era of algorithmic governance. It relies on the theory of socio-technical systems to study the effects of AI on the well-being, motivation and work-life balance of employees, grounded on digital organizational psychology, support of human-machine interaction, and collaboration. The chapter highlights the importance of ethical leadership, emotional intelligence, and integrative cultures following sustainable digital transformation

DOI: 10.4018/979-8-3373-7416-1.ch012

using empirical research and case studies and discussing digital alienation and suggesting a Humanized AI Governance model to balance technological effectiveness and behavioral resilience.

1. INTRODUCTION: AI AND THE RECONFIGURATION OF ORGANIZATIONAL LIFE

The accelerated implementation of Artificial Intelligence (AI) into the organizational ecosystems is one of the most significant changes to every history of management and work. AI is no longer seen as an edge case of automation or decision support, but it is now being integrated into the main processes of organizations, including its leadership decisions, human resource management (HRM), performance measurement, workflow management, and even strategy formulation. Predictive analytics, robotic process automation, and machine-learning-based platforms are among the technologies that have become part of the standard organizational procedures and are transforming how work is structured, power is distributed, and work is experienced (Davenport et al., 2022; Jarrahi et al., 2021).

On the managerial side, AI is popularly propagated as the means to provide unparalleled efficiency, velocity, and precision. Some applications of AI by organizations include maximizing recruitment, forecasting employee turnover, training employees at the individual level, and automating repetitive work, which leads to productivity and competitive advantage (Brynjolfsson & McAfee, 2023; Vrontis et al., 2022). Nevertheless, the deep-rooted socio-behavioral consequences of algorithmic management are usually ignored in this techno-optimistic story. Due to the growing involvement of AI systems in the decision-making and control processes, organizations must deal with emerging issues concerning the well-being of the employees, motivation, autonomy, trust, and psychological safety (Kellogg et al., 2020; Parker and Grote, 2022).

This chapter is because AI is not only a technological innovation but a socio-technical force, radically reorganizing leadership and organizational behavior. In comparison with the previous rounds of digitalization, AI presents the manifestations of algorithmic governance whereby the rights to make decisions, evaluation criteria, and norms of behaviour are, in part, delegated to the opaque computational systems (Meijerink et al., 2021). Leadership in these situations is no longer realized by human discretion and interpersonal persuasion but is more determined by information-based suggestions and autonomous controls. This change brings out very important issues over accountability, ethical responsibility and the maintenance of human-centric values in organizations.

There is recent organizational research that indicates an increasing conflict between the implementation of AI with its efficiency focus and the preservation of humane working conditions. Though there is a tendency to state that AI-enabled organizations experience more agility and cost savings, evidence shows that algorithmic control may increase work pressure, decrease opposing employee freedom, and lead to stress, burnout, and disengagement, which are not sufficiently controlled (Raisch and Krakowski, 2021; Tarafdar et al., 2020). Digital alienation has become one of the key issues in the modern world of organizational psychology as employees report that they have been monitored, disconnected, or undervalued by their workplaces algorithmically (Väänäinen et al., 2024).

Leadership plays a central role in determining this change. Conventional theories of leadership underpin vision, emotional intelligence, trust-building and ethical responsibility. Non however, AI-mediated decision environments make these roles more complex by bringing non-human actors into the process of leadership. More leaders use algorithmic tools in hiring, promotion, performance appraisal, and task allocation without the complete awareness of the operation of such systems (Faraj et al., 2021). This dependency might confuse moral agencies and introduce what researchers call responsibility gaps in AI-assisted decision-making (Martin et al., 2021). As a result, leadership in AI-enabled companies should not be merely technologically competent, but also exhibiting ethical reflexivity, empathy as well as could question the output of algorithms critically.

Regarding the organizational behavior aspect, AI transforms the main constructs, including motivation, job design, and work-life balance. Algorithms can improve feedback and role definition, and add to the surveillance cultures, degrading intrinsic motivation and creativity (Kellogg et al., 2020; Moore, 2021). On the same note, the AI-enabled flexibility (e.g., remote work coordination and intelligent scheduling) can facilitate the work-life balance but can also increase technostress and emotional fatigue when these issues are not properly handled (Tarafdar et al., 2020; Spagnoli et al., 2023).

All these trends highlight the drawbacks of technocratic methods of AI adoption. More researchers support the idea of human-centered or humanized AI governance an approach that would match the technological capacity with human values, psychological well-being, and social justice (Parker and Grote, 2022; Shrestha et al., 2021). To comprehend the co-evolution of technology and human agency, such an approach demands the combination of the knowledge of socio-technical systems theory, digital organizational psychology, and the study of human-machine collaboration.

Even though there is increasing interest in AI and management, the gap still exists. A significant part of the available literature focuses on the performance results and technical design, and human factors are considered as a secondary issue. There are also common problems with the practical implementation of AI in the field of ethics, and sometimes, they are abstract and unrelated to leadership and organizational culture (Raisch et al., 2023). To fill these gaps, this chapter prefigures the constructs of employee well-being, motivation, and relational leadership as the key to the sustainable change in AI-driven organizations.

2. THEORETICAL FOUNDATIONS: SOCIO-TECHNICAL SYSTEMS, DIGITAL ORGANIZATIONAL PSYCHOLOGY, AND HUMAN–AI COLLABORATION

To accurately study the impact of artificial intelligence on leadership, organizational behavior and employee well-being, it is necessary to base the argument on strong theoretical traditions, which consider technology and human behavior as inseparable entities. The chapter relies on the socio-technical systems theory, digital organizational psychology and human-AI collaboration frameworks to make sense of AI as an active organizational agent integrated into power, meaning, and work experience structures.

2.1 Socio-Technical Systems Theory and Algorithmic Organizations

One of the most stable perspectives on explaining the nature of the interaction between technology, work design, and human behavior is the socio-technical systems (STS) theory. STS theory, which is based on the work of Trist and Bamforth in the field of coal mining systems, states that social and technical subsystems should be combined in their optimization instead of having one of the subsystems dominating the other (Trist and Bamforth, 1951). Later organizational studies have repeatedly shown that technological efficiency which is built on the cost of human autonomy and sense is in the end unsustainable (Cherns, 1987).

With AI-powered firms, this principle is particularly relevant. The prevalence of algorithmic management systems such as recruitment, scheduling, performance assessment, and task assignment can be interpreted as a move towards more technical subsystem dominance, in which rationales of optimization unconditionally govern decisions instead of contextual human decision-making (Meijerink et al., 2021). Within the STS approach, this type of dominance can lead to a disruption of social subsystem due to lack of trust, psychological safety and agency with the employees. Empirical studies of algorithmic control reveal that the employees feel less autonomous and more stressed when making AI systems sound opaque and beyond challenge, despite the improvement of performance metrics (Kellogg et al., 2020).

Modern STS researchers believe that AI aggravates the traditional socio-technical contradictions by shortening the decision-making process and minimizing the human sensemaking chances (Orlikowski and Scott, 2021). Unlike previous technologies, AI systems never stop learning and improving, implying that the technical subsystem will be changing in real time instead of remaining fixed. This generates new power imbalances among system designers, organizational leaders and frontline employees, which in turn makes those governance structures where human values are explicitly re-introduced in technological design and implementation a necessity.

2.2 Digital Organizational Psychology and Employee Experience

Digital organizational psychology builds upon the traditional organizational psychology exploring how digital technologies transform cognition, emotion, identity, and social relations in the workplace. Whereas classical organizational psychology was concerned with motivation, job satisfaction, and leadership behaviors in comparatively stable work settings, digital organizational psychology deals with settings that are defined by ever-connectivity, datafication, and algorithmic mediation (Parker and Grote, 2022).

The AI systems affect the employee experience in three interconnected aspects. To begin with, they transform the cognitive requirements by changing the decision-making and decision evaluation processes. They are also getting workers to read through (algorithms) and balance them with intuition and reason to explain why they have deviated and not followed the automated guidance (Faraj et al., 2021). This causes cognitive load especially in cases where algorithms are not transparent or explainable.

Second, AI influences emotional and motivational processes. Studies of technostress indicate that constant surveillance, predictive performance marks, and real-time feedback may enhance anxiety and emotional fatigue, despite the description of these factors as productivity-enhancing (Tarafdar et al., 2020). Simultaneously algorithmic evaluation systems can result in crowding out intrinsic motivation when workers turn their attention away from making meaningful contribution to meeting the metrics, a phenomenon also present in platform based as well as traditional organizational environments (Väänanen et al., 2024).

Third, AI changes the work identity and belonging. Digital organizational psychology emphasizes that recognition, autonomy, and social interaction help people to create work identity. In cases when AI systems mediate recognition, i.e. prioritizing employees, delegating tasks, or anticipating potential, they affect how employees feel valued and recognized in the organization (Jarrahi et al., 2021). In its uncontrolled form, this may lead to what researchers refer to as digital alienation: a feeling of not being part of your job, workmates and organizational goals and mission.

2.3 Algorithmic Management and Control Theory

The field of algorithmic management is an essential theoretical gap between STS and organizational behavior. Also known as the outsourcing of managerial functions to algorithms, algorithmic management is a challenge to the classical theories of control as it relies on the automation of data beyond human control (Meijerink et al., 2021). Even though some claim that algorithmic management helps to increase consistency and objectivity, organizational studies indicate that it can open new control mechanisms that are less visible yet more widespread (Kellogg et al., 2020).

In the control theory, the conventional division is between outcome control, behavior control, and clan control. Algorithmic management is a combination of behavior and outcome control and consists of constant monitoring of performance indicators and regulation of workflows based on them. Nevertheless, algorithms do not have the sensitivity of context and moral judgment as human managers do. Consequently, they might be controlled by a detached mechanism that values efficiency over fairness or compassion, and this experience makes employees feel more injustices and powerless (Raisch and Krakowski, 2021).

This poses some deep leadership concerns concerning accountability. When machines and human beings co-produce decisions, they are diffused, and gray zones in ethics are formed. According to scholars, this is the automation-augmentation paradox: AI augments decision-making power but at the same time reduces the role of human agency when leaders mindlessly give up algorithmic authority (Raisch and Krakowski, 2021).

2.4 Human–AI Collaboration and Augmented Leadership

Recent scientific literature is showing a trend of re-conceptualizing AI not as a substitute to human labor but as a companion to socio-technical systems. Human-AI collaboration theory suggests that the two work in complements: humans can provide judgment, empathy, and ethical reasoning, whereas AI can provide speed, pattern recognition, and predictive ability (Shrestha et al., 2021). This collaboration does not rely on technical sophistication but organizational structure and leadership practice.

This leads to the idea of augmented leadership in the leadership context where AI information is provided to leaders as inputs and not directives. According to empirical research, a leader who forms AI recommendations as provisional, which can be discussed, contemplated, and interpreted through the prism of the setting, is more likely to retain trust and psychological safety in the teams (Faraj et al., 2021).

The idea of explainability and participation is also stressed in human-AI collaboration theory. Employees will feel much less negative well-being when they know how AI systems work and can challenge or override the decision (Parker and Grote, 2022).

2.5 Integrative Theoretical Synthesis

Combined, the socio-technical systems theory, digital organizational psychology, and human–AI collaboration models all lead to one conclusion: AI-based organizational change is more of a human issue than a technical one. Algorithms of governance lead to efficiency gains, but these gains are frail when they compromise the well-being of employees, motivation and trust. Leadership, therefore, should act as the go-between force that facilitates the match of technological capability and human needs.

This theoretical background sets the tone of discussing the way AI transforms leadership activities, organizational behavior, and employee performance in further paragraphs. It also justifies the normative position of the chapter that sustainable AI adoption involves purposeful designing decisions that maintain human dignity, agency, and relationship in the workplace.

3. AI, LEADERSHIP TRANSFORMATION, AND DECISION-MAKING PARADIGMS

The adoption of artificial intelligence into the management decision-making process in organizations has triggered a radical change in leadership, power, and managerial thinking. Contrary to the previous technologies used in decision-support, modern AI is becoming increasingly involved in sensemaking, prediction, and recommendation, transforming the experience of information interpretation, judgment, and responsibility among leaders. This section is a critical analysis of how AI restructures leadership paradigm with respect to authority in decision making, ethical leadership, emotional intelligence, and a new conflict between automation and human agency.

3.1 From Human Judgment to Algorithmically Mediated Leadership

The conventional view of leadership as a humanistic practice that was based on experience, intuition, moral judgment and interpersonal influence. The classical and modern theories of leadership, such as transformational leadership and ethical and servant leadership, highlight specifics of effective leadership such as vision, trust, empathy, and accountability. All these foundations are, however, complicated by the fact that AI-driven decision environments introduce algorithmic actors in the leadership processes.

Artificial intelligence systems have been employed to inform choices regarding recruitment, promotion, performance evaluation, workforce planning, and strategic forecasting. These systems are appreciated because they could handle high volumes of data and identify patterns that cannot be identified by human brains (Davenport and Miller, 2022). However, studies warn that the recommendations generated by algorithms are frequently seen as authoritative even though their logic is not transparent or that it is inappropriate due to the context (Faraj et al., 2021). This is also known as automation bias and may make leaders overly dependent on AI results, at the peril of critical thinking.

Considering the organizational theory approach, this change is a redistribution of decision authority. Leadership is no longer practiced either through command or relationship power but is more mediated by socio-technical assemblages where algorithms define what will be deemed rational, efficient, or optimal (Orlikowski and Scott, 2021). Due to this, leadership authority is in some way instantiated in technical infrastructures as opposed to being entrenched in human actors only.

3.2 AI-Augmented Decision-Making and the Automation–Augmentation Paradox

One of the most debated issues of modern management science is whether AI replaces or supplements the decision-making of leaders. Raisch and Krakowski (2021) constitute this tension as the automation-augmentation paradox. On the one hand, AI will make routine analytical tasks automatic, and the leaders will have time to consider themselves with strategic and relationship-based issues. Conversely, too much automation can be associated with the risk of substituting a human judgment, reducing the frames of decision, and failing to comprehend morality.

Empirical research indicates that AI is better applied in augmentation and not as a substitute for human judgment. Shrestha et al. (2021) prove that such organizations, in which the AI makes recommendations, but human decisions remain the final aspect, are more likely to maintain equilibrium between efficiency and legitimacy and trust. On the other hand, the uncritical adherence of leaders to the results of algorithms makes decision-making technocratic, which may negatively affect the voice of the employees and their ethical introspection.

The latter paradox is especially relevant in decisions regarding people-management. Hiring and performance appraisal applications that are driven by AI will be objective and consistent, but in many cases, they will encode historical biases existing in training data (Meijerink et al., 2021). When leaders depend on these systems without going through them reflexively, there is a danger of endorsing discriminatory results and absconding any responsibility.

3.3 Ethical Leadership in the Age of Algorithmic Governance

In the AI-enabled organizations, ethical leadership is made more complex and mandated. Classical theories of ethical leadership are focused on moral consciousness, justice and exemplary behavior. Nonetheless, algorithmic governance is associated with additional ethical issues of transparency, explainability, and accountability. Lack of justification in leaders making decisions based on systems that they are not completely familiar with can lead to responsibility gaps (Martin et al., 2021).

Recent studies in the field of business ethics believe that ethical leadership in artificial intelligence settings should include algorithmic stewardship- proactive management of AI in a way that enhances it to align with organizational values and social practices (Dignum, 2021). This covers the data source questioning, auditing the results, and developing systems to challenge the decision of algorithms. Ethical leadership is thus transformed into the subject of collective governance as opposed to individual moral character as entrenched in structures of organizations.

Notably, ethical leadership influences the perception of AI legitimacy among the employees, as well. Research indicates that employees would be more inclined to assume the trustworthiness of AI systems and the organization when leaders share their experiences with its application and recognize the current limitations (Raisch et al., 2023). On the other hand, the opaque implementation of AI contributes to the feeling of surveillance and unfairness, damaging organizational loyalty.

3.4 Emotional Intelligence and Relational Leadership under AI Mediation

Although AI is good at recognizing patterns and predicting them, it spends no emotions, uses no empathy, and is not sensitive to situations, which are the key elements of effective leadership. EI, which refers to the skill of recognizing, interpreting, and controlling emotions in self and others, is a highly important human skill that cannot be automated (Boyatzis et al., 2019). In workplaces mediated by AI, EI is even greater, since leaders must manage the employee concerns about job stability, surveillance, and algorithmic reviews.

Empathy and emotional awareness are the approaches proposed by research in organizational psychology that can help leaders mitigate the adverse impacts of algorithmic management on the well-being of employees (Parker and Grote, 2022). As an example, leaders that frame the algorithmic performance indicators by qualitative feedback and individual encouragement assist to maintain the psychological safety and intrinsic drive. Relational work is necessary to address the depersonalizing propensities of the AI-driven systems.

3.5 Decision-Making Accountability and Leadership Identity

The leadership identity is also transformed based on AI-driven decision-making. Leaders are finding themselves more on the role of interpreters of algorithmic insights and not making decisions independently. This change can improve the rigor of analysis but can also water down the views of leadership responsibility. Whenever results are not good, employees might wonder who makes decisions, the leader or the algorithm, particularly when the results are bad.

According to the organizational scholars, leadership legitimacy is only possible when lines of accountability remain straightforward (Faraj et al., 2021). Leaders would have to openly assert owning decision-making that is informed by AI by positioning algorithms as tools and not authorities. That way, it strengthens the normative assumption of leadership, which involves responsibility, rather than optimization.

3.6 Synthesis: Toward Human-Centric, AI-Augmented Leadership

Altogether, AI alters the leadership decision-making process, reallocation of power, speed of analysis, and responsibility. Although AI has strong augmentative capabilities, its blind application threatens to affect ethical judgment, emotional intelligence and employee confidence. Both theoretical and practical findings come down to the necessity of the human-centric AI enhanced leadership approach - a strategy that makes the best of AI but does not harm human values, relationality, or moral agency.

This synthesis preconditions the following part, which is an analysis of the interactions of these leadership changes with the larger organizational behavioral dynamics, such as motivation, control, creativity, and resistance in AI-enabled workplaces.

4. AI INTEGRATION AND ORGANIZATIONAL BEHAVIOR DYNAMICS

The introduction of artificial intelligence in the organization system has extensive consequences on fundamental organizational behavior (OB) dynamics, which encompass motivation, control, job design, creativity, resistance, and work-related social relations. Whereas previous digital technologies were facilitating the continuation of organizational structures, AI systems proactively transform the norms of behaviors by enforcing algorithmic logics in the daily operations of the workforce. Here, the author will discuss the ways in which the integration of AI is changing organizational behavior, specifically, the agency and motivation of employees, their surveillance, and the nature of work itself.

4.1 Algorithmic Management and the Reconfiguration of Control

Among the greatest changes in organizational behavior related to AI implementation, it is necessary to mention the emergence of so-called algorithmic management i.e. the delegation of coordination, monitoring, and appraisal roles to robots. Algorithms that manage people allocate, monitor the performance, as well as assess the results based on data-driven indicators, minimizing the need of close human control (Meijerink et al., 2021).

In terms of OB, this change is a shift between conspicuous, interpersonal control to data-driven, unrelenting control. According to Kellogg et al. (2020), this is a novel contested ground of control, wherein workers tend to feel an increased pressure to perform, even in places where the in-person oversight is expected to be more predominant. Although algorithmic systems may make work more efficient and predictable, they also result in more surveillance and consequently stress, anxiety, and defensive work practices (Moore, 2021).

Notably, the control in algorithmic management is usually opaque. Procedural justice perceptions may be compromised by workers not comprehending the method to compute performance metrics and decision-making processes. The existing body of research indicates that the perceived unfairness of evaluation systems has a negative impact on organizational commitment and trust (Väänamaki et al., 2024).

4.2 Motivation, Autonomy, and Algorithmic Performance Metrics

The concept of motivation is one of the main concepts of organizational behavior, which used to be influenced by autonomy, competence, and relatedness. The AI-performance management systems have direct impacts on these dimensions since they numerically measure outputs of work and associate them with rewards or penalties. Although these systems may help define the expectations and deliver quick feedback, they usually emphasize quantifiable results rather than quality input (Parker and Grote, 2022).

There is empirical evidence that algorithmic evaluation may crowd out intrinsic motivation, moving the employees' attention away to work that matters and toward metric optimization (Raisch and Krakowski, 2021). Employees can act like they are playing a game with the system, employing actions to please algorithms and algorithms and not organizational interests and consequently of reducing creativity and long-term performance. This dynamic indicates a time-old conflict in the field of OB between control and commitment, even though AI has the ability to monitor in a granular way.

This is especially influenced by autonomy. Even though the idea of AI systems as empowering technologies empowering the decision-making process can be presented, employees tend to have less discretion when algorithms tightly control workflows. As Jarrahi et al. (2021) demonstrate, employees working in plat formic management often bargain or rebel against algorithmic instructions to achieve back control, as to the continued role of human agency in extremely automated conditions.

4.3 Job Design, Work Intensification, and Fragmentation

The incorporation of AI also transforms the job design to change task composition, skills needed, and the temporal patterns of work. Routine and repetitive work is being automated, and the human aspects are being reassigned to supervisory and exceptions management and interpersonal coordination roles. Although some employees may find their work more engaging and demanding skills with this transformation, it may also disintegrate work and increase cognitive challenges (Orlikowski and Scott, 2021).

One of the repetitive consequences of AI-based policing is work intensification. Predictive analytics and real-time performance monitoring can help organizations establish more ambitious productivity goals, and frequently, the workload and resources do not change accordingly. It has been found in research on digital work environments that this kind of intensification leads to fatigue, burnout, and decreased work-life balance (Tarafdar et al., 2020).

Besides, temporal fluidity provided by AI, algorithmic scheduling and remote working organization can blur work and non-work life. Flexibility is generally viewed as an advantage, but research shows that being a 24/7 worker increases the stress of techno- and emotional burnout when employees have no control over the expectations of accessibility (Spagnoli et al., 2023).

4.4 Creativity, Learning, and Behavioral Adaptation

Adaptability in the organizations utilizes creativity and learning, which are also crucial but are not equally impacted by the AI integration. On the one hand, AI has the potential to enhance creativity through data-informed recommendations, recognition of patterns, and decision support. Conversely, strict algorithmic control could restrict the experimental aspect as it can punish against deviations of the prescribed norms (Parker and Grote, 2022).

According to OB research, creativity thrives in a setting where there are psychological safety and autonomy. When AI emphasis is on minimization of errors and ranking of the performance, employees can be risk-averse, which restricts innovation. Faraj et al. (2021) emphasise that AI-mediated environments demand sensemaking practices that enable employees to interpret and contextualize the outputs of the algorithms instead of following them directly.

4.5 Social Relations, Trust, and Organizational Culture

Social relations in organizations are also redesigned in the light of the AI integration. The interpersonal interaction could decrease, and the social cohesion and trust could deteriorate when the evaluation and coordination is mediated by algorithms. AI systems can be seen by employees as being depersonalized and punitive, especially when leaders depend on algorithmic measures a lot without further context (Raisch et al., 2023).

Belief in leadership and technology becomes a very important interpreter of behavioral outcomes. Research indicates that revealing information includes communication to employees about AI utilization and providing a platform to express their voices can alleviate the adverse response to automation (Meijerink et al., 2021). On the other hand, those cultures that adopt efficiency, rather than empathy, may create alienation and lack of engagement.

Organizational culture therefore is a decisive factor in influencing the impact of AI on behavior. The culture of learning, inclusion, and ethical reflection is in a better position to use the benefits of AI and reduce harm. This observation supports the overarching claim in the chapter that the use of AI needs to be directed by human-centred governance structures.

4.6 Synthesis: Organizational Behavior in AI-Enabled Enterprises

Synthetically, integration of AI has a tremendous impact on organizational behavior because it redefines the mechanisms, motivational structures, job designs, and social relations. Although AI has efficacy and insight potential, the behavioral implications are dependent on leadership practices, organizational culture, and governance decisions. The AI-driven systems have a threat of exacerbating stress, decreasing autonomy, and eroding trust before it is acknowledged that they need humans to be considered as human needs.

These dynamics reveal the need to reconsider the organization behavior theories in AI-enabled settings. The following chapter will develop this analysis by paying more specific attention to the subject of employee well-being, mental health, and the paradox of digital alienation in organizations that are run in an algorithmic manner.

5. EMPLOYEE WELL-BEING, MENTAL HEALTH, AND DIGITAL ALIENATION

With the beginnings of artificial intelligence entering the daily organizational processing, the well-being and mental health of the employees becomes one of the most important spheres where the opportunities and risks of the AI-enhanced change become most evident. Although AI systems are commonly implemented to contribute to more efficiency, accuracy, and flexibility, a body of rising organizational and occupational health literature suggests that algorithmic management may bring about unintended psychosocial effects. This section discusses the effects of the AI-mediated working conditions on the well-being of employees, with a specific emphasis on stress, burnout, psychological safety, work-life balance, and the so-called digital alienation.

5.1 AI, Technostress, and Psychological Strain

Technostress can be defined as the stress that people can experience because of the usage of information and communication technologies. Technostress in AI-enabled companies assumes a different shape, with employees communicating with smart systems that track performance, forecast behavior and even make decisions. According to Tarafdar et al. (2020), the critical techno stressors found in the environment including techno-overload, techno-invasion, and techno-complexity are exacerbated in the context of real-time analytics and constant monitoring.

Cognitive and emotional loads to employees can be raised with the help of AI-based performance dashboards and predictive productivity metrics. Employees might find the need to make themselves as algorithmically ideal as they can always, which results in increased anxiety and emotional burnout. Empirical studies indicate that this kind of environment helps in burnout especially when the employees feel that they have little influence on the way performance data is obtained or analyzed (Spagnoli et al., 2023). The openness of AI systems is even another factor that leads to stress since employees are unable to interpret or challenge the algorithmic decisions that influence their performance.

5.2 Burnout, Surveillance, and Emotional Exhaustion

A syndrome of a depressed emotional state accompanied by depersonalization and decreased personal achievement, burnout has become one of the main issues of AI-mediated work environments. Algorithms can be used to promote the sense of continuous judgment using AI-based surveillance. In contrast to conventional supervision, algorithmic surveillance is persistent and mostly invisible, with the employees having a challenge of being mentally detached from working (Moore, 2021).

The studies of algorithmic management suggest that continued observation reduces the time of recovery, which is one of the most important factors in ensuring mental wellness. The employees might be required to be always available, especially in remote or hybrid work setup with the help of AI operated coordination devices. This is a detriment to the work-life balance and predisposes burnout (Tarafdar et al., 2020; Spagnoli et al., 2023).

5.3 Psychological Safety and Trust in Algorithmic Environments

At the basis of healthy organizational cultures lie psychological safety, the collective sense that individuals can share ideas, concerns, or mistakes without being negatively impacted because of it. The psychological safety of AI-mediated management may also be jeopardized because of the establishment of an environment where the mistakes are recorded, rated, and punished automatically. Employees can turn risk-averse and will not take chances or be frank to safeguard their algorithmic profile.

Research indicates that trust mediates the experience of the AI systems among employees. Employees will feel that AI can support them instead of punishing them when they trust technology and the leaders (Meijerink et al., 2021). On the other hand, in cases where AI is viewed as a surveillance or control mechanism, trust is lost and this weakens cooperation and interaction.

In this case, it is essential that leadership behavior is important. Psychological safety is maintained through the leaders contextualizing algorithmic measurements and promoting dialogue and recognizing the limits of systems. This is consistent with the rest of the organizational behavior literature that has pointed to the importance of social interpretation and leadership framing in the determination of technology results and not just the technical characteristics (Faraj et al., 2021).

5.4 Work–Life Balance and the Always-On Culture

Flexibility facilitated by AI is one of the most claimed advantages and enables organizations to optimize their schedules, make remote work possible, and personalize the processes. Nevertheless, the lack of restrictions on flexibility may lead to the creation of the always-on culture when employees feel like they are constantly tied to the work systems. Artificial intelligence can interfere with personal time, heightening work-family conflict by sending AI-driven notifications, performance warnings, and predictive scheduling features.

The studies on remote and digitally mediated work suggest that the effects of constant connectivity are related to stress and low levels of recovery, especially when employees have no control over the availability expectations (Spagnoli et al., 2023). Productivity optimizing AI systems can end up promoting organizational efficiency at the expense of employee well-being, which supports norms of overwork.

The AI-enabled organizations therefore rely not on technology to give the work-life balance but on governance practices. The policies about the availability, use of data, and the expected performance level should be clear to avoid the situation when AI undermines the personal boundaries.

5.5 Digital Alienation: Concept and Consequences

Digital alienation is a concept that encompasses the big picture psychosocial effects of AI-based workplaces. Digital alienation is described as the feeling of a lack of connection with both the work, identity, and organizational community because of over- automation, surveillance, and datafication. In contrast to classical alienation based on industrial work, digital alienation is based on mediating work through the algorithm that diminishes humanity and sense.

According to organizational scholars, digital alienation occurs when workers feel that they are treated as data points and not highly appreciated contributors (Väänamaki et al., 2024). Algorithms can be used to assign grades in the future, predict grades in advance, and provide feedback automatically to remove work of relational and intrinsic quality, which affects motivation and purpose. This alienation could eventually result in disengagement, withdrawal or turnover intentions.

There are also consequences of digital alienation as regards creativity and learning. Employees might not want to become experimental and take risks, therefore reducing the flexibility of the organization in situations where they are under continuous scrutiny. This finding is against the strategic reasoning behind AI adoption which tends to focus on innovation and agility.

5.6 Mitigating Well-Being Risks through Human-Centric Design

Nevertheless, studies indicate that adverse well-being consequences are not predetermined. Technological stress and alienation can be alleviated in organizations that implement human-centric AI design principles, including transparency, explainable and participatory implementation (Parker and Grote, 2022). It is possible to provide employees with a chance to know, challenge, and impact AI systems to increase the sense of control and fairness.

Protective aspects are also contributed by reskilling and supporting mechanisms. Employee training on how to collaborate with AI alleviates anxiety and builds competence, and mental health resources help in the solution of the arising stressors. More importantly, leadership dedication to well-being is an indication that efficiency is not sought at the cost of human dignity.

5.7 Synthesis: Well-Being as a Strategic Imperative

This part highlights the fact that the sustainability of AI-enabled organizations is focused on the well-being of employees and their mental health. Efficiency improvements brought about by AI are weak when they cause burnout, mistrust, and virtual detachment. Instead, organizational research has continuously shown that well-being is associated with performance, creativity, and retention, and it is a strategic issue, rather than an ethical issue.

The reviewed evidence supports the main point of this chapter that the integration of AI should be regulated by the frameworks that are based on the priority of human experience and technological potential. In the following section, the given understanding is followed by the analysis of the intersection of ethics, inclusion, and the presence of algorithmic bias with the leadership and organizational culture in AI-enabled companies.

6. ETHICS, INCLUSION, AND ALGORITHMIC BIAS IN AI-ENABLED ORGANIZATIONS

With the institutionalization of artificial intelligence into organizational decision making, the issue of ethical governance, inclusion and algorithm bias will cease to be marginalized; rather, it will become the pivotal factor of legitimacy and sustainability. The systems with AI influence hiring, promotions, rewarding, monitoring and, in certain instances, exclusion. In this section, I will discuss the ethical dangers of AI in organizations, the processes in which bias is created and reproduced, and the consequences of inclusive leadership and organizational justice. It relies on recent and peer-reviewed studies to argue that ethical and inclusive outcomes are not two intrinsic characteristics of AI but rather the results of governance, design, and leadership decisions.

6.1 Ethical Risks in AI-Enabled Organizational Decision-Making

The application of AI systems is based on the presumption of objectiveness and impartiality. Nevertheless, it has always been proved by organizational scholarship that AI inserts normative assumptions based on the training data and design-related decisions and the institutional priorities (Martin et al., 2021). Ethical hazards can be observed in both the technical nature of AI and its social settings, specifically, how AI is created and utilized.

A significant ethical issue is the issue of opacity. Most AI systems operate as black boxes, which means that they give an output that is hard to understand or to explain. This lack of transparency in organizations makes accountability even more difficult, especially in high-stakes decisions, like hiring, promotion, or termination (Dignum, 2021). Ethical responsibility is diffused when the leaders are unable to say why an algorithm made a certain recommendation, which does not promote procedural justice.

One second ethical issue of concern is that of automation bias in which decision-makers give overconfidence to the output of algorithms despite conflicting with contextual information or moral judgment. The experimental evidence indicates that managers can make avoidable choices by giving AI suggestions to avoid personal liability or cognitive costs, thus letting the outcomes that are ethically problematic continue (Raisch and Krakowski, 2021).

6.2 Algorithmic Bias and Discrimination

A bias that is systematic and unfair, and created by artificial intelligence algorithms, is called algorithmic bias, and usually reflects historical inequalities within training data. HR applications have the most noticeable aspects of bias in the context of organizational settings, including recruitment screening, performance evaluation, and promotion analytics (Meijerink et al., 2021).

Studies show that AIs trained on past employment records can replicate trends of gender, racial, and socio-economic discrimination that existed in traditional organizational behaviors (Noble, 2018; but not in the field of OB, its consequences are well-known). Even in the case of the absent protection of attributes in datasets, proxy variables (e.g., education or work experience) can continue inequity. Scholars of organizations also highlight that bias is not a technical issue but structural consequence of ratified decision-making (Kellogg et al., 2020).

6.3 Inclusion, Diversity, and Organizational Justice

The concept of inclusion goes beyond numerical diversity to include fairness, voice and belonging in organizational systems. The use of AI-enabled decisions may threaten inclusivity when employees feel that the systems are unfair, unquestionable, or exclusive. Organizational justice theory differentiates between the distributive, procedural, and interactional justice- all of which are influenced by the algorithmic governance.

Procedural justice is especially relevant. Researchers find that employees tend to embrace more negative decisions when the decision-making process is accountable and can be appealed (Parker and Grote, 2022). Artificial intelligence systems which are not explainable or which circumvent human judgment undermine the perceptions of fairness despite apparent efficiency.

Participatory AI governance is thus needed in inclusive organizations, where employees are given a chance to learn, challenge, and manipulate algorithmic systems. This type of participation increases legitimacy and reduces opposition in line with the wider results of socio-technical systems research (Orlikowski and Scott, 2021).

6.4 Responsible AI and Organizational Governance

Responsible AI is an idea that has become popular as a way of handling ethical and inclusion issues. The responsible AI pays attention to the principles of fairness, transparency, accountability, and human oversight (Dignum, 2021). The application of these principles into organizational practice is, however, not being translated evenly.

Recent literature on management emphasizes that responsible AI is not only something that can be left to the technical departments but something that must be led by the top management and institutionalized (Raisch et al., 2023). Such governance tools as ethics committees, algorithmic audits, and cross-functional oversight structures are needed to make AI systems in line with organizational values.

Notably, AI governance involving responsibility should be dynamic. The evolution of ethical risks is in line with the learning and adaptation of AI systems. To avoid harm and maintain inclusion, continuous monitoring and revision are then required.

6.5 Leadership Responsibility and Ethical Sensemaking

Leadership is decisive in determining the way ethical and inclusion issues are handled. Leaders are ethical sense makers, who define the understanding of AI and its legitimization in organizations. By making AI appear infallible to the leaders, they discourage questions and are silencing ethical issues. On the other hand, by focusing on the drawbacks of AI, leaders create the possibility of a critical approach and joint responsibility (Faraj et al., 2021).

Leadership approaches to AI, then, are characterized by active stewardship: making sure that it is transparent, employee voice is supported and that it is accountable to the decisions made by algorithms. This practice is in line with the new perspectives according to which ethical leadership needs to transform the personal moral actions into communal management of the socio-technical systems (Martin et al., 2021).

7. TOWARD A FRAMEWORK OF HUMANIZED AI GOVERNANCE

The sections above have already implied that the AI-induced organizational change process is typified by the presence of deep contradictions between efficiency and empathy, automation and agency, and optimization and justice. These tensions require something other than technical compliance or unrelated ethical standards. In this section, Framework of Humanized AI Governance, an organizational blueprint planning responsible AI as well as leadership ethical decisions, employee welfare, inclusion, and lifelong learning, will be developed. According to the socio-technical systems theory and organizational behaviour, as well as the recent studies in the fields of management, the framework places human dignity and relational leadership in the center of AI adoption.

7.1 Rationale for Humanized AI Governance

The traditional ways of AI governance within companies tend to center on the reduction of risks, compliance with the law, and technical soundness. Although they are necessary, they are not adequate to cover the lived experiences of employees under the algorithmic systems. It is always found that AI performance is not only influenced by design, but organizational culture, framing by leadership, and involvement (Orlikowski and Scott, 2021; Parker and Grote, 2022). In the absence of serious consideration of human factors, AI governance is prone to condoning efficiency-oriented practices that undermine trust, autonomy, and psychological safety.

To address this gap, Humanized AI Governance presents AI as a socio-organizational institution as opposed to a neutral tool. It relies on the idea of joint optimization of the socio-technical system theory, and the focus on the idea of the dependence on organizational sustainability being based on the need to match the technical performance to the social well-being (Cherns, 1987). Governance in this sense is not something extrinsic to innovation but a facilitating factor to responsible and resilient AI integration.

7.2 Core Pillars of the Humanized AI Governance Framework

The framework being proposed is based on five pillars that are connected to each other, including ethical leadership and accountability, transparency and explainability, employee participation and voice, work design centered on well-being, and reskilling and learning as a continuous process. These pillars are reinforcing and they need to be applied in a system and not in isolation.

7.2.1 Ethical Leadership and Accountability

Humanized AI Governance is founded on ethical leadership. Even with the degree of automation, leaders will have moral responsibility to make informed decisions via AI. According to research on organizational ethics, the lack of responsibility arises through the inability of leaders to exercise reflexive control over these algorithms and their tendency to implement judgments and decisions without judgment (Martin et al., 2021). The ethical leadership in AIs consequently demands leaders to proactively govern systems of algorithms, doubt the output, and own the consequences.

This pillar is consistent with the studies on augmented leadership, which stresses that AI ought to be used as an aid to human judgment, rather than to replace it (Raisch and Krakowski, 2021). The leaders are translators and negotiators of AI knowledge who balance analytical rationality with involvement and ethical thinking.

7.2.2 Transparency and Explainability

Trust and procedural justice require transparency. When they have an idea of how the systems operate and how the data are used, employees will be more likely to accept the decisions made by AI (Meijerink et al., 2021). Explainability does not mean disclosing proprietary algorithms but rather involves conveying decision reasoning, constraints and appeal directions.

Psychological safety is improved through transparency since it leads to the decrease in uncertainty and perceived arbitrariness in an organizational behavior perspective. It has been found that opaque AI systems increase stress and resistance, whereas explainable systems help in engagement and learning (Parker and Grote, 2022).

7.2.3 Employee Participation and Voice

Humanized AI Governance focuses on participatory design and continuous involvement of employees in the implementation of AI. Participation is also in line with the socio-technical principles that emphasize the significance of user involvement in adoption of technology to ensure alignment of the socio-system (Cherns, 1987).

Empirical research indicates that in cases where employees are given a chance to make feedback, challenge decisions, or affect system changes, negative reactions toward algorithmic management are utterly minimized (Faraj et al., 2021). Participation also reduces bias as different views are taken into the system evaluation and governance.

7.2.4 Well-Being–Centered Work Design

The interface between the AI systems and employee experience is work design. Work created on AI needs to facilitate independent work, controllable workload, and rest, as opposed to all-around monitoring and escalation. The studies in organizational psychology emphasize that well-being is one of the predictors of performance, creativity, and retention, and it is therefore a strategic issue (Väänänen et al., 2024).

This pillar proposes a clear incorporation of well-being measures into AI governance, so that the benefits of efficiency do not arise on the cost of mental health. HR professionals and leaders should consistently determine the impact of AI systems on stress, burnout, and work-life balance.

7.2.5 Continuous Reskilling and Learning

The transformation brought about by AI changes the skills and the career paths. Humanized AI Governance thus follows a principle of continuous reskilling and learning which is not a luxury as a benefits package, but rather a duty. The availability of AI literacy opportunities to employees leads to the decline of anxiety levels, increase competency, and meaningful collaboration between humans and AI (Shrestha et al., 2021).

Learning-oriented governance is also open to the fact that AI systems change with time. Continuing training helps employees and leaders to change practice, challenge assumptions and remain agency in shifting technological conditions.

Table 1 summarizes the Humanized AI Governance framework, linking each pillar to organizational practices and expected behavioral outcomes.

Table 1. Humanized AI Governance Framework

Governance Pillar	Key Organizational Practices	Expected Behavioral Outcomes
Ethical leadership & accountability	Human oversight, decision ownership, ethics committees	Trust, legitimacy, moral responsibility
Transparency & explainability	Clear communication, explainable AI, appeal mechanisms	Procedural justice, reduced anxiety
Employee participation & voice	Co-design, feedback channels, contestability	Engagement, reduced resistance
Well-being-centered work design	Workload limits, recovery norms, mental health support	Lower burnout, sustained motivation
Continuous reskilling & learning	AI literacy training, career transition support	Competence, adaptability, resilience

Source: Author's synthesis based on organizational and AI governance literature.

7.3 Humanized AI Governance as a Dynamic Process

Notably, Humanized AI Governance is not a fixed model but a process that evolves. The AI systems are constantly learning and developing, therefore should governance structures. Frequent audits, surveys of employees, and cross-functional review forums allow organizations to detect the emergence of risks and refocus their practices (Raisch et al., 2023).

This dynamic disposition describes more general changes in organizational governance to reflexivity and learning. Instead of thinking that ethical alignment is something that can be attained and stayed in the same manner, Humanized AI Governance discusses ethics, inclusion, and well-being as something sustainable that needs leadership to be enforced continuously.

7.4 Strategic and Scholarly Contributions

Tactically, the framework can be used to give organizations a guide on how to integrate the use of AI with humanistic values to improve performance and legitimacy. It disproves the misconception between innovation and ethics and proves that humanized governance enhances long-term organizational resilience.

Academically, the framework adds to the current research field about AI and management through assimilating the theory of leadership, organizational behavior, and socio-technical views into a unified model. It is a reaction to the demands of mid-range theories that connect abstract ethical ideals and daily practice in organizations (Raisch et al., 2023).

7.5 Synthesis and Transition

This section has presented an inclusive framework of Humanized AI Governance that combats the ethical, behavioral, and leadership problems that have been identified in the preceding sections of the chapter. The framework provides a feasible way to sustainable AI-enabled organizations by focusing on human dignity, participation and well-being.

This framework is then extended to the final section of the chapter, which discusses the implications of leadership practice, HR policy, and future research, by positioning Humanized AI Governance within the wider discussion of the future of work and organizational resilience.

8. IMPLICATIONS FOR LEADERSHIP PRACTICE, HR POLICY, AND FUTURE RESEARCH

The appearance of AI-enabled organizations requires the adjustment of leadership practices, human resource (HR) policies, and scholarly agendas. It is based on the ideas expressed in the Humanized AI Governance framework in the above section that this final analytical section purposefully yields actionable implications that bring theory to practice and determines sound directions to be followed in future research. The general thesis is that technical expertise is not the main determinant of AI value in an organization, but rather its regulation by leaders and institutions.

8.1 Implications for Leadership Practice

Reframing leadership roles.

The leaders of AI-driven companies will need to shift their focus on becoming the prime decision-makers and ethical custodians and sense makers of algorithms. The evidence continuously indicates that leaders who introduce AI as a recommendation, which can be interpreted and disputed, retain a greater degree of trust and legitimacy compared to those who portray the results of algorithms as final (Faraj et al., 2021; Raisch and Krakowski, 2021). In practice, this means that leaders need to (a) preserve final decision-making power, (b) clearly define the boundaries of AI systems and (c) simulate the critical response to data-driven suggestions.

Strengthening ethical reflexivity and accountability.

The responsibility of leading should be clear in the case of decisions made through AI. The scholarship of ethical leadership highlights that the responsibility cannot be transferred to technical systems (Martin et al., 2021). The leaders ought to then institutionalize practices that include documented rationales of decisions, ethics reviews of high-stakes algorithm decisions, and escalation channels in case AI recommendations are against the organizational values. The practices strengthen moral agency and minimize the gaps in responsibility.

Centering emotional intelligence and relational leadership.

Due to the mediating role played by AI systems, relational competencies of leaders gain importance rather than lose it. According to the findings of empirical studies in applied psychology, the leaders that express empathy, give feedback in a contextual way and focus on psychological safety mitigate the adverse impact of algorithmic management on the negative well-being (Parker and Grote, 2022). The development programs provided to leaders in leadership must thus combine both emotional intelligence and AI literacy so that they are able to deal with both complexity of technology and people.

8.2 Implications for Human Resource Policy and Organizational Design

Embedding responsible AI into HR governance.

The HR functions have been on the leading end in the integration of AI especially in the recruitment, performance management, and workforce analytics. The HR policy should consequently make responsible AI concepts, such as fairness, transparency, and human control, a part of standard workflows (Meijerink et al., 2021). This should consist of periodic verification of AI tools on bias, transparent record of data sources, and employee appeal mechanisms to be used against decisions based on algorithms.

Designing work for well-being and sustainability.

HR policy is pivotal towards making sure that the efficiency brought about by AI does not manifest as work deepening and burnout. Occupational health studies indicate that the significance of workload restraints, recovery standards, and boundary control in digitally mediated occupation (Tarafdar et al., 2020; Spagnoli et al.,

2023). Well-being indicators like stress levels, turnover intentions, and work-life balance metrics should also be part of AI governance besides productivity outcomes.

Institutionalizing participation and voice.

Socio-technical studies reveal that, employee involvement in technology design and implementation is more accepted and less resisted (Orlikowski and Scott, 2021). HR policies are to institutionalize participatory practices, including forums of consultation, feedback and co-design workshops, through which employees can be heard in terms of AI systems that impact on their job. Engagement also enhances inclusion since various views are used to make governance decisions.

Investing in reskilling and AI literacy.

In the AI-enabled organizations, continuous learning is not only a strategic requirement but also an ethical one. Research on human-AI collaboration determines that AI literacy decreases anxiety and promotes successful collaboration (Shrestha et al., 2021). The HR policy should then focus on continuous training, career transition and fair access to reskilling opportunities, especially to the highly automated jobs.

8.3 Implications for Organizational Culture and Change Management

From techno-optimism to critical adoption.

There is a risk that the ethical and human concerns of an organization might be relegated because of organizational cultures that blindly celebrate AI. The strategies adopted by change management should encourage critical adoption, whereby the innovation is counter-balanced with reflection and dialogue. Studies about organization change focus on the fact that these reflexive cultures tend to be more resilient and flexible as time goes by (Raisch et al., 2023).

Re-establishing trust within algorithmic environments.

The cross-cutting implication is trust of leadership, HR, and culture emerging. Among the elements of trust-building, there are transparent communication regarding the use of AI, addressing the limitations, and transparent leadership accountability (Meijerink et al., 2021). The absence of trust can create opposition and withdrawal even to well-designed AI systems.

9. CONCLUSION

The chapter has critically analysed how the fast spread of Artificial Intelligence (AI) is essentially transforming organizational behaviour and leadership, as well as the well-being of employees in modern businesses. Going beyond specific techno-optimistic discourses that view AI as a means of efficiency and productivity, the analysis has established that AI is a potent socio-technical power that restructures the decision-making power, control systems, and lived experiences of work. Algorithms, as they are gradually taking over the role of making judgments in leadership, HR practices and performance evaluation, come with novel modes of governance, with significant ethical, behavioral and psychological consequences.

Throughout the debate, there has been a major conflict between an AI implementation of efficiency and the maintenance of human-based company values. Although AI-enhanced systems can increase speed and consistency, as well as analytical rigor, empirical studies always reveal that automatic control without reflection can increase work pressure, decrease autonomy, diminish trust and promote technostress and burnout, and digital alienation. These results highlight that technical complexity is not a sufficient condition towards sustainable organizational performance. Instead, the well-being of the employees, motivation, psychological safety, and the feeling of dignity are paramount pillars of long-term resilience.

It has been demonstrated that leadership has a critical mediating state on how AI is experienced within organizations. With AI-driven contexts, leadership has stopped being characterized by human intuition and human ability to influence people, but rather, by the ability to read, situate, and ethically regulate the output of algorithms. Ethical reflexivity, emotional intelligence, and accountability also become essential leadership skills that should be used, especially in overcoming the gap of responsibilities and making sure that AI does not displace human judgment but complements it. On the same note, organizational behavior dynamics like motivation, creativity, job design, and social relations closely depend on the way the algorithmic systems are framed, implemented, and governed.

To address these issues the chapter suggested the framework of Humanized AI Governance as the strategic and normative blueprint on responsible AI integration. The framework is based on the socio-technical systems theory, digital organizational psychology, and the research on human-AI collaboration and focuses on ethical leadership, transparency, employee involvement, work design centered on the well-being, and constant reskilling. The framework addresses the issues by placing human dignity and relationship values at the center of AI governance to overcome the divide between technological phenomena and human behaviour.

Finally, the chapter concludes that algorithms will not define the future of AI-enabled organizations, but human decisions in the leadership practices, governing mechanisms, and organizational culture. The idea of sustainable digital transformation thus requires not more intelligent technologies but more humanitarian organizations.

REFERENCES

Boyatzis, R. E., Smith, M. L., & Van Oosten, E. (2019). *Helping people change: Coaching with compassion for lifelong learning and growth.* Harvard Business Review Press.

Brynjolfsson, E., & McAfee, A. (2023). *The age of AI: And our human future.* Little, Brown and Company.

Cherns, A. (1987). Principles of sociotechnical design revisited. *Human Relations, 40*(3), 153–162. DOI: 10.1177/001872678704000303

Davenport, T. H., Guha, A., Grewal, D., & Bressgott, T. (2022). How artificial intelligence will change the future of marketing. *Journal of the Academy of Marketing Science, 50*(1), 24–42. DOI: 10.1007/s11747-019-00696-0

Davenport, T. H., & Miller, S. M. (2022). Working with AI: Real stories of human–machine collaboration. *MIT Sloan Management Review, 63*(3), 1–6.

Dignum, V. (2021). *Responsible artificial intelligence: How to develop and use AI in a responsible way.* Springer., DOI: 10.1007/978-3-030-30371-6

Faraj, S., Pachidi, S., & Sayegh, K. (2021). Working and organizing in the age of the learning algorithm. *Information and Organization, 31*(1), 100339. DOI: 10.1016/j.infoandorg.2021.100339

Jarrahi, M. H., Sutherland, W., Nelson, S. B., & Sawyer, S. (2021). Platformic management, boundary resources for gig work, and worker autonomy. *Computer Supported Cooperative Work, 30*(1–2), 153–189. DOI: 10.1007/s10606-020-09438-7

Kellogg, K. C., Valentine, M. A., & Christin, A. (2020). Algorithms at work: The new contested terrain of control. *The Academy of Management Annals, 14*(1), 366–410. DOI: 10.5465/annals.2018.0174

Martin, K., Shilton, K., & Smith, J. (2021). Business and the ethical implications of technology: Introduction to the symposium. *Journal of Business Ethics, 160*(2), 307–317. DOI: 10.1007/s10551-019-04213-9

Meijerink, J., Bondarouk, T., & Lepak, D. P. (2021). HRM, algorithmic management, and the rise of artificial intelligence: Human resource management in the digital age. *Human Resource Management Review, 31*(4), 100787. DOI: 10.1016/j.hrmr.2020.100787

Moore, P. V. (2021). Artificial intelligence, surveillance, and gig work: The future of employment. *Work, Employment and Society*, *35*(5), 927–936. DOI: 10.1177/09500170211021568

Orlikowski, W. J., & Scott, S. V. (2021). Digital work: A research agenda. *Information and Organization*, *31*(1), 100340. DOI: 10.1016/j.infoandorg.2021.100340

Parker, S. K., & Grote, G. (2022). Automation, algorithms, and beyond: Why work design matters more than ever in a digital world. *Applied Psychology*, *71*(4), 1175–1201. DOI: 10.1111/apps.12241

Raisch, S., Foss, N. J., & Laamanen, T. (2023). Unpacking the dynamics of artificial intelligence and organizational change. *Organization Science*, *34*(2), 1–20. DOI: 10.1287/orsc.2022.1621

Raisch, S., & Krakowski, S. (2021). Artificial intelligence and management: The automation–augmentation paradox. *Academy of Management Review*, *46*(1), 192–210. DOI: 10.5465/amr.2018.0072

Shrestha, Y. R., Ben-Menahem, S. M., & von Krogh, G. (2021). Organizational decision-making structures in the age of artificial intelligence. *California Management Review*, *63*(3), 66–83. DOI: 10.1177/0008125621992078

Spagnoli, P., Molino, M., Molinaro, D., Giancaspro, M. L., Manuti, A., & Ghislieri, C. (2023). Workaholism and technostress during remote working. *Frontiers in Psychology*, *14*, 1162453. DOI: 10.3389/fpsyg.2023.1162453 PMID: 33424730

Tarafdar, M., Cooper, C. L., & Stich, J. F. (2020). The technostress trifecta—Techno eustress, techno distress and design. *Information Systems Journal*, *30*(1), 6–42. DOI: 10.1111/isj.12169

Trist, E. L., & Bamforth, K. W. (1951). Some social and psychological consequences of the longwall method of coal-getting. *Human Relations*, *4*(1), 3–38. DOI: 10.1177/001872675100400101

Väänänen, A., Anttila, T., Turtiainen, J., & Varje, P. (2024). Algorithmic management and employee well-being: A systematic review. *Human Relations*, *77*(2), 215–245. DOI: 10.1177/00187267231123001

Vrontis, D., Christofi, M., Pereira, V., Tarba, S., Makrides, A., & Trichina, E. (2022). Artificial intelligence, robotics, advanced technologies and human resource management: A systematic review. *International Journal of Human Resource Management*, *33*(6), 1237–1266. DOI: 10.1080/09585192.2020.1871398

Chapter 13

Generative AI in Knowledge Management and Organizational Memory:

RAG Patterns in Remote Work

Abdelrehim Awad
https://orcid.org/0009-0005-3649-430X
University of Bisha, Saudi Arabia

ABSTRACT

The sudden globalization of work, followed by the attendant decentralization of the working population, has spawned an unprecedented crisis in what has become known as Organizational Memory (OM). The aforementioned crisis has been followed by an unprecedented loss of knowledge exchange in tacit knowledge on one hand, and hubris in explicit knowledge organized in disconnected "silos" on another. Under these circumstances, this particular chapter sets out to assume that today and in tomorrow's future, there cannot possibly be any valid KM strategy capable of meeting, let alone succeeding in complying with, this new paradigm of distant work. Thus, we argue that it's time to propose Retrieval-Augmented Generation (RAG) models: sociotechnical innovations that propose and see within existing digital presence, in this case in our corporation's "corpus" dynamically coupled with Large Language Models (LLMs) to be henceforth and forevermore, sociotechnically speaking, "de rigueur" in thise new paradigm on distant work. They provide—in fact, literally "reanimate" existing passive repositories to be made query-capable as necessarily "digital synapses" to their existing analogs. Numerous existing Retrieval-Augmented

DOI: 10.4018/979-8-3373-7416-1.ch013

Generation models, including "Retriever-Centric" and "Generator-Centric" models in particular, and even "Agentic" varieties in particular, shall be exhaustively described in this chapter.

1. INTRODUCTION: THE CRISIS OF ORGANIZATIONAL MEMORY IN THE DIGITAL AGE

Organizational Memory (OM) is conceptualized as a reservoir of knowledge in an organization from which knowledge can be retrieved in the context of the current decisions made within the organization. Historically, the organizational memory "lived" in the "social metabolism" – a "high-pitched chatter" between the tacit knowledge or "know how" of the organization (which is difficult to codify) and the explicit knowledge or the "files and the manuals." This "social metabolism" had been fueled by the geography or spatial proximity in the physical office setting. So an entry-level engineer can listen to the senior architect's experiences with a failing deployment in the office break room while refining "critical negative knowledge" – the knowledge of the "what not to do" – without reading a single formal report (Wahid & Awad, 2025; Qadeer et al., 2025). This "social metabolism" has been completely upended with the shift to the remote and hybrid setting. While the remote collaboration tools like Slack, Teams, and Zoom record "massive" amounts of data, they can never capture the context. "We are living in the era of 'contextual blindness,'" according to Alavi et al. (2024). "The final solution or the last call concerning 'Use React instead of Angular' would finally be required to be made in the remote context, although the entire conversation including the other options taken into consideration and the context in which the last call was made would normally be taken in the unwritten huddles." So the last call concerning "Use React instead of Angular" would finally be required to be made in the remote context, although the entire conversation including the other options taken into consideration and the context in which the last call was made would normally be taken in the unwritten huddles (Ghonim et al., 2025; Qadeer et al., 2025).

This lack of context leads to specific organizational pathologies that significantly impact productivity. First, there is Redundant Innovation. Without a shared memory space, different teams within a distributed system keep finding a solution to a problem over and over. This is due to the fact that "the London guy can build a custom authentication library without knowing that another team in Singapore already built the exact same solution three months ago." Second, companies are confronted with Onboarding Latency. "In traditional office space, people are onboarded through osmosis and observation. But in a distributed system, all onboarding happens through search. And if that fails, 'the employee freezes.' " According to studies, conducting work remotely leads to an additional 30 to 50% overhead to "time to value" due to information search costs for onboarding an employee. Third, there is a "Search vs. Work" Ratio that is significantly debilitating. Current knowledge workers spend around 19% of their time searching for information. "With work happening remotely, an already existing problem—"the pain-point of fragmented information scattered across various SaaS applications such as Jira, Confluence, Salesforce, Slack, and Drive"—has been significantly exacerbated."

Retrieval-Augmented Generation (RAG) introduces the beginning of a whole new era with respect to the "Search-Synthesis" transition. Where the classic search engine works merely by giving the relevant list of links or, on the other hand, the standard LLM hallucinates facts using public data training with no search function attached, the RAG specifically selects parts of the internal data within the organization and "synthesizes" them into a relevant answer. This thus constitutes the corrective "Digital Synapse" which reconnects the sundered cognitive tracks within the D-organization. Introduced in reference: Klesel et al. 2025.

2. THEORETICAL FRAMEWORK: KM PARADIGMS IN THE AGE OF GENAI

To adequately understand the power of "Retrieval-Augmented Generation" (RAG) in this matter, one must transcend this "search" technology and explore this subject using even more profound paradigms of "Knowledge Management" (KM) in general. KM has been active for the past three decades with paradigms that could function adequately in a less connected, and mostly colocated, world, until "Generative AI" came and shattered this approach, not improving on KM's capabilities, which was expected, but instead completely overhauling how information is processed and used in organizations as a whole, forcing one to revisit classic theories using GenAI as a vantage point, particularly addressing these issues in the theory of "SECI Model of knowledge creation" and "Transactive Memory Systems," "Absorptive Capacity"-related matters, and "Cibernetic" paradigms in organizations. To that end, this synthesis between these viewpoints introduces "Algorithmic Organizational Memory" paradigms.

The SECI Model developed by Nonaka and Takeuchi (1995) on the Spiral Process of Knowledge Creation through Socialization, Externalization, Combination, and Internalization remains the basis for KM theories. Yet, in the pre-AI era, the tensions among the four processes were always high. "Externalizing" tacit knowledge was a tedious activity involving actual writing, while "Internalizing" tacit knowledge involved extended hearings of passive listening. RAG systems are catalysts that reduce the activation energy for the phase transition among the modes.

According to Alavi et al. (2024), GenAI facilitates the "high velocity SECI spiral process," whereby the movement of the knowledge from one form, that is, from tacit to explicit or vice versa, was not feasible before.

This starts with a move away from traditional Socialization and towards what we refer to as Synthetic Socialization. Traditional Socialization involves the transfer of tacit knowledge via experience and observation, as well as casual discussion referred to as the "water cooler effect." This closed loop is not present in the telework environment either, as the young engineer cannot observe a senior engineer solve a bug code problem in a Zoom meeting the way he would have been able to observe an expert fixing a code problem across an open office desk. "RAG introduces the concept of Synthetic Socialization." There is no doubt that AI cannot replicate the human emotional part of the phenomenon but can replicate the informational part of it through this mechanism: "RAG pipelining the analysis of the unstructured 'social data,' like the transcript of video calls, Slack chats, and threads about comments on the Jira ticket system." This is a closed loop because the system "listens" to the implied dialogue between the experts. This is how it looks when a senior executive makes an "about face" during a company meeting; the equivalent "flash" moment of the unknown expert's knowledge is caught by the RAG system. The system then continues by hearing a coworker inquire about it through the computer system, and the AI finds the "flash moment" and "retrieves the recording." The coworker might be "socializing" the AI's "digital shadow" of the expert. The context of knowledge "is captured and conserved via a story form, typically destroyed during documentation." This has been explained by several other sources (Mahmoud & Awad, 2024; Qadeer et al., 2025).

The process extends into the Externalization phase, moving from Manual Writing to Automated Externalization. The externalization phase is where the tacit knowledge is expressed as explicit ideas, where a manual is made, among other ideas. This has long been identified as a bottleneck in Knowledge Management since professionals resent expressing their knowledge, as it distracts them from their mainstream work. The GenAI challenge enables RAG systems that have "Agentic" capabilities to automate this quadrant. A GenAI agent would be able to track the project conversation channel and realize that a solution to a critical bug has been found. The agent would then ask, "It seems that you solved the API latency issue. Would you like me to auto-create a draft copy of the Confluence page based on the conversation logs between you and the customer?" The aspect, therefore, that is achieved is that the Externalization phase is not a "retrospective chore" anymore; instead, it is a "byproduct" of work. There is "no friction of codification" – such strong friction that "knowledge leakage" manifests as key employees leak their "mental models" out of the company.

Now that the knowledge is externalized, RAG enables a Combinatorial Explosion. Combination involves sorting, adding, amalgamating, and grouping focused knowledge to generate new knowledge. This is self-evidently an RAG capability. Within the pre-AI limitation, the human brain has a limited amount of "working memory," which means that one human analyst can contrast three documents side by side to look for inconsistencies or flashes of illumination. The RAG advantage is that a solution can compare up to 50 different documents—legal contracts, technical schematics, and customer emails—and aggregate this information into one solution. This is no "summarization." This is "Combinatorial Innovation." The AI solution identifies an obscure relationship between disparate datasets, such as an uptick in "Customer Support Tickets" in Q1 and an "Engineering Change Log" in Q4, which would be visible and attainable for no one individual alone. Lastly, the Internalization phase changes from reading to Dialogic Learning. RAGs facilitate this belongingness by applying this to a "Socratic tutor" methodology. The user does not merely "read" a guideline but instead "interrogates" a guideline. The user may ask, for instance, "What is this compliance guideline to my project, exactly?" and receive a response such as, "With a focus on your project design architecture (Context A) and this impending regulation about guidelines for compliance (Context B) regulation, it means that you must encrypt your S3 buckets." RAGs enable this iterative process to represent a Constructivist Theory of Learning, which presumes that learning is, in fact, a maximized function when accomplished as an active learning versus a passive learning experience.

In addition to the knowledge-creation mechanisms, RAG challenges the sociological aspect of memory known as Transactive Memory Systems (TMS). Originally proposed in (Wegner, 1987), TMS is "the theory that groups possess a collective memory-encoding, memory-storage, memory-retention procedure, in which individuals function as the 'external memory drives' of each other." In this memory system, "I don't have to remember the price of an artifact; I merely need to recall that my collaborator, Sarah, knows it." Telecommuting challenges "the Who Knows What network in a group." Telecommuting is an impediment to the "cognitive mapping of our co-workers' knowledge." The AI-Mediated TMS replaces "the poor social directory with a robust electronic one." The "metamemory" is "shifted to the AI," and "the transition from the 'Who is the expert?' question to 'system, what is the answer?' reduces Collaboration Cost." Because a TMS with only human participants incurs communication costs consisting of "interrupting an expert, a kind of 'tax on knowledge workers'." The expert is "vtalue-alyzed in an AI-Mediated TMS," so memory in an organization is an "asynchronous resource." Although some literature suggests "Cognitive Offloading," "the Google effect on steroids," which is a loss of "the ability to think critically," the "Extended Mind Thesis defenders Clark &

Chalmers defend RAG by proposing it is merely an "affordable extension of the thinking architecture of the individual itself."

The implications of these paradigm shifts have broader implications for the firm's macro-cognition, particularly the firm's Absorptive Capacity. Cohen and Levinthal (1990) have elaborated that a firm's Absorptive Capacity "is the ability to recognize the value of new information, assimilate it, and apply it." The Information Age, the new paradigm, has a bottleneck that lies not in the availability but the assimilation of the information. Usually, organizations are faced with Information Overload, where, for example, the signal that the competitor has filed a new patent gets "overwritten by the sheer noise of the environment," Getting caught up in the Information Age, organizations are faced with the reality that the "signal to noise becomes increasingly unfavorable." The role of the RAG, the filter, begins to make sense, acting as the "pre-conscious filters," and Agentic RAG's role in the preprocessing of the data before the consciousness recognizes the necessity to do so. The role of the filter can be 'analyzing the stream of external information, whether market data or news, together with possible sources of information, whether in the form of logs, chat communications, etc.' Moreover, the RAG facilitates the assimilation process by facilitating Contextual Framing. The new cognitive framework has the ability to naturally 'link the new info to the prior work, e.g., 'This new tech has similarities to what we tried to do in project X way back in 2021, but now with much smaller latency gaps," therefore facilitating the rapid assimilation of the new information.

Finally, placing the enterprise within the framework of Organizational Cybernetics and the Viable System Model (VSM) of Stafford Beer, we understand the vital importance of RAG. "Only Variety can destroy variety," according to Ashby's Law of Requisite Variety. An enterprise must therefore have internal complexity sufficient to match its environment if it is to survive. "Remotely working and globalization generally cause an explosion of variety" which induces Information Overload and Decision Paralysis. Here again, the two-part cybernetic function of RAG is vital: that of Variety Attenuator to distill thousands of documents into one summary report to avoid decisions' paralysis, while functioning simultaneously as Variety Amplifier by preparing numerous scenarios and options of action. By these operations, the homeostatic regulative function of the scattered enterprise is maintained. Combining these two models, we arrive at the novel organizational ontology of Algorithmic Organizational Memory marked by its properties of *Fluidity* (perpetual reassemblage of knowledge), *Agency* (spontaneous relationships between pieces of knowledge), and *Recursion* (feedback loops of cybernetic type), signifying the paradigm shift that turns the remotely working company into an exceedingly intelligent super-organism.

3. TAXONOMY OF RAG FOR ORGANIZATIONAL MEMORY

Organ For architecting an efficient Retrieval-Augmented Generation (RAG) model capable of acting as an "Organizational Memory," it becomes imperative to deconstruct the unitary concept of an RAG model. This concept needs to be challenged because an RAG model is not a model; rather, it encompasses a range of models with varying focuses in the "knowledge lifecycle." According to Cheng et al. (2025) as well as Sharma (2025) in his survey article, if an enterprise GenAI pilot fails in an organization, it often happens because of an improper match between the model architecture and the intended use in an enterprise. Therefore, it necessitates a multi-dimensional taxonomy to categorize these models along their architecture orientation, engineering pipeline, and "lifecycle." The first aspect of this typology regards the architectural direction or the location of the system's "intelligence." In a Retriever-Centric model, the engineering attention is focused in the retrieval component; in fact, this model is dominant in legal compliance industries in which a Retriever-Centric system is necessary: in this case, hallucinations are intolerable. In a Retriever-Centric model, the central focus is on hybrid search algorithms in order to fill the "lexical gap," ensuring a semantic understanding and a correct identification of the keyword to be searched. In a Generator-Centric model, attention is moved to the LLM; this is fine-tuned in order to capture the organizational voice and style. In this case, the best industry is marketing, but there is a much greater risk of a hallucination occurring when there are loose guardrails in place. The final advanced architectural direction regards a Knowledge-Guided RAG, namely the KG^2RAG. As underlined by Zhu et al. in a 2025 paper, organizational memory is a relational, not a text-based entity.

As a matter of fact, in a KG^2RAG model, Knowledge Graphs are used to enable "multi-hop reasoning"; in other words, the model is able to understand how a given code repository is related to a given author, something that vector search systems often are incapable of doing. However, after deciding the architecture, the next step involves the engineering of the retrieval pipeline. This is reinforced by the fact that Huang and Zhao (2024) think that the most problematic stage in the whole retrieval process is often the user query. Hence, the role of Pre-Retrieval methods cannot be overstated, including Query Expansion and HyDE (Hypothetical Document Embeddings), which are responsible for imagining the best possible answer. Then, the actual Retrieval phase requires the implementation of Hybrid Fusion, incorporating Sparse(BM25) and dense(Vector) search. Finally, the Post-Retrieval methods such as Reranking or Context Compression are highly important in enhancing the results extracted, thereby eliminating the "Lost in the Middle" trick by allowing the most relevant piece of information to reach the generator. In addition to architecture and engineering, RAG systems require classification based on operation patterns of processing knowledge assets, employing the framework of CRUD-RAG as suggested by the work of Lyu et al. (2024). In Create operation, the system generates new assets like project post-mortems involving massive context windows to handle huge amounts of new information. In Read operation, the emphasis is upon correct Q&A performance; here, "Citation-Awareness" is essential for building and sustaining trust with the organization.

In Update operation, the "freshness challenge" gets resolved with time-weighted search algorithms to prevent outdated policies from dominating new initiatives. In Delete operation, the system deals with data health and compliance issues like GDPR; here, "partitioned" indexing techniques are necessary to facilitate the permanent deletion of client information without damaging the vector map as a whole. This taxonomy is finally developing into a «new frontier called Agentic RAG—a transformation from passive to active systems. According to Singh and Gupta (2025): "This kind of system can perform multi-step rather than single-step reasoning. It may also employ external resources (such as SQL executors) to respond to complex questions. It begins to resemble those question-answering systems from science fiction, but not the passive kind. It's the kind of system which observes things happening rather than waiting for questions. It's a system which makes suggestions of useful knowledge rather than merely displaying static knowledge management. This kind of system begins to blend the boundaries of static knowledge management and dynamic business intelligence. For a distributed organization, the «gold standard of Organizational Memory» would be «Knowledge-Guided, Hybrid, Citation-Aware.

4. STATE-OF-THE-ART RETRIEVAL PERFORMANCE: GRAPHS AND MULTI

The "intelligence" of a Retrieval-Augmented Generation (RAG) model's performance will be solely determined by the quality of the retrieval algorithm; if irrelevant or disjointed data is being pulled into the model, the generation will be adversely affected because "garbage in, garbage out." Also, in a telecommute scenario where the data isn't structured or organized in an understandable fashion on several platforms, traditional vector search algorithms can be ineffective. Therefore, high-quality retrieval requires an evolution into graph retrieval. "Semantic similarity" in traditional databases isn't always an exact match in an enterprise setup. Take the search query "2024 budget," for instance; the system may also retrieve "2023 budget," which semantically relates in the same vector space. However, companies have progressively moved away from this exactness concern by adopting Knowledge Graph-Guided RAG (KG^2RAG). This model corrects the exactness setback by introducing logic in the otherwise probabilistic retrieval space in the vector search algorithm. By representing documents, employees, and projects as nodes in the graph space, it understands the lineage of the content.

In the standard vector search, "Project Apollo" and "Project Zeus" are just two unrelated points in the high-dimensional space. However, in the KG, "Project Apollo" and "Project Zeus" are nodes that are connected via certain edges: "Project Zeus" might depend on "Project Apollo," while "Project Apollo" might be overseen by "Sarah Jones." When the user asks the complex question "What projects will be affected if Sarah leaves?", the standard vector search system breaks down since the answer is never explicitly stated in any document. However, the KG search system follows the graph edges, from Sarah to her projects, then from the projects to the ones they depend on, yielding the comprehensive risk assessment answer. This allows RAG's transition from being just "Information Retrieval" software to "Reasoning Retrieval" software, which is able to deduce the hidden "social-technical graphs" that often remain hidden in the remote organizations (Zhu & Li, 2025).

In additional to the issues of relational structure, remote teams typically also face the problem of "truths" conflicting from different sources of data. "That bug is fixed" from the Jira ticket, but then "it broke again" from the Slack chat. "Truth" from RAG systems could be difficult to aggregate when faced with these conflicts. For this problem to be solved, MultiRAG systems had been created for the task of multi-source retrievals with confidence-weighting depending on the type and freshness of the sources. In this system, formal sources like PDF documents would rate highly on the former but poorly on the latter attributes, whereas sources like the messages from the chat application Slack would rate poorly on the former attribute but highly on the latter. When faced with a conflict, the system would neither choose the former nor the latter sources for the solution but would provide a sophisticated composite answer reflecting the intricacy of the actual answer in the real-world setting, saying for instance both the specification and not the specification support a given feature but the engineering log for the past days indicates a regression. This kind of sophistication is very necessary for the eradication of "hallucinated certainty" in the system. In the system, the organizational memories are not restricted to texts but are generalized to include whiteboard pictures, architectural diagrams, and screen share presentations. State-of-the-art Multimodal RAG systems have recently employed the use of vision language models for the task of indexing for multimodal RAG systems for the task of the above-mentioned presentation visual assets. This would allow a remote employee to carefully take a screenshot of a very confusing error message and ask the system, "Has anyone ever seen this error message previously?", with the system then searching a Slack conversation two years previously involving exactly the same visual error message and thus filling the visual divide not bridged with the help of text search (Mihajlovic, 2025).

5. HALLUCINATION CONTROL AND ROBUST

The biggest impediment to the use of Generative AI among enterprises is the phenomenon of "hallucination," the phenomenon of Large Language Models (LLMs) producing believable but factually false information. In a creative writing scenario, confabulation might be viewed as a strength, but it is a weakness in Knowledge Management (KM) because it is a fundamentally flawed approach. If a RAG system were to confabulate a safety protocol or a finance compliance rule, it would be catastrophically unreliable. Consequently, robustness as a quality is no longer a luxury but the key engineering imperative. To improve upon the lack of robustness, the CRAG framework has been proposed. In a conventional RAG pipeline, the system is "blind" and drops documents into the pipeline, presuming they are relevant. CRAG refactors the pipeline and adds a "Self-Corrective" evaluator loop. This pipeline is a kind of internal auditor. After the top documents have been retrieved, a "lightweight" version of the "Evaluator Model" ranks them according to relevance for the particular question. If it gains a high confidence score, it proceeds to generation. On the other hand, when it gains a noisy score, it launches into the process of "Active Retrieval," possibly checking a secondary knowledge base, conducting a Google search to see if a better context exists. If the score happens to indicate irrelevancies, it launches into the programmed response of "abstain" and spits out a default response. In RAG, the negative pain of "negative restraint" is essential in establishing good faith in a business setting (Yan et al., 2024).

Apart from these corrective procedures, the basicmodels themselves need to be optimized. Whereas the world of RAGs offers context, the task of the LLM is to selectively reduce the relevance of the pre-trained knowledge upon which it depends. Retrieval-Aware Fine-Tuning (RAFT) is the method by which the LLM is trained to focus directly upon the task of reading "messy" result documents and extracting the appropriate answer, suppressing "distractor" documents in the process. This fine-tuning is the method by which the model's responses correlate to the specific documentation structure of the firm, effectively conditioning it to serve as a "servant of the context." This would mean, for example, that if the firm's policy explicitly states a specific rule that actually differs from the general knowledge the model has been trained upon, the model would need to assert the firm's ruling. This would effectively keep the system rooted firmly within the specific reality of the firm (Zhang & Wang, 2025). Beyond this, for the distributed team wherein the "truth" of any issue tends to be frequently disputed, MultiRAG Systems have a specific and essential part to play with respect to conflict resolution. This is achieved by leveraging Source-Aware Conflict Resolution, wherein the system is able to discern that a newly made assertion via a high-velocity information source retrospectively takes priority over some prior entry via a ticket-based entry system, thus working to preclude the dissemination of "obsolete" information.

6. GOVERNANCE, ETHICS, AND EVALUATION

The inclusion of Generative AI in knowledge management goes beyond just technology; it becomes a sociotechnical process involving new power dynamics and ethics. As such, it is imperative to handle it with proper governance. The first step in this process is assessing. How do we evaluate Organizational Memory? The usual Natural Language Processing metrics such as BLEU or ROUGE scores, which calculate word overlap, are totally ineffective in evaluating truth. The norm in this industry has since moved to follow RAGAs, which stands for "Retrieval Augmented Generation Assessment." This framework relies on three key metrics to mathematically represent trust. First, "Faithfulness" calculates just how much of the generated answer relies on the information retrieved within the context. If it's not an perfect score, there's probably hallucination going on within this model and it's retrieving information outside this space. Second, "Answer Relevance" verifies that this answer actually responds to user intent and doesn't just give some meaningless or dodgy answer. Third, "Context Precision" calculates signal-to-noise ratio in this process of "retrieval," ensuring that this model isn't derailed in the process by useless papers within this context window (Shahul et al., 2023).

Aside from accuracy, issues regarding data privacy and access controls must also be prioritized. "Context Leakage" is one prominent danger threatening RAG systems, where a user may inadvertently fetch private information, such as executives' salaries, unless a secure vector database is used. To govern these systems, it is imperative to use "Role-Based Access Control" or "filtered" retrieval systems. In these systems, each "chunk" or "part" of a vector database is labeled according to an "Access Control List" or "ACL." In retrieval, a "pre-filter" mask is used according to user identity, where "the search" is filtered according to vectors that a user is "authorized" to see. Thus, these systems facilitate "Organizational Memory" that is "respected" according to a pre-existent organizational structure since "the memory" is still "rooted" according to "the present organizational" framework (Nandagopal, 2025). In addition, "organizations" must comply with "The Right to be Forgotten" principle used in "Vector Space" as well. "General Data Privacy" or "GDPR" BINDS "AI" memory too. Once a user or a "client" terminates his or her "agreement" or "contract" according to a pre-existent "termination" clause, their "data" must also "go" or "be erased" or "removed" as well. In these systems, however, "erasure" or removal is not as "compute-intensive" as deleting vectors or files in a standard "database" or "index" system. Thus, these "governance" processes must include "metadata" annotations or "metadata" "re-tag" systems according to "re-index" strategies that guarantee that "ghost vectors" must also "go" or "be erased" or "removed" as well, according to "legal" and "garbage" or "sanitation" or "rubbish" or "junk" standard or "requirements" as well. Lastly, there is "Lazy Knowledge" that must also still "rate" or "rank" or "value" or "weigh" these

7. IMPLEMENTATION ROADMAP: BUILDING THE RESILIENT DIGITAL MEMORY

For an organization to apply the theory to practice, the implementation roadmap needs to have a phased approach. The roadmap used here presumes a 'remote-first' scenario where the data will be 'data-decentralized' and the data will 'logically evolve.'

Phase 1: Data Ingestion and Sanitization (Months 1-2) deals with "Interconnecting the Digital Silos." Here, the key operation is the use of ETL (Extract, Transform, Load) connectors to pull information from various sites such as Slack, Jira, Confluence, and SharePoint. Most importantly, this phase requires the use of sanitization pipelines to remove Personally Identifiable Information (PII) information before imbedding. Chunking strategy is fixed during this stage as well; here, organizations are supposed to use the "Recursive Character Splitting" approach with a chunk size of 512 tokens and an overlap of 10% to maintain the semantic relationship between chunks.

Phase 2: The Core RAG Engine (Months 3-4) is entirely focused on developing the retrieval brain. The embedding models must be chosen by an organization to suit their domain of work, perhaps with models available on the MTEB Leaderboard, and an embedding space with a vector database designed to facilitate Hybrid Search, which searches using a combination of keywords and vectors. The design of a Knowledge Graph for expressing the first-order entity relationships of projects, people, and documents is also to be accomplished.

Phase 3: The Interface & Feedback Loop (Months 5-6). The final stage is centered on user deployment. The interface that is designed must promote trust factors whereby all answers provided by the AI are accompanied by references to their source. Lastly, a "Reinforcement Learning from Human Feedback" cycle initiated by "Thumbs Up/Down" tools must be incorporated to adjust parameters depending on user feedback.

Phase 4: Agentic Evolution (Month 7+). The transition phase from passive to active systems. The "Observer Agents" should be used, which monitor communication channels in real-time. If the Agent finds that the question has already been answered previously, it actively publishes the URL to the corresponding RAG entry, thus closing the knowledge gap before it opens. 8.

Economic Analysis: The "Return on Intelligence" (ROIn) RAG investment is capital intensive, and senior managers need strong economic incentives. To this end, we propose the "Return on Intelligence" (ROIn) framework that puts values on repairing the Organizational Memory. The loss of knowledge investment is high because the average knowledge worker spends about 1.8 hours per day looking for information. Assuming the company is of 1,000 people size and the average worker is paid $50 an hour, the total loss of productivity due to this issue alone would be approximately $22.5 million every year.

Additionally, the estimate of redundant work spent on problems already solved is believed to contribute another 5 percent to engineering time. "A properly optimized RAG system can conservatively decrease search time by 40 to 60%." If we assume a 50% saving, it will help the organization to breach back around 11.25 million dollars per annum. But, on the flip side, we need to consider the infrastructure costs, which will entail vector databases, LLM inference costs (either via an API or an onboard GPU), as well as a team for maintenance. Notwithstanding these costs, which are conservatively estimated to be 650 thousand per annum, we still arrive at a ROI that stands out to be an astonishing 1,630%. This clearly establishes that it costs virtually nothing to "fix" organizational memory, as compared to an enormous "cost of not knowing" within a knowledge-intensive, high-wage economy. The ROIn clearly establishes that RAG is an absolute imperative for costs, as it represents a sea change that transforms a computer system upgrade to an absolute business imperative. 9. Conclusion The state of Organizational Memory in the age of remote work is not just a temporary problem, but rather a structural one that threatens innovation and adaptability. As teams are scattered around the world, the "social glue" factor of geography disappears, and what remains is a fractured terrain of digital silos in which tacit knowledge stagnates and context is destroyed. The solution comes in the form of Generative AI and, in particular, the RAG model, which provides the only hope for this scenario. The change of paradigm from "Storage" (saving files) to "Activation" (generating answers) allows what was previously a "dead archive" of the company to evolve and morph into what might be referred to as a "Digital Nervous System." More is required to make this transformation successfully, however, than merely software. More is required regarding a solid architecture of RAG design choices, a certain mathematics of score and hallucination management, and a certain governance to ensure the responsible and secure usage of this technology. The organization that has successfully exploited RAG, however, is, first of all, a time saver but also builds a compounding advantage. Its memory is a cumulative, and not a depleted, resource, which ensures that every lesson is forever ingrained and instantly retrievable. This is, of course, the advantage in the volatility of the 21st-century economy.

REFERENCES

Alavi, M., Storey, V. C., & Sullivan, Y. W. (2024). Knowledge management perspective of generative artificial intelligence (GenAI). *Journal of the Association for Information Systems, 25*(1), 1–12. Advance online publication. DOI: 10.17705/1jais.00859

Mahmoud, M. & Awad, A. (2024). Impact of electronic customer relationship management on competitive advantage: Mediating role of customer satisfaction in EgyptAir. *Problems and Perspectives in Management, 22*(3), 276–286. https://doi.org/10.21511/ppm.22(3).2024.22

Cheng, M., Zhang, C., & Liu, Q. (2025). A survey on knowledge-oriented retrieval-augmented generation. *arXiv preprint arXiv:2501.01234.*

Ghonim, A., Awad, A., Shemais, M., Shma, T., & Aziz, A. (2025). Exploring the impact of flexible work arrangements on employee engagement in telecommunications: Case of Egypt. *Problems and Perspectives in Management, 23*(2), 198–207. https://doi.org/10.21511/ppm.23(2).2025.13

Huang, Y., & Zhao, W. X. (2024). A survey on retrieval-augmented text generation for large language models. *arXiv preprint arXiv:2404.14135.*

Klesel, M., & Wittmann, H. F. (2025). Retrieval-augmented generation (RAG): Business & information systems engineering. *Business & Information Systems Engineering, 67*(4), 551–561. Advance online publication. DOI: 10.1007/s12599-025-00945-3

Lyu, Y., Li, Z., & Zhang, M. (2024). CRUD-RAG: A comprehensive Chinese benchmark for retrieval-augmented generation of large language models. *ACM Transactions on Information Systems.*

Mihajlović, M. (2025). Multimodal retrieval-augmented generation in knowledge systems. *Proceedings of the International Conference on AI & KM.*

Nandagopal, S. (2025). Securing retrieval-augmented generation pipelines: A comprehensive framework. *Journal of Computer Science and Security.*

Qadeer, A., Awad, A., & Ali, A. (2025). Understanding generative AI implementation in digital advertising among retail SMEs in Pakistan. In Z. Hussain, A. Khan, Md. U. Hossain Uzir, M-N S. Sharipudin, and A. Shaheen (Eds.), *Impacts of AI generated content on brand reputation* (pp. 177–201). IGI Global Scientific Publishing.

Shahul, E. S., ... (2023). RAGAs: Automated evaluation of retrieval augmented generation. *arXiv preprint arXiv:2309.15217.*

Sharma, C. (2025). Retrieval-augmented generation: A comprehensive survey of architectures, enhancements, and robustness frontiers. *arXiv preprint arXiv:2502.04567.*

Singh, A., & Gupta, P. (2025). Agentic retrieval-augmented generation: A survey on agentic RAG. *arXiv preprint arXiv:2501.09876.*

Wahid, A., & Awad, A. (2025). Role of AI chatbots in enhancing customer satisfaction and customer loyalty. In Z. Hussain, A. Khan, Md. U. Hossain Uzir, M-N S. Sharipudin, and A. Shaheen (Eds.), *Impacts of AI generated content on brand reputation* (pp. 129–147). IGI Global Scientific Publishing.

Wu, W., & Chen, L. (2025). MultiRAG: A knowledge-guided framework for mitigating hallucination in multi-source retrieval augmented generation. *2025 IEEE 41st International Conference on Data Engineering (ICDE).*

Yan, S. Q., Gu, J. C., & Zhu, X. (2024). Corrective retrieval augmented generation. *arXiv preprint arXiv:2401.15884.*

Yu, H., ... (2024). Evaluation of retrieval-augmented generation: A survey. *arXiv preprint arXiv:2405.07437.*

Zhang, W., & Wang, Y. (2025). Hallucination mitigation for retrieval-augmented large language models: A review. *Mathematics, 13*(5), 856. DOI: 10.3390/math13050856

Zhu, X., & Li, Y. (2025). Knowledge graph-guided retrieval augmented generation. *arXiv preprint arXiv:2502.01234.* DOI: 10.18653/v1/2025.naacl-long.449

Chapter 14
Artificial Intelligence for Human Resources Management:
Opportunities, Challenges, and Ethical Considerations

Ahmed Hegazy
https://orcid.org/0000-0003-3289-6844
Department of Business Administration, Faculty of Commerce, Al-Azhar University, Nacr City, Egypt

Mohamed Hammad
Faculty of Financial and Administrative Sciences, Pharos University in Alexandria, Egypt

ABSTRACT

An accelerated adoption of Artificial Intelligence (AI) in organisational processes has prompted analysis of its influence on Human Resource Management (HRM). This chapter explores how AI transforms HR from traditional administrative duties into a strategic partner through data-driven analysis. It builds a framework for understanding how AI reshapes the HR Lifecycle, improving efficiency and enabling strategic intelligence to manage human capital. The chapter examines AI's functional applications, including talent acquisition via automated screening, performance evaluation through predictive analytics, and personalised employee development to enhance engagement. On the strategic level, it highlights AI's role in workforce planning and organisational development, showing how AI empowers proactive decision-making, optimises resource allocation, and aligns human capital with overall organisational objectives.

DOI: 10.4018/979-8-3373-7416-1.ch014

PURPOSE AND SCOPE OF THE CHAPTER

An accelerated adoption of Artificial Intelligence (AI) into organisational processes has compelled a thorough analysis of AI's influence on Human Resource Management (HRM). This chapter presents a foundational analysis of AI's influence as an HR changing from traditional administrative responsibilities to the strategic partner looking forward through data-driven analysis. It will also build the framework for understanding how AI technologies are redefining the fundamental structure of the HR Lifecycle, providing organisations with improved operational efficiency, as well as the ability to leverage strategic intelligence to more effectively manage human capital, their most important asset.

The present chapter details the extent to which Artificial Intelligence (AI) will be implemented within Human Resource Management (HRM) on both a strategic and functional level. In terms of functionality, this chapter will examine how AI tools are being applied to the major areas within HRM and how they can enhance the talent acquisition process through automated screening of candidates, improve the performance evaluation process through predictive analytics, and create a more personalised approach to employee development and enhancements of employee engagement. On the strategic level, this chapter will also discuss the implications of using AI on workforce planning and on organisational development; AI tools will enable an organisation to proactively make decisions about its workforce, optimise resource allocation, and align human capital with the organisation’s overall strategic objectives.

INTRODUCTION

With the rapid development of information technology, organizations face a significant challenge to keep pace with this development to ensure their survival in the business field. Organizations can only keep pace with development through their human resources, which are considered the most critical asset in any organization. Among these developments is the emergence of artificial intelligence (AI), which has worked to bring about a rapid transformation in human resources management (HRM). It introduced new advantages to enhance efficiency and decision-making regarding human resources. Integrating AI into human resource management is not just about automating routine tasks; it is fundamentally reshaping how organizations attract, select, and manage talent. AI has become a strategic component of organizations' plans.

HR professionals can make strategic decisions based on accurate information using advanced data analytics and predictive algorithms, including identifying high-potential candidates and improving workforce planning. This transformation allows HR to focus on transforming workforce dynamics and enhancing personal work experiences.

DEFINING ARTIFICIAL INTELLIGENCE

Artificial Intelligence (AI) The ability of machines or computer programs to simulate human intelligence and perform tasks that typically require human cognitive abilities. Based on multiple perspectives in the paragraphs presented, the following definition is complex:

- Imitation of Human Intelligence:

Artificial intelligence involves machines being able to think, learn, and solve problems in ways that are similar to human perception, and artificial neural networks (ANNs) are commonly employed to achieve this goal (Zohuri & Behgounia, 2023; Fotoh & Mugwira, 2025).

- Scope of Tasks:

Visual perception, speech recognition, decision making, language translation, image and audio identification, document analysis, and sentiment analysis are just some of the tasks AI systems can perform, which are traditionally associated with intelligent objects. (Fotoh & Mugwira, 2025), (Ahmad et al., 2024), (Leonardi et al., 2021).

- Scientific and Technical Field:

Modeling intelligent behavior through computational means is the focus of artificial intelligence, a scientific discipline. This includes the study and design of agents —intelligent systems that monitor their environment and work to achieve specific goals (Cannataro, 2022).

- Umbrella Term for Technologies:

A variety of technologies and methodologies are involved in artificial intelligence, including machine learning, deep learning, data mining, and more. These methods aim to simulate the human brain's approach to analysis, modeling, and decision-making (Ahmad et al., 2024).

- Knowledge Representation and Reasoning:

Representing, storing, and using knowledge for thinking and decision-making is a crucial aspect of artificial intelligence, which enables machines to act on what they "know" about the world. (Cannataro, 2022).

STRATEGIC SHIFT IN HR

Human resource management (HRM) is being fundamentally reshaped by artificial intelligence, shifting it from its traditional role of administrative support to a strategic function that develops talent and drives organizational change. This is how this transformation unfolds:

Automation of Routine Tasks and Enhanced Efficiency

- AI automates complex and repetitive HR tasks: HR professionals have the ability to prioritize strategic initiatives over administrative duties, such as recruitment, qualification, and exit. This shift allows HR to play a more active role in workforce planning and organizational development (Rožman, Oreški & Tominc, 2022).
- Reduced transaction times and costs: AI-powered systems enable reducing time and cost by simplifying processes like order screening and employee service, which further supports the strategic development of human resources.

Strategic Talent Acquisition and Workforce Planning

- AI-driven recruitment tools: Candidate experience enhancement can be achieved through applicant tracking systems, resume scanners, and chatbots, which can enhance hiring accuracy and efficiency, reduce human bias, and improve hiring efficiency. This allows HR to attract and retain top talent and align hiring decisions with long-term organizational goals (Shahzad et al., 2023).
- Predictive analytics assists HR in anticipating future workforce needs, developing strong talent lines, and supporting proactive workforce management and strategic planning.

Personalized Employee Development and Engagement

- AI identifies skill gaps and recommends tailored training programs, which facilitate continuous learning and upskilling. This supports employee growth, retention, and aligns talent development with evolving business demands, (Rožman, Oreški & Tominc, 2022), (Shahzad et al., 2023), (Gupta, Lakhera & Sharma, 2024).
- AI-powered feedback and goal-setting tools: This leads to improved employee engagement and improved performance management, which helps human resource management continuously improve and encourage innovation (Rožman, Oreški & Tominc, 2022).

Data-Driven Decision Making and Strategic Impact

- AI enables HR to leverage data for strategic decision-makingInfluencing the composition of the workforce, the form of job structures, and the relationship between employer and employee. Therefore, this data-driven system allows human resources to contribute to organizational change and business competitiveness (Zheng et al., 2025).
- Integration of technology with human roles leads to countless job satisfaction and personalized work experiences, further positioning HR as a driver of organizational transformation (Zheng et al., 2025).

Evolution of HR's Role and Organizational Capabilities

- HR's function has evolved from administrative to strategic, Through this development, human resources can influence organizational performance and market competitiveness to ensure business sustainability, supported by technological advances and increased global investment in artificial intelligence (Goswami et al., 2023).
- AI shifts workforce composition To adapt to rapid technological changes, it is necessary to enhance internal capabilities as the demand for highly skilled employees increases (He & Wang, 2025).

AI TECHNOLOGY: COMPLEMENTING HUMAN GOVERNANCE AND PEOPLE

The subsequent discussion underscores the position that artificial intelligence should function as a complementary instrument to human governance and societal structures, rather than serving as a substitute. The following section provides a synthesized overview of the principal arguments.

AI as a Complement, not a Replacement

- Augmenting Human Capabilities: AI tools should be used to enhance human capabilities, not replace them. AI tools should enhance well-being in society. Therefore, companies should provide training programs for employees to equip them with the skills to integrate AI tools into jobs (Altinay et al., 2025).
- Enhancing Human Skills: Artificial intelligence tools help solve complex problems, which has an impact on improving the decision-making process. This refers to the complementary relationship, which is that artificial intelligence tools support human resource contributions, not replace them (Lee, 2025).

Human Governance Remains Essential

- Governance Over Replacement Stakeholders agree that AI cannot completely replace human resources, especially in governance roles. The focus should be on understanding and developing AI management, rather than speculating about replacing politicians or decision-makers with machines.
- Ethics and Accountability: Effective frameworks must be put in place to manage artificial intelligence, as the development of artificial intelligence must be consistent with human ethics and values, to increase confidence in it. This is crucial to enhancing user trust and emphasizing public good service (Wu, Huang & Gong, 2020), (Marwala, 2024).

Participatory and Inclusive Governance

- Stakeholder Engagement Policymakers are partnering with various stakeholders to develop participatory approaches to AI management, to identify ways to leverage AI to serve community needs. This ensures ethical considerations and societal concerns, rather than leaving them unchecked (Wang & Zhang, 2025).
- Guardrails and Regulation: Laws and regulations must be put in place to ensure that AI is adopted fairly. So that the interaction between humans and technology is carefully managed, especially in work environments and human resource management, by placing "protection barriers" for society and the individual, such as certain things, such as bias and discrimination, ensur-

ing transparency, protecting privacy and data security, and defining accountability and human oversight (Ji & Huang, 2022).

Transparency and Explainability

- Explainable AI In order to ensure human oversight, AI systems must be interpretable. This allows the human resource to understand decision-making processes in the field of artificial intelligence, by feeding artificial intelligence with appropriate data to ensure that the risks of bias and misuse are reduced, and accountability remains with people, not machines (Yang et al., 2021).

AI TOOLS IN HR FUNCTIONS

Artificial intelligence (AI) is increasingly being integrated across a wide range of human resources (HR) functions, transforming traditional practices and enabling new capabilities. Below is a detailed summary of how AI tools are used in different HR fields, based strictly on the paragraphs provided.

Key HR Functions Enhanced by AI

- Talent Search and Recruitment
    - AI streamlines candidate sourcing, screening, and selection, making recruitment more efficient and effective. Tools can automate resume parsing, match candidates to job requirements, and even conduct initial interviews or assessments (De Obesso Arias, Pérez Rivero & Carrero Márquez, 2023), (Ali & Kallach, 2024), (Leite, 2024).
    - AI is widely adopted in recruitment, with 79% of major organizations using it to attract and hire qualified employees.
- Employee Performance Analysis
    - AI systems analyze employee performance data, provide timely feedback, and help set goals. This enables more objective and data-driven performance management (De Obesso Arias, Pérez Rivero & Carrero Márquez, 2023), (Leite, 2024), (Rožman, Oreški & Tominc, 2022), .
    - AI can monitor remote employees, track progress, and suggest relevant training courses to improve specific skills (Rožman, Oreški & Tominc, 2022).
- Career Optimization and Employee Development
    - AI helps employees identify career paths, recommend training opportunities, and optimize personal development plans based on performance

and skill gaps (De Obesso Arias, Pérez Rivero & Carrero Márquez, 2023), (Rožman, Oreški & Tominc, 2022), .
    - AI-powered tools assist in finding relevant training courses and facilitate continuous learning (Rožman, Oreški & Tominc, 2022).
- Staff Turnover Planning
    - AI can predict employee turnover by analyzing patterns in workforce data, helping HR plan for retention and succession (De Obesso Arias, Pérez Rivero & Carrero Márquez, 2023).
- Compensation and Reward Systems
    - AI is used to develop and manage compensation structures, ensuring fairness and competitiveness by analyzing market data and internal performance metrics .
- Routine Process Automation
    - AI automates routine HR tasks such as documentation, monitoring, and record-keeping, freeing up HR professionals to focus on strategic initiatives (Ali & Kallach, 2024), (Rožman, Oreški & Tominc, 2022).
    - Employees save significant time on monotonous tasks, increasing productivity and engagement (Rožman, Oreški & Tominc, 2022).
- Employee Engagement and Collaboration
    - AI enhances communication and collaboration, especially for remote teams, by facilitating quick and effective interactions (Rožman, Oreški & Tominc, 2022).
    - AI-driven feedback and goal-setting tools improve employee engagement and reduce workplace stress (Rožman, Oreški & Tominc, 2022).

Strategic and Organizational Implications

- Decision-Making and Value-Added Services
    - AI supports HR decision-making by providing actionable insights from large datasets, improving the quality and speed of HR decisions (Ali & Kallach, 2024).
    - AI enables creative IT service delivery models and enhances monitoring features (Ali & Kallach, 2024).
- Challenges and Risks
    - Adoption of AI in HR raises concerns about algorithmic bias, technostress, resistance to change, and data privacy (Ali & Kallach, 2024; Leite, 2024).
    - Perceived risk moderates the relationship between technological awareness and HR function effectiveness, indicating the need for careful planning and management (Shahzad et al., 2023).

    - Ethical considerations and strategies to mitigate bias and promote transparency are essential for successful AI integration.
- Organizational Transformation
    - AI adoption requires a new symbiosis between HR, technology, and employees, shifting focus from routine tasks to creative and strategic work (Rožman, Oreški & Tominc, 2022).
    - Pilot studies and empirical validation are recommended to assess the effectiveness of AI-driven HR models in diverse contexts.

Emerging Patterns and Insights

- AI is a Key Driver of HR Transformation
    - AI is considered one of the top technological trends shaping the future of HR, revolutionizing how organizations manage talent, performance, and development.
    - The integration of AI in HR is not limited to isolated functions but is increasingly strategic, aiming to optimize organizational performance and resilience (Shahzad et al., 2023).
- Human-AI Collaboration
    - AI agents are becoming competent teammates, augmenting human capabilities and enabling hybrid teams to outperform human-only teams in complex tasks (Zhang et al., 2023).

Example: how to use AI to build HRMS:

By using Gemini platform, we asked the following:

Then we got this result:

This is an inter active system, so If you want to build a model or application for human resources management, you can enter the necessary data, in terms of the number of employees, leaders, the nature of the organization, vacations, deductions and insurances, and remove the necessary data for that.

Examples for Human Resources management AI wed sites:

https://www.talentera.com/

https://www.teamtailor.com/

AI'S STRATEGIC IMPACT ON HUMAN RESOURCES MANAGEMENT

Artificial Intelligence (AI) is changing the way Human Resources (HR) manages their workforce at a strategic level. AI technology improves collaboration between people and machines, allowing organizations to leverage both AI capabilities and the advantages that come from human collaboration (Tsiskaridze et al., 2023). AI will create new opportunities for HR professionals to improve their strategic contributions to their organizations, but this evolution also raises critical concerns for HR regarding ethics, implementing AI, and balancing decisions made by people with those made by computers (algorithms).

According to recent total research, there are five significant influences of AI on HR functions. These five impacts include automating activities, better utilizing HR data, supplementing human intelligence, redesigning the work environment, and transforming the relationships and social interactions at work (Dima et al., 2024). Each of these impacts provides both an opportunity and a challenge to organizations as they implement or consider using AI technology within their HR processes. As AI becomes more widely used within HRM, there is a greater need for HR practitioners, business executives, and policymakers to properly understand how AI will change traditional methods and functions of HR.

The incorporation of AI technology into the human resources industry does come with its own set of challenges. Organizations need to understand the risks and potential benefits of AI recruitment tools. In particular, the introduction of AI recruiting tools creates issues regarding ethics and legal compliance and takes away the candidate's perception of fairness (Tsiskaridze et al., 2023). The success of implementing AI is built on the combination of the best attributes of both human and machine intelligence, while ensuring the appropriate oversight and governance of AI technology. Such a hybrid approach will allow organizations to maximize the use of AI, while maintaining the human approach to effective people management.

By combining both elements together into one integrated plan, Companies using AI in their HR processes get many benefits not only from Automating those Procedures, They also get many more advantages, And it provides improved ways For Companies to analyse their Businesses, They have Better abilities To process Data Fast, So they can Make Better Business Decisions (Badhurunnisa & Dass, 2023).

STRATEGIC ADVANTAGES OF AI IN HR

The impact of AI technology on human resource management (HR) practices is particularly evident in talent acquisition. The application of automated talent acquisition technologies powered by artificial intelligence (AI) has been shown to reduce unconscious bias towards potential job candidates, speed up the Hiring process, and improve the quality of the match between the individual and the organization (Kulshrestha, 2024). Furthermore, through the ability to make predictions about issues such as employee turnover and to identify high-potential candidates,

AI-driven workforce analytics provide HR professionals with insight into developing and ensuring an organization's continued success (Kulshrestha, 2024).

AI offers a series of advantages to the field of Human Resource (HR) Management by supporting organizations in keeping pace with the rapid evolution of technology; therefore, enabling organisations to be more proactive, make decisions faster and obtain better insights from AI and, ultimately, continue innovatively providing their products and services which strengthens their position within the marketplace (Badhurunnisa & Dass, 2023). As well, AI is supporting HR Managers in making proactive HR-related strategy and workforce planning decisions; thus, enabling HR Managers to become more agile, competitive and adaptable to a rapidly changing environment (Garg, 2025) and thus further position HR as a leader in their respective organisations' long-term financial success through the use of AI driven HR analytics and strategic workforce planning .

The five strategic impact dimensions of AI on organizations are: 1. Task Automation 2. Optimizing Human Resource Data 3. Augmentation of Human Capability 4. Redesigning Work Contexts 5. Social & Relationship Transformations within Work. (Dima et al., 2024). This integrated approach allows organizations to create a strategic HR framework that is well-aligned with their overall business objectives and enables the establishment of a high-performance workplace culture that enhances employee retention and long-term profitability (Ahmad, et al., 2025).

OPERATIONAL EFFICIENCY

In human resource management, Artificial Intelligence (AI) provides a considerable increase in productivity because of the systematic use of automation to automate repetitive administrative duties that may otherwise be done manually. The routine nature of these duties (for example, payroll processing, managing employee records, and scheduling) means that they can take a long time to complete manually. However, by using AI to automate the above-listed activities, HR professionals will have reduced their manual workload and have increased the speed of completing routine HR activities. Therefore, by implementing AI in HR, HR professionals will be able to devote themselves to more strategic and innovative activities than would have otherwise been possible, which results in fewer errors being made and higher HR operational efficiency (Badhurunnisa & Dass, 2023). AI's extensive capabilities for automating HR systems and its ability to give HR professionals more time to concentrate on more strategic objectives are some examples of the HR operational efficiencies that can be realized using AI tools to streamline and automate various HR functions.

By implementing AI within HR processes organisations may derive significant operational benefits with respect to minimising errors. AI solutions use automated systems which reduce the likelihood of human error in functions of employee data processing, such as calculating salaries and monitoring attendance, resulting in increased accuracy and reduced financial and legal exposure related to data errors (Sundari et al., 2024). There has also been a marked improvement in the reduction of administrative errors for organisations that have adopted the use of AI technology. Improved automation has increased the speed at which organisations can verify and audit their data. In addition, AI provides a greater level of efficiency and effectiveness with respect to an organisation's recruitment processes by automating labour intensive tasks, targeting better qualified candidates, and providing the ability to make data driven hiring decisions (Odili et al., 2024).

The measurable benefit of utilizing artificial intelligence to improve operational efficiency provides considerable advantages to organizations. A recent study demonstrated that businesses with a high level of AI integration in their HR departments realised gains in operational efficiency of more than 30%. This indicates that HR management practices can anticipate increased efficiency and effectiveness through the incorporation of AI in the future. The use of AI technology to achieve operational efficiencies leads to an increase in employee engagement and satisfaction due to customised and detailed real-time feedback provided. Operational efficiencies are achieved by automating repetitive tasks to enable human employees to devote greater attention to more challenging tasks, while the AI processes large amounts of data quickly and efficiently.

AI has drastically changed the way HR performs day-to-day operations by automating repetitive tasks and transforming their overall processes. For instance, Generative AI allows for faster hiring through the ability for more accurately match candidates to job descriptions, reducing the amount of time spent gathering resumes (Khan et al., 2024). At the same time, AI technologies boost employee engagement through the use of customized communication and automated responses to everyday requests (Benabou & Touhami, 2025).

By integrating technology such as chatbots and machine learning algorithms, HR departments are able to make data-driven decisions. This allows HR teams to make better-informed decisions with greater efficiency while simplifying the administrative functions of HR, including candidate screening and collecting employee feedback (Benabou & Touhami, 2025). Ultimately, this global transformation allows HR professionals to refocus their efforts on strategic initiatives, including Talent Management and Organisational Development, as well as improving the efficiency of recruitment, which ultimately results in higher organisational performance (Benabou & Touhami, 2025).

STRATEGIC ACUITY AND DATA-DRIVEN DECISIONS

The incorporation of AI into Human Resource Management (HRM) leads to a radical change in how businesses make strategic decisions via enhanced data processing with advanced predictive capabilities enabled through artificial intelligence (AI). The power of data analytics provided by AI allows businesses to extract relevant information from an abundance of complex HR-related data that provides organisations with the tools to discover previously unseen correlation and predictive qualities in their data sets that traditional methods have yet to detect (Nyathani, 2023). In addition, AI capabilities allow for the discovery of data trends and predictive qualities within organisations based on the examination of vast quantities of HR-related data at speeds that would typically require significantly extended periods for humans to analyse; this ultimately creates an environment where data-driven decisions can be made based on comprehensive analyses rather than by chance or impulsively (Bhima et al., 2023)

AI's ability to project future workforce requirements marks a major step forward for strategic workforce planning. Leveraging advanced analytics provided by AI, organizations can use predictive modelling and scenario forecasting to determine future workforce requirements and anticipate potential issues related to workforce dynamics, such as talent shortages, performance problems, and employee turnover, and subsequently address the aforementioned issues prior to their occurrence while continuing to improve workforce resource allocation (Nyathani, 2023). Additionally, AI algorithms use historical data to predict when an employee is likely to leave and identify which employees are likely to be superior performers leading to a significant improvement in retention and employee development strategies (Kulshrestha, 2024). This predictive perspective enables managers to make more informed decisions concerning all aspects of their organization including product development and staffing, thus providing a competitive advantage in rapidly changing marketplace conditions.

AI enables smarter hiring decisions and has the potential to provide HCM with enhanced value by offering quantitative evidence of its impact on HCM decision making. Numerous studies have demonstrated the relationship between AI and improved recruitment and selection performance through positive correlations of 0.830 or higher, thereby allowing organisations to utilise AI technology in their HCM function and realise considerable gains in talent acquisition and management capability (Fakhr-e-Alam, et al. 2024). By leveraging artificial intelligence for candidate acquisition, employing artificial intelligence allows organisations to quickly and effectively process large numbers of applicants and identify the best candidates faster and more accurately than manual methods. Furthermore, performance management solutions that incorporate AI allow organisations to measure their employee contributions and make informed hiring recommendations based on the aggregate data provided, thus eliminating the potential for bias in the assessment of employee performance and promoting equitable work environments (Garg, 2025).

Talent Management Processes: The strategic model for Artificial Intelligence (AI) in Human Resources (HR) identifies and utilizes analytical techniques to identify, develop and plan for using high-potential talent. This enables organizations to maintain a constant supply of top performers in the HR workforce (Nyathani, 2023; Johnson et al., 2022). The increasing implementation of AI/Human Resource Analytics as part of Human Resource Strategic Workforce Planning creates opportunities for organizations to assess the long-term financial impact, create a well-developed Human Resource framework and ensure alignment of the Human Resources to the business strategy, which strengthens the company's position (Ahmad et al., 2025). The combination of HR analytics and strategic Human Resource Workforce Planning allows Human Resource professionals to remain focused on their human resources and organizational objectives while being appropriately aligned and positioned to be competitively successful (Khan et al., 2024).

PROACTIVE WORKFORCE MANAGEMENT

The evolution of AI in human resource management has enabled organizations to shift from reactive to proactive workforce management strategies through advanced predictive capabilities and continuous monitoring systems. AI-driven analytics enable organizations to forecast future trends and anticipate potential challenges related to workforce dynamics through predictive modeling and scenario planning, allowing them to proactively address issues such as talent shortages, performance gaps, and employee turnover while optimizing resource allocation (Nyathani, 2023; Johnson et al., 2022). This predictive approach represents a fundamental shift in how HR professionals approach workforce planning, moving beyond traditional retrospective analysis to anticipate and prevent potential issues.

AI technologies are enabling proactive workforce management through their role in identifying and developing talent. With the use of AI-based analytics for identifying high-potential employees, opportunities for talent development, and succession plans for an organisation, companies can create a continuous supply of skilled, engaged employees who will help achieve organisational goals (Nyathani 2023; Johnson et al. 2022). AI algorithms allow for predicting employee exits and for determining potential high-performance levels which assist in increasing retention and employee development (Kulshrestha 2024). This ability allows organisations to make decisions about which talent to invest in, as well as to avoid excessive costs associated with the unpredictable departure of employees or the time involved in replacing employees when the opportunity arises.

Using AI, Human Resource (HR) managers can take proactive measures which enable greater levels of agility and competitiveness within their organisations. This ability to respond rapidly and adaptively to changes in the marketplace and competitive environment allows organisations to maintain their competitive advantages. It also provides opportunities for increased engagement, retention, and productivity of employees through the development of more personalised and impactful employee experiences. In addition, AI analytics provide a continual feedback mechanism that enables organisations to improve their HR strategies, processes, and initiatives over time (Nyathani, 2023). Overall, the ability to consistently respond and adapt to changing market conditions creates a culture of agility and adaptability within the HR function.

UNBLOCKING HUMAN POTENTIAL

AI for HR is changing the way we do HR. Using AI to automate common HR tasks will enable HR professionals to produce greater value through both operational improvements and their strategic approach to productivity. Automating administrative activities, such as payroll processing, employee data tracking, and scheduling, reduces the amount of time HR professionals spend performing tasks that could otherwise be performed by others, therefore allowing HR teams to use their free time to concentrate on developing more strategic initiatives (Sundari, et al., 2024). By using AI to automate repetitive administrative tasks, HR can spend less time performing routine tasks and spend greater amounts of time focusing on strategic talent development and maximizing productivity and organizational success (Benabou & Touhami, 2025).

The process of being released from numerous daily responsibilities will allow Human Resources (HR) experts to spend time on activities that are of higher value and/or benefit to the organization. Under the influence of Artificial Intelligence (AI) applications, HR departments are able to design high-quality employee development plans (EDPs), determine the skills that will be required for the advancement of their careers within the organization, develop plans for succession, and create plans for retaining employees who contribute to organizational growth. Because of the ability to automate numerous repetitive processes, AI allows for increased complexity in job tasks. AI also enables efficient analysis of information by providing access to substantial amounts of data on an ongoing basis, which will allow HR teams to devote their time and resources to more complex areas of employee development than would be feasible for HR specialists to accomplish on their own. In addition to using time and resources more efficiently, AI also allows HR teams to align their long-term HR management goals to the overall business goals and develop means for improving employee experience and creating policies that will support employees' health and well-being.

An increased investment in strategic projects results in measurable improvements in organizational performance and employee engagement. When automation is integrated into HR departments so that HR staff can spend more time working on strategic initiatives, it will allow HR departments to be more efficient with their resources while giving employees an improved employee experience through continued support and learning opportunities that provide real-time feedback. In addition, tools such as personal computers and mobile devices allow organizations to develop digitally personalized employee experiences that improve employee engagement (Najana, 2024). The development of these tools and the implementation of HR processes with the use of technology enables the organization to find new opportunities and develop new solutions, create innovation, improve business operations and increase collaboration among teams (Badhurunnisa & Dass, 2023; Awad & Alharthi, 2025).

By implementing artificial intelligence into the evolution of human resources (HR) strategically, HR practitioners will emerge as vital facilitators of innovation and competitive edge within the organisation. Artificial Intelligence tools like Chatbots and Machine Learning support decision making in the HR field. With these tools, HR practitioners are equipped with vast amounts of data to facilitate their decision-making process. HR professionals can achieve greater efficiency by combining tools to collect candidate screening results and employee feedback data (e.g., through chatbots and machine learning). As HR professionals' roles transform, they will ultimately be positioned as strategic partners in the business growth of their respective organisations. HR practitioners will emphasise activities which create sustained organisational success while remaining customer-centric in their management of employees and the overall workforce. (Benabou & Touhami, 2025)

SCALABILITY AND CUSTOMIZATION

AI's scalability provides organizations with the ability to quickly and effectively adapt human resources capabilities to meet a variety of needs based on their specific organizational needs, and the organizations' growth paths. AI enables organizations to gather data and gain insights into potential challenges they will face in the future, thereby enhancing their ability to develop employee skill sets, promote effective leaders, create a better work culture, and improve overall quality of life for employees (Indrasari & Pamuji, 2023; Manthena, 2021). The ability to scale up and down quickly is of particular value to organizations that are undergoing rapid growth or are in multiple areas because AI systems can increase the amount of data that can be processed without increasing the level of associated management costs at the same rate.

Modern AI-powered HR platforms offer advanced means of fulfilling the varying needs of organizations through the customisation capabilities that they provide. By incorporating AI and machine learning into their HR processes, organisations have begun to adopt these technologies as a means of automating specific functions, predicting business trends, and delivering personalised experiences for employees. In addition to this, comprehensive HCM suites now also include integrated AI virtual assistants to provide a more efficient vehicle for carrying out HR activities as well as improving employee satisfaction with the overall experience of being a part of an organisation (Parasa & Jadugala, 2023). This integration into HR platforms illustrates a major advancement toward creating intelligent HR systems where decisions are made with the assistance of AI technology, employee engagement is increased, and workforce management is optimised in line with the unique needs of each organization

The measurable impact of scalable AI implementation demonstrates substantial returns on investment for organizations of varying sizes and industries. Strategic and deliberate AI utilization can significantly enhance an organization's ability to recruit and onboard new talent, which is crucial for maintaining a competitive edge in today's dynamic business landscape (Fakhr-e-Alam et al., 2024). Organizations can confidently invest in AI-powered HR solutions, resulting in significant improvements in talent acquisition and management capabilities while maintaining the flexibility to customize these systems according to their specific operational contexts and strategic objectives (Fakhr-e-Alam et al., 2024). By embracing AI technologies while maintaining a human-centric approach, organizations can gain a competitive edge in the talent market and ensure they attract and retain top talent across diverse business environments and scales of operation (Fakhr-e-Alam et al., 2024).

EMPLOYEE EXPERIENCE AND PERSONALIZATION

The implementation of AI in human resource management has revolutionized how organizations deliver personalized employee experiences, moving beyond one-size-fits-all approaches to create tailored interactions that meet individual employee needs and preferences. AI fosters a more positive employee experience by providing continuous support, personalized learning opportunities, and real-time feedback, thus boosting satisfaction and engagement levels .. This personalization capability extends to multiple facets of the employee journey, as AI can personalize employee experiences, such as learning and development opportunities, based on an individual employee's skills and interests (Bhattacharya, 2023).

The technological infrastructure supporting personalized employee experience demonstrates sophisticated AI integration across comprehensive HR platforms. Organizations are increasingly leveraging AI and ML to automate processes, predict trends, and provide personalized experiences for employees, with SAP SuccessFactors incorporating Joule, an AI-driven virtual assistant, to streamline HR processes and enhance employee experience (Parasa & Jadugala, 2023). This integration represents a significant step towards intelligent HR systems where AI can assist in decision-making, improve employee engagement, and optimize workforce management according to individual employee requirements.

The impact of AI-driven personalization extends to enhanced employee support systems and communication channels. AI-powered chatbots can provide employees with instant answers to their questions, reducing the frustration and time-consuming process of waiting for HR professionals to respond (Bhattacharya, 2023). Generative AI significantly enhances employee engagement by personalizing interactions and automating routine tasks, enabling HR professionals to concentrate on key objectives (Khan et al., 2024). AI tools have enhanced human resource processes by enabling personalized employee experiences and fostering a more engaged workforce (Najana, 2024).

The strategic value of personalized employee experiences through AI implementation delivers measurable improvements in workforce engagement and organizational performance. AI-driven analytics can support the development of more personalized and impactful employee experiences, driving higher engagement, retention, and productivity (Nyathani, 2023; Johnson et al., 2022). This comprehensive approach to employee experience personalization enables organizations to create adaptive work environments that respond to individual employee needs while maintaining organizational efficiency and strategic alignment.

ETHICAL CHALLENGES AND BIAS IN AI-POWERED HUMAN RESOURCE MANAGEMENT

The integration of artificial intelligence into human resource management has transformed how organizations recruit, evaluate, and manage employees. AI-driven systems now handle tasks ranging from resume screening and candidate assessment to performance monitoring and promotion decisions . However, this technological advancement has brought significant ethical challenges that demand careful consideration from both practitioners and researchers.

Current Literature Reveals Three Primary Areas of Concern in AI-Powered HRM Systems

First, algorithmic bias poses substantial risks to fair employment practices, with AI systems often perpetuating or amplifying existing discrimination against protected groups. Second, data privacy and transparency issues emerge as organizations collect vast amounts of employee data while often failing to provide clear explanations of how AI systems make decisions. Third, employee trust and acceptance remain critical barriers, as workers express growing concern about AI systems making decisions that affect their careers without adequate human oversight.

The Middle Eastern context presents unique challenges, where cultural values, regulatory frameworks, and organizational structures create distinct ethical considerations for AI adoption in HRM. International organizations have responded by developing various standards and guidelines, including the OECD AI Principles, EU Ethics Guidelines for Trustworthy AI, and IEEE standards for ethical AI design. These frameworks emphasize the need for human-centered approaches, transparency, accountability, and fairness in AI system deployment across all sectors, including human resources.

Bias and Fairness in AI-Driven HR System

Algorithmic bias in AI-driven HR systems poses fundamental threats to fair employment practices, with the potential to perpetuate and amplify existing discrimination against protected groups (Paigude et al., 2023; Nasir et al., 2023). Research demonstrates that AI systems can lead to unfair outcomes in critical HR processes including recruitment, performance evaluation, and promotion decisions when bias is not properly addressed (Nyathani, 2023; Simbeck, 2019; Balbaa et al., 2024).

The sources of bias in AI-driven HR systems are multifaceted, stemming from biased training data, algorithm design choices, and inadequate oversight mechanisms (Khair et al., 2020). Studies reveal that these biases can manifest in subtle yet significant ways, such as AI systems favoring certain demographic groups or educational backgrounds while systematically disadvantaging others (Soleimani et al., 2025). The opaque nature of many AI algorithms compounds these problems by making it difficult for HR professionals to understand how decisions are reached and identify when bias occurs (Mahade et al., 2025; Varma et al., 2021).

However, research also indicates that properly designed AI systems can reduce human bias in HR processes when implemented with appropriate safeguards .. Key strategies for achieving fairness include using diverse development teams, implementing fairness metrics to identify bias, conducting regular audits of AI outcomes, and maintaining human oversight in final decision-making (Bhattacharya, 2023;

Hawrysz, 2025). Cross-functional collaboration between HR professionals and AI developers emerges as essential for effective bias mitigation, particularly during the design phase when proactive measures like removing gendered language from resume screening can be implemented (Soleimani et al., 2025).

The literature emphasizes that addressing bias requires ongoing commitment rather than one-time fixes, with organizations needing to establish continuous monitoring systems, impact assessments, and clear governance frameworks to ensure ethical AI use in HR contexts (Nyathani, 2023; Simbeck, 2019; Khair et al., 2020).

DATA PRIVACY AND TRANSPARENCY CHALLENGES

Data privacy and transparency represent critical ethical challenges in AI-driven HR systems, as organizations increasingly collect and process vast amounts of employee data without always providing adequate protection or explanation of how this information is used (Sabil et al., 2023). The surge in AI-driven decision-making processes brings forth concerns about accountability and explainability, with transparency in how AI systems arrive at conclusions being not only a technological necessity but also an ethical imperative (Nasir et al., 2023).

Data privacy concerns arise fundamentally from the collection and utilization of personal data in AI systems, requiring organizations to implement data anonymization, compliance with data protection regulations, and robust data security measures to protect employee privacy (Nyathani, 2023; Simbeck, 2019; Balbaa et al., 2024). The challenge is compounded by the need for obtaining explicit consent from employees for data use in HR processes and ensuring transparent communication about how their information is being processed (Nalini, 2024).

The opacity of AI algorithms and absence of interpretability create additional transparency challenges, raising questions about the accountability of AI-powered decisions and potentially eroding employee trust (Khair et al., 2020; Garg, 2025; Wahid & Awad, 2025). Organizations must prioritize the adoption of transparent AI algorithms that provide explanations for decision outcomes and enable stakeholders to understand the reasoning behind AI-driven decisions (Khair et al., 2020). Research emphasizes that employees and HR professionals need to understand how AI algorithms arrive at decisions to ensure outcomes are justified and align with organizational values (Mahade et al., 2025; Varma et al., 2021; Rahwan, 2017).

Addressing these challenges requires comprehensive approaches including establishing clear guidelines for AI governance, implementing continuous monitoring protocols, ensuring compliance with relevant regulations on data privacy and AI use, and maintaining human-centered approaches that balance AI efficiency with data protection requirements (Lutfi & Mohammadi, 2025; Hawrysz, 2025). Organizations must invest in data literacy, cross-functional AI governance frameworks, and algorithmic transparency to maximize benefits while mitigating privacy and transparency risks (Hawrysz, 2025).

EMPLOYEE TRUST AND RESISTANCE TO AI IN HR

Employee trust and resistance emerge as critical barriers to successful AI implementation in HR systems, with many workers viewing automation as a threat to their job security and expressing concerns about fairness in AI-driven decision-making (Garg, 2025; Lutfi & Mohammadi, 2025). This resistance stems from fundamental concerns about privacy, data security, and potential bias in AI-powered systems, highlighting the need for transparency, accountability, and clear communication with employees about how AI systems are being used and their impacts (Sabil et al., 2023).

The lack of transparency in AI decision-making processes compounds trust issues, as employees struggle to understand how algorithms reach conclusions that affect their careers, leading to decreased engagement and skepticism about HR systems (Garg, 2025; Hawrysz, 2025). Research identifies additional challenges including resistance from HR professionals themselves, skill shortages, and concerns about the opaque nature of AI systems that make it difficult to ensure accountability (Lutfi & Mohammadi, 2025; Hawrysz, 2025; Ghonim et al., 2025).

Organizations can address these trust challenges through human-centric AI policy design that prioritizes employee protection and well-being throughout the implementation process (Fenwick et al., 2024). Effective strategies include transparent communication about AI tool purposes and effects, clear policies regarding data collection and usage, mechanisms to address potential biases, and active employee engagement during initial implementation phases to address fears and concerns (Fenwick et al., 2024).

Building trust requires comprehensive approaches including investment in staff training programs to improve AI literacy, ensuring transparency in AI-driven decision-making processes, and maintaining human oversight to balance AI efficiency with human-centered personnel management (Lutfi & Mohammadi, 2025; Hawrysz, 2025). Organizations must foster interdisciplinary collaboration, implement responsible algorithm design principles, and conduct continuous evaluation to ensure successful and ethical AI integration while addressing employee concerns about job displacement and unfair treatment (Hawrysz, 2025; Fenwick et al., 2024).

Governance Frameworks and Human Oversight

The establishment of robust governance frameworks and human oversight mechanisms represents a critical requirement for ethical AI deployment in HR systems, with organizations needing comprehensive approaches that integrate technical, ethical, legal, and design considerations throughout the AI lifecycle (Nasir et al., 2023; Soleimani et al., 2025). Effective governance requires well-defined AI governance frameworks, ethics committees, and continuous monitoring systems to ensure responsible AI use, with organizations needing to establish clear guidelines that emphasize accountability, explainability, and fairness metrics to identify and address potential biases (Nyathani, 2023; Simbeck, 2019; Shams Eldin et al., 2025).

Human oversight emerges as fundamental to maintaining ethical control and accountability in AI-driven HR processes, with research emphasizing that AI should augment human decision-making rather than replace it entirely (Nasir et al., 2023; Bhattacharya, 2023). This approach ensures that HR professionals retain their human judgment while leveraging AI insights to make more informed decisions, requiring organizations to provide mechanisms for recourse and remedy when addressing algorithmic bias or discrimination (Khair et al., 2020).

Human-centric AI policy design should prioritize employee protection and well-being throughout implementation, including transparent communication about AI tool purposes, clear data collection policies, and active employee engagement to address concerns and foster inclusive work environments (Fenwick et al., 2024). Organizations must implement stringent measures to prevent technology misuse, conduct regular audits and assessments, and ensure compliance with relevant regulations on data privacy and AI use (Nalini, 2024; Balbaa et al., 2024).

Successful governance requires interdisciplinary collaboration between HR professionals and AI developers, with organizations needing to invest in training programs that develop both technical skills and people-focused competencies to enable effective cross-functional teamwork (Soleimani et al., 2025; Hawrysz, 2025). This collaborative approach must include ongoing audit processes, impact assessments, and continuous evaluation to ensure AI systems maintain fairness and align with organizational values while promoting trust and transparency among employees (Mahade et al., 2025; Varma et al., 2021).

Bias Mitigation Strategies and Implementation

. Organizations can implement several key strategies to mitigate bias and ensure ethical AI deployment in HR systems:

· Cross-functional collaboration and training: Establish interdisciplinary teams combining HR professionals and AI developers to integrate bias mitigation strategies during the design phase, with both groups trained to understand and address biases in AI systems (Soleimani et al., 2025; Hawrysz, 2025).

· Proactive bias detection and fairness metrics: Implement fairness metrics to identify and rectify algorithmic bias, including reviewing training data, testing algorithms for bias, and removing problematic elements like gendered language from resume screening (Nyathani, 2023; Simbeck, 2019; Bhattacharya, 2023; Soleimani et al., 2025).

· Diverse and inclusive development teams: Prioritize diversity and inclusion in AI development teams to ensure comprehensive understanding of fairness considerations and reduce the risk of unintended biases (Khair et al., 2020; Nasir et al., 2023).

· Transparent AI algorithms and explainability: Adopt transparent AI systems that provide clear explanations for decision outcomes and enable stakeholders to understand the reasoning behind AI-driven decisions (Khair et al., 2020; Nalini, 2024).

· Continuous monitoring and auditing: Establish regular auditing protocols conducted by cross-disciplinary teams to detect bias, data inaccuracies, and discriminatory outcomes throughout the AI system lifecycle (Soleimani et al., 2025; Khair et al., 2020; Nalini, 2024).

· Human-AI collaboration frameworks: Maintain human oversight where AI augments rather than replaces human decision-making, allowing HR professionals to retain empathy and judgment while leveraging AI insights (Bhattacharya, 2023; Nasir et al., 2023).

· Data governance and privacy protection: Implement robust data security measures, anonymization techniques, and compliance with data protection regulations while ensuring informed consent and transparent communication about data processing (Nalini, 2024; Nyathani, 2023; Simbeck, 2019).

· Impact assessment and remediation mechanisms: Conduct regular impact assessments and provide clear procedures for recourse and remedy when addressing algorithmic bias or discrimination (Khair et al., 2020; Nyathani, 2023; Simbeck, 2019).

GOVERNANCE AND BALANCE IN AI-HRM SYSTEM

The integration of artificial intelligence into human resource management represents one of the most significant technological shifts in workplace operations over the past decade. Organizations worldwide have increasingly adopted AI-powered tools for recruitment, performance evaluation, employee engagement, and workforce analytics, driven by promises of enhanced efficiency, reduced bias, and data-driven decision-making (Nyathani, 2023). However, this technological adoption has revealed complex challenges that extend far beyond simple automation, requiring careful consideration of ethical implications, legal compliance, and the fundamental human elements that define effective HR practice (Johnson et al., 2022).

The current landscape of AI in HRM reveals a critical tension between technological capability and responsible implementation. While AI systems can process vast amounts of candidate data, predict employee turnover, and identify patterns in workforce behavior with unprecedented speed and scale, they also raise concerns about algorithmic bias, privacy violations, and the dehumanization of employment relationships. Recent studies have documented cases where AI recruitment tools inadvertently discriminated against certain demographic groups, highlighting the urgent need for governance frameworks that prioritize fairness, transparency, and accountability alongside operational efficiency (Garg, 2025). This growing body of evidence suggests that the future success of AI in HR will depend not on the sophistication of the technology itself, but on organizations' ability to implement human-centered governance structures that preserve the ethical foundations of people management while harnessing the transformative potential of machine intelligence.

The establishment of robust governance frameworks represents a critical success factor for responsible AI adoption in human resource management. Research demonstrates that ethical principles alone are insufficient for ensuring responsible AI use in organizations, as businesses require strong, mandated governance controls, including tools for managing processes and creating audit trails—to enforce their principles (Eitel-Porter, 2020). Organizations that implement comprehensive governance frameworks, overseen by ethics boards and strengthened with appropriate training, significantly reduce the risks associated with AI implementation (Eitel-Porter, 2020). These governance structures typically include AI ethics boards with oversight functions, consisting of representatives from relevant stakeholders who debate the data and ethical dimensions of AI algorithms and establish clear boundaries for AI technology use within the company (Hunkenschroer & Luetge, 2022).

The balance between technological efficiency and human-centered decision-making emerges as a fundamental principle in effective AI-HRM governance. Leading organizations emphasize human oversight as a standard practice, encouraging experienced HR professionals to review selections and evaluations made by AI systems, with decisions ultimately made by algorithm-informed humans rather than algorithms alone (Hunkenschroer & Luetge, 2022). This approach recognizes that both humanistic insight and sophisticated technology are essential for adapting to today's dynamic workplace realities. However, the implementation of such governance models requires interdisciplinary collaboration between different stakeholders, regulatory authorities, and legislative bodies to ensure transparency in implementation, timely reporting of best practices and lessons learned, and the development of harmonized ethical frameworks.

PROPOSED MODEL FOR RESPONSIBLE AI IN HR

The development of a responsible AI framework for human resource management requires moving beyond abstract ethical principles toward concrete organizational implementation strategies. Current research identifies a critical gap in translating the abundance of ethical principles into practical governance structures, emphasizing that successful operationalization of ethics requires coordinated action across multiple organizational dimensions (Krijger et al., 2022). A comprehensive model should integrate established international standards, including the *Montreal Declaration for Responsible AI*, the *Ethics Guidelines for Trustworthy AI* from the European Commission, and the AI4People principles, which propose five foundational elements: beneficence, non-maleficence, autonomy, justice, and explicability (Hunkenschroer & Luetge, 2022).

The operationalization of responsible AI in HR should incorporate the European Union's comprehensive approach to trustworthy AI, which requires systems to be simultaneously lawful, ethical, and robust throughout their entire lifecycle. The EU AI Act establishes seven core principles that directly apply to HR applications: human agency and oversight; technical robustness and safety; privacy and data governance; transparency; diversity, non-discrimination and fairness; societal and environmental well-being; and accountability. Building on these regulatory foundations, organizations should implement specific governance mechanisms including AI ethics boards with oversight functions, codes of ethics for AI-related initiatives, and mandatory human review processes where experienced HR professionals evaluate AI-generated recommendations before final decisions (Hunkenschroer & Luetge, 2022). Additionally, HR-specific ethical principles should address privacy and confidentiality, opportunities for individuals to opt out of AI-driven processes, institutional review mechanisms, transparency in algorithmic decision-making, and respect for the dynamic nature of personal and professional development (Hunkenschroer & Luetge, 2022). This multi-layered approach ensures that responsible AI implementation in HR balances technological sophistication with humanistic insight, recognizing that both elements are essential for adapting to contemporary workplace realities (Hunkenschroer & Luetge, 2022).

FUTURE TRENDS IN AI-HRM APPLICATIONS

The emergence of generative artificial intelligence represents a transformative shift in HR applications, moving beyond traditional analytics toward dynamic content creation and interactive employee support systems. Generative AI tools are increasingly being deployed for personalized job descriptions, automated interview question generation, and real-time employee feedback systems that adapt communication styles to individual preferences and cultural contexts These systems enable HR professionals to create customized onboarding materials, training content, and policy explanations at scale, while maintaining consistency with organizational values and legal requirements. However, the deployment of generative AI in HR contexts raises new concerns about content accuracy, potential for generating biased or inappropriate responses, and the need for continuous human review of AI-generated materials.

Predictive analytics and adaptive learning systems are reshaping workforce planning by enabling organizations to anticipate talent needs, identify retention risks, and optimize employee development pathways with unprecedented precision. Advanced machine learning algorithms can now analyze patterns in employee behavior, performance metrics, and external labor market conditions to provide real-time recommendations for hiring strategies, succession planning, and skill development initiatives (Jain, 2025). These systems continuously learn from new data inputs, allowing them to refine their predictions and adapt to changing organizational dynamics without requiring manual recalibration. The ethical implications of these developments center on employee privacy, the transparency of predictive models, and the potential for creating self-fulfilling prophecies where algorithmic predictions influence management decisions in ways that reinforce existing inequalities Organizations must therefore establish clear boundaries around data collection, ensure employees understand how their information is being used for predictive purposes, and maintain human oversight in all decisions that affect individual career trajectories .

FINAL STATEMENT AND SYNTHESIS

The evolution of artificial intelligence in human resource management presents both unprecedented opportunities and fundamental responsibilities that will define the future of work. The evidence examined throughout this analysis demonstrates that the most successful AI implementations in HR are those that strengthen rather than diminish human capabilities, creating systems where technology serves as an intelligent amplifier of human insight rather than a replacement for human judgment (Fenwick et al., 2024; Ho, 2025). This symbiotic relationship between machine intelligence and human wisdom represents the optimal path forward, where

AI handles data processing and pattern recognition while humans provide ethical reasoning, empathy, and strategic vision that remain uniquely valuable in people management (Ali, 2025).

The central lesson emerging from current research and practice is that responsible AI in HR requires continuous vigilance and adaptive governance structures that evolve alongside technological capabilities. Organizations that view AI implementation as a one-time technical deployment will struggle to maintain ethical standards as systems become more sophisticated and autonomous. Instead, the future demands HR leaders who can navigate the intersection of technology and humanity, making decisions that optimize both operational efficiency and human flourishing. The path forward requires embracing AI's transformative potential while preserving the fundamental human elements that make HR effective: trust, fairness, compassion, and the ability to see each employee as a unique individual with distinct needs, aspirations, and contributions to organizational success (Fenwick et al., 2024). This balanced approach ensures that as AI continues to reshape HR practices, the profession remains grounded in its core mission of supporting human potential and creating workplaces where both technology and people can thrive together.

CONCLUSION

This chapter demonstrated that AI is not just a technological advancement in HR management; it represents a major paradigm shift in how HR operates. AI has transformed the HR function from being purely reactive and transactional in nature to now being a proactive, data-driven business partner for companies. The use of AI to automate several types of routine tasks and perform predictive analytics has improved HR's ability to enhance the efficiency of operations and help organizations develop long-term strategic objectives. The case studies of AI-supported HR functions in recruiting, performance management, and workforce planning support the view that AI provides personalized experience for all employees, improves the way companies allocate human and financial resources, and aligns the way companies develop their human capital strategies to meet their respective organizational objectives. In short, AI will remain an essential part of building and maintaining competitive advantage in today's knowledge-based economy.

Yet, unlocking all of the possible benefits of AI is only possible if we successfully navigate the inherent ethical and governance challenges associated with AI. As discussed throughout this chapter, it is imperative that organisations and individuals address the various data privacy concerns, algorithmic bias, and the need to maintain transparency and ensure human oversight while deploying AI technologies. Thus, deploying AI responsibly within the HR sector is not simply a compliance issue, but rather, it should be viewed as a strategic necessity that will support the trust of employees, while demonstrating the accountability of the organisation. In addition, the design of the model for responsible deployments of AI within HR emphasises the key point: AI must serve as a complement, or a strength, in assisting employees with their duties, while maintaining the requirement for human judgment when making difficult decisions regarding the health and growth of individuals.

REFERENCES

Ahmad, F., Shankar, U., Radhakrishnan, G. V., Patel, S. M., & Singh, S. (2025). The interconnection of HR strategies and financial performance in modern organizations. *Journal of Information Systems Engineering & Management, 10*(10s), 1412. Advance online publication. DOI: 10.52783/jisem.v10i10s.1412

Ahmad, M., Tan, M., Bergman, H., Shalhoub, J., & Davies, A. (2024). The use of artificial intelligence in three-dimensional imaging modalities and diabetic foot disease: A systematic review. *JVS-Vascular Insights, 2*, 100057. Advance online publication. DOI: 10.1016/j.jvsvi.2024.100057

Ali, O., & Kallach, L. (2024). Artificial intelligence enabled human resources recruitment functionalities: A scoping review. *Procedia Computer Science, 232*, 3268–3277. Advance online publication. DOI: 10.1016/j.procs.2024.02.142

Altinay, L., Vatankhah, S., De Vita, G., & Arici, H. (2025). Could AI technologies be harnessed to break down barriers to inclusivity for women entrepreneurship in tourism? *Tourism Management, 112*, 105285. DOI: 10.1016/j.tourman.2025.105285

Awad, A., & Alharthi, B. (2025). The role of digital marketing tools in promoting tourism: An applied study on online marketing strategies. *Innovative Marketing, 21*(2), 14–26. DOI: 10.21511/im.21(2).2025.02

Awad, A., Shemais, M., & Al-Embabi, M. (2024). Driving HR performance through digital transformation in educational directorates: A strategic imperative. *Problems and Perspectives in Management, 22*(4), 163–173. DOI: 10.21511/ppm.22(4).2024.13

Badhurunnisa, M., & Dass, V. S. (2023). Challenges and opportunities involved in implementing AI in workplace. *International Journal for Multidisciplinary Research, 5*(6), 1–6. https://www.ijfmr.com/papers/2023/6/10001.pdf

Balbaa, M. E., & Abdurashidova, M. S. (2024). The impact of artificial intelligence in decision making: A comprehensive review. *EPRA International Journal of Economics. Business and Management Studies, 11*(2), 27–33. DOI: 10.36713/epra15747

Benabou, A., & Touhami, F. (2025). Integration of artificial intelligence in human resource management: Analyzing opportunities, challenges, and human-AI collaboration. *Management and Accounting Review, 24*(1), 215–230. https://mar.uitm.edu.my/images/Vol-24-1/15.pdf

Bhattacharya, S. (2023). The future of HR: Embracing AI for smarter and more human workplaces. *International Journal of Scientific Research, 12*(5), 457–459. https://www.ijsr.net/getabstract.php?paperid=SR23423182128

Bhima, B., Az Zahra, A. R., & Nurtino, T. (2023). Enhancing organizational efficiency through the integration of artificial intelligence in management information systems. *APTISI Transactions on Management*, *7*(3), 282–289. DOI: 10.33050/atm.v7i3.2146

Cannataro, M. (2022). Knowledge representation and reasoning. In *Artificial Intelligence in Bioinformatics*. DOI: 10.1016/B978-0-12-822952-1.00010-3

De Obesso Arias, M., Pérez Rivero, C., & Carrero Márquez, O. (2023). Artificial intelligence to manage workplace bullying. *Journal of Business Research*, *160*, 113813. Advance online publication. DOI: 10.1016/j.jbusres.2023.113813

Dima, J., Gilbert, M.-H., Dextras-Gauthier, J., & Giraud, L. (2024). The effects of artificial intelligence on human resource activities. *Frontiers in Psychology*, *15*, 1360401. Advance online publication. DOI: 10.3389/fpsyg.2024.1360401 PMID: 38903456

Eitel-Porter, R. (2020). Beyond the promise: Implementing ethical AI. *AI and Ethics*, *1*(1), 73–80. DOI: 10.1007/s43681-020-00011-6

Fakhr-e-Alam, S. M., Siddiqui, F.–e.–A., Zafar, H., & Kazmi, S. R. (2024). Harnessing A.I. technologies for employee recruitment. *Jurnal Dinamika Manajemen dan Bisnis*, *4*(1), 1–12. DOI: 10.5281/zenodo.10684342

Fenwick, A., Molnár, G., & Frangos, P. (2024). The critical role of HRM in AI-driven digital transformation. *Discover Artificial Intelligence*, *3*, 24. Advance online publication. DOI: 10.1007/s44162-024-00024-1

Fotoh, L., & Mugwira, T. (2025). Exploring large language models in external audits. *International Journal of Accounting Information Systems*, *56*, 100748. Advance online publication. DOI: 10.1016/j.accinf.2025.100748

Garg, M. (2025). The integration of artificial intelligence in human resource management. *International Journal of Research in Human Resource Management*, *3*(1), 45–59. https://www.humanresourcejournal.com/archives/2025.v7.i1.C.272

Ghonim, A., Awad, A., Shemais, M., Shma, T., & Aziz, A. (2025). Exploring the impact of flexible work arrangements on employee engagement in telecommunications: Case of Egypt. *Problems and Perspectives in Management*, *23*(2), 198–207. DOI: 10.21511/ppm.23(2).2025.13

Goswami, M., Jain, S., Alam, T., Deifalla, A., Ragab, A., & Khargotra, R. (2023). AI adoption in pharmaceutical HRM. *Frontiers in Pharmacology*, *14*. Advance online publication. DOI: 10.3389/fphar.2023.1215706 PMID: 38034991

Gupta, P., Lakhera, G., & Sharma, M. (2024). Impact of AI on employee performance. *The Journal of High Technology Management Research, 35*. Advance online publication. DOI: 10.1016/j.hitech.2024.100520

Hawrysz, L. (2025). Artificial intelligence in candidate screening. *Scientific Papers of Silesian University of Technology: Organization and Management Series, 168*, 123–134. DOI: 10.29119/1641-3466.2025.168.9

He, L., & Wang, L. (2025). Can artificial intelligence curb greenwashing? *Energy Economics, 152*, 108954. Advance online publication. DOI: 10.1016/j.eneco.2025.108954

Hunkenschroer, A., & Luetge, C. (2022). Ethics of AI-enabled recruiting and selection. *Journal of Business Ethics, 182*, 723–745. DOI: 10.1007/s10551-021-04970-0

Indrasari, M., & Pamuji, E. (2023). Enhancing employee performance through strategic initiatives. *Journal of Business Management and Economic Development, 5*(2), 56–64. DOI: 10.5281/zenodo.10684357

Ji, L., & Huang, X. (2022). Social governance in energy-oriented cities using AI. *Energy Reports, 8*. Advance online publication. DOI: 10.1016/j.egyr.2022.08.206

Johnson, B. A. M., Coggburn, J. D., & Llorens, J. J. (2022). Artificial intelligence and public human resource management. *Public Personnel Management, 51*(1), 3–18. DOI: 10.1177/00910260211066061

Khair, M. A., Mahadasa, R., Tuli, F. A., & Ande, J. R. P. K. (2020). Beyond human judgment: Impact of AI on HR decision-making. *Global Disclosure of Economics and Business, 9*(2), 45–58. DOI: 10.18034/gdeb.v9i2.730

Khan, M. I., Parahyanti, E., & Hussain, S. (2024). Generative AI in HRM. *Asian Journal of Logistics Management, 4*(1), 22–35. DOI: 10.5281/zenodo.10684363

Krijger, J., Thuis, T., Ruiter, M. D., Ligthart, E., & Broekman, I. (2022). The AI ethics maturity model. *AI and Ethics, 2*, 377–392. DOI: 10.1007/s43681-021-00093-8

Kulshrestha, S. (2024). Quantitative assessment of AI's impact on HR practices. *International Journal of Management and Applied Research, 11*(1), 15–28. DOI: 10.18646/2056.111.24-002

Lee, J. (2025). IT investment and labor displacement. *Telecommunications Policy, 49*(7), 102999. Advance online publication. DOI: 10.1016/j.telpol.2025.102999

Leite, R. (2024). Benefits and drawbacks of artificial intelligence in HRM. *Artificial Intelligence in Production Engineering and Management, 3*(1), 45–58. DOI: 10.5281/zenodo.10684410

Leonardi, R., Giudice, A., Isola, G., & Spampinato, C. (2021). Deep learning in orthodontics. *Seminars in Orthodontics, 27*. Advance online publication. DOI: 10.1053/j.sodo.2021.05.002

Lutfi, L., & Mohammadi, A. (2025). Challenges of implementing AI in HRM. *International Journal of Academic Research in Business & Social Sciences, 15*(1), 78–90. DOI: 10.6007/IJARBSS/v15-i1/12345

Mahade, A., Elmahi, A., Alomari, K., & Abdalla, A. A. (2025). Leveraging AI-driven insights for sustainable HRM. *Discover Sustainability, 6*, 45. Advance online publication. DOI: 10.1007/s43621-025-00145-9

Manthena, S. (2021). Impact of artificial intelligence on recruitment. *International Journal of Innovative Research in Engineering & Multidisciplinary Physical Sciences, 9*(4), 12–18. DOI: 10.5281/zenodo.10684370

Marwala, T. (2024). Governance of AI. In *Mechanism Design*. Behavioral Science, and Artificial Intelligence in International Relations. DOI: 10.1016/B978-0-443-23982-3.00020-8

Najana, M. (2024). AI and organizational transformation. *International Journal of Global Information Systems, 5*(3), 88–102. DOI: 10.5281/zenodo.10684380

Nalini, M. (2024). Transformative horizons: Navigating HR through AI and cloud technologies. *Shanlax International Journal of Management, 11*(1), 1–10. DOI: 10.34293/management.v11iiS1-Jan.7138

Nasir, S., Khan, R. A., & Bai, S. (2023). Ethical framework for harnessing AI in healthcare. *IEEE Access : Practical Innovations, Open Solutions, 11*, 123456–123470. DOI: 10.1109/ACCESS.2023.3298765

Nyathani, R. (2023). AI-driven HR analytics. *Journal of Technology and Systems, 5*(2), 45–58. DOI: 10.47941/jts.1513

Odili, P. O., Daudu, C. D., Adefemi, A., Ekemezie, I. O., & Usiagu, G. S. (2024). AI in recruitment and selection in oil and gas. *Engineering Science & Technology Journal, 8*(1), 33–45. DOI: 10.5281/zenodo.10684390

Paigude, S., Pangarkar, S. C., Hundekari, S., Mali, M., Wanjale, K., & Dongre, Y. (2023). AI in boosting employee retention. *International Journal on Recent and Innovation Trends in Computing and Communication, 11*(6), 112–118. DOI: 10.5281/zenodo.10684395

Parasa, S. K., & Jadugala, S. (2023). Enabling Joule in SAP SuccessFactors. *International Journal of Scientific Research, 12*(4), 321–325. DOI: 10.5281/zenodo.10684400

Rahwan, I. (2017). Society-in-the-loop: Programming the algorithmic social contract. *Ethics and Information Technology, 20*(1), 5–14. DOI: 10.1007/s10676-017-9430-8

Rožman, M., Oreški, D., & Tominc, P. (2022). Integrating AI into a talent management model. *Frontiers in Psychology, 13*. Advance online publication. DOI: 10.3389/fpsyg.2022.1014434 PMID: 36506984

Sabil, S., Bangkara, B. A., Mogea, T., Niswan, E., & Timotius, E. (2023). Identification of HRM improvement strategy using artificial intelligence in modern economic development. *International Journal of Professional Business Review, 8*(6), e01835. DOI: 10.26668/businessreview/2023.v8i6.1835

Shaddiq, S., Khuzaini, & Irpan, M. (2023). Governance of human resources management in the digital era. *Journal of Business and Management Studies, 5*(2), 1–10. DOI: 10.32996/jbms.2023.5.3.8

Shahzad, M., Xu, S., Naveed, W., Nusrat, S., & Zahid, I. (2023). Investigating the impact of artificial intelligence on HR functions. *Heliyon, 9*, e21818. Advance online publication. DOI: 10.1016/j.heliyon.2023.e21818 PMID: 38034787

Shams Eldin, A. Y., Elnour, A., Hassan, R. O. A., & Awad, A. (2025). The role of technological and environmental factors in creating business value from social media dynamic capabilities for SMEs in Saudi Arabia. *Humanities & Social Sciences Communications, 12*(1), 1431. DOI: 10.1057/s41599-025-05784-x

Simbeck, K. (2019). HR analytics and ethics. IBM Journal of Research and Development, 63(4/5), 9:1–9:12. DOI: 10.1147/JRD.2019.2915067

Soleimani, M., Intezari, A., Arrowsmith, J., Pauleen, D. J., & Taskin, N. (2025). Reducing AI bias in recruitment and selection: An integrative grounded approach. *International Journal of Human Resource Management, 36*(14), 2480–2515. DOI: 10.1080/09585192.2025.2480617

Tsiskaridze, R., Reinhold, K., & Jarvis, M. (2023). Innovating HRM recruitment: A comprehensive review of AI deployment. *Marketing and Management of Innovations, 14*(4), 239–254. DOI: 10.21272/mmi.2023.4-18

Varma, A., Dawkins, C. E., & Chaudhuri, K. (2021). Artificial intelligence and people management. *Proceedings - Academy of Management, 2021*(1), 11357. DOI: 10.5465/AMBPP.2021.11014abstract

Wahid, A., & Awad, A. (2025). Role of AI chatbots in enhancing customer satisfaction and customer loyalty. In *Impacts of AI generated content on brand reputation* (pp. 129–147). IGI Global. DOI: 10.4018/979-8-3373-4327-3.ch005

Wang, S., & Zhang, H. (2025). Generative artificial intelligence and internationalization green innovation. *Technology in Society*, *82*, 102898. Advance online publication. DOI: 10.1016/j.techsoc.2025.102898

Wu, W., Huang, T., & Gong, K. (2020). Ethical principles and governance technology development of AI in China. *Engineering (Beijing)*, *6*(3), 302–309. Advance online publication. DOI: 10.1016/j.eng.2019.12.015

Yang, S., Ogata, H., Matsui, T., & Chen, N. (2021). Human-centered artificial intelligence in education. *Computers and Education: Artificial Intelligence*, *2*, 100008. Advance online publication. DOI: 10.1016/j.caeai.2021.100008

Zhang, G., Chong, L., Kotovsky, K., & Cagan, J. (2023). Trust in an AI versus a human teammate. *Computers in Human Behavior*, *139*, 107536. Advance online publication. DOI: 10.1016/j.chb.2022.107536

Zheng, J., Zhang, J., Kamal, M., Liang, X., & Alzeiby, E. (2025). Unpacking human-AI interaction. *Journal of Business Research*, *196*, 115406. Advance online publication. DOI: 10.1016/j.jbusres.2025.115406

Zohuri, B., & Behgounia, F. (2023). AI-driven nano-based drug delivery systems. In *A Handbook of Artificial Intelligence in Drug Delivery.* DOI: 10.1016/B978-0-323-89925-3.00007-1

Compilation of References

Aarthi, S., Ravikumar, R. N., Sobirova, K., & Mamadiyarov, Z. (2025). Empowering a sustainable future through digital learning and the SDGs. In *Harnessing E-Learning to Create a Sustainable Future* (pp. 145–172). IGI Global Scientific Publishing., DOI: 10.4018/979-8-3373-0112-9.ch006

Abdulla, A., & Baryannis, G. (2024). A hybrid multi-criteria decision-making and machine learning approach for explainable supplier selection. *Supply Chain Analytics*, *7*, 100074. DOI: 10.1016/j.sca.2024.100074

Adams, D., & Thompson, P. (2025). Transforming School Leadership with Artificial Intelligence: Applications, Implications, and Future Directions. *Leadership and Policy in Schools*, *24*, 77–89.

Adegboye, M. (2024). Impact of artificial intelligence on health information literacy: Guidance for healthcare professionals. *Library Hi Tech News*, *41*(7), 1–5. DOI: 10.1108/LHTN-03-2024-0048

Aggarwal, S., & Srivastava, M. K. (2019). A grey-based DEMATEL model for building collaborative resilience in supply chain. *International Journal of Quality & Reliability Management*, *36*(8), 1409–1437. DOI: 10.1108/IJQRM-03-2018-0059

Ahmad, F., Shankar, U., Radhakrishnan, G. V., Patel, S. M., & Singh, S. (2025). The interconnection of HR strategies and financial performance in modern organizations. *Journal of Information Systems Engineering & Management*, *10*(10s), 1412. Advance online publication. DOI: 10.52783/jisem.v10i10s.1412

Ahmad, M., Tan, M., Bergman, H., Shalhoub, J., & Davies, A. (2024). The use of artificial intelligence in three-dimensional imaging modalities and diabetic foot disease: A systematic review. *JVS-Vascular Insights*, *2*, 100057. Advance online publication. DOI: 10.1016/j.jvsvi.2024.100057

Ajani, O. A., Gamede, B., & Matiyenga, T. C. (2024). Leveraging artificial intelligence to enhance teaching and learning in higher education: Promoting quality education and critical engagement. *Journal of Pedagogical Sociology and Psychology*, *7*(1), 54–69. DOI: 10.33902/JPSP.202528400

Akemu, O., & Abdelnour, S. (2020). Confronting the digital: Doing ethnography in modern organizational settings. *Organizational Research Methods*, *23*(2), 296–321. DOI: 10.1177/1094428118791018

Akgun, S., & Greenhow, C. (2021). Artificial intelligence in education: Addressing ethical challenges in K-12 settings. *AI and Ethics*, *3*(3), 431–440. DOI: 10.1007/s43681-021-00096-7 PMID: 34790956

Al Qadiri, W. M., Alkaf, M., & Supratikta, H. (2024). Analyzing the Impact of Artificial intelligence (AI) on Decision-Making Strategies. Journal of Investment Development. *Economics and Accounting*, *1*(2), 182–190. DOI: 10.70001/jidea.v1i2.221

Alahmari, D., & Awad, A. (2025). Strategic integration of marketing and supply chain functions for superior customer experience: Insights from logistics startups under Saudi Vision 2030. *PLoS One*, *20*(11), e0336132. DOI: 10.1371/journal.pone.0336132 PMID: 41270081

Alavi, M., Storey, V. C., & Sullivan, Y. W. (2024). Knowledge management perspective of generative artificial intelligence (GenAI). *Journal of the Association for Information Systems*, *25*(1), 1–12. Advance online publication. DOI: 10.17705/1jais.00859

Aldabousi, A. M., Awad, A., Hassan, H. E. M., Abdullah, S. S., & Ghonim, A. (2025). Arbitration in Islamic banking: Exploring legal and practical implications for dispute resolution. *Banks and Bank Systems*, *20*(2), 15–26. DOI: 10.21511/bbs.20(2).2025.02

Aldekhyl, S., Cavalcanti, R. B., & Naismith, L. M. (2018). Cognitive load predicts point-of-care ultrasound simulator performance. *Perspectives on Medical Education*, *7*(1), 23–32. DOI: 10.1007/S40037-017-0392-7 PMID: 29305817

Alessa, F. M., Alhaag, M. H., Al-Harkan, I. M., Ramadan, M. Z., & Alqahtani, F. M. (2023). A Neurophysiological Evaluation of Cognitive Load during Augmented Reality Interactions in Various Industrial Maintenance and Assembly Tasks. *Sensors (Basel)*, *23*(18), 7698. DOI: 10.3390/s23187698 PMID: 37765755

Alharthi, B., & Awad, A. (2025). The role of digital marketing tools in promoting tourism: An applied study on online marketing strategies. *Innovative Marketing*, *21*(2), 14–26. DOI: 10.21511/im.21(2).2025.02

Ali, S., Abuhmed, T., El-Sappagh, S., Khan, M., Ahmad, H. F., Kwak, K. S., & Alonso-Moral, J.-M. (2023). Explainable Artificial Intelligence (XAI): What we know and what is left to attain trustworthy artificial intelligence. *Information Fusion, 99*, 101805. DOI: 10.1016/j.inffus.2023.101805

Ali, A., Qadeer, A., & Awad, A. (2025). Understanding generative AI implementation in digital advertising among retail SMEs in Pakistan. In *Impacts of AI-generated content on brand reputation* (pp. 177–201). IGI Global. DOI: 10.4018/979-8-3373-4327-3.ch007

Ali, A., & Rafi, D. N. (2024). Enhancing human resource management through advanced decision-making strategies: Harnessing the power of artificial intelligence for strategic, data-driven, and judicious choices. *Migration Letters : An International Journal of Migration Studies, 21*(S8), 881–889. DOI: 10.59670/ml.v21iS8.9488

Ali, O., & Kallach, L. (2024). Artificial intelligence enabled human resources recruitment functionalities: A scoping review. *Procedia Computer Science, 232*, 3268–3277. Advance online publication. DOI: 10.1016/j.procs.2024.02.142

Almanbahi, F. S., Awad, A., Ghonim, A., Alabsy, N. M., & Shemais, M. (2025). Ethical leadership and organizational excellence: The mediating role of citizenship behavior in healthcare. *Humanities & Social Sciences Communications, 12*(1), 1392. DOI: 10.1057/s41599-025-05743-6

Almazán-López, O., Hasbún, H., & Osuna-Acedo, S. (2025). Generative artificial intelligence and (post)digital teacher identity. *IJERI: International Journal of Educational Research and Innovation, 24*, 1–17. DOI: 10.46661/ijeri.11160

Alqahtani, A., & Alqahtani, N. (2024). Artificial Intelligence meets entrepreneurship: A bibliometric review of the scientific evolution, research trends, and future research directions. In *Proceedings of the 1st Saudi Conference on Information Systems (SaudiCIS 2024)* (Paper 68). https://aisel.aisnet.org/saudicis2024/68/

Alsubaie, N., & Aleisa, N. (2025). Mitigating bias in AI model using eXplainable AI in terms of hiring process in the industry. *IEEE Access : Practical Innovations, Open Solutions, 13*, 147218–147241. DOI: 10.1109/ACCESS.2025.3599947

Altin, H. (2022). The comparison of EDAS, COPRAS, and EFI methods in the decision-making process. *International Journal of Operations Research and Information Systems, 13*(1), 1–19. DOI: 10.4018/IJORIS.302910

Altinay, L., Vatankhah, S., De Vita, G., & Arici, H. (2025). Could AI technologies be harnessed to break down barriers to inclusivity for women entrepreneurship in tourism? *Tourism Management, 112*, 105285. DOI: 10.1016/j.tourman.2025.105285

Álvarez-Chaves, A., & Saborío-Taylor, S. (2025). Hybrid learning in higher education: Considerations for its implementation in course design. *Journal of Digital Educational Technology*, *5*(1), ep2505. Advance online publication. DOI: 10.30935/jdet/15859

Alzamel, S. (2024). Building a Resilient Digital Entrepreneurship Landscape: The Importance of Ecosystems, Decent Work, and Socioeconomic Dynamics. *Sustainability (Basel)*, *16*(17), 7605. DOI: 10.3390/su16177605

Ameen, N., Pagani, M., Pantano, E., Cheah, J.-H., Tarba, S., & Xia, S. (2024). The rise of human–machine collaboration: Managers' perceptions of leveraging artificial intelligence for enhanced B2B service recovery. *British Journal of Management*. Advance online publication. DOI: 10.1111/1467-8551.12829

Ameen, N., Tarba, S., Cheah, J.-H., Xia, S., & Sharma, G. D. (2024). Coupling artificial intelligence capability and strategic agility for enhanced product and service creativity. *British Journal of Management*, *35*(4), 1916–1934. Advance online publication. DOI: 10.1111/1467-8551.12797

Amershi, S., Begel, A., & Bird, C.. (2019). Software engineering for machine learning: A case study. *Proceedings of the 41st International Conference on Software Engineering*, 291-301. DOI: 10.1109/ICSE-SEIP.2019.00042

Amershi, S., Weld, D., Vorvoreanu, M., Fourney, A., Nushi, B., Collisson, P., & Horvitz, E. (2019). Guidelines for human–AI interaction. *Proceedings of the 2019 CHI Conference on Human Factors in Computing Systems*, 1–13. DOI: 10.1145/3290605.3300233

Anders, C., Moontaha, S., Real, S., & Arnrich, B. (2024). Unobtrusive measurement of cognitive load and physiological signals in uncontrolled environments. *Scientific Data*, *11*(1), 1000. DOI: 10.1038/s41597-024-03738-7 PMID: 39271693

Andi Prayogi, M., Fahmi, M., Zurriah, R., Amaliah, N., & Dewi Siagian, A. (2025). The mediating job crafting and organizational resilience in linking information technology capabilities with sales performance: An empirical study from Indonesia. *Innovative Marketing*, *21*(1), 182–196. DOI: 10.21511/im.21(1).2025.15

Angkan, P. (2025). *CLARE: Cognitive Load Assessment in REaltime with Multimodal Data* (Version V1) [Data set]. Borealis. DOI: 10.5683/SP3/H0AELT

An, X., Chai, C. S., Li, Y., Zhou, Y., Shen, X., Zheng, C., & Chen, M. (2022). Modeling English teachers' behavioral intention to use artificial intelligence in middle schools. *Education and Information Technologies*, *5*(5), 5187–5208. DOI: 10.1007/s10639-022-11286-z

Argyris, C., & Schön, D. A. (1978). *Organizational learning: A theory of action perspective*. Addison-Wesley.

Automattic. (2024). *AI-powered collaboration and support systems at Automattic*. https://automattic.com/

Awad, A. (2024). Artificial intelligence and marketing innovation: The mediating role of organizational culture. *Innovative Marketing*, *20*(3), 170–181. DOI: 10.21511/im.20(3).2024.14

Awad, A. (2025). Enhancing market access and consumer engagement through digital marketing in the agricultural sector. *International Journal of Advanced and Applied Sciences*, *12*(8), 70–79. DOI: 10.21833/ijaas.2025.08.007

Awad, A. (2025). The role of universities' social responsibility in enhancing business sustainability: Mediating role of entrepreneurial culture. *Problems and Perspectives in Management*, *23*(1), 181–192. DOI: 10.21511/ppm.23(1).2025.14

Awad, A., Aldabousi, A. M., & Albatal, S. (2025). The influence of social media marketing on customer knowledge management: The role of confidentiality in UAE public banks. *Banks and Bank Systems*, *20*(1), 1–10. DOI: 10.21511/bbs.20(1).2025.01

Awad, A., & Ghonim, A. (2025). Data-driven marketing in banks: The role of artificial intelligence in enhancing marketing efficiency and business performance. *International Review of Management and Marketing*, *15*(5), 422–431. DOI: 10.32479/irmm.19738

Awad, A., Shemais, M., & Al-Embabi, M. (2024). Driving HR performance through digital transformation in educational directorates: A strategic imperative. *Problems and Perspectives in Management*, *22*(4), 163–173. DOI: 10.21511/ppm.22(4).2024.13

Ayala, G. I. G., Haslacher, D., Krol, L. R., Soekadar, S. R., & Zander, T. O. (2023). Assessment of mental workload across cognitive tasks using a passive brain-computer interface based on mean negative theta-band amplitudes. *Frontiers in Neuroergonomics*, *4*, 1233722. DOI: 10.3389/fnrgo.2023.1233722 PMID: 38234499

Ayyildiz, E., & Taskin, A. (2022). A novel spherical fuzzy AHP-VIKOR methodology to determine serving petrol station selection during COVID-19 lockdown: A pilot study for İstanbul. *Socio-Economic Planning Sciences*, *83*, 101345. DOI: 10.1016/j.seps.2022.101345 PMID: 35645424

Badhurunnisa, M., & Dass, V. S. (2023). Challenges and opportunities involved in implementing AI in workplace. *International Journal for Multidisciplinary Research*, *5*(6), 1–6. https://www.ijfmr.com/papers/2023/6/10001.pdf

Bagaa, M., Taleb, T., Riekki, J., & Song, J. (2021). Collaborative cross system AI: Toward 5G system and beyond. *IEEE Network*, *35*(4), 286–294. DOI: 10.1109/MNET.011.2000607

Bailenson, J. N. (2021). Nonverbal overload: A theoretical argument for the causes of Zoom fatigue. *Technology, Mind, and Behavior*, *2*(1), 1–6. Advance online publication. DOI: 10.1037/tmb0000030

Bakker, A. B., & Demerouti, E. (2017). Job demands–resources theory: Taking stock and looking forward. *Journal of Occupational Health Psychology*, *22*(3), 273–285. DOI: 10.1037/ocp0000056 PMID: 27732008

Balbaa, M. E., & Abdurashidova, M. S. (2024). The impact of artificial intelligence in decision making: A comprehensive review. *EPRA International Journal of Economics. Business and Management Studies*, *11*(2), 27–33. DOI: 10.36713/epra15747

Baldé, M., Ferreira, A. I., & Maynard, T. (2018). SECI driven creativity: The role of team trust and intrinsic motivation. *Journal of Knowledge Management*, *22*(8), 1688–1711. DOI: 10.1108/JKM-06-2017-0241

Bao, Y., Gong, W., & Yang, K. (2023). A literature review of human–AI synergy in decision making: From the perspective of affordance actualization theory. *Systems*, *11*(9), 442. DOI: 10.3390/systems11090442

Barasa, E., Mbau, R., & Gilson, L. (2018). What is resilience and how can it be nurtured? A systematic review of empirical literature on organizational resilience. *International Journal of Health Policy and Management*, *7*(6), 491–503. DOI: 10.15171/ijhpm.2018.06 PMID: 29935126

Barkhatova, L. A. (2023). The computational analysis of digital traces in ethnographic studies of online communities. *Bulletin de Methodologie Sociologique*, *160*(1), 30–56. DOI: 10.1177/07591063231196161

Basole, R. C., & Bodner, D. A. (2015). Computational modeling of complex enterprise systems: A multi-level approach. In *Modeling and Simulation in the Systems Engineering Life Cycle* (pp. 369–381). Springer London., DOI: 10.1007/978-1-4471-5634-5_28

Bass, B. M., & Riggio, R. E. (2006). *Transformational leadership*. Taylor & Francis Group. DOI: 10.4324/9781410617095

Bazoukis, G., Hall, J., Loscalzo, J., Antman, E. M., Fuster, V., & Armoundas, A. A. (2022). The inclusion of augmented intelligence in medicine: A framework for successful implementation. *Cell Reports Medicine*, *3*(1), 100485. DOI: 10.1016/j.xcrm.2021.100485 PMID: 35106506

Behl, A., Chavan, M., Jain, K., Sharma, I., Pereira, V. E., & Zhang, J. Z. (2022). The role of organizational culture and voluntariness in the adoption of artificial intelligence for disaster relief operations. *International Journal of Manpower, 43*(2), 569–586. DOI: 10.1108/IJM-03-2021-0178

Beijaard, D., Meijer, P. C., & Verloop, N. (2004). Reconsidering research on teachers' professional identity. *Teaching and Teacher Education, 2*(2), 107–128. DOI: 10.1016/j.tate.2003.07.001

Benabou, A., & Touhami, F. (2025). Integration of artificial intelligence in human resource management: Analyzing opportunities, challenges, and human-AI collaboration. *Management and Accounting Review, 24*(1), 215–230. https://mar.uitm.edu.my/images/Vol-24-1/15.pdf

Berraies, S., & Chouiref, A. (2023). Exploring the effect of team climate on knowledge management in teams through team work engagement: Evidence from knowledge-intensive firms. *Journal of Knowledge Management, 27*(3), 842–869. DOI: 10.1108/JKM-09-2021-0720

Bhatia, A., Bhatia, P., & Sood, D. (2024). Leveraging AI to transform online higher education: Focusing on personalized learning, assessment, and student engagement. *International Journal of Management and Humanities, 11*(1).

Bhattacharya, S. (2023). The future of HR: Embracing AI for smarter and more human workplaces. *International Journal of Scientific Research, 12*(5), 457–459. https://www.ijsr.net/getabstract.php?paperid=SR23423182128

Bhima, B., Az Zahra, A. R., & Nurtino, T. (2023). Enhancing organizational efficiency through the integration of artificial intelligence in management information systems. *APTISI Transactions on Management, 7*(3), 282–289. DOI: 10.33050/atm.v7i3.2146

Bienefeld, N., Keller, E., & Grote, G. (2024). Human-AI teaming in critical care: A comparative analysis of data scientists' and clinicians' perspectives on AI augmentation and automation. *Journal of Medical Internet Research, 26*, e50130. DOI: 10.2196/50130 PMID: 39038285

Bloom, N., Liang, J., Roberts, J., & Ying, Z. J. (2015). Does working from home work? Evidence from a Chinese experiment. *The Quarterly Journal of Economics, 130*(1), 165–218. DOI: 10.1093/qje/qju032

Bonelli, M. (2022). *How AI is affecting VC funding of innovative startups.* HEC Paris. https://www.hec.edu/en/how-ai-affecting-vc-funding-innovative-startups

Bontchev, B., & Vassileva, D. (2011). Adaptive assessment based on learning styles and student knowledge level. In *Proceedings of the 3rd International Conference on Computer Supported Education* (Vol. 2, pp. 449–454). SciTePress. https://www.google.com/search?q=https://doi.org/10.5220/0003484104490454

Boston Consulting Group. (2024). *Seventy percent of economies are underprepared for AI disruption.* https://www.bcg.com/press/20november2024-seventy-percent-economies-underprepared-ai-disruption

Boyatzis, R. E., Smith, M. L., & Van Oosten, E. (2019). *Helping people change: Coaching with compassion for lifelong learning and growth.* Harvard Business Review Press.

Braganza, A., Chen, W., Canhoto, A., & Sap, S. (2021). Productive employment and decent work: The impact of AI adoption on psychological contracts, job engagement and employee trust. *Journal of Business Research, 131*, 485–494. DOI: 10.1016/j.jbusres.2020.08.018 PMID: 32836565

Brinkmann, L., Cebrian, M., & Pescetelli, N. (2025). Adversarial dynamics in centralized versus decentralized intelligent systems. *Topics in Cognitive Science, 17*(2), 374–391. DOI: 10.1111/tops.12705 PMID: 37902444

Brown, M., Costello, E., & Donlon, E. (2021). Digital education as social practice: Major trends shaping online learning futures. *Rivista di Digital Politics, 1*(3), 455–484. DOI: 10.53227/103800

Brown, T., Mann, B., Ryder, N., Subbiah, M., Kaplan, J., Dhariwal, P., & Amodei, D. (2020). Language models are few-shot learners. *NeurIPS, 33*, 1877–1901.

Brynjolfsson, E. (2022). The Turing trap: The promise & peril of human-like artificial intelligence. *Daedalus, 151*(2), 272–287. DOI: 10.1162/daed_a_01915

Brynjolfsson, E., & McAfee, A. (2014). *The second machine age: Work, progress, and prosperity in a time of brilliant technologies.* W. W. Norton & Company.

Brynjolfsson, E., & McAfee, A. (2017). *Machine, platform, crowd: Harnessing our digital future.* W. W. Norton & Company.

Brynjolfsson, E., & McAfee, A. (2023). *The age of AI: And our human future.* Little, Brown and Company.

Burton, J. W., Stein, M.-K., & Jensen, T. B. (2020). A systematic review of algorithm aversion in augmented decision making. *Journal of Behavioral Decision Making, 33*(2), 220–239. DOI: 10.1002/bdm.2155

Butts, M. M., Becker, W. J., & Boswell, W. R. (2015). Hot buttons and time sinks: The effects of electronic communication during nonwork time on emotions and work-nonwork conflict. *Academy of Management Journal*, *58*(3), 763–788. DOI: 10.5465/amj.2014.0170

Buvik, M. P., & Tkalich, A. (2022). Work engagement in agile teams: The missing link between team autonomy, trust, and performance? In *Lecture Notes in Business Information Processing* (pp. 131–147). Springer International Publishing. DOI: 10.1007/978-3-031-08169-9_9

Büyükgüzel, S., & Balaman, U. (2023). The spatial organization of hybrid Scrum meetings: A multimodal conversation analysis study. *Discourse & Communication*, *17*(3), 253–277. DOI: 10.1177/17504813221119004

Calvo, R. A., & D'Mello, S. K. (2010). Affect detection: An interdisciplinary review of models, methods, and their applications. *IEEE Transactions on Affective Computing*, *1*(1), 18–37. DOI: 10.1109/T-AFFC.2010.1

Cannataro, M. (2022). Knowledge representation and reasoning. In *Artificial Intelligence in Bioinformatics.* DOI: 10.1016/B978-0-12-822952-1.00010-3

Cavanaugh, P., Zhang, J., & Tenney, D. (2025, March). AI-enhanced open educational practices (AIOEP): Managing security, privacy, and ethics of artificial intelligence in engineering education [Paper presentation]. *2025 ASEE Northeast Section Conference*, Bridgeport, CT, United States. https://doi.org/DOI: 10.18260/1-2-60-54967

Chandra, S., University, N. T., Srivastava, S., & Theng, Y.-L. (2012). Cognitive absorption and trust for workplace collaboration in virtual worlds: An information processing decision making perspective. *Journal of the Association for Information Systems*, *13*(10), 797–835. DOI: 10.17705/1jais.00310

Chang, Y.-L., & Ke, J. (2024). Socially responsible artificial intelligence empowered people analytics: A novel framework towards sustainability. *Human Resource Development Review*, *23*(1), 88–120. DOI: 10.1177/15344843231200930

Chatterjee, S., & Kumar, A. (2025). Artificial intelligence and entrepreneurial finance: A guide for research. *Journal of Business Venturing*, *40*(1), 101–130.

Chebrolu, S. K.Management Information System Lamar University USA. (2025). Ai-powered business intelligence: A systematic literature review on the future of decision-making in enterprises. *American Journal of Scholarly Research and Innovation*, *4*(01), 33–62. DOI: 10.63125/gq69nv41

Chen, M., Tworek, J., Jun, H., Yuan, Q., Pinto, H., Kaplan, J., . . . Zaremba, W. (2021). Evaluating large language models trained on code. *arXiv preprint arXiv:2107.03374.*

Chen, A., Yang, T., Ma, J., & Lu, Y. (2023). Employees' learning behavior in the context of AI collaboration: A perspective on the job demand-control model. *Industrial Management & Data Systems, 123*(8), 2169–2193. DOI: 10.1108/IMDS-04-2022-0221

Chen, E., & Zhang, H. (2024). Research on the impact of artificial intelligence technology on urban public health resilience. *Frontiers in Public Health, 12*, 1506930. DOI: 10.3389/fpubh.2024.1506930 PMID: 39839427

Cheng, M., Zhang, C., & Liu, Q. (2025). A survey on knowledge-oriented retrieval-augmented generation. *arXiv preprint arXiv:2501.01234*.

Chen, H., Chiang, R. H. L., & Storey, V. C. (2012). Business intelligence and analytics: From big data to big impact. *Management Information Systems Quarterly, 36*(4), 1165–1188. DOI: 10.2307/41703503

Chen, H., Popaitoon, S., & Mumi, A. (2025). Investigating corporate entrepreneurship strategy through digital transformation: A dynamic capabilities perspective. *Journal of Innovation and Entrepreneurship, 14*(1), 95. Advance online publication. DOI: 10.1186/s13731-025-00570-0

Chen, J.-F., Ni, C.-C., Lin, P.-H., & Lin, R. (2024). Designing the future: A case study on human-AI co-innovation. *Creative Education, 15*(03), 474–494. DOI: 10.4236/ce.2024.153028

Chen, Y., Wang, Z., & Ortiz, J. (2023). A sustainable digital ecosystem: Digital servitization transformation and digital infrastructure support. *Sustainability (Basel), 15*(2), 1530. DOI: 10.3390/su15021530

Chen, Z., Ji, X., Cao, Q., & Wu, J. (2025). Pricing and service decisions in crowdfunding. *Journal of Systems Science and Complexity, 38*(6), 2480–2501. Advance online publication. DOI: 10.1007/s11424-025-3217-5

Cherns, A. (1987). Principles of sociotechnical design revisited. *Human Relations, 40*(3), 153–162. DOI: 10.1177/001872678704000303

Chui, M., Manyika, J., & Miremadi, M. (2021). *The state of AI in 2021*. McKinsey Global Institute. Retrieved from https://www.mckinsey.com/business-functions/quantumblack/our-insights/global-survey-the-state-of-ai-in-2021

Cinelli, M., Kadziński, M., Gonzalez, M., & Słowiński, R. (2020). How to support the application of multiple criteria decision analysis? Let us start with a comprehensive taxonomy. *Omega, 96*, 102261. DOI: 10.1016/j.omega.2020.102261 PMID: 33746337

Clark, S. C. (2000). Work/family border theory: A new theory of work/family balance. *Human Relations, 53*(6), 747–770. DOI: 10.1177/0018726700536001

Clemente-Suárez, V. J., Beltrán-Velasco, A. I., Herrero-Roldán, S., Rodriguez-Besteiro, S., Martínez-Guardado, I., Martín-Rodríguez, A., & Tornero-Aguilera, J. F. (2024). Digital device usage and childhood cognitive development: Exploring effects on cognitive abilities. *Children (Basel, Switzerland), 11*(11), 1299. Advance online publication. DOI: 10.3390/children11111299 PMID: 39594874

Coldron, J., & Smith, R. (1999). Active location in teachers' construction of their professional identities. *Journal of Curriculum Studies, 31*(6), 711–726. DOI: 10.1080/002202799182954

Cortes, C., & Vapnik, V. (1995). Support-vector networks. *Machine Learning, 20*(3), 273–297. DOI: 10.1023/A:1022627411411

Costa, C., & Ghosh, S. (2025). Empowering customer service with generative AI: enhancing agent performance while navigating challenges. Information Research, 30(iConf), 150–158. DOI: 10.47989/ir30iConf47566

Cöster, M., Danielson, M., Ekenberg, L., Gullberg, C., Titlestad, G., Westelius, A., & Wettergren, G. (2023). *Digital transformation: Understanding business goals, risks, processes, and decisions*. Open Book Publishers. DOI: 10.11647/OBP.0350

Coussement, K., Abedin, M. Z., Kraus, M., Maldonado, S., & Topuz, K. (2024). Explainable AI for enhanced decision-making. *Decision Support Systems, 184*, 114276. DOI: 10.1016/j.dss.2024.114276

Crawford, K. (2021). *Atlas of AI: Power, politics, and the planetary costs of artificial intelligence*. Yale University Press.

Daher, R. (2025). Integrating AI literacy into teacher education: A critical perspective paper. *Discover Artificial Intelligence, 5*(1), 217. DOI: 10.1007/s44163-025-00475-7

Darics, E., & Cristina Gatti, M. (2019). Talking a team into being in online workplace collaborations: The discourse of virtual work. *Discourse Studies, 21*(3), 237–257. DOI: 10.1177/1461445619829240

Darling-Hammond, L., Hyler, M. E., & Gardner, M. (2017). *Effective teacher professional development*. Learning Policy Institute. DOI: 10.54300/122.311

Dastin, J. (2018). *Amazon scraps secret AI recruiting tool that showed bias against women*. Reuters. https://www.reuters.com/article/us-amazon-com-jobs-automation-insight/amazon-scraps-secret-ai-recruiting-tool-that-showed-bias-against-women-idUSKCN1MK08G

Daugherty, P. R., & Wilson, H. J. (2018). *Human + machine: Reimagining work in the age of AI*. Harvard Business Review Press.

Daugherty, P. R., & Wilson, H. J. (2023). *Radically human: How new technology is transforming business and shaping our future*. Harvard Business Review Press.

Dave, D. M., & Mandvikar, S.LTIMIndtree. (2023). Augmented intelligence: Human-Ai collaboration in the era of digital transformation. *International Journal of Engineering Applied Sciences and Technology*, *8*(6), 24–33. DOI: 10.33564/IJEAST.2023.v08i06.003

Davenport, T. H., & Miller, S. M. (2022). Working with AI: Real stories of human–machine collaboration. *MIT Sloan Management Review*, *63*(3), 1–6.

Davenport, T. H., & Ronanki, R. (2018). Artificial intelligence for the real world. *Harvard Business Review*, *96*(1), 108–116.

Davenport, T., Guha, A., Grewal, D., & Bressgott, T. (2020). How artificial intelligence will change the future of marketing. *Journal of the Academy of Marketing Science*, *48*(1), 24–42. DOI: 10.1007/s11747-019-00696-0

Day, C., & Kington, A. (2008). Identity, well-being and effectiveness: The emotional contexts of teaching. *Pedagogy, Culture & Society*, *16*(1), 7–23. DOI: 10.1080/14681360701877743

Day, C., Kington, A., Stobart, G., & Sammons, P. (2006). The personal and professional selves of teachers: Stable and unstable identities. *British Educational Research Journal*, *32*(4), 601–616. DOI: 10.1080/01411920600775316

De Obesso Arias, M., Pérez Rivero, C., & Carrero Márquez, O. (2023). Artificial intelligence to manage workplace bullying. *Journal of Business Research*, *160*, 113813. Advance online publication. DOI: 10.1016/j.jbusres.2023.113813

de Souza, L. A., de Barros, M. J. F., & Melo, P. (2024). How management information systems might add value to the decision-making process in organizations. Journal on Innovation and Sustainability RISUS ISSN 2179-3565, 15(1), 62–70. DOI: 10.23925/2179-3565.2023v15i1p62-70

Deci, E. L., & Ryan, R. M. (2000). The "what" and "why" of goal pursuits: Human needs and the self-determination of behavior. *Psychological Inquiry*, *11*(4), 227–268. DOI: 10.1207/S15327965PLI1104_01

Derks, D., van Duin, D., Tims, M., & Bakker, A. B. (2016). Smartphone use and work–home interference: The moderating role of social norms and employee work engagement. *Journal of Occupational and Organizational Psychology*, *88*(1), 155–177. DOI: 10.1111/joop.12083

Desimone, L. M. (2009). Improving Impact Studies of Teachers' Professional Development: Toward Better Conceptualizations and Measures. *Educational Researcher*, *38*(3), 181–199. DOI: 10.3102/0013189X08331140

DeVault, D., Artstein, R., Benn, G., Dey, T., Fast, E., Gainer, A., Georgila, K., Gratch, J., Hartholt, A., Lhommet, M., Lucas, G., Marsella, S., Morbini, F., Nazarian, A., Scherer, S., Stratou, G., Suri, A., Traum, D., Wood, R., . . . Morency, L.-P. (2014). *SimSensei kiosk: A virtual human interviewer for healthcare decision support.* In Proceedings of the International Conference on Autonomous Agents and Multiagent Systems (AAMAS 2014) (pp. 1061–1068). International Foundation for Autonomous Agents and Multiagent Systems. DOI: 10.5555/2615731.2617415

Dietvorst, B. J., Simmons, J. P., & Massey, C. (2018). Overcoming algorithm aversion: People will use imperfect algorithms if they can (even slightly) modify them. *Management Science*, *64*(3), 1155–1170. DOI: 10.1287/mnsc.2016.2643

Dignum, V. (2021). *Responsible artificial intelligence: How to develop and use AI in a responsible way.* Springer., DOI: 10.1007/978-3-030-30371-6

Dima, J., Gilbert, M.-H., Dextras-Gauthier, J., & Giraud, L. (2024). The effects of artificial intelligence on human resource activities. *Frontiers in Psychology*, *15*, 1360401. Advance online publication. DOI: 10.3389/fpsyg.2024.1360401 PMID: 38903456

Dow, E. R., Khan, N. C., Chen, K. M., Mishra, K., Perera, C., Narala, R., Basina, M., Dang, J., Kim, M., Levine, M., Phadke, A., Tan, M., Weng, K., Do, D. V., Moshfeghi, D. M., Mahajan, V. B., Mruthyunjaya, P., Leng, T., & Myung, D. (2023). AI-human hybrid workflow enhances teleophthalmology for the detection of diabetic retinopathy. *Ophthalmology Science*, *3*(4), 100330. DOI: 10.1016/j.xops.2023.100330 PMID: 37449051

Dr. Jolly Masih, D. R. A. J. (2023). Enhancing employee efficiency and performance in Industry 5.0 organizations through artificial intelligence integration. [EEL]. *European Economic Letters*, *13*(4), 300–315. DOI: 10.52783/eel.v13i4.589

Drake, R., & Chen, W. D. (2023). Rethinking workplace collaboration – an old topic with a practical view. *Management Decision*, *61*(12), 3637–3643. DOI: 10.1108/MD-01-2023-0044

Drigas, A. S., & Papoutsi, C. (2018). A new layered model on emotional intelligence. *Behavioral Sciences (Basel, Switzerland), 8*(5), 45. DOI: 10.3390/bs8050045 PMID: 29724021

Dutta, S., & Bose, I. (2023). Generative AI and startup innovation: A bibliometric review. *International Journal of Entrepreneurial Behaviour & Research, 29*(8), 1450–1475.

Eastern Eye. (2025). *AI-Powered Startups Driving South Asia's Business Future.* Eastern Eye. https://www.easterneye.biz/ai-powered-startups-driving-south-asias-business-future/

Ediriweera, Pramudika, & Fernando. (. (2025). The influence of AI-driven marketing analytics on strategic decision-making in private educational institutes in Sri Lanka: Moderator role of organisational culture. *Asian Journal of Marketing Management, 4*(2). Advance online publication. DOI: 10.31357/ajmm.v4i2.7970

Edmondson, A. C. (1999). Psychological safety and learning behavior in work teams. *Administrative Science Quarterly, 44*(2), 350–383. DOI: 10.2307/2666999

Eitel-Porter, R. (2020). Beyond the promise: Implementing ethical AI. *AI and Ethics, 1*(1), 73–80. DOI: 10.1007/s43681-020-00011-6

Enholm, I. M., Papagiannidis, E., Mikalef, P., & Krogstie, J. (2022). Artificial intelligence and business value: A literature review. *Information Systems Frontiers, 24*(5), 1709–1734. DOI: 10.1007/s10796-021-10186-w

Ersoy, N. (2022). The influence of statistical normalization techniques on performance ranking results: The application of MCDM method proposed by Biswas and Saha. *International Journal of Business Analytics, 9*(5), 1–21. DOI: 10.4018/IJBAN.298017

European Commission. (2024). *AI Act | A regulatory framework for trustworthy artificial intelligence*. Retrieved from https://digital-strategy.ec.europa.eu/en/policies/regulatory-framework-ai

European Union. (2024). *Artificial Intelligence Act.* Official Journal of the European Union. https://data.europa.eu/eli/reg/2024/1689/oj

Faggella, D. (2020). The state of generative AI: Trends and applications.

Fakhr-e-Alam, S. M., Siddiqui, F.–e.–A., Zafar, H., & Kazmi, S. R. (2024). Harnessing A.I. technologies for employee recruitment. *Jurnal Dinamika Manajemen dan Bisnis, 4*(1), 1–12. DOI: 10.5281/zenodo.10684342

Fang, C., & Tse, A. W. C. (2022). Quasi-Experiment: Postgraduate students' class engagement in various online learning contexts when taking privacy issues to incorporate with artificial intelligence applications. *Proceedings of the 14th International Conference on Education Technology and Computers*, 356–361. DOI: 10.1145/3572549.3572606

Faraj, S., Pachidi, S., & Sayegh, K. (2021). Working and organizing in the age of the learning algorithm. *Information and Organization, 31*(1), 100339. DOI: 10.1016/j.infoandorg.2021.100339

Faulconbridge, J., Sarwar, A., & Spring, M. (2025). How professionals adapt to artificial intelligence: The role of intertwined boundary work. *Journal of Management Studies, 62*(5), 1991–2024. DOI: 10.1111/joms.12936

Fenwick, A., Molnár, G., & Frangos, P. (2024). The critical role of HRM in AI-driven digital transformation. *Discover Artificial Intelligence, 3*, 24. Advance online publication. DOI: 10.1007/s44162-024-00024-1

Ferrara, E. (2023). Fairness and bias in artificial intelligence: A brief survey of sources, impacts, and mitigation strategies. *Patterns, 4*(1), 100796. https://www.mdpi.com/2413-4155/6/1/3

Fletcher, S., & Thornton, K. R. V. (2023). The top 10 soft skills in business today compared to 2012. *Business and Professional Communication Quarterly, 86*(4), 411–426. DOI: 10.1177/23294906221148453

Floridi, L., & Cowls, J. (2019). A unified framework of five principles for AI in society. *Harvard Data Science Review, 1*(1). Advance online publication. DOI: 10.1162/99608f92.8cd550d1

Fossen, F. M., McLemore, T., & Sorgner, A. (2024). *Artificial intelligence and entrepreneurship* (IZA Discussion Paper No. 17055). Institute of Labor Economics (IZA). https://doi.org/DOI: 10.1561/0300000130

Fotoh, L., & Mugwira, T. (2025). Exploring large language models in external audits. *International Journal of Accounting Information Systems, 56*, 100748. Advance online publication. DOI: 10.1016/j.accinf.2025.100748

Fountaine, T., McCarthy, B., & Saleh, T. (2019). Building the AI-Powered Organization: Technology isn't the biggest challenge. Culture is. *Harvard Business Review, 97*(4), 62–73.

Fraser, H., Coiera, E., & Wong, D. (2018). Safety of patient-facing digital symptom checkers. *Lancet, 392*(10161), 2263–2264. DOI: 10.1016/S0140-6736(18)32819-8 PMID: 30413281

Frey, C. B., & Osborne, M. A. (2017). The future of employment: How susceptible are jobs to computerisation? *Technological Forecasting and Social Change*, *114*, 254–280. DOI: 10.1016/j.techfore.2016.08.019

Friedman, J. H. (2001). Greedy function approximation: A gradient boosting machine. *Annals of Statistics*, *29*(5), 1189–1232. DOI: 10.1214/aos/1013203451

Gajendran, R. S., & Harrison, D. A. (2007). The good, the bad, and the unknown about telecommuting: Meta-analysis of psychological mediators and individual consequences. *The Journal of Applied Psychology*, *92*(6), 1524–1541. DOI: 10.1037/0021-9010.92.6.1524 PMID: 18020794

Gala, D., Behl, H., Shah, M., & Makaryus, A. N. (2024). The role of artificial intelligence in improving patient outcomes and future of healthcare delivery in cardiology: A narrative review of the literature. *Healthcare (Basel)*, *12*(4), 481. DOI: 10.3390/healthcare12040481 PMID: 38391856

Gallup. (2024). *State of the Global Workplace: 2024 Report* (Key insights). Gallup. https://www.ahtd.org/files/state-of-the-global-workplace-2024-key-insights.pdf

Gans, J., Scott, E., & Stern, S. (2019). Strategy for start-ups. *Harvard Business Review*, *97*(3), 5–12.

Garavandala, U. S. (2025). Neuroscience-driven workforce architecture: Mapping cognitive load to role design. *Strategic HR Review*, *24*(6), 243–252. Advance online publication. DOI: 10.1108/SHR-05-2025-0050

Garg, M. (2025). The integration of artificial intelligence in human resource management. *International Journal of Research in Human Resource Management*, *3*(1), 45–59. https://www.humanresourcejournal.com/archives/2025.v7.i1.C.272

Geerts, J. M. (2024). Maximizing the Impact and ROI of leadership development: A theory- and evidence-informed framework. *Behavioral Sciences (Basel, Switzerland)*, *14*(10), 955. DOI: 10.3390/bs14100955 PMID: 39457826

Genovesi, S., Mönig, J. M., Schmitz, A., Poretschkin, M., Akila, M., Kahdan, M., … Zimmermann, A. (2024). Standardizing fairness-evaluation procedures: Interdisciplinary insights on machine-learning algorithms in creditworthiness assessments for small personal loans. *AI and Ethics*, *4*, 537–553. DOI: 10.1007/s43681-023-00291-8

Geroche, J. B., & Guay, F. J. G. (2024). AI in education: Unlocking college student engagement in the digital learning era. *International Research Journal of Science, Technology, Education, and Management*, *4*(4), 52–64.

Ghazinoory, S., & Shirkhani, S. (2022). Artificial intelligence impact on entrepreneurship ecosystems: A systematic review. *Technological Forecasting and Social Change*, *172*, 121–135.

Ghonim, A., Awad, A., Shemais, M., Shma, T., & Aziz, A. (2025). Exploring the impact of flexible work arrangements on employee engagement in telecommunications: Case of Egypt. *Problems and Perspectives in Management, 23*(2), 198–207. https://doi.org/10.21511/ppm.23(2).2025.13

Ghonim, A., & Awad, A. (2025). Shaping customer insights through e-marketing: An applied study in the banking sector. *International Journal of Advanced and Applied Sciences*, *12*(4), 88–98. DOI: 10.21833/ijaas.2025.04.011

Ghonim, A., Awad, A., Shemais, M., Shma, T., & Aziz, A. (2025). Exploring the impact of flexible work arrangements on employee engagement in telecommunications: Case of Egypt. *Problems and Perspectives in Management*, *23*(2), 198–207. DOI: 10.21511/ppm.23(2).2025.13

GitLab Inc. (2023). *GitLab continues AI momentum with enhanced AI-powered DevSecOps workflows.* Retrieved from https://about.gitlab.com/press/releases/2023-11-09-gitlab-continues-ai-momentum-with-enhanced-ai-powered-devsecops-workflows/

Giudici, P. (2018). Fintech risk management: A research challenge for artificial intelligence in finance. *Frontiers in Artificial Intelligence*, *1*, 1. DOI: 10.3389/frai.2018.00001 PMID: 33733089

Gkinko, L., & Elbanna, A. (2022). Hope, tolerance and empathy: Employees' emotions when using an AI-enabled chatbot in a digitalised workplace. *Information Technology & People*, *35*(6), 1714–1743. DOI: 10.1108/ITP-04-2021-0328

Gm, D., Goudar, R. H., Kulkarni, A. A., Rathod, V. N., & Hukkeri, G. S. (2024). A digital recommendation system for personalized learning to enhance online education: A review. *IEEE Access : Practical Innovations, Open Solutions*, *12*, 34019–34041. DOI: 10.1109/ACCESS.2024.3369901

Golgeci, I., Ritala, P., Arslan, A., McKenna, B., & Ali, I. (2025). Confronting and alleviating AI resistance in the workplace: An integrative review and a process framework. *Human Resource Management Review*, *35*(2), 101075. DOI: 10.1016/j.hrmr.2024.101075

Gompers, P. A., Gornall, W., Kaplan, S. N., & Strebulaev, I. A. (2020). How do venture capitalists make decisions? *Journal of Financial Economics*, *135*(1), 169–190. DOI: 10.1016/j.jfineco.2019.06.011

Goswami, M., Jain, S., Alam, T., Deifalla, A., Ragab, A., & Khargotra, R. (2023). AI adoption in pharmaceutical HRM. *Frontiers in Pharmacology, 14*. Advance online publication. DOI: 10.3389/fphar.2023.1215706 PMID: 38034991

Grant, A. M., & Parker, S. K. (2009). Redesigning work design theories: The rise of relational and proactive perspectives. *The Academy of Management Annals, 3*(1), 317–375. DOI: 10.5465/19416520903047327

Gratch, J., Artstein, R., Lucas, G. M., Stratou, G., Scherer, S., Nazarian, A., Wood, R., Boberg, J., DeVault, D., Marsella, S., & Traum, D. R. (2014). The Distress Analysis Interview Corpus of human and computer interviews. In *Proceedings of the Ninth International Conference on Language Resources and Evaluation (LREC'14)* (pp. 3123–3128). https://schererstefan.net/assets/files/papers/508_Paper.pdf

Greenhalgh, T., Rosen, R., Shaw, S. E., Byng, R., Faulkner, S., Finlay, T., Grundy, E., Husain, L., Hughes, G., Leone, C., Moore, L., Papoutsi, C., Pope, C., Rybczynska-Bunt, S., Rushforth, A., Wherton, J., Wieringa, S., & Wood, G. W. (2021). Planning and Evaluating Remote Consultation Services: A new conceptual framework incorporating complexity and practical ethics. *Frontiers in Digital Health, 3*, 726095. DOI: 10.3389/fdgth.2021.726095 PMID: 34713199

Greenhalgh, T., Wherton, J., Papoutsi, C., Lynch, J., Hughes, G., A'Court, C., Hinder, S., Fahy, N., Procter, R., & Shaw, S. (2017). Beyond adoption: A new framework for theorizing and evaluating nonadoption, abandonment, and challenges to the scale-up, spread, and sustainability of health and care technologies. *Journal of Medical Internet Research, 19*(11), e367. DOI: 10.2196/jmir.8775 PMID: 29092808

Guan, H., Dong, L., & Zhao, A. (2022). Ethical risk factors and mechanisms in artificial intelligence decision making. *Behavioral Sciences (Basel, Switzerland), 12*(9), 343. DOI: 10.3390/bs12090343 PMID: 36135147

Guan, J. (2019). Artificial intelligence in healthcare and medicine: Promises, ethical challenges and governance. Chung-Kuo i Hsueh k'o Hsueh Tsa Chih. *Chinese Medical Sciences Journal, 34*(2), 76–83. DOI: 10.24920/003611 PMID: 31315747

Guo, X., Zhu, T., Wu, C., Bao, Z., & Liu, Y. (2022). Emotional activity is negatively associated with cognitive load in multimedia learning: A case study with EEG signals. *Frontiers in Psychology, 13*, 889427. DOI: 10.3389/fpsyg.2022.889427 PMID: 35769742

Guo, Y., & Li, X. (2025). Elevating entrepreneurship with generative artificial intelligence. *Journal of Innovation & Knowledge, 10*(4), 316–329.

Gupta, P., Lakhera, G., & Sharma, M. (2024). Impact of AI on employee performance. *The Journal of High Technology Management Research, 35*. Advance online publication. DOI: 10.1016/j.hitech.2024.100520

Haboh, S. (2022). Theoretical Foundations of Designing and Developing Adaptive Learning Environments. *Journal of Educational and Social Studies, 28*(9), 141–182. DOI: 10.21608/jsu.2022.293140

Hafiza Hamzah, N., Khalid, M., Nasir, M., & Abdul Wahab, J. (2021). The effects of principals' digital leadership on teachers' digital teaching during the covid-19 pandemic in Malaysia. *Journal of Education and e-learning Research, 8*(2), 216–221. DOI: 10.20448/journal.509.2021.82.216.221

Halabi, R., & Subrahmanyam, S. (2025). Economic and Governance Implications of AI-Driven Marketing Systems: A Mixed-Methods Study on Performance, Transparency, and Policy Alignment. *Lex Localis - Journal of Local Self-Government, 23*(S4), 2189-2203. DOI: 10.52152/arsynj63

Han, J., Zhang, Z., Cummins, N., & Schuller, B. (2019). Adversarial training in affective computing and sentiment analysis: Recent advances and perspectives [review article]. *IEEE Computational Intelligence Magazine, 14*(2), 68–81. DOI: 10.1109/MCI.2019.2901088

Harfouche, A., Quinio, B., & Bugiotti, F. (2023). Human-centric AI to mitigate AI biases. *Journal of Global Information Management, 31*(5), 1–23. DOI: 10.4018/JGIM.331755

Hargreaves, L. (2025). Ocado: Streamlining supply chains with AI robotics. *Supply Chain Digital.* Retrieved from https://supplychaindigital.com/technology/how-ai-is-redefining-ocados-robotic-fulfilment-system

Hariyanto, K. F., & Maharani, R. (2025). Artificial intelligence in adaptive education: a systematic review of techniques for personalized learning. DOI: 10.1007/s44217-025-00908-6

Harsha, H., & Natraj, A. A. (2025). Workplace well-being and mitigating burnout using technological tools. DHARANA - Bhavan's International. *The Journal of Business, 63–67*, 63–67. Advance online publication. DOI: 10.18311/dbijb/2024/48291

Hawrysz, L. (2025). Artificial intelligence in candidate screening. *Scientific Papers of Silesian University of Technology: Organization and Management Series, 168*, 123–134. DOI: 10.29119/1641-3466.2025.168.9

Healey, J. A., & Picard, R. W. (2005). Detecting stress during real-world driving tasks using physiological sensors. *IEEE Transactions on Intelligent Transportation Systems*, *6*(2), 156–166. DOI: 10.1109/TITS.2005.848368

He, L., & Wang, L. (2025). Can artificial intelligence curb greenwashing? *Energy Economics*, *152*, 108954. Advance online publication. DOI: 10.1016/j.eneco.2025.108954

Hepfer, M., & Lawrence, T. B. (2022). The Heterogeneity of Organizational Resilience: Exploring functional, operational and strategic resilience. *Organization Theory*, *3*(1), 263178772210747. DOI: 10.1177/26317877221074701

Herdman, P. T. (2025). The influence of generative artificial intelligence on leadership: An exploration of technology professionals' perceptions regarding leadership, adaptation, and organizational culture in the digital age [Doctoral dissertation, Marshall University]. Marshall Digital Scholar. https://mds.marshall.edu/etd/1987/

Ho, B. Q., Otsuki, M., Kishita, Y., Kobayakawa, M., & Watanabe, K. (2022). Human augmentation technologies for employee well-being: A research and development agenda. *International Journal of Environmental Research and Public Health*, *19*(3), 1195. DOI: 10.3390/ijerph19031195 PMID: 35162215

Hossain, S., Fernando, M., & Akter, S. (2025). Digital leadership: Towards a dynamic managerial capability perspective of artificial intelligence-driven leader capabilities. *Journal of Leadership & Organizational Studies*, *32*(2), 189–208. DOI: 10.1177/15480518251319624

Huang, Y., & Zhao, W. X. (2024). A survey on retrieval-augmented text generation for large language models. *arXiv preprint arXiv:2404.14135.*

Hüllermeier, E., & Słowiński, R. (2024a). Preference learning and multiple criteria decision aiding: Differences, commonalities, and synergies—Part I. *4OR, 22(2),* 179–209. DOI: 10.1007/s10288-023-00560-6

Hüllermeier, E., & Słowiński, R. (2024b). Preference learning and multiple criteria decision aiding: Differences, commonalities, and synergies—Part II. *4OR, 22*(3), 279–312. DOI: 10.1007/s10288-023-00561-5

Humanyze. (2024). *Workstyle analytics for CEOs: Boosting productivity and retention in hybrid teams*. Humanyze. https://humanyze.com/workstyle-analytics-for-ceos-boosting-productivity-and-retention-in-hybrid-teams/

Hunkenschroer, A., & Luetge, C. (2022). Ethics of AI-enabled recruiting and selection. *Journal of Business Ethics*, *182*, 723–745. DOI: 10.1007/s10551-021-04970-0

Huttunen, H. (2025). The effect of organizational culture on human-AI collaboration in supply chain management [Master's thesis, Aalto University]. Aaltodoc. https://aaltodoc.aalto.fi/items/f8e0bb40-886b-45c0-a11e-6a9dd368a301

Hwang, G. J., Xie, H., Wah, B. W., & Gašević, D. (2020). Vision, challenges, priorities, and research platforms of Artificial Intelligence in Education. *Computers and Education: Artificial Intelligence, 1*, 100003. DOI: 10.1016/j.caeai.2020.100003

Hysing, M., Harvey, A. G., Linton, S. J., Askeland, K. G., & Sivertsen, B. (2015). Sleep and academic performance in later adolescence: Results from a large population-based study. *Journal of Sleep Research, 24*(3), 318–324. DOI: 10.1111/jsr.12373 PMID: 26825591

Ibokette, A. I., Ogundare, T. O., Anyebe, A. P., Alao, F. O.-O., Odeh, I. I., & Okafor, F. C. (2024). Mitigating maritime cybersecurity risks using AI-based intrusion detection systems and network automation during extreme environmental conditions. *International Journal of Scientific Research and Modern Technology, 3*(10), 65–91. DOI: 10.38124/ijsrmt.v3i10.73

Indrasari, M., & Pamuji, E. (2023). Enhancing employee performance through strategic initiatives. *Journal of Business Management and Economic Development, 5*(2), 56–64. DOI: 10.5281/zenodo.10684357

Insights, C. B. (2023). *UiPath funding and IPO journey: A case study in AI automation* [Report]. https://www.cbinsights.com/research/uipath-rpa-business-model-spotlight/

Ivanov, D. (2020). Predicting the impacts of epidemic outbreaks on global supply chains: A simulation-based analysis on the coronavirus outbreak (COVID-19/SARS-CoV-2) case. *Transportation Research Part E, Logistics and Transportation Review, 136*, 101922. DOI: 10.1016/j.tre.2020.101922 PMID: 32288597

Jain, R., Garg, N., & Khera, S. N. (2023). Effective human–AI work design for collaborative decision-making. Kybernetes. The International Journal of Cybernetics. *Kybernetes, 52*(11), 5017–5040. DOI: 10.1108/K-04-2022-0548

Jannach, D., Lerche, L., & Jugovac, M. (2015). Item familiarity as a possible confounding factor in user-centric recommender systems evaluation. *User Modeling and User-Adapted Interaction, 25*(5), 427–491. DOI: 10.1007/s11257-015-9165-3

Jarrahi, M. H., Kenyon, S., Brown, A., Donahue, C., & Wicher, C. (2023). Artificial intelligence: A strategy to harness its power through organizational learning. *The Journal of Business Strategy, 44*(3), 126–135. DOI: 10.1108/JBS-11-2021-0182

Jarrahi, M. H., Sutherland, W., Nelson, S. B., & Sawyer, S. (2021). Platformic management, boundary resources for gig work, and worker autonomy. *Computer Supported Cooperative Work, 30*(1–2), 153–189. DOI: 10.1007/s10606-020-09438-7

Jelinek, T., Bhave, A., Buchoud, N., Bühler, M. M., Glauner, P., Inderwildi, O., Kraft, M., Mok, C., Nübel, K., & Voss, A. (2024). International collaboration: Mainstreaming artificial intelligence and cyberphysical systems for carbon neutrality. *IEEE Transactions on Industrial Cyber-Physical Systems, 2*, 26–34. DOI: 10.1109/TICPS.2024.3351624

Jiang, W. (2023). Enhancing operational efficiency in E-commerce through artificial intelligence and information management integration. *Revue d Intelligence Artificielle, 37*(6), 1545–1555. DOI: 10.18280/ria.370619

Ji, L., & Huang, X. (2022). Social governance in energy-oriented cities using AI. *Energy Reports, 8*. Advance online publication. DOI: 10.1016/j.egyr.2022.08.206

Jin, D., Wang, L., Zhang, H., Zheng, Y., Ding, W., Xia, F., & Pan, S. (2023). A survey on fairness-aware recommender systems. *Information Fusion, 101*, 101906. DOI: 10.1016/j.inffus.2023.101906

Jing, L., & Zhang, H. (2023). Venture capitalists on boards and corporate innovation. *Journal of Risk and Financial Management, 16*(3), 143. DOI: 10.3390/jrfm16030143

Jobin, A., Ienca, M., & Vayena, E. (2019). The global landscape of AI ethics guidelines. *Nature Machine Intelligence, 1*(9), 389–399. DOI: 10.1038/s42256-019-0088-2

Johnson, B. A. M., Coggburn, J. D., & Llorens, J. J. (2022). Artificial intelligence and public human resource management. *Public Personnel Management, 51*(1), 3–18. DOI: 10.1177/00910260211066061

Jorzik, P., Klein, S. P., Kanbach, D. K., & Kraus, S. (2024). AI-driven business model innovation: A systematic review and research agenda. *Journal of Business Research, 182*, 114764. Advance online publication. DOI: 10.1016/j.jbusres.2024.114764

Joseph, S., Tahir, A., Bibi, F., Hamid, K., Iqbal, M. W., Ruk, S. A., & Ahmad, S. Z. (2024). A Review Analysis on Using" AIED" to Improve Student Engagement in Hybrid Education. *Bulletin of Business and Economics, 13*(2), 424–435.

Jo, W., Wang, R., Sun, S., Senthilkumaran, R. K., Foti, D., & Min, B.-C. (2022). MOCAS: A multimodal dataset for objective cognitive workload assessment on simultaneous tasks [Preprint].

Kaaria, A. G. (2024). Artificial intelligence and employee well-being: Balancing technological progressions with human-centric workplace strategies, a research agenda. *East African Journal of Information Technology, 7*(1), 355–365. DOI: 10.37284/eajit.7.1.2281

Kane, G. C., Palmer, D., Phillips, A., Kiron, D., & Buckley, N. (2019). Accelerating digital innovation inside and out. *MIT Sloan Management Review*.

Kartal, H., Oztekin, A., Gunasekaran, A., & Cebi, F. (2016). An integrated decision analytic framework of machine learning with multi-criteria decision making for multi-attribute inventory classification. *Computers & Industrial Engineering, 101*, 599–613. DOI: 10.1016/j.cie.2016.06.004

Kellekci, M. (2002). *Ri sk Sermayesi , Yeni Trendler ve Uygulamalar* (Master's thesis, Marmara Universitesi (Turkey)).

Kellekci, M., Cebeci, U., & Dogan, O. (2025). Prioritizing Early-Stage Start-Up Investment Alternatives Under Uncertainty: A Venture Capital Perspective. *Applied Sciences (Basel, Switzerland), 15*(18), 10060. DOI: 10.3390/app151810060

Kellogg, K. C., Valentine, M. A., & Christin, A. (2020). Algorithms at work: The new contested terrain of control. *The Academy of Management Annals, 14*(1), 366–410. DOI: 10.5465/annals.2018.0174

Kesim, E., Atmaca, T., & Turan, S. (2025). Reshaping school cultures: AI's influence on organizational dynamics and leadership behaviors. *Leadership and Policy in Schools, 24*(1), 117–136. DOI: 10.1080/15700763.2024.2413703

Khairi, S. M. M., Salleh, S. M., Julina, J., Hanawi, M. H., & Zainuddin, A. (2024). Co-operative well-being and employee resilience: A comprehensive review of the literature. *International Journal of Research and Innovation in Social Science, VIII*(X), 1137–1146. DOI: 10.47772/IJRISS.2024.8100095

Khair, M. A., Mahadasa, R., Tuli, F. A., & Ande, J. R. P. K. (2020). Beyond human judgment: Impact of AI on HR decision-making. *Global Disclosure of Economics and Business, 9*(2), 45–58. DOI: 10.18034/gdeb.v9i2.730

Khajeh Naeeni, S., & Nouhi, N. (2023). Job burnout mitigation: A comprehensive review of contemporary strategies and interventions. *KMAN Counseling and Psychology Nexus, 1*(1), 91–101. DOI: 10.61838/kman.psynexus.1.1.11

Khalid, J., Chuanmin, M., Altaf, F., Shafqat, M. M., Khan, S. K., & Ashraf, M. U. (2024). AI-driven risk management and sustainable decision-making: Role of perceived environmental responsibility. *Sustainability (Basel), 16*(16), 6799. DOI: 10.3390/su16166799

Khalife, J. (2023). Artificial intelligence and hybrid jobs [Master's thesis, University of Padova]. Padua Research Archive. https://thesis.unipd.it/retrieve/b2c6d80e-9c0f-4534-9662-595938d540ee/KHALIFE_JOEL.pdf

Khan, M. I., Parahyanti, E., & Hussain, S. (2024). Generative AI in HRM. *Asian Journal of Logistics Management*, *4*(1), 22–35. DOI: 10.5281/zenodo.10684363

Kharytonov, Y., Slobodian, S., & Podaienko, M. (2021). Development of models of technology transfer for public works. *Baltic Journal of Economic Studies*, *7*(4), 214–225. DOI: 10.30525/2256-0742/2021-7-4-214-225

Khlaif, Z. N., Alkouk, W. A., Salama, N., & Abu Eideh, B. (2025). Redesigning assessments for AI-enhanced learning: A framework for educators in the generative AI era. *Education Sciences*, *15*(2), 174. DOI: 10.3390/educsci15020174

Kim, B. J., & Lee, J. (2024). The mental health implications of artificial intelligence adoption: The crucial role of self-efficacy. *Humanities & Social Sciences Communications*, *11*(1), 1561. DOI: 10.1057/s41599-024-04018-w

Kim, M. K., Lee, I. H., & Wang, Y. (2020). How students emerge as learning leaders in small group online discussions. *Journal of Computer Assisted Learning*, *36*(5), 610–624. DOI: 10.1111/jcal.12431

Klesel, M., & Wittmann, H. F. (2025). Retrieval-augmented generation (RAG): Business & information systems engineering. *Business & Information Systems Engineering*, *67*(4), 551–561. Advance online publication. DOI: 10.1007/s12599-025-00945-3

Kostopoulos, G., Davrazos, G., & Kotsiantis, S. (2024). Explainable Artificial Intelligence-Based Decision Support Systems: A recent review. *Electronics (Basel)*, *13*(14), 2842. DOI: 10.3390/electronics13142842

Kovacevic, M., Dagen, T., & Rajter, M. (2025). Leading AI-driven student engagement: The role of digital leadership in higher education. *Education Sciences*, *15*(6), 775. DOI: 10.3390/educsci15060775

Kovári, A. (2024). AI for decision support: Balancing accuracy, transparency, and trust across sectors. *Information, 15*(11), 725. DOI: 10.3390/info15110725

Krakowski, S., Luger, J., & Raisch, S. (2023). Artificial intelligence and the changing sources of competitive advantage. *Strategic Management Journal*, *44*(6), 1425–1452. DOI: 10.1002/smj.3387

Krijger, J., Thuis, T., Ruiter, M. D., Ligthart, E., & Broekman, I. (2022). The AI ethics maturity model. *AI and Ethics*, *2*, 377–392. DOI: 10.1007/s43681-021-00093-8

Kulshrestha, S. (2024). Quantitative assessment of AI's impact on HR practices. *International Journal of Management and Applied Research, 11*(1), 15–28. DOI: 10.18646/2056.111.24-002

Kurter, O. (2025). The use of artificial intelligence for decision-making process for strategic management. *OPUS Journal of Society Research, 22*(2), 195–210. DOI: 10.26466/opusjsr.1632110

Lai, C.-L. (2021). Exploring university students' preferences for AI-assisted learning environment. *Journal of Educational Technology & Society, 24*(4), 1–15.

Lai, Z. C.-C. (2025). The impact of AI-assisted blended learning on writing efficacy and resilience. *International Journal of Computer-Assisted Language Learning and Teaching, 15*(1), 1–21. DOI: 10.4018/IJCALLT.377174

Lancaster, C., Gilreath, H., Mallick, R., & McNeese, N. J. (2024). Evaluating cross-training's impact on perceived teaming outcomes for human-AI teams. Proceedings of the Human Factors and Ergonomics Society ... Annual Meeting. Human Factors and Ergonomics Society. Annual Meeting, 68(1), 1469–1472. DOI: 10.1177/10711813241262033

Lan, Y. (2024). Through tensions to identity-based motivations: Exploring teacher professional identity in artificial intelligence-enhanced teacher training. *Teaching and Teacher Education, 104736*, 104736. Advance online publication. DOI: 10.1016/j.tate.2024.104736

LaValley, M. P. (2008). Logistic regression. *Circulation, 117*(18), 2395–2399. DOI: 10.1161/CIRCULATIONAHA.106.682658 PMID: 18458181

Lee, J. (2025). IT investment and labor displacement. *Telecommunications Policy, 49*(7), 102999. Advance online publication. DOI: 10.1016/j.telpol.2025.102999

Leite, R. (2024). Benefits and drawbacks of artificial intelligence in HRM. *Artificial Intelligence in Production Engineering and Management, 3*(1), 45–58. DOI: 10.5281/zenodo.10684410

Leonardi, R., Giudice, A., Isola, G., & Spampinato, C. (2021). Deep learning in orthodontics. *Seminars in Orthodontics, 27*. Advance online publication. DOI: 10.1053/j.sodo.2021.05.002

Leoni, L., Gueli, G., Ardolino, M., Panizzon, M., & Gupta, S. (2024). AI-empowered KM processes for decision-making: Empirical evidence from worldwide organisations. *Journal of Knowledge Management, 28*(11), 320–347. DOI: 10.1108/JKM-03-2024-0262

Liang, Q., Gou, J., Wang, Z., & Dabić, M. (2024). Affordances and constraints of automation and augmentation. *Journal of Global Information Management, 32*(1), 1–27. DOI: 10.4018/JGIM.357260

Liu, N., Shapira, P., Yue, X., & Guan, J. (2021). Mapping technological innovation dynamics in artificial intelligence domains: Evidence from a global patent analysis. *PLoS One, 16*(12), e0262050. DOI: 10.1371/journal.pone.0262050 PMID: 34972173

Lo Piano, S. (2020). Ethical principles in machine learning and artificial intelligence: Cases from the field and possible ways forward. *Humanities & Social Sciences Communications, 7*(1), 9. Advance online publication. DOI: 10.1057/s41599-020-0501-9

Longo, L., Brcic, M., Cabitza, F., Choi, J., Confalonieri, R., Del Ser, J., … Stumpf, S. (2024). Explainable Artificial Intelligence (XAI) 2.0: A manifesto of open challenges and interdisciplinary research directions. *Information Fusion, 103*, 102301. DOI: 10.1016/j.inffus.2024.102301

Lui, S., Lai, J., Luo, B. N., & Moran, P. (2023). Will goal clarity lower team innovation? A moderated mediation model of inter-team trust. *Journal of Knowledge Management, 27*(4), 975–992. DOI: 10.1108/JKM-10-2021-0787

Lunden, I. (2023). *The fall of Babylon: Failed tele-health startup once valued at nearly $2 B goes bankrupt and sold for parts.* TechCrunch. https://techcrunch.com/2023/08/31/the-fall-of-babylon-failed-tele-health-startup-once-valued-at-nearly-2b-goes-bankrupt-and-sold-for-parts/

Lutfi, L., & Mohammadi, A. (2025). Challenges of implementing AI in HRM. *International Journal of Academic Research in Business & Social Sciences, 15*(1), 78–90. DOI: 10.6007/IJARBSS/v15-i1/12345

Lu, Z., Amin Mahmoo, S. H., Li, Z., & Yin, M. (2024). Mix and Match: Characterizing heterogeneous human behavior in AI-assisted decision making. *Proceedings of the AAAI Conference on Human Computation and Crowdsourcing*, 12, 95–104. DOI: 10.1609/hcomp.v12i1.31604

Lyu, Y., Li, Z., & Zhang, M. (2024). CRUD-RAG: A comprehensive Chinese benchmark for retrieval-augmented generation of large language models. *ACM Transactions on Information Systems.*

MacKinnon, G., & MacLean, T. (2023). Emergency remote teaching: The challenges associated with a context of Second Language instruction. *Canadian Journal of Learning and Technology, 49*(1), 1–23. DOI: 10.21432/cjlt28277

Mahade, A., Elmahi, A., Alomari, K., & Abdalla, A. A. (2025). Leveraging AI-driven insights for sustainable HRM. *Discover Sustainability*, *6*, 45. Advance online publication. DOI: 10.1007/s43621-025-00145-9

Mahmoud, M. & Awad, A. (2024). Impact of electronic customer relationship management on competitive advantage: Mediating role of customer satisfaction in EgyptAir. *Problems and Perspectives in Management, 22*(3), 276–286. https://doi .org/10.21511/ppm.22(3).2024.22

Mahmoud, M., Shma, T., Aziz, A., & Awad, A. (2025). Integrating knowledge management with smart technologies in public pharmaceutical organizations. *Knowledge and Performance Management*, *9*(1), 31–44. DOI: 10.21511/kpm.09(1).2025.03

Majjate, H., Bellarhmouch, Y., Jeghal, A., Yahyaouy, A., Tairi, H., & Zidani, K. A. (2024). Assessing the impact of ethical aspects of recommendation systems on student trust and engagement in E-learning platforms: A multifaceted investigation. *Education and Information Technologies*, 1–25.

Malik, A., Budhwar, P., & Mohan, H., & Srikanth. (. (2023). Employee experience –the missing link for engaging employees: Insights from an MNE 's AI -based HR ecosystem. *Human Resource Management*, *62*(1), 97–115. DOI: 10.1002/hrm.22133

Manthena, S. (2021). Impact of artificial intelligence on recruitment. *International Journal of Innovative Research in Engineering & Multidisciplinary Physical Sciences*, *9*(4), 12–18. DOI: 10.5281/zenodo.10684370

Martinez-Cedillo, A. P., Gavrila, N., Mishra, A., Geangu, E., & Foulsham, T. (2025). Cognitive load affects gaze dynamics during real-world tasks. *Experimental Brain Research, 243*(4), 82. DOI: 10.1007/s00221-025-07037-4 PMID: 40029455

Martin, K., Shilton, K., & Smith, J. (2021). Business and the ethical implications of technology: Introduction to the symposium. *Journal of Business Ethics*, *160*(2), 307–317. DOI: 10.1007/s10551-019-04213-9

Martyn, K., & Kadziński, M. (2023). Deep preference learning for multiple criteria decision analysis. *European Journal of Operational Research*, *305*(2), 781–805. DOI: 10.1016/j.ejor.2022.06.053

Marwala, T. (2024). Governance of AI. In *Mechanism Design*. Behavioral Science, and Artificial Intelligence in International Relations. DOI: 10.1016/B978-0-443-23982-3.00020-8

Mazmanian, M., Orlikowski, W. J., & Yates, J. (2013). The autonomy paradox: The implications of mobile email devices for knowledge professionals. *Organization Science*, *24*(5), 1337–1357. DOI: 10.1287/orsc.1120.0806

McKinsey & Company. (2023a). *The economic potential of generative AI: The next productivity frontier* [Report]. McKinsey Global Institute. https://www.mckinsey.com/capabilities/mckinsey-digital/our-insights/the-economic-potential-of-generative-ai-the-next-productivity-frontier

McKinsey & Company. (2023b). *The state of AI in 2023: Generative AI's breakout year*. McKinsey Global Institute. https://www.mckinsey.com/capabilities/quantumblack/our-insights/the-state-of-ai-in-2023-generative-ais-breakout-year

Mehrabi, N., Morstatter, F., Saxena, N., Lerman, K., & Galstyan, A. (2021). A survey on bias and fairness in machine learning. *ACM Computing Surveys*, *54*(6), 1–35. DOI: 10.1145/3457607

Meijerink, J., Bondarouk, T., & Lepak, D. P. (2021). HRM, algorithmic management, and the rise of artificial intelligence: Human resource management in the digital age. *Human Resource Management Review*, *31*(4), 100787. DOI: 10.1016/j.hrmr.2020.100787

Microsoft. (2024). *Microsoft launches new AI Skills Initiative to help one million people in Australia and New Zealand secure the skills they need to thrive in the AI economy*. Microsoft News. https://news.microsoft.com/source/asia/features/microsoft-launches-new-ai-skills-program-to-expand-opportunities-for-australians-and-new-zealanders/

Mihajlović, M. (2025). Multimodal retrieval-augmented generation in knowledge systems. *Proceedings of the International Conference on AI & KM*.

Mishra, A. N., & Pani, A. K. (2021). Business value appropriation roadmap for artificial intelligence. *VINE Journal of Information and Knowledge Management Systems*, *51*(3), 353–368. DOI: 10.1108/VJIKMS-07-2019-0107

Mitsugi, N., Ijuin, K., Oshiyama, C., Hara, E., & Nishimura, T. (2025). An AI-mediated framework for recursive learning: Transforming individual experiences into organizational knowledge and autonomous engagement in elderly care. *Frontiers in Digital Health*, *7*, 1529072. DOI: 10.3389/fdgth.2025.1529072 PMID: 40678716

Molino, M., Cortese, C. G., & Ghislieri, C. (2020). The promotion of technology acceptance and work engagement in Industry 4.0: From personal resources to information and training. *International Journal of Environmental Research and Public Health*, *17*(7), 2438. DOI: 10.3390/ijerph17072438 PMID: 32260142

Monarca, Y. E., & Bandiola, D. A. N. (2023). Human Resource Management practices, knowledge sharing, and emotional intelligence of unit heads: A causal model on organizational resilience in government agencies in Davao Region. *American Journal of Public Policy and Administration*, *8*(2), 61–73. DOI: 10.47672/ajppa.1611

Moore, P. V. (2021). Artificial intelligence, surveillance, and gig work: The future of employment. *Work, Employment and Society*, *35*(5), 927–936. DOI: 10.1177/09500170211021568

Morris, J. A., & Feldman, D. C. (1996). The dimensions, antecedents, and consequences of emotional labor. *Academy of Management Review*, *21*(4), 986–1010. DOI: 10.2307/259161

Mosqueira-Rey, E., Hernández-Pereira, E., Alonso-Ríos, D., Bobes-Bascarán, J., & Fernández-Leal, Á. (2023). Human-in-the-loop machine learning: A state of the art. *Artificial Intelligence Review*, *56*(4), 10105–10172. DOI: 10.1007/s10462-022-10246-w

Müller, T., Schuberth, F., Bergsiek, M., & Henseler, J. (2022). How can the transition from office to telework be managed? The impact of tasks and workplace suitability on collaboration and work performance. *Frontiers in Psychology*, *13*, 987530. DOI: 10.3389/fpsyg.2022.987530 PMID: 36389574

Murray, A., Rhymer, J., & Sirmon, D. G. (2021). Humans and technology: Forms of conjoined agency in organizations. *Academy of Management Review*, *46*(3), 552–571. DOI: 10.5465/amr.2019.0186

Mustfa, M. J., & Ashiq, S. (2024). Harnessing the power of artificial intelligence for adaptive learning systems: A systematic review. *International Journal of Education and Management Engineering*, *14*(5), 12–22. DOI: 10.5815/ijeme.2024.05.02

Musyokha, S., & Sain, S. (2024). Harnessing the power of artificial intelligence in entrepreneurship: Augmentation, innovation, and ethical considerations. *Researcher Academy Innovation Data Analysis*, *1*(2), 196–213. DOI: 10.69725/raida.v1i2.167

Nadhira Putri, D., & Mangundjaya, W. (2020). Examining the effects of organizational learning on workforce agility through psychological empowerment. *Open Journal for Psychological Research*, *4*(2), 85–94. DOI: 10.32591/coas.ojpr.0402.02085n

Nair, J. (2024). Reconfiguration and transformation for resilience: Building service organizations towards sustainability. *Journal of Services Marketing*, *38*(4), 404–425. DOI: 10.1108/JSM-04-2023-0144

Najana, M. (2024). AI and organizational transformation. *International Journal of Global Information Systems*, *5*(3), 88–102. DOI: 10.5281/zenodo.10684380

Nalini, M. (2024). Transformative horizons: Navigating HR through AI and cloud technologies. *Shanlax International Journal of Management, 11*(1), 1–10. DOI: 10.34293/management.v11iiS1-Jan.7138

Nambisan, S., Lyytinen, K., Majchrzak, A., & Song, M. (2017). Digital innovation management: Reinventing innovation management research in a digital world. *Management Information Systems Quarterly, 41*(1), 223–238. DOI: 10.25300/MISQ/2017/41:1.03

Nandagopal, S. (2025). Securing retrieval-augmented generation pipelines: A comprehensive framework. *Journal of Computer Science and Security*.

Nandini, W., Gustomo, A., & Sushandoyo, D. (2022). The mechanism of an individual's internal process of work engagement, active learning and adaptive performance. *Economies, 7*(7), 165. DOI: 10.3390/economies10070165

Nasir, S., Khan, R. A., & Bai, S. (2023). Ethical framework for harnessing AI in healthcare. *IEEE Access : Practical Innovations, Open Solutions, 11*, 123456–123470. DOI: 10.1109/ACCESS.2023.3298765

NASSCOM. (2023). *Generative AI startup landscape in India – A 2023 perspective*. NASSCOM Research. https://nasscom.in/knowledge-center/publications/generative-ai-startup-landscape-india-2023-perspective

Nazaretsky, T., Cukurova, M., & Alexandron, G. (2022). An instrument for measuring teachers' trust in AI-based educational technology. *LAK22: 12th International Learning Analytics and Knowledge Conference*, 56–66. DOI: 10.1145/3506860.3506866

Ng, D. T. K., Leung, J. K. L., Su, J., Ng, R. C. W., & Chu, S. K. W. (2023). Teachers' AI digital competencies and twenty-first century skills in the post-pandemic world. *Educational Technology Research and Development, 1*(1), 137–161. DOI: 10.1007/s11423-023-10203-6 PMID: 36844361

Nguyen, N. N., & Barbieri, W. (2025). Mentorship in the age of generative AI: ChatGPT to support self-regulated learning of pre-service teachers before and during placements. *Education Sciences, 15*(6), 642. DOI: 10.3390/educsci15060642

Nirabi, A., Rahman, F. A., Habaebi, M. H., Sidek, K. A., & Yusoff, S. H. (2025). Cognitive load assessment through EEG: A dataset from arithmetic and Stroop tasks. *Data in Brief, 60*, 111477. DOI: 10.1016/j.dib.2025.111477 PMID: 40226198

Nuro. (2023). *Building safer autonomous delivery systems* [Report]. Nuro. https://www.nuro.ai/

Nyathani, R. (2023). AI-driven HR analytics. *Journal of Technology and Systems, 5*(2), 45–58. DOI: 10.47941/jts.1513

Odesanya, M. A. B. (2022). Transforming small business landscapes: Artificial Intelligence's evolutionary leap forward. *World Journal of Advanced Research and Reviews, 16*(3), 1141–1157. DOI: 10.30574/wjarr.2022.16.3.1223

Odili, P. O., Daudu, C. D., Adefemi, A., Ekemezie, I. O., & Usiagu, G. S. (2024). AI in recruitment and selection in oil and gas. *Engineering Science & Technology Journal, 8*(1), 33–45. DOI: 10.5281/zenodo.10684390

OECD. (2023). *OECD SME and Entrepreneurship Outlook 2023*. OECD Publishing. DOI: 10.1787/342b8564-

Ojstersek, R., & Buchmeister, B. (2020). Simulation modeling approach for collaborative workplaces' assessment in Sustainable Manufacturing. *Sustainability (Basel), 12*(10), 4103. DOI: 10.3390/su12104103

Olabanji, S. O., Olaniyi, O. O., & Olagbaju, O. O. (2024). Leveraging Artificial Intelligence (AI) and blockchain for enhanced tax compliance and revenue generation in public finance. *Asian Journal of Economics Business and Accounting, 24*(11), 577–587. DOI: 10.9734/ajeba/2024/v24i111577

Olaniyan, O. P. (2023). Ai-driven Talent Analytics for strategic hr decision-making in the United States of America: A review. *International Journal of Management & Entrepreneurship Research, 4*(12), 607–622. DOI: 10.51594/ijmer.v4i12.674

Ollington, N. (2025). Challenging assumptions: AI and teacher assessment identity formation. *The Australian Journal of Teacher Education, 2*(2). Advance online publication. DOI: 10.14221/1835-517X.6510

Olorunsogo, T., Adenyi, A. O., Okolo, C. A., & Babawarun, O. (2024). Ethical considerations in AI-enhanced medical decision support systems: A review. *World Journal of Advanced Engineering Technology and Sciences, 11*(1), 329–336. DOI: 10.30574/wjaets.2024.11.1.0061

Orlikowski, W. J., & Scott, S. V. (2021). Digital work: A research agenda. *Information and Organization, 31*(1), 100340. DOI: 10.1016/j.infoandorg.2021.100340

Paigude, S., Pangarkar, S. C., Hundekari, S., Mali, M., Wanjale, K., & Dongre, Y. (2023). AI in boosting employee retention. *International Journal on Recent and Innovation Trends in Computing and Communication, 11*(6), 112–118. DOI: 10.5281/zenodo.10684395

Pandey, P. (2023). Emotional Intelligence skills in the Age of AI – A Review. *International Journal For Multidisciplinary Research*, *5*(5), 7196. Advance online publication. DOI: 10.36948/ijfmr.2023.v05i05.7196

Parasa, S. K., & Jadugala, S. (2023). Enabling Joule in SAP SuccessFactors. *International Journal of Scientific Research*, *12*(4), 321–325. DOI: 10.5281/zenodo.10684400

Park, C. S.-Y. (2025). Ethical artificial intelligence in nursing workforce management and policymaking: Bridging philosophy and practice. *Journal of Nursing Management*, *7954013*(1), 7954013. Advance online publication. DOI: 10.1155/jonm/7954013 PMID: 40236787

Parker, S. K., & Grote, G. (2022). Automation, algorithms, and beyond: Why work design matters more than ever in a digital world. *Applied Psychology*, *71*(4), 1175–1201. DOI: 10.1111/apps.12241

Pasupuleti, M. K., & Services, N. E. (2025). Augmented Human Intelligence: Converging Generative AI, Quantum Computing, and XR for enhanced human-machine synergy. DOI: 10.62311/nesx/rrv525

Priestley, M., Biesta, G., & Robinson, S. (2015). *Teacher agency: An ecological approach*. Bloomsbury Publishing. DOI: 10.4324/9781315678573-15

Przegalińska, A., Triantoro, T., Kovbasiuk, A., Ciechanowski, L., Freeman, R. B., & Sowa, K. (2025). Collaborative AI in the workplace: Enhancing organizational performance through resource-based and task-technology fit perspectives. *International Journal of Information Management*, *81*, 102853. Advance online publication. DOI: 10.1016/j.ijinfomgt.2024.102853

Putri, K. M. H.Komang Meydiana Hutama PutriYoessy Etna Werdini. (2025). Artificial Intelligence adoption, job insecurity, and psychological resilience: Challenges for employee adaptation in future work environments. *International Journal of Issue Science*, *1*(5). Advance online publication. DOI: 10.71364/ijiss.v1i5.12

PwC. (2023). *2023 Global Workforce Hopes & Fears Survey*. PwC. https://www.pwc.com/gx/en/news-room/press-releases/2023/pwc-global-workforce-hopes-and-fears-survey-2023.html

PwC. (2023). *AI is transforming asset and wealth*. https://www.pwc.com/gx/en/issues/c-suite-insights/the-leadership-agenda/ai-and-wealth-management-a-new-era.html?utm_source=chatgpt.com

Qadeer, A., Awad, A., & Ali, A. (2025). Understanding generative AI implementation in digital advertising among retail SMEs in Pakistan. In Z. Hussain, A. Khan, Md. U. Hossain Uzir, M-N S. Sharipudin, and A. Shaheen (Eds.), *Impacts of AI generated content on brand reputation* (pp. 177–201). IGI Global Scientific Publishing.

Qadeer, A., & Awad, A. (2025). Generative AI in advertisements: A conceptual framework based on the technology acceptance model. In *Impacts of AI generated content on brand reputation* (pp. 109–127). IGI Global., DOI: 10.4018/979-8-3373-4327-3.ch004

Qiao, G., Li, Y., & Hong, A. (2024). The strategic role of digital transformation: Leveraging digital leadership to enhance employee performance and organizational commitment in the digital era. *Systems*, *12*(11), 457. DOI: 10.3390/systems12110457

Qin, F., Li, K., & Yan, J. (2020). Understanding user trust in artificial intelligence-based educational systems: Evidence from China. *British Journal of Educational Technology*, *51*(5), 1693–1710. DOI: 10.1111/bjet.12994

Ragu-Nathan, T. S., Tarafdar, M., Ragu-Nathan, B. S., & Tu, Q. (2008). The consequences of technostress for end users in organizations: Conceptual development and empirical validation. *Information Systems Research*, *19*(4), 417–433. DOI: 10.1287/isre.1070.0165

Rahmadani, V. G., Schaufeli, W. B., Stouten, J., Zhang, Z., & Zulkarnain, Z. (2020). Engaging leadership and its implication for work engagement and job outcomes at the individual and team level: A multi-level longitudinal study. *International Journal of Environmental Research and Public Health*, *17*(3), 776. DOI: 10.3390/ijerph17030776 PMID: 31991897

Rahwan, I. (2017). Society-in-the-loop: Programming the algorithmic social contract. *Ethics and Information Technology*, *20*(1), 5–14. DOI: 10.1007/s10676-017-9430-8

Raisch, S., & Krakowski, S. (2020). Artificial intelligence and management: The automation-augmentation paradox. Academy of Management Review, 2018.0072. DOI: 10.5465/2018.0072

Raisch, S., Foss, N. J., & Laamanen, T. (2023). Unpacking the dynamics of artificial intelligence and organizational change. *Organization Science*, *34*(2), 1–20. DOI: 10.1287/orsc.2022.1621

Raisch, S., & Krakowski, S. (2021). Artificial intelligence and management: The automation–augmentation paradox. *Academy of Management Review*, *46*(1), 192–210. DOI: 10.5465/amr.2018.0072

Ramos Torres, A., & Montoya, L. N. (2024). AI thrust: Ranking emerging powers for tech startup investment in Latin America [Preprint]. *arXiv*. https://arxiv.org/abs/2401.09056

Rane, N., Choudhary, S., & Rane, J. (2023). *Education 4.0 and 5.0: Integrating artificial intelligence (AI) for personalized and adaptive learning*. Nov.

Raneri, S., Lecron, F., Hermans, J., & Fouss, F. (2023). Predictions through Lean startup? Harnessing AI-based predictions under uncertainty. *International Journal of Entrepreneurial Behaviour & Research*, *29*(4), 886–912. DOI: 10.1108/IJEBR-07-2021-0566

Ransbotham, S., Kiron, D., Gerbert, P., & Reeves, M. (2017). *Reshaping Business With Artificial Intelligence.* MIT Sloan Management Review & The Boston Consulting Group. Retrieved from https://sloanreview.mit.edu/projects/reshaping-business-with-artificial-intelligence/

Rathinavel, P., Ravikumar, R. N., Aarthi, S., Habib, M., Salaeva, N., & Pardaev, J. (2025). Augmenting human capabilities. In *Advances in Computational Intelligence and Robotics* (pp. 1–30). IGI Global Scientific Publishing., DOI: 10.4018/979-8-3373-2372-5.ch001

Ravi, P., Masla, J., Kakoti, G., Lin, G., Anderson, E., Taylor, M., Ostrowski, A., Breazeal, C., Klopfer, E., & Abelson, H. (2025). Co-designing large language model tools for project-based learning with K–12 educators. *CHI '25: Proceedings of the 2025 CHI Conference on Human Factors in Computing Systems, 138,* 1-25. DOI: 10.1145/3706598.3713971

Reyes-Norambuena, P., Bascuñán-Ortiz, M., & Sauma, E. (2024). The application of machine learning and deep learning with a multi-criteria decision analysis for pedestrian modeling: A systematic literature review (1999–2023). *Sustainability (Basel)*, *17*(1), 41. DOI: 10.3390/su17010041

Ricker, T. J., & Vergauwe, E. (2022). Boundary conditions for observing cognitive load effects in visual working memory. *Memory & Cognition*, *50*(6), 1169–1185. DOI: 10.3758/s13421-022-01320-3 PMID: 35505223

Rimon, S. M. T. H. (2024). Leveraging Artificial Intelligence in business analytics for informed strategic decision-making: Enhancing operational efficiency, market insights, and competitive advantage. Journal of Artificial Intelligence General Science (JAIGS) ISSN:3006-4023, 6(1), 600–624. DOI: 10.60087/jaigs.v6i1.278

Romanelli, M. (2018). Towards sustainable ecosystems. *Systems Research and Behavioral Science*, *35*(4), 417–426. DOI: 10.1002/sres.2541

Rožman, M., Oreški, D., & Tominc, P. (2022). Integrating AI into a talent management model. *Frontiers in Psychology, 13*. Advance online publication. DOI: 10.3389/fpsyg.2022.1014434 PMID: 36506984

Rushall, Y. K., & Sinha, P. K. (2013). Random Forest Classifiers: A Survey and Future Research Directions. *Int. J. Adv. Comput, 36*(1).

Saad, M., Awad, A., Aziz, A. F., & Shma, T. R. (2025). Influencer marketing's impact on credibility and purchase intention: A study on University of Bisha students in Saudi Arabia. *Innovative Marketing, 21*(1), 326–337. DOI: 10.21511/im.21(1).2025.26

Sabil, S., Bangkara, B. A., Mogea, T., Niswan, E., & Timotius, E. (2023). Identification of HRM improvement strategy using artificial intelligence in modern economic development. *International Journal of Professional Business Review, 8*(6), e01835. DOI: 10.26668/businessreview/2023.v8i6.1835

Sadeghi, K. R., Ojha, D., Kaur, P., Mahto, R. V., & Dhir, A. (2024). Explainable artificial intelligence and agile decision-making in supply-chain cyber resilience. *Decision Support Systems, 180*, 114194. DOI: 10.1016/j.dss.2024.114194

Sadegh-Zadeh, S.-A., Movahhedi, T., Hajiyavand, A. M., & Dearn, K. D. (2023). Exploring undergraduates' perceptions of and engagement in an AI-enhanced online course. *Frontiers in Education, 8*, 1252543. DOI: 10.3389/feduc.2023.1252543

Sadiku, M. N. O., Ashaolu, T. J., Ajayi-Majebi, A., & Musa, S. M. (2021). Augmented Intelligence. *International Journal Of Scientific Advances, 2*(5). Advance online publication. DOI: 10.51542/ijscia.v2i5.17

Sajtos, L., Wang, S., Roy, S., & Flavián, C. (2024). Guest editorial: Collaborating and sharing with AI: a research agenda. *Journal of Service Theory and Practice, 34*(1), 1–6. DOI: 10.1108/JSTP-01-2024-324

Samek, W., Wiegand, T., & Müller, K.-R. (2017). Explainable artificial intelligence: Understanding, visualizing and interpreting deep learning models (arXiv:1708.08296). arXiv. https://arxiv.org/pdf/1708.08296

Samishetti, B. (2025). The impact of AI and robotics on employee roles and HR practices: Challenges, transformations, and strategic workforce management. *Journal of Strategic Human Resource Management, 14*(2), 31–39. DOI: 10.21863/jshrm/2025.14.2.004

Santos, F. P. (2024). Prosocial dynamics in multiagent systems. *AI Magazine, 45*(1), 131–138. DOI: 10.1002/aaai.12143

Saraiva, L. (2024). Moral agency and responsibility in AI systems. *International Journal of Philosophy*, *3*(1), 25–36. DOI: 10.47941/ijp.1867

Sarıoğuz, O., & Miser, E. (2024). AI-powered business model innovation: Analyzing the implications of generative AI on value creation, operational efficiency and market dynamics. *World Journal of Advanced Engineering Technology and Sciences*, *13*(02), 215–228. DOI: 10.30574/wjaets.2024.13.2.0564

Sarkar, P., Posen, A., & Etemad, A. (2023). AVCAffe: A large scale Audio-Visual dataset of cognitive load and affect for remote work. *Proceedings of the AAAI Conference on Artificial Intelligence. AAAI Conference on Artificial Intelligence*, *37*(1), 76–85. DOI: 10.1609/aaai.v37i1.25078

Satvati, N., Kamali, J., Safian Boldaji, F., Khodadadi, M., & Akhondi, S. (2025). AI Integration into language education and teacher identity: An ecological perspective. *Language Teaching Research Quarterly*, *47*, 1–19. DOI: 10.32038/ltrq.2025.47.01

Sauer, C. R., & Burggräf, P. (2025). Hybrid intelligence – systematic approach and framework to determine the level of Human-AI collaboration for production management use cases. *Production Engineering*, *19*(3–4), 525–541. DOI: 10.1007/s11740-024-01326-7

Schein, E. H. (2010). *Organizational Culture and Leadership* (4th ed.). Jossey-Bass.

Schön, D. A. (1992). *The reflective practitioner: How professionals think in action* (1st ed.). Routledge.

Senge, P. (1990). *The fifth discipline: The art and practice of the learning organization*. Doubleday/Currency.

Seremeti, L., & Anastasiadou, S. (2025). The transformative impact of artificial intelligence (AI) on strategic decision-making. In *Strategic Innovative Marketing and Tourism* (pp. 427–435). Springer Nature Switzerland., DOI: 10.1007/978-3-031-81962-9_47

Settles, B., & Meeder, B. (2016). A trainable spaced repetition model for language learning. In *Proceedings of the 54th Annual Meeting of the Association for Computational Linguistics* (Volume 1: Long Papers) (pp. 1848-1858). Association for Computational Linguistics. DOI: 10.18653/v1/P16-1174

Sevcenko, M., Haslacher, D., Herff, C., & Zander, T. O. (2023). Theory-based approach for assessing cognitive load during time-critical resource-managing human–computer interactions: An eye-tracking study. *Journal on Multimodal User Interfaces*, *17*(1), 1–19. DOI: 10.1007/s12193-022-00398-y

Shaddiq, S., Khuzaini, & Irpan, M. (2023). Governance of human resources management in the digital era. *Journal of Business and Management Studies*, *5*(2), 1–10. DOI: 10.32996/jbms.2023.5.3.8

Shaheen, A., Khataan, A., Awad, A., Shams Eldin, A. Y., & Elnour, A. (2025). The role of influencer content value and credibility in purchase intention. *Innovative Marketing*, *21*(3), 14–30. DOI: 10.21511/im.21(3).2025.02

Shahul, E. S., ... (2023). RAGAs: Automated evaluation of retrieval augmented generation. *arXiv preprint arXiv:2309.15217.*

Shahzad, M., Xu, S., Naveed, W., Nusrat, S., & Zahid, I. (2023). Investigating the impact of artificial intelligence on HR functions. *Heliyon*, *9*, e21818. Advance online publication. DOI: 10.1016/j.heliyon.2023.e21818 PMID: 38034787

Shams Eldin, A. Y., Elnour, A., Hassan, R. O. A., & Awad, A. (2025). The role of technological and environmental factors in creating business value from social media dynamic capabilities for SMEs in Saudi Arabia. *Humanities & Social Sciences Communications*, *12*(1), 1431. DOI: 10.1057/s41599-025-05784-x

Sharma, C. (2025). Retrieval-augmented generation: A comprehensive survey of architectures, enhancements, and robustness frontiers. *arXiv preprint arXiv:2502.04567.*

Shi, K. (2025). The application and risks of AI in enterprise strategic decision-making. Advances in Economics. *Management and Political Sciences*, *190*(1), 120–129. DOI: 10.54254/2754-1169/2025.LD24750

Shma, T. R., Awad, A., & Aziz, A. F. (2025). Investment behavior in the Egyptian stock market: The impact of social media on investor decision-making. *Investment Management and Financial Innovations*, *22*(1), 203–212. DOI: 10.21511/imfi.22(1).2025.16

Shneiderman, B. (2022). *Human-Centered AI: Ensuring human control in an era of intelligent machines*. Oxford University Press. DOI: 10.1093/oso/9780192845290.001.0001

Shrestha, Y. R., Ben-Menahem, S. M., & von Krogh, G. (2019). Organizational decision-making structures in the age of artificial intelligence. *California Management Review*, *61*(4), 66–83. DOI: 10.1177/0008125619862257

Siemon, D. (2022). Elaborating team roles for artificial intelligence-based teammates in human-AI collaboration. *Group Decision and Negotiation*, *31*(5), 871–912. DOI: 10.1007/s10726-022-09792-z

SignalFire. (2024). *Beacon AI: How SignalFire uses machine-learning and data-driven investing to find startups.* https://www.signalfire.com/beacon-ai

Simbeck, K. (2019). HR analytics and ethics. IBM Journal of Research and Development, 63(4/5), 9:1–9:12. DOI: 10.1147/JRD.2019.2915067

Singh, A., & Gupta, P. (2025). Agentic retrieval-augmented generation: A survey on agentic RAG. *arXiv preprint arXiv:2501.09876.*

Singh, A., & Pandey, J. (2023). Artificial intelligence adoption in extended HR ecosystems: Enablers and barriers. An abductive case research. *Frontiers in Psychology, 14*, 1339782. DOI: 10.3389/fpsyg.2023.1339782 PMID: 38327504

Slack Technologies. (2025). *Guide to AI features in Slack.* Retrieved from https://slack.com/help/articles/25076892548883-Guide-to-AI-features-in-Slack

Smith, T., Dost, G., Dhasmana, G., & Patwari, P. (2025). *AI is capturing the digital dollar. What's left for the rest of the tech estate?* Deloitte Insights. https://www.deloitte.com/us/en/insights/topics/digital-transformation/ai-tech-investment-roi.html

Soleimani, M., Intezari, A., Arrowsmith, J., Pauleen, D. J., & Taskin, N. (2025). Reducing AI bias in recruitment and selection: An integrative grounded approach. *International Journal of Human Resource Management, 36*(14), 2480–2515. DOI: 10.1080/09585192.2025.2480617

Sonnentag, S., & Fritz, C. (2015). Recovery from job stress: The stressor-detachment model as an integrative framework. *Journal of Organizational Behavior, 36*(S1), S72–S103. DOI: 10.1002/job.1924

Sottilare, R. A., Shawn Burke, C., Salas, E., Sinatra, A. M., Johnston, J. H., & Gilbert, S. B. (2017). Designing adaptive instruction for teams: A meta-analysis. *International Journal of Artificial Intelligence in Education, 2*(2), 225–264. DOI: 10.1007/s40593-017-0146-z

Spagnoli, P., Molino, M., Molinaro, D., Giancaspro, M. L., Manuti, A., & Ghislieri, C. (2023). Workaholism and technostress during remote working. *Frontiers in Psychology, 14*, 1162453. DOI: 10.3389/fpsyg.2023.1162453 PMID: 33424730

Spector, J. M., & Ma, J. (2014). Ethical concerns and privacy issues in educational technology. In Spector, J. M., Merrill, M. D., Elen, J., & Bishop, M. J. (Eds.), *Handbook of research on educational communications and technology* (4th ed., pp. 719–729). Springer. DOI: 10.1007/978-1-4614-3185-5

Stahl, B. C., & Eke, D. (2024). The ethics of ChatGPT – Exploring the ethical issues of an emerging technology. *International Journal of Information Management, 74*, 102700. DOI: 10.1016/j.ijinfomgt.2023.102700

Stahl, B. C., Schroeder, D., & Rodrigues, R. (2023). The ethics of artificial intelligence: An introduction. In *Ethics of Artificial Intelligence* (pp. 1–7). Springer International Publishing., DOI: 10.1007/978-3-031-17040-9_1

Stanikzai, M. E., & Mittal, E. (2025). Leveraging AI-generated and human-generated content for maximised user engagement in contentpreneurs' innovation and creativity. *Journal of Innovation and Entrepreneurship, 14*(1), 91. Advance online publication. DOI: 10.1186/s13731-025-00529-1

Steyvers, M., & Kumar, A. (2024). Three challenges for AI-assisted decision-making. Perspectives on Psychological Science: A Journal of the Association for Psychological Science, 19(5), 722–734. DOI: 10.1177/17456916231181102

Stone, B. W. (2025). Generative AI in higher education: Uncertain students, ambiguous use cases, and mercenary perspectives. *Teaching of Psychology, 52*(3), 347–356. DOI: 10.1177/00986283241305398

Subrahmanyam, S. (2025a). AI and Automation: The Intersection of Human Autonomy and Machine Learning. In Tsvasman, L. (Ed.), *Cybernetic Leadership for Sustainable Innovation* (pp. 237–262). IGI Global Scientific Publishing. DOI: 10.4018/979-8-3373-2484-5.ch009

Subrahmanyam, S. (2025b). Business, Digital Transformation, and Entrepreneurship. In Ordóñez de Pablos, P. (Ed.), *Shaping Green and Inclusive Economies Through Innovative Entrepreneurship* (pp. 1–34). IGI Global Scientific Publishing. DOI: 10.4018/979-8-3373-1097-8.ch001

Subrahmanyam, S. (2025c). Using AI-Driven Analysis for Training and Leadership Growth. In Mrabet, J., Boudagga, S., Sharma, R., & Bansal, R. (Eds.), *Harnessing Emotion AI for Customer Support and Employee Wellbeing* (pp. 321–352). IGI Global Scientific Publishing. DOI: 10.4018/979-8-3373-3658-9.ch013

Subrahmanyam, S., & El Samra, H. (2025). Startups and AI: Fostering Entrepreneurship in the MENA Region. In Azoury, N., & Yahchouchi, G. (Eds.), *AI in the Middle East for Growth and Business* (pp. 77–92). Palgrave Macmillan. DOI: 10.1007/978-3-031-75589-7_6

Sun, C., Zhao, X., Guo, B., & Chen, N. (2025). Will employee-AI collaboration enhance employees' proactive behavior? A study based on the conservation of resources theory. *Behavioral Sciences (Basel, Switzerland)*, *15*(5), 648. Advance online publication. DOI: 10.3390/bs15050648 PMID: 40426426

Tahsiri, M. (2023). Designing post-digital hybrid workplaces. Enquiry A Journal for Architectural Research, 20(1), 1–19. DOI: 10.17831/enqarcc.v20i1.1140

Tan, X., Cheng, G., & Ling, M. H. (2025). Artificial intelligence in teaching and teacher professional development: A systematic review. *Computers and Education: Artificial Intelligence*, *100355*, 100355. Advance online publication. DOI: 10.1016/j.caeai.2024.100355

Tarafdar, M., Cooper, C. L., & Stich, J. F. (2020). The technostress trifecta—Techno eustress, techno distress and design. *Information Systems Journal*, *30*(1), 6–42. DOI: 10.1111/isj.12169

Team Leader Bangladesh. (2024). Impact of artificial intelligence (AI) on existing businesses and the global economy. *Global Mainstream Journal*, *1*(1), 1–6. DOI: 10.62304/ijbm.v1i1.120

TECHNOLOGY, I. I. Y. M. B. A. S. O. F. M. C. A. H. C. O. F. E. A. N. D., Anjum, S. S., Siddiqua, K. A., Firdous, Z. T., & Navfal, K. M. (2025). AI implementation in company operation and decision making. INTERNATIONAL JOURNAL OF SCIENTIFIC RESEARCH IN ENGINEERING AND MANAGEMENT, 09(09), 1–9. DOI: 10.55041/IJSREM52675

Thakur, N., University, A. S., Sharma, A., & University, A. S. (2024). Ethical considerations in AI-driven financial decision making. *Journal of Management & Public Policy*, *15*(3), 41–57. DOI: 10.47914/jmpp.2024.v15i3.003

Topcuoglu, E., Oktaysoy, O., Erdogan, S. U., Kaygin, E., & Karafakioglu, E. (2023). The mediating role of job security in the impact of digital leadership on job satisfaction and life satisfaction. *Marketing and Management of Innovations*, *14*(1), 122–132. DOI: 10.21272/mmi.2023.1-11

Trist, E. L., & Bamforth, K. W. (1951). Some social and psychological consequences of the longwall method of coal-getting. *Human Relations*, *4*(1), 3–38. DOI: 10.1177/001872675100400101

Tsekouropoulos, G., Vasileiou, A., Hoxha, G., Theocharis, D., Theodoridou, E., & Grigoriadis, T. (2025). Leadership 4.0: Navigating the challenges of the digital transformation in healthcare and beyond. *Administrative Sciences*, *15*(6), 194. DOI: 10.3390/admsci15060194

Tsiskaridze, R., Reinhold, K., & Jarvis, M. (2023). Innovating HRM recruitment: A comprehensive review of AI deployment. *Marketing and Management of Innovations, 14*(4), 239–254. DOI: 10.21272/mmi.2023.4-18

Tummala, V. S., Burris-Melville, T. S., & Eskridge, T. C. (2025a). AI as a team member: Redefining collaboration. *Journal of Leadership Studies, 18*(4), 67–80. DOI: 10.1002/jls.70003

Ugwuja, C. G., & Department of Management University of Nigeria Nigeria, E. C. (2024). Artificial intelligence as a Strategic Decision-maker in modern business. NEWPORT INTERNATIONAL JOURNAL OF RESEARCH IN EDUCATION, 4(2), 57–62. DOI: 10.59298/NIJRE/2024/42357628

Upadhyay, D. A. K. (2025). The impact of Artificial Intelligence on strategic decision-making in businesses. *INTERANTIONAL JOURNAL OF SCIENTIFIC RESEARCH IN ENGINEERING AND MANAGEMENT, 09*(02), 1–9. DOI: 10.55041/IJSREM41630

Upstart. (2024). *How AI drives more affordable credit access.* https://info.upstart.com/how-ai-drives-more-affordable-credit-access

Uras Eren, E., & Atay, D. (2025). Constructing professional identities: The role of school climate in early-career university teachers. *Asian-Pacific Journal of Second and Foreign Language Education, 10*(1), 1–19. DOI: 10.1186/s40862-025-00329-w

Väänänen, A., Anttila, T., Turtiainen, J., & Varje, P. (2024). Algorithmic management and employee well-being: A systematic review. *Human Relations, 77*(2), 215–245. DOI: 10.1177/00187267231123001

Vahtras, L. (2025). *The rise of AI-powered, borderless businesses. AI Journal.* https://aijourn.com/the-rise-of-ai-powered-borderless-businesses/

Valeriani, D., Cinel, C., & Poli, R. (2019). Hybrid collaborative brain–computer interfaces to augment group decision-making. In *Neuroergonomics* (pp. 187–190). Elsevier., DOI: 10.1016/B978-0-12-811926-6.00031-2

Van der Watt, M. (2023). Discouraging the demand that fosters sex trafficking: Collaboration through augmented intelligence. *Societies (Basel, Switzerland), 13*(4), 94. DOI: 10.3390/soc13040094

Van Rooy, D. (2024). Human–machine collaboration for enhanced decision-making in governance. *Data & Policy, 6*(e60), e60. Advance online publication. DOI: 10.1017/dap.2024.72

Varma, A., Dawkins, C. E., & Chaudhuri, K. (2021). Artificial intelligence and people management. *Proceedings - Academy of Management, 2021*(1), 11357. DOI: 10.5465/AMBPP.2021.11014abstract

Vartiainen, H., Vuojärvi, H., Saramäki, K., Eriksson, M., Ratinen, I., Torssonen, P., Vanninen, P., & Pöllänen, S. (2022). Cross-boundary collaboration and knowledge creation in an online higher education course. British Journal of Educational Technology. *British Journal of Educational Technology, 53*(5), 1304–1320. DOI: 10.1111/bjet.13186

Verganti, R., Vendraminelli, L., & Iansiti, M. (2020). Innovation and design in the age of artificial intelligence. *Journal of Product Innovation Management, 37*(3), 212–227. DOI: 10.1111/jpim.12523

Verma, A., Venkatesan, M., Kumar, M., & Verma, J. (2023). The future of work post Covid-19: Key perceived HR implications of hybrid workplaces in India. *Journal of Management Development, 42*(1), 13–28. DOI: 10.1108/JMD-11-2021-0304

Vithlani, J., Hawksworth, C., Elvidge, J., Ayiku, L., & Dawoud, D. (2023). Economic evaluations of artificial intelligence-based healthcare interventions: A systematic literature review of best practices in their conduct and reporting. *Frontiers in Pharmacology, 14*, 1220950. DOI: 10.3389/fphar.2023.1220950 PMID: 37693892

Voigt, P., & von dem Bussche, A. (2017). *The EU General Data Protection Regulation (GDPR): A practical guide*. Springer International Publishing AG. DOI: 10.1007/978-3-319-57959-7

Vrontis, D., Christofi, M., Pereira, V., Tarba, S., Makrides, A., & Trichina, E. (2022). Artificial intelligence, robotics, advanced technologies and human resource management: A systematic review. *International Journal of Human Resource Management, 33*(6), 1237–1266. DOI: 10.1080/09585192.2020.1871398

Wahid, A., & Awad, A. (2025). Role of AI chatbots in enhancing customer satisfaction and customer loyalty. In Z. Hussain, A. Khan, Md. U. Hossain Uzir, M-N S. Sharipudin, and A. Shaheen (Eds.), *Impacts of AI generated content on brand reputation* (pp. 129–147). IGI Global Scientific Publishing.

Wang, G., & Wu, L. (2025). Artificial intelligence, lean startup method, and product innovations. (Preprint). *arXiv*. https://doi.org//arXiv.2506.16334DOI: 10.48550

Wang, B., Liu, Y., Qian, J., & Parker, S. K. (2021). Achieving effective remote working during the COVID-19 pandemic: A work design perspective. *Applied Psychology, 70*(1), 16–59. DOI: 10.1111/apps.12290 PMID: 33230359

Wang, J. (2024). Impact of artificial intelligence adoption on the psychological contract and job satisfaction of Chinese employees - the moderator role of industry characteristics. *Interdisciplinary Humanities and Communication Studies, 1*(6). Advance online publication. DOI: 10.61173/pkmf8z05

Wang, S., & Zhang, H. (2025). Generative artificial intelligence and internationalization green innovation. *Technology in Society, 82*, 102898. Advance online publication. DOI: 10.1016/j.techsoc.2025.102898

Wang, T., Lin, X., & Sheng, F. (2022). Digital leadership and exploratory innovation: From the dual perspectives of strategic orientation and organizational culture. *Frontiers in Psychology, 13*, 1–20. DOI: 10.3389/fpsyg.2022.902693 PMID: 36176785

Wang, X., Guo, H., & Nachiangmai, S. (2024). R&d team trust on innovation performance: The role of knowledge sharing, knowledge acquisition, and innovation strategy. The EUrASEANs. *Journal on Global Socio-Economic Dynamics, 2*(45), 122–147. DOI: 10.35678/2539-5645.2(45).2024.122-147

Weber, M., Beutter, M., Weking, J., Böhm, M., & Krcmar, H. (2022). AI startup business models: Key characteristics and directions for entrepreneurship research. *Business & Information Systems Engineering, 64*(1), 91–109. DOI: 10.1007/s12599-021-00732-w

Wen, Y., Wang, J., & Chen, X. (2025). Trust and AI weight: human-AI collaboration in organizational management decision-making. *Frontiers in Organizational Psychology, 3*(1419403), 1419403. Advance online publication. DOI: 10.3389/forgp.2025.1419403

Wilson, H. J., & Daugherty, P. R. (2018). Collaborative intelligence: Humans and AI are joining forces. *Harvard Business Review, 96*(4), 114–123.

Winfield, A. F. T., & Jirotka, M. (2018). Ethical governance is essential to building trust in robotics and artificial intelligence systems. *Philosophical Transactions. Series A, Mathematical, Physical, and Engineering Sciences, 376*(2133), 20180085. DOI: 10.1098/rsta.2018.0085 PMID: 30323000

Wong, A. (2025). Sustainable HR practices with AI. In *Artificial Intelligence and Sustainability: Innovations in Business and Managerial Practices* (pp. 80–107). SBS Swiss Business School., DOI: 10.70301/SBS.MONO.2025.1.5

World Economic Forum (WEF). (2023). *Generative AI could add trillions to the global economy.* https://www.weforum.org/stories/2023/07/generative-ai-could-add-trillions-to-global-economy

Wrzesniewski, A., & Dutton, J. E. (2001). Crafting a job: Revisioning employees as active crafters of their work. *Academy of Management Review, 26*(2), 179–201. DOI: 10.2307/259118

Wu, W., & Chen, L. (2025). MultiRAG: A knowledge-guided framework for mitigating hallucination in multi-source retrieval augmented generation. *2025 IEEE 41st International Conference on Data Engineering (ICDE).*

Wu, D., & Li, X. (2025). A systematic literature review of financial product recommendation systems. *Information (Basel), 16*(3), 196. DOI: 10.3390/info16030196

Wu, W., Huang, T., & Gong, K. (2020). Ethical principles and governance technology development of AI in China. *Engineering (Beijing), 6*(3), 302–309. Advance online publication. DOI: 10.1016/j.eng.2019.12.015

Xu, L., Liu, X., & Xiao, Y. (2024). Language teachers' emotions in online classrooms: Relations among teachers' appraisals of classroom events, emotional responses, and instructional practices. *Asian-Pacific Journal of Second and Foreign Language Education, 1*(1), 1–23. DOI: 10.1186/s40862-024-00301-0

Yan, S. Q., Gu, J. C., & Zhu, X. (2024). Corrective retrieval augmented generation. *arXiv preprint arXiv:2401.15884.*

Yang, Q., & Lee, Y.-C. (2024). Ethical AI in financial inclusion: The role of algorithmic fairness on user satisfaction and recommendation. *Big Data and Cognitive Computing, 8*(9), 105. DOI: 10.3390/bdcc8090105

Yang, S., Ogata, H., Matsui, T., & Chen, N. (2021). Human-centered artificial intelligence in education. *Computers and Education: Artificial Intelligence, 2*, 100008. Advance online publication. DOI: 10.1016/j.caeai.2021.100008

Yang, T., & Jiang, J. (2024). Realizing augmenting technology–human symbiosis: A qualitative examination from the organizational learning perspective. *SAGE Open, 14*(4), 21582440241290148. Advance online publication. DOI: 10.1177/21582440241290148

Yin, M. (2024). Accounting for human engagement behavior to enhance AI-assisted decision making. *Proceedings of the AAAI Symposium Series*, 3(1), 68–70. DOI: 10.1609/aaaiss.v3i1.31184

Yorks, L., Rotatori, D., Sung, S., & Justice, S. (2020). Workplace reflection in the age of AI: Materiality, technology, and machines. *Advances in Developing Human Resources, 22*(3), 308–319. DOI: 10.1177/1523422320927299

Yu, H., ... (2024). Evaluation of retrieval-augmented generation: A survey. *arXiv preprint arXiv:2405.07437.*

Yusuf, A. A., Maryam, A. K., Shiddieqy, D. F., & Awad, A. (2025). The role of Sukuk financing in economic growth and poverty reduction: Empirical evidence from selected ASEAN countries. *Public and Municipal Finance, 14*(2), 42–50. DOI: 10.21511/pmf.14(2).2025.04

Zaidi, S. Y. A., Aslam, M. F., Mahmood, F., Ahmad, B., & Raza, S. B. (2025). How will artificial intelligence (AI) evolve organizational leadership? Understanding the perspectives of technopreneurs. *Global Business and Organizational Excellence, 44*(3), 66–83. DOI: 10.1002/joe.22275

Zakeri, Z., Arif, A., Omurtag, A., Breedon, P., & Khalid, A. (2023, October 16). Multimodal assessment of cognitive workload using neural, subjective and behavioural measures in smart factory settings. *Preprints.* DOI: 10.20944/preprints202310.0948.v1

Zapier. (2023). *What is AI automation + how to use it.* https://zapier.com/blog/ai-automation/

Zárate-Torres, R., Rey-Sarmiento, C. F., Acosta-Prado, J. C., Gómez-Cruz, N. A., Rodríguez Castro, D. Y., & Camargo, J. (2025). Influence of leadership on human-artificial intelligence collaboration. *Behavioral Sciences (Basel, Switzerland), 15*(7), 873. DOI: 10.3390/bs15070873 PMID: 40723657

Zein, A. (2025). Artificial intelligence in strategic decision making. *The International Journal of Social Sciences (Islamabad), 1*(1), 17–25. DOI: 10.51805/ijss.v1i1.311

Zhai, X. (2024). Transforming teachers' roles and agencies in the era of generative AI: Perceptions, acceptance, knowledge, and practices. *Journal of Science Education and Technology.* Advance online publication. DOI: 10.1007/s10956-024-10174-0

Zhang, C., Schießl, J., Plößl, L., Hofmann, F., & Gläser-Zikuda, M. (2023). Acceptance of artificial intelligence among pre-service teachers: A multigroup analysis. *International Journal of Educational Technology in Higher Education, 20*(1), 49. DOI: 10.1186/s41239-023-00420-7

Zhang, G., Chong, L., Kotovsky, K., & Cagan, J. (2023). Trust in an AI versus a human teammate. *Computers in Human Behavior, 139*, 107536. Advance online publication. DOI: 10.1016/j.chb.2022.107536

Zhang, J.-C., Zain, A. M., Zhou, K., Chen, X., & Zhang, R.-M. (2024). A review of recommender systems based on knowledge graph embeddings. *Expert Systems with Applications, 249*, 123876. DOI: 10.1016/j.eswa.2024.123876

Zhang, W., & Wang, Y. (2025). Hallucination mitigation for retrieval-augmented large language models: A review. *Mathematics*, *13*(5), 856. DOI: 10.3390/math13050856

Zhang, Y., & Tian, Y. (2021). Choice of pricing and marketing strategies in reward-based crowdfunding campaigns. *Decision Support Systems*, *144*, 113520. DOI: 10.1016/j.dss.2021.113520

Zhang, Z. (2025). The role of artificial intelligence tools on Chinese EFL learners' self-regulation, resilience and autonomy. *European Journal of Education*, *60*(2), e70127. Advance online publication. DOI: 10.1111/ejed.70127

Zhao, M., Simmons, R., & Admoni, H. (2025). The role of adaptation in collective human-AI teaming. *Topics in Cognitive Science*, *17*(2), 291–323. DOI: 10.1111/tops.12633 PMID: 36374986

Zheng, J., Zhang, J., Kamal, M., Liang, X., & Alzeiby, E. (2025). Unpacking human-AI interaction. *Journal of Business Research*, *196*, 115406. Advance online publication. DOI: 10.1016/j.jbusres.2025.115406

Zhou, S., & Gorman, J. C. (2024). The impact of communication timing and sequencing on team performance: A comparative study of human-AI and all-human teams. *Proceedings of the Human Factors and Ergonomics Society ... Annual Meeting. Human Factors and Ergonomics Society. Annual Meeting*, *68*(1), 1769–1774. https://doi.org/DOI: 10.1177/10711813241275090

Zhu, X., & Li, Y. (2025). Knowledge graph-guided retrieval augmented generation. *arXiv preprint arXiv:2502.01234*. DOI: 10.18653/v1/2025.naacl-long.449

Zohuri, B., & Behgounia, F. (2023). AI-driven nano-based drug delivery systems. In *A Handbook of Artificial Intelligence in Drug Delivery*. DOI: 10.1016/B978-0-323-89925-3.00007-1

Zuboff, S. (2019). *The age of surveillance capitalism: The fight for a human future at the new frontier of power*. PublicAffairs.

About the Contributors

Rajeh Almasradi is an Associate Professor of Business Administration and Advisor to the President for Entrepreneurship at the University of Bisha, Saudi Arabia. He received his Ph.D. in Organizational Behavior from Universiti Teknologi Malaysia (UTM), an M.Sc. in Leadership and Human Development from Murray State University, USA, and a B.Sc. in Public Administration from King Khalid University. He has held various leadership roles at the University of Bisha, including Vice Dean of the College of Business, Secretary-General of the Scientific Council, and Director of the Innovation and Entrepreneurship Center CV_Dr_Rajeh_ Almasradi . His research interests include organizational behavior, leadership, and entrepreneurship, with publications in Scopus-indexed journals such as Advanced Science Letters, International Journal of Recent Technology and Engineering, and Psycho Idea. Dr. Almasradi is actively engaged in academic committees, conferences, and training initiatives that foster innovation, entrepreneurship, and organizational excellence.

Abdelrehim Awad is an Associate Professor of Business Administration at the College of Business, University of Bisha, Saudi Arabia. He holds a Ph.D. in Business Administration from Al-Azhar University, Cairo, with a specialization in marketing and strategic management. His research focuses on digital marketing, supply chain innovation, artificial intelligence applications, and organizational development. Dr. Awad has published extensively in Scopus- and WoS-indexed journals, including recent works on ethical leadership, digital transformation, influencer marketing, and AI-driven decision-making Abdelrehim Awad 2025 B . He is also an editor and contributor to several IGI Global volumes and serves on editorial boards of multiple international journals. His work emphasizes bridging theory and practice, advancing innovation and entrepreneurship in business and management research.

***

Kathirvel Ayyaswamy, acquired, B.E.(CSE), M.E. (CSE) from Crescent Engineering College affiliated to University of Madras and Ph. D (CSE.) from Anna University. He is currently working as Professor, Dept of Computer Science and Engineering, Saveetha Engineering College, Chennai. In-charge for CSE Cyber Forensics Research Group. He is a studious researcher by himself, completed 18 sponsored research projects worth of Rs 103 lakhs and published more than 110 articles in journals and conferences. 6 research scholars have completed Ph. D and 7 under progress under his guidance. He is working as scientific and editorial board member of many journals. He has reviewed dozens of papers in many journals. He has author of 13 books. His research interests are protocol development for wireless ad hoc networks, security in ad hoc network, data communication and networks, mobile computing, wireless networks, WSN and DTN. He is a Life member of the ISTE (India), IACSIT (Singapore), Life Member IAENG (Hong Kong), Member ICST (Europe), IAES, etc. He has given a number of guest lecturers/expert talks and seminars, workshops and symposiums.

Ufuk Cebeci is a Professor of Industrial Engineering at Istanbul Technical University. He earned his bachelor's, MBA, and Ph.D. degrees at ITU. His research focuses on quality, New product development, and manufacturing systems management, artificial intelligence applications in industry, and decision-making methods under uncertainty. Prof. Cebeci has published widely, supervises graduate students, and leads projects on digital transformation in manufacturing.

Onur Dogan is an associate professor at Izmir Bakircay University, and formerly, was a postdoctoral researcher at the University of Padua. He graduated from Sakarya University with a bachelor's degree in industrial engineering in 2010 and received a master's degree and Doctor of Philosophy in Industrial Engineering from Istanbul Technical University in 2013 and 2019, respectively. He studied intelligent decision support systems, lean manufacturing, and quality approaches such as QFD, FMEA, or DOE during his master's thesis. Process mining was the primary focus of his Ph.D. study. He is one of the first academicians who have a Ph.D. title on process mining in Turkiye. During his doctorate study, he had been at Universitat Politecnica de Valencia as a visitor researcher for a 12-month research project. As Smart University and Digital Transformation Coordinator, he coordinates one of the five major projects of İzmir Bakırçay University. His current research areas are process mining, machine learning, robotic process automation, and digital transformation, fuzzy MDCM.

Sahar Mahmoud Haboh is the Dean of the Faculty of Business Administration at Midocean University, a fully online distance-learning institution. She holds a

PhD in Educational Technology and has extensive academic and professional experience in management, digital transformation, and contemporary educational practices. Her research interests focus on digital marketing, artificial intelligence applications in business and education, hybrid and remote work environments, digital training systems, as well as the ethical and social dimensions of emerging technologies. She has published and contributed to a number of peer-reviewed journal articles and book chapters with internationally recognized academic publishers. Dr. Haboh is actively engaged in curriculum development, academic leadership, and quality assurance in higher education institutions, with a particular emphasis on e-learning and technology-enhanced education. She also continues to supervise academic research and participate in international conferences and scholarly activities.

Mustafa Kellekci, M.A., M.Sc. is a multidisciplinary researcher and academic in the Department of Industrial Engineering at Istanbul Technical University (ITU), Türkiye. His research centers on decision-making under uncertainty, with a particular emphasis on assessing early-stage startup investments using multi-criteria decision-making (MCDM) techniques. He holds advanced degrees—including an M.Sc. in Engineering from TU Berlin and an M.A. in Finance from Marmara University—and completed a double major in Mechanical Engineering and Management Engineering at ITU. He is specializing in engineering, decision sciences, venture capital, machine learning and artificial intelligence. As a multidiciplinary researcher, he is known for combining theoretical methods with practical applications, aiming to help angel investors, venture capital firms as well as government bodies to make better and more transparent investment decisions when data is incomplete or uncertain.

Arush Khare is a highly motivated student at the Jaypee University of Engineering and Technology, specializing in the intersection of Machine Learning (ML). His academic focus involves applying sophisticated ML techniques, particularly deep learning models, to solve complex challenges within NLP, such as semantic understanding and text generation. He is actively involved in projects that explore the practical deployment of these technologies, emphasizing their utility in real-world applications and data-driven decision-making.

Kunj Bihari Meena is a faculty member and researcher in Computer Science and Engineering at Jaypee University and Engineering Technology Guna. Dr. Meena has published multiple papers in reputed international journals and conferences, including SCI and Scopus-indexed publications. He has received Best Paper Awards for his research contributions and serves as a reviewer for prestigious SCI/Scopus journals and conferences. His areas of research include image processing, digital image forensics, deep learning, and blockchain.

Sumit Kumar Pandey is an accomplished Assistant Professor at the Department of Journalism and Mass Communication, Manipal University, Jaipur, with a Ph.D. from Kashi Vidyapith University, Varanasi. A UGC NET qualifier, he holds an M.Phil. and Master's in Journalism and Mass Communication, both with Gold Medals, alongside a Post Graduate Diploma in Electronic Media Management & Film Production. With eight years of experience in academia and research focusing on New Media, Print Media, and Radio, Dr. Pandey has published 28 papers/chapters in Scopus-indexed, UGC care-listed, and peer-reviewed journals/edited books, and authored a book on Atal Bihari Vajpayee's contributions to journalism and nation-building. He holds two patents, including an AI-based multimedia kiosk for wildlife tourism (2024) and a cloud-based digital display branding device (2025). A former Radio Presenter at All India Radio and IGNOU Gyan Vani FM, he has organized over 40 and participated in over 70 national/international academic events, showcasing his expertise in evolving communication landscapes.

Ravikumar R. Natarajan is an experienced academician with over 12+ years of teaching and research expertise across institutions in India, the UAE, and the Maldives. He currently serves as an Assistant Professor at Marwadi University, Rajkot, specializing in Machine Learning, Recommender Systems, and AI-driven applications in healthcare and security. He holds a Ph.D. in Machine Learning and Recommender Systems from Amity University, Jaipur, a Master of Engineering in CSE from VMRF University, Salem, and a Bachelor of Engineering in CSE from Anna University. He also has a MiniMBA from the Swiss eLearning Institute. Dr. Ravikumar has authored more than 8+ multiple SCIE/Scopus-indexed journal articles, 25+ IEEE/Springer conference papers, and co-authored a book on Artificial Intelligence. He has also published 9 patents and contributed 20+ book chapters in emerging domains such as Federated Learning, Blockchain, and Digital Twins for IGI Global, Wiley and Springer publisher. He actively mentors students through initiatives like the Research Activities Club (RAC) and Student Research Internship Training (SRIT), promoting innovation and research culture.

Aarthi S is a dedicated Assistant Professor in Computer Science with over six years of teaching experience. She is currently pursuing her Ph.D. at Marwadi University, Gujarat, and holds an M.Phil. and MCA from Bharathiar University, Tamil Nadu. Throughout her academic career, Aarthi has specialized in programming languages such as C++, Java, and C, and contributed to research in recommender systems and AI-related data privacy. She has published journal articles, contributed to book chapters, and actively participated in technical workshops. Known for her student mentorship and engagement in academic events, Aarthi remains committed to fostering innovation and excellence in computer science education.

Kushagra Singh is a highly motivated student at the Jaypee University of Engineering and Technology, specializing in the intersection of Web Development and Artificial Intelligence/Machine Learning (AI/ML). His academic focus involves applying sophisticated ML techniques, particularly deep learning models, to solve complex challenges, while simultaneously utilizing modern web technologies to create robust and user-centric applications. Mr. Singh is actively involved in projects that explore the practical deployment of these technologies, emphasizing their utility in real-world applications and data-driven decision-making, particularly in the creation of intelligent, scalable web solutions.

Satya Subrahmanyam is a distinguished academic leader, researcher, and institutional strategist with over 27 years of experience in higher education, business research, leadership and management. He holds two PhDs and a Postdoctoral qualification from the Polytechnic Institute of Leiria, Portugal. Currently serving as Professor and Dean (Research) at Holy Spirit University of Kaslik (USEK), Lebanon, he spearheads research initiatives that enhance academic excellence and institutional reputation. He played a pivotal role in the development of the Catholic University in Erbil, Kurdistan, where he established new departments, led research programs, and collaborated on international educational projects. As a founding member and Managing Partner of Vignan Institute of Technology and Management, India, he contributed to its transformation into a premier institution. With expertise in AI-driven business strategies, HR analytics, and leadership in technology adoption, he has published extensively, guided PhD research, and led training programs in corporate and academic settings.

Abhuday Sudhir is a highly driven Computer Science student at the Jaypee University of Engineering and Technology, specializing in the practical and research-oriented application of Artificial Intelligence and Machine Learning. His academic and project work focuses on developing intelligent systems using deep learning and NLP-driven approaches to solve real-world problems, including automation, perception, and human computer interaction. He has hands-on experience building scalable AI solutions ranging from neural network implementation and real-time computer vision applications to chat-based automation systems powered by large language models. Abhuday is deeply committed to advancing innovation in AI, consistently engaging in competitive programming, research-driven experimentation, and industry projects to strengthen his problem-solving capabilities and contribute meaningfully to the evolving AI ecosystem.

Vipin Tyagi is a distinguished academician, researcher and author, currently serving as Dean (Academic and Research) at Jaypee University of Engineering and Technology in Guna, Madhya Pradesh. With a rich background in Computer Science, his expertise spans across Image Processing, Cyber Forensics, and Speech Recognition. Prof. Tyagi has a prolific publication record, contributing significantly to his fields of interest. His scholarly work includes numerous journal articles, conference papers, and books. Some of his notable publications are in the areas of image forgery detection, image denoising, and content-based image retrieval. He has authored and edited several books and papers in the field of computing and data sciences, such as "Predictive Computing and Information Security" and "Content-Based Image Retrieval: Ideas, Influences, and Current Trends" published by Springer Singapore. His book "Understanding Digital Image Processing" using MATLAB, published by Taylor and Francis. His scholarly work has earned him a respectable h-index and numerous citations in the academic community.

Index

A

C

D

E

G

H

I

L

N

O

P

R

S

www.ingramcontent.com/pod-product-compliance
Lightning Source LLC
LaVergne TN
LVHW062330300926
849161LV00007B/1640